# Learning to Be LITERACY TEACHERS in Urban Schools

## Stories of Growth and Change

### ALTHIER M. LAZAR

Saint Joseph's University
Philadelphia, Pennsylvania, USA

**INTERNATIONAL Reading Association**

800 BARKSDALE ROAD, PO BOX 8139
NEWARK, DE 19714-8139, USA
www.reading.org

The International Reading Association attempts, through its publications, to provide a forum for a wide spectrum of opinions on reading. This policy permits divergent viewpoints without implying the endorsement of the Association.

**Editorial Director, Books and Special Projects**   Matthew W. Baker
**Managing Editor**   Shannon T. Fortner
**Permissions Editor**   Janet S. Parrack
**Acquisitions and Communications Coordinator**   Corinne M. Mooney
**Associate Editor, Books and Special Projects**   Sara J. Murphy
**Assistant Editor**   Charlene M. Nichols
**Administrative Assistant**   Michele Jester
**Senior Editorial Assistant**   Tyanna L. Collins
**Production Department Manager**   Iona Muscella
**Supervisor, Electronic Publishing**   Anette Schütz
**Electronic Publishing Specialist**   R. Lynn Harrison
**Proofreader**   Elizabeth C. Hunt

**Project Editors**   Sara J. Murphy and Shannon T. Fortner

**Cover Design**   Linda Steere; cover photos (from left): Skjold, Skjold, Fotosearch.com

Web addresses in this book were correct as of the publication date but may have become inactive or otherwise modified since that time. If you notice a deactivated or changed Web address, please e-mail books@reading.org with the words "Website Update" in the subject line. In your message, specify the Web link, the book title, and the page number on which the link appears.

**Library of Congress Cataloging-in-Publication Data**
Lazar, Althier M.
  Learning to be literacy teachers in urban schools : stories of growth and change / Althier M. Lazar.
     p. cm.
  Includes bibliographical references and index.
  ISBN 0-87207-542-7
  1. Language arts. 2. Poor children--Education--United States. 3. Children with social disabilities--Education--United States. 4. Education, Urban--United States. 5. Multicultural education--United States. 6. Student teachers--United States. I. Title.
  LB1576.L373 2004

                                                              2004010049

For Mitch, Zachary, and Aaron
and to my mother,
Patricia,
who loved a good story.

# CONTENTS

# FOREWORD

In 1998, I first heard Althier Lazar talk about the culturally responsive early field experiences she had developed for her interns. It was immediately apparent that she was one of few white teacher educators who were critically addressing the plight of white as well as black interns in urban settings. In fact, Lazar was already passionately addressing a 2003 challenge proposed by Tyrone C. Howard:

> Teachers must face the reality that they will continue to come into contact with students whose cultural, ethnic, linguistic, racial, and social class backgrounds differ from their own. In short, U.S. schools will continue to become learning spaces where an increasingly homogeneous teaching population (mostly White, female, and middle class) will come into contact with an increasingly heterogeneous student population (primarily students of color, and from low-income backgrounds). Thus, teacher educators must reconceptualize the manner in which new teachers are prepared, and provide them with the skills and knowledge that will be best suited for effectively educating today's diverse student population. In order to provide more meaningful knowledge and skills for teaching in today's cultural context, teacher educators must be able to help preservice teachers critically analyze important issues such as race, ethnicity, and culture, and recognize how these important concepts shape the learning experience for many students. More specifically, teachers must be able to construct pedagogical practices that have relevance and meaning to students' social and cultural realities.

*Learning to Be Literacy Teachers in Urban Schools: Stories of Growth and Change* is a trailblazing text, one in which we as literacy educators will learn a great deal. I particularly like the manner in which Lazar details how she helped interns to (a) confront their preconceptions of children and their caregivers, (b) understand the complex facts (including their own responsibility as teachers) that shaped literacy achievement in the urban community in which they taught, and (c) develop knowledge about culturally relevant teaching. Lazar provides poignant examples of how teachers who face children each morning from lives far from their own can successfully teach these children as well as learn to communicate effectively with their caregivers. Lazar's text is one of few texts that I have read that addresses with breadth and depth a suggestion offered by Courtney Cazden (1999), who believes that teachers [need] to learn *experientially* about students and families, and in the process to reflect on their own personal and cultural background instead of unthinkingly living it as an unexamined norm. But saying that only changes the terms of the problem; solving it is now up to each teacher. (p. viii)

Through Lazar's analyses of her interns' autobiographies, attitude-knowledge surveys, lesson plans, and observations and field notes, we hear in her own words that

stories that illuminate teachers' changing attitudes about children and communities are important for education students, who need to make decisions about preparing to teach *all* children. Such stories also are important for practicing teachers, who need to make better connections with their students, and they are important for teacher educators, who need to design programs that support teacher development. Knowing more about the process of becoming culturally sensitive helps education students and practicing teachers find ways to enrich their own cultural understandings. These stories also help teacher educators design courses and K–12 teacher preparation curricula to increase future teachers' cultural sensitivity. (p. 5)

Culturally relevant pedagogy has been described by a number of researchers as an effective means of meeting the academic and social needs of culturally diverse students (Gay, 2000; Ladson-Billings, 1994; Shade, Kelly, & Oberg, 1997). Gay (2000) asserts that culturally relevant pedagogy uses

the cultural knowledge, prior experiences, frames of reference, and performance styles of ethnically diverse students to make learning more relevant to and effective [for students].... It teaches to and through strengths of these students. It is culturally validating and affirming. (p. 29)

More recently, researchers like Ladson-Billings (2001) have described the journeys taken by novice teachers who have made a commitment to teaching in urban communities. In *Learning to Be Literacy Teachers in Urban Schools*, Lazar argues that "what is still not well known is what happens prior to a teacher's making such a commitment" (p. 4). This book clearly uncovers what happens prior to a teacher's making a commitment to culturally relevant pedagogy.

Lazar's depiction of how teachers make a commitment to culturally relevant pedagogy is yet another reason I like this book. She provides breadth and depth with an emphasis clearly on self-reflection, making the point repeatedly that teachers are enriched by their ability to reflect on what they are thinking and doing in classrooms as well as how they value the input of their students' caregivers. The book is a strong scaffold for teachers wanting to try, or get better at, working in culturally diverse urban settings. What Althier Lazar has done in this book is lower the diving board so that, for all of us, holding our nose and jumping into culturally relevant pedagogy is a much safer bet. And, Lazar's book helps us to begin our journey toward increasing the academic achievement of culturally diverse students—a goal some would argue is the most important goal of culturally relevant pedagogy.

Patricia A. Edwards
Michigan State University
East Lansing, Michigan, USA

## References

Cazden, C.B. (1999). Foreword. In C. Ballenger, *Teaching other people's children: Literacy and learning in a bilingual classroom* (pp. vii–viii). New York: Teachers College Press.

Gay, G. (2000). *Culturally responsive teaching: Theory, research, & practice*. New York: Teachers College Press.

Howard, T.C. (2003, Summer). Culturally relevant pedagogy: Ingredients for critical teacher reflection. *Theory Into Practice*. Retrieved June 18, 2004, from http://articles.findarticles.com/p/articles/mi_m0NQM/is_3_42

Ladson-Billings, G. (1994). *The dreamkeepers: Successful teachers for African-American children*. San Francisco: Jossey-Bass.

Ladson-Billings, G. (2001). *Crossing over to Canaan: The journey of new teachers in diverse classrooms*. San Francisco: Jossey-Bass.

Shade, B.J., Kelly, C., & Oberg, M. (1997). *Creating culturally responsive classrooms*. Washington, DC: American Psychological Association.

# ACKNOWLEDGMENTS

First and foremost, I want to thank the undergraduate students to whom these stories of growth and change belong. I could not have written this book without their cooperation and hard work. I also want to thank the principals who graciously allowed my students into their schools and the cooperating teachers who helped to mentor them. To the hundreds of children who worked with us, I thank you for helping us learn to be better teachers.

I would like to thank those who inspired me to carry out my research work in urban public schools, especially my former professors at the University of Pennsylvania—Susan Lytle, Morton Botel, and Fred Erickson. I owe special thanks to Fred Erickson for introducing me to the concepts and methods of ethnographic research. I also am indebted to Rene Weisberg, a former colleague and National Research Council dinner partner, whose interest in the area of caregiver communication led me to incorporate two-way caregiver communication projects into the internship.

Several colleagues at West Chester University supported this work. I want to thank Tom Gill, who spearheaded our partnership with Philadelphia Public Schools. His commitment to Philadelphia's school children is an inspiration. I owe a great deal to my department chairperson, Sharon Kletzien, who supported my teaching efforts and whose work with the Kids Around Town project inspired me to integrate social action projects into the literacy internship. I owe enormous thanks to Dan Darigan for providing me with many book titles to use in the internship. I am grateful to Tony Johnson, Dean of the School of Education at West Chester University, who read one of the final drafts of the book and offered words of support. I want to thank Madeline Wing Adler, President of West Chester University, for spending time with my students and me in our partner schools and recognizing the significance of university involvement in urban education.

I wish to extend my gratitude to the summer research grant committee at Saint Joseph's University for providing the funds to allow me to finish this book. I also want to thank my colleagues at Saint Joseph's University who have contributed to my thinking and growth as a teacher educator. I am energized by your commitment to urban education.

In the preparation of this book, many thanks go to Matt Baker at the International Reading Association for steering this manuscript through the review process. I also acknowledge with much appreciation the thoughtful suggestions made by the reviewers who read the first and second drafts of this manuscript. Their keen insights helped me to strengthen the text in many ways. I owe a special thanks to Sara Murphy, who helped bring this book to fruition through her careful editing work.

I owe so much to my parents, John and Patricia Pino, who have always supported me. I feel fortunate to have such wonderful friends, Barbara Reville and Helen Aster, who listen with genuine interest to all of my work stories. Finally, I want to thank my sons—Aaron and Zach—and my husband, Mitch. Their love, patience, encouragement, and good humor keep me going.

# INTRODUCTION

*It is simply unacceptable that a vastly disproportionate number of minority students fail to learn to read. It is unacceptable that we have so few teachers of color in our schools. It is even more unacceptable that so many majority teachers possess so little knowledge about cultural and linguistic diversity.*

—James Hoffman & P. David Pearson, "Reading Teacher Education in the Next Millennium: What Your Grandmother's Teacher Didn't Know That Your Granddaughter's Teacher Should," p. 41

After having spent more than a decade preparing literacy teachers for work in high-poverty urban communities, I am convinced that we teachers and teacher educators need to learn as much as we can about the children who attend these schools so that we can help them achieve in literacy. I discovered how important this was when I brought groups of preservice teachers—interns, if you will—to teach children in Philadelphia public schools as part of a literacy internship. Many of the interns I assigned to these schools did not believe that these children had the same inherent potential to achieve in reading as children who lived just a few miles away in the suburbs. Many of the interns also assumed that the children's caregivers were irresponsible. These assumptions—based on racial stereotypes and a fundamental disconnect from people in high-poverty communities—prevented interns from being able to truly serve these children. To challenge these views, I began what would be a six-year effort to shape the literacy internship experience in a way that would best prepare interns to teach in high-poverty communities.

My first revision of the internship attempted to address interns' negative attitudes toward parents because these attitudes were the most blatant. Most of the interns blamed caregivers for children's failures to satisfy grade-level expectations, even though interns knew very little about these caregivers. In the internship, the interns read articles on parents and parent–teacher communication and learned about some of the reasons caregivers may have difficulty interfacing with school (Henry, 1996), including that they may not have had

1

positive and quality educational experiences themselves. Most important, we communicated directly with caregivers. Many interns came to know how much caregivers valued their children's academic success.

Even though this inquiry exposed interns to the perspectives of caregivers, most of the interns continued to focus on caregivers' inabilities to prepare children for the demands of school. These interns could not understand why caregivers would not want to improve their own children's chances to achieve in school. This viewpoint exposed interns' assumptions about the relation between home and school. They perceived grade-level standards for literacy as absolute and neutral, reasonably applied to all children despite their very different social and historical circumstances. The interns did not yet see that literacy standards are set according to mainstream lifestyles and uniformly applied to those who have historically had access to the same high levels of literacy education.

Further, interns perceived public schools to be fairly uniform in their delivery of educational services. They assumed most teachers were well educated to serve children's educational needs and that children would do well if caregivers only prepared them for the school experience in kindergarten and supported their children's efforts along the way. Interns did not acknowledge vast inequalities in public schooling, nor did they recognize that home–school differences in literacy, language, and school expectations also shaped students' achievement. I knew I could not simply focus on issues of parenting but also needed to open up dialogues about relations between schools and communities, and embed these dialogues in other conversations about hegemony, racism, and poverty.

Over the next few years, I decided to increase our studies of diversity in the internship. We read, wrote, and talked about white privilege, institutional racism, African American history and culture, language diversity, culturally relevant teaching, and the factors that affect literacy achievement in high-poverty communities. In conjunction with these studies, I wanted to challenge interns' views about children's literacy potential. I arranged for them to tutor children in high-poverty communities, using texts and tasks that were meaningful and that fit with the children's abilities. Interns used multicultural literature in their literacy lessons, especially texts that reflected the lifestyles of the children in these communities, and texts that contained important themes about cultural differences. Instruction focused on inviting children's critical responses to this literature and involving children in social action projects related to the themes in these books (Banks, 1999). (See the appendix, page 152, for more information about how the internship was structured and what literature was studied.) Over time, I began to see changes in the interns' attitudes and understandings about these children, caregivers, and communities.

Restructuring the internship meant that I had to change, too. When I began this project, I asked myself how a white, middle class teacher educator like myself could help white, middle class preservice teachers serve the children in urban schools, who were primarily poor and black. I had experienced success as an elementary school teacher but had felt disillusioned by my involvement with school programs that stripped meaning and authenticity from the process of learning to read. By attending a graduate program, I constructed understandings about the conditions needed to inspire and nurture children's literacy growth. The program also emphasized social responsibility, and many of my research projects involved work in urban schools. Upon graduation, I was committed to preparing future teachers for these schools, but I felt that my understandings about the children in these communities—and specifically, the children's cultural heritage, language, and family lifestyles—were not extensive enough. The work of reforming the internship meant, then, that I needed to better understand children, caregivers, and schooling in this community. It required that I work with children in our field-site classrooms, meet with their caregivers, join multicultural organizations, work with teachers and principals, and participate in school district partnerships. These engagements mediated my own growth as a teacher educator.

After spending several semesters restructuring the internship to include cultural diversity content, I decided to study how the experience helped interns to (a) confront their preconceptions of children and their caregivers, (b) understand the complex factors (including their own responsibility as teachers) that shaped literacy achievement in this community, and (c) develop knowledge about culturally relevant teaching. This book discusses the interns' growth in these areas.

In order to make some assertions about the impact of the internship on interns' attitudes and knowledge, I collected and analyzed interns' autobiographies, attitude-knowledge surveys, lesson plans, and observations and field notes. I used an interpretive, ethnographic methodology (Erickson, 1990) that involved gathering data over a long period of time (one year); collecting and analyzing data from multiple sources; collecting information about participants' actions and perspectives; triangulating the data; and explaining key linkages between participants, their backgrounds, and the contexts in which they were operating. Conscious that I have a vested interest in making claims about the effectiveness of the internship, I have been careful to examine and report on both the successes and limitations of the internship. I have used pseudonyms for all names of schools and teachers in an effort to protect the identities of those who shared their perspectives so candidly.

## Why This Book?

This book comes at a time when there is agreement among literacy experts about what constitutes good literacy teaching (Flippo, 2001). Yet there are still too many children who are not learning how to read and write successfully. There is an ongoing need in the field of literacy education to look at this problem as one of bridging cultural differences between teachers and students. This means describing the process of becoming culturally sensitive and discussing how this matters in literacy teaching. In short, it is time for teachers to share stories of their growth.

Ladson-Billings's book, *The Dreamkeepers: Successful Teachers of African American Children* (1994), provides an important framework for understanding the characteristics of successful teachers of African American children. Delpit's book, *Other People's Children: Cultural Conflict in the Classroom* (1995), focuses on issues of language and literacy in the education of children of color and offers important insights about the need for teachers to recognize the talents these children bring to the classroom. Both of these texts identify directions for teacher growth. What is needed now is more information about how teachers evolve to be successful teachers. Ladson-Billings addresses this topic in her latest book, *Crossing Over to Canaan: The Journey of New Teachers in Diverse Classrooms* (2001), which describes some of the journeys taken by novice teachers who have made a commitment to teaching in these communities.

What is still not well known, however, is what happens prior to a teacher's making such a commitment. That is where this book's stories fit. In this book, I describe preservice teachers who participated in an urban internship even though they were not committed to teaching in high-poverty urban communities. I share how their internship experiences helped to prepare them for this responsibility and even inspired some to envision urban teaching careers.

This journey is an important piece of the teacher growth puzzle because most people who enter the teaching profession fit a white, middle class demographic profile (Cochran-Smith, 1995b), and many of these teachers prefer to teach in suburban schools like those they once attended (Chisholm, 1994).

Yet teachers are needed to serve the growing numbers of children of color and non–English-speaking children, many of whom live in high-poverty urban communities. How do all teachers come to care about these children, believe in their inherent language and literacy abilities, and see their own responsibility to teach them?

## Who Should Read This Book

Stories that illuminate teachers' changing attitudes about children and communities are important for education students, who need to make decisions about preparing to teach *all* children. Such stories also are important for practicing teachers, who need to make better connections with their students, and they are important for teacher educators, who need to design programs that support teacher development. Knowing more about the process of becoming culturally sensitive helps education students and practicing teachers find ways to enrich their own cultural understandings. These stories also help teacher educators design courses and K–12 teacher preparation curricula to increase future teachers' cultural sensitivity. My hope is that our stories will inspire educational reform around these goals.

The 30 preservice teachers who participated in the internship during the year I conducted the study were white and had been raised in middle class communities in Pennsylvania and New Jersey. Most of my assertions about the nature of teacher change are drawn from studying these teachers' responses during the internship. But this book is not just for white teachers; it is for all teachers, teacher educators, and preservice teachers who need to better understand the children they serve. Often, this requires working through differences across several dimensions of identity, including race, class, culture, and language.

In the three years of the internship prior to my study, preservice teachers of color had participated in the internship, although their numbers were quite small. Out of the eight total semesters I did this internship, I taught only four black interns. Two were raised in middle class suburbs, and two were raised in Philadelphia. Interestingly, some of these black interns revealed the same prejudices about children living in the city as were reflected in white interns' written comments during the study. These black education students criticized children's oral and written language and caregivers' lifestyles. In retrospect, I believe that the black interns had absorbed some of the views and values of the dominant Eurocentric culture. This—the fact that one can even have some misconceptions about people of one's own race—is one reason why it makes better sense to frame a discussion about teacher change around cross-cultural differences—differences of orientation and perceptions—rather than differences of race.

Your reading of this book about the process of becoming more culturally sensitive will take place through the lens of your own social reality. As you read, think about the dimensions of difference that separate you from the children you serve or hope to serve. White teachers serving a largely black high-poverty community reflected our reality in the study, but the underlying principles of becoming culturally sensitive can be applied to teachers of other cultural communities. If you are a teacher in Albuquerque, New Mexico, USA, for example, you are more likely to serve children who affiliate with Mexican and Pueblo cultures. Examining racial prejudices, understanding how children's language and literacy practices fit with school expectations, and finding out about the history and culture of children are processes that apply cross-culturally.

Stories about my growth and the growth of interns can serve as templates to help you think about the significance of culture in literacy teaching. I invite you to walk in our shoes as I share stories about our developing awareness of culture and its importance in the literacy classroom.

## Organization of the Book

I begin in chapter 1 by describing the crisis of losing children to literacy failure, and the historical, sociological, and cultural factors that have contributed to this problem. Fortunately, recent research (Pressley, 2002; Taylor, Pressley, & Pearson, 2000) dictates that schools can do much more to reverse the cycle of literacy failure for children in high-poverty communities. This research describes how teachers in high-achieving, high-poverty schools can work together in supportive school environments to help children succeed. These teachers believe in children and see themselves as responsible for teaching them. Unfortunately, though, relatively little is known about how these teachers came to think and act in these successful ways. Being more explicit about how these growth processes happen will help teachers understand the need to self-educate and select programs that will help them develop understandings about the children they teach and the communities that surround their schools.

I demonstrate one such path toward cultural sensitivity by sharing my own cultural autobiography in chapter 2. This chapter includes the pivotal experiences that have shaped my thinking about children and caregivers in one urban community.

Chapter 3 focuses on teachers and teacher education. I address the problems of teachers' low expectations of poor children of color and how these have a negative impact on teaching behaviors. I present research on the characteristics of successful teachers who believe in children's inherent potential and work toward children's academic success. These teachers are better able to do their excellent work with children if they are immersed in a positive school climate that is invested in student learning. The problem is that we do not know as much as we ought to about how teachers come to be successful, and so I look at the limitations and possibilities of teacher education.

In chapter 4, I present the interns' beliefs about children and caregivers who live in high-poverty urban communities. This is an account of the ways the interns underestimated children's intelligence, behavior, language abilities, and interest in literacy before they met the children. The interns primarily targeted urban caregivers for the problems they perceived children to have. This account reveals the need to address teachers' assumptions about children and caregivers. I also look at the roots of prejudice by tracing the histories of two interns whose experiences with diversity were very different and by examining how these experiences shaped their ways of seeing themselves and others.

Each of the next three chapters focuses on the pivotal experiences in the literacy internship that helped interns become more culturally sensitive and see their own responsibility to teach. Chapter 5 is a description of interns' changed understandings about themselves and others as they learned about white privilege, racism, and inequalities in public schooling through course readings and discussions. Chapter 6 focuses on interns' communication with caregivers and how gathering caregiver stories (Edwards, 1995) helped them understand caregivers' perspectives and the out-of-school lives of the children they taught. In chapter 7, I describe how various teaching experiences revealed children's literacy potential and helped interns gain understandings about culturally responsive teaching.

Chapter 8 explores the implications of this text for readers' own growth as culturally sensitive literacy educators. There are several ways that literacy educators, including teachers and teacher educators, can continue the journey of cultural sensitivity begun in this book. Based on my and the interns' experiences, I propose specific areas for this ongoing study and inquiry.

Becoming more culturally aware requires deliberate reflection and action. The Reflection and Inquiry section at the end of each chapter is designed to help you extend your thinking. Use this section as a stopping point to consider how the ideas in the chapter relate to your own insights, experiences, and circumstances. You also might use this section to facilitate group discussions about each chapter. Using the Reflection and Inquiry section in these ways will help you to guide your own development.

The appendix provides a description of the internship and explains the methodology I used for this study. It discusses the data collection process, sequence of the internship, and other important information.

## Clarifying Language

Much of the language related to cultural diversity can be misinterpreted; this necessitates clarification of certain terms used in this book. For instance, I use the word *urban* frequently. The word *urban* is often misused as a euphemism for poor African Americans, as in "the urban family" or "the urban child." Writing about urban education, urban schools, or urban communities requires unpacking the word *urban* because it is often used to denote conditions of concentrated poverty and violence. Life within city borders is much more economically and socially complex, however, than this usage implies. Affluent African Americans live within city boundaries but have very different lifestyles from poor individuals in the same city who claim the same heritage. Conversely, poor African Americans live in rural and suburban areas as well as in urban areas, as do other people of color and whites.

According to Weiner (2000), degrees of "urban-ness" exist on a continuum with characteristics that vary depending on whether cities are very large (e.g., New York City) or significantly smaller (e.g., Allentown, Pennsylvania). When I use the word *urban*, I am referring to the characteristics that define school districts in large metropolitan cities like Philadelphia. These characteristics are as follows:

1. service to a large, highly diverse population

2. centralized decision making isolated from communities

3. chronic underfunding that affects decisions about teaching and learning

4. high concentrations of linguistic minorities and "voluntary minorities" (Ogbu, 1987, p. 321)—people who chose to come to the United States, expecting a better life

5. high concentrations of "involuntary minorities" (p. 321)—people who were incorporated into U.S. society against their will—whose cultural

model is often different from and in conflict with the dominant cultural model

6. attempts at curriculum uniformity with student performance measured primarily by standardized tests

I sometimes use *African American* and sometimes use *black* to describe children and the community when I want to make a specific point about race as a factor in literacy achievement or schooling. Site documents containing information about the demographics of the schools in the study described the majority of the student body as African American. This is significant in that we served a highly segregated community. In working directly with the children, we realized that a few of the children affiliated with particular countries of origin (e.g., Nigeria, Sudan, Jamaica). The term *African American* did not apply to all of these children, and, therefore, the term *black* is more appropriate in its inclusiveness. In fact, *black* would more appropriately describe almost all the children we served.

What complicates matters, though, is that people have very different opinions about the use of these descriptors. Once, I used the expression *African American* in speaking to one of my colleagues, and she told me quite clearly how much she disliked the term: "What's this African American stuff? I'm black!" Yet one teacher told me she did not particularly care for the term *black* and preferred instead to be called African American. In this book, I use *black* as a more general term for people who affiliate as African Americans and people of African or Caribbean descent. I use the term *African American* when I want to specify that the people being discussed are Americans of African heritage.

*Children of color* is a more inclusive term that embraces the majority of the world's children who do not trace their ancestry to Europe. I use this term when relating findings about teacher change to other populations of children beyond those we served in the internship—populations whose relation to the mainstream is similar to that of the children in our field placement schools.

*Culture* is another term that is often misunderstood. In the past, *culture* was used to describe the patterns of behavior of those affiliating with particular ethnic or language groups. This view, however, does not capture the dynamic and shifting nature of the ways diverse people cross ethnic and language borders constantly and are then transformed by these experiences (Florio-Ruane & McVee, 2000). What has replaced a static view of culture is a more interpretive one that sees culture as "webs of significance," or meanings partially shared and manipulated by groups of people (Eisenhart, 2001). *Cultural sensitivity* is the awareness that cultural differences exist and have an impact on the meanings, values, perceptions, and behaviors of particular groups of people. *Culturally relevant* and *culturally responsive* describe ways of teaching that are informed by a knowledge of the shared meanings, values, perceptions, and behaviors of particular communities.

*Diversity* refers to differences among people along several dimensions of identity, including class, race, ethnicity, religion, language, gender, age, sexual orientation, and physical capacities. All of these differences are included in discussions of diversity, in recognition that each difference brings with it particular challenges of securing equal treatment in a society that gives preference to those who possess certain attributes. In the United States, for instance, those who are rich, white, Anglo-Saxon, Christian, English-speaking, young, male, heterosexual, and healthy can generally count on certain privileges that others who do not possess these attributes cannot. The problem is that categories of "otherness"—black, white, Asian, female—are often expressed and interpreted as static categories of identity (M.E. Dyson, 2003). Dyson argues that the rhetoric of multiculturalism (and the labeling of differences) often ignores the hierarchy of difference within difference itself:

> It ignores, for instance, how in the politicization of multicultural rhetoric through affirmative action, white women have fared far more successfully in employment and education opportunities than black women and men. It also ignores how, on the representational front created by multicultural struggles to combat stereotypes, blacks have done far better, especially on television and on the silver screen, than Latinos. It ignores how, in the empirical terms of economic advantage and social status, gay white men have been able to leverage considerable clout within domains—particularly corporate life and Hollywood production—closed to most minorities. The point is simple: Social differences within the ideology of difference make a material difference in how the politics of difference are conceived and expressed. (pp. 52–53)

The concept of race is a construct invented fairly recently in human history. It is often misunderstood to mean actual genetic differences between people. I consider race to be a social construct that gives people different access to opportunities and resources. *Racism* is discrimination based on the belief that some "races" are by nature superior to others.

Although race and class are two important factors in discussions about preparing preservice teachers for high-poverty urban schools, other dimensions of identity also shaped the interns' responses to the internship. For example, in chapter 6 I describe how one intern's identity as a mother shaped her perceptions of children and caregivers.

Finally, research for this book was based on experiences with senior-level preservice teachers. The phrase *preservice teachers* is rather cumbersome to use repeatedly, so I use *preservice teachers* to indicate education students in general and use *interns* to indicate education students who participated in my urban literacy internship.

## Conclusion

If we really want to do something about the high rates of literacy failure among children of color in high-poverty urban communities, expert knowledge of literacy teaching is essential but not sufficient. We—teachers and teacher educators—must focus on children, and that means understanding their social, historical, and cultural places within the local community. It also means interrogating our own views about people who we do not yet know. This book adds to the existing knowledge base about the process of understanding these concepts. My hope is that these stories of growth and change will inspire conversations about what it takes to serve all children.

# CHAPTER 1

# Historical, Social, and Cultural Factors Shaping Literacy Achievement

*The hands of none of us are clean if we bend not our energies to righting these great wrongs.*

—W.E.B. DuBois, *The Souls of Black Folk: Essays and Sketches*, p. 94

A t a recent convention of the International Reading Association, about 100 concerned educators of African American students gathered to listen to Candace Dawson Boyd speak. Dawson Boyd introduced herself as one of the few African American professors at St. Mary's College of California in Moraga, California, USA, and one who has spent a career educating teachers to teach reading. What she said that day needs yet another audience.

Dawson Boyd placed a transparency of a child's writing on the overhead projector and invited those of us in the audience to examine it and think about the age of the author. The piece contained three lines of print with a simple message about a friend. Many of the words were spelled phonetically, with a mix of uppercase and lowercase letters. Having worked with elementary school children for some time, I had seen hundreds of pieces of writing like this, created by children younger than eight. Dawson Boyd looked at us and shouted, "Seventh grade! Black boy!" She asked us to sit for a moment and think about what it means to approach high school with the literacy skills of a first grader. Then she showed us a page from a seventh-grade textbook. It was appropriately dense, with a mix of complex sentences and high-level vocabulary.

Dawson Boyd looked at us again and said,

> Think of how humiliated and angry this boy must feel when he sees something like this! It is no wonder he acts out in class. It is no wonder he drops out of school. And when this happens, where will he go? We live in the age that demands high levels of literacy. He will not have a place in this world. He will not be able to reap the personal and social benefits that literacy can bring. He will

be living on the margins of society. We have lost him! This has got to stop! (Dawson Boyd, 2003)

I was not surprised to see an African American woman waging war on a system that fails poor children of color. Right now, too many of these children arrive in middle school without the literacy skills needed to achieve in high school, participate in higher education, contribute to a technologically advanced society, and participate fully as citizens and intellectuals. They are lost. This *does* have to stop.

Stopping this trend of literacy failure requires that educators understand how, when, and where the phenomenon started and what the recurring problems are in today's educational system. In this chapter, I present an overview of the history that has given rise to problems of literacy achievement among African Americans. I also present a complicated picture of why the educational playing field remains uneven for many children in this cultural community.

## Past and Present Access to Literacy

From 1619, when the first African captives were brought to Virginia, to the present day, African Americans have been adaptive and resilient in the face of denied access to literacy and education. For most of the 19th century in many parts of the United States, it was against the law to teach African Americans to read. Recognizing the value of mastering print, though, they learned to read despite the threat of beatings and even death. Myers (1991) crystallizes why African slaves were so determined to learn to read and why their owners fought hard to prevent them from succeeding:

> Africans understood that being able to read gave them abilities that the owners did not want them to have, but they took the chance of being punished as they read by candlelight at night or took whatever books they could find into the forests. The planters certainly did not want the Africans thinking about ideas of freedom and equality, ideas that their own sons and daughters were exploring in school. They didn't want them to read newspaper articles about the debates in Congress over the expansion of slavery, or to realize how many white Americans thought Africans should be free. Nor did they want them to read about other Africans who were free in Northern states, or who had escaped to Canada. (p. 41)

The Thirteenth, Fourteenth, and Fifteenth Amendments to the U.S. Constitution respectively abolished slavery, permitted Africans to become citizens of the United States, and allowed African Americans the right to vote, but the fight for equality had just begun. In 1896, the U.S. Supreme Court upheld the "separate but equal" doctrine mandated in the *Plessy vs. Ferguson* decision, in which facilities were supposed to be equal but remained essentially unequal and inferior for African Americans. Along with the physical separation from whites that was sanctioned by the U.S. government, different education paths were envisioned for African Americans than for whites. Fears about African American liberation through education prevailed among members of the dominant class, giving rise to the prevalence of vocational education for African Americans.

One historical account of African Americans living in Calhoun, Alabama, USA, during the post–Reconstruction era (1892–1945) revealed how education at Calhoun Colored School was based on a vocational model in which minimal access to literacy was made available to students (Willis, 2002). Offered as a path to liberation, literacy in this school nevertheless focused on the skills needed for graduates to function primarily as farmers, servants, and laborers. Based on the Hampton-Tuskegee education model that stressed industrial training over academic learning, African Americans were specifically groomed for the southern farm in ways that would "not upset the economic balance of the South built on black labor, to appease the African American laborers through elementary education, and to keep African American families working the land" (p. 22). Despite a campaign against industrial education for African Americans, led by DuBois (1903) and others, the Hampton–Tuskegee model shaped the educational experiences of many thousands of African Americans for generations.

Racial segregation existed in the public schools until the mid 1950s. African Americans' hard-fought struggle for educational equality led to a pivotal U.S. Supreme Court decision in 1954, *Brown vs. Board of Education*, ruling segregation to be unconstitutional. In many parts of the United States, however, whites resisted school integration. African American children attending white schools for the first time had to be escorted to school, often under police and military guard. To integrate schools, many districts across the country began busing children to schools outside their home neighborhoods, which led to violent protests.

A half century later, African Americans are still struggling to enforce the full intent of the *Brown* decision. Today, many African American children attend public schools that are effectively still racially segregated. Sociologists find that African Americans, unlike other groups, have not been able to translate socioeconomic gains into improved residential mobility (Charles, 2000). Between 1980 and 1990, African Americans remained substantially more isolated than either Asians or Hispanics (Farley & Frey, 1994). De facto segregation was evident in the schools I visited in the six years prior to 2001, as each of them served a population of children that was more than 95% African American.

The schools I visited also were chronically underfunded, which is typical of large metropolitan school districts (Weiner, 2000). Affluent communities have the means to spend almost double what poor communities spend to educate children. In the 1997–1998 school year, per-pupil spending in Philadelphia was $6,969, compared with $13,287 in the nearby community of Radnor (Nicholas, 2000). Such funding differences between schools in affluent and poor communities influence a range of factors including class size, materials, and professional development support for teachers.

However, before looking at the impact of these school-related factors on literacy achievement, I need to address the core expectations of school literacy achievement and the home and community factors that affect how well children are prepared to meet these expectations.

## The Mastery of Print

Despite vast differences in public school funding, all U.S. children are held to a similar standard of understanding and using print-based decontextualized language skills (Snow, Burns, & Griffin, 1998). Children are expected to decode, interpret, and compose written language within the first few years of school. School success is tied to the degree to which children's experiences with print outside school match the expectations for mastering print in school (Heath, 1983). Children who enter kindergarten without prior engagement in story reading or language play begin the schooling process at a clear disadvantage. Unless the discrepancy is corrected within the first few years of school, the likelihood is that children will lag further behind in their ability to meet school literacy expectations.

Certain groups of children tend to fall behind in literacy achievement. According to one study, these include children living in high-poverty communities, children whose parents did not graduate from high school, and children of teenage mothers (Grissmer, Kirby, Berends, & Williamson, 1994). However, the same study defied the stereotype that children of single-parent homes also are at risk. Single-parent homes and homes in which two parents work were not found to significantly affect children's achievement.

15

Another view exposes the differences between lower and middle class communities in the skills and resources available to parents to support children's academic achievement (Lareau, 1989). One study looked at the relative impact of in-school versus out-of-school influences on academic performance (Entwisle, Alexander, & Olsen, 1997) and found that differences in experiences outside of school accounted for, in part, the gains made in reading by middle class children and the stagnation of reading growth for many children in low-income households. These researchers found that middle class children made many of their reading gains over the summer as they were exposed to books, travel, and camp experiences, while children in poor communities either stayed the same or fell further behind in reading. By the sixth grade, the cumulative advantages of summer reading and experiences contributed to a two-year gap between poor and more affluent children's reading scores. Although these researchers found that children in high-poverty communities can make literacy gains during the school year similar to children who attend schools in more affluent communities, they do not comment on how schools can and should address this achievement gap.

Although these studies show relations between certain factors, particularly between income and achievement, they do not account for the unique ways each family, irrespective of income or the caregivers' marital status, relates to print at home. There is wide variation among low-income families in their use of print and ways of engaging in print experiences associated with school success, such as book reading (Purcell-Gates, L'Allier, & Smith, 1995). Compton-Lilly (2003) reports that the African American parents whom she interviewed in one low-income urban community interacted with print in a variety of ways and recognized the significance of reading for personal satisfaction and social mobility. They also rejected poverty and poor parenting as legitimate reasons for reading failure, but because these explanations conflicted with mainstream explanations, they had difficulty supporting their views. The parents also reported that the stresses and pressures of their lives made it difficult for them to find time to read. What is important in this research is the need to resist assumptions about parenting and the nature of school literacy activity outside of school.

The question of children's exposure to print outside of school is also tied to the availability of print in the local environment (Neuman & Celano, 2001). In their study comparing the availability of texts across neighborhoods of different socioeconomic levels, Neuman and Celano found vast differences in the availability of books and other forms of print in local libraries and stores. These researchers also found differences in the quality of signage in poor versus more affluent communities. The number of public library books available to children in the primarily white affluent neighborhood averaged almost 12 books per child, about 10 books more than what was available to a primarily African American population of children in the poorest, most segregated neighborhood. Similarly, the numbers of available children's texts found in stores in the two poorest neighborhoods totaled 358 in one and 55 in the other. The number of children's texts found in stores in the most affluent community totaled 16,453, presenting a striking example of unequal access to texts.

The availability of well-stocked and expertly staffed school libraries also makes a difference in children's literacy achievement, regardless of the socioeconomic and education levels of their caregivers. Krashen (1995) reports that children get a substantial percentage of their reading material from the school library and that the libraries that produce children with higher reading achievement are the ones that have larger, quality collections; offer longer hours of availability; provide comfortable and relaxing reading environments; and are staffed with qualified school librarians. He found that children in a school with no library averaged 3.8 books read over a four-week period, but children from a school with a library averaged 7.6 books. The urban schools I visited in my study did not have fully functioning school libraries, thereby limiting children's access to books and to librarians—professionals who play a key school role in motivating children to read.

Many history and science books found in urban school libraries in Philadelphia and across the country are outdated and, consequently, inaccurate (Hall, 2003). For example, in Philadelphia's public school libraries, the average copyright date of books is 1980. Crystal Patterson (as cited in Hall, 2003), lead coach for library programs for the Philadelphia School District said,

> It's worst for seventh graders and up, especially in the areas of science, history, geography and biography. For example, we've found (our collections) very lacking in information since the Persian Gulf War, what's going on there now. We've found books that still have Russia the way it was in 1980 to 1985, before they broke up. One book we pulled said Nelson Mandela was killed. (p. A15)

In science, Patterson found books to be grossly outdated: "There's no reference to issues like cloning. And we actually pulled science books that said, 'Someday, man will go to the moon'" (p. A15).

## Access to Literacy Education

Children's ability to access print in the environment is another condition that affects their familiarity with the print activities valued in school. Whether or not schools in high-poverty communities compensate for the lack of environmental print is dependent on many factors. Children, even those who struggle with reading, can develop as readers when they are given lots of texts they can read and when they have highly knowledgeable teachers to guide their progress (Allington, 2001).

Instruction must be targeted within a child's Zone of Proximal Development (Vygotsky, 1934/1978), or between what a child can do independently and with assistance from a more capable peer or adult. Children must be given texts they can read almost independently so they can easily draw from meaning, structural, and visual cues to figure out unknown words and make meaning (Fountas & Pinnell, 1996). Children who are constantly given texts that are too difficult for them cannot do this and, therefore, do not gain the problem-solving strategies to advance in reading. Children from the lower socioeconomic strata tend to have this experience more because they are often the ones who struggle with reading to begin with. Above all, reading must be presented as a purposeful and meaning-centered experience.

Reading instruction in school tends to be more aligned with the abilities of the most successful readers: Children in the top quartile in reading are given school materials in which they make, at most, 2 errors per 100 words, whereas the weakest readers make at least 18 errors per 100 words using these same materials (Shannon, 1988). Reading errors, or miscues, interfere with understanding the text. If struggling readers are miscuing so much, how can they make as much sense of these texts as those who do not miscue as often? These miscuing children are less able to make gains in reading because they are being given texts that are too difficult. These children fall increasingly behind those who can read grade-level texts, creating what Stanovich (1986) calls the Matthew effect: The differences between good and poor readers become magnified over time.

Reading progress is dependent on a knowledgeable teacher who selects texts carefully, based on observations of children's reading, and who is able to provide individualized and small-group instruction for children (Tharp & Gallimore, 1989). The larger the number of children in the classroom, the more expert the teacher must be to figure out how to provide such individualized instruction. Urban public school classrooms are chronically overcrowded

(Weiner, 2000). Problems of teacher retention and the emergence of emergency certification of teachers for these classrooms suggest that many teachers may not have the expertise needed to continually assess children's abilities, determine flexible grouping routines, and teach children within disparate groups in developmentally appropriate ways. It takes an expert teacher to do this.

Furthermore, children who share a heritage of denied access to education may not know how to play the game called school. There are ways of behaving and interacting among those belonging to what Delpit (1995) calls the "culture of power," to which most teachers and mainstream children belong, that may be different from the ways of behaving and interacting among many low-income, racially diverse, or immigrant children and their families. Children enter schools where they are also expected to talk about print and relate to others using mainstream linguistic codes and patterns of interaction (Cazden, 1986; Erickson & Mohatt, 1982; Heath, 1983; Philips, 1972). If children do not behave and communicate according to these expectations, they may be seen as deficient (lacking understanding), defiant (unwilling to play by the rules of school), or both.

There are also curriculum issues that can have an effect on how children view themselves in relation to school. The absence of their culture in the school curriculum can have an alienating effect on children (Ladson-Billings, 1994). If children of color are placed in a school curriculum that reflects the dominant middle class Anglo/Western European culture, they do not see their own history, culture, beauty, language, or accomplishments reflected in school. When teachers do not respect children or take into account the perspectives and lifestyles of children's cultural communities, children will have more difficulty identifying with school culture (Delpit, 1995).

## Academic Resistance

Some educators see academic resistance as a major problem that contributes to the achievement gap between white and African American children. Linguist McWhorter (2000) asserts that academic failure stems from a culture of anti-intellectualism that he believes is pervasive in the African American community. He questions how poverty could be such a central factor of school failure if (a) African American children who attend schools in affluent communities sometimes do not perform to their full potential and (b) recent immigrants manage to succeed in school despite attending schools in high-poverty com-

19

munities. According to McWhorter, the real problem is a culture that actively resists intellectualism.

But McWhorter does not adequately address why some African American children might resist intellectualism in the first place. Resistance theory posits that children can actively choose not to learn after a sustained pattern of school failures and misunderstandings (Erickson, 1993). Resisting learning then becomes a form of political protest (Giroux, 1994). Relevant to this psychology of resistance is the perception that "school success" means acting white (Fordham & Ogbu, 1986). According to Tatum (1999), "Doing well in school becomes identified as trying to be white. Being smart becomes the opposite of being cool" (p. 62). This view reflects a dual-identity dilemma in which children see intellectualism as being at odds with having a strong community identification. If children of color perceive achievement as being associated with being white, they may resist it for fear that becoming academically successful may lead to peer rejection.

A recent study of African American children in an affluent community attempts to explain why so many of these children do not do as well academically as they could (Ogbu & Davis, 2003). In an ethnographic study of the affluent suburb of Shaker Heights, Ohio, USA, Ogbu and Davis investigated the factors that shaped academic achievement in this community. Patterns of academic disengagement from school were noted among African American children, especially those in middle school and high school. The researchers stated that these children did not put forth as much effort in school as their white counterparts did, nor did most choose to take more academically challenging honors or advanced placement classes. The caregivers of these children had high academic aspirations for their children, but they did not show their children how to succeed in school. Caregivers' lack of attendance at school functions and limited assistance with schoolwork were found to be factors in these children's lower academic achievement.

Ogbu and Davis uncovered many factors that influenced these students' academic disengagement. Many of the African American students they interviewed expressed self-doubts about their academic abilities, reflecting internalized beliefs about their own intellectual inferiority. The researchers pointed to generations of racial inequality as a major factor in shaping these beliefs. Not trying in school was in accord with the African American students' perceptions of themselves as learners: Because these children were concentrated in the lower academic tracks, the school's expectations were lower for these children, and the children responded to these expectations, reinforcing perceptions (held by themselves and by others) that they were academically less capable than white children. The causal relationship between these two phenomena—children not achieving and teachers expecting that children will not achieve—remains unclear.

Also according to these researchers, caregivers' relations with the schools were contradictory. Caregivers entrusted the schools with doing the job of educating their children and worked hard to pay for the higher cost of living in the community. They cared a great deal about their children's grades in school and dispensed rewards and punishments based on report card grades. Some caregivers attended school meetings and made sure their children took academically challenging classes. At the same time, however, Ogbu and Davis found that many other caregivers were disengaged from their children's academic experiences. These caregivers did not have time to attend to children's schoolwork at home, primarily because of job commitments and the need to prove themselves as exceptional employees to secure their places in the workforce.

Ogbu and Davis also found that many caregivers who had not achieved academic success wanted their children to do better than they did, but they did not know how to help their children achieve. Some caregivers lacked awareness about their roles in their children's academic success and about how much caregiver involvement mattered in this success. They themselves had not had caregivers who set the example of monitoring homework, pushing them into higher academic tracks, or attending school meetings. Parents also felt the financial burden of being in the community was sacrifice enough and that it was the school's job to ensure their children's academic success.

Ogbu and Davis's study suggests that resistance toward school is deeply entwined in a history of racial inequity that has shaped educational and employment opportunities for members of this community. In other words, the act of resisting school is not a matter of rejecting intellectualism as much as it is an outcome given the history of this community's relations with the dominant culture. Resistance is too limited an explanation for why African American students in an affluent community disengage from school. Also, it does not account for the reality that academically successful African American children can be both successful and oppositional (O'Connor, 1997). Nonetheless, I found it necessary to look at the idea of resistance because it often is used to explain academic failure among African American children across socioeconomic levels.

What is clear in the current research, however, is that literacy achievement is dependent on a range of interrelated factors.

It also is clear that researchers have approached the problem of literacy achievement through particular ideological lenses. Failure to achieve in school has been seen in the context of one group's domination over another (Giroux, 1994), manifested by the expectation that all children should master school-based literacies within the same time period, despite the fact that many who live in poverty have not had equal access to texts and educational opportunities and, therefore, cannot compete in the same academic arena as those who have (Kozol, 1991, 2000). Some believe the problem of achievement lies squarely with caregivers' and students' willingness to embrace school-based literacies and that the responsibility lies within the marginalized culture to liberate itself through academic achievement (McWhorter, 2000). Others have centered the problem of literacy achievement on the differences between home and school expectations and discourses (Delpit, 1995; Heath, 1983) and believe that schools must change to successfully serve all children.

What I take up in this book is the last view, that educators can and must work toward solving the problem of helping all children achieve in literacy. First, we bear the responsibility of understanding the factors that have an impact on children's literacy achievement. Mapping out the history and culture of a community, relative to the standards and expectations of its schools, is a first step toward understanding our responsibility to act within this complex web of influences. We need to realize that children's ways of using language and print outside school are not deficient, but different, and that our job is to help children acquire the additional discourses of school literacy (Gee, 2000). Teachers who know about children's limited access to texts and literacy education, both historically and in contemporary society, can work to offset these challenges by helping children access books, finding out more about children's communities and enriching literacy teaching in the classroom as a result, listening to caregivers and teaching them about school literacy expectations, and recognizing the knowledge that children bring to school as being valid.

## Conclusion

We can learn about and acquire the characteristics that help us to be successful teachers in these communities. Among these attributes are the beliefs that children are capable of success and that we have the power and responsibility to help children become successful. What does this process look like?

For the preservice teachers who participated in my urban internship, their change process largely depended on mine. In the next chapter, I will describe my own evolution as a literacy educator. I will share many life experiences that have put me on a path toward taking responsibility for the literacy education of children in high-poverty communities.

## REFLECTION AND INQUIRY

1. Consider the cultural community in which you teach. Write about your understandings of the following aspects of the community:

- the literacy potential of children
- caregivers and home environments
- differences between home and school literacy/language
- issues that specifically relate to this community
- the history and culture of community members
- ways to bridge any gaps that may exist between home and school cultures
- children's and caregivers' relationships with teachers in the community

2. Think about your history. In what ways has your history affected your own access to education and literacy?

CHAPTER 2

# Knowing Ourselves Culturally

*Because European dominance has been so broadly and effectively established, it is important to ask ourselves as White educators how our own social positionality and history of dominance might be implicated in the disproportionate distribution of privilege and penalty in contemporary educational systems.*

—Gary Howard, *We Can't Teach What We Don't Know: White Teachers, Multiracial Schools*, p. 34

Understanding children and their social worlds requires that we understand ourselves. According to Florio-Ruane (Florio-Ruane & McVee, 2000), "The work of understanding and describing others' lives is inevitably mediated by our own autobiographies" (p. 160). Tracing our own histories relative to particular communities of people exposes the critical experiences that have influenced who we are and how we see others. Writing about this history is an important beginning point for confronting assumptions about ourselves and others (Schmidt, 2001).

I present my own cultural autobiography in this chapter for two reasons. First, I hope my story will help you evoke your own memories about the critical experiences that have shaped your views about yourself and others. As you read, think especially about yourself in relation to others. Because my university's placement schools served African American children in high-poverty urban neighborhoods, my search was to understand myself in relation to these children and their community.

As you read my story, think about the communities you are most likely to serve, would like to serve, or already do serve. Consider how your views about the children and their caregivers in these communities have been shaped. Jot down these ideas. These notes are seeds; use them to write your own cultural autobiography. At the end of this chapter, I will provide specific ideas to guide your writing.

Second, my story is for those who are not sure that change is necessary. When I first taught elementary school students 20 years ago, I probably would have denied the need for this kind of introspection. I considered myself to be a hard-working, dedicated teacher who felt pretty confident about how to teach reading. Have things ever changed! Over time, I realized how little I knew then and how little I know now. In reading my cultural autobiography, I hope you will see the relevance of taking your own journey.

## Cultural Isolation

Raised in southeastern Massachusetts during the 1960s and 1970s, I was surrounded by white people of western European ancestry. Many of the families I knew were second-generation Portuguese, Italian, and Irish immigrants. My classmate Susan lived in a dilapidated two-room house on the outskirts of town. Her father was an alcoholic who left her mother. My best friend Debbie lived in a small ranch house, typical of those found all over town. Her father was a postal worker and her mother was a homemaker. Another friend, Donna, lived in a house filled with books near the town's center. Her parents taught at the local college. I also remember Terry, the daughter of an executive who lived in a big house with a tennis court. Class and education were the most salient differences among people in this predominantly white Christian community. In the absence of racially different others, I did not identify as a white person. Nor did I understand the significance of whiteness in this society.

I did not know many people of color while growing up. Only two black families lived in my town of 13,000, but for a brief time, I knew one of these families personally. Mr. Allen became my seventh-grade math teacher when he and his family moved to my neighborhood from Virginia. He was refined and soft-spoken. Some of the mean-spirited boys in my math class mocked him, and, when provoked enough, Mr. Allen usually asked them to leave class. These interruptions continued throughout the school year. Meanwhile, I became friends with Mr. Allen's 11-year-old daughter, Angela. We visited each other after school, but we never talked about what it must have been like for her to be the only black student in a class of 150. I imagined that it was difficult for her and her family to adjust to my town, where there was not much room for difference. They moved away after just one year, and I never heard from Angela again.

I knew that most African Americans in the area lived 30 miles to the north in Boston, in the segregated communities of Mattapan and Roxbury. On trips through these communities, I saw children jumping rope on sidewalks and sitting on the doorsteps of the run-down brownstones that lined Massachusetts Avenue. I was told that these "colored" children and their parents were desperately poor. My mother described slavery and the laws of the South that kept blacks separated from whites. Her occasional commentary about the unfairness of these things left the impression that we, as northern whites, were not to blame for the dire circumstances of these black families.

The media also played a part in shaping my social consciousness. Lawyers, doctors, teachers, business executives, police officers, and judges on television were white. White men delivered the news each night, and white actors sold us everything from cigarettes to detergent. In the 1970s, there was an increasing number of black and Latino faces on television—Redd Foxx, Freddie Prinze, Flip Wilson, Bill Cosby—but television still largely reflected a white United States.

The curriculum to which I was exposed in the 1960s and 1970s almost exclusively emphasized European achievement, history, and culture. I had virtually no exposure to Asian, Middle Eastern, Latin, or African cultures. I read about Anglo characters, from Dick and Jane to Young Goodman Brown. My classmates and I drew pictures of Columbus's three ships and chanted the famous "1492" song. History teachers tiptoed over the topic of slavery. We never seemed to get to the Civil Rights chapter in our history book before school let out in June. I went to high school during the Cold War years and spent a lot of time talking about the horrors of communism and the virtues of democracy. I graduated from high school knowing very little about the experiences and contributions of other cultures.

This trend continued in college in the early 1980s, where I read books by white, primarily male, authors. I dutifully generated pages of recounted facts about our system of government, told from an Anglo perspective. In psychology class, I studied the normal and abnormal ways in which whites behave. My education courses taught me to view all children, regardless of social or cultural influences, as moving through "stages" of development. My college's survey of children's literature included primarily white authors. In all these courses, information was transmitted during the semester and then regurgitated on exam days. My higher education did not teach me about cultural differences.

I cannot recall whether I took the course I did on black religion because I was curious about the topic or because it happened to fit my need for a humanities course at the time. The course was taught by the Reverend Charles Stith, a former pastor of the United Methodist Church in Boston who later became an ambassador to Tanzania. He was the only African American professor I had ever met in college. Through him, I learned about the significance of religion in the black community.

## Culturally Unresponsive Teaching

After college, I took a job at a boarding school in New England that served elementary school students with reading problems. Ours was a primarily white, affluent clientele, but we also taught many foreign students. We tutored children using a phonics-based, tactile–kinesthetic approach. The books we used contained lists of words grouped by rhyme patterns (e.g., *lid*, *rid*, *bid*, *Sid*), followed by the words used in context:

> Sid hid a kid in a big bag.
>
> Did a cat bat at Sid?
>
> Can Sid tap at a cat?
>
> Sid did. Bad Sid.

Children were asked to read the word lists first, then the text. They were required to spell the words they missed by moving their fingers across a rough board. I saw many students learn to decode using this method, but few seemed to enjoy our regimented tutoring sessions.

This was particularly true for one of my students, Manuel, a boy from Nicaragua. I knew virtually nothing about his home, family, or community, nor did it occur to me to find out. Talking with students about their lives was discouraged at this school. We were specifically asked not to "psychologize" with students, which meant, "Don't spend time getting to know these students. Just teach them to read!" My tutoring sessions with Manuel were difficult. He resisted using the rough board and hated the reading passages. He often became frustrated, and at times, he cried. Relief came at the end of each of our sessions, when we had a few moments to chat. Our most pleasant conversations were about his pet armadillo, but I never used his stories about home to construct any meaningful teaching experiences with him.

I concentrated on helping Manuel decode words. Although he gained skill in decoding, this method did not help him fall in love with books. I knew I needed a better arsenal of teaching tools than the fragmented, skills-driven approach I currently used. I needed to understand literacy teaching and learning. At the crest of the movement toward whole language, I began a doctoral program.

## Confronting Prejudice

In graduate school, I was immersed in conversations about race, class, culture, and gender as factors that influenced everything from text interpretation to literacy achievement. My expectations and assumptions were challenged constantly. In my first year in the program, I wrote about how low-income African American children could not get enough educational support at home because their parents were too busy working to make ends meet. In response, my professor wrote, "How do you know this is true? Have you lived in this community? How would you know how these families respond to life's challenges to get their children educated?" This was the first time anyone had ever confronted my beliefs about these children and their caregivers. Somehow, I had thought I was incapable of stereotyping others, but my written words were proof that I presumed much on the basis of few real experiences. This professor did not leave me to wallow in my ignorance. She gave me a direction instead. At the bottom of my paper, she wrote, "Please read the book *Growing Up Literate* and you may have a different view."

Books like *Growing Up Literate: Learning From Inner-City Families* (Taylor & Dorsey-Gaines, 1988) had a profound effect on my thinking. Now considered a classic, the book captures the literacy practices of four African American families living in urban poverty and the ways children in these families learned to read and write despite the economic hardships in their lives. The obstacles these families faced, from arranging public transportation to dealing with government agencies for the poor, revealed their determination and strength and their need to master the print that affected their lives. Life outside of school contrasted with the decontextualized, disconnected ways children were taught literacy in school. In reading the field notes of the authors as they observed classroom life, it became clear to me that the schools underserved the needs of the children in these families. The book helped me recognize that families of all races and classes want the best for their children and that one's race, class, gender, or setting does not determine one's ability to read and write.

*Ways With Words: Language, Life, and Work in Communities and Classrooms* (Heath, 1983), another classic written five years earlier, was based on a 10-year study of three different families: one middle class white, one working class white, and one working class black. Language and interactions around print between caregivers and children in these families were distinctively different. Heath found that school expectations, curricula, and teaching methods matched best with middle class families' ways of talking, reading, and writing. When Heath worked with teachers to adjust for the children's different ways of approaching print, she and the teachers observed improvements in children's responses to school and school literacy tasks.

Over time and after reading these books, I began to see literacy achievement as a social construct. Literacy objectives are usually based on the values and experiences of those in charge. If children do not meet these objectives, they may be sorted, ranked, and marginalized, often along lines of race and class. I realized that teachers needed to do a better job of adjusting literacy instruction to match the needs of children in high-poverty communities, whose ways of using language and print do not always match school expectations. I also realized that teachers needed much more support to inquire about children's ways of using language and print, to teach in culturally congruent ways, and to identify and challenge the policies and practices interfering with literacy learning.

## The Uneven Playing Field

Upon graduation, I accepted a position at West Chester University, a Pennsylvania state university located about 25 miles west of Philadelphia. In my first year there, I taught a literacy practicum at a public elementary school in the affluent community of Radnor. At that time, I believed that it was the perfect setting for a field experience: The teachers were highly educated and modeled current literacy teaching practices, the physical environment was pleasant, and the children came from "good" homes. Each classroom looked like an exciting learning laboratory—full of class pets, museum artifacts, computers, math manipulatives, globes, maps, and lots of books. The library was state-of-the-art, stocked, and organized. An experienced librarian read to young children and helped older children with their research projects. Boys played football. Girls jumped rope and played hopscotch. Children climbed on shiny new playground equipment. Hearing children laugh and seeing them romp on the green, rolling hills reminded me of a Norman Rockwell painting.

Although my interns and I enjoyed this public school paradise, I became increasingly uncomfortable. I started to wonder about my priorities: Was I really helping to prepare my students to teach *all* children? Would they be prepared to teach reading and writing in an environment with many obstacles? In choosing this placement, did I reinforce the idea that teachers should strive to work in affluent suburban settings? By choosing this setting in which to mentor future teachers, what messages did I convey about whom to teach and where to teach? I knew I was not helping my students develop a consciousness about serving children of diverse backgrounds and cultures.

The following semester, I made arrangements to bring my students to Philadelphia public elementary schools. These schools were just a few miles' drive from my home west of the city. I lived in Lower Merion, a community well known for its excellent school district. City Line Avenue is a major thoroughfare that separates Philadelphia from Lower Merion.

When I had first moved to Philadelphia, the city had seemed more racially integrated than my home city of Boston. Traveling back and forth over City Line Avenue, however, I came to realize that Philadelphia contains many more racially isolated neighborhoods than racially integrated ones. Ninety-five percent of the residents in the community surrounding our two placement schools in West Philadelphia were black, and so the student population in these schools reflected the segregated status of the area.

After spending one semester working with these schools, I discovered similarities among them. African American women served as principals in these schools. Secretaries, cafeteria workers, and custodial staff were primarily black. About 60% to 80% of the teachers were white, depending on the school. None of these schools employed a librarian, and only one had a reading specialist (who often served as the assistant principal). The libraries contained shelves of books, but many of these books were old and their arrangement on the shelves was chaotic. Computers were decrepit, and classrooms did not have Internet access. Every classroom overflowed with children, sometimes more than 30. Children ate lunch in dimly lit basements and played on concrete playgrounds. There were no swings or jungle gyms.

But there were many bright spots within these schools. I found them when I asked principals to recommend the most successful teachers to serve as cooperating teachers to the interns. One teacher invited her students' families to her classroom for "cultural feasts," and nearly all of them came. This teacher was something of a scavenger: She acquired a copy machine to generate more print for her third graders to read, and she collected many books for her class library. Another teacher's classroom was alive with fish, hamsters, reptiles, and guinea pigs. She differentiated instruction using a large assortment of her own leveled books, purchased at yard sales and libraries. A group of teachers in another school collaborated after school to weave Afrocentric themes throughout the curriculum. All of these excellent teachers invested considerable time, energy, and money to do their jobs well.

Other teachers either did not or could not devote much of themselves to their work. I met several new teachers who seemed overwhelmed by their jobs. Few had mentors to help them through their first few years of teaching, and those who were assigned mentors had little time to meet with them. Some made it known that they were going to teach in the city for a few years and then get out.

I also met some veteran teachers who appeared worn down by the system. It was not unusual to hear these teachers yelling at children in classrooms and hallways. Often, these teachers blamed caregivers for the academic failures of children. They sometimes looked flustered as they marched passed me with lines of children following. I saw one teacher shove a child against a wall. I began to realize that teacher quality varied in these schools. Some children had excellent teachers, and some did not. I imagined that teachers in more affluent suburban schools who yelled at students or shoved students would be dismissed immediately. Teacher shortages in the city, however, meant that ineffective teachers would likely stay.

Juxtaposing my son's school in Lower Merion with the schools in Philadelphia crystallized for me the injustices of U.S. public schooling. His classroom was stocked with everything from Big Books to listening centers. The teacher, Mrs. Ray, was one of many who had applied for the position, and she had just been hired. She was an experienced teacher with a master's degree. One day, I arrived early to my son's classroom and found a "technology manager" sitting next to Mrs. Ray, helping her to learn the new computer system installed by the school district over the summer. My son would be able to use the Internet and an assortment of software on new computers. He would have a librarian, a reading specialist, and many highly educated support staff. Comparing his school experience with the experiences of those who attended our Philadelphia field placement schools, I began to understand how one's home address could make such a difference in the everyday school life of a child.

# Reinforcing Prejudice

Another revelation made me think about my responsibility to do something about the inequalities in education through teacher preparation. The first year I brought preservice teachers into the city for the internship, I discovered that just placing them in these classrooms was not the answer. One intern told me that he had just spoken with a teacher at one of the placement schools, who told him all about the children in his classroom and their caregivers. He explained, "I think I now know about the parents in that school. They don't care about their kids. They are either on drugs or in jail. You can't expect anything from them." This teacher had not developed positive relationships with parents, as I knew other teachers did.

I was stunned. It occurred to me that the experience of bringing interns into the city could actually reinforce misperceptions about the caregivers of children who lived there. I began to research ways teachers could better understand the caregivers of the children they tutored. Epstein (1988), a prominent researcher in the field of caregiver–teacher collaboration, studied how teacher outreach enhanced caregiver participation among primarily African American communities in Baltimore, Maryland, USA. Her research convinced me that there was much more we could do to prepare teachers to work in collaboration with caregivers and to learn from them. The question was how to help preservice teachers communicate with caregivers in a relaxed, nonintrusive way so as to learn more about their children and share some ways of helping caregivers help their children read at home. I drew from Edwards's (1995) research on caregiver–teacher conversations to design a caregiver communication project for the interns. Edwards writes about the significance of listening to caregivers and asking them relevant questions about children and their engagements with literacy.

The following semester, I arranged for interns to contact caregivers by telephone, and "caregiver stories" became part of our initial and final assessments of the children the interns tutored. About two thirds of the interns who were able to reach caregivers and talk about children came away with a much better sense of caregivers' perspectives and the out-of-school lives of children. Those who contacted caregivers and had successful conversations with them believed that these caregivers cared about their children, and these interns were less critical about caregivers' level of literacy support at home.

However, when caregivers were difficult to contact or did not return calls, it left interns with lingering doubts about caregivers' ability to nurture children's literacy at home. Perceptions of caregiver neglect, combined with observations of crowded classrooms and poor teaching, left many interns with a sense of hopelessness about children's literacy and their own ability to do anything about a system that produces so much failure. Although the interns shed some stereotypes about caregivers' ability to care, they still were caught up in a cycle of blaming both the school and the community at large for the literacy failures of children. Although enlightened by the process of working with these children, most interns saw themselves as permanent outsiders. Few opted for urban teaching after they graduated. Many times, I wondered if my efforts to prepare preservice teachers for urban schools were misplaced.

## Immersing in Culture

Even though I felt committed to the idea of educating teachers for urban schools, I had to admit that I was part of the problem. Most of my educational experiences did not help in this regard. I knew I had to place myself in situations in which I could learn more about the children and caregivers in this community.

I became motivated to learn about the ancestral heritage of children in the placement schools after attending a caregiver workshop at which book publisher Derrick Gantt spoke. He explained about the significance of reconstructing black heritage in storybooks so that black children will become aware of the rich ancestral heritage that is theirs. Gantt took the audience back to 350 B.C. to learn about Queen Candace of Ethiopia and her military prowess. He told us about Mansa Musa, who ruled Mali (now Ghana) beginning in 1312 and forged one of the largest and wealthiest empires in the world. After Gantt's talk, I began to scrutinize what I knew about the ancestral heritage of the children with whom I worked in the city. It was embarrassingly little.

During this time, I tried to learn as much as I could about the history, experiences, and perspectives of African Americans. This involved reading lots of books on my own, including fiction, poetry, folk tales, and biographies and other nonfiction works. I spent a lot more time sitting with the children in the field placement schools, talking to them about reading, writing, and life outside of school. I sat in many classrooms, observing excellent teachers relating to children. I talked with teachers of color in the city, who shared with me their perspectives on children and families. I put myself in closer contact with children's caregivers by facilitating caregiver workshops on reading at home.

Through these experiences, I learned about some of the concerns that united the primarily African American community in which we worked.

Poverty and racism underlie many of the problems that plague this community, including inequalities in health care, education, housing, and jobs. I also learned about the strength and significance of the church in the black community, the resilience and determination of black citizens and community leaders to make positive changes, and caregivers' concern about the education of their children. At the same time, I came to understand the divergent voices of this community in matters of integration, affirmative action, school vouchers, and language. For instance, the African American teachers in the graduate classes I taught were almost equally divided over whether teachers should learn about the linguistic derivations of Ebonics. One group took a vehement stand against it: "Why waste our time with this? What we need is to help kids speak standard English!" The other group countered: "But we need to have teachers who don't discount the language kids come to school with!" Although many in this community shared perspectives based on common historical and contemporary experiences, this was a community with many voices.

## Discovering Whiteness

At this time, I also joined various diversity-related committees and met educators who were committed to diversity awareness. I learned that many whites, like myself, can open our knapsack of unearned privileges—everything from walking into a store without being followed to living in any neighborhood we choose without the threat of harassment—simply because we are white (McIntosh, 1990). Whites can wear tattered jeans, misspell words, and snap gum in people's faces without anyone attributing these behaviors to the inferiority of their race. When I first talked to my education students about white privilege, I was not prepared for the resistance I met. I recall a student who rejected the idea completely: "My family is not rich. How have I been privileged? No one has handed me anything. In fact, my brother was denied a job because of affirmative action. If anything, whites don't have a chance these days!" Like her, many of my working class students did not *feel* privileged.

When I thought about my own family history and discovered the extent of my white privilege, I shared this history with the interns. For example, my grandfather, an Italian immigrant who came to the United States in the early 1900s, left school in the sixth grade to earn money for his family. Like other immigrants, he and his family believed that anything was possible if one worked hard enough. My grandfather worked in a woolens mill alongside other immigrants and a few African Americans. He was promoted to foreman within his first few years on the job. His dream was to own his own business, and so with the money he accumulated working in the mill, he secured a loan to buy a restaurant.

I asked my interns to consider these questions: What percentage of people of color would have been promoted to supervise white men in the 1940s? How likely would it have been for a person of color to secure a business loan in the 1950s? White privilege made it easier for my grandfather to establish financial independence and to pass along to his descendants the idea that hard work can make things possible.

The interns and I talked about why knowing all of this matters. I told them how I have benefited from the cultural, educational, and financial capital passed down to me by my grandparents and parents. Although we lived modestly, I cannot deny that white privilege improved my chances of achievement and that it has made generational progress more secure for my children. Revealing my own white privilege, inviting my (mostly white) students to reflect on their own family histories, and pointing out the unencumbered choices they make each day has helped my students acknowledge the phenomenon of white privilege.

## Discovering Racism

The realization that racism is a system of advantage based on race helped me understand my own responsibility in doing something about the problem. My students asked, Aren't things a lot better for black people today? I explained that although U.S. society has evolved from the days of separate drinking fountains, racism still permeates the society. I challenged my students to read *The Philadelphia Inquirer* for one week and to count the number of articles that addressed the topic of racism. They usually found at least five articles each week. I also told my students stories about my own experiences with racism.

For example, in 1997, I vacationed in New Hampshire with my family and stayed at a moderately priced hotel in Concord. I recalled passing through the hotel lobby on my way to my room as a young black couple entered and asked if there were any vacancies. I thought nothing of it when the hotel clerk told them the hotel was full. After all, it was Christmas vacation week. When I walked back to my room, it occurred to me that the hotel did not seem very full. In fact, my brother-in-law was able to get a room at the last minute. The incident smacked of discrimination, but I could not be sure. I picked up the phone and dialed the front desk. When the clerk answered, I said I had a brother in

Massachusetts who would drive up tonight if there was an available room. He said the hotel had several vacancies and asked if I would prefer a smoking or nonsmoking room. I said I would get back to him and hung up the phone. Even though the incident bothered me, I did not seek to do anything about it. This story shows a time in my life when I did not acknowledge racism as an institutionalized phenomenon that limits opportunities for certain people, nor did I see my own responsibility to do something about the problem.

My studies in this area eventually helped me to see racism as being institutionalized through policies and practices that determine one's access to social, cultural, and economic resources (Tatum, 1999). Any policy, however unofficial, of refusing people based on race is an example of racism. As an institutionalized force, racism often is concealed under a cloak of "procedure": "This is the way we do business." "This is the way we run our club." "This is the way we make hiring decisions."

When I ask my students to notice policies and practices that systematically favor one group over another, they often report on that which is observed readily. For instance, a few students have mentioned that while shopping, black customers seem to be supervised more closely than whites. Yet these students often miss the subtle—and more insidious—forms of institutional racism. One semester, I took a group of students to hear a lecture by Temple University professor Charles Blockson, who spoke about the accomplishments of black people throughout Philadelphia's history. At the end of the lecture, he reminded my students that if they lived in Chester County, Pennsylvania, they ought to know about the significance of southeastern Pennsylvania as a major route for those traveling the Underground Railroad. Afterward, some of my students told me they felt cheated by their own education. They had been completely unaware of the contributions made by black citizens to Pennsylvania's history and about the local geography related to this history. My students began to see how the official school curriculum had limited their awareness of so many kinds of people who did not claim a European heritage. They realized that seemingly innocuous tasks, such as selecting textbooks and designing curricula, are affected by racial and class-based privilege.

## Being a Perpetual Learner and Change Agent

According to Ladson-Billings (2001), most teacher educators tend to be white, middle class professors who resist change because they perceive it as difficult, time-consuming, and risky. In *Crossing Over to Canaan* (2001), Ladson-Billings states, "They (teacher educators) often work hard at reproducing the same kinds of teachers they have had for decades" (p. 6). I was one of these teacher educators. In accepting responsibility for preparing teachers for urban communities, I have worked hard at changing my views. My goal now is to work with others to press for changes in the ways teachers are being educated, as part of a larger social action mission.

I do this work even though I have not yet arrived at the enlightened state to which I aspire. No matter how many children and caregivers I have met, or how many diversity workshops I have given and attended, I am still learning. Every once in a while, I trip on my own naïveté. At a recent literacy conference, for example, I met a Latino researcher who told me about the first time she had attended that conference: "I looked around at the sea of white faces and I wanted to cry. I didn't want to be here. There was nobody who looked like me or spoke like me. I told myself I didn't belong." Why was I surprised to learn that this woman, who held a doctoral degree and a teaching position at a major university, felt awkward at this conference? I took for granted that all of "us educated folk" are a welcoming bunch. I did not imagine that the prevalence of whites would be so unsettling for the few educators of color who had similar credentials.

This means I still have a lot to learn. The conversation described above with the Latino educator affirmed for me the importance of being in the company of others and of interrogating my own assumptions and knowledge. As Howard (1999) writes, "As white educators, we cannot fully know or experience the struggles of our students and colleagues of color, but we can work to create an empathetic environment in which their stories and experiences can be acknowledged and shared" (p. 75).

Looking back at my journey, several qualities of my growth now stand out: (1) It is continually evolving, (2) it is difficult and risky, (3) it requires personal motivation fueled by a desire for social justice, and (4) it is nurtured through external means (people, programs, settings). The significance of this last point is huge. Had it not been for certain educational opportunities, I may not have taken this path. This is why I am convinced that teacher education and professional development hold so much promise for those who have not yet committed themselves to see teaching as an act of social justice.

You may have a better head start than I did. I grew up in a much more racially and culturally segregated world than many who are now teachers or are learning to be teachers. Also, there are many more opportunities today for teachers to grow in their cultural sensitivity than I was afforded as a young adult. The presence of poor children of color in public school classrooms is a much larger reality now than it was 20 years ago. How well you serve these children will depend on your beliefs about their potential to learn and on your capacity to nurture their growth. Both of these require that you examine your own perceptions about children in particular cultural communities and place yourself in settings where you can learn to be an effective teacher of these children.

## Conclusion

In the next chapter, I present a rationale for the need for us to be culturally sensitive literacy teachers. First, I look at the ways in which low expectations of children have a negative impact on teaching behaviors. Then, I contrast these ways of looking at children with those of successful teachers of children in high-poverty schools. Successful teachers work collaboratively with colleagues in schools that are invested in student learning. They also believe in children's inherent capacity to learn, and work hard at knowing what to do to support children's development. This requires knowing much more about children and their cultural communities, and as part of this inquiry, scrutinizing one's prejudicial views about children and caregivers in high-poverty communities.

---

## REFLECTION AND INQUIRY

1. Begin to write your own cultural autobiography. Include your thoughts on the following:

- your earliest memories of noticing racial or cultural differences
- how your views about your own and others' cultures have been shaped through family, community, school, work, the media, and society
- the times your understandings about yourself and others have been challenged
- your discoveries about people who are culturally different from you

# CHAPTER 3

# Cultivating Culturally Sensitive Literacy Educators

*A primary source of stereotyping is often the teacher preparation program itself. It is in these programs that teachers learn that poor students and students of color should be expected to achieve less than their "mainstream" counterparts.*

—Lisa Delpit, *Other People's Children: Cultural Conflict in the Classroom*, p. 172

Underestimating or misjudging children's intellectual potential can have a permanent effect on the ways they are educated in school. For instance, disproportionate numbers of black children have been placed in special education classes, even though only a small percentage of these children have the neurological or perceptual problems that would justify their need for this kind of placement (Coles, 1987). Many of these children are permanently placed in low-ability tracks as they continue in school, with negative consequences for realizing their own academic potential (Bartoli & Botel, 1988).

In general, teachers cannot serve children well if they fail to see children's fullest potential, or if they believe something is inherently wrong with a child's culture (Ladson-Billings, 1994). Many teachers blame children's caregivers for neglecting their responsibility to prepare their children for the demands of school (Ascher, 1988). Assumptions about alternative family structures also have an impact on teachers' perceptions of children's literacy potential (Jones & Blendinger, 1994; Midkiff & Lawler-Prince, 1992). Foster families, single-parent families, or families headed by grandparents or other extended family members are often perceived as less likely to offer the same range of home literacy experiences as those of traditional nuclear families. Also, teachers tend to assume that single and working caregivers cannot be approached or relied on (Epstein, 1986).

Low expectations of children can create two counterproductive teaching styles that emerge from different perspectives on caring about children (Brophy, 1998). Sometimes, teachers who perceive children as being at risk show they care by applying a "law and order" teaching style in which controlling children's behavior is the primary goal. In this approach, children are rewarded or punished based on adherence to teachers' rules for specific outcomes: perfect papers, sitting up straight, standing in line. In these classrooms, processes of learning that involve making approximations and constructing knowledge are undervalued. The underlying premise is that children need to be controlled because they lack the intrinsic ability to make reasonable decisions for themselves.

The other counterproductive teaching style is the sympathetic stance, in which the teacher feels sorry for the children and tries to compensate for the children's perceived lowered abilities by reducing expectations, reinforcing incorrect answers, and accepting low-quality work. In time, children realize that the teacher is disingenuous, and their intrinsic desire to learn is reduced. In both situations, children internalize the messages "I am one who needs to be controlled," "I am one who is unable to do high-quality work," or "I am one who cannot be trusted."

One problem with focusing on teachers' low expectations is that it shifts the blame for literacy failure onto teachers and, consequently, diminishes the importance of other factors that contribute to low achievement (Nieto, 2000). It also does not make sense to blame teachers when the programs that are charged with educating them have not done enough to help them see the academic potential of children who live in high-poverty urban neighborhoods. Many new teachers continue to become certified without the critical experiences needed to understand these children, their caregivers, and their communities. Although cultural diversity education is making a big impact on teacher education, these programs do not and cannot provide all of what is needed for teachers to understand children and their communities. Teachers need to self-educate in areas where these programs fall short.

Lacking an understanding of the complexity of literacy achievement leaves teachers vulnerable to this blaming of children and caregivers for low literacy achievement. Consequently, in this chapter I describe some of the attributes and actions of successful teachers in high-poverty urban communities, including knowledge of literacy teaching and knowledge of children and their communities. I will focus on this latter category of teacher expertise throughout this book and argue that many teachers, especially those who are outsiders to these communities, need time and support to gain this community knowledge.

## Looking at Teachers and Schools That Make a Difference

Teachers who achieve success with children in high-poverty communities can serve as our models in this discussion. The highly qualified, expert teacher is a key factor in the literacy achievement formula. Children learn to read when they attend schools that are filled with teachers who expect excellence and who give children the support they need to achieve it (Adler & Fisher, 2001; Bartoli, 2001; Taylor, Pearson, Clark, & Walpole, 1999).

Research that looks at the differences between most- and least-accomplished teachers has found that most-accomplished teachers had higher student engagement, provided more small-group instruction, coached children during reading, asked more high-level comprehension questions, engaged children in more independent reading, and communicated more with caregivers (Taylor, Pearson, Clark, & Walpole, 2000). Similarly, Pressley et al. (1998) found that the best elementary literacy teachers kept children engaged in reading and writing tasks for much of the school day, taught literacy skills through meaningful reading-writing events, monitored student progress, tailored instruction to students' needs, and encouraged children's growth.

Although the individual teacher has a powerful influence in the classroom, it takes more than a few expert teachers to affect literacy achievement. Communities of effective educators also need to work together to make a difference. Taylor, Pressley, and Pearson (2000) looked at five large-scale studies of high-performing schools in moderate to high-poverty communities and found six factors common to these schools:

1. Prioritizing student learning (found in four out of the five studies)—Teachers, caregivers, the principal, and the school staff worked together to realize their goal of substantially improved student learning.

2. Strong school leadership (found in three of the five studies)—Leadership, often from the principal, galvanized the school community toward improvement, engendered a collective sense of responsibility, and supported school staff by providing professional education and collaboration opportunities.

3. Strong teacher collaboration (found in four of the five studies)—Teachers were given time to work together to support student learning.

4. Assessment-based teaching (found in four of the five studies)—Student assessment information was used to tailor instruction to children's needs.

5. Professional development (found in four of the five studies)—Ongoing professional development and experimentation with new research-based ideas and practices was encouraged.

6. Caregiver communication/collaboration (found in all five studies)—School staffs made efforts to reach out to caregivers and work with them to improve student achievement.

These schoolwide factors reveal much about the particular characteristics and attitudes of those who are employed in these schools. These schools function well because they are staffed by educators who prioritize student learning, assume responsibility for this outcome, respect children and their caregivers, believe in children's literacy potential, and are willing to work with others (including caregivers) to achieve success. In order to act in these ways, teachers need to believe in children and do what is necessary to support their development. These ways of thinking and acting require qualities that extend beyond knowing how to teach children to read and write.

## The Culturally Sensitive Literacy Teacher

The teachers in a study by Ladson-Billings (1994) saw their roles as critical to improving children's academic achievement, and so they expected and aimed for children's academic excellence. These teachers respected children and their families, viewed knowledge as being critical and as being constructed jointly by teachers and students, knew about students' cultures and used this information to teach the children, respected the teaching profession and their own professional worth, and challenged school policies they believed interfered with children's learning. These behaviors required teachers to believe in children and to value their cultures.

Literacy teachers who are culturally sensitive know about and respect children's home languages, validating these languages through the classroom use of associated literature, poetry, and song. They also recognize children's need to use ways of speaking and writing for certain settings and purposes

(Perry & Delpit, 1998). These teachers teach literacy skills explicitly in the context of meaningful, purposeful reading and writing experiences (Delpit, 1995). They carefully choose activities most conducive to helping children try standard ways of using language, such as writing and formal oral presentations, because these events allow for preparation and reflection. These teachers also know that correcting dialect-related miscues during reading aloud could produce children who resist reading (Delpit, 1995). They use multicultural texts in the classroom and invite critical responses to this literature (Wolf, 2000). These teachers also engage children in social action projects that help children realize their own power to change the world (Banks, 1999).

Culturally sensitive literacy teachers see caregivers and others in the community as resources for supporting children's literacy achievement (Cairney & Munsie, 1995). As teachers invite the perspectives of caregivers and other community members, they continue to understand more about children's home language and literacy practices (Edwards, Pleasants, & Franklin, 1999; Lazar, 1998; Lazar & Weisberg, 1996; Shockley, 1994; Shockley, Michalove, & Allen, 1995). Extending themselves beyond the classroom is also critical for teachers in understanding the immediate (home, school) and larger (poverty, racism) systems that influence school achievement.

These ways of thinking and acting align with a diverse constructivist orientation (Au, 1998). Based on Cummins's (1986) theoretical framework for empowering minority students, a diverse constructivist orientation considers "the links between events in the school and conditions in the larger society, the centrality of the teacher's role in mediating learning, the inseparability of affective or motivational factors and academic achievement, and the connections between schooled knowledge and personal experience" (Au, p. 304). Au drew from Cummins's work to construct a conceptual framework that specifically addresses literacy education. She proposed that students from diverse backgrounds could achieve in literacy if educators would do the following:

1. establish students' ownership of literacy as the overarching goal (p. 309)

2. recognize the importance of students' home languages and come to see biliteracy as an attainable and desirable outcome (p. 310)

3. use materials that present diverse cultures in an authentic manner, especially through the works of authors from diverse backgrounds (p. 310)

4. become culturally responsive in their management of classrooms and interactions with students (p. 311)

5. make stronger links to the community (p. 312)

6. provide students with both authentic literacy activities and a considerable amount of instruction in specific literacy skills needed for full participation in the culture of power (pp. 312–313)

7. use forms of assessment that eliminate or reduce sources of bias (such as prior knowledge, language, and question type) and more accurately reflect students' literacy achievement (p. 313)

Within this framework, successful educators' actions are focused on leveling the playing field for culturally diverse children by validating what they bring to the classroom and empowering students to take control over their learning. We can admire and learn from these excellent teachers. But the big question, and one that cannot be answered by watching them teach, is how they came to be such great teachers. How did they come to care about children, believe in children's inherent abilities, and see their own responsibility to teach these children? Can these qualities be taught to teachers who have little cultural connection to their students?

## A Disconnect Between Teachers and Children and Communities

The questions mentioned above become important because of the cultural differences between those who teach and those who are taught. Although the teaching force is largely white, students are becoming more culturally diverse. Between 1986 and 1996, the number of whites in public schools nationwide increased by just 3%, but the number of black students increased by 14% and the number of Hispanic students rose by 45% (Clotfelter, 2001). In many school districts across the United States, African Americans and Hispanic Americans now represent the majority, challenging the very notion of "minority" status. In all probability, most teachers will someday work with students whose cultural backgrounds are different from their own. Teachers' beliefs about the language and literacy potential of these children will have an impact on how they will serve these children in the classroom.

Most teachers, as well as students of education, prefer to teach in suburban public schools like those they once attended (Chisholm, 1994; Gay, 1993).

My experiences with undergraduates suggest that fears about violence and the challenges of teaching in financially strapped school districts keep many teachers from pursuing jobs in high-poverty communities. Assumptions about the children and families in these communities have an impact on teachers' decisions about choosing field placements during the teacher education program. This was certainly true for a former student of mine, Melissa.

Melissa sat in my office after the first day of class. All the other "nonurban" sections of the literacy internship had been filled and she was "stuck" with the one I taught in the city of Philadelphia. I had assigned her to intern in a school that served mostly African American and some Asian children in a working-class section of the city. Her scowl and crossed arms at this meeting suggested that something was wrong. She began, "You know, I have serious concerns about going to the Flemming Elementary School. It's dangerous around that school. A guy was shot in that neighborhood last week. Is there another school I could go to? How about in the suburbs? My parents would definitely have a problem with this whole arrangement. You understand, don't you?"

Melissa was not ready to accept her role as one who could learn to be a teacher in this community. The problem was, Melissa and others in the program who felt as she did would be certified to teach *all* children in a few months. Their fears would prevent them from even considering teaching careers in high-poverty urban communities. My experience indicates that even if they decide to teach in such communities, students like Melissa often bring with them misconceptions about children's language and literacy potential that prevent them from serving the children well.

There are also teachers who, through various experiences, have been able to question their assumptions about children in high-poverty communities and are seeking to learn more about these children and their communities in order to form stronger connections between themselves and the children they teach. Because everyone brings a spectrum of experiences and attitudes to the classroom, one cannot assume anything about people's assorted cultural understandings. What is known for sure, though, is that cultural sensitivity education for literacy educators has largely been left to chance and, although they are being certified to teach all children, most teachers are not ready for this responsibility.

Deeply entrenched views, such as Melissa's, about African Americans living in high-poverty urban communities are a natural consequence of breathing the racist air that surrounds us, as Tatum (1999) suggests. African

Americans have been targets of racial stereotyping for generations. Television news flashes and newspaper photos featuring urban crime have influenced America's social consciousness. Even that which is identified as social science has contributed to the misrepresentation of African Americans. Only one generation ago, Baratz and Baratz (1970) examined the available research on black children's achievement that focused on the deficits of their home and community environments. This research suggested that children raised in impoverished environments lacked the verbal stimulation needed for language development and abstract thinking.

Although the ideas of biological deficit and cultural deprivation have been largely dismissed over the past few decades, there are still some who continue to resurrect deficit theories to explain why black children do not achieve as their white counterparts do. In their book, *The Bell Curve: Intelligence and Class Structure in American Life* (1996), Herrnstein and Murray try to establish African Americans' genetic predisposition to academic failure, suggesting that inequalities stem from these inherited deficits, and contend that society should accept this as a fact of life. Unfortunately, news reports of African American children failing at school only appear to support such assumptions of these children's intellectual and linguistic inferiority.

These theories have been replaced by new understandings. Black English is grammatical, rule-bound, complex, capable of expressing abstract thought, and acquired through day-to-day immersion in one's language community (Labov, 1972; Perry & Delpit, 1998; Rickford & Rickford, 2000). Old assumptions that African American children lack familiarity with written language are now challenged through ethnographic studies that find that literacy is deeply embedded in the culture of low-income African American families and communities, functioning primarily as an aspect of pragmatic human activity rather than isolated skills (Taylor & Dorsey-Gaines, 1988).

## Teacher Education

Having taught many preservice teachers over the years, I am convinced of the need for educators to examine how perceptions of children and families evolve. How have educators been influenced by media representations of the urban poor and by research that reflects deficit views of particular communities? To what extent have societal messages about children's language and environments shaped our expectations of children's literacy achievement? We must respond to these questions so that we do not perpetuate a history of blaming children and families, but instead see our own responsibility for making achievement in high-poverty schools possible.

I have presented research that shows teachers in successful high-poverty schools taking responsibility for children's academic success because they believe in the inherent potential of these children and work with others in their schools to develop it. I look to teacher education as a powerful influence for helping teachers to think and act in these ways. The past decade produced an explosion of literature that is now used to guide teacher education programs in the area of multiculturalism (Banks, 1999; Bennett, 1999; Howard, 1999; Ladson-Billings, 1994; Nieto, 2000; Sleeter, 1991; Smith, 1998), including literature that specifically looks at culturally responsive literacy teaching (Delpit, 1995; Schmidt & Mosenthal, 2001; Xu, 2000). Based on this body of work, several programs have evolved to educate literacy teachers for urban and high-poverty communities through cultural immersion experiences (Hinchman & Grace, 2002; Leland & Harste, 2002; Lenski, Crawford, Crumpler, & Stallworth, 2002; Schmidt, 2002). The problem is that programs like these are not available to all education students and teachers.

Haberman (1996) reports that teacher preparation programs have made efforts to add multicultural content but that these are little more than add-on programs, not integral to the design of the teacher education program. He charges that universities have made only superficial commitments to preparing graduates for urban classrooms and that diversity education happens more by chance than by a deliberate plan. Research has found that preservice teachers require programs that treat diversity education in a systematic and thoughtful way, as these students tend to hold to racial stereotypes (Gomez, 1993; Guillaume, Zuniga, & Yee, 1998), particularly toward black English (Bowie & Bond, 1994; Harber, 1979). Wiggins and Follo (1999), for example, found that their efforts to explicitly address diversity issues in one field-based urban practicum produced more confident preservice teachers. Many preservice teachers, however, continued to underestimate children's abilities and to express doubts about teaching in urban schools.

Given the variation among teacher education programs, many graduates of these programs have not been helped to confront their biases toward children of color in high-poverty communities. It is no wonder, then, that so many teachers decide not to teach in these communities. Of those who do choose to begin careers in these schools, about one half exit them within the first five years of teaching (Darling-Hammond & Sclan, 1996), leaving disproportionate numbers of children with emergency-certified or noncertified teachers. High rates of teacher turnover in high-poverty schools leave the children who need the most support in literacy with less access to high-quality, experienced teachers.

There are many reasons why teachers leave these schools, and it is difficult to uncover truths about why so many do so after a few years. I have wondered whether this exodus reflects a cultural disconnect between these teachers and their students. Although there is no reliable research that correlates teachers' decisions to leave these classrooms with their levels of cultural sensitivity, I have found that preservice teachers have many misconceptions about children, caregivers, and communities, despite their different experiences with cultural diversity.

Strengthening teacher education programs to include more intensive, systematic, and meaningful studies of cultural diversity will help graduates, but it is only a start. There is only so much room in undergraduate programs to help preservice teachers become culturally sensitive. Issues such as racism and privilege, language variation, sociocultural influences of literacy achievement, culturally responsive teaching, elements of culture, and social action require a lot of thoughtful study and are made meaningful through immersion in high-poverty communities (Smith, 1998). Teacher education programs are already crowded with other important curricula, including general education courses and professional education courses. Even the most solid program cannot deliver what teachers really need to become the exemplary culturally sensitive literacy teachers discussed earlier.

So, although teacher education programs must strive to offer cultural diversity curricula to their students, the responsibility also lies with teachers themselves to become more culturally literate. As one who grew up with little connection to poverty or people of color, I have been struck by how much time it takes to get to know some fundamental things about a community and the children and caregivers who live there and by how much more I need to know. My experience leads me to believe that this kind of growth must extend well beyond teacher education programs, although it is important that these programs inspire this growth.

In the next chapter, I will discuss the interns' initial perceptions of children and caregivers before they began the internship. Their perceptions provide a picture of attitudes and assumptions that mirror those of many preservice teachers.

# REFLECTION AND INQUIRY

1. Do you know any teachers who are working successfully in high-poverty schools? What are some of their qualities?

2. Think about why you prefer to teach in a particular community. In what ways has your background or culture shaped your choice?

3. Assess the ways you have been educated to serve children in high-poverty communities. How has your education helped or hindered your ability to do this?

# CHAPTER 4

# Revealing Preconceptions of Children, Caregivers, and Classrooms

*When I walked into that classroom, I had already judged everyone. I didn't give anyone a chance. I knew no one there before I started, but I believed the stereotypes that we have all heard over and over again.*

—Jason, intern

*I expected some kind of war zone when I found out I would be in Philadelphia:* Stand [and Deliver] *meets* Apocalypse Now. *All the horror stories I had seen on television and all that were told to me by fellow students helped to cement this image in my head. I envisioned uncaring teachers trying to cope with undisciplined students who went home to uncaring parents.*

—Dawn, intern

Jason, Dawn, and most of the other interns I worked with who were setting foot in urban classrooms for the first time had already formed impressions about the children and caregivers in this community, even though most of the interns had not spent time in urban communities or interacted with people of color. Their low expectations of children's intellect, literacy and language abilities, and social/emotional adjustment revealed ingrained prejudices. These students were only one semester away from being certified as teachers. Unless they confronted these prejudices, these soon-to-be teachers would most likely carry them into the classroom, and bringing these attitudes to the classroom would prevent them from seeing children's literacy potential.

# A Framework for Examining Perceptions

How we see ourselves and others is a reflection of several socially defined dimensions of identity: race, class, gender, language, religion, sexual orientation, intelligence, physical ability/attractiveness, age, and so forth. Identity is made even more complex by the idea that these dimensions of identity can be seen as either dominant (holding the power and authority in society) or subordinate (targeted by the dominant group as substandard) (Tatum, 1999). For example, men have traditionally held positions of power in many societies around the world. But power and authority are not conferred to all men equally. Each man will see himself and others according to the other dimensions of identity that make up his total self and according to the power invested in these dimensions by members of particular societies. In the United States, a poor, uneducated, male senior citizen may see himself (and be seen) as subordinate to a wealthy, college-educated, younger man because affluence, education, and youth are viewed as assets in mainstream U.S. society.

According to Tatum (1999), almost everyone experiences some form of subordination, and this makes it easier to share experiences cross-culturally: "To the extent that one can draw on one's own experience of subordination— as a young person, as a person with a disability, as someone who grew up poor, as a woman—it may be easier to make meaning of another targeted group's experience" (p. 27). Problems arise when members of dominant groups do not acknowledge their power and privilege, or when they simply see themselves as "normal." When this is the case, they cannot really know about the experiences of "others" or acknowledge the existence of inequality.

Race (as a social construct) and class were two salient dimensions of identity for the interns in this study. The interns were white, and they came from mostly suburban, middle class homes. They did not see the relative privileges conferred on them by being members of these social groups. They did not understand the experiences of racially different others, nor did they understand quite how race and class shaped others' access to literacy education. Their explanations for literacy failure were grounded in racist notions about the deficits of children and caregivers. This undermined their ability to serve children in the literacy classroom. To serve children well, they needed to learn to see their own dominance (e.g., their own opportunities to access education, etc.) and the dominance of a school curriculum in which the ground rules for literacy achievement are set by those in power. This is the point at which we could begin to unravel ideas about children's literacy capacity and about the interns' own capacity to teach.

As a framework for looking at interns' shifting ways of seeing themselves and others from the perspectives of race and culture, I drew from Howard's (1999) work in the area of white identity. According to Howard, the ignorance, confusion, and fear underlying racial prejudice reflects a fundamentalist orientation toward diversity. Fundamentalists have a Western-centric view of what is right and true. Although they may not be openly hostile toward people of color, they believe that whites are inherently superior. Many avoid cross-cultural interactions. Fundamentalists also tend to be oblivious to their own whiteness and its significance, and, therefore, they tend to see themselves as "typical" or "normal" and others as "abnormal" or "different." They may react with anger, denial, or defensiveness when confronted with the issue of their own racism, a stance that a few students in each of my classes took. Fundamentalist teachers often adopt a "colorblind" attitude and assert that they do not see color in the classroom, or at least that they do not pay attention to it.

Howard, in his research, distinguishes between fundamentalists and integrationists. Integrationists are those who are beginning to acknowledge diverse perspectives. This stage of cultural awareness is characterized by a beginning awareness of racism but a lack of depth in understanding it, its sociohistorical influences, and its relation to Western hegemony. Integrationists' feelings about multiculturalism often are characterized by curiosity about others. Integrationists can exhibit ambivalence, guilt, shame, denial, and other forms of dissonance when they make discoveries about racial inequality and whites' culpability in it. Even though they may acknowledge that whites perpetuate racism, they tend not to accept personal responsibility for racism.

# Existing Misconceptions

## *Choosing an Urban Placement*

Before discussing the interns' perceptions about children and the community, it is important to discuss some of their purposes for taking the internship. My internship course section was clearly identified in the university's master schedule as an urban placement. Some students signed up for the internship because they believed it would help them be better teachers for all children. Others were less invested in their own learning and more anxious about their job prospects after graduation; these interns believed that an urban placement would look great on their resumes. Others felt curious about inner-city schools and wanted to see for themselves what they were like. None of these interns had specific intentions to teach in these schools after graduation.

For some interns, the urban placement was not a first choice. A few were "stuck" with the urban placement because other sections of the course were filled by the time they were allowed to register for courses. Yet they needed to take the internship in order to student teach the following semester. A subset of these students reacted with fear and avoidance, an emotional response to differences that fits with a fundamentalist orientation toward diversity. A few students later shared these concerns in retrospective accounts of their growth in the course:

> When I scheduled last semester for this class I tried my best to get it without an urban experience. I even tried to talk with a professor I had heard didn't have a class going to Philadelphia. My efforts were obviously useless, so I spent the summer worrying about going to a school in the city. I was concerned about issues such as race, violence, lack of motivation, and just not enjoying the experience. —Amy

> My thoughts about coming to this school were not very enthusiastic. I pictured myself slaving over a map, trying to figure out different ways to drive into the city without going through the ghettos. For a (very) brief moment, purchasing a bulletproof vest came to mind. And trying to think of ways to contact the mother of my students (because who knows where the father may be?) was also a challenge I wondered if I was going to have to face. —Joyce

Only a few interns wrote about their fears and concerns in taking the urban literacy placement, and they did so at the end of the course. I reasoned that those who felt this way might have previously been reluctant to share their concerns in a class where cross-cultural understanding was valued.

## Initial Views of the Children

Although fundamentalist views were not openly expressed by most interns, expressions of prejudice surfaced in their anonymous written statements and surveys. In a survey filled out by the interns prior to meeting children in the field, 79% of the interns agreed that white children were "emotionally well adjusted," yet only 26% believed this to be true of black children. The interns believed that their cooperating teachers would need to spend a lot of time disciplining unruly children:

> I expect the children to be less disciplined in the urban schools—less likely to do as they are told. Children in the inner city tend to have less parental guidance at home, therefore, they are more prone to behavior problems at school. —Beth
>
> Students are not motivated and have an attitude. —Lynne
>
> The teachers cannot really teach because they are dealing with too many discipline problems. —Maggie
>
> Some teachers can be stressed out because of the lack of discipline of the students, the heavy load of students per teacher, the lack of resources, and the lack of parental involvement. —Rachel
>
> Teachers often have to deal with more behavioral problems than any other aspect in the classroom. —Joshua

Although behavioral concerns topped most interns' lists of perceptions about the children with whom they were about to work, many interns anticipated that the children would have academic difficulties, particularly in learning to read and write. Across almost every category of literacy and language engagement, children in these Philadelphia schools were assumed to be less interested in books, less proficient in acquiring language and communicating, less apt to read for pleasure and meaning, less apt to read on grade level, less able to think critically and creatively, and less apt to have favorite authors or books than suburban students. This assertion also was supported by interns' comments after just one visit to the schools, when many of them discovered that most of the children enjoyed reading and writing experiences: Many interns responded with some variation of "I was surprised to see that these children really do enjoy reading."

## Initial Views of the Caregivers

For the most part, the children were assumed to be victims of bad parenting. When interns wrote about their expectations of the caregivers of children in their placement schools, many made direct statements linking caregivers' behavior with children's poor school performance:

> Many are not simply around much so there is not much parental influence for the children. —Monica
>
> The parents are not involved in their children's education so children suffer. —Anne
>
> The children are mostly from families who either care or don't care about the education needed for a child to grow. So it may be frustrating when the support from home is not there. —Andrea

I do believe there will be a high number of parents in the lower socioeconomic status because of the urban setting. This may cause them not to be as interested in their children's schoolwork. —Christina

I have heard that the parents do not seem to give their children encouragement to do well in school. —Kim

Of the interns, about three fourths expected minimal academic support for children at home. Most interns blamed poor economic conditions and caregivers' need to work long hours:

Both parents need to work so it can be difficult to have them involved with the classroom. —Beth

Some parents may work long hours to support the family and hence have little time to help children with school. Some parents may not value education highly and pass those opinions on to their kids. —Dawn

However, a few interns saw economic hardship as a factor that might enhance caregivers' desire to support their children in school:

I would assume that as a working class–middle class parent, they [caregivers] would be fairly involved with their children's progress. Most people of working class [status] would rather their children have a better life that is made easier by education. —Kelly

More often though, interns assumed a lack of caregiver support because of the depressed economic environment and because they believed there would be many single-parent households in the community. Many interns felt that these single parents would be too inundated with problems and responsibilities to support their children's academic needs:

I think that when there is a two-parent family, involvement in education is easier because while one parent works, the other can help the children. —Jason

Most interns believed that caregivers were primarily responsible for neglecting children's early literacy needs (reading to children from an early age, teaching the alphabet, pointing out environmental print). These interns perceived urban and suburban caregivers very differently in the levels of literacy support they give to their children. For instance, 90% of the interns believed that white caregivers provided books at home for their children, yet only 10% believed that black caregivers did. Likewise, most interns thought that white caregivers read to their children, but only 14% felt that black caregivers read to their children. Across other categories of home literacy activity, black caregivers were thought to be less supportive than white caregivers in the categories of teaching children to read, bringing children to the library, pointing out environmental print to children, and serving as models to the children by reading for themselves. Despite these results, interns believed that black caregivers wanted their children to read just as much as white caregivers did. Also, most interns surveyed believed that caregivers would like to help their children to read but did not necessarily know how to do this.

Some comments received from interns reflected a belief that caregivers simply did not care about their children's literacy success. The following statement by one intern clearly reveals this attitude:

> In Philadelphia, there will be little to no parent involvement [in helping children learn to read]. Some will care but due to work will be unable to participate. There will be the rest who just won't bother. Education will not be a factor for these children. —Joyce

Comments such as this revealed an impression that urban caregivers undermined children's literacy achievement through socioeconomic circumstances, negligence, or a blatant disregard for academic success. It was the general belief among the interns that children came from homes where caregivers did not, could not, or would not support children's academic achievement.

The interns were far more critical of caregivers than they were of schools. In fact, many of the interns expected that urban schools would meet children's literacy needs. Their written comments focused on the positive qualities of urban teachers, especially their dedication and their concern for children. Although many interns anticipated shortages of texts and supplies and overcrowded classrooms, they did not see these as primary constraints to children's literacy achievement. Rather, caregivers were held responsible for the literacy achievement of children. The interns' impressions about literacy failure for black children were simplistic: poverty causes poor caregiving, and a lack of caregiver support at home causes literacy failure.

## The Roots of Prejudice

I found that when the interns worked with children who read below grade level, they either assumed that caregivers were negligent in teaching children to read or that children were too cognitively deficient to develop "normally" in literacy. The interns' limited exposure to issues of race and culture left them with few other explanations about children's academic failures. In tracing back over their own cultural histories (see the Appendix), many interns realized that growing up in predominantly white communities and knowing few African Americans had fueled these misconceptions. Many commented that family members and the media influenced their perceptions. Such was the case with Marie, an intern whose experiences prior to coming to the university had shaped her views about the children she would someday meet in Philadelphia.

## Marie

Marie was like many of the young women who joined my internship to learn about urban classrooms. A 19-year-old white woman, she was one of the approximately 90% of my students who had lived in an Anglo-centered world prior to coming to college. While growing up in a large suburban community in eastern Pennsylvania, Marie had associated almost exclusively with whites. She believed that her isolation from people of color limited her opportunities to think much about the issues of race.

Marie formed impressions of African Americans through the descriptions of others—her parents, other relatives, community members, and the media. Marie claimed to have been oblivious as a child to racist comments about people of color, but said she had grown more aware of the prejudices of her parents and extended family members:

> I did not realize until I went to high school that my family was very prejudiced against African American people. I guess they never really said anything in front of me when I was younger because I never heard anyone talk badly about other races. Throughout my high school career, I began noticing racial comments, jokes, and slurs made by my relatives, but I did not do anything about it. I grew up thinking that this behavior was normal.

Marie also believed that her views about African Americans had been shaped by the media:

> When I watched the news, almost every crime or felony has occurred in some part of Philadelphia. The boarded up houses, graffiti on the scenery, and run down homes gave me a feeling that the neighborhoods are not safe. Movies were one of the biggest things that scared me about going into the city. Movies that depicted kids in gangs, killing people, robbing people…just plain out of

control. These same movies show the parents as not caring, on drugs, and living in poverty.

Marie said that the schools she attended did not provide many opportunities to know students of color, even though she graduated from a racially integrated high school:

> I was raised in an all white middle-class neighborhood; I attended elementary and middle school with almost all white middle class children. There may have been one or two non-white students in the entire school. I am not saying that black students were not allowed in my school, or even that they were shunned away from the school. They didn't live in my neighborhood, and therefore were not in my school. They mostly lived in a low-class slum neighborhood, known as the "projects." There was an elementary and middle school in their neighborhood which they attended. Not until I attended high school, and all of the middle school students from the general area were combined, were large numbers of black students in my classes, and in the school itself. (I think the ratio was about two thirds white and one third black.) And the black students always seemed to be the trouble-makers, the ones who were in the principal's office every day for detention. In high school, the kids of different races tended to sit with each other at lunch and hang out together after school. There was not a lot of integration. I never paid much attention to them.

Most interns agreed that they learned very little about the views, experiences, and histories of people of color in their schools. Discussions of black history were relegated to a day or two during Black History Month. Like Marie, most did not talk about black issues or racism in school:

> In school, race was never something I talked about with others or even thought about to myself. The only real time we talked about "Black people" was on MLK [Martin Luther King, Jr.] day, for a period during social studies.

When I invited the interns to write about some of the pivotal events in black history, Marie recalled two time periods: slavery and the Civil Rights era. She knew about Harriet Tubman and the Underground Railroad, and Martin Luther King, Jr., and his "I Have a Dream" speech. She did not know about Africa prior to American colonization or about contemporary life in Africa. Nor did she understand the events that led to the enslavement of African Americans or the African American experience following Reconstruction.

When Marie moved to the university campus as a first-year student, she lived on a residential floor with black women. This was an eye-opening experience for her, a time when she first confronted issues of race:

> Once I came to college, my race was something that stood out to me. I was now living in a dorm, sharing bathrooms and personal space with people of color. It did not bother me, however, I actually thought, "Wow, now this is what it is like to live outside of my home town." Just seeing the things associated with Black people made me stop and think how sheltered I was. For example, before the cleaning people came, hair weaves or extensions would be left on the bathroom floor, hair sheen on the shelves, and occasionally we would see hair beads and rubberbands. But, hey, this is life and this is what it is like to live in the world with people who are different from me.

Notice how Marie defines racial differences according to surface features such as hair styling. Also, the remark "it did not bother me" suggests that she anticipated some conflict in her dealings with black students. She, like many white students on campus, did not cultivate many friendships with black students or deeper understandings of race and culture through living arrangements that placed just a few black students among many whites. Marie's campus living experiences did help her recognize her own cultural isolation, though.

The themes that surfaced in Marie's autobiographical essay also surfaced for the majority of the other interns: few experiences with people of color, family prejudices either tacitly or overtly displayed, community and school segregation of a small population of people of color, a Euro-focused school curriculum, and the presence of negative portrayals of blacks in the media. I found, however, that some of these factors were more influential than others in shaping interns' attitudes toward black children and caregivers. Even those interns who claimed to have had experiences with cultural diversity had developed prejudices about the children they would meet in the internship. This suggests that some background factors were more powerful in shaping their attitudes than others. To illustrate my point, I present the case of Allison.

## Allison

Allison's tongue ring, tie-dyed shirts, and baggy jeans suggested that she led a kind of counterculture lifestyle. She seemed out of place in the skirts and nylon stockings she wore to the elementary school where we held the internship. In her essay, Allison wrote about having had many experiences with cultural diversity while growing up:

> I grew up in several culturally mixed areas bordering Philadelphia. The neighborhood I would classify as working class (it wasn't dirt poor but it wasn't a middle class neighborhood by a long shot) and was made up of very racially mixed people. My neighborhood had many different cultural and ethnic backgrounds present. I had many childhood friends that were of a different race than I am and my parents never tolerated any form of racism.

Note Allison's reference to her parents' example of racial tolerance. Allison also maintained friendships with African Americans and saw how racism shaped their lives. She reported that these experiences helped her to develop an understanding of racial inequality:

> I have had and presently have close relationships with people of color and I saw how racism affected them. It has also been my experience that racism can get pretty blatant in poorer racially mixed neighborhoods like the ones I grew up in. I do feel some shame and guilt because of my race and things that have been done. I used to hang out with a lot of "sharp" skin heads (skin heads against racial prejudice) and because of them, I got into a lot of arguments with white power and Nazi skin heads. This probably wasn't the best way to confront racism.

Allison acknowledged acts of racism, admitted to being a member of a race of people who treated people of color unfairly, and engaged in antiracist activity. One might assume that a student like Allison would resist stereotyping children of color and their caregivers because doing so would conflict with her identity as a racially tolerant person. Yet this was not the case. Allison admitted to having several prejudices about children of color and their caregivers:

> I didn't have high expectations for these kids, parent involvement, the school and the neighborhood. I believed the students would all be reading drastically below grade level, and parents would not be taking an interest in their children's education. I can't think of why I would have these low expectations for students, parents, and a school and a neighborhood I've never been to if not for various media images and ideas from my past.

Despite the fact that Allison was raised in an atmosphere of racial tolerance, had been exposed to diversity in her home community, and even had involved herself in antiracist activities, she held the same low expectations of black children and caregivers that Marie did. It is noteworthy that both of these interns commented on media images of the urban poor and on how these images influenced their thinking about urban black children and care- givers. Their attitudes were shaped by news stories about high urban crime rates, images of gang shootings, and headlines about teenage pregnancies. They saw these snapshots as truths about most low-income African Americans, and these assumptions further translated into doubts about caregivers' abilities to nurture their children's literacy growth. Allison believed that the media played a particular role in her thoughts about high-poverty urban communities.

Both interns eventually changed their outlooks in response to the course experiences, albeit in different ways. Marie, who came to the internship with few experiences with cultural diversity, began to recognize and question her racial biases, and in doing so experienced the emotional dissonance (guilt, anger) that is often associated with this discovery (Tatum, 1999). Allison rec- ognized her biases, and while she regretted them, she did not struggle with guilt in the same way that Marie did. Instead, she focused on developing her knowl- edge and skills so she could better serve her students.

## Conclusion

Without direct access to high-poverty urban communities or opportunities to question stereotypes and learn about African Americans and other people of color, and with a history of exposure to racist language and images since child- hood, many of the interns with whom I worked viewed the students they would teach in the city and their caregivers through prejudicial lenses. What is of particular interest is that despite Allison's background in diversity, she still viewed these children and caregivers negatively. As mentioned previously, living in racially diverse neighborhoods and having friends of color—and even joining an antiracist group—did not prevent her from underestimating the children and caregivers in this community. Interns' prejudices affected their expectations about literacy achievement in this community—that children would not perform well in literacy classes because their immediate home envi- ronment did not support this growth.

My previous work with other interns had taught me that these interns' negative views of children and caregivers would interfere with their ability to ac- cept responsibility for the children's literacy achievement. I believed that a more comprehensive view that described the multiple factors making an impact on literacy achievement, including the roles of teachers and schools, would help interns see themselves and their places within the literacy achievement formula. Reading, writing, and talking about diversity issues during the internship did help interns locate themselves in the sociology of literacy achievement. The next chapter describes interns' responses to diversity issues and how they related new insights about privilege and racism to literacy teaching and achievement.

## REFLECTION AND INQUIRY

1. How do these interns' perceptions of children and caregivers compare to your own?

2. How have your family, your friends, the media, and school influenced your thinking about the children and caregivers in high-poverty communities? Add these insights to your cultural autobiography.

3. Read texts that provide information about caregiving and families in the cultural communities that you serve or would like to serve. The Recommended Resources list at the end of this book (pp. 177–179) suggests some texts that focus on serving children of different cultural groups and their families.

CHAPTER 5

# Constructing Understandings About Race, Culture, and Literacy Achievement

*I came into this practicum thinking it was the parents' fault that these kids are below level in reading, but I leave with a different opinion. I feel now, that the fault cannot really be put on one specific thing, for it is a problem with society as a whole. I am no longer looking for someone to place the fault on, for as a teacher I want to make a difference in the student's lives.*

—Monica, intern

*I could not believe the children really wanted to learn when I initially thought they did not care. I always thought it was the lack of parental support at home that was a major factor as to why so many children failed. I felt I needed to throw my negative attitude out the window because I knew the effort and dedication I would put into teaching these children would be so vital to their lives.*

—Beth, intern

Monica's and Beth's words above reveal their changed beliefs about literacy achievement in urban classrooms. They transformed from first blaming children and caregivers for literacy failure to eventually seeing literacy teaching within a complex web of social and historical influences. Most important, they began to see themselves as key players within this web.

In this chapter, I focus on the ways in which the interns constructed understandings about themselves in relation to the children they taught. They

63

did this through reading, writing, and talking about issues of cultural diversity. In order to understand power relations among themselves, children, and caregivers and between home and school, my students and I studied the notions of white privilege and institutional racism. This investigation helped the interns to see their own prejudices, acknowledge some of the social realities of urban schooling, understand the complexity of literacy achievement within these classrooms, and recognize their own responsibility for nurturing children's literacy achievement.

The interns' growth was not orderly or linear. The interns zigzagged toward and away from higher levels of understanding as each new discovery led to more questions, tensions, and sometimes regressions. I will report in this chapter on general patterns of growth and will specifically highlight how two of the interns presented in chapter 4, Marie and Allison, explored the notions of white privilege and institutional racism. As you read about their growth, consider your own responses to the reading material that is summarized in this chapter. Also, think about how your past has shaped your current understandings about these issues as they apply specifically to literacy teaching and achievement.

## A Framework for Looking at Growth

One of my goals in this study was to help interns recognize their own privileges as a way of scrutinizing their assumptions about the children they served in the internship. Access to quality public schools, well-stocked libraries, or neighborhood bookstores are privileges, but few people recognize these as privileges until they are pointed out as such. Howard (1999) asks white educators to consider how their "own social positions and history of dominance might be implicated in the disproportionate distribution of privilege and penalty in contemporary educational systems" (p. 34).

Most whites are not aware that they operate from a platform of advantage, and they believe that their achievements are based on merit alone: A common attitude is "I succeed because I work hard." This perspective leaves whites susceptible to believing that people who have not achieved according to mainstream markers of success are, therefore, inherently deficient. Many interns who entered urban classrooms for the first time during this internship viewed schoolchildren from such a deficit vantage point: "Something must be wrong with these kids and their parents if they can't succeed in school." This way of seeing caregivers and children reflects the fundamentalist orientation toward diversity described in chapter 4.

To explore interns' developing understandings of white privilege, racism, and sociohistorical influences on literacy achievement among African Americans, I return to Howard's description of the integrationist orientation toward diversity. Recall from chapter 4 that integrationists become aware of social inequality but do not accept personal responsibility for it. Translated into teaching terms, interns with integrationist orientations toward diversity are constructing understandings about society and the ways it has influenced the literacy achievement of children, although they have not taken responsibility for changing the status quo through their acts as literacy teachers. According to Howard, those teachers who take such responsibility assume a transformationist orientation toward diversity.

According to Howard (1999), transformationists accept multiple perspectives and multidimensional realities. They are self-reflective, interrogating their assumptions about whiteness and about what is considered normal. They see their own responsibility for racism, yet they maintain a positive racial identity. Transformationists feel positive about their growth in racial identity development and show patience and support for whites who have not yet reached this state of awareness. They seek roles as social reformers, attacking institutional policies and systems that marginalize people. Their teaching focuses on dismantling social injustices through changing the curriculum to enable students to view ideas and problems from diverse perspectives and engage in social action projects. Few interns exited from the urban literacy internship exhibiting behaviors that fit with the transformationist orientation toward diversity.

However, some of the reading, writing, talking, and observing experiences in the internship helped interns construct more sophisticated understandings of cultural diversity. These new understandings were critical to helping interns to see their own responsibilities as teachers. The interns and I began by looking at the notion of white privilege.

## Constructing Understandings of White Privilege

Reading McIntosh's (1990) article "White Privilege: Unpacking the Invisible Knapsack" put to rest assumptions by the interns that the problem of racism has been solved. Interns were uniformly shocked to discover that they could cash in, as McIntosh explains, on a number of privileges just because they are white. Below is a partial listing of the privileges McIntosh mentions:

1. I can, if I wish, arrange to be in the company of people of my race most of the time.

2. If I should need to move, I can be pretty much assured of renting or purchasing housing in an area I can afford and in which I would want to live.

3. I can be pretty sure that my neighbors in such a location will be neutral or pleasant to me.

4. I can go shopping alone most of the time, pretty well assured that I will not be followed or harassed.

5. I can turn on the television or look at the front page of the paper and see people of my race widely represented.

6. When I am told about the United State's national heritage or about "civilization," I am shown that people of my color made it what it is.

7. I can be sure that my children will be given curricular materials that testify to the existence of their race.

8. If I want to, I can be pretty sure of finding a publisher for this piece on white privilege.

9. I can go into a music shop and count on finding the music of my race represented, into a supermarket and find the staple foods that fit with my cultural tradition, into a hairdresser's shop and find someone who can cut my hair.

10. Whether I use checks, credit cards, or cash, I can count on my skin color not to work against the appearance of financial reliability.

11. I can swear, or dress in secondhand clothes, or not answer letters, without having people attribute these choices to the bad morals, the poverty, or the illiteracy of my race.

12. I can be pretty sure that if I ask to talk to the "person in charge," I will be facing a person of my race. (pp. 10–11)

Upon reading this list, the interns recognized the significance of white privilege and came to recognize how subtly it can operate by restricting the behaviors of people of color. A few students related this list to the news stories that they had been reading about New Jersey police being investigated for using race as a criterion for stopping motorists on the highway. This discussion led to other realizations by the interns about differential treatment of blacks and whites. Most of the interns rejected the notion that they were personally involved in racist acts, but they often believed that other whites were involved. Jennifer's written account reflects this attitude:

I did not think that I was racist. I went to school in a predominantly white setting and thought of myself as part of the racial norm. I had advantages, but was not conscious of them. Then I became more aware of racism, not within myself, but among other people. An incident while I was shopping really made me realize this. I was in a store and I was waiting to try on something in the fitting room. There were two African American girls in front of me in line. When they went into the dressing room the salesperson called on her headset to place someone at the exit of the store because she thought that they were going to steal something. They were just standing there waiting just like I was but because they were black, the staff was more cautious of them.

Even though most of the interns could identify instances when whiteness had worked in their favor, it was difficult for some, such as Marie, to accept this idea. Marie resisted the notion of white privilege and felt that racial inequality was not her fault because she did not choose her race:

I did not want to acknowledge the privileges that I had as a white person. When I learned these things in this class I got angry in the beginning. I remember thinking that I could not help being white and I thought I was anything but a prejudice [sic] person. After reading a few of the passages, I began to realize what white privilege meant to me—like the passage that talked about the dolls being the same as my race, or the bandages matching my skin color. However, I did not work to be white, I came into this world as white and I will leave the same. No one asked to be a certain race, so no one should be judged because of this. A person should be judged from what is on the inside, rather than the outside.

Marie was clearly defensive about her white privilege. This stance was very different from Allison's response. She recognized the significance of white privilege and racism, and she felt ashamed for never having done anything about it. In her writings, Allison demonstrated her own complicity in racism and a willingness to take action against racism:

I can be in the company of white people most of the time if I want to. I can perform well in a challenging situation without being called a "credit to my race." I can swear or dress in second-hand clothes if I want to without worrying what people think. The twenty-six examples [of white privilege] would definitely cause trouble in my life if I couldn't count on these privileges. I never really considered my white privilege and attitudes buried deep beneath the surface. I am beginning to see just how much my apathy has contributed to racism as well as many other problems around me and in the world.

The challenge for me was to help the interns relate the problem of unfair advantage to one of conferred dominance—the idea that racism is institutionalized through the policies and practices that allow whites to dominate in U.S. society (Tatum, 1999). Most of the interns understood white privilege as something that affects people's personal choices, but they did not see how it might affect school achievement. One intern commented that blacks could avoid the heavily policed white communities known for their "driving while black" violations. She reasoned that blacks simply should find alternative driving routes. The implication was that blacks could somehow avoid this injustice and reach their destinations, although she did not explain how this could happen. Her example suggested that she saw the barriers imposed by racism as mere inconveniences to be avoided, but tolerated nonetheless. Related to literacy achievement, her implication was that racial discrimination was inconvenient but that it should not prevent a student from doing well in school.

## Understanding Racism and Unequal Schooling

After weeks of comparing their own schooling experiences in the suburbs to the school experiences of the children they taught in their urban field placements, the interns began to see how public schools did not offer equal opportunities for all children. Interns' work with individual children and conversations with cooperating teachers confirmed that at least half of these children did not meet grade-level standards in reading. Many interns realized that struggling readers would not get the help they needed to perform at grade level unless they received rigorous supplemental instruction.

The interns and I discussed how exemplary reading instruction called for differentiated instruction, tailored to the needs of each child. The interns found out, however, that providing this kind of instruction would be difficult with 30 children in a classroom and more than half of them reading below grade level. It would require knowledgeable teachers, the use of a wide selection of books for children with very different reading needs, and a low teacher-student ratio. The interns noticed that many children who needed supplemental reading instruction did not have access to reading specialists, specialized tutors, or librarians who could provide it. The interns also believed that the absence of fully functioning libraries prevented children from being exposed to a wide enough variety of books. Furthermore, substitute teachers were in short supply, so when the regular teachers were absent, their students were distributed to other classrooms. On many days, cooperating teachers had to take time from regular classroom duties to accommodate these extra children. Interns saw this situation as time taken away from literacy instruction.

Having spent years in suburban schools and knowing about the excellent facilities and resources contained in them, the interns now began to see how the differences between urban and suburban schools could translate to achievement differences. They began to see why so many children remained below grade level in reading and why they fell further behind each year that they spent in school. Marie became more conscious of the differences in urban and suburban public schooling when she compared her experiences growing up in the suburbs to the experiences of children in the urban school of her field placement:

> When I arrived, I was absolutely shocked at the condition of the school. From the outside, the school looked to be in okay condition but once I went inside, I had immediate feelings of guilt. I would not believe that children were expected to learn in the conditions such as the ones I saw. The hallways and classrooms were dark and dingy. The bathroom toilets didn't work well. The teachers had to sometimes provide their own paper for the copy machine. There was no school librarian. The temperature in the classrooms was at one extreme or another. I was also surprised that there was such a shortage of teachers and overcrowding of classrooms. There were about thirty kids to every teacher in the beginning of the year. I was surprised to see that every student was African American. One thing was clear to me at this point; these were not the proper conditions for students to work up to their potential.

Marie questioned children's differential access to literacy education in the United States. Notice her changed views about public schooling in the following statement:

> I know that I may sound naïve, but I guess that I automatically thought that all public schools were the same. I believed that all schools at least had the basics. I never knew that growing up in the suburbs provided me with such an advantage. Why is this a fair situation? I didn't know that the wealthier one is the better the education. I always heard that education is the key to a good life, but does that mean if you live in a middle class area?

Marie's doubts about the equality of public schooling led to other questions. She, like many of the interns, reasoned that if children could not get adequate literacy instruction in school—unless, perhaps, they had extraordinary teachers—then why didn't caregivers realize this and take matters into their own hands? Some interns argued that if caregivers took greater responsibility for children's literacy learning at home, children would be able to achieve anyway, despite the problems of urban schools. They suggested that caregivers could compensate for the deficiencies of schools if they read to children more and taught their children to read. These interns wondered why caregivers simply didn't save up enough money to buy a modest home in the affluent suburbs a few miles away. Like the other interns, Marie's tendency was to blame caregivers. New understandings of white privilege and institutional racism, however, were beginning to complicate her views. One of her written comments reflects a new belief that caregivers' ways of responding to school may be shaped by factors such as racial inequality:

> I am seeing how much the lives of blacks have been affected by racism. But I did wonder, are these parents not trying hard enough to make a better life for their children or is it our society that is not letting them become better people?

The overall tendency among the interns was to see unequal schooling as being separate from good caregiving. Many felt that even if people are affected by racism, they can still teach their children to read. My response to this idea was not one of defending caregivers, but one of helping the interns to formulate a position based on reliable evidence. I emphasized that we could not assess what caregivers were or were not doing with their children unless we spent considerable amounts of time with children outside of school and carefully recorded caregivers' interactions with children around print. I also pointed out to the interns that this step would be only the beginning. We also would have to compare literacy and language practices in these homes with the practices expected at school, and we would need to explore the sociology that shapes these differences.

Conceptions of unequal schooling as a separate issue from caregiving also could be addressed, in part, by taking a broader, sociohistorical view of schooling in urban communities and of African Americans' access to quality education. This was difficult because the interns lacked knowledge about African Americans, their culture, and their history, and, consequently, the interns operated under several misconceptions. One misconception that was common among the interns was that African Americans have historically chosen to live in hypersegregated urban communities because they like it that way. Marie, for instance, wrote,

> African Americans ended up in these communities and schools because they wanted to be with their own kind.

Marie recast the problem of unequal schooling as one of personal preference for segregation, thereby absolving whites of any responsibility for the problem. Part of my challenge was to help her and the other interns to see how white people have been implicated in the problem of segregation and how blacks historically have fought for better schooling opportunities. Reading the story of Ruby Bridges (Coles, 1987), one of the first black children to attend an all-white elementary school in New Orleans, Louisiana, USA, was particularly effective in helping interns to understand the struggles that African Americans faced to integrate schools during the Civil Rights era. The story shows whites' resistance to school integration and African Americans' willingness to take risks to achieve equality in education.

I explained to the interns that great waves of blacks migrated north during the early decades of the 20th century in search of better employment opportunities and equal rights. Thousands settled in cities like Baltimore, Philadelphia, Washington, New York, and Chicago, where many found low-wage work and racial discrimination. With the influx of blacks to urban areas, many white residents of these cities relocated to the suburbs, both because they feared a reduction of their property values with the influx of poor black residents, and because they wanted to live in high-status middle class communities. I explained that relocation to the suburbs was not an easy option for many blacks at this time. Blacks faced discrimination in the housing market in many places, which limited their mobility. I showed the interns a copy of the original bylaws for a housing development established in the 1950s in the Philadelphia suburb of Lower Merion. It specifically states, "No Negroes will be permitted to buy properties in the subdivision." The interns began to realize that the economic and social realities of the time often limited African Americans' choices of which schools they attended.

The interns studied the reading material I gave them that addressed the social, historical, and economic conditions affecting African Americans. They wrote responses to these articles and our seminar discussions about the articles, but I could tell that they needed an even more thorough grounding in this history, which I could not easily give them within the scope of the internship. Allison's writing below, for example, shows a beginning understanding of some of the important historical factors that shaped the current conditions of Philadelphia public schools, but it also shows gaps in her understanding. She wrote,

> The conditions in Philadelphia schools are bad because of the system that funds them. The schools rely on taxes from citizens in the area who for the

most part are unable to pay them or have them raised. After slaves were emancipated, they still were tied to their former enslavers' plantations through sharecropping. Since many poor blacks, migrated to northern cities where there was industrial work, many areas of the city stayed poor to this day and can't really afford to support the schools. Heavy suppression of black citizens' civil rights until the 1960's and more subtle oppression today keeps positive change away from our Philadelphia schools.

Allison recognized the economic exploitation that blacks experienced through sharecropping and the suppression of black civil rights. Her explanation of the reduced tax base for Philadelphia city schools was based on the influx of poor blacks migrating northward but not on the simultaneous exodus of whites out of the cities and the prejudices underlying this movement. As Allison and her classmates brought little prior knowledge of African American history and sociology to the course, they lacked a nuanced understanding of how urban schools came to be essentially segregated and lacking in the conditions needed to promote high levels of literacy achievement.

I also wondered if there were gaps in interns' understandings about black resistance and power. Concerned that interns would focus on blacks as victims in our studies of institutional racism, I touched upon the ways in which blacks have fought and won many battles for social justice in public schooling. Yet I was not sure how interns made sense of this idea because they did not refer to it in their writing. Upon further reflection, I realized that I did not point out the ways in which black resistance operated locally, and in our placement schools specifically. Since the study, I have made it a point to discuss resistance at the local level by sharing with preservice teachers news about parent groups that have rallied for various causes such as eliminating education management organizations from city schools. Now, I make a conscious effort to share news articles about the resistance efforts of the black community in the area of school reform.

At the time I conducted the study, I struggled with the need to help interns construct richer understandings of black history and contemporary local issues in the black community, while at the same time helping them develop understandings about literacy teaching. I realized, however, that the internship exposed my students to perspectives they could explore more deeply someday. The experience of integrating two curricula strands—diversity and literacy education—helped me understand the importance of inquiry-based teaching and the need to help students (whether they be children or graduate students) develop their own questions and methods for finding out, rather than merely providing them with information.

## Understanding Race in the Classroom

By reading Ladson-Billings's book *The Dreamkeepers: Successful Teachers of African American Children* (1994), the interns and I also explored how racism can operate within classrooms. This book helped the interns to see how ignoring or minimizing racial differences in the classroom actually underserves children of color. In the book, Ladson-Billings draws from a study of preservice teachers, the majority of whom believed that current educational disparities between blacks and whites could be attributed to the enslavement of blacks in the 1600s–1800s. This belief, she argues, leads preservice teachers to adopt a "colorblind" view of children. She explains,

> According to this view, the past alone determines the future of a people. A more fundamental problem with this point of view in the classroom context is the following: If a teacher looks out at a classroom and sees the sons and daughters of slaves, how does that vision translate into her expectations for educational excellence? How can teachers who see African American students as mere descendants of slaves be expected to inspire them to educational, economic, and social levels that may even exceed their own?
>
> The usual antidote for this persistent view of African American children is for the viewer to pretend that he or she does not see the color that once forced their ancestors into slavery. Thus the teacher claims to be color-blind. However, such claims cannot be valid. Given the significance of race and color in American society, it is impossible to believe that a classroom teacher does not notice the race and ethnicity of the children she is teaching. Further, by claiming not to notice, the teacher is saying that she is dismissing one of the most salient features of the child's identity and that she does not account for it in her curricular planning and instruction. (pp. 32–33)

In reading these words, many of the interns began to think about colorblindness more critically. Marie, for instance, was surprised to discover that ignoring race and acting colorblind would be unfair to children:

> I never realized that it was bad to have a color-blind attitude. I always thought that it would be good if everyone had that attitude. Now I understand that there is a difference between being colorblind and accepting differences of color. When a teacher or administrator say they are colorblind, they are basically stating that they are not concerned with the different cultures, traditions,

races, or ethnicity within their classroom or school building. When this takes place, students of color will feel that they are not important, because the teacher will not incorporate their culture into the classroom. This might lead to low achievement and a lack of motivation from these students. I feel teachers say that they are colorblind so they do not have to worry about being unfair to children of color. However, these teachers don't realize that everyday that they enter the classroom they are being one hundred percent unfair to children of color. Teachers need to realize that differences are good and rather than acting blind to them, they should incorporate these differences into everyday learning.

While reading Ladson-Billings's book, Marie began to see how acknowledging color and validating cultural differences could inspire learning and help confront racism:

> I feel that it is very important that there are programs that capitalize on students' own social and cultural backgrounds. Each child should be given the feeling that where they come from is very important and is worth learning about. Maybe if we could get people to feel comfortable and proud of their own race, we could cut racism down a bit. I feel racism has a lot to do with ignorance of [the black] race and other races.

Allison also saw how acknowledging color and culture could help teachers to battle racism. Allison drew from another university course to further her understanding of the significance of colorblindness. This course also focused on the study of cultural diversity, and it involved the tutoring of Mexican migrant workers' children. Allison already had read Paley's *White Teacher* (1979) for a previous course, and so she drew from this text and Ladson-Billings's book *The Dreamkeepers* to see colorblindness as itself being a form of racism:

> Teachers who claim to have a "color-blind" view of their students are lying to themselves and the people that they come in contact with. This attitude, which I must admit I was guilty of having until I read "White Teacher" a year ago, hurts the students, their parents, and the teachers who claim the philosophy. As Paley points out, the difference between black and white children's skin is "a comfortable and natural one." Recognizing this is part of the "journey toward acknowledging and valuing differences." Teachers that say they don't see a child's color as part of what makes up that child contribute to a racist system. They use an "uncritical habit of mind that justifies inequity and exploitation by accepting the existing order of things as given." As Ladson-Billings notes, a person can only be pretending to not see color when a little more than a hundred years ago that same color forced people into slavery. Personally, I'm begin-

ning to see how a person's skin color impacts who she is and I, for one, won't ignore it. I've come to grips with the idea that differences in skin color are beautiful. Diversity should be taught that way.

One thing I learned about differences is never to ignore them. I want to create a classroom where everyone is equal, not despite their differences, but because of their differences. I want to make my students feel like every aspect of who they are is special and beautiful. Claiming that you can't see color usually means a person is not dealing with the issue of diversity. I will help my students from other cultures realize the specific obstacles they will have because of their difference and work to overcome these obstacles.

While reading *The Dreamkeepers*, Allison was struck by the notion that teachers do have the power to raise achievement and, simultaneously, to confront the problem of racism in their own classrooms:

Ignoring social and cultural backgrounds of the kids is a form of systematic racism. When any kid's background and experiences are used positively and celebrated, they feel better and more at home at school. I think that just makes sense for any student. I can use culturally responsive teaching by making sure my kids see other kids and adults who look like them in books we read and have elements of their culture in them that are accurate and positive. Also, allowing kids to focus on comprehension and putting stories in words and ways of speaking that are familiar to them. I can be a good teacher by knowing kids can be great readers and writers and by assuming my share of the responsibility to help them get there. These can be done by not lowering standards, giving constant support and encouragement, and expressing my faith in them. I've got to let the students know they are, as Ladson-Billings says "capable of excellence."

Allison's willingness to validate cultural differences, aim for excellence, and accept responsibility for teaching are attributes of successful teachers. Yet she, like most of the other interns, faced some challenges in trying to translate these beliefs into practice.

# The Price of Knowledge

Our inquiries about race evoked new understandings and questions, but most of the interns were not completely comfortable with these ideas. By the end of the semester, Marie felt shameful about her own whiteness. Although she accepted responsibility for white privilege, she was mired in guilt and felt the need to prove to African Americans that she was no longer prejudiced:

Now I have realized how wrong I was and I am now at a point where I feel ashamed of my whiteness. I feel like I have to prove to any African American I meet who does not know me personally that I am not prejudice [sic]. I feel like I owe the black community something to make up for all the persecution they have endured from my race. They are a minority and some people blame them for that. If these people just drove into the city and sat with these children like I did, I know they would change their thinking.

In the last two statements of this response, Marie acknowledges the existence of racism and the need to challenge other whites to learn what she had learned about some of the social realities of African American children. Note how she challenged "other whites" to bear the burden of racial prejudice. Although she accepted responsibility for racism during the internship, the guilt and shame she expressed aligned with an integrationist orientation toward diversity. Marie would need continued support to work through these feelings to construct a positive white identity, a characteristic that fits with a transformationist orientation toward diversity.

Unfortunately, she was unable to get this kind of support from home. Talking to family members about some of the problems African Americans faced produced stress for her. Conversations with her uncle were especially difficult for her, as she explained in the following entry:

My uncle would be at Sunday Dinner and make racist comments about blacks and I would start to argue with him, but there was no way I could win. I just didn't know how to tell him about the way things are. What can I say to him?

Like Marie, some other interns had family members whom they felt were part of the problem. These students wanted to do something about the problem of racism, yet they were not ready to break ties with family members over the issue of racism. These conversations also produced anxiety when interns realized that they could not defend their new ideas easily. Although they knew some new things about the nature of the racism in public schooling, they still had difficulty articulating these views in the company of friends and family members. They were, however, able to measure their own growth in becoming more racially sensitive by comparing their new views to the existing ones of their family members. Marie's account exemplifies this:

I was telling my Dad, a teacher of history about my experiences (in the city), and he would, without realizing it, make comments that offended me. He was not even trying to offend, but I realized that he has had so little contact with African

Americans (living in the same town his entire life and teaching in a mostly white school), that he didn't think twice about what he was saying. My point is that before, I didn't even realize he was talking the way he was talking.

Other interns noticed similar kinds of stress between themselves and family members as a result of their studying issues of race during the internship. One intern actually broke up with her boyfriend because, among other things, she could not accept his racist views. For most of the interns, their new understandings about themselves and others were worth the personal and emotional costs that accompanied the journey.

Allison did not have to pay such a price for coming to understand the significance of race in literacy teaching. Although she described herself as "not being one hundred percent comfortable with race issues," her written statements revealed her growth:

> Although I may never understand the extent of the systematic discrimination against black people in this country, since I don't live it every day nor does my family have to endure it day in and day out, yet I am now beginning to see more of the truth. Now, the best way I've found to confront it is to stop people in the middle of a racist joke to tell them their [sic] not doing a good thing and they're being unoriginal, uncreative, and ugly. I am beginning to understand why there is so much pain, frustration, hopelessness, rage, and, fortunately, determination for change in many African Americans, young and old.

This statement shows Allison's emergence as a culturally sensitive teacher. First, she describes herself as a learner, someone who will continue to inquire about issues of race. Second, she takes responsibility for resisting racism by challenging those who make racial slurs and jokes. Finally, her last statement in the excerpt reflects her ability to understand the perspectives of African Americans by recognizing both their struggles and their resolve to overcome them.

## Understanding Interns' Development

The study of racism during this internship had a profound effect on interns' attitudes toward themselves, children, caregivers, teaching, schools, and the communities in which they taught. Their different interpretations of the material we studied were, in part, based on their distinctive experiences with diversity. Many of Marie's responses to the course were similar to those of other interns who grew up either in white communities or in homes where they were exposed to prejudicial views of African Americans. Her case provides an example of how teachers with few prior experiences with racial diversity might interpret issues of privilege and racism. She, like most of the interns, acknowledged that there are unequal schooling opportunities for children of color in high-poverty urban communities and began to see how teachers could confront racism through validating all children's cultures in the classroom. Marie was able to learn this new viewpoint by relating new information acquired in the internship to her own schooling experiences and the experiences of other schoolchildren in both urban and suburban communities. By the end of the semester, Marie and several other interns became receptive to the idea of teaching in an urban school someday.

Challenging their own racist beliefs was not easy for most of the interns, and Marie's journey was no exception. Her journey began with her first awareness of white privilege and her denial that racial inequality was her fault. After facing the issues of white privilege and unequal schooling for the children in her charge, she was consumed by guilt. Her insights about "the way things are for African Americans" conflicted with the racist beliefs of some of her family members, intensifying her doubts. Her ways of constructing whiteness and racism corresponded with an integrationist orientation toward diversity, in which a new awareness about diversity is confounded by shame, guilt, and confusion (Howard, 1999). Marie will need support to continue the journey to a transformationist orientation toward diversity. She will need to learn much more about her own and others' history and culture to see her own responsibility for teaching and to put into practice the ideals of culturally relevant teaching. Marie's case shows that those who grow up with demonstratively racist family members, little formal education in multiculturalism, and few experiences with race or class differences may have a longer and more emotionally risky journey toward cultural sensitivity than those who bring many diversity experiences to their teacher training.

Allison's case, on the other hand, exemplifies the changes that can take place when teachers come to the study of diversity with important precursors for success: growing up in a racially mixed community with caregivers who did not tolerate prejudice and having previous exposure to diversity studies in college. Many of Allison's statements fit with a transformationist orientation toward diversity because she (a) accepted responsibility for the problem of racism, (b) considered ways of challenging racial inequality through confronting others who made racist jokes and through pluralistic teaching,

(c) regarded her own privileged situation honestly, (d) positioned herself as a learner, and (e) considered others' perspectives. Also consistent with a transformationist orientation toward diversity was Allison's appreciation, joy, and genuine respect for the children she taught. Yet her comment that she still was not comfortable with issues of race reflects an integrationist orientation toward diversity. Allison's profile suggests that people who are beginning to make sense of diversity issues may not demonstrate one identity orientation for all modalities of growth but may simultaneously display characteristics of two orientations. Her growth also demonstrates the potential for teachers to achieve high levels of understanding if they commit themselves to change.

How does understanding issues of diversity relate to being a good literacy teacher? Most of the interns were able to see the complexity of the problem of literacy achievement for African American children in high-poverty urban schools. They began to understand a number of factors that shaped literacy achievement for these children. The lists below show some of the questions that emerged from our studies about diversity as they applied to literacy teaching. Notice the difference in complexity between interns' queries at the beginning of the semester and those generated during the internship.

Questions before the internship
- What's the matter with these children?
- What's the matter with these caregivers?
- Why don't caregivers work harder to help their children succeed?
- Why can't caregivers save to buy a house in the suburbs?

Questions generated during the internship
- How was I privileged in gaining access to the literacies of school?
- How did my opportunities to learn to read compare to those of children in urban schools?
- How have schooling opportunities been historically different for blacks than for whites?
- How can teachers counteract the problems of urban schools?
- How can caregivers counteract the problems of urban schools?
- What's my responsibility as a teacher to make the playing field more even for these children?

# Conclusion

Understanding how race fits into the literacy achievement equation is only one part of being a successful literacy teacher in urban schools. These interns, and any other teachers interested in urban teaching, need to understand the theories and practices of literacy development and instruction and classroom management in order to navigate around the problems of overcrowded classrooms and limited support staff. They will need to work with caregivers in the community to help children achieve. Their chances of success in these schools also will be highly dependent on the level of educational and administrative support they receive and on their sustained commitment to urban education, a topic I will address in chapter 8.

Studying issues of white privilege, colorblindness, racism, and culturally relevant teaching helped these interns to construct more sophisticated explanations about literacy achievement. These inquiries helped interns see the children in their placement schools in the context of several sociohistorical and sociocultural factors. The inquiries also helped interns see that these factors influenced schooling opportunities and caregivers' ways of supporting children's academic success. These investigations provided an important backdrop for communicating with caregivers directly. Interns were given opportunities to communicate with caregivers in an effort to further understand children's home literacy experiences and caregivers' ways of supporting children's literacy growth outside school.

In the next chapter, I share the ways in which interns communicated with caregivers and how this project was significant for informing interns' understandings about children, caregivers, and the communities surrounding each of the field placement schools.

## REFLECTION AND INQUIRY

1. What privileges do you have relative to the children you will teach or currently teach? How does knowing about these privileges help you understand children's access to texts and literacy education?

2. Apply Howard's (1999) identity framework—discussed in this chapter and chapter 4—to your own views about cultural difference. Where do you fit? What are the limitations of this framework for you?

**3.** What kinds of investigations about race, class, and culture would help you to become a better literacy teacher?

**4.** How has the study of diversity issues affected your relationships with your own family members?

# CHAPTER 6

# Communicating With Caregivers

*To my surprise, the parents by far proved my initial thoughts to be false. The parents of many children were extremely involved and concerned about their child's academic welfare.*

—Andrea, intern

*The parents who were very difficult to get hold of made me think...are these parents ever home to help their children with school work? I still believe that some parents do not put their child's education on their list of top priorities. I believe the number one problem for the low academics of African Americans is because of the environment and the lack of support and concern from their parents.*

—Julia, intern

These contrasting remarks about parents were written by interns who experienced very different communications with the caregivers of the children they taught. Interns' views of parents and other caregivers were shaped primarily by their ability to contact caregivers and engage in positive dialogue with them. After discussing the importance of two-way communication and describing the process of preparing interns for conversations with caregivers, this chapter will present some actual conversations between interns and caregivers.

## Why Two-Way Communication?

Teacher preparation programs generally do not offer specific courses on working with caregivers to support children's literacy needs. Teachers usually are not educated to see caregivers as resources for knowing children and their ways of relating to print at home. School-centered, one-way communication models dominate in schools (Henry, 1996). Think about what you may imagine as a typical teacher–caregiver conversation: Caregivers usually remain silent while teachers tell them about their children's performance in school. This model fits many caregivers' expectations for communication with teachers. Caregivers, especially those in low-income communities, tend to view teachers as authority figures and assume a subordinate status to teachers (Burke, 1985; Henry, 1996). Communication, therefore, generally flows from teachers to caregivers (Fuller & Olsen, 1998), a model of communication often reproduced through teacher education programs.

I wanted the interns to experience a different model of communication with parents and other caregivers. I asked them to conduct two-way telephone conversations with caregivers in order to better understand children's out-of-school lives and literacy experiences and the roles caregivers played in them. Through these projects, the interns began to understand how school literacies are interpreted by caregivers, how literacy activities vary across families, and how some life circumstances sometimes can prevent caregivers from supporting school literacy goals.

## Preparing Interns for Caregiver Communication

My earliest attempts to help interns communicate with children's caregivers were challenging. Interns expressed a lot of anxiety about talking with caregivers. They asked caregivers only the questions they had prepared in advance, avoiding deeper, more informative conversations about the children. When interns asked caregivers to describe their children, many interns reported being so preoccupied with trying to think of more questions that they did not even listen to caregivers' responses. Consequently, the interns' follow-up questions had little connection to caregivers' descriptions of their children. These conversations, therefore, remained superficial.

Based on these experiences, I realized that I needed to do more to prepare the interns in this study for two-way conversations with caregivers. I began by asking the interns to identify what they thought were features of successful communication between caregivers and teachers. The interns responded by saying that listening and asking good questions were important when speaking to caregivers. I then asked them, "How might you help caregivers know they have been heard?" and "How could you respond to caregivers when they voice a concern about their children's reading?" Few had thought about how to communicate with caregivers to learn from them and build relationships with them to support children's literacy growth. We then spent time talking about the significance of two-way conversations, practicing two-way dialogues with peers who assumed the role of caregivers, and reflecting on the interns' own dialogues with these "mock" caregivers. Our discussions began by exploring the importance of active listening.

## Teacher as Interviewer

When I think about conversations that invite caregiver input, I am reminded of National Public Radio interviewer Terry Gross. Gross has a talent for asking open-ended questions that yield specific and powerful details about interviewees' lives. She actively listens to a person's responses and formulates relevant follow-up questions based on some provocative idea, issue, or experience the person mentions. With each follow-up prompt, "Tell me more about...," listeners are led down a particular path until an element of an interviewee's life is fully explored. As one question begets another, Gross's interviews seem to flow naturally, like a real-life conversation, rather than a formal interview.

Teachers probably rarely think of themselves as interviewers. Yet the strategies suggested in the professional literature for teachers are very similar to those used by interviewers such as Gross. These suggested strategies often begin with open-ended questions and involve active listening and reflective questioning by the teacher (Fuller & Olsen, 1998; Studer, 1994). Open-ended questions invite caregivers to describe and explain. They direct caregivers to tell what they notice going on at home and to discuss their feelings about what they see happening. Examples might include questions such as, What have you noticed about Jason's reading at home? What kinds of reading does Jason do? What do you think about Jason's reading? Notice how none of these questions would be likely to yield a yes, no, or other one-word response.

Teachers also can imagine themselves as researchers during these conversations, mining for significant bits of information and assessing whether what is being said needs further clarification. I asked my interns to role-play conversations with a peer "caregiver," keeping the following guidelines in mind: As soon as the caregiver speaks, listen actively to his or her response, being mindful to listen for evidence of successes or dilemmas in a child's experiences. For example, active listeners capture information about children while asking themselves, What seems important about what is being said? What do

I need to know more about? What seems unclear about what the caregiver is saying? Focus on the most significant parts of the conversation, such as children's dilemmas or successes or caregivers' difficulties or successes in helping children at home. Then, to use reflective questioning, rephrase what the caregiver says in the form of a question, and invite the caregiver to say more. For example, a teacher might say, "Your daughter refuses to read with you? Can you tell me more about that?" Rephrasing caregivers' comments and reshaping them into questions lets caregivers know they have been heard, and relevant follow-up questions invite more information about why certain events happen and in what context they happen.

## Learning How to Actively Listen and Respond: Rachel's Self-Assessment

One of the interns, Rachel, agreed to be videotaped while she conducted a face-to-face conference with Mrs. Williams, the mother of a first grader named Naomi. Rachel tutored Naomi twice each week and had become very familiar with Naomi's literacy abilities and needs. Rachel had had opportunities to speak with Mrs. Williams before this conference and felt comfortable communicating with her about Naomi. The purpose of the conference was to ask Mrs. Williams for information about Naomi's reading habits at home and to share some of the things Rachel and Naomi had been doing in the tutorial. Following the conference, I asked Rachel to review the videotape and evaluate her ability to actively listen to Mrs. Williams and generate relevant questions and responses based on what this parent said. What follows is a section of Rachel's conversation with Mrs. Williams:

Rachel: What have you noticed about Naomi's reading and writing at home?

Mrs. Williams: Her writing has changed. The reading...not too much...because now she knows how to skip a space after you finish a word. If you look at her homework book it's much better. Before it was really sloppy.

Rachel: You said her reading hasn't really changed?

Mrs. Williams: I've been trying to read the *Jump In* book to her. She recognizes, like, one or two words, but she doesn't read.

Rachel: Does she show any interest in books? Does she want to look at them?

Mrs. Williams: Yes, she does this with her sister. But if I say, "Come here," she figures that I'm getting ready to teach her and that's boring, so she'd rather do it with her sister. Maybe I don't do it the proper way...I think I bore her sometimes. I can't keep her attention. She's looking around somewhere.

Rachel: I've noticed in school, when I take a book out of my book bag, she'll want me to read it immediately and she wants to know what it is....

In response to Mrs. Williams's description of Naomi's at-home literacy experiences, Rachel rephrases the mother's concern about her daughter's reading progress with the question, "You said her reading hasn't really changed?" Note how Rachel turns Mrs. Williams's statement into a question to prompt more information about Naomi's reading. This yields more details about Naomi's ability to read the book *Jump In*: "She recognizes, like, one or two words, but she doesn't read." *Jump In* (Sterling, 1999) was a text sent home by the classroom teacher and was part of the basal text series being used in Naomi's first-grade class. Judging from this parent's description, one might suspect that the book was too difficult for Naomi, but it is difficult to tell for sure. More specificity is needed; Rachel might have asked, "You say she cannot read the *Jump In* book?" or "How do you think she feels about the *Jump In* book?" or "Can you tell me more about how she reads the *Jump In* book?" Questions such as these may have drawn out more information about Naomi's reading at home. This additional information could have helped Rachel assess whether this text was a good match for Naomi, and, if not, helped Rachel suggest other books that better fit Naomi's reading ability.

At this point in the conversation, however, Rachel decides to focus on Naomi's interest in books. She asks two questions of a type that tend to solicit yes or no answers. These questions prompt Mrs. Williams to reveal two important pieces of information about literacy events at home: (1) Naomi enjoys reading with her sister, and (2) when Mrs. Williams requests that Naomi read with her, Naomi hesitates, and Mrs. Williams presumes that it is because Naomi sees reading with Mom as a teaching activity.

In the same response, Mrs. Williams expresses doubts about her ability to motivate her daughter to read. She also describes her daughter's disengagement during these at-home reading events: "She's looking around somewhere." At this juncture, the teacher or intern would want to know Mrs. Williams's approach to getting her daughter to read. The teacher or interns conducting the conference might ask, "You say you think you bore her? Tell me more about this." Yet Rachel bypasses this parent's concerns and instead discusses Naomi's enthusiastic response to the books Rachel brought to school. In reviewing this taped conversation, Rachel noticed that she had overlooked an opportunity to ask Mrs. Williams these follow-up questions. Doing so may have helped Rachel understand more about Naomi's reading at home. One possibility for Naomi's lack of interest in reading at home was that Naomi's miscues were frequent, violating the text's meaning so much that Mrs. Williams became visibly frustrated and that this, in turn, caused Naomi to disengage.

Reflecting on her conversation with Mrs. Williams, Rachel identified other instances when she could have listened to Mrs. Williams more carefully and responded to her in ways that may have yielded more information about Naomi's reading. In addition, Rachel was displeased with her use of jargon at select points during the conference. When critiquing her performance during this conference, Rachel once commented, "Can you believe I used the term *word sort* and I didn't even explain or demonstrate it to her?" Rachel emerged from this reflection experience with a much clearer vision of how to approach the next caregiver conference. Viewing and discussing Rachel's videotaped conversation with Mrs. Williams also helped other interns to think about active listening as a critical element in conducting two-way conversations.

## Addressing Fears About Caregiver Communication

Despite my efforts to help prepare the interns for conversations with caregivers, many expressed nervousness about calling caregivers. They felt that they did not know enough about the children they taught or about literacy teaching, and they believed that caregivers would see them as incompetent. They were especially worried that caregivers would ask them for advice and they would not know what to say. They wanted to come across in the conferences as articulate, poised, and confident and to have all the answers. I explained that even experienced teachers do not know so much about individual children at the beginning of the school year and that, for this reason, many teachers resist giving advice until they learn more about the children and the ways they respond to print. I pointed out to the interns that it was all right to admit to being learners and to have caregivers teach them about their children.

To allay interns' fears about calling caregivers, I explained that most of the caregivers I have known supported teachers. I acknowledged that there could be differences between the ways some caregivers thought that literacy ought to be taught and the ways literacy actually is taught in many classrooms today, and that these different ways of seeing literacy instruction would need to be addressed. However, I mentioned that with major paradigm shifts in literacy instruction over the past 20 years, many adults are unfamiliar with recent approaches to literacy instruction. Many caregivers remember schools using round-robin reading and skill sheets, and contemporary practices are sometimes misunderstood by parents and other caregivers who want to make sure their children are getting what they had in school. I pointed out to the interns that teachers need to understand that caregivers are not simply out to criticize them. What caregivers need and deserve is useful information about why literacy instruction has evolved in certain ways.

The first step in the intern–caregiver conferences involved sending home a letter introducing the intern to caregivers and outlining the intern's tutoring responsibilities with the caregivers' child. Each letter indicated that the intern would telephone the caregivers to share information about their child. Attached to this letter was a list of questions to help prepare caregivers for this conversation. One week later, interns contacted caregivers to decide how—via telephone or in person—and when the conversation about the child could take place. When interns telephoned caregivers, they briefly introduced themselves and asked if it was a convenient time to talk. Any hesitation was taken as a sign that the caregiver could not easily talk, so interns asked if there was a more convenient calling time. If a caregiver indicated that now was a good time to talk, interns initiated the conference with open-ended questions and tried to continue the conversation in the manner described previously, soliciting as much information as possible about the child through active listening and by asking relevant follow-up questions. To facilitate active listening, I directed the interns to have a pen and piece of paper ready for note taking as caregivers spoke. I also provided interns with a guide (see Figure 1) to help them focus on primary areas for their questioning.

Following their conversations with caregivers, interns were asked to respond to the following questions and prompts:

1. What were the highlights of your conversation with your student's caregiver? What comments did the caregiver make that really stood out for you?

2. How might you use the information provided by the caregiver?

# FIGURE 1
## Parent Conference Guide

Please read the following questions in advance to get a feel for the wording so that you can sound as though you are asking the questions naturally, rather than reading them from a prepared list. Begin by asking a general question, then listen to the caregiver's response to formulate the next follow-up question.

These questions are only a guide in case you cannot think of a question to ask. Use the right-hand side of this sheet to take notes about the information the caregiver shares with you.

| Questions | Notes |
|---|---|
| 1. Can you tell me about your child? | |
| Specific Questions | |
| • What are some of his or her interests? | |
| • What seems to motivate him or her? | |
| • How do you think he or she reacts to reading (to writing, to school)? | |
| • How do you think he or she learns best? | |
| • What do you think are his or her particular learning needs? | |
| • What do you think he or she likes/dislikes about learning to read and write? | |
| 2. How do you think I, as his or her teacher, can best help your child to learn? | |
| Specific Questions | |
| • Can you suggest ways to help me communicate with him or her? | |
| • Can you offer specific suggestions to help me interest him or her in reading and writing? | |

3. Describe the tone of the conversation, including how you felt just before communicating with the caregiver and how you felt while you talked with the caregiver.

4. Evaluate your own performance in talking to the caregiver. Comment on how you listened to the caregiver, elicited information from the caregiver, and kept the conversation moving. What were your strengths and weaknesses during this conversation? What would you change about the way in which you related to the caregiver?

5. Comment on the value of this experience to you.

Based on interns' responses to these questions and their comments in class, about two thirds of the interns believed that they had successful two-way conversations with caregivers. Although many interns initially were nervous about speaking to caregivers, they reported feeling at ease once they found that caregivers seemed receptive to speaking with them. A few interns believed that they could have listened better and asked more relevant follow-up questions. These interns challenged themselves to apply these communication skills during their next conversations with caregivers. Many of these interviews yielded specific information about caregivers' ideas for supporting their children's literacy and about the out-of-school circumstances that influenced their children's literacy development. This kind of detailed caregiver input helped many of the interns understand the children's attitudes, behaviors, and literacy performance at school.

## Learning From Caregiver Conferences: Two Interns' Experiences

Through caregiver conferences, the interns learned about children's favorite home activities; about their relationships with significant family members and friends; and about families' trips, gatherings, and celebrations. These insights about children were particularly valuable for helping the interns to work with reluctant student writers. The information they received gave the interns starting points for helping children to talk about their experiences outside of school, and these conversations often led to writing topics that the children found very engaging. For instance, when interns learned from caregivers that a child had a particular interest in a subject, they often invited the child to talk about what he or she knew and how he or she felt about a topic. These "rehearsals" led to helping children write little "teaching" books to tell their classmates about a topic. This process worked especially well for children who felt that they could not write or had nothing to write about, such as one first grader, formerly reluctant to write, who eventually wrote and illustrated a 15-page story about his dirt bike.

One intern who learned this type of important information about her students' needs was Kim.

## Kim and Mrs. Jones

Kim reflected on and wrote about her conversation with the parent of a second grader, Tyeshia, including information about this child's relationship with family members and how her mother tried to help her learn to read and write. Kim made an effort to explore and process this information:

> At school Tyeshia never raises her hand, or even calls out an answer. [I think] she fears being wrong she would rather say nothing at all. Tyeshia's mother reports much the same behavior at home. She says Tyeshia frustrates easily and will give up when reading a book to her mother. Her mother said that when she or Tyeshia's older sister read books to her, her mind seems to wander. If she stumbles when reading, her mother says she will put the book down and refuse to read. Because she is the youngest child in her family, her mother feels that she is used to having her siblings "baby" her and do things for her. Her mother bought her a small V-tech computer to help with her phonics skills, but Tyeshia also becomes frustrated while using it. Tyeshia closes it and walks away. Mrs. Jones says she provides many books for Tyeshia, but Tyeshia puts them in her closet and doesn't read them. She recently bought Tyeshia a book which has a tape to go along with it. Mrs. Jones is exasperated because Tyeshia listened to the tape but will not follow along in the book. Mrs. Jones is very concerned that Tyeshia cannot identify the sounds of letters, especially consonant blends. Mom reports that Tyeshia has to be "pushed" to get her to read (or do anything). I think Tyeshia appears to be retaliating against this push.

The information provided by Mrs. Jones provided a great deal of insight into understanding Tyeshia's disengagement from reading. The telephone conversation helped Kim became aware of some of Mrs. Jones's beliefs: Tyeshia was too pampered (being the youngest), she had to be pushed to read and write, her literacy skills were underdeveloped, and she needed explicit instruction in phonics. Kim felt that Mrs. Jones was passionate about helping

Tyeshia, but Kim also believed that Tyeshia was unable to perform according to her mother's expectations.

Tyeshia seemed to be experiencing similar frustrations with reading at school. Kim noticed that Tyeshia was given reading materials that were too difficult for her, and, according to Mrs. Rice, Tyeshia's classroom teacher, Tyeshia was not able to get the individual help she needed in a classroom of 32 children, many of whom also struggled with classroom literacy tasks. Compounding the problem, Mrs. Rice felt pressured by the school district to keep children reading grade-level materials (whether they could read such materials proficiently or not) that satisfied the school district's literacy standards. Furthermore, the school had no reading specialist or other support teacher to offer individualized help for children who needed it.

Kim felt that Tyeshia's inability to meet both home and school expectations partially explained why this child did not appear confident in the classroom. In a later paper, Kim wrote about encouraging Tyeshia's risk taking during the literacy tutorials:

> I fear that Tyeshia is hindered greatly by her fear and uncertainty. I deliberately make mistakes and talk about them to help her become comfortable with errors. I really want her to know that mistakes are great—we learn from them!

Kim also focused on helping Tyeshia learn to enjoy reading and writing: "I would like Tyeshia to begin enjoying reading and writing. All the other work is almost pointless if she views literacy as a chore."

Mrs. Jones provided Kim with a direction for making tutorial reading more enjoyable for Tyeshia by describing how Tyeshia loved playing with dolls. Based on this idea, Kim had Tyeshia dictate a series of adventure stories that included Tyeshia's dolls as characters. Kim wrote these stories down, and Tyeshia read them both at home and in tutorial sessions. Kim and I also discussed ways to assist Tyeshia at home by providing her with books she had read successfully in tutorial sessions so that she could reread them to her mother and other family members with confidence. Occasionally, Kim attached notes to these books for Mrs. Jones, explaining that these were examples of books Tyeshia would be able to read by herself. Kim felt that this would be an unobtrusive way to help Mrs. Jones select other reading materials that Tyeshia could read at home.

What also is important about Kim's conversation with Mrs. Jones is that Kim gained knowledge that contrasted with the image of the uninvolved, unsupportive caregiver. The other interns and I also communicated with some other caregivers like Mrs. Jones, who tried to help improve their children's literacy performance because they did not feel that school alone would meet their children's literacy needs. A few caregivers even talked about purchasing the *Hooked on Phonics* program and sending their children to Sylvan Learning Center after school and during the summer.

## Cynthia and Mrs. Fine

Many interns enjoyed the personal relationships they established with caregivers. Cynthia, a nontraditional university student and mother of two girls, saw her initial conversation with Mrs. Fine, Blossom's grandmother, as a way to open up an ongoing dialogue with this caregiver:

> The conversation went really well. We both related to each other. I think when I told Blossom's grandmother that I have two children of my own, we connected. Right before we talked I was a little nervous because I didn't know what to expect. She could have been warm and receiving like she was or she could have felt I was intruding and not really want to talk to me. So I was pleased with the outcome of the conversation. I felt I listened well to Mrs. Fine. The conversation flowed easily. We talked, really talked, it wasn't just me reciting questions and her answering them. I think the strengths were relating to her one on one, letting her see I really cared. This was a valuable experience because it gave me a clearer understanding of Blossom's home life, the support she receives at home, interests she has that I can use in the classroom in teaching her. I feel anytime the connection is made between home and school, it can only be beneficial for the child.
>
> The major highlight from the conversation with Blossom's grandmother was the connection that was made. I feel like I know them better now and they know me better now. By having the conversation, relating information back and forth we are both more "human" to each other now, not just names any longer. Mrs. Fine seems like a warm, caring person. She is doing her best in raising these girls. Comments she made about wanting to do her best for them, make more time to read with them and help them with their homework, shows me how much she cares about their education. Knowing that Blossom's grandmother is willing to work with her at home is encouraging. The tape recorder and books I am sending home, I know will be used. This will help Blossom in her reading. Also anything I send home with Blossom to help her, she will receive support from her grandmother.

To Cynthia, establishing a relationship with Mrs. Fine was the most important part of the conference experience. She believed that this dialogue helped establish a connection, as a result of which she could call Mrs. Fine periodically and send home literacy materials for Blossom. She saw Mrs. Fine as a caring person who believed she was doing her best for all her granddaughters. Cynthia thought that Mrs. Fine did not read to her granddaughters but that she was willing to help them with literacy projects sent home from school. Cynthia believed that the bond she established with Mrs. Fine increased the possibility that this caregiver would follow through with literacy support at home.

Interns who successfully communicated with caregivers felt that the caregivers generally supported their children's literacy development, especially if they were given specific ideas or directions from the teacher or intern. Given most of the interns' initial expectations that caregivers would be generally unsupportive, these kinds of dialogues were critical for helping interns confront their assumptions about caregivers. More important, though, was the interns' growing recognition of the fact that each home is distinct in the ways it shapes a child's literacy learning.

## Raising Questions About Caregiver Involvement

About one third of the interns believed that factors at home limited their students' literacy development. These factors varied considerably. Often, the inability to contact caregivers prompted interns to wonder if children had consistent contact with their caregivers after school. Interns occasionally found that the phone numbers children or cooperating teachers gave them were disconnected. A few persistent interns called several times before reaching a caregiver at home. They found that some caregivers worked in the evenings and, therefore, were less available to talk to interns, but occasionally, caregivers gave interns their work phone numbers. Once, a mother returned an intern's call at 5:30 a.m. because this was the most convenient time this caregiver could make the call.

The interns also learned about lifestyles and circumstances of some children and their families that limited caregivers' abilities to support children's literacy at home. One intern learned that a first-grade student of hers, Jason, had eight older siblings who took turns caring for him in the evenings, which sometimes made it difficult for him to get consistent help with his homework. She reported that Jason's mother was very concerned about her son's progress but could not spend much time helping him. Other interns learned about some of their students being in foster homes, and they noted how some caregivers in these temporary arrangements did not seem to know the children well.

Some interns learned information about children's health, or the health of children's family members, that also had an impact on home literacy activity. One intern, Judy, learned that a second-grade student, Kyle, suffered from sickle cell anemia and was frequently too ill to attend school or do homework. Prior to learning about Kyle's illness, Judy had felt that his mother was irresponsible for not sending him to school each day. Following the conversation with Kyle's mother, Judy researched sickle cell anemia and began to understand more about the nature of the disease and its impact on Kyle and his family. Judy, like other interns, developed more accurate understandings about her students and their families in the course of having conversations with caregivers.

A few interns reported having awkward conversations with caregivers. These interns reported that the caregivers shared very little information about their children. For example, Jaime did not feel that her first conversation with Tyreek's mother went well. In her reflection, she wrote,

> The tone of the conversation was dry. Mrs. Wilson gave one-word answers and didn't seem interested. I felt I tried to be upbeat and keep the conversation flowing. The positive comment she gave was that Tyreek likes to read and that he likes everything about school. I listened to the parent, but she talked very little. I asked if I should call at a better time, but she said it was fine. I felt my weakness was not knowing how to continue the conversation after I got the feeling she did not want anything to do with me. I would change the way I related to the parent by not letting my feelings get in the way and focus on positive points.

Even though Jaime tried to be friendly and offered to call this parent at a more convenient time, she believed that Mrs. Wilson was not interested in sharing information about her son. Using this conversation as an example, I cautioned interns not to conclude from this conversation that this parent is not interested in her child. This is an assumption the interns often made when caregivers provided them with little information. The interns and I discussed the possibility that caregivers like Mrs. Wilson are sometimes too busy to talk, yet too polite to tell a teacher this.

We also considered the idea that some caregivers' reluctance to talk might have reflected a mistrust in teachers and schools. We talked about how teachers and school administrators sometimes can play a role in perpetuating caregiver mistrust. Most teachers in the schools we visited called caregivers primarily when children were having problems in school. A call from the teacher, therefore, might have signaled to Mrs. Wilson that something was wrong with her child, and so she responded guardedly. I explained that caregivers need to be reassured that gathering information about a child helps a teacher do his or her job better and that it does not signal that the child is in trouble. Finally, the interns suggested that some caregivers might not see preservice teachers as "real" teachers, and, therefore, some caregivers may have questioned the need for these conversations.

A few interns (less than 5%) reported that caregivers seemed hostile over the phone, as in the following case of an intern named Maggie:

> When I contacted Jordan's mother, I reintroduced myself. I explained the nature of my call and asked if she had time to talk about Jordan. This is when a sense of frustration came. I first asked her if I caught her at a bad time and she said "No" so I then proceeded to ask her if she could tell me a little about Jordan. I hate to say it, but she was the rudest person and she did not answer my question. I was shocked and frustrated. She did not even have the manners to say "I choose not to discuss this," or "Now is not a good time." Before I could say any more, I got the hint that this conversation needed to be over and fast.

Maggie was so upset by this experience that she refused to have any further contact with this parent, and it also left her feeling doubtful about conversations with other caregivers. Notice how Maggie blamed this parent for the failed conversation: "she was the rudest person." The goal I had for the interns, however, was to move beyond blaming the caregivers because such a stance might dissuade interns like Maggie from seeing other caregivers as approachable. I encouraged the interns to consider the larger scale social realities of caregivers' lives and to look for alternative explanations for these failed conversations.

## Changing Attitudes

Almost all the interns in the study spoke with caregivers at least twice, and many had three or more conversations in addition to other written or face-to-face exchanges with caregivers. The interns' final discussions and written reports from the caregiver project revealed changes in their ideas about caregivers. Their original tendency to blame caregivers for not meeting their children's literacy needs was replaced by a more informed understanding of caregivers' viewpoints, family circumstances, and, especially, concern for their children. By the end of the semester, the interns were more cautious in describing caregivers, taking into consideration caregivers' perspectives and circumstances. Marie's perspective at the end of the semester reflected a more complex view of caregivers:

> Children came from a variety of home situations, with parents involved in different ways. Some parents were really involved with helping their children with school. Some parents were not as involved with their children and sometimes this was because they held many jobs and raised more than one child by themselves.

The fact that Marie and other interns described varieties of home situations and different kinds of caregiver involvement was a noteworthy change from their earlier views, which tended to pigeonhole caregivers. Also, the interns' increased awareness of the social realities of these families was extremely important, given that one of the goals of diversity education is to understand others. End-of-semester survey data did not reflect the subtleties of the interns' new understandings about the complexities of families and urban life, but these data did reveal changes in the ways some interns viewed caregivers. The percentage of interns who believed that caregivers read to children or provided books for them increased almost threefold, to about 40% of the interns. The rest of the interns did not believe caregivers actively supported their children's literacy growth at home, but many believed that caregivers cared about their children.

It is important to note that the interns communicated with only a handful of caregivers, usually caregivers of children targeted by the cooperating teacher for needing extra help in reading. Therefore, the interns did not contact a representative sample of caregivers. Although many of the interns changed their minds about caregivers, this change primarily was based on the caregivers they contacted. Interns' beliefs about "other" caregivers were based on observing caregivers, observing children's homework, asking children about their homes and caregivers, and talking to cooperating teachers about the children's caregivers. By the end of the semester, about one quarter of the interns admitted that they had stereotyped urban caregivers at the beginning of the semester, a realization that prompted embarrassment and guilt:

> I believed the stereotypes that we have all heard over and over again. It angers me at how naïve I was and still am today. —Marie
>
> I feel like a fool. I could not have been more prejudice [sic]. —Amy

# Conclusion

Communicating with these caregivers helped many of the interns to envision ways to build relationships with their future students' caregivers and to learn from them. Through this project, the interns built more accurate understandings about children, home literacy events, caregivers' roles, and the circumstances that influence literacy achievement outside of school. Interns' opinions about caregivers, however, were shaped by the limitations of these communication projects; having only two telephone conversations with a given caregiver limited the amount of information available to the interns.

Also, the interns and I may have concentrated too narrowly on school-related literacy events at home, and caregivers may have gotten the impression that interns were interested only in children's school-related literacy activities. We did not fully explore the complexity of home-related literacy events and their influence on children's literacy growth. This aspect of literacy needs to be built into future caregiver communications in the internship.

The next chapter focuses on interns' work with children in school. Interns' teaching projects helped them develop understandings about children's literacy potential and the classroom conditions that support it. Of particular importance is their realization of the teacher's role in developing readers and writers, especially how much teachers need to know about assessment, instruction, literature, classroom management, and culturally relevant pedagogy. In constructing a complicated picture of literacy achievement, this inquiry had a significant impact on interns' understandings about their future roles as teachers.

---

## REFLECTION AND INQUIRY

1. Ask the caregivers of the children you teach to tell you about their children. (See the Parent Conference Guide on p. 89 for sample questions.) What insights did you derive from these interviews? How might you use this information to support each child's literacy development?

2. Experiment with different forms of caregiver communication. What modes of communication maximize caregiver input?

**3.** Consider why caregiver communication is significant for your teaching. How can you build caregiver communication/collaboration projects into your professional practice?

**4.** Read more about caregiver collaboration. See page 179 for a list of suggested readings.

CHAPTER 7

# Making Cultural Connections
# in Literacy Instruction

*I assumed my students (in the city) would barely be able to read and have little motivation to learn. I was completely wrong. My individual students, as well as the others I taught, were able to read and were eager to better their skills.*

—Randi, intern

*I thought that it would be a struggle to get children to read and write. I thought that they would only know a few words and that most would be illiterate. I had lower expectations due to stereotypes on TV. I learned that the students loved to read and write as long as the book or topic interests them.*

—Ashley, intern

*The children from the city were just as capable of learning as those from the affluent suburbs. What disturbed me the most was that I was able to realize how I expected less of these children based on their culture and where they were from.*

—Sarah, intern

At first, I smiled when I read these statements, thinking about the power of the internship to change interns' perceptions about the children they taught. But the statements also made me wonder why so many teachers have to *discover* that these children are academically capable. Why is it such a surprise to learn that these children like to read and can learn to read well? This chapter describes an awakening among the interns on two levels. First, it is about the interns discovering children's capacity to develop as readers and writers when literacy experiences are meaningful and are appropriately matched to their abilities. Second, it is about the interns discovering their own capacity to create learning environments that nurture children's literacy growth.

In the internship, we approached teaching from a diverse constructivist orientation (Au, 1998), which includes providing children with authentic, assessment-based literacy instruction. Authenticity includes the idea of drawing from children's lives to construct literacy lessons and giving children ownership over their literacy learning. Constructivist teaching also includes using multicultural literature and validating children's home language. In this chapter, I focus on interns' work with children in three areas: (1) using authentic, assessment-based literacy instruction, (2) using multicultural literature, and (3) validating children's home language. As with most new adventures, trying out new ways of teaching was exciting and challenging for the interns. Questions surfaced about managing classrooms and coping with less-than-optimal school resources, but these obstacles did not prevent many interns from considering taking urban teaching jobs someday.

# Child-Centered Literacy Instruction in the Tutorial Setting

## Experimenting With Authentic, Assessment-Based Instruction

The most convincing evidence in the internship that children could achieve in literacy came from the interns' direct observations of children's growth in the tutorial setting. The instructional goals followed a diverse constructivist orientation in that interns relied most heavily on authentic assessment (observations) to inform instruction, provided children with authentic literacy activities as well as instruction in specific literacy skills, and invited children to take ownership over their tutorial experiences.

The interns began by interviewing children about their attitudes and interests, and they gathered information about children's literacy abilities through running records (i.e., notations of a child's reading), spelling assessments, and writing assessments. Although information from these assessments provided teachers with general plans for selecting books and beginning instruction, the most valuable assessment information came from interns' own observations of children responding to instruction during the tutorials. In their teaching records, the interns recorded detailed notes about children's literacy behaviors, and they referred to these notes when forming instructional plans for individual children. They often included these instructional plans in their notes as well. To demonstrate the significance of matching instruction to ability, I will present Julia's work with Dante.

Julia, one of the interns, tutored Dante, a mid-year first grader who was just beginning to read books with one line of print (four to eight words) per page. Dante could identify all the letters of the alphabet, and his knowledge of most initial consonant sounds was good. He still confused some letter sounds, especially visually similar letters (e.g., *b*/*d*) and letters that represented similar sounds (e.g., *f*/*v*). Dante could automatically identify 12 of 20 words on the preprimer-level sight word list provided in *The Howard Street Tutoring Manual: Teaching At-Risk Readers in the Primary Grades* (Morris, 1999). He needed a lot of encouragement to write, and in fact he refused to write during Julia's initial assessment. When he was asked to write words as part of a spelling assessment, Dante included beginning and ending consonants but omitted or confused vowels. Dante enjoyed listening to stories read aloud and could identify the major story elements in the books Julia read aloud to him during the initial weeks of her assessment. Julia's instructional plan for Dante included both shared and guided (assisted) reading, writing tasks, word study, and making sense of stories read aloud, with the largest concentration of time being spent reading and writing whole texts.

Julia's first challenge was to find books for Dante's guided reading instruction. These texts would be ones he could read almost independently but that would give him an opportunity to draw from his knowledge of language and print to solve problems at the word and sentence levels. To find these texts for Dante, Julia selected from a large bank of leveled readers stored in the college library. She followed the guided reading format described by Fountas and Pinnell (1996), which included a story introduction and a modeling of strategies. After a few sessions with Dante, Julia felt more comfortable selecting leveled readers that were a good fit for him, but she monitored his reading constantly to inform her text selection. When Dante read these books, Julia recorded the strategies Dante used to identify unknown words, and from this information, she designed goals for helping him enhance his ability to use reading strategies effectively.

To strengthen Dante's knowledge of consonant sounds, Julia organized picture sorting activities using the text *Words Their Way: Word Study for Phonics, Vocabulary, and Spelling Instruction* (Bear, Invernizzi, Templeton, & Johnston,

1996) as a guide. At first, she wanted to make sure he could distinguish between frequently confused consonants. She modeled saying the names of the items pictured, emphasizing the initial consonant sounds of these words and placing the picture cards in columns under the letters that represented these initial consonant sounds.

Julia also read Dante picture books with rich vocabulary and interesting plots. She planned to help him make sense of these stories through various writing, talking, and role-playing experiences. She was most interested in building Dante's understanding of story characters. Through reading aloud to him, Julia hoped she could inspire Dante to write stories about his own life outside of school. Table 1 shows a sample of her observations and reflective notes during their third tutoring session; this sample shows Julia's ability to observe and reflect on Dante's responses to the guided reading, word study, and read-aloud experiences she planned for him.

Over time, Julia became more and more proficient in recording observations and adjusting plans for Dante. As she targeted her instruction within his Zone of Proximal Development (Vygotsky, 1934/1978), she observed how

### TABLE 1
### Reflective Notes—Julia Tutoring Dante

| Anecdotal Notes | Reflection |
| --- | --- |
| Assisted Reading: During echo reading, he read with me some parts of the story and seemed to rely on picture cues. | I think I should show him several reading strategies. I need to remind him that what he reads needs to make sense—[I should say] go back, reread, [and] ask, Does that make sense? |
| Word Study: He did the closed *p/s/m* picture sort with ease. | He can distinguish between these three sounds, so I'll try a sort next time with *b/d*. |
| Making Sense of Stories Read Aloud: He needed a lot of scaffolding to determine which events were important in the story. | I need to keep guiding/scaffolding until he can pick out the events that are important in stories. Next time, I will make the story circle [a circle-shaped graphic organizer with one section for each story event] bigger, perhaps with more sections so he can write more and break down the story more. |

well he responded to instruction. Within two months, Dante was reading predictable pattern books with two and three lines of print per page (10–20 words), and he also used pictures and sense-making strategies more often while reading. In the area of word study, Dante could now sort consonant blends and was working on vowel picture sorts. His sight word knowledge increased to about 40 words. He included many more vowel sounds accurately in his invented spelling, and, on occasion, he now became excited to write, a point I will discuss in more depth later.

Almost all of the interns observed progress with their individual tutoring students, and in noting this progress, the interns realized they had the ability to advance children's development. By mid-semester, I began to see many comments such as the following on interns' teaching records:

> I feel more confident now. I better understand how to give my student what he needs to improve his reading abilities. —Anne

> I feel very confident with tutoring my individual student. He is always happy to see me and I have observed his progress. —Lynne

I cannot emphasize enough how important these words are. These comments reflected a fundamental change in interns' ways of seeing children and of seeing themselves as literacy teachers. By semester's end, 90% of the interns felt confident about their ability to help children grow as readers and writers in the tutorial. Success in the tutorial enhanced their self-images as teachers, as each intern added a new dimension to his or her emerging identity—the dimension of "I am one who can teach successfully." Notice the language Anne and Lynne used to describe students. Instead of saying "this" student, each intern wrote "my" student. In this close tutorial space, interns began to assume their responsibility as literacy teachers. By the end of the semester, I found them boasting about what *their* students could do.

## Tapping Into Children's Interests and Culture

For the interns in the study, individualizing instruction also meant bringing children's out-of-school experiences into the tutorial. This was done primarily through writing, but engagements in writing also were enriched by meaningful reading and talking experiences. At the start of the semester, I gathered together all of the children tutored by interns and told them that there would be an author's party at the end of the semester. I explained that they would have an opportunity to create their own books during their tutorials, which they then would share at the end of the semester with all the interns and with the children involved in our tutoring program.

The interns began this project by helping the children choose relevant topics drawn from their own lives. Interns also shared their own writing with children, and these pieces reflected the infinitely interesting world (from the children's viewpoint) of the college student—university life, exams, friends, parties, music, shopping, studying, and families. Some interns shared their poetry, songs, travel notes, and jokes with the children. The interns discussed why they wrote these pieces and where they might "publish" their writing once they felt it was ready to be shared publicly. This writing gave interns a place to begin conversations with children about the children's interests, families, friends, and communities and about the children's plans for writing. The interns found most children eager to talk about their lives, as one intern, Amy, reported: "They wanted to tell me all about their families (and their) likes and dislikes outside of the classroom. I listened carefully to the children because I knew how important it was to connect with their lives."

There were initial snags, however, when some children did not reveal much about themselves. Rebecca's student Tamika was one of these children. Rebecca complained that Tamika wouldn't "open up" during the first few days of the tutorial, despite Rebecca's many attempts to invite dialogue. Rebecca worried that she wouldn't be able to inspire this child to write. We noticed, though, that Tamika always joined another child, Rayana, after each tutorial. They'd often sing as they skipped back to their classroom together. Being a big fan of hip-hop music, Rebecca downloaded some song lyrics from the Internet and brought them in to share with Tamika. Music became the focus of their literacy work together; Rebecca brought in lyrics for Tamika to read and sing, which led to other explorations of poetry and songwriting. As I checked in with Rebecca to monitor her progress with Tamika, I couldn't help but notice the solid rapport they had developed through their mutual interest in music. To the interns' last class session with the children, I brought a microphone and amplifier so that the children could read aloud their "published books" to all of the interns and other children. Tamika and Rayana kicked off the event by singing one of their favorite songs.

Throughout the semester, the interns observed children's positive responses toward personally relevant literacy lessons, but they also realized a continuing need to create literacy experiences for children that were both meaningful and developmentally fit. For most interns, designing instruction that was both engaging and appropriate for each child was very challenging at first. Julia's experience with Dante shows that the process of constructing successful literacy experiences for children requires lots of experimentation and reflection.

As I mentioned earlier, Julia's student Dante did not want to write at the outset of the tutorial. In an effort to inspire him to write about his home city of Philadelphia, Julia read him Lenski's (1987) *Sing a Song of People* (a poem picture book about the comings and goings of people in the city) and Dorros's (1995) *Isla* (a picture book about a grandmother who returns to her native Caribbean islands to show her granddaughter the old city, the tropical rain forest, and her home). After reviewing the pictures in both stories and discussing the differences between Philadelphia and the settings described in the two books, Julia asked Dante to write about his own city of Philadelphia. She then suggested that he make a travel brochure that would help readers learn about his city. To begin, she asked Dante to jot down a list of the things he had seen and done in the city.

Dante did not respond to this experience in the ways Julia had expected. She wrote in her notes, "He really struggled with the writing. He seemed constantly to be distracted, frustrated or uninterested. I had to keep pulling for ideas, asking him to write his thoughts and asking him questions." Julia believed that her lesson had not gone well because Dante did not want to write about Philadelphia, nor did he have much to say about the city. She also questioned the relevance of having Dante make a travel brochure:

> I think generally, I need to make writing assignments more personalized and meaningful for Dante. No matter how appropriate or enjoyable the books I choose are, they won't be effectively integrated with writing unless Dante really takes an interest in what he is writing.

The next week, Julia read Dante the book *Uncle Jed's Barbershop* (1993) by Margaree King Mitchell. It is the story of Uncle Jed, who gives up his savings to pay for his niece's surgery and then later loses his money again when the bank closes down during the Great Depression. Despite these losses, he continues to pursue a dream by working hard to save up enough money to own a barbershop. As she read aloud, Julia stopped to talk to Dante about how Uncle Jed worked hard to make his dream come true. She then invited Dante to write about a dream that he wanted to make come true, or to write about a family member of his who had such a dream.

According to Julia's notes, Dante responded very positively to being given a choice, and he chose to write about being a basketball player:

He really liked being given a choice today. He chose to write about his dream of being a basketball player. He ended up writing about his new sneakers and Michael Jordan and the movie about Jordan. He was very excited as he began numbering and listing (on the brainstorming sheet), but then began to write in paragraph form. This is the most and probably the best he has ever written for me.

Julia's book selection, theme discussion, and invitation to choose a topic inspired Dante to write about something that mattered to him.

Dante's choice to write about a sports hero was typical among the boys that the interns taught in the internship. For example, some boys' topics focused on The Rock, a heavyweight wrestling champion; Allen Iverson, the Philadelphia 76ers basketball star; and Donovan McNabb, the Philadelphia Eagles quarterback. The boys wrote "mini" biographies about these men, as well as fictionalized accounts of teaming up with them to defeat "bad guys." The boys loved writing about these and other sports figures, and so we saw these topics as catalysts for helping reluctant readers and writers to join the literacy "club" (Smith, 1988). We also found that children's interests often were divided along gender lines, with girls generally writing about best friends, family members, events (sleepovers, birthday parties, and trips), and television characters, rather than sports heroes.

In the internship, we wanted to create literacy experiences that would not only engage children but also empower them. In one of my class meetings with the interns, we talked about what it meant for children to write about being sports superstars or rap artists, another popular topic for children. Allison commented that these children's fascination with superstars was nothing unusual; it only reflected U.S. society's obsession with money and celebrity. This conversation led to another about the importance of teachers selecting books with characters who displayed virtues such as integrity, intellectualism, bravery, honor, and diligence. We also talked about expanding children's sense of their own cultural heritage by bringing into the tutorial some stories about men and women of color who, by their own wit and determination, overcome obstacles to attain their dreams. This was Julia's original intent in using *Uncle Jed's Barbershop* with Dante. Uncle Jed sacrificed for his family, pursued a goal over a long period of time, and worked hard to achieve it. These are topics that show readers and writers how to recognize "heroes" within their own families and communities. Julia was not able to help Dante extend this theme into his own writing, however, which showed me that I needed to help the interns make these themes more explicit for children.

In their tutorials, the interns used many biographies of famous African Americans across a wide range of fields. They brought in picture books about Richard Wright, Phyllis Wheatley, Ida B. Wells, Sarah Breedlove Walker, and many others. The positive responses these books received from the children affirmed that the interns were on the right track, as Anne noticed when she planned a unit on famous African Americans for her fourth-grade student Rasheem. Rasheem was so excited about these stories that he asked Rebecca to make copies of them so that he could have them in his notebook at home. When she completed her internship, Rebecca wrote, "The attitudes children had towards us had taken a total 180 turn. Even those students who were not thrilled with us in the beginning of the semester had been turned onto us and our methods of teaching."

What had taken a big turn were the interns' attitudes toward children and toward themselves as literacy teachers. Creating experiences that inspired children to really read and write demonstrated to the interns that they could be effective teachers. Seeing themselves as successful teachers of *their* tutorial students was an important beginning that I hoped would carry over to the interns' work in the regular classroom. However, this transference proved more difficult.

When teaching in the regular classroom, interns realized how difficult it was to design literacy experiences that were fit for each child. Each intern was placed in a grade-level classroom with a peer partner to teach lessons around multicultural themes, a component I describe later in the chapter. Interns also spent time observing and assisting their cooperating teachers. In both situations, interns observed firsthand how challenging it was to organize the literacy classroom to serve children's individual needs. Most cooperating teachers were using guided reading groups, writer's workshop, and word study centers to differentiate instruction, but many were just becoming proficient in organizing the classroom around these literacy events. Cooperating teachers also provided children with time for independent reading using the 100 Book Challenge program (in which children read books they selected from clearly marked bins of leveled readers). Through the school–university partnership that allowed for my study, the classroom teachers were given a wide range of leveled books to use with children who read below grade level. Many of the interns began to see that children could realize their potential in these classrooms if teachers organized learning environments toward this goal, as Marie discovered: "I witnessed outstanding teachers and instruction in these classrooms, and quickly discovered that despite the poor conditions, these children were learning and the teachers were making it all possible."

The interns observed how demanding it was to create these classroom climates. Anne and others discovered how much time teachers spent to make these classrooms work:

> It was not until I spent time with the whole class did I see the desire and passion these teachers had to develop children's learning. The time and endless efforts [teachers devoted] for the children to learn was truly limitless. For example, Miss ___ would spend hours planning lessons because so many of her children were on different levels.

Anne and other interns wondered about their own ability to individualize instruction. The interns believed that they would need much more time to work out systems for individualizing instruction in the regular classroom in order to be effective teachers.

## Using Multicultural Texts

The use of multicultural literature is one of seven recommendations for improving the literacy achievement gap of children of color:

> The use of literature that accurately depicts the experiences of diverse groups may improve the literacy achievement of students of diverse backgrounds by increasing their motivation to read (Spears-Bunton, 1990), their appreciation and understanding of their own language and cultural heritage (Jordan, 1988), and their valuing of their own life experience as a topic for writing. (Au, 1998, p. 311)

The presence of multicultural literature is important for helping children see themselves reflected in the school curriculum, but the significance of this literature lies in how teachers help children interact with it. In the internship, I modeled three different ways of transacting with texts through personal, literary, and critical responses. Personal response helps children make text-to-self connections. For example, the interns would ask children to compare themselves with the main character and tell how they felt about the character's decision. Interns were very comfortable with this mode of response. Literary response demands that children explore the literary elements found in narrative texts, such as characters, problem, solution, setting, and theme. For example, the interns might ask children to tell how a character changed during a story or to describe the setting of the story and explain how it influences what happens. Most interns were able to help children examine the literary features in multicultural literature, but sometimes they needed help interpreting the major themes contained in these stories and discussing the themes with the children. This may be one reason why many interns had difficulty with the expectation that they help children transact with texts critically.

Critical reading demands that we actively question the messages contained in literature. I explained that reading critically helps children look beyond what is in the text, to examine the values, assumptions, and beliefs underlying the messages or images being represented. Although many interns realized that reading critically is essential for helping children form opinions about what they read and make sound decisions based on these opinions, most interns were not able to apply this notion when they used multicultural literature in the classroom. This is consistent with the research that suggests that preservice teachers resist critical readings of multicultural literature (Apol, Sakuma, Reynolds, & Rop, 2003). Initially, the interns in my study even resisted using multicultural books with children.

## *Locating and Incorporating Multicultural Texts*

Beginning in 1997, I asked the interns in my university classes to weave multicultural literature into their teaching. I provided them with lists of picture books with culturally diverse characters and with multicultural themes. Some interns complained that they couldn't find much multicultural literature in libraries and bookstores. Others indicated that they preferred to use "raceless" picture books—that is, ones in which characters' physical features were rendered abstractly (collages, stick figures) so that the characters could not be identified by race. Our university library contained some, but not many, Big Books, leveled books, and picture books that would be considered multicultural. Some interns, such as Amy, reported having trouble locating enough of these materials, even in bookstores:

> I've tried to stick with culturally relevant books. I've spent hours in the library and books stories [sic] looking for books that include different cultures, especially African American, Cambodian, and Spanish cultures. Sometimes I would just bring books with animal characters because I did not want to make black and white an issue.

If a piece of literature did not feature white characters, the interns reasoned that the text satisfied the "multicultural" requirement. At this point I recognized interns' use of these "culturally neutral" texts had something to do with their difficulty finding multicultural texts. I did wonder, however, if they preferred to use these books because they were uncomfortable with using multicultural literature. I knew limited quantities of such books were kept in the college library and were more readily available in local bookstores. Nevertheless, this prompted me to be much more explicit about how interns could find and use this literature in the future. The following semester, I demonstrated how to construct a teaching unit that specifically addressed multicultural themes, particularly themes that mirrored the experiences and histories of their own students from different cultures. I connected our treatment of multicultural literature to Banks's (1999) transformation and social action approaches, asking the interns how we could use literature to help children (a) view concepts, issues, and events from the perspective of others (transformation); and (b) take a stance on important social issues and take action to solve social problems (social action). I modeled before-, during-, and after-reading experiences that would help children think critically about the themes contained in these multicultural books. I talked with the interns about the images represented in the literature and about the ways in which the language and themes validated the experiences and heritages of children across many cultural communities.

After I began these more in-depth discussions with interns about using multicultural literature, all of the interns in these groups located and used multicultural literature that contained realistic images of people of color. Interns' treatment of this literature, however, varied. I return to the two interns discussed in chapter 5, Marie and Allison, to illustrate the different stances that interns took when using multicultural literature.

**Marie**. Marie was struck by the ways in which the successful teachers of black students in *The Dreamkeepers* (Ladson-Billings, 1994) challenged children to critically examine the literature they read. In response to Ladson-Billings's book, she wrote the following:

> It is very easy to read a book to a child and ask him/her questions about what happened. However, these teachers want to know why something happened and why the students feel that this is what they should believe or if they should research these topics further. The traditional ways knowledge is conceived in

the classroom is by reading a book, and memorizing what they have read. I feel it is important to emphasize critical thinking because this is a way to get children involved in their reading. They will have a say in what they believe in and reasons to back up their beliefs.

Even though Marie appreciated the ways in which expert teachers helped children to interact critically with literature, she herself did not help children respond critically to books. She and her teaching partner developed a "world tour" thematic unit, in which they taught about a different cultural community each day through the use of picture books in the historical fiction genre. This approach did not allow for deep exploration of any one community anyway, but within the limitations of this format, Marie and her partner also resisted engaging the children in critical discussions of these books. As one example, I draw from notes taken on the day I observed Marie teaching a group of third graders about the Japanese American experience the World War II. Her aim was to help the children understand how Japanese Americans suffered during the time of internment, when they were identified as being sympathetic toward the Japanese while the United States was at war with Japan. Clearly, her objective aligned with Banks's (1999) transformation approach to teaching, but she was not able to reach this goal.

Marie began by reading aloud the book *My Hiroshima* (Morimoto, 1992), a story about a boy who recalls growing up peacefully in Japan until the United States dropped an atomic bomb on the city of Hiroshima. After Marie read aloud the book, a few children raised their hands and asked, "Did that really happen?" "Did our country really bomb those people?" "Why did we do that?" Marie explained that Hiroshima and Nagasaki were bombed to end World War II. Marie also explained to the children that during this part of the war, Japanese American families were forced to move to internment camps. She showed the children illustrations of these camps from another picture book. Following this discussion, she taped a picture of a suitcase to the blackboard. Inside the suitcase were words describing what she would take if she had to suddenly leave her home, as the Japanese Americans did. She asked the children to think about what they would put in a suitcase if they were told they had a day to pack only a few of their belongings. The children were then given construction paper and asked to "make their own suitcases" and to fill them with words representing things they would take with them.

Marie's intent was to simulate what it must have been like for Japanese Americans to leave their homes during the time of internment. But the suitcase activity did not help the children to think about race as a factor in the internment campaign. Marie did not emphasize that Japanese Americans were *forced* to leave and were held captive because they looked like the enemy. Her students actually presented her with opportunities to talk about these more significant issues when they asked, "Why did we bomb those people?" This question could have led to discussions about racial prejudice, but this did not happen. Instead, Marie answered this question by defending the U.S. bombing campaign against Japan: "It was the only thing we could do to stop the war."

In my conference with her afterward, Marie seemed very pleased with the lesson: "The kids really paid attention and did what I asked them to do." This was true. Her students were captivated by these stories, and they were very cooperative throughout the lesson. I wondered if, having gained confidence in attracting the children's attention, Marie could move on to staging critical discussions about this literature. I asked her to think about how she could extend the lesson into another day and address the theme of racial prejudice using the book *My Hiroshima* and how she could build on what the children might know about judging people on the basis of physical characteristics. Marie indicated that she already had planned another lesson with her teaching partner for the next day.

I hoped that Marie might consider my suggestion, but I later realized that without having opportunities to think critically about these stories herself, she would be on shaky ground with these kinds of discussions. I also sensed that she needed more information about these historical events and that she needed to be immersed in critical discussions that would help her look at these events from alternative perspectives. These were not "safe" topics, and I realized that I was asking her and other interns to do things they simply were not ready to do.

**Allison**. Allison's approach to multicultural literature was more transactional (Rosenblatt, 1978) in that she helped readers relate their own life experiences to the themes contained in books. However, like Marie, she did not engage children in critical discussions about these themes. In response to teaching a semester-long unit using African American folk tales, Allison developed a strong appreciation for using this literature to make important connections with children: Allison felt that African American writers can make a true connection with an African American child because of a shared experience and shared history.

The story of John Henry, as written by Lester (1994) and illustrated by Pinkney, was an example.

I observed Allison reading aloud this book to a group of third graders. As with most tall tales, Lester's version of the John Henry story captures important themes about human nature. John Henry is presented as a folk hero with superhuman strength who builds a railroad in the hills of West Virginia. John Henry uses strength and determination to beat a steam engine in a contest to dig out a railroad tunnel. Sadly, he dies after completing the tunnel. Following his death, a whisper is heard among those who mourn his death: "Dying ain't important. Everyone does that. What matters is how well you do your living" (p. 33).

Upon finishing the book, Allison invited the children to tell the class what they thought about John Henry. Some children raised their hands and said that John Henry was strong, hardworking, and powerful. Allison then prompted the children to think more deeply about the character: "Okay, that's true. Now think about the kind of person it takes to do what he did."

In response, one student said, "John Henry didn't let no one stop him." Allison extended the conversation:

> That's right. Even though John Henry was tired and had to compete against a machine, he still hung in there and didn't let anyone stop him. Do you know any people who stick with something even though it's hard to do?

She asked them to think about the kinds of people in their lives who persevered in the face of big challenges, and she gave them time to write down a list of such people. Every child in the classroom began to write.

Allison helped the children to make sense of an important theme that figures prominently in African American literature: struggle and perseverance. She helped the children to think about the traits that made John Henry such a noble character and helped them to see these traits in others. A more critical discussion of this text might involve helping the children see that even though John Henry's power and determination helped him triumph over the steam engine, the effort he expended to do so probably killed him. I also could imagine a discussion that would help children connect the power of the steam engine to the technologies of today: What happens when people are replaced by machines? Who owns the technologies of today? How can everyone own these technologies?

Allison and the other interns enjoyed using multicultural literature that depicted realistic images and themes from different cultural communities. These stories captivated the children and reinforced the power of this literature to inspire reading, writing, and discussion. The interns helped children to connect with texts on a personal and aesthetic level, but, as mentioned previously, they did not help children view these texts critically. There was no evidence to suggest that this omission was intentional, but the interns themselves had had few prior experiences interacting with texts critically.

## Validating Home Language and Teaching the Language of Power

Prior to this school experience, I viewed Ebonics as a kind of slang. Therefore if African American children "refused" to speak "correctly"—they obviously didn't want to be literate adults. We viewed these students as uncaring because of their use of "slang." I discovered that Ebonics is a language and a huge part of the African American culture. These children need to be taught that standard English is a second language. —Amy

Nearly all of the children the interns and I served in the internship spoke African American Vernacular English (AAVE) (Rickford & Rickford, 2000), also referred to as Ebonics. As previously stated, there were a few children who came from different cultures, some of whom may have spoken a language other than English at home. Because the overwhelming majority of students were AAVE speakers, I focused on interns' understanding of this language. Our discussions about language were centered on the book *The Real Ebonics Debate: Power, Language, and the Education of African American Children* (Perry & Delpit, 1998). After reading and discussing this book, the interns suggested that the children's home language should be validated in the classroom and that bilingualism ought to be a goal of their instruction. Many interns wrote about teachers' capacity to marginalize children by continually correcting dialect-related miscues rather than acknowledging children's meaning-making attempts during reading (Delpit, 1995). The interns began to see how difficult it was for children of a nondominant culture to perform in a classroom where standard English was expected, in the company of teachers who lacked awareness about the significance of the children's home language:

Put yourself in their position...what if we went to school and the teacher made us speak Ebonics. Just put yourself in their place for a second! —Marie

I would be resentful of a culture that didn't respect me and wanted me to speak differently. —Cynthia

I had no idea...we don't understand that they are able to comprehend if they put it into their own language. If you stop them (and say) "What is that word?" you are breaking up their development. —Amy

By continually correcting students you are taking away the meaning of reading and it comes to a point where they don't want to read anymore. Then there will be silence. —Julia

The interns became absorbed in our discussions about the origins of the children's home language. Having lived in culturally mixed neighborhoods, Allison brought to her reading many past experiences with language. She already was familiar with some features of African American vernacular and was fascinated to learn about the origins of the language:

Reading about Ebonics cleared up some mysteries for me. I learned that "be" and "been" is rooted in Niger-Congo languages. It is an expression that means "recurring or habitual state of affairs" ([Perry & Delpit, 1998], p. 31). These examples show that Ebonics is not a chaotic dialect. Another interesting fact I found was the reason for the /r/ sound deletion in many words. A lot of friends I have do this as well as my kids in the practicum. As Smitherman (1998) points out, it results from "a phonological pattern derived from the influence of West African languages" which doesn't have this sound (p. 31). I think its cool too that these influences have still survived and fought back against "colonization." Something that was totally new to me was the word *signifyin*. Although the concept and different details of signifyin are more than familiar to me from growing up (I personally know a billion or so yo mamma jokes) the label itself is new. I heard people call it "playin the Dozens" though.

In this journal entry, Allison expresses a belief that African Americans have actively resisted "colonization" of African American vernacular, but she fails to indicate that the language also has been sustained over time through segregation and that racism has contributed to the social isolation of its speakers (Rickford & Rickford, 2000).

Allison's appreciation for children's language really stood out in much of her writing. In another entry, she acknowledges a need to help children code switch—that is, switch from standard English to Ebonics or vice versa when the conditions warrant it—but she then questions why anyone would want to groom children for a life in the corporate world:

I think as a teacher I definitely have to respect the language of my students' local environment while still helping them achieve competency in standard code for when they need it. I think it's all about respect and letting kids know their language is beautiful but they'll need some other code, not because the other codes are better, but because it is the language of business and politics, and is needed for higher success. The key is helping kids to understand when they have to switch between codes and they don't have to forsake the code of their loved ones. Does it ever bother anyone when people talk about how standard English is the language of business and the corporate world and how we need our kids to be able to use this form of English to get jobs in these fields? Who wants to be in business and the corporate world all their lives? Talk about a miserable existence. Why are we measuring "success" with money? When I have kids, whatever color they end up being, I'm definitely steering them away from any corporate life.

Allison's anti-establishment identity influenced the ways in which she viewed language and literacy. She articulated a need to help children become biliterate, but her critical views of corporate America suggest that she would resist teaching standard forms to her own children, "whatever color they end up being." Judging from her statements shown above, Allison did not appear to account for the perspectives of African Americans who do feel that it is necessary to teach children how to code switch when the situation warrants it. After reading more of *The Real Ebonics Debate*, Allison recognized the need to help children code switch. In her cultural autobiography (see the Appendix), she wrote about the teacher's role as one of preserving culture through validating the language children bring to school. Further, she defended the use of Ebonics among her friends:

The children at _____ school and *The Real Ebonics Debate* have shown me how beautiful, fluid, structural, and grammatical Ebonics actually is despite ignorant criticisms. I have used many points discussed in the book in arguments with friends and won them over to appreciating and conceding the worth of Ebonics. I know that language is more than just words but that is [sic] a part of us. [It is] a living, changing part of our lives. Language unites us with others. When a teacher takes shots at a student when he/she uses Ebonics, the teacher is actually taking shots at her/the family, neighborhood, and the essence of the student themselves. I see that code switching must be emphasized, but that there is a time and place for Ebonics.

Allison's comments about Ebonics contrasted with those of Marie, who, prior to taking the internship, was less familiar with the speech patterns of

African American children. Marie realized the need to value children's home language, but she did not know how to do this while teaching children standard forms:

> I found it difficult to explain to them certain sounds, vowels, spellings, etc. because I didn't want to make them feel like they were wrong for the way they speak. Sounds such as *a, e, i, o, u, th, fl, d*, etc., seemed to be exceptionally hard for them to speak and for me to explain. We learned Ebonics is a language and should be recognized as one. Before this class I had no idea that there was a big controversy over Ebonics. I realize now how uneducated I was about this topic and all the misconceptions people have about it. It is important for classroom teachers to understand Ebonics in order to help their students learn and grow in their culture. I will accept that my African American students speak a second language and [I] will not always correct their use of this language. Instead I will try to help them to see the difference between Ebonics and standard English and help them to switch between the two languages.
> —Marie

Marie articulated the need to honor the children's home language and help children code switch, but she worried that the children might be offended by her explanation that standard English ought to be used at certain times. Being an outsider to the culture and realizing that language and identity are entwined, Marie felt uncomfortable about approaching language differences with the children.

Other interns helped the children translate from Ebonics to standard English, but they did not talk to children directly about how code switching might help them. Also, although they appropriated some of the language that linguists used to describe the legitimacy of Ebonics (from reading *The Real Ebonics Debate*), their spontaneous remarks about Ebonics revealed deeply rooted prejudices about the language:

> In their published pieces we stressed Standard English—we never told the children they were wrong, rather we asked for ways to say it differently. —Kelly
>
> I did not constantly correct her writing or her speech. I would point out some things in her writing, but not rip it apart and tell her everything that was wrong. —Kristina

Note how both of these interns described the children's home language as "wrong," reflecting a deficit view of Ebonics. They had not learned to see Ebonics as a legitimate language form, despite their reading of *The Real Ebonics*

*Debate* and our discussions of this book. They refrained, however, from correcting children's speech and instead concentrated on helping children use standard forms in their written communication.

Although none of the interns constructed a lesson that specifically helped children to explore language differences, a few interns considered how they might use literature this way. Allison considered using *John Henry* to help children study differences between the African American vernacular that Lester uses in the book and standard forms of English:

> While the majority of the sentences are written in standard English, Lester uses Ebonics to spice up the tale. For instance, he uses a double negative to emphasize a point: "She wasn't going to have none of that" or "Didn't nobody see John Henry." The students and I could discuss different possibilities pertaining to its meaning. We could write down those sentences in other ways—some with other double negatives and some with standard English phrasings. We could talk about when it's better to use the different forms of these sentences when you, for instance, write a letter to your brother or cousin (Ebonics), write a letter to Mayor John Street or the principal (standard English). Other examples of Ebonics include "It ain't gon' rain," and "I don't know about none of that." I think the important point is getting kids to realize when it's appropriate and beautiful to use Ebonics, and when it's good to use standard English.

Allison did not have an opportunity to use Lester's book in this way, but her plans suggest a willingness to help children explore language through the medium of children's literature.

Some interns believed that children's home forms of oral communication would interfere with their literacy development, despite my argument that pronunciation does not determine one's mastery of literacy. I explained that speakers of alternative forms of English eventually learn to read, write, and spell words in the English lexicon through reading, writing, and spelling instruction. For example, my Massachusetts relatives do not pronounce the final consonant sound in words ending with *r* so they say *bettah* for *better*, but they can read and spell the word correctly. The interns also raised concerns that speaking Ebonics would prevent children from achieving success in school, especially if teachers were not sensitive to language issues. Anne, for instance, continued to frame Ebonics as a problem to be overcome:

> I know that we say that Black dialect is grammatical and all that but when I heard them use it and saw it in their writing and I just know it's wrong. My friends and family say the whole Ebonics thing is nuts, and I know I couldn't

get anywhere talking like that. My English teachers jumped on my mistakes. That's the way I learned. And these kids are making lots of mistakes. I just don't see how they're going to learn to read, write, and spell talking like that.

Direct successful teaching experiences with children, and reading and discussing *The Real Ebonics Debate*, still left about half of the interns believing that the children spoke ungrammatically (76% of the interns, on the other hand, felt that suburban children spoke grammatically). These interns believed that standard English was grammatical, but they couldn't ascribe this quality to Ebonics, even though we discussed the idea that all languages are grammatical in that they are rule-governed and based on the norms of particular discourse communities. It was as if the interns could accept the fact in the abstract that nonstandard dialects were grammatical, but when placed in discourse contexts, they regressed to judging the children's language negatively because it deviated from their own.

# Can I Do This Job?

## *Questions About Classroom Management*

Most interns team-taught with another intern in the regular classroom with their cooperating teacher's assistance, so, given all this help, few interns had difficulty with managing children in whole-class settings. But because the interns did not have opportunities to teach the whole class by themselves, I wondered about their capacity for whole-class teaching. I also wondered if those interns who talked the talk of multiculturalism would be able to interact well in the regular classroom with children in high-poverty schools. I could not assume that knowing about multiculturalism would translate to excellent teaching of these children. For example, I have highlighted Allison's growth in cultural sensitivity, including her activist stance, her capacity to select and convey important cultural themes in books, and her appreciation of children's home language—yet I wondered about her ability to be an effective teacher because of her difficulty in managing the classroom when she worked with her partner.

Allison's cooperating teacher had a large class of 29 children. She frequently worked with children out in the hallway when Allison and her partner taught the class. Two weeks into the semester, Allison wrote, "I love all of my kids and feel very comfortable with them, but I do have some management problems I can't seem to deal with in the most effective way." I visited Allison's classroom that week and noted how politely and sweetly she asked her students to attend to directions. The children attended for a few moments, but I noticed that some of the children in the back of the room soon began to tune out. When I had a chance to speak with Allison later, I described how she had spoken to the children in a respectful, pleasant manner but that some children in the back of the room were not paying attention. I asked her to tell me what she thought about her ways of communicating with the class. Allison said that she wanted to speak respectfully to the children because, she believed, "They hear too much yelling already in this school." Then she looked at me and asked, "What do you think I should do? I don't want to yell."

Mainstream discourses (including those at the university level) teach preservice teachers that intellectual growth and motivation are born in a democratic classroom. Preservice teachers often are groomed to invite children to make good choices about how they will conduct themselves in the classroom. Many students of education view authoritative teaching as an approach that places limits on children's responsibility and decision making, and they feel that these ways of teaching do not communicate to children that they should want to learn and that they can be trusted. Current literacy pedagogy aims toward self-regulation—helping a child select his or her own books during independent reading time or having children work independently and cooperatively during reading and writing workshop time. This paradigm shaped Allison's thinking about how she should communicate with children.

Allison did not know that other cultural communities have different ideas about the role of a teacher. Delpit (1995) makes the case that people of color expect authority figures to act with authority. Delpit contends that one's title alone does not confer authority, as it often does in mainstream middle class communities, but that children instead make judgments about a teacher's authority based on his or her words and deeds. Teachers who act like the students will not be viewed as having authority in the classroom. Delpit also contrasts the indirect questioning style of many white teachers with the kinds of directive more typically used by black teachers. She refers to the indirect questioning style of the middle class teachers in Heath's study (1983), for example, "Is this where the scissors belong?" To most middle class white students, this would mean, "Put the scissors away where they belong." Poor and working class children may misinterpret such a request because their caregivers are more apt to use directives in the form of statements, such as, "Put those scissors on that shelf."

When I explained all this to Allison, she noted that she would like to pay more attention to her ways of talking to children, but she didn't quite know how best to adjust her approach in order to show children that she was the authority figure in the classroom. She feared that the damage already had been done; the children already did not see her as the person in charge. Fortunately, Allison was working with a strong and effective cooperating teacher whose communication style was firm, direct, and respectful. I suggested that Allison observe her cooperating teacher more carefully and focus on the ways in which she sustained the children's attention and helped them stay on task. I also invited Allison to talk to the cooperating teacher about some of her ways of communicating with students.

In my subsequent visits to Allison's classroom, I noticed some changes. She learned to clap in rhythm to get students' attention, and they clapped back. She read and talked to the class more effectively by moving around the classroom, projecting her voice, and directing her attention to children who did not seem to be on task. She also used more directives in the form of statements, such as "Please go to your seat." In time, she became more proficient in accomplishing her teaching goals, although she continued to have difficulty in getting some students to attend to her. By the end of the semester, she was able to read a book to the class, conduct thoughtful literature discussions about the book, and lead the children in a writing activity based on these discussions. She recognized that she needed continued help with her classroom management approach, but she felt capable of becoming successful at it someday.

## Stepping Up to the Challenges of Urban Schools

I had hoped that by having interns experiment with culturally relevant teaching during the internship, they would recognize children's literacy potential and their own potential to be successful teachers in urban schools. Although the interns realized that children could learn well in the tutorial when they were provided with instruction tailored to their needs and interests, some interns did not believe that the children had the same potential as their suburban counterparts for becoming fully literate. This was not because they believed that urban children lacked the ability, but because they believed that the schools did not provide enough support for urban children to reach their literacy potential. These interns saw their cooperating teachers as dedicated and effective, but they realized that these teachers did not have control over resources such as special education services and libraries or over the numbers of children placed in their classrooms. The interns also saw how taxing it was for teachers to deliver individualized instruction to so many children with such varied literacy needs. They wondered about children's ability to thrive in these schools:

> The intelligence and talent that I see in the students at _____ is overwhelming, but I feel that in a way their brilliance is being wasted, for they are not getting the support, guidance, and special attention that is needed [to succeed]. It is extremely frustrating to see students with so much potential being stuck in a situation that seems unlikely to improve. —Cynthia

> I discovered how little the children had. There wasn't a library and the students didn't even have their own reading books. They wrote letters to other schools asking for donations and used what they could. No one is really willing to be there for permanent support and extra help. —Joshua

Many interns were not only concerned about how schools functioned to help children reach their potential but also wondered about some children's emotional well-being and whether it might hinder their ability to achieve academically. Some interns reported that children craved the attention of adults, but with so many children in a classroom, teachers could not devote a lot of time to each child's emotional needs. A few interns witnessed children who had a great deal of difficulty controlling their behavior in the classroom. Some had heard reports from teachers about children striking their peers, throwing furniture, using obscenities, and hurting themselves—all with little provocation. By the end of the semester, many more interns believed children were emotionally well adjusted than they did at the beginning of the semester, but still only about half of the interns felt this way at the end of the internship.

Achieving successes with children, studying multiculturalism, and observing examples of excellent teaching could not counter the concerns some of the interns had about someday teaching in urban schools. Of 30 interns, 4 declared that they would not seek jobs in an urban school district because they believed that the lack of resources in urban schools undermined children's development and made teaching more difficult. One of these interns said that she would probably apply to a suburban school district because she believed it would be more supportive:

> I think it is natural to want to work in a suburban school—not that teaching there is easier but you know when your [sic] going into an inner city school you're going to be dealing with a lot of things. You would want to go somewhere where the district has enough money to do all kinds of things in the school. —Anne

Despite their new knowledge about the demands of teaching in urban classrooms, though, most interns stated that they would be more inclined than they were before to teach in the city, with five interns stating that they actually would apply for teaching jobs in the city. The reasons most frequently offered by interns for this desire related to their sense of being able to serve children and, in return, to see children grow as readers and writers. The most frequently cited reason for considering an urban teaching job was that interns felt needed in these classrooms.

> I saw a big difference when I did my Theory and Field [course] in [a suburban district]. Not to say that the kids weren't happy and warm and loving and stuff but when I went to Philadelphia and when we left that day, I don't know how many kids like gave us hugs and told us that they would miss us and at the other [suburban] school, the kids loved us too but they didn't show it and that brought a new light to where I want to teach...before I did this practicum, I really didn't want to do inner city [teaching] at all because I was scared about what I was going to see and just the way I would teach there. Now I have a totally different view. I would not mind at all if I would teaching [sic] in the inner city. —Lynne

> Every child in that school wants to learn and they truly want a structured and organized classroom setting. My students will know that I believe in them and I will establish a personal connection with them and their families so they know they are cared for and supported both in and out of the classroom. I have gained a new heart for teaching in the inner city. There is a need for good teachers there that I no longer have a fear of tackling. —Beth

> People give up on these kids too easily. I just think a lot of people are ignorant about kids in the city and the city in general. I want to teach in the city and help these children. Taking this course made me realize how much more I want to give to the community and give to the kids. —Marie

> What makes me extremely happy to see is the way these children look at their teachers. Not to say suburban children don't completely look up to and respect their teachers, but here on some level it seems to be more intense. I would love the opportunity to be an influence such as that in someone's life. —Karen

## Conclusion

Culturally sensitive teachers must set high expectations for children, and, to do so, they first must recognize that children are inherently capable. First and foremost, the interns in this study needed to recognize children's capacity to grow as readers and writers. The interns became more familiar with ways of inspiring children to read and write by learning more about children's out-of-school lives and by using multicultural literature. The interns also became familiar with the characters, themes, plots, and language in this literature. By studying about Ebonics, most of the interns began to value children's home language and to see their own roles in helping children acquire standard English.

We did not have as much time as we needed to experiment with transformative teaching, which is directed toward raising children's social consciousness and helping them see things from another person's perspective, or to help children interact with texts critically and involve them in social action projects connected to the themes contained in these texts. There also were not enough opportunities in the internship to help children explore language differences and examine the power of using different types of language in specific discourse communities. The interns needed a deeper exploration of second-language speakers and the sociopolitical aspects of language. There also were other areas of "unfinished business," such as helping all the interns acquire successful classroom management strategies and helping them to understand how to work with others in the school district to get children what they need to succeed.

Despite these shortcomings in the internship, the interns in this study came one step closer to realizing their potential to teach in urban classrooms. Teachers can learn much from their stories. In the next chapter, I will draw from our experiences to discuss what literacy educators need to do to prepare to serve the needs of children in high-poverty urban communities. I discuss ways to revise internship experiences, and teacher preparation programs in general, around the ideals of transformative and social action teaching, transacting critically with literature, and successfully applying classroom management techniques to urban classrooms.

## REFLECTION AND INQUIRY

1. The interns realized that children had great potential to be successful readers and writers when instruction was targeted to children's development and when it was engaging. How might you individualize instruction in your classroom? How might you learn about children's worlds outside of the classroom and use this information to inform your literacy teaching?

2. Teaching from a diverse constructivist orientation aims to empower children. How might you empower children in the literacy classroom?

3. Investigate the kinds of characters children like to write about. How might you expose children to multiple dimensions of character through children's literature and through your own writing?

4. Assess your knowledge about multicultural literature. How comfortable are you in drawing out the important themes contained in this literature? How comfortable are you in helping children to understand these themes? To what extent do you use literature to help children see issues from the perspectives of others? To what extent do you engage children in social action projects that allow them to use literacy to make the world a better place to live?

5. What do you know about the home language(s) of your students or students you would like to teach? What is the political status of this language relative to standard English? How do you validate children's home languages while also helping children acquire more mainstream ways of using language?

6. What can you learn about your students' communication patterns that would help you best manage your classroom?

# CHAPTER 8

# Continuing to Grow as Culturally Sensitive Literacy Educators

*The question is not, Is it possible to educate all children well? but rather, Do we want to do it badly enough?*

—Deborah Meier, *The Power of Their Ideas: Lessons for America From a Small School in Harlem*, p. 4

I am a little skeptical about recent efforts to improve the literacy performance of children who live in high-poverty communities. Billions of dollars go to publishing companies that churn out scripted, one-size-fits-all programs that aim toward "teacher proofing" the literacy curriculum (Allington, 2002). But no script can help a teacher figure out what to do with 29 very different children on Monday morning.

For-profit educational management companies are getting big contracts to run inner-city schools, based on promises of raising children's test scores. But will these companies really spend what affluent suburban districts can spend to help struggling readers achieve? To do this, they would have to pay highly educated teachers a decent wage, reduce class size, flood the classrooms with texts and materials, and support teacher education and school reform. There is little financial profit in this, especially if the tax base in the community does not support these initiatives. Lost in these "reform" efforts is the need to create expert teachers who are committed to children's academic success. People in the United States have a better shot at achieving social equality if they invest heavily in preparing teachers to serve *all* children. I will use the example of school privatization to illustrate my point.

Some Philadelphia public schools are now under the management of private companies. Privatization of schools does not guarantee an improvement in teacher quality and academic achievement. The management of FitzSimons Middle School by a private company is one example. Of particular concern was the fact that the average reading level of FitzSimons's students in September

2002 was reported to be mid-second grade. Although the company's plan to separate girls from boys helped students to concentrate on learning rather than flirting, the company had trouble attracting and keeping teachers (Snyder, 2003). Faced with the challenges of overcrowded classrooms and a disproportionate number of academically needy students, several teachers left the school because they were not adequately prepared for these responsibilities:

> More than half of this year's staff do not have teaching degrees, and many are in their first year or two of teaching. They have been thrust into classrooms with as many as 33 students, many of them with troubled backgrounds. One-fifth of the students—a rate far higher than in most schools—are in special education. It was too much to handle for about a half-dozen of the new teachers, who have since quit. In their place have come a succession of substitutes, many of whom stay only a day or a week. The unsurprising result for students in such classrooms has been stalled improvement. (p. 13)

How could FitzSimons's students make up the four-, five-, or six-year gap in their reading performance if they didn't have qualified teachers to help them? What these students needed were knowledgeable, culturally sensitive teachers who could address students' divergent literacy needs within a supportive school culture. The company provided FitzSimons with some support for professional development, but more still needs to be done to attract teachers to FitzSimons and other urban schools and to help the teachers succeed. Most teachers can learn to teach these underserved children to read, but they have to want to accept this challenge, and they need support to meet it. I will devote this chapter to looking at ways educators can make a difference in the literacy achievement of children in high-poverty communities.

## Growth and Continuing Needs

The interns in this study changed their understandings about urban children and about their own capacity to teach children in urban schools to read and write. Many began the internship with fears about the urban community—fears that dissipated once the interns became regular visitors to the schools. Many entered the internship blaming urban caregivers for their children's failures to read at grade level, but these initial misconceptions were lifted once the interns talked to caregivers and gained some insight both into caregivers' concerns and hopes for their children and into the social realities of urban families. Through studies of diversity, the interns discovered that literacy achievement is influenced by a broad social ecology. Most of the interns began the internship with low expectations of these children, until they saw their young pupils grow as readers and writers in one-on-one tutorials. At first, most of the interns saw children's speech as sloppy slang, until we explored the history of black English and began our own investigation of the children's speech patterns.

With each leap forward, the interns confronted new challenges. Marie's growing awareness about diversity issues was accompanied by shame, guilt, and intellectual dissonance. Marie was interested in learning about herself and others, but her inability to challenge Eurocentric perspectives fit with an integrationist orientation toward diversity (Howard, 1999; see chapter 4). Allison's primary difficulty, on the other hand, centered on translating her views about diversity into classroom practice in the area of classroom management. Although she demonstrated a transformationist orientation toward diversity (Howard, 1999) with regard to children and urban teaching, she needed more time and support to develop as a culturally sensitive literacy teacher.

Specific evidence that the interns reached an integrationist orientation toward diversity can be seen by looking at five areas of their growth: (1) knowledge about children and their caregivers, (2) knowledge about literacy achievement, (3) knowledge of culture and community, (4) knowledge of culturally relevant literacy teaching, and (5) the realization of one's responsibility to teach.

## Knowledge About Children and Their Caregivers

Most of this study's interns, irrespective of their backgrounds in cultural diversity, at first underestimated caregivers' ability to support children's literacy growth. Factors influencing these misconceptions included the media, family, and prior schooling experiences. Caregiver contact helped the interns to see many caregivers as caring advocates for their children. Caregivers who could not be contacted or did not respond positively to interns' communication efforts, however, left some of the interns concerned about the amount of academic support available to some children at home.

## Knowledge About Literacy Achievement

The interns' explanations for children's literacy failures initially were simplistic: Poverty causes poor caregiving, and a lack of caregiver support at home causes poor literacy achievement. All of the interns later learned to see literacy achievement within a complex web of sociohistorical influences, but some deficit views of "unresponsive" caregivers continued to exist. Most interns acknowledged the existence of white privilege and institutional racism and acknowledged how these social, historical, and political factors translated into unequal opportunities for children to access literacy education within public schools.

## Knowledge of Culture and Community

The interns' knowledge about children's history, culture, and experiences grew during the internship. To increase this knowledge, the interns drew from articles and book chapters on black history, culture, and language; children's literature written and illustrated by Africans and African Americans; and conversations with children and their caregivers. Although the interns' knowledge of culture expanded, however, there continued to be gaps in their understandings about Ebonics; African American history, culture, and contemporary perspectives; contributions of African Americans to mainstream U.S. society; and local community issues. Most interns remained outsiders with respect to the black community, but they realized that their effectiveness as teachers would depend on establishing cultural knowledge and community affiliations.

## Knowledge of Culturally Relevant Literacy Teaching

The interns admired the skills and traits of those described as culturally sensitive teachers, and they identified some of the key perspectives of these teachers: (a) recognizing the limitations of a colorblind perspective, (b) realizing the importance of setting high expectations for children, (c) seeing the significance of culture represented in the classroom, and (d) validating children's home language. Although the interns could articulate these perspectives, more time and effort was needed to translate these beliefs into classroom practices. Specifically, the interns needed more time to organize classrooms to help children realize their potential; teach children to think and read critically; infuse children's home culture into the curriculum; explore children's home language, including its roots, structure, and relationship to literacy; and teach explicitly the codes and discourses of power.

## The Realization of One's Responsibility to Teach

All the interns in the study came to recognize the existence of racism, their own privileged status, and children's unequal access to literacy education, but some contended that these inequalities were not their fault. Some interns had difficulty admitting personal responsibility for these social problems, and others accepted responsibility for them and saw culturally relevant teaching as a way to ensure greater equality for children. Most interns left the internship being willing to work in urban schools, but it remained unclear whether this new interest would result in their accepting actual employment in urban schools.

Knowing what could and could not be accomplished in an urban-based literacy internship helped me to consider what literacy educators can do to serve children of color in high-poverty communities. In the following sections of this chapter, I draw from my own growth experiences and those of the interns to inform paths of growth for students of education, practicing teachers, and teacher educators.

## Growing as Students of Education

### Course Selection

Most of the interns I have discussed in this book had virtually no experience in urban schools or communities prior to participating in the internship. A few were exposed to diversity issues prior to taking the internship, through experiences in local communities and by participating in a college course that included a strong diversity component. This course allowed them to tutor the children of Mexican migrant workers and to study diversity issues. These experiences prepared Allison to appreciate children's intellectual talents and home language and accept responsibility for teaching. Her experience shows that there are ways to prepare for work in different cultural communities well in advance of participating in an internship.

For undergraduate students of education, preparing for internship experiences means scrutinizing required and elective university courses for their diversity content. Education students should do some homework before scheduling their courses. Based on my own experience, individual professors bring their own expertise and interests to their courses, so students will find some variation across sections of the same course. Preservice teachers can ask their advisors which professors emphasize diversity issues within their courses. Choosing these courses will give preservice teachers additional exposure to cultural diversity through reading and through participating in service learning experiences similar to Allison's tutoring project.

Preservice teachers also should realize that no matter how rich their course experiences are, one course alone will not make them culturally sensitive literacy teachers. Successful teachers need to know how to teach literacy, and they need to believe that all children can succeed. This takes a long time; teachers' educations will extend throughout their entire teaching careers.

Most of the outstanding teachers I have known have attended graduate school to earn a master's degree or to become certified in a specialty area. Many teachers enroll in reading specialist certification programs, not because they want to be reading specialists per se, but because they want to better serve the literacy needs of children in the regular classroom. Also, teachers who want to learn more about the history, culture, literature, and language of particular communities have many options to learn about cultural diversity. Programs in diversity education and multiculturalism are now offered at many universities. Teachers can take advantage of workshops and courses that address topics of cultural difference from varied perspectives: racial identity development, race relations, peace and social justice, urban vs. rural communities, and dialect/language differences. There also are major and minor study programs that explore Asian, black, Middle Eastern, and Latino cultures.

The programs I have described so far fall under the domain of either literacy studies or diversity studies. My findings, though, suggest a need for programs that fuse these two areas. The question is not, How do I teach reading and writing? Rather, it is, How do I teach *my students* to read and write? The addition of the words *my students* here emphasizes that children bring with them particular experiences in using language, interacting with print, perceiving school, and acting in the world that are shaped by their particular cultural communities, and these experiences may be different from their teachers' experiences. These differences can have a major impact on how teachers perceive children and teach them. This state of affairs suggests a need to understand language and literacy issues from a sociocultural perspective. Below are some areas of study that consider language and literacy issues through the lens of culture:

- anthropological studies of literacy and learning within specific communities
- foundations of social constructivism, racism, culture, classism, sexism
- literacy as a social construct; home–school literacies and dissonance
- sociohistorical contexts for literacy acquisition
- learning styles of children in specific communities
- literacy, language, and sociolinguistics
- communication and collaboration with caregivers

- family literacy and parenting/caregiving
- culturally responsive literacy teaching/learning
- culturally responsive assessment
- methods of reflective practitioners and teacher researchers; methods of teacher-as-reformer

Courses that address language and literacy from a sociocultural perspective might also be offered in university departments other than education or literacy. The courses may be listed under anthropology, sociology, social psychology, history, political science, English, or the arts. The important thing for educators is immersing themselves in conversations that consider literacy and language as culturally situated practices (Scribner & Cole, 1981; Street, 1995).

Education students need to take advantage of opportunities to work in schools in high-poverty communities to work with children, communicate with caregivers, and get to know the school climate. They should capitalize on opportunities to learn as much as they can about both literacy teaching and cultural diversity. The university experience is an opportune time to meet and get to know individuals who do not share the same cultural experiences or perspectives and who can, therefore, offer new outlooks to education students.

## Securing Professional Growth After Graduation

When applying for a teaching job, teachers should scrutinize what opportunities for professional development different school districts have to offer. Currently, for example, public schools in Philadelphia are quite varied in the kinds of professional development available to teachers. Some schools are run by for-profit companies or nonprofit organizations, and some schools are charter schools that are independently run but operate with school district funds or through affiliations with universities. Applicants to Philadelphia public school districts can explore which schools offer the most opportunities for teachers to grow. It is important to identify those schools that support teacher inquiry, invest in teacher development, and invite teacher input. Such schools are more likely to foster a climate of professionalism than those that do not value these ideas.

Teachers who are considering applying to large urban school districts should do some research. Teachers can gather information about a school district's plans for supporting teachers by asking such questions as, What does this school district offer in the way of professional development? How does the school district mentor new teachers? How can I learn from successful teachers in the school district? How might this school district support my decision making about instruction, assessment, curriculum design, and the needs of specific children? How would you describe the professional climate in this school district?

# Growing as Teachers

As mentioned previously, teacher certification programs often do not provide opportunities to study the issues of literacy, diversity, communities, and parenting/caregiving in great depth. The interns who exited my internship received the equivalent of four literacy courses, two of which involved direct contact with children in urban classrooms. Because most of the interns had not spent time in an urban setting before, the internship provided a way for them to begin a study of these relevant issues. Still, the interns had only begun to understand how to approach children's divergent literacy needs. This is why teacher certification programs often are the beginning point of teacher professionalism, not the end point.

Teachers need to nurture and sustain their professional growth, and they can do so through thoughtful study, collegial collaboration, and inquiry projects.

## *Dog and Pony Shows Versus Thoughtful Study*

Pritchard and Marshall (2002) report that teachers' professional growth depends on the amount of time teachers are given to implement changes, the control teachers have over the ways in which they implement changes, and their school district's commitment to teacher growth. The researchers found that the occasional after-school workshop delivered by an outside expert is the predominant professional development model, although it is largely ineffective in supporting teachers' growth. Further, workshops that focus on one or two lessons, or those that have teachers "make and take" materials for particular lessons, are temporarily helpful to teachers, but these "training" sessions are not enough to help novice teachers succeed in schools that serve high-poverty urban communities. In fact, the word *training* is inaccurate. The term *teacher education* more appropriately captures the processes by which teachers grow intellectually and professionally. How teachers educate themselves and what is offered to teachers in the way of education varies widely, but there is much teachers can do to control their own professional growth. Teachers can choose on their own to (a) participate in programs that address literacy and culture, (b) join with colleagues who are interested in learning more about serving the literacy needs of children in particular cultural communities, and (c) establish their own research agendas.

## Collegial Collaboration

Outside formal programs of study, there are many ways for teachers to grow professionally by being in the company of others who are committed to professional development. Many teachers who are invested in their own professional growth belong to professional reading or literacy organizations such as the National Council of Teachers of English (NCTE) and the International Reading Association (IRA) and its regional organizations. See page 179 for information about these professional literacy organizations.

Also, networks of teachers can come together on a regular basis to talk about the children they teach. The Teachers' Learning Collaborative (TLC) in Philadelphia is one example of a teacher-led effort to improve student achievement through collaboration and inquiry. Participants in the TLC meet weekly during the school year to participate in a "descriptive review" of one student at each meeting (Carini, 2001). The review begins with one teacher's description of a student's physical presence and gestures, disposition and temperament, social activity, interests and preferences, and ways of thinking and learning. Artifacts produced by the student (drawings, constructions, and writings) are passed around for the other participants to examine. The teacher responds to participants' questions about the student, and only after a portrait of the student has been fully rendered do participants offer suggestions for how the school and teacher might build upon the student's strengths. The discussion provides the student's teacher with a deepened insight into the student and into ways of nurturing his or her development. The rest of the teachers in the group get an opportunity to exercise their observational and reflective skills through this process.

Similar processes of inquiry could be brought to cross-grade or grade-level teacher meetings. I have found that the most enthusiastic teachers are those who are socially connected to others in the school and are supported by a network of friends and colleagues. However, I also have found that schools differ in their ways of organizing teacher teams, so some teachers I know do not meet regularly with other teachers. Worse, some teachers who do meet find that such gatherings are unproductive because they turn into gripe sessions. In schools where teachers do not come together regularly to discuss students and teaching in meaningful ways, motivated teachers should find out why. These teachers can begin a dialogue with other teachers about the possibilities of coming together on a consistent basis to talk about how to best support each other and the students about whom they are concerned. Teachers who find their meetings to be unproductive should reestablish meeting objectives to focus on children and ways to support them.

## Inquiry Projects for Teachers

My findings from the internship point to many areas of inquiry that are available to teachers who would like to improve their teaching practices as they specifically relate to teaching in high-poverty urban areas. Based on my experiences with the internship, I have identified three areas of teacher inquiry related to this goal: (1) assessment-based teaching, (2) culturally relevant teaching, and (3) work with caregivers. In each of these areas, there are some specific questions that merit further exploration. Teachers should select from these questions to guide their own research paths.

**Focus of Inquiry: Assessment-Based Teaching**. Matching development to instruction requires knowledge of how to use and interpret assessments. Teachers especially need information about assessment practices that take into account large numbers of children of varied abilities. Observational notes, running records, and spelling and writing samples are informal means of finding out what children know about print. Tutoring children and basing teaching practices on observations of children's literacy behaviors during the tutorials helped the interns in my study to see the importance of assessment-based teaching for realizing children's literacy potential. When children did not respond well to instruction, the interns often recognized that it was because the texts they selected were too easy or too difficult, or that they did not scaffold instruction enough for the children. The interns learned how to adjust their instruction for next time so it was more in keeping with children's abilities. The interns also noticed that the more closely they matched their instruction to children's abilities, the better the children responded—both in their willingness to engage in classroom tasks and in the observable learning that took place in the tutorial setting.

Applying the principle of assessment-based learning is easier to do with one child than it is with 30. Tharp and Gallimore (1989), in *Rousing Minds to*

*Life: Teaching, Learning, and Schooling in Social Context*, comment on the difficulty of using assessment-based teaching in a traditional whole-class setting:

> To provide assistance in the ZPD [Zone of Proximal Development], the assistor must be in close touch with the learner's relationship to the task. Sensitive and accurate assistance that challenges but does not dismay the learner cannot be achieved in the absence of information. Opportunities for this knowledge, conditions in which the teacher can be sufficiently aware of the child's actual, in-flight performing, simply are not available in classrooms organized, equipped, and staffed in the typical American pattern. There are too many children for each teacher. (p. 42)

From this excerpt, the following words deserve another mention: *The assistor must be in close touch with the learner's relationship to the task.* U.S. classrooms do not allow for the teacher to be aware of "the child's actual, in-flight performing" and to assist in ways that advance learning for each child, primarily because there are too many children of varied abilities. The greatest concern among the urban teachers I meet is how to address the varied literacy needs of all the students in their classes. In the urban schools in which my interns and I have worked, children in the same grade are often are up to four years apart in reading levels when they first enter school, and this spread increases as children make their way through school (Gill, 2003). This means that whole-class teaching is instructionally ineffective: If all children in the classroom are given the same text to read or the same phonics worksheet to complete, only some of the students will actually benefit from completing the task. Traditionally, teachers have tried to differentiate instruction through ability grouping, but there are challenges to this practice that need to be addressed by the teacher. These include the practical matter of organizing and monitoring groups and dealing with the stigmatization of low-ability group placement.

*Ability Grouping.* It is possible to arrange classrooms so that instruction is more directed to each child's Zone of Proximal Development (Vygotsky, 1934/1978), or the difference between what a child can do alone and what he or she can do with assistance. What teachers need are classroom arrangements that help them gather information about what children can do successfully and where their performance begins to break down. They also need classroom structures that allow them to build on children's different capabilities. This can be done by organizing small groups of students who have similar literacy needs and setting up activity centers where children can either spend more individual time with the teacher or perform independently or with peers tasks that match their development level. Ability grouping is especially recommended for activities such as guided reading (Fountas & Pinnell, 1996) and word study (Bear et al., 1996) so the teacher can use the books and materials that children with similar abilities need.

To avoid the possible stigmatizing effects of ability grouping, many teachers group children flexibly using ability-based and non-ability-based groups. If ability-based groups are used, they should change according to the children's development, based on the teacher's assessment of children's progress. Reading and writing workshops also allow for individualized instruction. These workshops involve direct, explicit instruction through minilessons, a period of time for individualized reading and writing, and a time for sharing (Calkins, 1994; Keene & Zimmermann, 1997). By using individual instruction, teachers can better assess what students need instructionally.

Questions for teachers to ask themselves when setting up such a system would include, How do I organize the classroom for assessment-based teaching? What do I know about using ability-based and non-ability-based groups, activity centers, and workshops in the literacy classroom? Are student groupings based on ability appropriate? Are the tasks performed within the groups well matched to students' needs? How do I gather information about children's literacy behaviors in order to revise groups and centers? For instance, teachers need to carefully monitor how members of each guided reading group approach the texts they are given. If some children move quickly ahead in their ability to read texts of a particular complexity level, teachers may need to change the composition of groups to keep instruction at the cusp of children's development.

Assessment informs teachers not only about grouping and structuring for individualized learning but also about how instruction is delivered. Teaching within children's Zones of Proximal Development demands that teachers are mindful of the level and type of assistance they provide to children. Tharp and Gallimore (1989) refer to this "help" as *assisted performance*, or the ways in which teachers scaffold learning for children through modeling, questioning, and providing feedback. Teachers need to ask themselves how they mediate children's growth through the types of questions they ask and the kinds of feedback they give to children, and if and how they demonstrate to children what successful readers and writers do. Teachers also need to organize the classroom to maximize children's risk taking—because making approximations is a necessary condition for learning—and their engagement.

*Choosing Texts.* Finding suitable texts for instruction required the interns in the study to carefully observe and record children's reading behaviors. Through observations many interns discovered that the children could not read the grade-level basal text, so they provided the children with other texts that they could read with relative ease and with which they could employ predicting and questioning as well as decoding strategies for identifying unknown words. It took time for the novice teachers to find the right text–ability matches for the children they tutored. For emergent and beginning readers, the interns were able to tailor instruction well through the use of leveled readers organized from least to the most linguistically sophisticated.

The interns and I imagined that selecting appropriate texts for each of 29 children in one classroom would require the teacher to develop organized assessment procedures to monitor children's reading behaviors. We agreed that the grade-level basal would not be suitable for all of the children in one classroom, even though the school district mandated its use for all students. Texts used for reading instruction ought to be ones that children can read well but have not mastered. The rule of thumb is 90% accuracy in word recognition and fluency that is not halting or labored and the ability to make sense of much of the text (Fountas & Pinnell, 1996). The teacher's job is to demonstrate how to use strategies to recognize unknown words and make sense of texts and to guide children to employ these strategies when they read independently. If texts are too difficult, children will not be able to draw from their store of strategies to make sense of them. At each instructional occasion, teachers need to monitor whether children can employ these strategies successfully or if the book is too linguistically complex for children to read and understand independently. Texts that are above children's reading abilities should be read aloud to children for enjoyment and for development in understanding text and concepts.

For further exploration of the text selection process, teachers might ask themselves, How can I gather information about children's varied reading behaviors in order to make informed decisions about text selection? What are the best texts to use for independent reading, guided reading, and reading aloud to children? How do I help children to select texts that allow them to develop as readers?

*Writing.* When the children taught by the interns in the study were willing to write, their writing yielded a treasure trove of information about their worlds outside of the classroom as well as their understandings about print. When the interns and I periodically examined children's first drafts (when they chose their own writing topics), we were struck by the variation among children's top-ic choices, their ways of conveying messages, and their understandings of how print works. Examining these samples provided us with information on how to enhance children's writing by selecting literature that complemented and extended their knowledge and by modeling features of writing (how to use di-alogue, what makes a good lead, how a character is described, how conventions are used, etc.). Writing samples also informed our word study instruction: Information about children's spelling patterns helped us to create word study activities that were appropriate to children's needs. For example, children who included beginning and ending consonants accurately, but who also confused vowels, were given picture sorts that helped them discriminate between those vowels they often confused in their invented spelling.

In using children's writing to inform instruction, teachers might ask them-selves, What does children's writing reveal about their experiences outside of the classroom? What does it suggest about what they know and what they need to know about the world? What does it suggest about children's ability to com-municate clearly and powerfully? In what ways does children's writing inform reading and word study instruction?

*Putting It All Together.* The interns wondered how teachers orchestrated all of these bits of "exemplary practice" into a unified whole. I stressed that it is im-portant to observe how teachers create classrooms that inspire and nurture lit-eracy learning. Observing other teachers provides a look at multiple dimensions of exemplary practice within one classroom. In their own research, teachers might want to locate other educators who have been successful in helping children achieve in literacy.

In observing these exemplary educators, other teachers might ask them-selves, How do they structure class time? What literacy events are provided in their daily class routine? How do they apportion time for each literacy event? How do they individualize instruction? In what ways do they invite risk tak-ing, choice, and ownership? How do they validate children's home language and culture and still teach the "codes of power"? How do they work with col-leagues and caregivers? What do they do when school policies are not in keep-ing with their own views of what children need to succeed in school?

*Additional Considerations.* There are also alternative ways of looking at lit-eracy development that the interns and I did not consider in the internship. The lens we used focused mainly on school-based literacies. Although we did open the lens a bit to look at children's ways of interacting with print at home and at what they did when using print among friends (e.g., reading jump-rope rhymes, writing about sports heroes), we did not capture the breadth of children's reading, writing, talking, and listening behaviors that were shaped by their social worlds. A.H. Dyson (2003) reminds us of how children appropriate language from a variety of popular media—radio, videos, compact discs, television, computer games, and so on. The language children use among friends and others, often expressed away from their teachers, reflects how children have taken these forms and transformed them through play. When teachers think about development, and about matching instruction to it, they also need to consider how children are able to adapt, improvise, and reconfigure the popular symbols that surround them. If teachers are serious about bringing children's lives into closer alignment with school, they need to know more about children's worlds. To consider this, teachers might ask themselves, What popular cultural forms are expressed in children's play? How do children translate their experiences with popular culture through oral and written language? How do I organize the classroom in a way that would tap children's cultural literacy? For teachers to answer these questions, they will need to learn more about culturally relevant teaching.

**Focus of Inquiry: Culturally Relevant Teaching**. The interns' initial expectations for literacy failure of children in urban classrooms were based on limited firsthand contact with African Americans in contexts construed as negative, and on family members' and the media's accounts of inner-city lifestyles that portrayed these communities negatively. These conditions gave rise to the interns' simplistic ideas about the cause–effect relationship regarding literacy failure among urban children of color: Bad parenting or caregiving causes literacy failure. Interns did not really "see" children when they entered the field site because they arrived with stereotypes about children of color who live in urban communities.

When the interns were given opportunities to read about white privilege and to unearth their own cultural histories and experiences, they began to recognize their prejudicial views. When they studied the factors that have an impact on literacy achievement in schools and communities, they realized that children's development is not solely determined by poverty and caregiver support. They found that children's development is shaped by many factors related to society, school, teachers, caregivers, and childhood. When they provided assessment-based, child-centered instruction, the interns saw children move ahead in their development. Through these experiences, the interns confronted their views that these children were predisposed to literacy failure and that their caregivers were primarily responsible for this failure. With this knowledge, the interns were better able to see how important it is to believe in all children of color and set high expectations for them.

*Teacher Expectations for Children of Color.* Believing in children is central to a diverse constructivist orientation that focuses on respect and empowerment (Au, 1998), and it is a core belief of those teachers who have been successful with children of color (Ladson-Billings, 1994). What is more controversial is the way cultural relevance is interpreted and translated to classroom teaching practices. Delpit (1995), for instance, believes that teachers must know children and their worlds outside of schools, but she questions the perspectives of liberal educators who ignore or de-emphasize teaching "mainstream" ways of reading, writing, and speaking as a way of not making students feel bad about their home and community discourses. Educators must heed this argument and pay careful attention to the balance between giving children what they need to achieve within the mainstream and, at the same time, addressing children's disconnectedness from the school curriculum through language and literacy experiences that integrate and validate local knowledge. Children who are alienated from school will not want to learn, but children who are not explicitly taught what they need will not learn either.

Others, like Ogbu and Davis (2003), do not see culturally relevant pedagogy as a solution to the problem of academic failure among black students:

> Our research findings in Shaker Heights suggest that culturally responsive pedagogy is not an adequate solution to the academic disengagement and low achievement of Black students. In fact, culturally responsive pedagogy is problematic as a theory and in practice. As a theory, culturally responsive pedagogy implies that in order to educate minority students successfully, the public school must teach the students from each minority group according to their own indigenous pedagogic style. But it cannot explain why immigrant minority students from Africa and Asia in Shaker Heights were doing better than Black Americans under the same conventional public school pedagogy. (pp. 271–272)

After asking why African Americans need a special pedagogical style when many immigrant minority students from Africa and Asia do well academically without it, Ogbu argues that instead of changing a teacher's pedagogical style to accommodate African American students, a variety of other factors should be changed. These include caregiving practices that are oppositional to school success, schooling practices that slot black students into low academic tracks, and teacher practices that underestimate students' potential. I agree with Ogbu, to a point. Achievement requires that literacy educators be mindful of all of these factors, not just of pedagogical style. Indeed, seeing children's inherent talents and intellectual potential is more critical to their achievement than knowing about pedagogical style (Steele, 1992). But aiming expectations high is a critical element of culturally relevant pedagogy.

However, graduates of teacher preparation programs may not always subscribe to this core belief. Indeed, having low expectations of children is not a teacher problem per se, but a problem with U.S. society as a whole. Teachers who care about students and have devoted their lives to working with children in high-poverty communities should not be targets of blame. However, when it is the case that teachers' expectations get in the way of teachers' seeing and serving children well, teachers and teacher educators must work toward solving the problem.

Ogbu and Davis (2003) suggest that the problem of low expectations should be addressed by giving teachers periodic workshops devoted to this topic. However, based on the interns' ingrained underestimations of urban children and caregivers of color, I contend that addressing the problem of low expectations deserves a more comprehensive solution. It should involve addressing racism in primary school classrooms and throughout the school curriculum, within teacher preparation programs, in professional organizations, during teacher certification programs, and in local communities.

The interns with whom I worked started to unlearn many of the messages U.S. society had taught them about those who have been targets of racism for generations. In the internship, interns learned respect for children by reflecting on their own cultural and racial privileges, studying how different cultural groups have historically been positioned in society, learning about the contributions of marginalized communities, communicating with caregivers, and, most important, seeing children learn in response to individually appropriate instruction.

Based on these findings, teachers can ask themselves the following questions during their own explorations of this topic: What do I know about my own cultural experiences and history relative to this community? What are my assumptions and cultural biases, and how have these shaped my perceptions about and treatment of students? How does my communication style affect children's ways of seeing themselves as readers, writers, and thinkers? In what ways do I communicate high expectations for all of my students? (See also the Reflection and Inquiry section of each chapter of this book.)

*Teaching in Multicultural Classrooms.* On a practical level, Ogbu and Davis (2003) question the feasibility of applying culturally responsive teaching in classrooms that contain children from several cultural communities. Given the highly segregated classrooms in which the interns and I found ourselves during the internship, this question of serving multiple cultural groups in one classroom did not surface. Some elementary schools in the greater Philadelphia area and other urban areas, however, do serve children who affiliate with many cultures. The teachers in these schools also can apply culturally relevant pedagogy in their literacy teaching practices by setting high expectations for all children, respecting children's out-of-school experiences, and inviting children to bring their social worlds into the classroom through reading, writing, and talking experiences.

For teachers, applying a culturally relevant pedagogy in the literacy classroom means asking themselves many questions such as the following:

- What do I know about the everyday worlds of the children in my classroom?

- What do I know about the histories, languages, and cultures of the students I serve?

- What kinds of expectations do I have for children in particular social groups?

- What do I know about each cultural group's pedagogic style?

- How can I invite children to read, write, and talk about their out-of-school experiences in ways that will empower them?

- What are the ways I can validate both home cultures and codes of power in my classroom?

- How can I learn more about the history and culture of the community in which I teach?

- What do I know about the texts that have been written and illustrated by members of the cultural community that I serve?

- How can I bring the language and literacy experiences that are valued in the community into the classroom?

144

- How can I use my knowledge of culture to help children acquire new literacies?

**Focus of Inquiry: Communicating and Collaborating With Caregivers**. A recent conversation with Ms. Johnson, a cooperating teacher, left me feeling uneasy about the prospect that teachers in general will be able to work cooperatively with all caregivers. She said, "I have a parent who actually tells their kids not to do the homework that I assigned." Exasperated, Ms. Johnson has given up trying to work with this parent. I, too, would be angry if my teaching efforts were undermined by parents. Ms. Johnson doesn't give up on all caregivers, however; her efforts to reach out to caregivers usually pay off. Nearly all of her students' caregivers come to her parent conferences, and she attributes this response, in part, to the work she has put into establishing relationships with them.

The same is true for Ms. Campbell, a kindergarten teacher I know who recruits and educates parent and grandparent volunteers (as well as university students) to work with her kindergarteners during a writer's workshop activity. She requests caregiver help with much enthusiasm during her open house meeting and follows up with phone calls to the children's homes. I often have walked into her classroom to find 5 volunteers for her class of 25 children, reducing the student–teacher ratio from 25:1 to 5:1. Reducing this ratio is particularly effective because many of the children need adult assistance when they spell during writer's workshop, when they read in guided reading groups and independently, and when they sort picture cards as part of a word study lesson. Over the past few years, this teacher has been able to help most of her kindergarten students attain grade-level or higher proficiency in literacy.

Based on my visits to many urban classrooms, I have found that this kind of caregiver outreach effort does not happen as much as it could. This is not the fault of teachers as much as it is a problem with teacher education (a point I will address later). Many teachers who prefer to work alone seem to have a Herculean view of teaching: I should be able to tackle any classroom challenge without anyone's help. To them, a request for help is a sign of weakness. Some teachers see additional adult help as interference or intimidation. Whether a teacher invites additional adult help into the classroom is heavily dependent on the teacher's feelings of efficacy. Ms. Campbell is a veteran teacher and, although she sees herself as a continual learner, she is secure about her role as a teacher. Some teachers, especially inexperienced ones, are less secure about their teaching and, therefore, are less willing to have other adults in the classroom when they themselves still are experimenting with teaching. These are, unfortunately, the very teachers who could benefit from additional help.

It also is a challenge to help caregivers to support their children's literacy growth at home when the caregivers do not have a background in literacy teaching and do not have easy access to texts. An example is Mrs. Jones's failed attempts to get her daughter, Tyeshia, to read at home (see chapter 6). One problem was that the materials Mrs. Jones purchased were too difficult for her daughter. I have worked with many caregivers in Philadelphia who, with all good intentions, waste their money on phonics or reading comprehension workbooks that are not instructionally appropriate for their children. This is an area where teachers need to work with caregivers more closely to show them the kinds of texts and literacy experiences that would benefit their individual children most.

Improving literacy achievement depends on bridging home and school cultures. Successful communication with caregivers is dependent on the energy teachers put into exploring and improving such communication. Teachers might be able to secure some caregivers' permission to videotape conferences with them, which will provide an excellent opportunity to examine both teachers' nonverbal and verbal transactions with caregivers. If videotaping is not feasible, teachers can try to capture as much of their conferences as possible in writing. Then, they can look over their notes after each conference and think about the important aspects of the experience and ways they might improve communication with the parent or caregiver in the future.

The following questions can guide teachers' understandings about working with caregivers:

- How often do I communicate with caregivers?
- What is the nature of my communications with caregivers?
- Do I project a welcoming presence to caregivers?
- What choices do I give caregivers about the ways in which they communicate with me?
- What are caregivers' impressions of their roles in providing literacy support?
- How accessible are caregivers during the day and evening?
- What can I do to help caregivers know about the school's literacy expectations?

- What can I do to learn more about the home-based literacy practices being used by my students' families?
- How can I learn more about children's cultures and community through talking with their caregivers?
- How can I improve my communication with caregivers?

Teachers need to seize professional development opportunities in order to grow as educators. They can no longer see themselves as lone heroes; successful teaching demands that teachers collaborate with colleagues, caregivers, and community members. Teachers need to interrogate the school curriculum, policies, routines, and practices to see if they meet children's literacy needs, and join forces with their colleagues to reform school practices and policies that seem to undermine student achievement (Cochran-Smith, 1991). Teachers also can direct their own learning by asking questions—such as the ones suggested in this chapter— about the children they serve and the teaching practices they employ. Teachers who are successful with children in high-poverty communities could spread the wealth of their knowledge and experience by mentoring apprentice teachers and contributing to their knowledge base through research projects (Cochran-Smith & Lytle, 1993). New, and even experienced, teachers need the support of colleagues and teacher educators to grow as professionals.

# Growing as Teacher Educators

Teacher educators have a lot to do to prepare future teachers to teach successfully in high-poverty communities. In thinking about this issue, I am reminded of Ladson-Billings's (2001) statement about the glacial pace of change within universities and departments of education. Based on my own growth over many years and my observations of education students in internships, I offer several suggestions for reforming teacher education at a more rapid pace.

## *Knowing Ourselves and Culturally Different Others*

Teachers' growth in the area of literacy and diversity studies is a reflection of the growth of teacher educators. How much do we teacher educators scrutinize our assumptions and biases? How much do we know about others? It is important that as teacher educators we ask ourselves these questions; otherwise, we cannot be as successful as we might in mentoring education students and teachers.

We need to be able to guide uncomfortable and risky conversations about topics such as racism and language diversity (Cochran-Smith, 1995a, 1995b). Teaching at universities usually means that we are removed from traditional classrooms and community schools. Sometimes we may be accused of not being in touch with the real problems of teachers in high-poverty urban schools. This was true for me until I actually spent time in these schools and communities. It took time to understand the culture of these schools, and I did so by sitting with children and looking at instruction from their perspective, as well as talking with teachers and principals. Time spent in these schools has enabled me to understand much more about the ways in which the school district and the community shape the experiences of children, teachers, and administrators at a given school.

Also, we must realize that knowledge about urban teaching is local. One cannot gain insights into the local realities of schools unless one spends time in them. By reading Kozol's books (1991, 2000), for instance, I was "taken" to public schools in high-poverty communities where many issues of schooling overlapped with those that I have encountered in Philadelphia. But there were local issues of teaching children to read and write at the Philadelphia schools that were determined by the policies and practices of the local school district and the needs of the local community; I could not have learned about these issues from reading Kozol's books. In fact, each time I visit a new school in Philadelphia, I see that it has its own culture based on the surrounding neighborhood, the physical setting of the building, and what the students and school staff bring to the school. Because of the unique features of each school and school district, we as teacher educators need to know about the districts and schools in which new teachers make their careers so we can mentor these teachers successfully.

## Knowing About Education Students

Teacher educators need to understand the backgrounds and views of education students, some of whom, like Marie (see chapter 4), may come to the university without many experiences with cultural differences, and some of whom, like Allison, may come with many experiences within culturally diverse communities. But teacher educators cannot assume that education students raised in urban or culturally diverse neighborhoods are culturally sensitive. We also cannot assume that those raised in affluent communities are culturally insensitive. We should, instead, spend some time finding out about the views and attitudes that all of our education students bring to the university.

Even though the interns became more culturally aware through my internship, some refused to consider teaching positions in high-poverty urban schools. Some could not see how they could be successful teachers in the city because they felt too inexperienced to solve the problems they would encounter in urban classrooms. Many others cultivated an interest in urban teaching through face-to-face interactions with children—in the swapping of family stories, in the exchanges of hugs, and in the personal gratification the interns felt when they helped a child read a book or write a story. These were the emotionally charged human connections that the interns referred to when explaining why they became interested in teaching in the city. These interns were so moved by the experience of working with the children that they overlooked their inexperience and the limits of urban schools and focused on what they could do to serve these children.

These experiences remind me that we, as teacher educators, need more information about what it takes to inspire passion for this kind of work. One way is to help teachers feel confident in their abilities, but we can only do this if we know what is required of teachers to work successfully within particular schools and with particular children. We need to ask, What qualities attract teachers to work in high-poverty communities? What sustains their commitment to these communities? What can I do to attract more teachers to careers as urban educators? What can I find out about schools and children that can inform my instruction on the college or university campus?

## Reforming Teacher Preparation Programs

We teacher educators need to scrutinize our teacher certification curricula to find out where there are programming gaps. For instance, I found in my research that schools of education and professional development programs previously have not done a very good job of preparing teachers to talk with parents and other caregivers or work with these people collaboratively. The fears and anxieties that surfaced among the interns around the caregiver communication project suggest that preservice teachers need much more support in this area. From my experiences teaching at four universities, I know that few courses for working with caregivers currently exist in teacher preparation programs. However, there are many books and research studies that provide excellent advice for working with caregivers (see the recommended resources on pages 177–179). Seeing caregivers and community members as information resources requires that teachers understand more about diversity, cross-cultural communication, and alternative perspectives of caregivers.

Like teachers, teacher educators cannot work alone in this regard. We need to collaborate with educators in other university departments to make a full complement of cultural diversity curricula available to students of education. Those who teach literacy education courses need to see how discussions of language, culture, and the sociology of literacy achievement can be integrated with discussions about literacy development, assessment, and instruction. We also need to work with other educators and with university administrators to recruit education students and faculty members of color to our universities so that conversations among preservice teachers about children in various cultural communities can be richer and better informed. Finally, we as teacher educators need to focus research on the processes of preparing teachers to teach reading (Anders, Hoffman, & Duffy, 2000), especially in the contexts of different cultural communities.

# Conclusion

I began this study by asking what literacy educators can do to influence literacy achievement for children in high-poverty urban communities. For my interns and me, getting to know one cultural community and aligning our literacy teaching practices with the needs of the children in this community gave us some information to address this question. To learn about this community, we needed to learn more about our own cultural identities, and we needed know more about the children and caregivers in the community we served. We needed to see literacy teaching through a broad perspective that captured the sociopolitical and sociohistorical influences on achievement in the community. But we also needed to take a more focused look at the ways particular children responded to print during tutorial sessions.

Through these experiences, the majority of the interns changed the ways they viewed children, caregivers, literacy achievement, and their own capacities to be effective teachers in urban schools. As discussed in previous chapters, the interns' writings provided the best evidence of this change. Most of the interns replaced their deficit descriptions of children with a new vocabulary of understanding and hope.

Literacy teachers need to know how to teach well, and they must believe that all children are capable of learning. The internship discussed in this book placed preservice teachers on a path toward excellence in both of these areas. It is not the only path, however. My journey is unique, and other teachers' journeys will be, too. But the ultimate goal is essentially the same—making the playing field more equal for all children through our roles as literacy educators. Many experienced and inspired teachers are already doing this. The aim should be to support all literacy educators in this humbling and important responsibility.

Having expert, culturally sensitive literacy teachers in schools that serve children in high-poverty urban communities is a worthy goal. Getting there requires a lot from everyone involved in education. But consider the price that teachers, teacher educators, and students of education pay for not being the best professionals they can be for all children: Thousands of children who do not achieve in reading at the primary level fall further behind as they approach middle school and high school. They will be less able to secure a future as enlightened, productive, and socially responsible citizens. They will be less able to find jobs that pay a decent wage, and they will not be able to experience the fulfillment that literacy brings.

There are few social problems that are more important than literacy failure. All education professionals can learn to teach children who are socially and culturally different from themselves. We now know much more about what it takes to do this kind of work. The big question is, Are we willing to make changes to teacher education programs in order to get there?

# Study Methodology

## Context and Participants

This book is drawn from my work with preservice teachers at West Chester University (WCU) in West Chester, Pennsylvania. WCU is a large, state-supported university located in southeastern Pennsylvania, about 25 miles west of Philadelphia. The internship, identified in the university's master schedule as the Reading Practicum, is a requirement for all those seeking elementary teaching certification at WCU. Two literacy teaching courses are required before taking the internship: One is focused on the teaching of reading, and the other is focused on the teaching of writing. Connections between all language and literacy processes are emphasized in both courses. Teaching students often take the internship in their senior year, just prior to doing their student teaching.

The internship section that I taught was identified as an urban experience in the master. Seniority status at the time of course registration allowed education students the option of choosing which internship they wanted. Because taking the internship was a requirement, students sometimes were forced to choose the urban section of the course if the suburban and rural sections were filled. To my knowledge, this was the situation for some of my students each semester, although this information was difficult to ascertain.

Although I worked with preservice teachers in the urban literacy internship between the years 1996–2001, I have chosen not to identify the particular year my study took place, in order to protect the identities of those students involved in the study. I have used pseudonyms throughout the book for the same reason. Thirty preservice teachers—three men and 27 women— agreed to participate in this study. All were senior undergraduate students who had taken most of their prerequisite professional courses, including the two previously mentioned literacy education courses and a course in children's literature.

The demographics of the students in the internship reflected the larger reality of the ratio of white students to students of color who attended WCU and were enrolled in its teacher education program during this time. Students of color represented only 6% of those who participated in the internship between 1996 and 2001. Despite campaigns to create more cultural diversity at the university, WCU did not attract large numbers of black students from the region. The underrepresentation of black students in WCU's teacher education program may have been because WCU is located within a few miles of Cheyney University, a state-supported, historically black university that also offers a teacher education program and that draws many African American students from the greater Philadelphia area.

As stated in chapter 2, the internship was based in two public elementary schools in Philadelphia that serve primarily African American children. About 85% of the children were eligible for subsidized school meals, but this percentage does not accurately represent the economic diversity within the neighborhoods surrounding the schools. Some blocks contained abandoned or boarded-up homes, but many residential neighborhoods contained well-maintained row homes on tree-lined streets. In the commercial areas of these communities, there were locally operated businesses and a few national chain stores. There also were many churches, small and large, scattered throughout these neighborhoods.

Two interns were placed in each classroom of the 10 cooperating teachers who were participating in the second year of a three-year reading specialist certification program at WCU. All cooperating teachers had taken three WCU graduate courses that focused on assessment-based reading and writing instruction. Although they were all receiving similar exposures to the university program, their levels of teaching experience were different, as were their teaching styles. The cooperating teachers' participation in the WCU graduate program reflected their common investment in improving their knowledge and instructional practices.

## The Internship

The 6-hour-per-week internship included seminar and teaching time each Tuesday and Thursday morning during the 13-week semester. Interns were required to participate in the following course experiences:

1. *Twenty-five hours of on-campus seminar discussions that addressed literacy education from a diverse constructivist orientation* (Au, 1998): Seminars addressed literacy pedagogy as well as topics in cultural diversity, including white privilege, racism, African American history and culture, Ebonics and language variations, culturally relevant teaching, and literacy achievement theories (see Table A1 for a reading list).

## TABLE A1
## Internship Literature and Topics

| Text | Major Themes Addressed |
|---|---|
| McIntosh, P. (1990, Winter). White privilege: Unpacking the invisible knapsack. *Peace and Freedom*, pp. 10–12. | • White privilege as unearned advantage <br> • Racism as a system of dominance |
| Tatum, B.D. (1999). *Why are all the Black kids sitting together in the cafeteria? And other conversations about race* (Rev. ed.). New York: Basic Books. | • Prejudice vs. racism <br> • Domination and subordination <br> • White identity development |
| Ladson-Billings, G. (1994). *The dreamkeepers: Successful teachers of African American children.* San Francisco: Jossey-Bass. | • Segregation and schooling <br> • Teacher attitudes and behaviors <br> • Culturally relevant teaching <br> • Conceptions of knowledge |
| Bennett, C.I. (1999). Conflicting themes of assimilation and pluralism among African Americans. In C.I. Bennett, *Comprehensive multicultural education: Theory and practice* (4th ed., pp. 115–127). Boston: Allyn & Bacon. | • African American history <br> - enslavement <br> - emancipation and sharecropping <br> - northern migration <br> - solidarity and civil rights |
| Perry, T., & Delpit. L.D. (Eds.). (1998). *The real Ebonics debate: Power, language, and the education of African-American children.* Boston: Beacon Press. | • Ebonics debate defined <br> • Language and identity <br> • Teacher attitudes toward Ebonics <br> • Dialect, reading, and writing <br> • History of Ebonics <br> • Myths and realities of Ebonics <br> • Classroom practices <br> - investigating language <br> - code switching |
| Nieto, S. (2000). Toward an understanding of school achievement. In S. Nieto, *Affirming diversity: The sociopolitical context of multicultural education* (pp. 230–247). New York: Longman. | • Deficit theories <br> • Economic and social reproduction <br> • Cultural incompatibilities theory <br> • Resistance theory |

2. *Tutoring one child for one hour each Tuesday and Thursday throughout the semester*: Cooperating teachers selected children in grades K–4 who ranged from emergent readers (i.e., children who "pretend read" and have not achieved phonemic awareness) to beginning readers (i.e., children who can read primer

and first-grade texts), and these were the children the interns tutored. Interns were shown how to assess children's literacy abilities using interviews, writing and spelling samples, running records, and retellings. Interns also were taught how to craft literacy lessons that (a) were directed toward the child's Zone of Proximal Development (Tharp & Gallimore, 1988; Vygotsky, 1934/1978); (b) were balanced within the tutorial setting, including assisted reading, listening to read-alouds, independent reading, writing, and word study (Morris, 1999); (c) emphasized the real communicative functions of print (Altwerger, Flores, & Edelsky, 1991; Goodman, 1986); (d) were explicit, with direct modeling of strategies that successful readers (Fountas & Pinnell, 1996) and writers (Calkins, 1994; Tompkins, 1994) use; and (e) were closely monitored and reflected on (Schon, 1983). On the last day of the internship, the interns, cooperating teachers, and I celebrated the children's writing with a party. The children were asked to read aloud from the books they had made in their tutorial sessions.

Tutoring individual children was an idea suggested to me by my colleague Tom Gill, who also taught an urban section of the internship at WCU. He understood that preservice teachers needed to see how well children responded to "ideal" assessment-based teaching conditions. It was important to both of us that children's literacy potential be revealed to preservice teachers within the relatively short, 13-week semester, and so we organized our internships around one hour of one-on-one tutoring, and the interns spent the remaining time in the regular classroom.

3. *Coteaching with both a peer and a cooperating teacher in a regular classroom on Tuesdays and Thursdays for six weeks*: Instruction focused on using multicultural literature, especially texts that mirrored the lifestyles and themes of the children and families in the school's community and those that contained important themes about cultural differences. Instruction also focused on reading aloud to children and inviting children's written responses to literature. To prepare interns for these activities, I demonstrated personal, literary, and critical ways of responding to literature.

4. *Initiating communication with children's caregivers*: Interns sent home a list of open-ended questions about the children's attitudes, interests, and literacy behaviors. Interns also were shown how to conduct two-way, reciprocal conversations with caregivers (Edwards et al., 1999) and then were asked to conduct phone conversations with caregivers about children's progress.

5. *Responding to readings about cultural diversity in two ways*: First, after reading a chapter or article, interns were given a deadline to send a written

response to me via e-mail. I responded back to each intern via e-mail, acknowledging the interns' critical and insightful comments. Second, the interns also responded verbally to readings in the seminars, both on campus and in the field.

## Semester Calendar

The first three seminars were all devoted to preparing the interns to meet the children, collecting observational information about children and schools, and assessing the children's literacy abilities. In preparation for these seminars, I asked the interns to read selections from the book *Words Their Way: Word Study for Phonics, Vocabulary, and Spelling Instruction* (Bear et al., 1996) so they could understand the development of orthographic knowledge and the analysis of invented spellings. I also required the interns to read chapters from *Guided Reading: Good First Teaching for All Children* (Fountas & Pinnell, 1996) to learn about reading processes and to review the procedures for taking running records. I also pulled information from *The Art of Teaching Writing* (Calkins, 1994) and *Teaching Writing* (Tompkins, 1994) for seminar discussions about writing instruction and assessment. Some of the seminar time also was devoted to interns responding to the first few reading assignments related to white privilege and racism (see McIntosh, 1990; Tatum, 1999, for information related to cultural diversity).

The fourth and fifth class sessions were held at the placement site. The interns met the children and cooperating teachers in the field and spent much of their time learning about the children who they would tutor individually. During his or her first meeting with the children, each intern shared a personal story and invited the children to tell a story about themselves also. Then, the interns interviewed the children about their interests outside of school and their attitudes toward literacy, asking questions such as the following:

- Do you read?
- Are you learning to read? Who is helping you?
- Do you like to read? Why?
- Who reads to you?
- What kind of stories do you like?
- Do you write?
- Do you like to write?
- What do you like to write about?

The interns were shown a battery of assessments that required children to identify upper- and lowercase letters, memorize a short jingle and track it, spell words using the Spelling-by-State Inventory (Bear et al., 1996), listen to a story and retell it, read an unfamiliar text (preprimer, primer, first grade) and retell it, and—after a short demonstration of how to select meaningful topics—write about a self-selected topic. Interns were asked to use the assessment guidelines flexibly, based on their observations of children. Interns who tutored children in kindergarten and grade 1 began with the letter identification and continued until the children showed signs of frustration with the assessments. Children in grades 2 and higher began with the spelling assessment. If they did not use correct consonants in the spelling battery, interns asked them to identify upper- and lowercase letters and track the memorized jingle.

During the sixth and seventh seminars, I helped the interns to draw from their assessment information to plan tutoring instruction for their first week of teaching individual students. I emphasized that their assessments would be on-going, based on their observations of children's "in-flight" (Tharp & Gallimore, 1989, p. 42) responses to instruction. I demonstrated how to take observational and reflective notes and how to use these notes to plan further instruction.

At this time, I informed the interns that they would work with partners to create lessons for children in the regular classroom. I used the multicultural curriculum framework proposed by Banks (1999) and demonstrated how to construct a themed unit using multicultural texts in order to (a) enrich children's understandings about African American culture and history; (b) help children view concepts, issues, and events from the perspective of those who are culturally different from themselves; and (c) take a stance on important social issues and take actions to solve social problems. I helped the interns identify important themes from multicultural children's books, although I realized that the interns would need further assistance with this task (see chapter 7). I also demonstrated reading and writing experiences that would help children think critically about the themes contained in these books.

After our seventh class meeting, the interns returned to their assigned public schools for the rest of the semester, working with children individually, assisting the classroom teacher, and teaching lessons with a partner. The interns spent one day during the last week of the internship assessing children's literacy skills, selecting from the same battery of assessments used at the beginning of the semester. I asked the interns to summarize children's progress in reading (fluency, word identification, strategy use, and comprehension), writing (process, conventions, and message), and word study (spelling patterns and sight words). After I reviewed these assessment summaries, I asked the intern tutors to share them with their cooperating teachers, the children, and the children's caregivers.

Throughout the semester, much of my time in the field was spent watching the interns work with children, taking field notes, demonstrating instruction, and leading seminars. I observed tutoring sessions and modeled an instructional approach for each intern to use with each child. I usually visited each intern at least one time per week.

I scheduled classroom visits ahead of time with the interns. During these visits, I observed and took notes, but I did not interrupt an intern's teaching to model instruction. After each visit, I met with the intern and asked him or her to comment on the lesson I had observed. I shared with each intern my observations and often directed him or her to reflect on the lesson from the perspectives of particular students. In 20-minute "debriefing" sessions following each day of classroom visits, I drew from my own field notes to address particular teaching issues during the seminars. Many of these seminars focused on translating observational information into instructional goals and lessons.

## Cultural Diversity

Throughout the internship, the interns were asked to read and respond to professional literature that addressed several topics related to cultural diversity. Table A1 on page 154 lists the articles and the major topics addressed in these articles. I have included in chapter 4 responses from two interns profiled in this study.

## Data Gathering

I acted as participant–observer in this interpretive, inductive study to *explore what preservice teachers' internship experiences meant to them and specifically how they constructed attitudes and understandings about themselves, children, caregivers, literacy achievement in an urban community, and culturally relevant literacy teaching.* I was not only interested in understanding how interns' views and actions evolved during the internship but also how these were shaped by social factors beyond the internship (e.g., media, schooling, family, etc.). I drew my findings from the triangulation of the following data sources: cultural autobiographies, written responses to questions, surveys, caregiver communication reports, teaching records, interns' e-mail responses to the articles and chapters they read, and my own field notes. In an attempt to enhance interns' candor in responding to sensitive questions about race and culture, I asked them to respond anonymously to the surveys and questions.

According to Erickson (1990), the materials collected in the field are not data themselves but resources for generating data based on some formal means of analysis. The following section explains the procedures I used for converting the documents to the data that I then used as evidence to build key assertions.

## Cultural Autobiographies

The cultural autobiography served as my primary data source for developing assertions about the impact of the internship on preservice teachers' perspectives and teaching behaviors. At the beginning of each semester, I discussed the components of the cultural autobiography and provided written directions in the syllabus. In the first section of the autobiography, interns were asked to describe their cultural backgrounds, including where they grew up, their involvement with cultural differences, family communication around cultural diversity, and their schooling (primary, high school, university) experiences related to cultural diversity. In the second section, interns were asked to describe their own growth in racial identity development and their emerging understandings about children, caregivers, schooling, and society. The third section of the paper focused on cultural diversity within literacy teaching. I asked students to describe their understandings about culturally relevant teaching and how this notion translates to classroom teaching practices. The final section of the paper directed interns to describe issues they struggled to understand and what they will need to do to continue to learn about these issues. My sense was that most interns waited until the end of the semester to complete this assignment. Two interns took extended time to complete their autobiographies, so I did not include these autobiographies in the analysis.

I read each intern's cultural autobiography at least twice, making analytic notes in reference to each of the four categories previously mentioned. For example, for the category of "intern's background," I wrote about the extent to which each intern had been exposed to cultural diversity prior to the internship and the nature of this exposure. For "racial identity development," I noted how interns saw themselves in relation to the children they served in the placement schools. This included whether they included whiteness as a dimension of identity, or whether they examined their own racial biases and, if so, how they came to terms with these biases. I noted any statements that indicated an intern's interest in urban teaching (positive or negative). Under "understanding literacy achievement," I recorded the factors that interns' assigned to literacy achievement (e.g., home, class, teacher, district policies, district funding, society). Under the category of "culturally relevant teaching," I noted the different ways interns interpreted this approach in their tutoring and whole-class teaching practices.

After generating notes about each cultural autobiography, I eliminated four autobiographies from further analysis because they were missing descriptions of one of the six categories. For the remaining papers, I drew from the notations to generate a list of typical responses (e.g., "realizing the importance of validating culture/language in literacy teaching") and calculated the percentage of interns who included these responses in their papers (see Table A2).

### TABLE A2
### Common Themes in Autobiographies ($N$ = 24)

| Themes (in descending order of occurrence) | Percent of Papers Addressing Theme |
|---|---|
| Realizing the importance of validating culture/language in literacy teaching | 96% |
| Reporting limited background experiences with cultural diversity | 88% |
| Realizing prejudices toward children, caregivers, community | 79% |
| Realizing the need to learn more about children, community, culture, and or language | 66% |
| Realizing the importance of setting high expectations | 56% |
| Recognizing own assumptions about race (white privilege, colorblindness) | 54% |
| Realizing that I (intern) can teach children | 54% |
| Recognizing that children have the potential to do well academically | 54% |
| Realizing the importance of using books that mirror experiences of children | 54% |
| Realizing cooperating teachers provided positive learning environments | 42% |
| Realizing the importance of respecting children and caring for children | 36% |
| Realizing that factors of racism and poverty impact schooling | 33% |
| Recognizing the challenges of urban schooling | 33% |
| Acknowledging guilt, shame, regret, or paranoia about prejudices | 33% |

## Questions

Although the cultural autobiographies provided rich descriptions of interns' views and experiences, some parts of these papers were more developed than others, and the parts that were more detailed varied from intern to intern. For example, some interns focused on background information while others wrote in greater detail about their teaching practices. To correct for this difference, I added a short list of focus questions to the data corpus the following semester to ensure that interns would respond to specific areas of inquiry.

Interns were asked to respond to the following three questions at the beginning and midpoint of the semester:

1. How would you describe your interest and confidence in teaching literacy in urban classrooms?
2. How would you describe your cultural identity?
3. What factors do you think contribute to the literacy achievement of the children you teach in the internship?

They were asked to respond to a fourth question at midsemester:

4. How would you describe your efforts to teach in culturally relevant ways?

One student was absent on the day the midsemester questions were given, resulting in 13 interns responding to the questions. I drew from interns' responses to these questions to generate charts that showed interns' confidence in teaching (see Table A3), descriptions of cultural identity (see Table A4), their understandings of factors contributing to literacy achievement (see Table A5), and their interpretations of culturally relevant teaching in the internship (see Table A6).

### TABLE A3
### Confidence in Tutoring at Weeks 1 and 7 (*N* = 13)

| Confidence Levels | Week 1 | Week 7 |
| --- | --- | --- |
| High | 2 | 1 |
| Moderately high | 5 | 12 |
| Moderately low | 4 | - |
| Low | 1 | - |

## TABLE A4
## Descriptions of Cultural Identity at Weeks 1 and 7 (*N* = 13)

| Description of Cultural Identity | Week 1 | Week 7 |
|---|---|---|
| No previous exploration of whiteness; cultural descriptions center on ethnicity (Irish, Italian, Polish) | 12 | - |
| Use of "white" to describe identity | 1 | - |
| Awareness of white privilege | - | 13 |
| Awareness of white complicity in racism | - | 8 |
| Desire to know more about self and others culturally | - | 2 |
| Desire to be openly antiracist | - | 1 |

## TABLE A5
## Identifying Factors That Affect Literacy Achievement at Weeks 1 and 7 (*N* = 13)

| | Week 1 | | Week 7 | |
|---|---|---|---|---|
| Category | # of Mentions | Factors Cited by Interns | # of Mentions | Factors Cited by Interns |
| Parents | 20 total | | 6 total | |
| | 11 | • Parents do not provide literacy support to children. | 6 | • Parents have difficulty supporting children's literacy. |
| | 4 | • Single parents raise children. | | |
| | 3 | • Homes contain few books. | | |
| | 2 | • Parents discourage learning. | | |
| Schools | 11 total | | 30 total | |
| | 2 | • Low teacher salaries | 7 | • Crowded classrooms |
| | 2 | • Low expectations | 7 | • Low expectations |
| | 2 | • Crowded classrooms | 7 | • Limited funding |
| | 1 | • Poor school funding | 4 | • Poor instruction |
| | 1 | • Limited technology | 3 | • Irrational promotion policy |
| | 1 | • Unqualified teachers | | |
| | 1 | • Limited materials | 2 | • Insufficient faculty |
| | 1 | • Irrational promotion policy | | |
| Society | 4 total | | 7 total | |
| | 2 | • Poverty | 5 | • Poverty |
| | 1 | • Limited city budget | 2 | • History of oppression/racism |
| | 1 | • Crime | | |

## TABLE A6
### Implementing Culturally Relevant Teaching at Week 7 by Intern Number (*N* = 13)

|  | 1 | 2 | 3 | 4 | 5 | 6 | 7 | 8 | 9 | 10 | 11 | 12 | 13 |
|---|---|---|---|---|---|---|---|---|---|---|---|---|---|
| Using information about students' lives in literacy lessons |  |  |  | x |  | x | x |  |  |  |  |  | x |
| Using books reflecting multicultural themes | x | x | x | x | x |  |  | x |  |  |  |  |  |
| Using books reflecting lifestyles of children |  | x | x |  |  | x |  | x |  | x | x | x | x |
| Emphasizing children's cultural uniqueness |  | x | x |  |  | x |  |  |  |  |  |  | x |
| Modeling standard English (versus correcting child's language) |  |  |  |  |  | x |  |  | x |  |  | x |  |
| Validating use of dialect for story character (dialogue) |  |  |  |  |  |  |  |  | x |  |  |  |  |
| Teaching about standard English in writing lessons |  |  |  |  |  |  |  |  | x |  |  | x |  |

## Surveys

Interns responded to a survey (a modified version of Cultural Diversity Awareness Inventory [Henry, 1985]) twice at the beginning of the internship and once at the end. One intern was absent the first day the survey was given, resulting in 29 surveys in the data corpus. Interns responded to statements about children, caregivers, and teachers in reference to a particular community. Using a four-point Likert scale (strongly agree, agree, disagree, strongly disagree), interns completed the first survey in reference to a primarily African American urban community in which the annual income averages $35,000. These demographics reflected the community surrounding the placement schools. The interns completed the second survey in reference to a primarily white suburban community in which the average annual income is $100,000. At the end of the semester, interns completed the same survey in reference to the African American urban community and also responded to statements about their own comfort level with respect to particular areas of teaching.

I collapsed the survey responses into two categories—"agreement" and "disagreement"—and calculated the percentage of interns who strongly and moderately disagreed with an item (Likert items 1 and 2). Then, I calculated the percentage of interns who strongly and moderately agreed with each item (Likert items 3 and 4) (see Table A7). Once these percentages were computed, I noted differences in how interns responded to items related to each community and differences in their views about the urban community before and after their participation in the internship. I also looked at the degree to which interns changed their views about their own comfort level with assessing children; tutoring, teaching, and differentiating instruction in the regular classroom; and integrating information about children's lives into literacy lessons.

## Caregiver Communication Reports

Interns' notes about caregiver input indicated the nature and frequency of the communication between caregivers and interns. Immediately after interns communicated with caregivers, they were asked to describe (a) highlights of the conversation, recording as much about the specific language used as possible; (b) how the information provided by the caregiver might be useful in lesson planning; (c) the tone of the conversation; (d) how well they listened to the caregiver and maintained the conversation; and (e) the value of communicating with the caregiver.

Three interns did not complete the communication project because they could not get in touch with caregivers, and one report was incomplete. I read the remaining 26 reports and made notations about the topics discussed by interns and caregivers (e.g., children's interests, homework, school work, caregivers' expectations, and caregivers' support), the conversational tone of the communication (e.g., positive, neutral, or negative), the information interns gleaned about the child (e.g., family issues; literacy activity at home; school- and non–school-related hobbies and interests; homework habits; and relationships with siblings, friends, and caregivers), and ways of using parental information (e.g., writing instruction, reading instruction, and conversations with the child). I counted the numbers of "positive," "neutral," and "negative" responses, categorized the amount of information received by interns into the categories

## TABLE A7
## Survey Results (*N* = 29)

| I think most caregivers | Suburban | Pre-urban | Post-urban |
|---|---|---|---|
| Provide reading materials for children. | 90 | 14 | 41 |
| Read to children. | 86 | 14 | 41 |
| Try to teach their children to read. | 86 | 41 | 41 |
| Want their children to read well. | 86 | 86 | 90 |
| Read magazines or newspapers. | 90 | 52 | 80 |
| Read books. | 83 | 14 | 48 |
| **I think most children** | | | |
| Want to learn to read. | 93 | 90 | 97 |
| Read for pleasure. | 72 | 27 | 52 |
| Have acquired oral language commensurate with their ages. | 83 | 48 | 83 |
| Speak grammatically. | 76 | 48 | 59 |
| Who are not on grade level by third grade have the potential to read high school level texts. | 79 | 44 | 59 |
| Think critically. | 80 | 59 | 76 |
| Think creatively. | 86 | 76 | 83 |
| Are emotionally well-adjusted. | 79 | 26 | 52 |
| **I think most teachers in this community** | | | |
| Design lessons to meet students' needs. | 83 | 72 | 52 |
| Select appropriate reading materials for students. | 83 | 66 | 44 |
| Keep current on trends in literacy instruction. | 83 | 72 | 48 |
| Treat students respectfully. | 83 | 90 | 60 |
| Invite student decisionmaking/ownership. | 83 | 72 | 44 |
| **I feel confident in my understanding of** | | | |
| How to assess children's literacy needs. | N/A | 17 | 100 |
| How to help children grow as readers. | N/A | 24 | 90 |
| Tutoring children individually. | N/A | 62 | 100 |
| Teaching in the regular classroom. | N/A | 55 | 90 |
| Differentiating instruction in the regular classroom. | N/A | 34 | 55 |
| Integrating information about children's lives into instruction. | N/A | 48 | 86 |

"none," "little," "some," and "very much," and generated a list of the types of information provided by caregivers and what the interns would do with the information. Based on these notations, I identified four types of communication and listed the number of reports that reflected each type (see Table A8).

**TABLE A8**
**Communication Types Identified in Caregiver Communication Reports**
**(*N* = 26)**

| Description | Number |
|---|---|
| Positive communication: Caregivers were willing to talk to interns and expressed concern about their children. | 10 |
| Positive communication: Caregivers shared information about how they supported children's literacy learning. | 7 |
| Neutral communication: Caregivers answered interns' questions but did not supply additional information. | 6 |
| Negative or awkward communication: Caregivers seemed resistant to communicating with interns. | 3 |

## Teaching Records, E-mail Journal Entries, and Field Notes

I also collected interns' teaching records, e-mail journal entries, and field notes. I did not use these items to generate typical patterns but to construct narrative vignettes of teaching and to convey interns' views and ways of interpreting the professional literature.

Teaching records described interns' teaching activities with children and their reflections on these activities. Each record was divided into four columns. Column 1 contained interns' teaching plan, including the major areas of literacy instruction (reading aloud, guided/assisted reading, writing, and word study) and the specific activities and materials used for instruction. Column 2 contained a rationale for selecting these activities and materials. In column 3, interns wrote anecdotal notes of how children reacted to each section of the teaching plan. I explained to interns that reflective comments could include children's ability to accomplish the task, their attitudes about the task, and their interest in the task. Column 4 included interns' reflections on each teaching section. In this space, interns evaluated their own teaching efforts and the extent to which they succeeded in motivating children, engaging children in the lesson, and teaching children within their Zones of Proximal Development. They also identified problems, concerns, and questions about their teaching practices and suggested specific ways they could improve their instruction for next time.

E-mail responses to the chapters and articles are described on page 159.

Field notes included interns' questions and comments that arose during seminars and my office hours, and interns' teaching activities in the field. I recorded my own observations of field activity, summaries of conversations with interns, and commentary and questions about these observations and conversations. I drew from these notes to construct the narrative vignettes I use in the book.

## Building Assertions

I developed assertions about the impact of the internship on the interns based on positive relationships between data sets (triangulation). For instance, both the questions and survey data indicated that interns became more critical of urban schools and, simultaneously, less critical of caregivers during the semester. Interns' positive reports of communication with caregivers and their written critiques of urban school conditions (in their cultural autobiographies) give some insight as to why their perceptions shifted during the semester. In addition, the question responses and survey data together show positive change in interns' comfort levels with tutoring individual students, which also correlated with autobiographical reports of interns' statements about their ability to teach children in urban schools.

From these data, I was able to profile particular interns who demonstrated either typical or atypical reactions to the internship. I chose reports written by Kim and Cynthia to represent the many positive conversations interns had with caregivers (see chapter 6). In the same chapter, Maggie's negative experience talking to a parent illustrates a less typical response. Julia typified the use of observations to tailor instruction to their student's literacy needs (see chapter 7). In the same chapter, Rebecca's use of music to inspire a child to write was less typical. As much as possible, I combined information from the data sets to construct narrative vignettes of interns' activity with children and communication with caregivers.

Another layer of analysis involved looking for relations between interns' interests in urban teaching and their backgrounds. Five of the eight students who indicated they would be interested in teaching in urban schools also indicated that they had tutored the children of migrant workers and studied diversity issues as part of a foundations course taken one semester before the internship. Three of these interns reported having some exposure to cultural diversity before attending college, and one had been raised in different racially integrated neighborhoods surrounding Philadelphia. A few of the interns who showed an interest in teaching in urban schools had very little experience with cultural diversity prior to taking the internship. All interns who stated they would not seek urban jobs indicated they had little prior experience with cultural diversity. From this evidence, it appeared to me that prior experiences with cultural diversity related positively to having an interest in urban teaching, but I could not state that prior experiences with cultural diversity were *necessary* for this interest to develop because two of the interns who conveyed interest in urban teaching stated that they had had very little exposure to cultural diversity prior to the course.

This path of analysis led me to focus on how interns with little prior exposure to cultural diversity left the internship experience being receptive to urban school teaching. I wondered, What understandings and skills did these interns acquire to help them take on this responsibility? Answering this question demanded that I take a close-up look at two interns who reported that they would teach in urban schools, including one with many prior experiences with cultural diversity (Allison) and one with few (Marie). By drawing extensively from their autobiographies and their e-mail journals, I was able to show how each evolved in her understandings about children, caregivers, schools, teaching, and the community. Both interns arrived to the internship with doubts about children's literacy potential, despite their very different background experiences with respect to cultural diversity. Allison (atypical) was able to construct more sophisticated understandings about cultural diversity than Marie (most typical).

Analyzing patterns of response to the internship prompted a search for theoretical lenses that would help me make sense of interns' understandings about cultural diversity. My search led me to Howard's (1999) book *We Can't Teach What We Don't Know: White Teachers, Multiracial Schools*. Howard's White Identity Orientations framework was helpful for looking at how interns' reactions to the course projects aligned with particular orientations toward cultural diversity: fundamentalist, integrationist, and transformationist. I found that Howard's description of the integrationist orientation toward diversity described most of the interns in the course who were just beginning to understand issues of whiteness, cultural dominance, and culturally relevant teaching.

I concluded that the interns made some fundamental shifts in their thinking about themselves, children, caregivers, teaching, and the sociology of literacy achievement, but I also found that interns would need continued support to develop their understandings beyond the internship. It became evident that interns would need to learn more about caregivers and caregiver communication, children's language and ways of helping children code switch, applications of culturally relevant teaching, critical responses to literature, and working toward a positive white identity. I concluded that a much more comprehensive system of university and professional development supports would be needed to help teachers serve children in high-poverty urban communities.

In the tradition of ethnographic reporting, I used particular description, general description, and my own analytic commentary to support my assertions about how interns responded to the internship (Erickson, 1990). Particular description, in the form of written quotations from interns' writing and narrative vignettes of interns' activities from my field notes, bring the reader in close contact with interns' views and actions. I used general description to convey some of the typical and atypical patterns of interns' perspectives and teaching behaviors. I wove analytic commentary throughout the chapters to describe my own participation in the internship and my interpretation of interns' reactions to course projects.

## Reflections on Data Collection, Research Design, and Future Research

There are a few caveats to using autobiographical writing, despite the level of detail they provide. The researcher must be mindful that this kind of writing, especially if it is not delivered anonymously, may not convey the actual perspectives of the participants, but instead the perspectives that participants think they should convey. Given that I took a strong stance on valuing cultural diversity, some interns may have identified themselves as having a greater commitment to cultural diversity and urban education than they actually did. A few interns, however, exposed their racial biases even though they were not required to do so, suggesting they felt they could communicate openly about their prejudices. I wondered, however, if their ability to do this was related to my being white, with the underlying assumption that I would understand their perspectives. Positive correlation between the data completed anonymously (surveys and questions) and the cultural autobiographies suggests that most views expressed in these documents were valid.

In reporting on the general patterns of growth among interns and focusing on the experiences of some, questions remain about the impact of the internship on each intern. Presenting several complete intern cases would have provided a more individualized picture of interns' views and experiences, even though doing so would have resulted in some redundancies. More individualized representations of what the internship meant to each intern are warranted so that alternative models of teacher growth can be developed. A focus on Allison's case, for instance, showed that not all interns' comments aligned neatly into one of the three orientations described by Howard, prompting the need to develop a model of growth that captures the nuances of developing as cultural sensitive teachers.

One area I felt needed much more attention in this study was the role of the cooperating teacher in preparing interns to teach in urban schools. I described cooperating teachers as building their expertise in the area of literacy teaching but did not address the impact of their efforts on the interns. This would require asking cooperating teachers about their views related to mentoring preservice teachers and observing their ways of mentoring the preservice teachers. It would also require interviews with preservice teachers about the influence of their cooperating teachers on their views and actions.

The assertions I present are a small piece of the overall puzzle of understanding the impact of a literacy internship that is infused with cultural diversity experiences. More research is needed to better understand how teacher education programs shape teacher development over the long term and how cultural sensitivity education for the teacher affects academic achievement. A valuable research effort would be to find out the ways in which high expectations of children and a validation of students' culture affect literacy achievement. Studies that link teachers' cultural sensitivity with achievement gains are needed to justify the inclusion of cultural sensitivity education into all teacher preparation programs.

# REFERENCES
## AND RECOMMENDED RESOURCES

## References

Adler, M.A., & Fisher, C.W. (2001). Early reading programs in high-poverty schools: A case study of beating the odds. *The Reading Teacher, 54*, 616–619.

Allington, R.L. (2001). *What really matters for struggling readers: Designing research-based programs.* New York: Longman.

Allington, R.L. (2002). *Big brother and the national reading curriculum: How ideology trumped evidence.* Portsmouth, NH: Heinemann.

Altwerger, B., Flores, B., & Edelsky, C. (1991). *Whole language: What's the difference?* Portsmouth, NH: Heinemann.

Anders, P.L., Hoffman, J.V., & Duffy, G.G. (2000). Teaching teachers to teach reading: Paradigm shifts, persistent problems, and challenges. In M.L. Kamil, P.B. Mosenthal, P.D. Pearson, & R. Barr (Eds.), *Handbook of reading research* (Vol. 3, pp. 719–742). Mahwah, NJ: Erlbaum.

Apol, L., Sakuma, A., Reynolds, T.M., & Rop, S.K. (2003). "When can we make paper cranes?" Examining pre-service teachers' resistance to critical readings of historical fiction. *Journal of Literacy Research, 34*(4), 429–464.

Ascher, C. (1988). Improving the school-home connection for poor and minority urban students. *Urban Review, 20*(2), 109–123.

Au, K.H. (1998). Social constructivism and the school literacy learning of students of diverse backgrounds. *Journal of Literacy Research, 30*(2), 297–319.

Banks, J.A. (1999). *An introduction to multicultural education.* Boston: Allyn & Bacon.

Baratz, S., & Baratz, J. (1970). Early childhood intervention: The social science base of institutional racism. *Harvard Educational Review, 40*(1), pp. 29–50.

Bartoli, J. (2001). *Celebrating city teachers: How to make a difference in urban schools.* Portsmouth, NH: Heinemann.

Bartoli, J., & Botel, M. (1988). *Reading/learning disability: An ecological approach.* New York: Teachers College Press.

Bear, D.R., Invernizzi, M., Templeton, S., & Johnston, F. (1996). *Words their way: Word study for phonics, vocabulary, and spelling instruction.* Upper Saddle River, NJ: Merrill.

Bennett, C.I. (1999). *Comprehensive multicultural education: Theory and practice* (4th ed.). Boston: Allyn & Bacon.

Bowie, R.L., & Bond, C.L. (1994). Influencing future teachers' attitudes toward Black English: Are we making a difference? *Journal of Teacher Education, 45*(2), 112–118.

Brophy, J.E. (1998). *Motivating students to learn.* New York: McGraw-Hill.

Brown v. Board of Educ., 347 U.S. 483 (1954).

Burke, C. (1985). Parenting, teaching, and learning as a collaborative venture. *Language Arts, 62*(8), 836–843.

Cairney, T.H., & Munsie, L. (1995). Parent participation in literacy learning. *The Reading Teacher, 48*, 392–403.

Calkins, L.M. (1994). *The art of teaching writing.* Portsmouth, NH: Heinemann.

Carini, P.F. (2001). *Starting strong: A different look at children, schools, and standards.* New York: Teachers College Press.

Cazden, C.B. (1986). Classroom discourse. In M.C. Wittrock (Ed.), *Handbook of research on teaching* (3rd ed., pp. 432–463). New York: Macmillan.

Charles, C.Z. (2000). Neighborhood racial-composition preferences: Evidence from a multiethnic metropolis. *Social Problems, 47*(3), 379–407.

Chisholm, I.M. (1994). Preparing teachers for multicultural classrooms. *The Journal of Educational Issues of Language Minority Students, 14*, 43–68.

Clay, M.M. (1985). *The early detection of reading difficulties* (3rd ed.). Portsmouth, NH: Heinemann.

Clotfelter, C.T. (2001). Are whites still "fleeing"? Racial patterns and enrollment shifts in urban public schools, 1987–1996. *Journal of Policy Analysis and Management, 20*, 199–221.

Cochran-Smith, M. (1991). Learning to teach against the grain. *Harvard Educational Review, 61*(3), 279–310.

Cochran-Smith, M. (1995a). Color blindness and basket making are not the answers: Confronting the dilemmas of race, culture, and language diversity in teacher education. *American Educational Research Journal, 32*(3), 493–522.

Cochran-Smith, M. (1995b). Uncertain allies: Understanding the boundaries of race and teaching. *Harvard Educational Review, 65*(4), 541–570.

Cochran-Smith, M., & Lytle, S.L. (1993). *Inside/outside: Teacher research and knowledge.* New York: Teachers College Press.

Coles, G. (1987). *The learning mystique: A critical look at "learning disabilities".* New York: Pantheon.

Compton-Lilly, C. (2003). *Reading families: The literate lives of urban children and their families.* New York: Teachers College Press.

Cummins, J. (1986). Empowering minority students: A framework for intervention. *Harvard Educational Review, 56*(1), 18–36.

Darling-Hammond, L., & Sclan, E.M. (1996). Who teaches and why. In J.P. Sikula, T.J. Buttery, & E. Guyton (Eds.), *Handbook of research on teacher education: A project of the Association of Teacher Educators* (2nd ed., pp. 67–101). New York: Simon & Schuster.

Dawson Boyd, C. (2003, May). *Empowering literacy in the 21st century.* Paper presented at the 48th annual convention of the International Reading Association, Orlando, FL.

Delpit, L.D. (1995). *Other people's children: Cultural conflict in the classroom.* New York: New Press.

DuBois, W.E.B. (1990). *The souls of black folk: Essays and sketches.* New York: Signet Classic. (Original work published 1903)

Dyson, A.H. (2003). *The brothers and sisters learn to write: Popular literacies in childhood and school cultures.* New York: Teachers College Press.

Dyson, M.E. (2003). *Open Mike: Reflections on philosophy, race, sex, culture, and religion.* New York: Basic Books.

Edwards, P.A. (1995). Empowering low-income mothers and fathers to share books with young children. *The Reading Teacher, 48*, 558–564.

Edwards, P.A., Pleasants, H.M., & Franklin, S.H. (1999). *A path to follow: Learning to listen to parents.* Portsmouth, NH: Heinemann.

Eisenhart, M. (2001). Changing conceptions of culture and ethnography methodology: Recent thematic shifts and their implications for research on teaching. In V. Richardson (Ed.), *Handbook of research on teaching* (4th ed., pp. 209–225). Washington, DC: American Educational Research Association.

Entwisle, D.R., Alexander, K.L., & Olson, L.S. (1997). *Children, schools, and inequality.* Boulder, CO: Westview.

Epstein, J.L. (1986). Parents' reactions to teacher practices of parent involvement. *The Elementary School Journal, 86*(3), 277-294.

Epstein, J.L. (1988). How do we improve programs for parent involvement? *Educational Horizons, 66*(2), 58-59.

Erickson, F. (1990). *Qualitative methods of research in teaching and learning.* New York: Macmillan.

Erickson, F. (1993). Transformation and school success: The politics and culture of educational achievement. In E. Jacob & C. Jordan (Eds.), *Minority education: Anthropological perspectives* (pp. 27–51). Norwood, NJ: Ablex.

Erickson, F., & Mohatt, G. (1982). Cultural organization of participation structures in two classrooms of Indian students. In G. Spindler (Ed.), *Doing the ethnography of schooling: Educational anthropology in action* (pp. 133–174). New York: Holt, Rinehart and Winston.

Farley, R., & Frey, W.H. (1994). Changes in the segregation of whites from blacks during the 1980s: Small steps toward a more integrated society. *American Sociological Review, 59*(1), 23–45.

Flippo, R.F. (2001). *Reading researchers in search of common ground.* Newark, DE: International Reading Association.

Florio-Ruane, S., & McVee, M. (2000). Ethnographic approaches to literacy research. In M.L. Kamil, P.B. Mosenthal, P.D. Pearson, & R. Barr (Eds.), *Handbook of reading research* (Vol. 3, pp. 153–162). Mahwah, NJ: Erlbaum.

Fordham, S., & Ogbu, J.U. (1986). Black students' school success: Coping with the "burden of 'acting white'." *Urban Review, 18*(3), 176–206.

Fountas, I.C., & Pinnell, G.S. (1996). *Guided reading: Good first teaching for all children.* Portsmouth, NH: Heinemann.

Fuller, M.L., & Olsen, G. (1998). *Home-school relations: Working successfully with parents and families.* Boston: Allyn & Bacon.

Gay, G. (1993). Building cultural bridges: A bold proposal for teacher education. *Education and Urban Society, 25*(3), 284–299.

Gee, J.P. (2000). Discourse and sociocultural studies in reading. In M.L. Kamil, P.B. Mosenthal, P.D. Pearson, & R. Barr (Eds.), *Handbook of reading research* (Vol. 3, pp. 195–207). Mahwah, NJ: Erlbaum.

Gill, T. (2003, May). *A Philadelphia story: An urban research- and assessment-based literacy program that made a difference.* Paper presented at the 48th annual convention of the International Reading Association, Orlando, FL.

Giroux, H.A. (1994). *Border crossings: Cultural workers and the politics of education.* New York: Routledge.

Giroux, H.A. (2001). *Theory and resistance in education: Towards a pedagogy for the opposition.* New York: Bergin & Garvey.

Gomez, M.L. (1993). Prospective teachers' perspectives on teaching diverse children: A review with implications for teacher education and practice. *Journal of Negro Education, 62*(4), 459–474.

Goodman, K.S. (1986). *What's whole in whole language: A parent guide to children's learning.* Portsmouth, NH: Heinemann.

Grissmer, D.W., Kirby, S.N., Berends, M., & Williamson, S. (1994). *Student achievement and the changing American family.* Santa Monica, CA: RAND.

Guillaume, A., Zuniga, C., & Yee, I. (1998). What difference does preparation make? Educating preservice teachers for learner diversity. In M.E. Dilworth (Ed.), *Being responsive to cultural differences: How teachers learn* (pp. 143–159). Thousand Oaks, CA: Corwin.

Haberman, M. (1996). Selecting and preparing culturally competent teachers for urban schools. In J.P. Sikula, T.J. Buttery, & E. Guyton (Eds.), *Handbook of research on teacher education: A project of the Association of Teacher Educators* (2nd ed., pp. 747–760). New York: Simon & Schuster.

Hall, B. (2003, February 26). City's school libraries search for funds to update holdings. *The Philadelphia Inquirer*, p. A15.

Harber, J.R. (1979). *Prospective teachers' attitudes toward black English.* (ERIC Document Reproduction Service No. ED181728)

Heath, S.B. (1983). *Ways with words: Language, life, and work in communities and classrooms.* Cambridge, UK: Cambridge University Press.

Henry, G.B. (1985). *Cultural diversity awareness inventory.* Hampton, VA: Hampton University Mainstreaming Outreach Services.

Henry, M.E. (1996). *Parent-school collaboration: Feminist organizational structures and school leadership.* Albany: State University of New York Press.

Herrnstein, R.J., & Murray, C.A. (1996). *The bell curve: Intelligence and class structure in American life.* New York: Simon & Schuster.

Hinchman, K.A., & Grace, T. (2002, December). *Constructing culturally responsive literacy teacher education: Exploring the practices of two teacher educators.* Paper presented at the 52nd annual meeting of the National Reading Conference, Miami, FL.

Hoffman, J., & Pearson, P.D. (2000). Reading teacher education in the next millennium: What your grandmother's teacher didn't know that your granddaughter's teacher should. *Reading Research Quarterly, 35*, 28–44.

Howard, G.R. (1999). *We can't teach what we don't know: White teachers, multiracial schools.* New York: Teachers College Press.

Jones, L.T., & Blendinger, J. (1994). New beginnings: Preparing future teachers to work with diverse families. *Action in Teacher Education, 16*(3), 79–86.

Jordan, J. (1988). Nobody mean more to me than you and the future life of Willie Jordan. *Harvard Educational Review, 58*(3), 363-374.

Keene, E.O., & Zimmermann, S. (1997). *Mosaic of thought: Teaching comprehension in a reader's workshop.* Portsmouth, NH: Heinemann.

Kozol, J. (1991). *Savage inequalities: Children in America's schools.* New York: Crown.

Kozol, J. (2000). *Ordinary resurrections: Children in the years of hope.* New York: Crown.

Krashen, S.D. (1995). School libraries, public libraries, and the NAEP reading scores. *School Library Media Quarterly, 23*(4), 235-237.

Labov, W. (1972). *Sociolinguistic patterns.* Philadelphia: University of Pennsylvania Press.

Ladson-Billings, G. (1994). *The dreamkeepers: Successful teachers of African American children.* San Francisco: Jossey-Bass.

Ladson-Billings, G. (2001). *Crossing over to Canaan: The journey of new teachers in diverse classrooms.* San Francisco: Jossey-Bass.

Lareau, A. (1989). *Home advantage: Social class and parental intervention in elementary education.* New York: Falmer Press.

Lazar, A.M. (1998). Helping preservice teachers inquire about caregivers: A critical experience for field-based courses. *Action in Teacher Education, 19*(4), 14–28.

Lazar, A.M., & Weisberg, R. (1996). Inviting parents' perspectives: Building home-school partnerships to support children who struggle with literacy. *The Reading Teacher, 50*, 228–237.

Leland, C.H., & Harste, J.C. (2002, December). *Doing what we want to become: Preparing new urban teachers.* Paper presented at the 52nd annual meeting of the National Reading Conference, Miami, FL.

Lenski, S.D., Crawford, K., Crumpler, T., & Stallworth, C. (2002, December). *Preparing literacy teachers in a diverse world*. Paper session presented at the 52nd annual meeting of the National Reading Conference, Miami, FL.

McIntosh, P. (1990, Winter). White privilege: Unpacking the invisible knapsack. *Peace and Freedom*, pp. 10–12.

McWhorter, J. (2000). *Losing the race: Self-sabotage in black America*. New York: Free Press.

Meier, D. (1995). *The power of their ideas: Lessons for America from a small school in Harlem*. Boston: Beacon Press.

Midkiff, R.B., & Lawler-Prince, D. (1992). Preparing tomorrow's teachers: Meeting the challenge of diverse family structures. *Action in Teacher Education*, 14(3), 1–5.

Morris, D. (1999). *The Howard Street tutoring manual: Teaching at-risk readers in the primary grades*. New York: Guilford.

Myers, W.D. (1991). *Now is your time! The African-American struggle for freedom*. New York: Scholastic.

Neuman, S.B., & Celano, D. (2001). Access to print in low-income and middle-income communities: An ecological study of four neighborhoods. *Reading Research Quarterly*, 36, 8–26.

Nicholas, P. (2000, May 30). Fattah vows to keep fighting for schools. *The Philadelphia Inquirer*, p. A1.

Nieto, S. (2000). *Affirming diversity: The sociopolitical context of multicultural education*. New York: Longman.

O'Connor, C. (1997). Dispositions toward (collective) struggle and educational resilience in the inner city: A case analysis of six African-American high school students. *American Educational Research Journal*, 34(4), 593–629.

Ogbu, J.U. (1987). Variability in minority school performance: A problem in search of an explanation. *Anthropology and Education Quarterly*, 18(4), 312–334.

Ogbu, J.U., & Davis, A. (2003). *Black American students in an affluent suburb: A study of academic disengagement*. Mahwah, NJ: Erlbaum.

Paley, V.G. (1979). *White teacher*. Cambridge, MA: Harvard University Press.

Perry, T., & Delpit. L.D. (Eds.). (1998). *The real Ebonics debate: Power, language, and the education of African-American children*. Boston: Beacon Press.

Philips, S.U. (1972). Participant structures and communicative competence: Warm Springs children in community and classroom. In C.B. Cazden, V.P. John, & D.H. Hymes (Eds.), *Functions of language in the classroom* (pp. 370–394). New York: Teachers College Press.

Plessy v. Ferguson, 163 U.S. 537 (1896).

Pressley, M. (2002). Effective beginning reading instruction. *Journal of Literacy Research*, 34(2), 165–187.

Pressley, M., Wharton-McDonald, R., Allington, R., Block, C.C., Morrow, L.M., Tracey, D., et al. (1998). *The nature of effective first-grade literacy instruction* (Research Report No. 11007). Albany, NY: National Research Center on English Learning and Achievement.

Pritchard, R.J., & Marshall, J.C. (2002). Professional development in "healthy" vs. "unhealthy" districts: Top ten characteristics based on research. *School Leadership and Management*, 22(2), 113–141.

Purcell-Gates, V., L'Allier, S., & Smith, D. (1995). Literacy at the Harts' and the Larsons': Diversity among poor, inner-city families. *The Reading Teacher*, 48, 572–578.

Rickford, J.R., & Rickford, R.J. (2000). *Spoken soul: The story of Black English*. New York: Wiley.

Rosenblatt, L.M. (1978). *The reader, the text, the poem: The transactional theory of the literary work*. Carbondale: Southern Illinois University Press.

Schmidt, P.R. (2001). The power to empower: Creating home/school relationships with the ABCs of cultural understanding and communication. In P.R. Schmidt & P.B. Mosenthal (Eds.), *Reconceptualizing literacy in the new age of multiculturalism and pluralism* (pp. 389–433). Greenwich, CT: Information Age.

Schmidt, P.R. (2002, December). *Literacy teacher education for the appreciation of diversity.* Paper presented at the 52nd annual meeting of the National Reading Conference, Miami, FL.

Schmidt, P.R., & Mosenthal, P.B. (2001). *Reconceptualizing literacy in the new age of multiculturalism and pluralism.* Greenwich, CT: Information Age.

Schon, D.A. (1983). *The reflective practitioner: How professionals think in action.* New York: Basic.

Scribner, S., & Cole. M. (1981). *The psychology of literacy.* Cambridge, MA: Harvard University Press.

Shannon, P.W. (1988). *Broken promises: Reading instruction in twentieth-century America.* Glenview, IL: Greenwood.

Shockley, B. (1994). Extending the literate community: Home-to-school and school-to-home. *The Reading Teacher, 47*, 500–502.

Shockley, B., Michalove, B., & Allen, J. (1995). *Engaging families: Connecting home and school literacy communities.* Portsmouth, NH: Heinemann.

Sleeter, C.E. (Ed.). (1991). *Empowerment through multicultural education.* Albany: State University of New York Press.

Smith, F. (1988). *Joining the literacy club: Further essays into education.* Portsmouth, NH: Heinemann.

Smith, G.P. (1998). *Common sense about uncommon knowledge: The knowledge bases for diversity.* Washington, DC: American Association of Colleges for Teacher Education.

Smitherman, G. (1998). Black English/Ebonics: What it be like? In T. Perry & L.D. Delpit (Eds.), *The real Ebonics debate: Power, language, and the education of African American children* (pp. 29–37). Boston: Beacon Press.

Snow, C.E., Burns, M.S., & Griffin, P. (Eds.). (1998). *Preventing reading difficulties in young children.* Washington, DC: National Academy Press.

Snyder, S. (2003, April 27). The big test. *The Philadelphia Inquirer Magazine*, pp. 9–13.

Spears-Bunton, L.A. (1990). Welcome to my house: African American and European American students' responses to Virginia Hamilton's "House of Dies Drear." *Journal of Negro Education, 59*(4), 566–576.

Stanovich, K.E. (1986). Matthew effects in reading: Some consequences of individual differences in the acquisition of literacy. *Reading Research Quarterly, 21*, 360–407.

Steele, C.M. (1992). Race and the schooling of black Americans. *The Atlantic Monthly, 269*(4), 68-78.

Street, B.V. (1995). *Social literacies: Critical approaches to literacy development, ethnography, and education.* New York: Longman.

Studer, J.R. (1994). Listen so that parents will speak. *Childhood Education, 70*(2), 74–76.

Tatum, B.D. (1999). *Why are all the Black kids sitting together in the cafeteria? And other conversations about race* (Rev. ed.). New York: Basic Books.

Taylor, B.M., Pearson, P.D., Clark, K.F., & Walpole, S. (1999). *Beating the odds in teaching all children to read.* Ann Arbor, MI: Center for the Improvement of Early Reading Achievement.

Taylor, B.M., Pearson, P.D., Clark, K.F., & Walpole, S. (2000). Effective schools and accomplished teachers: Lessons about primary-grade reading instruction in low-income schools. *The Elementary School Journal, 101*(2), 121–165.

Taylor, B.M., Pressley, M., & Pearson, P.D. (2000). *Research-supported characteristics of teachers and students that promote reading achievement*. Washington, DC: National Education Association.

Taylor, D., & Dorsey-Gaines, C. (1988). *Growing up literate: Learning from inner-city families*. Portsmouth, NH: Heinemann.

Tharp, R.G., & Gallimore, R. (1989). *Rousing minds to life: Teaching, learning, and schooling in social context*. New York: Cambridge University Press.

Tompkins, G.E. (1994). *Teaching writing: Balancing process and product*. New York: Merrill.

Vygotsky, L.S. (1978). *Mind in society: The development of higher psychological processes* (M. Cole, V. John-Steiner, S. Scribner, & E. Souberman, Eds. and Trans.). Cambridge, MA: Harvard University Press. (Original work published 1934)

Weiner, L. (2000). Research in the 90s: Implications for urban teacher preparation. *Review of Educational Research, 70*(3), 369–406.

Wiggins, R.A., & Follo, E.J. (1999). Development of knowledge, attitudes, and commitment to teach diverse student populations. *Journal of Teacher Education, 50*(2), 94–105.

Willis, A.I. (2002). Literacy at Calhoun Colored School 1892–1945. *Reading Research Quarterly, 37*, 8–44.

Wolf, S. (2000, December). *"Only connect!" Cross cultural connections in the literacy engagement of a preservice teacher and the child who taught her*. Paper presented at the 50th annual meeting of the National Reading Conference, Scottsdale, AZ.

Xu, S.H. (2000). Preservice teachers in a literacy methods course consider issues of diversity. *Journal of Literacy Research, 32*, 505–531.

## Children's Literature Cited

Coles, R. (1995). *The story of Ruby Bridges*. Ill. G. Ford. New York: Scholastic.

Dorros, A. (1995). *Isla*. Ill. E. Kleven. New York: Dutton.

Lenski, L. (1987). *Sing a song of people*. Ill. G. Laroche. Boston: Little, Brown.

Lester, J. (1994). *John Henry*. Ill. J. Pinckney. New York: Dial.

Mitchell, M.K. (1993). *Uncle Jed's barbershop*. Ill. J.E. Ransome. New York: Simon & Schuster.

Morimoto, J. (1992). *My Hiroshima*. New York: Penguin.

Sterling, S. (1999). *Jump in*. Scarborough, ON: ITP Nelson Thomson Learning.

## Recommended Resources

### General

Au, K.H., & Kawakami, A.J. (1994). Cultural congruence in instruction. In E.R. Hollins, J.E. King, & W.C. Hayman (Eds.), *Teaching diverse populations: Formulating a knowledge base* (pp. 5–23). Albany: State University of New York Press.

Avery P.G., & Walker, C. (1993). Prospective teachers' perceptions of ethnic and gender differences in academic achievement. *Journal of Teacher Education, 44*(1), 27–37.

Davis, K.C. (1995). *Don't know much about history: Everything you need to know about American history but never learned*. New York: Avon.

Foster, J.E., & Loven, R.G. (1992). The need and directions for parent involvement in the 90s: Undergraduate perspectives and expectations. *Action in Teacher Education, 14*(3), 13–18.

Foster, M. (1994). Effective black teachers: A literature review. In E.R. Hollins, J.E. King, & W.C. Hayman (Eds.), *Teaching diverse populations: Formulating a knowledge base* (pp. 225–241). Albany: State University of New York Press.

Garcia, J., & Pugh, S. (1992). Multicultural education in teacher education programs: A political or an educational concept? *Phi Delta Kappan, 74*(3), 214–219.

Gentemann, K.M., & Whitehead, T.L. (1983). The cultural broker concept in bicultural education. *The Journal of Negro Education, 52*(2), 118–129.

Gill, T., & Nelson-Gill, L. (1994). Dialect and reading revisited. *Reading Research and Instruction, 34*(1), 1–4.

Giroux, H.A. (1988). *Schooling and the struggle for public life: Critical pedagogy in the modern age.* Minneapolis: University of Minnesota Press.

Glaser, B.G., & Strauss, A.L. (1967). *The discovery of grounded theory: Strategies for qualitative research.* Hawthorne, NY: Aldine de Gruyter.

Goldenberg, C. (1994). Promoting early literacy development among Spanish-speaking children: Lessons from two studies. In E.H. Hiebert & B.M. Taylor (Eds.), *Getting reading right from the start: Effective early literacy interventions* (pp. 171–199). Boston: Allyn & Bacon.

Haycock, K. (2001). Closing the achievement gap [Electronic version]. *Educational Leadership, 58*(6), 6–11.

Helms, J.E. (1990). *Black and white racial identity: Theory, research, and practice, Vol. 129.* Westport, CT: Greenwood.

Hoover-Dempsey, K.V., & Sandler, H.M. (1997). Why do parents become involved in their children's education? *Review of Educational Research, 67*(1), 3–42.

Lazar, A. (2001). Preparing white preservice teachers for urban classrooms: Growth in a Philadelphia-based literacy practicum. In J.V. Hoffman, D.L. Schallert, C.M. Fairbanks, J. Worthy, & B. Maloch (Eds.), *50th yearbook of the National Reading Conference* (pp. 367–381). Chicago: National Reading Conference.

Shannon, P. (1998). *Reading poverty.* Portsmouth, NH: Heinemann.

Strickland, D., & Snow, C. (2002). *Preparing our teachers: Opportunities for better reading instruction.* Washington, DC: National Academy Press.

Taylor, D. (1994). *From the child's point of view.* Portsmouth, NH: Heinemann.

Teale, W.H. (1986). Home background and young children's literacy development. In W.H. Teale & E. Sulzby (Eds.), *Emergent literacy: Writing and reading* (pp. 173–206). Westport, CT: Greenwood.

Zeichner, K.M. (1993). *Educating teachers for cultural diversity.* East Lansing, MI: National Center for Research for Teacher Learning.

## Children and Families

Compton-Lilly, C. (2003). *Reading families: The literate lives of urban children and their families.* New York: Teachers College Press.

Hale-Benson, J.E. (1986). *Black children: Their roots, culture, and learning styles.* Baltimore, MD: Johns Hopkins University Press.

Hill, S.A. (1999). *African American children: Socialization and development in families.* Thousand Oaks, CA: Sage.

McAdoo, H.P. (2001). *Black children: Social, educational, and parental environments* (2nd ed.). Thousand Oaks, CA: Sage.

McCubbin, H.I., Thompson, A.I., Thompson, E.A., & Fromer, J.E. (1998). *Resiliency in Native American and immigrant families.* Thousand Oaks, CA: Sage.

Rodriguez, G. (1999). *Raising nuestros niños: Bringing up Latino children in a bicultural world.* New York: Simon & Schuster.

Taylor, R.J., Jackson, J.S., & Chatters, L.M. (Eds.). (1997). *Family life in black America*. Thousand Oaks, CA: Sage.

Zhou, M., & Bankston, C.L. (1999). *Growing up American: How Vietnamese children adapt to life in the United States*. New York: Russell Sage.

## Collaborating With Caregivers

Cairney, T.H., & Munsie, L. (1995). *Beyond tokenism: Parents as partners in literacy*. Portsmouth, NH: Heinemann.

Edwards, P.A., Pleasants, H.M., & Franklin, S.H. (1999). *A path to follow: Learning to listen to parents*. Portsmouth, NH: Heinemann.

Epstein, J., Coates, L., Salinas, K.C., Sanders, M.G., & Simon, B.S. (1997). *School, family, and community partnerships: Your handbook for action*. Thousand Oaks, CA: Sage.

Fuller, M.L., & Olsen, G. (1997). *Home-school relations: Working successfully with parents and families*. Boston: Allyn & Bacon.

Goldberg, S. (1997). *Parent involvement begins at birth: Collaboration between parents and teachers of children in the early years*. Boston: Allyn & Bacon.

Henry, M. (1996). *Parent-school collaboration: Feminist organizational structures and school leadership*. Albany: State University of New York Press.

Vopat, J. (1994). *The parent project: A workshop approach to parent involvement*. York, ME: Stenhouse.

## Teacher Organizations

International Reading Association (IRA)
www.reading.org
800-336-7323

National Council of Teachers of English (NCTE)
www.ncte.org
877-369-6283

179

# A

# B

Burke, C., 83
Burns, M.S., 15

# C

Cairney, T.H., 43
Calkins, L.M., 138, 155–156
caregivers: intern attitudes toward, 1–2, 32, 54–56, 94–97; knowledge of, in integrationist orientation, 129; relations with schools, 20–21
caregiver–teacher communication, 32, 82–99; fears about, addressing, 87–90; guide for, 89f; inquiry project on, 145–147; learning from, 90–94; reflection and inquiry on, 98–99; reports on, in teacher preparation study, 164–165, 166t; and school effectiveness, 42
Carini, P.F., 134
Cazden, C.B., 19
Celano, D., 16
change agent: teacher as, 36–38
Charles, C.Z., 15
child-centered literacy instruction: in tutorial setting, 101–109
children of color: curriculum and, 19; interests of, in literacy instruction, 104–109; intern attitudes toward, 53–54; knowledge of, in integrationist orientation, 129; term, 9
Chisholm, I.M., 4, 44
Clark, K.F., 41
class: and identity, 51
classroom: intern practice in, 108–109; management of, intern questions on, 120–122; race in, 73–75
Clotfelter, C.T., 44
Cochran-Smith, M., 4, 147–148
code switching, 116–117
Cole, M., 133
Coles, G., 39
Coles, R., 71
colorblind view, 73–75
communication: with caregivers, 32, 42, 82–99; two-way, need for, 82–83
community: cultural, reflection and inquiry on, 23; knowledge of, in integrationist orientation, 130
Compton-Lilly, C., 16
course selection: growth and, 131–133
Crawford, K., 47
critical reading: and multicultural texts, 110
cross-cultural differences, 5–6; and literacy education, 44–46; validation of, 74
Crumpler, T., 47
cultural autobiography: of author, 24–38; reflection and inquiry on, 38; in teacher preparation study, 159–160, 160t
cultural community: reflection and inquiry on, 23
cultural factors: affecting literacy achievement, 12–23
culturally relevant: definition of, 10
culturally relevant literacy teaching, 100–126; inquiry project on, 141–145; knowledge of, in integrationist orientation, 130; reflection and inquiry on, 125–126

room management, 120–122; development of, understanding, 77–79; teacher educators and, 148–149; term, 11; and urban schools, 122–124

SPEARS-BUNTON, L.A., 109
STALLWORTH, C., 47
STANOVICH, K.E., 18
STEELE, C.M., 143
STERLING, S., 86
STITH, CHARLES, 27
STREET, B.V., 133
STUDER, J.R., 84
STUDY: thoughtful, for professional growth, 134–135
SUBORDINATION: experience of, 51
SYMPATHETIC TEACHING STYLE, 40

# T

TATUM, B.D., 20, 36, 45, 51, 61, 68, 154, 156
TAYLOR, B.M., 6, 41
TAYLOR, D., 28, 46
TEACHER(S): disconnect with children and communities, 44–46; effective, characteristics of, 41–44; growth as, 134–147; inquiry projects for, 136–147; as interviewer, 84–85; power of, 75; responsibility of, realization of, 130–131; roles of, 36–38, 121; turnover among, 48
TEACHER COLLABORATION: for professional growth, 135–136; and school effectiveness, 42
TEACHER COMMITMENT: precursors to, 4–5
TEACHER EDUCATORS: growth as, 147–150
TEACHER EXPECTATIONS, 39–40, 142–144; interns on, 100; racial tolerance and, 60–61
TEACHER EXPERTISE: and learner access, 18–19
TEACHER PREPARATION, 1–11, 46–48; on caregiver communication, 83–87; on cultural connections in literacy instruction, 100–126; for cultural sensitivity, 39–49; growth in, 131–134; reflection and inquiry on, 49; reform of, 149–150
TEACHER PREPARATION STUDY: context of, 152–153; data gathering in, 158–167; internship in, 153–156; literature and topics in, 154t; methodology of, 152–170; participants in, 152–153; reflections on, 169–170; semester calendar for, 156–158; surveys in, 163–164, 165t
TEACHER QUALITY: in urban schools, 30–31
TEACHING RECORDS: in teacher preparation study, 166
TEACHING STYLES: African Americans and, 120–122, 142–143; types of, 40
TEMPLETON, S., 102, 138, 156–157
TEXTBOOKS: comparison of, 17
TEXT SELECTION: in assessment-based teaching, 139; multiculturalism and, 109–115
THARP, R.G., 18, 136, 138, 155, 157
TOMPKINS, G.E., 155–156
TRACEY, D., 41
TRANSFORMATIONIST ORIENTATION: to diversity, 65, 78–79

# U–V

UNEQUAL SCHOOLING, 29–31; constructing understandings of, 68–73
URBAN: term, 8–9
URBAN PLACEMENT: intern attitudes toward, 52–53

URBAN SCHOOLS: challenges of, 122–124; conditions in, 15; constructing understandings of, 68–73; effective, characteristics of, 41–42; privatization of, 127–128; teacher preparation for, 1–11; teacher quality in, 30–31

VOCATIONAL EDUCATION, 14

VOLUNTARY MINORITIES, 8

VYGOTSKY, L.S., 18, 103, 137, 155

# W

WALPOLE, S., 41

WEINER, L., 8, 15, 19

WEISBERG, R., 43

WHARTON-McDONALD, R., 41

WHITENESS: discovering, 34–35

WHITE PRIVILEGE, 34–35; constructing understandings of, 65–68; invisibility of, 51–52; resistance to, 34, 64–65, 67

WIGGINS, R.A., 47

WILLIAMSON, S., 15

WILLIS, A.I., 14

WOLF, S., 43

WRITING: assessment-based teaching and, 139–140

# X–Z

XU, S.H., 47

YEE, I., 47

ZIMMERMAN, S., 138

ZONE OF PROXIMAL DEVELOPMENT, 18, 137

ZUNIGA, C., 47

# THE WOUNDED HEART OF GOD

# THE WOUNDED HEART OF GOD

## THE ASIAN CONCEPT OF HAN AND THE CHRISTIAN DOCTRINE OF SIN

Andrew Sung Park

ABINGDON PRESS
Nashville

THE WOUNDED HEART OF GOD:
THE ASIAN CONCEPT OF HAN AND THE CHRISTIAN DOCTRINE OF SIN

*Copyright © 1993 by Abingdon Press.*

Library of Congress Cataloging-in-Publication Data

Park, Andrew Sung
    The wounded heart of God: the Asian concept of han and the Christian doctrine of sin. / Andrew Sung Park.
      p.    cm.
    ISBN 0-687-38536-9
    1. Han (Psychology)   2. Sin.   I. Title.
    BF75.H26P37    1992                            92-32182
    241'.3—dc20

Printed in the United States of America on recycled, acid-free paper.

# CONTENTS

# ACKNOWLEDGMENTS

Dorothee Soelle shares the story of her divorce in her book *Death by Bread Alone* because she believes that theology is not only an intellectual endeavor, but also a sharing of the life of the theologian. In her work, I find the courage to share the story of my own family life.

My family has experienced the reality of han. My parents were born during the Japanese occupation of Korea (1910–1945) and suffered the hardship of exploitation at the hands of the Japanese. My father was drafted into the Japanese Army toward the end of World War II. The defeat of Japan saved his life. When Korea became independent of Japan in 1945, the North Korean communist government confiscated the land, the house, and all the possessions my parents had inherited from their ancestors. By crossing the Imjin River, where they were shot at by the border patrols, they barely escaped to South Korea. When the Korean War broke out in 1950, our family once more escaped from the communists by walking from Inchon to Pusan, a distance of more than 300 miles. On the way, we lost our grandfather. As refugees, our life was miserable, a fact made all the worse by our father's occupation as a countryside preacher. After a long struggle, our family finally emigrated to the United States in January 1973. We expected a stable life, but in December of that same year our parents were killed in an automobile accident in Colorado. That was the darkest time of my life.

Among our family members, my mother had suffered the most: patriarchal suppression and repression, the wars, and the hardship of a preacher's wife. Her life was a series of tragedies and human anguish. She was born in han and died in han. She is the reason I write about han, so that fewer people might have to suffer as she did.

The deep pain of human agony has been a primary concern for my theological reflection. The issue of han has been more significant in my life than the problem of sin. Accordingly, my theological theme has been how to resolve the human suffering which wounds the heart of God. This book is an attempt to grapple with the problem of han in relation to sin.

I would like to take this opportunity to express my deepest gratitude to my spouse, Sun-Ok Jane Myong, who has fully supported the publication of this project by taking care of the lion's share of the housework. I am grateful most of all for her unfailing love and patience through the long process of writing a book. I am also thankful for the understanding and patience of my two sons, Amos (6) and Thomas (3). They often wanted to play with "Daddy" a little longer, but when "Daddy" had to study, they understood and let him go. This book was a family project and was written with the help of the whole family.

Without the ardent support of Dr. Rex Matthews, senior editor of academic books at Abingdon Press, the publication of this project would not have been possible. I thank him for taking the initiative to publish this project. Dr. Robert A. Ratcliff, associate editor of academic books, has done an excellent job of editing. I am deeply indebted to him.

I also would like to extend my sincere appreciation to my colleagues at the School of Theology at Claremont: Prof. John Cobb as my teacher and colleague inspired me in various ways and lured me to sharpen the definition of han; Prof. Marjorie Suchocki was my insightful dialogue partner. Prof. Dan Rhodes helped me to outline the structure of the book; Prof. Cornish Rogers and Prof. Mary Elizabeth Moore assisted me by providing useful resources. I am also grateful to Dr. Philip Anderson, Dr. Carol Voisin, Mr. Jeff Irish, and Mr. Barry Gannon who read parts of the book and provided valuable suggestions. I would like to thank my students at the School of Theology at Claremont for their useful feedback and comments, for they were indeed my teachers.

# INTRODUCTION

Raising a question relevant to the present world is crucial to the task of constructing a theology. As Reinhold Niebuhr says, "Nothing is so incredible as an answer to an unasked question. One half of the world has regarded the Christian answer to the problem of life and history as 'foolishness' because it had no questions for which the Christian revelation was the answer and no longings and hopes which that revelation fulfilled."[1] In light of Niebuhr's remarks, Christian theologians need to analyze well the problems of the world before seeking to answer them.

The present work raises the dual questions of whether the doctrine of sin relevantly addresses the issues Christians face in today's world and whether the doctrine can contribute to leading the world to the reign of God on earth. The world is full of such personal, social, and global problems as child abuse,[2] family, sexual, and racial violence,[3] labor exploitation, drug abuse, human rights violations, crimes of corporations, animal cruelty, and environmental crises. Some problems, caught in the vicious cycle of escalated violence and hatred, grow continually worse. Racial or religious violence increases between Israelis and Palestinians, Azerbaijanis and Armenians, Afrikaners and the native peoples of South Africa, Serbs and Croats, Sikhs and Hindus, and between Christians and Jews. Making matters yet worse, sometimes these victims direct their misguided resentment to individuals and groups other than to those responsible for the original offense.

Is the doctrine of sin capable of responsibly diagnosing and constructively dealing with these kinds of issues? Has Christianity effectively grappled with them with a serious commitment to the establishment of God's reign on earth?

Right questions precede right answers. The way we raise questions determines the way we receive answers. Good diagnosis indicates good healing. Since the doctrine of sin is Christianity's primary means of describing and addressing the wrongs of the world, its diagnosis is pivotal to the doctrine of personal and corporate salvation.

## SIN AND HAN

Throughout its history, the church has been concerned with the sin of people, but has largely overlooked an important factor in human evil: the pain of the *victims* of sin. The victims of various types of wrongdoing express the ineffable experience of deep bitterness and helplessness. Such an experience of pain is called *han* in the Far East. Han can be defined as the critical wound of the heart generated by unjust psychosomatic repression, as well as by social, political, economic, and cultural oppression. It is entrenched in the hearts of the victims of sin and violence, and is expressed through such diverse reactions as sadness, helplessness, hopelessness, resentment, hatred, and the will to revenge. Han reverberates in the souls of survivors of the Holocaust, Palestinians in the occupied territories, victims of racial discrimination, battered wives, children involved in divorces, the victims of child-molestation, laid-off workers, the unemployed, and exploited workers.

Sin and han must be treated together, if we are to grasp a more comprehensive picture of the problems of the world than that delineated by the doctrine of sin alone. In brief, the traditional doctrine of sin has been one-sided, seeing the world from the perspective of the sinner only, failing to take account of the victims of sin and injustice. A brief review of the history of the doctrine of sin will reveal this to be the case.

The Greek view of sin is more liberal than the Latin dogmatic view. The greater part of the Eastern Church Fathers before Augustine denied any real original sin. They acknowledged a propagated corruption in humankind resulting in mortality, but asserted that this is not sin, for it does not involve humanity in guilt. While upholding the solidarity of the human race in its physical connection with Adam, they believed that the will of humans is free and spontaneous in its action.[4] A different picture emerges from the Western Church, in which speculation with regard to the Fall and the inheritance of guilt proceeded steadily along lines laid down by Tertullian until it culminated in Augustine's idea of original sin.[5] He perceives the essence of this original sin as pride and concupiscence. Although Scholasticism shifted the balance somewhat with its greater emphasis on human autonomy, the Reformers, particularly Luther and Calvin, regressed to a rigid Augustinian doctrine of depravity, instead of progressing toward more openness. Their view is rather pessimistic about human nature.

In a modern view, Hegel's absolute idealism views sin as "alienation." Such alienation is a necessary step toward union with the divine spirit, defying the pessimistic mood of the Reformation and replacing it with an optimistic view, which suavely connects sin and salvation, alienation and union. Schleiermacher's intuitive notion of sin and God contradicts Hegel's rational concept of sin. Schleiermacher's romanticist understanding of sin as the "world-consciousness" endeavors to surpass the rational bias of Idealism. He attenuated the idea of sin by regarding it as a shortcoming on the road to perfection. Kierkegaard denounced the smooth dialectical process of the Hegelian idea of alienation by presenting the discontinuous dialectical discrepancy between God and sin. Sin, according to Kierkegaard, is our existential, irrational, and illogical leap into absurdity. Rauschenbusch, a spokesperson for the Social Gospel movement, transcended the individualistic interpretation of sin and described it at a collective level, regarding it as social disorder based on "selfishness."

For Reinhold Niebuhr, sin is crucial to Christian theology. In the condition of anxiety, we either deny our limits of human finitude or attempt to escape our anxious state of insecurity by giving up our opportunity to exercise freedom. The denial of our finitude by asserting ourselves beyond our limits is the sin of *pride*, which is a more fundamental sin to human beings. The renunciation of the exercise of our freedom by indulging ourselves in physical pleasure is the sin of *sensuality*. This sin is derived from pride. With either pride or sensuality, Niebuhr claimed that it is not *necessary* that we commit sin, but it is *inevitable*. In all these different perspectives from the history of Christian thought, the focus of the doctrines of sin and salvation has fallen firmly on the moral agency of the sinner and his or her standing before God. The role played in human salvation by the victims of sin has rarely been considered.

In certain recent theological developments, however, we can find some indications of how to overcome the one-sidedness of the notion of sin. Feminist and liberation theologians have developed under-

11

standings of "sin" which reject its traditionally male-dominated and individualistic interpretations.

Valerie Saiving has rejected Reinhold Niebuhr's concept of sin on the basis of its male-centered interpretation. For Saiving, *pride* is the sin of men, not of women. Women, she says, suffer from a different set of problems: "triviality, distractibility, and diffuseness, lack of an organizing center or focus, dependence on others for one's own self-definition."[6] Saiving holds that even though women are capable of sinning in other ways, they generally suffer from lack of pride, low self-esteem, and lack of self-assertiveness.

Gustavo Gutiérrez, an exponent of Latin American liberation theology, rejects the exclusively individualistic interpretation of sin which Western theologies have customarily espoused. For him, sin has a threefold nature. First, sin is the social, economic, and political oppression which exploits the oppressed, particularly the poor. Second, sin is the historical determinism which discourages the oppressed from determining their own destiny in history. Third, sin is a breach of communion with God and neighbor. This last Gutiérrez calls "spiritual sin."[7] He insists that these three dimensions of sin are interconnected, thus debunking the interpretation of sin as solely an individual act before God.

Even though I appreciate these efforts to transcend the male-centered and individualistic interpretations of sin, I would nonetheless raise questions about Saiving's and Gutiérrez's positions. Van Harvey defines sin (actual) in *A Handbook of Theological Terms* as "any act, which includes thoughts as well as deeds, done in conscious and deliberate violation of God's will as expressed in the revealed or natural law."[8] Sin is a conscious offense committed against God or neighbors. *The Westminster Dictionary of Christian Theology* confirms this notion of sin: "'Sin is any word or deed or thought against the eternal law' (Augustine)."[9] Quoting Augustine's saying, the dictionary affirms the intrinsic involvement of the human will in sin.

Although Saiving says that women's sin is distractibility, triviality, and low self-esteem, I would question whether these are indeed really *sins* for women. Sin involves volition. Since there is no act of volition in those characteristics Saiving mentions, these characteristics are not the sins, but rather the *han* of women. Sin is the volitional act of sinners (oppressors); han is the pain of the victim of sin. Thus, women's sin as "diffuseness" and "triviality" is a misnomer. *Women's lack of an organizing center is not sin but han.* This fact proves that the proper analysis of sin and han is crucial to bringing forth the healing (salvation) of the world.

In the same way, Gutiérrez's social and historical dimensions of sin are wrong designations. Since social, economic, and political oppression and historical fatalism are impediments to the fulfillment of the human potential of the oppressed, I would point out that these are not so much sin as they are the han of the oppressed. Gutiérrez, for lack of better terminology, has mixed the sin of the oppressors (the breach of fellowship with God and others) with the han of the oppressed (economic, social, and political oppression, and historical determinism).

The church has developed the doctrine of sin and other related theological ideas with the sinner, but not the victim of sin, in mind. I consider this unchristian. To bring the good news to the poor and the downtrodden, we need to develop a proper analysis of the problems of the world viewed from the perspectives of both the sinner and the victim. The notion of han will help us to see the side of the victim. Moreover, when we make this change, certain other doctrines—repentance, justification, salvation—will be revised as well. The doctrine of *repentance*, which has focused on the sinner/oppressor, will be complemented with the doctrine of *forgivingness* which is for the victim/oppressed. The doctrine of *justification* for the oppressor will be underpinned by the doctrine of *justice* for the oppressed. The doctrine of *salvation* for sinners will be complemented by the doctrine of the *resolution of han* for the victims of sin.

The notion of han necessitates a perspectival change in how we formulate the doctrines of sin and salvation. It shifts the discussion from an exclusive focus on the sinner/oppressor to a viewpoint that includes the victims/oppressed as well. The present state of theological discussion needs such an overhaul in favor of the oppressed.

It is important for this discussion to remember that sin and han are complex, entangled realities. While sin and guilt belong to oppressors, and han and shame belong to the oppressed, the two realities often overlap. Frequently—indeed, probably most of the time—they exist side by side in individuals. The oppressed can be oppressors and vice versa; sometimes we commit sin and sometimes we experience han. For example, a victim of racism can be a sexist. This fact, however, should not diminish the distinction between sin and han, oppressors and oppressed.

One notable feature of the discussion of han is its multidisciplinary character. We can only fully understand han on the basis of data collected from such various disciplines as psychology, sociology, philosophy, economics, ecology, and physics. The suffering of humanity and creation is neither exclusively theological, psychological, sociological, political, nor economic. Any reductionist approach fragments the interpretation of the reality of world-pain. To heal the wound of the world, all the disciplines must cooperate to diagnose the pain of the world and to cure its diseases, envisaging together the world's wholeness. One of my objectives in this book is thus to free theology from its parochial enclave. With a vision of theology as part of an interdisciplinary whole, we can more fully utilize God's abundant gifts of life in bringing forth God's reign on earth.

# The Reality of Han

Han is an Asian, particularly Korean, term used to describe the depths of human suffering.[1] Han is essentially untranslatable; even in Korean, its meaning is difficult to articulate. Han is the abysmal experience of pain. It has two aspects: active and inactive. Active han is closer to aggressive emotion, while inactive han is similar to an acquiescent spirit. Of the two, inactive han is more common in human experience. In this chapter I will endeavor to define the meaning of han; in the next, its structure.

## THE DEFINITIONS OF HAN

### Frustrated Hope

There is hope at the very foundation of our existence. The meaning of the English word *existence* is "standing out," out (*ex*) of standing (*sistentia*). We exist because we stand out. The essence of human existence is hope. Hope is the window of the soul. That is, when we look out and look forward, we can exist. When it is frustrated, hope turns into han, a psychosomatic pain. Han produces sadness, resentment, aggression, and helplessness.

According to Chi Ha Kim, a *minjung* poet, "Han is the *minjung's* angry and sad sentiment turned inward, hardened and stuck to their hearts. Han is caused as one's outgoingness is blocked and pressed for an extended period of time by external oppression and exploitation."[2] It is the hardened heart that is grieved by oppression and injustice.

15

One way to understand han is to compare it with Peter Burke's frustration-aggression hypothesis of social psychology. This hypothesis holds that human beings, as organic social beings, have goals. As major and minor frustrations assail them, people seldom move smoothly toward the goals they set for their lives. Their opponents, their own inability, their own personality, and natural forces—e.g., illness, accidents, disasters—block their will to fulfill these goals. Also, people may have mutually contradictory goals, some of which have to be foiled. Thus they develop frustration.[3]

Burke's research further suggests that the impediment of goal-achievement results in hostile impulses in people.[4] Sometimes, people's hostility cannot be steered directly to the source of frustration, because the culprit is unknown or too powerful to strike back against. In this situation, frustration may be produced by self-contradictory tendencies within the individual. The culprit may be an in-group member, a friend, or an advocate, making it difficult to recognize him or her as the culprit of frustration. If the relationship is between child and parent, the hostility can be accumulated or directed toward oneself or some other target that is safer to accuse and lash out at.

The hostility accumulated due to frustrated hope in the frustration-aggression hypothesis points to the reality of han. Han begins when goals are blocked. The formation of han takes time. The intensity of a traumatic experience depends upon the duration of tension and trauma.

Moltmann says, in his *Theology of Hope*, that hope is a key to understanding history, for the hope that flows from the promise of God creates history. His idea of hope takes its stand on faith in God, claiming that hope is the "inseparable companion" of faith. For him, the other side of pride is hopelessness, resignation, and melancholy. These comprise "the sin of despair."[5]

Thus, Moltmann says that despair is sin![6] However, when people are betrayed by those they have trusted, they become hopeless and experience despair. Children who have been abused often mistrust their parents and fall into hopelessness and despair. This hopelessness is not sin but han.

## The Collapsed Feeling of Pain

Han can be further defined as the collapsed pain of the heart due to psychosomatic, interpersonal, social, political, economic, and cultural oppression and repression. The reality of han is the emotional, rational, and physical suffering of pain rooted in the anguish of a victim.

Han can be compared to the black hole theory in astrophysics. When a star ten times more massive than the sun grows old, it will expand and grow to become what is called a red giant. When the red giant surpasses its maximum point of expansion, the inner core of the star implodes and its exterior rebounds, and then a supernova phenomenon transpires.[7] After this explosion, the star collapses to "singularity." It is called a black hole. Whatever a black hole touches, it swallows up. Its gravity is so strong that nothing, not even light, can escape it.[8] Like a black hole, when suffering reaches the point of saturation, it implodes and collapses into a condensed feeling of pain. This collapsed feeling of sadness, despair, and bitterness is han.[9] In the life of han-ridden people, the mode of han overwhelms the other types of human emotion and becomes a domineering spirit.

This collapsed feeling is more than a psychological phenomenon. Such a feeling encompasses all dimensions of human existence. It controls our physical mode of expression, producing bodily pain or sickness. It shows through the interpersonal social, cultural, and religious aspects of life. Like repression, han is submerged in the unconscious, forcing us to bury our oppressed feelings. Han, however, controls our ways of thought, emotion, and behavior. Unlike unconsciousness, the actuality of han exposes its oppressed feelings at the various emotional levels of life. Han, the condensed feeling of pain, thus denotes the quality, not the quantity, of oppressed feelings.

## Han as "Letting Go"

When people receive too much stress or pressure from outside, they come to a breaking point where they lose their center of control. From that point, they can no longer control their own feeling, and therefore let go of all feelings.

There are two types of such letting go—one positive, the other negative. Meister Eckhart, a medieval mystic, experienced the positive letting go. For him, letting the will go was necessary to letting be, which is the authentic mode of human existence (being); letting the intellect go was necessary to experiencing pure ignorance and a transformation of knowledge. Letting go is the way of the *via negativa* by which we come to emptiness, the fruitful release of the self so that God can take away all our suffering and pain.[10]

The other letting go is negative. While positive letting go requires self-control, its negative form derives from the loss of self-control.

Negative letting go is resignation, self-renunciation, and self-abnegation. Han is a negative letting go which is desolate, barren, bitter, and meaningless. In a sense, han is not a true letting go, since it is forced upon self and impinged upon it by oppression, which destroys the self's organizing center.

Erik Erikson states this truth in a slightly different way in his *Childhood and Society,* in which he asserts that the ability to hold on and to let go with discretion is an important step in childhood development.[11] Firmness or holding must protect the child against any potential anarchy. In human social interaction, these two social modalities, holding on and letting go, must maintain a balance. According to Erikson, "to hold can become a destructive and cruel retaining or restraining, and it can become a pattern of care: to have and hold. To let go, too, can turn into an inimical letting loose of destructive forces, or it can become a relaxed 'to let pass' and 'to let be'."[12]

Han is the inimical letting go produced by destructive forces. Han arises when the equilibrium of holding on and letting go is broken and the weight tilts toward letting go. When han is appropriately dissolved, a more relaxed letting go will take place. The han of destructive letting go conjures up a sarcastic, pessimistic, and scornful spirit.

A poem by Chang Yan So expresses the han of letting go. In spite of this letting-go spirit, there is a glimpse of holding on in his faint smile, which indicates that the waiting is for a "Godot."[13]

> Waiting need not be for meeting;
> If my heart hurts, let it ache;
> If the wind blows,
> let it carry away my faint smile,
> as I hold my head
> high . . . [14]

The spirit of han echoes "let it go," "let it ache," "let it blow," and "let it rain." The mind of han does not quiver before pain. Let it hurt and hurt until it is incapable of being hurt. This concretion of pain tends to nihilism or fatalism without totally giving in; there still remains the will to existence expressed as "holding the head high"— the spirit of defiance against the source of one's han, the negation of the negation.

18

## Resentful Bitterness

Han is resentment plus bitterness. Bitterness is intense animosity, while resentment is a feeling of indignation resulting from injury or insult. Han is the intensive, indignant sense of repulsion by the present state of affairs, usually caused by offense and insult. For Chi-ha Kim, a *minjung* poet, the han of bitterness can be sublimated as the dynamic form of energy for revolution.[15] Sung Woo Yang, another *minjung* poet, expresses this form of han in his "Slaves Notebook"—one of his underground classics which caused his incarceration by the South Korean government in 1977 after a printing in Japan.

> Curse, curse, you mountains,
> rivers, trees and grass!
> cry, beating your breast;
> because you will be able to live
>     billions of years;
> To curse the offspring of the
> offspring of those who bear
>         swords . . .[16]

Yang articulates the resentful bitterness of the oppressed *minjung* against any ruling power by forces, including the oppressors and those who rule with swords. Here we find the notion of han as "something akin to martyred, unresolved, bitterness."[17] It is a righteous grudge against brutal military dictators, abusive authoritarian officials, or unscrupulous business people.

For Nam Dong Suh, a *minjung* theologian, han is "a deep feeling that rises out of the unjust experience of the people" or a "just indignation."[18] There is a common denominator of the feeling of the powerless *minjung*: han.[19] When the suppressed experiences of people accumulate, han appears.

Another *minjung* theologian, Younghak Hyun, depicts han as something created by the burden of the governmental policy of blind development: "Han is a sense of unresolved resentment against injustices suffered, a sense of helplessness because of the overwhelming odds against oneself, a feeling of the total abandonment ('Why hast thou forsaken me?'), a feeling of acute pain of sorrow in one's guts and bowels making the whole body writhe and wiggle, and an obstinate urge to take 'revenge' and to right the wrong—all these combined."[20] An unresolved resentment against injustice epitomizes the state of han, which is expressed through the feeling of abandonment and helplessness.

C. S. Song, a Taiwanese theologian, clarifies the meaning of han as "the rhythm of passion welling out of restless souls in the world of the dead, the wrongs done to them unrequited. Han is the rhythm of passion crying from the hearts of those who have fallen victim to social and political injustices."[21] Song holds that the experience of han is not unique to the Korean people, but is universal for souls experiencing suppression. In Asian culture, where dominance-subordination has persisted for centuries, such an experience of han is particularly evident. It appears in folktale, folk songs, folk music, and folk plays, releasing people's sorrow, frustration, and anger.[22] The universality of han is also confirmed by most Korean *minjung* scholars.[23]

When people undergo traumatic experiences, they survive the experiences through the han of self-defense mechanisms. Like the water of *marah* mentioned in the book of Exodus in the Old Testament, the han of resentful bitterness wells up in victims. Unless it is treated like the water of *marah*, its bitterness will not stop welling up.[24]

## Han as the Wounded Heart

A wound is "a hurt caused by the separation of the tissues of the body."[25] It usually involves division of tissue or rupture of membrane, due to external violence. Han is the division of the tissue of the heart caused by abuse, exploitation, and violence. It is the wound to feelings and self-dignity.[26]

When the heart is hurt so much, it ruptures symbolically; it aches. When the aching heart is wounded again by external violence, the victim suffers a yet deeper pain. The wound produced by such repeated abuse and injustice is han in the heart.

For instance, Korean women's pain becomes acute when they are hated or abandoned by husbands or by lovers. Their dignity is trampled and their hearts broken. Few social systems exist to protect or advocate for their rights in a patriarchal society. Consequently pain develops within and their hearts are broken. Patriarchy breaks their broken hearts yet further, thus producing han, the deep wound of the heart and the soul.

## STORIES OF HAN

I am skeptical of the capability of language to express deep human experiences. Han is one of these experiences which language cannot sufficiently explain. I do believe, however, that stories are one of the best means by which language can be used to convey its meaning. Stories communicate the heart of han without confining it to the boundary of definition. Below are some stories of han from Korea and other parts of the world.

## Tae-il Chun: Exploited Worker

Tae-il Chun's is the story of a twenty-two-year old Korean man whose death became the focal point of the contemporary Korean *minjung* movement, the liberation movement for the down-and-out. Tae-il was born in 1948, the son of a family so poor that during his early years one of Tae-il's brothers died of malnutrition. Having very little formal education, by the time he was eight he was working such jobs as shoeshine boy and rear-cart pusher. When he was sixteen he began work as an apprentice in a sewing shop in the Peace Market. The working conditions in this mile-long, three-story building were miserable. Neither fresh air nor sunlight ever penetrated its window-less walls. His coworkers were nearly all young people like himself; the average age was eighteen, with nearly 40 percent between the ages of twelve and fifteen. They worked fifteen-hour days with only two days off a month, to earn a daily wage of only seventy to one hundred Won—when a typical lunch for the shop owners was two hundred Won. The grueling schedule laid waste their young bodies; many developed tuberculosis, bronchitis, irregular menstruation, and so on.

> One day, seeing a young sewing machinist vomiting blood, Tae-il was so shocked that he could not sleep for a few days afterward. The incident compelled him to study labor laws and organize a labor union. In March 1969, he was fired by his employer because he was starting a labor union. In his deep frustration, he retreated into the prayer house of his church, which was under construction in Mt. Samkak. During the day he worked on the construction as a volunteer and at night meditated. While spending six months there, he deter-mined to protest unto death against the subhuman treatment which the laborers at the Peace Market had borne. His diary reveals his resolution to sacrifice his life for the cause of his fellow laborers: 'I must go back to you, my poor brothers and sisters . . . I am willing to give my life for you . . . the Saturday of August, the day of resolution . . . Dear God, have mercy upon my effort to be a morning dew-drop'. In the same year, Tae-il found a sewing machinist job at the Peace Market again, and began to organize a labor union gradually. On 13 November 1970, Tae-il and 500 other laborers peacefully marched into the Peace Market with the placard: 'We are not machines'. When

21

a special police unit was dispatched and dispersed this lawful demonstration, Tae-il immolated himself. While dying, he cried aloud, 'Do not exploit the young lives! Don't make my death futile!' At the age of twenty-two, Tae-il presented his body and soul as a living sacrifice before God for the sake of his suffering sisters and brothers at the Peace Market.[27]

Tae-il's han was the suffering of his follow workers due to outrageous injustice. His death voiced the groaning han-cry of many exploited young laborers. The han of exploited laborers, especially young ones, has filled the space of the Korean sweatshops and factories and has demanded justice. As the first person to try to organize a labor union, Tae-il was the voice of the han of these laborers. His death points to the han of the crucifixion Jesus Christ underwent for the salvation of others.[28]

The perspective of han offers a fresh understanding of the vicarious suffering and death of Jesus and Tae-il. The doctrine of sin alone is insufficient to bring out the full meaning of Jesus' vicarious suffering. Scripture stresses that Jesus suffered not only to remit sinners' transgressions but also to heal victims' pain, i.e. han (Mt. 8:17; Lk. 4:18-21; I Pet. 2:21, 24). In the Ebed-Yahweh songs (Servant of Yahweh), we find a similar theme of vicarious suffering: "Surely he has borne our griefs and carried our sorrows . . . But he was wounded for our transgressions, he was bruised for our iniquities" (Is. 53:4-5). Contradicting the traditional idea that suffering is a punishment decreed by Yahweh, the Servant took upon himself the suffering and griefs of others.[29] Tae-il was wounded for the transgressions of the shop owners and bore the laborers' han. Like Jesus, Tae-il vicariously suffered death in order to resolve the young laborers' han.

## Elie Wiesel: Survivor of the Holocaust

A "Wailing Wall" exists in the heart of Jewish people. The Jews have continually suffered from discrimination, persecution, hate crime, and holocaust in history. Elie Wiesel, a 1988 Nobel Prize laureate, attempts to describe the unutterable experience of the concentration camp at Auschwitz, where he witnessed the last moments of his father's life, who suffered from dysentery and was struck to death by a German officer.[30] In an autobiographical statement, he speaks of his and his people's han:

A Time of Despair
It was only later, upon leaving the nightmare, that I underwent a prolonged crisis, painful and anguished, questioning my past certain-

ties. I began to despair of humanity and God; I considered them as enemies of one another, and both as enemies of the Jewish people. I didn't express this aloud, not even in my notes. I studied history, philosophy, psychology; I wanted to understand. The more I learned, the less I understood.

I was angry at the Germans: How could they have counted Goethe and Bach as their own and at the same time massacred Jewish children? I was angry at their Hungarian, Polish, Ukrainian, French and Dutch accomplices: How could they, in the name of a perverse ideology, have turned against their Jewish neighbors to the point of pillaging their houses and denouncing them? I was angry at Pope Pius XII: How could he have kept silent? I was angry at the heads of the Allied countries: How could they have given Hitler the impression that, as far as the Jews were concerned, he could do as he wished? Why hadn't they taken action to save them? Why had they closed all doors to them? Why hadn't they bombed the railroad line to Birkenau, if only to show Himmler that the Allies were not indifferent?

And—why not admit it?—I was angry at God too, at the God of Abraham, Isaac and Jacob: How could he have abandoned his people at the moment when they needed him? How could he have delivered them up to the killers? How could one explain, how could one justify the deaths of a million Jewish children? For months and months, for years, I lived alone. I mistrusted my fellow humans; I suspected them. I no longer believed in the word as a vehicle of thought and of life; I shunned love, aspiring only to silence and madness. Disgusted with the West, I turned toward the East. I was attracted by Hindu mysticism; I was interested in Sufism; I even began to explore the occult domains of marginal sects here and there in Europe. . . .

### Making the Ghosts Speak

And yet, there has been a change in our behavior. First of all, we express ourselves. I force myself to share the secret that consumes me. I try to make the ghosts within me speak. Does that mean that the wound has healed over? It still burns. I still cannot speak of it. But I can *speak*—that's the change. . . .

The problem is that the essential will never be said or understood. Perhaps I should express my thought more clearly: it's not because I don't speak that you won't understand me; it's because you won't understand me that I don't speak.

That's the problem, and we can do nothing about it: what certain people have lived, you will never live—happily for you, moreover. Their experience has set them apart: they are neither better nor worse, but different, more vulnerable and at the same time more hardened than you. The slightest arrow wounds them, but death does not frighten them . . . God himself cannot change the past; even he cannot negate the fact that the killer has killed 6 million times. How could he redeem himself? I don't know. I suppose that he cannot.

23

> Those who claim that this or that constitutes a response to the holocaust are content with very little. . . . [31]

Wiesel states the fact that his and his people's experience is indescribable. What he has profoundly portrayed can be called han. The open wound of his burning anger at humanity and God warps into the abyss of silence, yet he speaks of the experience in order to protect the silence. The incommensurability of his experience on the boundary of human suffering with our experience may be the source of his silence which cannot be intruded by words. The depth of han cannot be spoken, but only cried out or groaned. Han resides in the empty soul of a victim. Wiesel is the incarnation of the uniquely deep han of his people.

## Violet Masuda: Internee

There is another kind of han that the U.S. government forced upon Japanese-Americans during World War II. The government had anticipated the war with Japan and premeditated modest plans to intern some "dangerous" first-generation Japanese. This plan was carried out by the Department of Justice in the days immediately following the Pearl Harbor attack.[32] It involved 110,000 Japanese in the continental United States.[33] Japanese-Americans from the three west-coast states—both aliens and citizens—were evacuated to ten "relocation centers," surrounded by barbed wire and watched over by armed guards, located in inaccessible and largely barren areas often in the interior of the United States.[34]

Here is the story of Mrs. Masuda. a second generation Japanese-American woman, a mother, grandmother, and Sunday school teacher:

> Without any warning, like a cancerous growth, my frustrations began to grow slowly but surely deep down inside, developing a vague, uneasy dissatisfaction. . . .
>
> When World War II brought the evacuation of 110,000 Japanese Americans to life in concentration camps, I felt the loss of dignity, the shame of my race, the guilt of being Japanese for 'sins' I had not committed. I was married during that period of turmoil—living in the most remote parts of this land, behind barbed wire fences, under military guard (ironically, with our sons, husbands, and brothers in service to this country). The scar that I bury in my heart is Manzanar, a desolate area in southern California. This is one of the 'whys' of my life. My husband spent four and a half years in the service, yet after he had returned from Europe, he was not allowed to attend his father's funeral in the concentration camp in Amanche, Colorado.

> At that time, we would not have dared to look at our true feelings,
> for that would have revealed a part of us that would not have been
> acceptable—it would not have been good Americanism.[35]

The "frustrations" growing like a cancer "deep down inside" and the "scar" buried in the hearts of Violet Masuda and her people are *han*. She felt ashamed of her ethnic background. Her *han* lies in the fact that she was made to feel responsible for the "sin" she had not committed.[36] For years, she had denied the existence of her own feelings and had buried them in her unconscious anguish. The unforgettable tragic element of her life can be expressed by the term *han*. For the internees, the illegal dislocation was painful enough, yet the anti-Asian racism of the administration, which did not intern Germans—even though the United States was waging war against Nazi Germany at that time—had aggravated their pain. This complex ironical fact of the unfair treatment of Japanese-Americans is the reality of *han*.

Furthermore, she questioned the validity of religion in America. The church was silent and did not raise its voice for the voiceless and the defenseless. She had been a Christian throughout her life, yet when she suffered from injustice, the church, to which she gave all loyalty, did little against the injustice. She experienced a deep spiritual crisis and felt "self-hate" and "disenchantment."[37] That self-hatred is part of her *han* of being a Christian.

## Soe-Ryoeng Kang: Korean A-bomb Victim

As Japanese-Americans have unjustly suffered in the United States, Koreans in Japan have suffered as well. The approximately 667,000 Koreans in Japan are the frequent victims of discrimination.[38] For instance, the Japanese impose mandatory fingerprinting every five years for all non-Japanese residents, of whom the largest majority are Koreans. Fingerprinting is also required of criminals in Japanese society.

Ronald Rujiyoshi, a Japanese-American missionary, was indicted in 1982 for refusing to be fingerprinted, an action he took for two reasons. First, fingerprinting has been associated from the beginning with indicted criminals and thus has been a mark of shame and disgrace. Its requirement is a clear encroachment of human rights. Second, fingerprinting is a symbol of the Japanese government's assimilation policy toward long-term Asian residents in Japan. Eighty percent of the Koreans residing in Japan were born there, but this does not automatically entitle them to Japanese citizenship. They can

25

become naturalized citizens only when they change their Korean names to Japanese names. This means that the Japanese law forces them to renounce their ethnic heritage.[39] As Mahatma Gandhi fought against the legislation of required fingerprinting during his stay in South Africa, Koreans in Japan and their supporters have resisted this discriminatory legislation as well.[40]

Even worse are the living conditions of the Korean victims of the atomic bomb. During the war, many Koreans were drafted for work at military industrial factories in Hiroshima and Nagasaki. There was a total of 70,000 Korean casualties in both cities; 40,000 were killed and 30,000 were exposed to the A-bomb radiation. Out of 30,000, 23,000 returned to Korea after the war.[41] While 7,000 victims remained in Japan, only 2,000 of them have received medical treatments. The remaining 5,000 Koreans, not having the right kind of visas or hiding their identity, were excluded from treatment.[42] The survivors and their descendants have lived in subhuman conditions. These people are reticent about their disease, because it affects their employment, their marriage, and their children's future. Speaking of the A-bomb disease has become a social taboo, effectively burying them alive in a society that ignores them.

The Korean A-bomb victims are thus treated as criminals, condemned eventually to die for the "crime" of being Korean victims. Soe-Ryoeng Kang was exposed to the A-bomb while he was working for the supply depot of the army in Hiroshima. The left half of his body was severely burned. His father and nine brothers and sisters died from the explosion. His oldest brother, who survived, became involved in the anti-Korean War movement and was ordered by a court-martial of the U.S. occupation army to be deported to Korea. He died of radiation disease just before he was to be sent back. This interview was conducted in 1966 in Hiroshima when Kang was forty-three.

> My age? Well, I was called up for the first reserve so I was twenty then. . . . Thanks to the bomb, my face doesn't get old, ha, ha. . . . Well, I don't think I'll live until I'm sixty, but I'm not going to have lies on my face you know (it was a mysterious face. Not only when he was laughing, but also when he spoke angry words, the face just stayed young and it looked like a *Noh* mask with no expression whatsoever). . . .
>
> Well, my father came to Hiroshima when he was just about twenty, and he died a day laborer. The life of laborers hasn't changed since the old days. Well, we can work only half a month at best. The Koreans in Hiroshima are much poorer than other Koreans in Japan, aren't they? It's because we have no jobs other than manual labor or relief

work—that's about 80%. . . .

Last year I worked at a regular construction site at night all summer, because my older son was going on a school trip . . . If they find out that you are doing regular day work instead of relief work, you'll get automatically disqualified, you see. Well if only my body were normal I bet I'd become a general manual laborer. But how can a dying man like me do it, when your body looks healthy from outside, but in fact you are half dead. . . . The flesh from my shoulders to my back is dead because of the burn from the bomb. That part *doesn't perspire* even in summer. *It itches so much and if I scratch it, it festers.* My body must be half rotten inside. I can't handle things like manual labor, you know.[43]

The burned part of his body that festers if scratched symbolizes the reality of han. The part of the body that does not perspire epitomizes han! His mask-like face, unable to express anger and happiness, is *the face of han,* burying all his sorrow and that of other Korean A-bomb victims. He buries the grief of the loss of his parents and nine brothers and sisters behind that expressionless face. Physical suffering from A-bomb disease and the inability to do hard labor are a constant source of han-accumulation. In addition, the double discrimination he experiences as a Korean and an A-bomb victim intensifies his han. Living in such a social system, his wrath has "festered" more than twenty-two years.

Furthermore, there is no country that will advocate his rights. Japan has neglected its responsibility to provide for him and other victims. Korea has done little for them.[44] Even the Korean residents have been divided by two organizations, *Cho-Chong-Ryun* (an organization supporting the North Korea government) and *Min-Dan* (an organization supporting the South Korean government). With a divided homeland their han has been deepened.

These people survived a hell on earth. As survivors they are experiencing an inner hell in which they envy those who died during the explosion. They have withdrawn in silence to a bottomless pit where no one has access. Their han can be called "the dark night of the soul."[45] They have experienced a dark night indeed, expecting no dawn to break.

## Virginia: Incest Victim

Child sexual abuse is another experience of han. Little has been revealed on the numbers involved in the sexual abuse of children because the data is basically dependent on cases reported to the police or social service agencies.[46]

27

In his book *Sexually Victimized Children* (1979), David Finkelhor has put together a comprehensive and empirical work on sexual abuse of children in the United States. His main study focused on students of sociology, psychology, social work, and human sexuality at six New England colleges. Child sexual abuse cases were reported by 19 percent of the 530 female and 8.6 percent of the 266 male respondents. The most common experiences were genital fondling (38 percent of female and 35 percent of male experiences) and exhibitionism (20 percent of female and 14 percent of male experiences).[47] In another report using a sample from the general population, 28 percent of female respondents reported some abusive sexual experience when they were under 14.[48]

In September 1982, a popular British teenage magazine, *19*, invited readers to fill in a questionnaire on their experiences of sexual abuse.[49] Of the over 3,000 respondents, 36 percent said they had been sexually abused as children or adolescents.[50] Half of the cases were incestuous, probably due to the characteristics of the questionnaire angled toward intrafamilial relations. The following is the story of Virginia, an account of an incestuous abuse case drawn from another source:

> It started off, as I say, when I was quite young. We lived in a really big house, and my father had a separate room which was like an office, off my mother's bedroom. It was at the other end of the house from where the kitchen and activity things went on.
>
> My first memory of what happened would be that I'd be in summer pajamas, like shortie pajamas: I'd be in my father's office with my father and he'd get me sitting on his knee and start feeling my breasts. I know I was very young then. That became a regular kind of thing—it happened quite frequently, quite a lot. I felt really guilty about it happening. And of course it always stopped when anyone approached—so that reinforced the feeling that it shouldn't have been happening, which I kind of knew.
>
> Then, I'm not sure when, it became a thing of when I was going to bed—I suppose he was meant to be doing the good fatherly thing of putting me to bed—and he would come and fondle me in bed. He'd touch my breasts and my vagina. That became an ongoing thing—it happened over a really long period of time. I was in a state of constant fear because I never knew when it was going to happen. . . .
>
> The worst part of that was the guilt; and also the feeling so *powerless*. I'd just lie there, absolutely petrified. I'd be totally, utterly powerless. And it would go on for a few minutes . . . and then I'd kind of find the strength to fight him off . . . and he'd go away.
>
> Understanding it as a power thing has resolved the guilt for me. I certainly don't remember it as enjoyable: I was literally unable to

move or respond. . . .

I was the only daughter; I had four brothers—three of them much younger than me. But I was very much the only girl and there was always the big thing about me being "Daddy's little girl". . . .

I was a very mopey teenager. I always thought that I was just so put down, so not allowed to be myself, that was why I was so unhappy! But fear was there, as part of the incest thing. But anger I'm not sure of, not consciously, not till later, and then I found it!

There's also a lot of stuff to do with my brothers. When I was about twelve, my elder brother and I were having a bit of a wrestle—we hadn't had that kind of contact for a while—and he started trying to touch my vagina. He actually put his hand inside my pants . . . [voice very low] . . . they were sort of tight . . . I think that was the only time. . . .

The other thing that happened was that one of my younger brothers, when he was six or seven (I was sixteen I guess), started this thing of peeping through keyholes and things like that . . . But again I felt totally powerless: it was just something that went on.

. . . I became aware one day when I was having a shower that he was in the ceiling looking down through the exhaust fan. I got really angry and went and told my mother he was there—and nothing was made of it at all. It was just kind of covered up . . . which absolutely confirmed my fears of what would have happened if I'd complained of the others when I was younger. His doing that went on, I think, till I left home. . . .

I actually told him, that brother, last year, why I didn't go to see my father, why I wouldn't have anything to do with him. I told him about the ongoing molesting; I felt really good about telling him—and he was just speechless when I told him! I'm sure part of that was his own guilt. . . . [51]

Virginia, like a single tree standing on a windy hill, had no one on whom she could lean in the family. She felt powerless and groundless. Her han grew as everyone in the family wanted only to use her. She did not have anyone in the family in whom she could put her trust; her fundamental trust of her parents was betrayed. Although her parents were present, she was fatherless and motherless. This han of parentlessness is shared by many other abused children. She was unaware of her anger until much later and thus she decided to have a baby without an "involved" father.[52]

The enormous burden of holding the family together was her perceived role.[53] For the sake of family unity, she was silent about her sexual molestation for many years. The family was no less than a true self-prison, from which she could only escape when she left. Her han is different from that of a rape victim; it is within her own flesh and soul. In such a case as this, her anger and blame are not directed toward her parents and her brothers without passing through her first. The han of incest eats one's own heart out first. A child's total identification with parents makes his or her necessary distance from them extremely difficult, and thus his or her han is incarnated in the flesh.

Once silence on the taboo of speaking of incest broke in the 1980s, more cases of buried incest have come to the fore. The han of the dark night of the soul is exposed in its naked form. The reality of incest han indicts not only involved family members, but also humanity—primarily men—for their proclivity to selfish love, and demands justice which will bring healing.

# The Structure of Han

We have defined han as *frustrated hope, the collapsed feeling of pain, letting go, resentful bitterness,* and *the wounded heart.* Frustrated hope, the collapsed feeling of pain, letting go, and the wounded heart characterize the acquiescent nature of han, whereas resentful bitterness demonstrates its aggressive nature.

To understand the reality of han, we need to know its structure, something which is however sufficiently complex to make it difficult to unfold its meaning to the full extent. Han must be seen as a whole; it cannot simply be reduced to isolated levels. Yet if one is to grasp the meaning of han, one must first gain perspective on its constituent elements. The main division of han is between individual and collective dimensions.[1] In addition, han exists in conscious vs. unconscious and active vs. passive expressions, both in individuals and groups.

## THE HAN OF INDIVIDUALS: CONSCIOUS HAN

### Active: The Will to Revenge

When there is a person or object which serves as a clear source of an individual's suffering, one's han is directed against that person or object. When there is no visible or identifiable person or object toward which to direct one's han, that han retreats into resignation.

Active individual conscious han may take a form of *fury* and *vengefulness.* Until it is resolved, such han relentlessly seeks gratification by retaliation for injuries suffered. This han is like an inner fire blazing in the soul. The following story of a rape victim epitomizes this sort of han:

> Bu-Nam Kim was born as the fifth daughter in a normal farmer's family. One day Bu-Nam (9 yrs) was on the way to one of her friends' and bumped into Mr. Song (30 yrs). She knew him well. He said, 'Bu-Nam, can you run errands for me? Why don't you wait for me in my room?' She obeyed him and waited for him in his room. He came in and abruptly raped her. She felt a rupturing pain and was petrified by fear and terror. For ten days, she could not speak. From that time, she became quiet. Meeting any male made her heartbeat momentarily suspend. Unaware that this happening, her mother used to say, 'Like a cow, Bu-Nam is taciturn'.
>
> At twenty-three, she married Mr. Choi, a farmer. But from the beginning, she had trouble in making love with him because of anxiety, guilt, and phobia created by the rape. One day, her husband asked the reason why she had been that way and she confessed the past incident. She was hospitalized and was divorced two months after the confession.
>
> Later, she married Mr. Lee, a truck driver, and had a son between them. When her husband was incarcerated due to an automobile accident and her life became miserable again, her paranoia came back.
>
> Last June, while visiting her family at Nam-Won-Kun, she met Mr. Song and demanded compensation for her misery. Mr. Song avoided dealing with her directly but only with her elder brother. Excluding her, they settled the issue with the compensation of 400,000 Won ($ 570). When she revisited him to demand a suitable recompense, he reviled at her; in return, she took the revenge into her own hands by killing him. The han of a rape victim, which had been brooded over twenty years, took the rapist's life for its price. After the killing, she did not show any remorse.[2]

Her personal han exploded negatively, causing her to kill the guilty party. After the rape incident, she became fearful of the offender and other men. Her fear became a silence of fright, the silence grew into deep anger, and the anger erupted in retaliation. Her vengeful han was too intense to regret the killing.

The active personal conscious han is expressed in dread, horror, anger, resentment, hatred, and even killing. But the reality of this conscious han is deep-seated in unconscious han. Han in the unconscious never sleeps. Until they retaliate against their attackers, victims are engrossed with revenge or "revenge fantasies": "I wanted to get my hands on the guy . . . I just want to take him apart."[3] The longer one broods over han, the deeper han becomes.

Active individual conscious han is visible, recognizable, and restless. The active respondents to victimization generate *the will to revenge.* The mind of vengeance is the *destructive-instinct* in Kleinian theory.[4] While the death-instinct involves a desire to dissolve oneself, the destructive-instinct includes a wish to kill others. Victims react to violence with an initial anger and shame, and then blame someone. Finally, they reach the volitional state of retaliation. "Vengeance" is the desire of victims to inflict injury, harm, and humiliation on the victimizers. Most victims express their resentment, quite often to the wrong persons (misplaced resentment). When the resentment of victims is directed to their attackers, it is termed *revenge.*[5]

## Passive: Resignation

Depending on the circumstances of an incident and the characteristics of a victim, the han of the victim becomes active or passive. When the culprit of han is unidentifiable, han tends to be passive. When the offender is either too vulnerable or too formidable to blame, a victim's han turns into *resignation.* Virginia,[6] the incest victim whose story was discussed in chapter one, tried to bear all the burden of the sexual abuse in order to save the family. Her han had withdrawn into herself during her childhood and adolescence, but later evolved into a more active one.

If one's resigned han is deep seated, it can hurt one even to the point of death. *Self-denigration, low self-esteem, self-withdrawal, resignation,* and *self-hatred* are conspicuous marks of passive han. The following is an extreme example:

> A seventeen-year-old adolescent female was transferred from a substance abuse program to St. Vincent's adolescent unit after a serious suicide attempt. Initial screening revealed a depressed, anxious youth with a long-standing history of substance abuse and poor self-esteem. Intensive assessment efforts to identify a precipitant to the suicide attempt led to the disclosure of previous sexual abuse by a neighbor (a sixteen-year-old male) when the patient was 12 years old. After several weeks of inpatient treatment, in which the patient appeared to be making progress, her suicidal ideation resurfaced. At that point she reported that her oldest brother had also sexually abused her. The patient expressed many reservations about returning home, though the brother no longer lived there. After two months, the patient was transferred to a long-term treatment facility. After another serious suicide attempt, she finally reported that her alcoholic father had abused her since she was six.[7]

The layers of this victim's han are manifold and are hidden from outsiders. She hesitated to reveal the depths of han because of embarrassment, shame, guilt, and repression. Instead of seeking revenge against the guilty parties, she took revenge against herself. This is the sad han of many victims; they try to harm themselves. In this case fear of retaliation led her to believe that there was no benefit in seeking revenge, and thus she directed her anger toward herself. Passive han emerges as victims negate the self already negated by offenders, sometimes even to the point of self-extermination.

Passive han takes the form of heart-rending resignation. It lets go of everything, including the self. The self is so poorly developed that its organizing center is diffuse, and the soul moves toward self-disintegration. This *resignation* involves Freud's *death-instinct* which postulates a wish to annihilate oneself.[8]

# THE HAN OF INDIVIDUALS: UNCONSCIOUS HAN

## Active: Bitterness

Most victims of abuse feel mournful about their experiences. When han in the unconscious takes an active form, *bitterness* wells up from the depth of the soul. When it is passive, *helplessness* appears to be the victim's attitude.

Questions may arise whether bitterness is something that resides in the unconscious and whether something in the unconscious can be active. I employ the term *unconscious* here according to its usage in the Freudian tradition. For Freud, there are two types of unconscious: the *preconscious* and the *unconscious* proper. The preconscious is those portions of memory that are "capable of reaching consciousness."[9] Its excitations take place according to the observance of certain rules. The unconscious is "incapable of consciousness" "except through the preconscious."[10] That which resides in the unconscious is not lost but is blocked to memory. Some types of bitterness are conscious, and others are unconscious. The bitterness that is discussed in this section has both preconscious and unconscious dimensions; it is partially accessible to our consciousness. *Also, in spite of its preconscious and unconscious dimensions, the form of bitterness as a whole feeling retains active and passive aspects.*

Victims with active responses to traumatic situations become bitter toward those responsible for their victimization. These victims feel unfairly treated and develop *resentment* against the offending individuals, institutions, or social systems. Whereas anger is immediate emotion provoked by a wrong, resentment is the strong and lasting ill-will of the injured against the persons who caused the pain. While victims' resentment can be expressed directly, bitterness also appears in disguised forms such as indifference, subservience, humor, or even (according, at least, to Nietzsche) love.[11]

Soe-Ryoeng Kang, a victim of the A-bomb, expressed his resentment toward the Japanese government, which had neglected the treatment of the Korean A-bomb victims. Behind his keloid skin lay a deep well of many resentments: the Japanese occupation of Korea, his father's hard labor, and the deaths of his father and nine brothers and sisters by the A-bomb. His conscious and unconscious levels of resentment actively erupted during his many years of living in Japan. Although he verbalized his resentment to a certain extent, he retained the *bitterness* that could not be fully expressed with words. As the conscious memory of a trauma fades away, its han is deeply engraved in one's unconscious.

## Passive: Helplessness

*Helplessness* is a noticeable sign of passive unconscious han. When han-causing persons or objects are too close or important to oneself for the expression of the han, the victim blames and punishes herself or himself. In this paradoxical condition in which the victim cannot hate the offenders without hating him or herself, the victim despairs and enters into a state of helplessness. The seventeen-year-old suicidal youth discussed above shows this state of helplessness; she could not alleviate her painful situation by blaming her offenders. Instead, she attempted suicide three times. Outsiders could offer no help to her completely sealed off, inaccessible world of han. By entering there, she evoked the spirit of the unconscious han and found no exit. To avoid prolonged wandering in the horrifying darkness, she endeavored to escape through a short cut—the termination of her life.

When a transgressor is either too potent to revolt against or unidentifiable, a victim's unconscious han is likely to become self-pity or helplessness. Child-molestation victims often undergo this unconscious process. As they assume that their voice would not be heard or would not make any difference in an unfavorable situation, but rather would incur the retaliation of powerful molesters, they retreat into themselves. The case of Virginia exemplifies this passive han of helplessness. Even after she was sexually manipulated or exploited by her father and brothers, she could do little about the situation; she

35

believed that telling it to her mother would not improve things. This assumption was verified by her mother's disbelief when she reported a younger brother's peeping. After that, she no longer confided in her mother. Her unconscious state was that of helplessness. She used the term "powerlessness" in her retrospective interview. Her anger and resentment were swallowed up by the unconscious experience of helplessness.

Violet Masuda's case also sheds light on passive unconscious han. The United States government was too powerful for her to resist; she knew any attempt would do little good. So she retreated into silence and brooded at the conscious and unconscious levels over her han of *helplessness* for years. Toward the church, she had a love-hate relationship. She had dedicated her life to the church, yet felt betrayed by it in time of her need. Her church was too important to reject and hate. Thus she experienced "disenchantment" and "self-hate," developing a spiritual crisis.

## THE HAN OF GROUPS: CONSCIOUS HAN

Collective han can be interpreted in two ways. One is the collective reality of individual experiences of han. The other is the experience of a group of people. The collective han referred to here means both, but the latter is emphasized.

### Active: The Corporate Will to Revolt

This han can be seen in street demonstrations, citizen uprisings, and revolutions. It arises when a group of people experience oppression, exploitation, and injustice, either directly or indirectly. Such han takes place when public wrath and rage respond to any oppressive public policies and unjust work.

This active collective conscious han is also known as *collective will to revolt*. According to Camus, the world is absurd and sanity means to revolt against the world. This han is not the symptom of insanity, but rather the sign of sanity in an insane world. Active collective han is disclosed as people resist the oppressive systems of the world.

The fall of communist regimes which took place in Eastern Europe in the late 1980s displays this active collective will. It ended Nicholae Ceausescu's brutal rule in Romania in 1989 and brought down the Berlin wall. This active collective han led Filipinos to topple Marcos's dictatorial regime in 1986 and African-Americans to transmute their oppressed experience into the civil rights movement in the 1960s.

This han has been sizzling in China since the Tiananmen Square massacre in 1989.[12] The pro-democracy protesters are quiet now, but that does not mean that they have lost their will to revolt. They wait for the right timing. The active collective conscious han that initiated the demonstrations has been intensified by the aftermath of the violent suppression. A poem, carrying a hidden message, appeared in the March 20 overseas edition of the official *People's Daily* in 1991. If one reads it diagonally from top right to lower left (rather than the customary order from top right to lower right), it says: "Li Peng step down to assuage the people's anger." The final line alludes to a new future: "Wait, sacred land, spring is everywhere."[13] Premier Li Peng is a key advocate for using violence to suppress the demonstrations. The people's fury is still felt in the air of Tiananmen Square and against Li Peng, the representative of oppression.

This active han continues to erupt in South Africa, the old Soviet republics, Palestine, El Salvador, Northern Ireland, Cambodia, and elsewhere. Sometimes it explodes negatively, killing innocent people, and at other times positively, transforming the oppressive society. However, whether its eruption is negative or positive, a violent eruption results in forming another han. Under a state of the violent eruption of han, passive corporate han grows within a victimized group.

## Passive: Corporate Despair

*Corporate despair* is the distinctive mark of passive collective conscious han. It is a feeling which resides within victims who have been oppressed for a long period without any hope. As Elie Wiesel perceived, this despair is despair before humanity. This despair is different from the absolute despair which indicates the impossibility of restoration. It can yet transform itself into the active collective will to resistance if circumstances allow.

The Jewish victims and survivors of the Holocaust have brooded over this passive collective despair. They suffered the inhumane atrocities of the Nazi regime. They are angry not only at the Nazis but at humanity. Their anger is the expression of despair. After Auschwitz, it is very difficult for them to trust humanity again. Their image of humanity was irrevocably broken by the incredible cruelty of human beings toward fellow human beings. The outcome of the

Holocaust is the broken covenant of humanity, a brokenness which forms the central basis of passive collective han.

In the case of Wiesel and others, anger at God was also present. Richard Rubenstein has declared that there is no God after Auschwitz, for God is dead.[14] The God of Abraham, Isaac, and Jacob died at Auschwitz.[15] Furthermore, han is also engendered by the persistence of anti-Semitism in history. Time has slowly begun to erase the memory of this unforgettable crime and anti-Semitic practices are gradually resurfacing. The survivors protest but people pay little attention. This reinforces the passive collective han of the survivors and their supporters.

Unfortunately we do not learn the lessons of history. These horrible crimes against humankind have been repeated in recent memory. When the Jewish population in Nazi-ruled Europe had dwindled from almost 10 million in 1939 to 3.5 million in 1945, people's excuse was that they did not know what went on in Auschwitz, Belsen, Buchenwald, Dachau, and the other camps. When another 6 million people—Poles, Czechs, Russians, and others—had been decimated by the Nazis,[16] people said they did not know. This type of atrocity was repeated before our eyes in Cambodia in the 1970s. Out of a population of 8 million, 3,314,786 people were killed or driven away by the Pol Pot regime from 1975 to 1979.[17] This dictator and his followers also destroyed 1,200 villages, 5,857 schools, and 796 hospitals and clinics.[18] If it happened in the United States, what would be the world's response? Since it happened in an "insignificant" country such as Cambodia, the world did not know and did not want to know about the genocide. Here cries the collective han of Cambodians: one insane person killed millions of their people, and the world has paid scant attention. Even worse, some countries like the United States supported the Pol Pot regime during his cruel reign and turned their faces away from its outrageous acts.

## THE HAN OF GROUPS: UNCONSCIOUS HAN

At the unconscious level, han is immersed in the ethos of group or racial mourning. Many years of social injustice, political oppression, economic exploitation, or foreign invasions create collective unconscious han. The victims who experience unjust suffering over many generations develop collective unconscious han deep in the soul.

This han is similar to Jung's "collective unconscious." He holds that we are endowed with a psychological heritage as well as with a biological heritage: "Our unconscious mind, like our body, is a storehouse of relics and memories of the past."[19] The han of a race is inherited through a form of psychosomatic proclivity. Unlike Jung's "collective unconscious," however, this han does not take over the content of the han of a previous generation, but the structure of han-memory. The structure of collective unconscious han is transmittable to another generation through the framework of ethnic ethos, tradition, and culture. Empiricists such as John Locke, David Hume, and B. F. Skinner suppose that we are born with a blank sheet of paper, a *tabula rasa*, and experiences make memories. Rationalists like Descartes assert that reason instead of experience initiates knowledge. Immanuel Kant integrates empiricism and rationalism by saying that we are born with an *a priori*, something existing in the mind prior to experience, but that knowledge arises from our experience. Jung espouses the idea of an *a priori*, claiming that we all share something universal in the mind independent of experience, and that such an unconscious reality is owned by all.

> The collective unconscious . . . are not individual acquisitions, are essentially the same everywhere, and do not vary from man to man. This unconscious is like the air, which is the same everywhere, is breathed by everybody, and yet belongs to no one. Its contents (called archetypes) are the prior conditions or patterns of psychic formation in general.[20]

While Jung claims no individual differentiation of the collective unconscious, I believe that the han of collective unconscious varies according to racial diversity. That is why we have the variety of racial ethos. Furthermore, Jung's "collective unconscious" is impersonal,[21] but the collective unconscious han is personal, including rational and emotional dimensions accumulated in the ethnic ethos. Moreover, this hereditary aspect of han denies neither the empiricist's view, the rationalists', nor Kant's. Distinctive from the universality of an *a priori*, this idea holds that some are born with the structure of han and others are not. There is no uniform state of the mind among individuals and among races.

## Active: Racial Resentment

When the active collective conscious han toward a person, a group, or a race accumulates for a long time, it becomes the unconscious han of the group or race. This han is *subliminal collective*

39

*resentment.* The historical conflicts between Turks and Armenians and between Israelis and Palestinians exemplify this aspect of han. In a series of brutal campaigns, Armenian massacres were conducted by Sultan Abdul-Hamid of the Ottoman Empire in 1894–96 and by the Young Turk Government in 1915. In 1914–18, one million Armenians were killed or died of starvation, and thousands were forced into exile.[22] A deep-seated antagonism is rooted in their unconscious ethos and sometimes such han explodes in the form of violence between the two groups. The strife between Israelis and Palestinians also has a long history of struggle. The Jewish people have been persecuted throughout history since the fall of the Northern Kingdom (721 B.C.E.) and of the Southern Kingdom (597 B.C.E.). The Holocaust was the critical point of the Jewish racial han-formation; thereafter, since the establishment of the modern state of Israel their collective han-ridden mind has sometimes exploded at Palestinians. Palestinians are a long-suffering people as well. They too have been dominated by various groups. Their han has exploded toward Israelis. The present conflict between them is the result of the negative explosion of the active collective conscious and unconscious han in each group.

The relation between Japan and Korea has been antagonistic since Japan invaded Korea in 1592. Since Japan annexed Korea in 1910, the unconscious collective animosity of the Koreans towards the Japanese has become active and has dominated the Korean substructure of consciousness. As a consequence Koreans have subconsciously related to Japanese in terms of han.

## Passive: The Ethos of Racial Lamentation

Passive collective unconscious han signifies *the ethos of racial lamentation.* Hundreds and thousands of years of oppression mold a race into a certain mode of moaning spirit—the dark soul where the suffering people share their agony. The crucible which melts the anguish of a certain people into this unconscious solidarity expresses itself in art: music, poetry, and pictures.

The blues and Negro spirituals of African-Americans epitomize this passive sad collective unconscious han. The frequent minor intervals and the repetition of the first line in the usual three-line stanza evoke the deep melancholy of their collective soul. The Negro spirituals also touch upon the buried experience of collective suffering resonating in the hallowed space of the soul. These are the products of passive sad collective unconscious han, the other side of the rage of Harlem or Watts—sad, melancholic, and fatalistic.

The songs of the Jewish people are quite melancholic as well. Many songs end in minor keys, communicating their mournful spirit. The motifs of the songs and the music point to the long suffering of people who have undergone inhumane treatment. In Israel's psalms and their traditions, we see this more clearly. The most frequent type of psalm next to that of hymns is the lament.[23] The communal lament is verbalized in psalms and prophecies, i.e., Jer. 3:21-25; 14:7-9, 19-22; Hos. 6:1-3; 14:3b-4.[24] For the last two millennia, Jews have suffered as strangers in a strange land. The underlying ethos of the Jewish people is han.

Likewise, Koreans all throughout history have been continually invaded by surrounding countries. As a relatively small country, Korea has been the prey of its powerful neighbors. As a result Koreans have acquired a dejected spirit of life. Their music, poetry, drama, and linguistic expression indicate a han-filled spirit. In the English expression, "a bird sings," but in Korean, "a bird cries." There are other comparable terms: in English, "the whistle of a steam-engine blows" while in Korean, "the whistle of a steam-engine cries." In Korean, many things in nature cry, i.e., the wind, a mountain, a river, a cloud. Koreans have experienced numerous foreign invasions, tyrannical oppression, and patriarchal suppression. As a result, racial unconscious despair, which is almost fatalistic, is imbedded in the Korean consciousness. To a certain extent, this racial despair, combined with a Buddhist worldview, has turned into racial nihilism in Korea.[25] This is the abyss which lies within the dark soul of being Korean, a soul which has been engulfed by all the sorrow of historical tragedies. Its power is strong enough to swallow up other types of feelings. This sad passive collective unconscious han, accumulated through the memory of the past, controls Korea's present state of affairs and its future direction.

Passive collective unconscious han is a predominant phenomenon among those social groups and races which have been oppressed for a long time with little hope. It is like the spirit which possesses us and dictates to us how we are to think and act. This spirit of han mourns for the fateful tragedies inside the structure of the unconscious world beyond individual identity. Although it is passive, the spirit of han is not static, but rather dynamic in nature, continually creating new han-ridden consciousness.

Below all the diversity of han lies *world han,* a common denominator of all world sorrow and grief. The world han is the dark side of

41

the world soul.[26] It is the world grief which recollects all the tragic memories of the past. No single tragic event is lost forever; all are retained in the world grief that is the han of the world. From time to time, this world grief discloses itself through world tragedies. It rolls below all occasions with sullenness.

## THE HAN OF NATURE

Beyond human han there is the han of animals and nature. Animals and nature suffer from abusive treatment by humans, yet cannot protest against it. They can only groan over their lot. There is no other term to describe this miserable condition of animals and nature except the word *han*. Han is their inexpressible pain at being maltreated. Paul well describes this form of han:

> For the creation waits with eager longing for the revealing of the sons of God; for the creation was subjected to futility, not of its own will but by the will of him who subjected it in hope; because the creation itself will be set free from its bondage to decay and obtain the glorious liberty of the children of God. We know that the whole creation has been groaning in travail together until now; not only the creation, but we ourselves, who have the first fruits of the Spirit, groan inwardly as we wait for adoption as sons, the redemption of our bodies. (Rom. 8:19-23)

The creation has been forced to serve human whims and has suffered the pain in silence. The creation was not meant to be subjected to human exploitation.

According to a Worldwatch Institute report, we have crossed one threshold—the limit of nature. If we cross a second threshold, there will be an unprecedented and irreversible change in climate. We can still prevent that from happening.[27] Crossing these thresholds creates nature's han. Nature tries to cope with all the stress it receives but is unable to bear the stress any more. It collapses. That is han.

The environmental stress caused by technological advancement is so tremendous that we face natural catastrophe. The atmosphere is being irrevocably damaged before our eyes. Every year power plants, automatic machines, furnaces, and other equipment which burn fossil fuel emit five billion tons of carbon dioxide into the atmosphere, a global rate of one ton per person.[28]

Tree cover is one of the primary signs of the earth's health, but an estimated 11 million hectares of forests are being cleared annually in 76 tropical countries, while 31 million hectares in industrial countries are damaged by air pollution or acid rain.[29] In the early 1980s, 11.3 million hectares were annually cleared in tropical regions, whereas only 1.1 million hectares of plantations were established. That is, 10 hectares were cleared for every 1 planted. In Africa, the ratio was 29 to 1.[30] In 1990 it could be said that "forests are vanishing at a rate of some 17 million hectares per year, an area about half the size of Finland."[31] Deforestation triggers a chain reaction. Wild animals are losing their natural habitats and are quite rapidly being eliminated, mainly through deforestation. Species are rapidly becoming extinct: "A minimum of 140 plant and animal species are condemned to extinction each day."[32] In the past two decades, about one million species have vanished from the world's tropical forests.[33] "By the year 2000, 20% of all Earth's species could be lost forever."[34]

Desertification is another problem. Some 6 million hectares of new desert are formed each year by land mismanagement.[35] Excessive soil-loss is produced by the crisis of farming. An estimated 26 billion tons of topsoil are being washed or blown off cropland each year.[36]

The depletion of the ozone layer due to chlorofluorocarbon (CFC) production has created an ozone "hole" twice the size of the continental United States over Antarctica.[37] A similar ozone hole about the size of Greenland opened in the Arctic, perhaps draining ozone from the Northern Hemisphere.[38] More disturbing, the latest data indicate that an ozone hole could soon open above Russia, Scandinavia, Germany, Britain, Canada, and northern New England.[39]

Thousands of lakes in the industrial north are now biologically dead; underground water tables are falling in parts of Africa, China, India, and North America as water usage rises above aquifer recharge rates; some 50 pesticides contaminate groundwater in 32 American states while 2,500 U.S. toxic-waste sites need cleanup. Mean temperature is projected to rise between 1.5 and 4.5 degrees Celsius by 2050; sea level is projected to rise between 1.4 and 2.2 meters by 2100.[40]

Animal factory farming causes a great deal of immoral animal suffering. To raise chickens or cows most effectively, factory farmers use compact cages or pens, in which these animals spend most of their lives with insufficient space in which to move around. Factory farming manufactures meat by treating animals as mere meat-producing machines. Although the abolition of factory farming might be impractical in this urbanized civilization, we must find some way to alleviate animal suffering. Silent pain and suffering felt by animals turn into their han.

43

Trees, water, air, and soil have been destroyed, one might say, against their will.[41] Human actions which contradict the will of nature and animals produce han, and nature groans under the weight of this oppression. Whether it is organic life or an inorganic thing, there is will, and thus there is han. Unlike han in the organic world, han in the inorganic sphere is always unconscious. This han cannot be overlooked as in the past. The han of the inorganic realm is deeply connected with that of the organic world. Primitive religions have been intuitively aware of this han so as to respect and honor the order of nature. Furthermore, the Bible has taught this idea of the han of all the creation (Rom. 8:19-23), yet we have not taken it seriously. We have ignored the han-ridden cry of nature and animals and have been judged by them in the form of ecological disasters. It is time for the human race to repent its sin of anthropocentrism against nature and animals. In order to achieve a holistic vision of the global welfare, the human race must move with the will to dissolve the han of animals and nature. Then the complete reign of God Isaiah envisioned will be fulfilled on earth: "The sucking child shall play over the hole of the asp, and the weaned child shall put his hand on the adder's den. They shall not hurt or destroy in all my holy mountain; for the earth shall be full of the knowledge of the Lord as the waters cover the sea" (11:8-9).

# The Major Roots of Han

The various structures of han have their roots in the diverse structures of sin. In general, individual han results from personal sin, and collective han derives from collective sin, but they are entangled in cause-effect relationships. Collective sin, however, generates a great deal of personal han as well as collective han.

In the course of history, sin has produced more sin, which has created corporate expressions of evil at the socioeconomic, political, and cultural dimensions of life.[1] The diverse modes of sin as the vortex of evil have produced sin and han in the world. There have been many structural bastions of sin throughout the years; while some of them have been destroyed by the forces of history or have disintegrated by themselves, the rest still remain. A few can be named: neocolonialism, totalitarianism, hierarchical social structures, provincialism, racism, sexism, handicappism, ageism, religious exclusivism, and militarism.

Although it is difficult to single out the root causes of han in the world because they are interrelated, we can say that there are at least three which have regularly generated han in the world: the capitalist global economy, patriarchy, and racial and cultural discrimination.

## CAPITALIST GLOBAL ECONOMY

One of the major sources of han can be found in the capitalist global economy. Capitalism has instigated over-urbanization; the desolation of the family farm; environmental deterioration; immigration; the conflict between immigrants and local workers; the unequal distribution of resources, wealth, and income in society; and animal cruelty. Not only does capitalism promote these sources of han, it actually needs them to survive.

As U.S. capitalism develops, transnational corporations destroy local businesses by absorbing them or by relocating their factories. There are roughly four major reasons why multinational corporations relocate: (1) the search for cheap labor, (2) the search for cheap raw materials, (3) the search for foreign markets, and (4) the search for investment opportunities.[2]

The primary reason for the cheap labor in less developed countries is due to the character of precapitalist modes of production. In such systems, capitalist employers need not pay the full benefits for the employed, including health care, education, and housing, because the employed at first work basically for supplementary income only. Another major reason for cheap labor in less developed countries is a lower standard of living. Thus, capitalist employers harvest extraordinary rates of surplus value and outmaneuver their competitors who use proletarianized labor only.[3]

Another reason for cheaper labor in these countries is the presence of cheap raw materials, the expansion of markets to sell manufactured goods, and better investment opportunities than in their home countries. To prevent a declining rate of profit, capitalist corporations search for ways to cheapen the means of production. Raw materials in third-world countries attract them because those resources are more likely to be less depleted and less expensive to extract or grow in those countries than their own.

In terms of market conditions, the companies of advanced capitalist countries can make great profits in less developed countries. Owing to automated mechanization in the advanced countries, the productivity of labor increases, requiring less labor time. For less developed countries, it takes more labor to produce the same items. Thus companies of the industrial countries bring their technologically advanced products to third-world countries and undersell local producers, including those who deal in agribusiness items. Most of the time, despite charging more than these companies do in their home countries, they undercut the price of local markets in the third-world countries. In this situation, complete free trade between more advanced and less developed countries results in benefit to the former.[4] This is the reason many less developed and European countries oppose the negotiation of the Uruguay Round imposed by the United States and its sympathizers. The impact of the liberalization of market systems proposed by the Uruguay Round on less developed, less commercialized, and smaller countries will be so tremendous that many of their local businesses must be liquidated, and thousands of farmers and laborers must suffer great loss.

Finally, companies in advanced capitalist countries move to poor countries in search of investment opportunities. The simple reason is that the rate of profit is higher for doing business in these rather than in their own countries because of cheap surplus labor. In these third-world countries, governments crack down on labor union movements in order to attract foreign investments.

What happens when companies in advanced capitalist countries invest or move to third-world countries? When transnational corporations invest and build factories in third-world countries, they choose their sites in urban areas for cheap labor and the accessibility of transportation. This attracts farmers to cities and causes over-urbanization. This over-urbanization produces a so-called surplus population along with a depression of farms. The surplus population results in surplus labor which attracts more foreign investments.

Further, the relocation of transnational companies to the third world damages advanced capitalist countries' local businesses, leaving unemployed workers behind. The products of these transnational corporations are imported back to the advanced capitalist countries and are used to undersell the competition, resulting in the additional destruction of local entrepreneurship. Furthermore, the surplus population created by over-urbanization in third-world countries become available for emigration.

To see this process in action, one need only look at U.S. investment in South Korea. This example will explain the frequent conflict between African-Americans and Korean immigrants, which is not an accident but rather the necessary outcome of the capitalist global economy. Ivan Light and Edna Bonacich in their book *Immigrant Entrepreneurs: Koreans in Los Angeles 1965–82* elaborate on how U.S. capitalism attracts Korean immigrants and how they come into conflict with local laborers.[5]

In the 1960s, when large U.S. corporations invested or constructed factories in major cities in Korea, farmers and laborers relocated to the cities to find jobs. Concentration of labor forces in the cities triggered over-urbanization and the depression of farms. In fact, farms had already been so depressed that farmers would have desired to leave them anyway. The decline of farms was due to various factors—importation of some agricultural items, national policy to espouse industrial developments, and so forth. The over-urbanization

47

due to the relocation of farmers produced a so-called surplus population. The surplus population brought forth surplus labor which attracted more foreign companies. The relocation of U.S. companies to Korea damaged U.S. local businesses, leaving unemployed workers behind. The products of these U.S. multinational corporations were imported back to the U.S. and were undersold, resulting in the additional destruction of U.S. entrepreneurship. Further, some labor forces created by over-urbanization in Korea became available for emigration, incited by the liberalization of U.S. immigration policy.[6] As Korean immigrants poured into the U.S. labor market, they helped resuscitate its declining entrepreneurship.[7]

Since Korean immigrants could not find jobs on account of their language barrier and racial discrimination, they started their own small businesses.[8] They succeeded in beginning their small business by using family labor, while other small business owners lost out in competition with small stores operated by Korean immigrants. The immigrant small business owners who hired immigrant workers could survive in a tough competitive market, contributing to sustaining cheap immigrant labor. This benefited U.S. businesses in terms of lowering the cost of the production of merchandise.

The roles that immigrant entrepreneurs and immigrant workers played in the labor market created the conflict between local workers, immigrant entrepreneurs, and immigrant workers.[9] As employment opportunities for local laborers were lost to immigrant laborers, local people became enraged at these immigrant store owners.

This view sheds light on the present conflict between African-Americans and Korean immigrants in the major cities in this country, particularly in New York and Los Angeles. This inevitable conflict has come to light since the late 1980s. The work of global capitalism may be diagrammed as follows:[10]

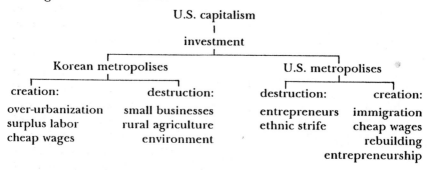

U.S. capitalism
|
investment

Korean metropolises    U.S. metropolises

creation:          destruction:        destruction:     creation:
over-urbanization  small businesses    entrepreneurs    immigration
surplus labor      rural agriculture   ethnic strife    cheap wages
cheap wages        environment                          rebuilding
                                                        entrepreneurship

We have seen how U.S. capitalism has participated in the devastation of entrepreneurship and its reconstruction through immigrant labor force, and how it has aroused racial strife between local workers and new immigrants in the United States. The capitalist structure of economy has promoted the devastation of farms and over-urbanization in the third world and has contributed to the crackdown on labor movements in order to lower labor costs. Above all, it has obstructed the third-world countries' establishment of their own self-sustainable system of economy and has forced them to subordinate themselves to more advanced capitalist countries. Whereas the capitalist structure of the world order has bestowed benefits on the rich—who are, after all, minorities in the world—it has produced the tears, perspiration, and outcries of the poor. It has also brought forth animal cruelty via animal factory farming and has devastated nature. In short, the capitalist structure of world economic order is the matrix of the han of many humans, animals, and nature.

## Reflection

The economic structure of capitalism is a demonic structure. It is the ruling power in the present world and a source of all kinds of han and sin. The New Testament is explicit about the spirit of capitalism as the source of evil:

> But those who desire to be rich fall into temptation, into a snare, into many senseless and hurtful desires that plunge men into ruin and destruction. For the love of money is the root of all evils; it is through this craving that some have wandered away from the faith and pierced their hearts with many pangs. (I Tim. 6:9-10)

Money is not the root of evils, but the love of money is. The capitalist system fosters a milieu of the *love of money*. In such a system, many people's ultimate concern is profit. Their God is not the God who was crucified on the cross, but the god of Mammon. This idolatry of Mammonism produces han. As the above paragraphs mention, the love of money lures people to serve the idol of capitalism, distorting the meaning of the Christian faith. It is ironic that Christianity, which supposedly rejects the idolatry of Mammon, embraces the capitalist system. As Jesus said, we cannot serve two masters: God and Mammon.

According to Max Weber, Protestant ethics caused the rise of modern capitalism. He contends that modern capitalism is derived from the work ethic of Calvinists and other Protestant groups.[11] Their vocational ethic held that even though works are futile as a means of earning salvation, hard and successful work is a mark of election and a sign of salvation; that although work which arises out of craving for wealth is evil, the procurement of wealth as the result of the exercise of one's divine vocation is the fruit of God's grace. If Weber's theory is valid, the Protestant ethic ironically twists the reality of the Christian gospel. On the one hand, Christianity condemns the principle of capitalism which provides motivation for the the accumulation of capital. On the other it underpins the pursuit of wealth by Christians through capitalism, claiming such wealth as the outcome of God's blessing. Christianity, caught in these ambivalent values, has been rather quiet about the vice of capitalism. This marriage between Christianity and capitalism is strange and absurd. The church must challenge not only the rich who exploit the poor, but also the demonic capitalistic economic order that enforces people to worship profit. Borrowing Niebuhr's terms, the system makes "moral" people "immoral."

# PATRIARCHY

To unravel han, we must understand that patriarchy is one of the major matrixes in which the han of the world is produced. Patriarchy, distorting the image of humanity, has oppressed, exploited, maimed, and killed women. Women's told and untold stories of suffering have cried out for the resolution of their han everywhere in the world throughout history. In the following, we will look into the principles of patriarchy and patriarchal traditions in the East and the West.

## The Principles of Patriarchy

### The Asymmetry of Yin and Yang

Asian women have suffered under the teaching of Confucianism for approximately two thousand five hundred years. Confucianism teaches five basic types of human relationships: king and ministers, husband and wife, the older and younger, men and women, and friends. One is always superior to the other except "friends." Women are seen as inferior to men. This imbalance is based on a deontological ethic which justifies the inferiority of women to men by invoking "divine mandate"—categorical imperative in Kant's phrase—rather than logical principle.[12]

The Confucian teaching on the status of women is the distortion of the principle of the Yin and Yang found in the *I Ching*, an ancient Chinese classic which is older than Confucian texts. In fact, Confucius said, "If some years were added to my life, I would give fifty to the study of the *Yi* (*I Ching*), and might then escape falling into great errors."[13]

Yin is the negative, dark, and feminine principle, and Yang is the positive, bright, and masculine principle. These two principles produce and reproduce all things in the universe in their interaction. In the Yin and Yang philosophy there is no hierarchical value system, only the principle of dynamic complementarity:

> Anciently, when the sages made the Yi, it was with the design that (its figures) should be in conformity with the principles underlying the natures (of men and things), and the ordinances (for them) appointed (by Heaven). With this view they exhibited (in them) the way of heaven, calling (the lines) yin and yang; the way of earth, calling (them) the weak (or soft) and the strong (or hard) . . . A distinction was made of (the places assigned) to the yin and yang lines, which were variously occupied, now by the strong and now by the weak forms, and thus the figure (of each hexagram) was completed.[14]

When Yin expands and Yang recedes, a union occurs. When Yin and Yang expand, a disharmony takes place. Their unity is possible in a harmonious interaction within. The weak and the strong are distinguished, but are not posited in a superior-inferior relationship. Their dynamic relationship aims at *equity* rather than *equality*. *Equity* is concerned with the quality of life based on fairness, while *equality* connotes the quantity of life based on numerical balance.

Patriarchy is a violation of the harmonious Yin and Yang principle. Women are treated as inferior to men in patriarchy. This denotes the force of Yang subduing the force of Yin, thus yielding disharmony. The unbalance between male and female brings forward their distorted images and obstructs them from being themselves.

The Confucian ethic of patriarchy perverts the Yin and Yang principle of the *I Ching,* which is a part of the Confucian canon. Taoism, which is founded on the Tao of Yin and Yang dynamics, is not sexist in principle. Buddhism tends to be non-sexist in asserting the interpenetration of all being. Shamanism, a religion which consoles the han-ridden people, is a strong advocate of women.

In spite of the principles of these religions, patriarchy prevails in the East. This indicates that religions have not created patriarchy, but that patriarchy has had an impact on the ideological formations of these religions. Thus, in rectifying patriarchy, I would not suggest deprogramming people of their religious convictions. The transvaluation of culture is more urgent than transmuting religious values for social transformation. Culture and religion are, however, closely interwoven.

### Hierarchical Dualism

Philosopher Karen Warren characterizes Western patriarchal ideas as consisting of three traits: value-hierarchical thinking, a logic of domination, and conceptual dualism.[15] Value-hierarchical thinking measures differences between male and female, the haves and the have-nots, and humans and nature with the criteria of "up" and "down." This type of thinking underpins hierarchical value at the cost of depreciating the great value of diversity. A logic of domination derived from value-hierarchical thinking justifies the value system of superiority and inferiority by providing various grounds of presumptive prejudice. Conceptual dualism bifurcates items of mind and body, self and other, history and nature, reason and emotion. It perceives these dualities in terms of either/or instead of both/and, in the frame of mutual exclusion.

Rosemary Ruether rejects the Augustinian interpretation of original sin, but perceives that one may slip into the real fall which occurs in the dehumanization of woman. She points out in her early work *Liberation Theology* that apocalyptic-Platonic dualism has alienated the mind from the body, the individual from the social community, the spirit from nature.[16] To her, sexism is the basic paradigm of dualism. In *New Woman/New Earth*, Ruether becomes aware that sin is more than the simple nature of dualism; it is the misappropriated dualism based on "the hierarchical symbolism of masculinity and femininity."[17] The dialectics of human existence—mind/body, spirituality/carnality, being/becoming, truth/appearance, life/death—are identified as male and female and are socially projected upon men and women as their natures.[18] In her later work *Sexism and God-Talk*, she underpins the hierarchical nature of dualism as the root of sexism, concurring with Sherry Ortner's postulation of "a universal devaluation of women based on a cultural assumption of the hierarchy of culture over nature."[19] Expanding the sin of hierarchical dualism to the relationship between humans and nature, she refines the chief connotation of dualism into the domination of relationship. This alienation from nature is derived from the transcendent consciousness of the male mind expanded through capitalism and colonialism, engendering a new form of hierarchicalism. Furthermore, Ruether defines sin as a "self-other dichotomy," separating between the human and the non-human and between our kind of humans and others. Evil exists precisely in such false naming of evil—projection and exploitation. In projection, the inferior group usually internalizes the dominant idea while the superior group rationalizes exploitation of the inferior group on the ground of their lesser value.[20] Evil arises from the distortion of the self-other relationship into superior-inferior and good-evil dualism.

Dualism has projected a distorted view of humanity. By bifurcating dominant and subservient sexes, men distort themselves in the framework of oppressive stereotypes, which confirm their dominating role. They do not know what the true image of humanity is, for the dehumanizers dehumanize themselves first.

*Power to Control: Perfection of Freedom*

The disharmony of Yin and Yang, value hierarchical thinking, hierarchical dualism, and the logic of domination are the marks of patriarchy. The power to control others is its source. To explain the power to control others, Reinhold Niebuhr's analysis of anxiety will be helpful. For Niebuhr, there are two kinds of anxiety: "anxiety about insecurity" and "anxiety about perfection." He illustrated this with the simile of a sailor who climbs the mast, with the abyss of the waves beneath him ("anxiety about insecurity") and the "crow's nest" above him ("anxiety about perfection").[21] The sailor's double anxiety arises from his fear of falling into nothingness (meaninglessness) and his ambition for actualizing his potential.[22] Patriarchy makes women develop the anxiety about falling into nothingness, and assigns to men the anxiety of ambition for actualizing one's potential. The power to control others derives from the anxiety of ambition. The boys of patriarchy and capitalism are trained in a hierarchical value system to control others, through which they desire to perfect their freedom at the expense of others' loss of freedom. Such drive to control others generates the domain of patriarchy. Its historical examples in Asia are Chinese foot-binding, the relationship between daughters-in-law and mothers-in-law, women's three virtues of obedience, and the rite of the *Sati*. This deep-seated desire to control others operates in human relationships and in our relationship with animals, nature, and space.

The insanity of humanity has been demonstrated in the shameful history of the inhumane treatment of women, the mothers of all. The oppression of women has affected humanity in a unique way by creating the primary milieu—the family—in which the human mind has been formed.[23] The han of women is the deep root of all human unconsciousness, in which we all participate. Until the human family fully restores the humanity of women, the restoration of all of humanity will tarry. In this section, we will briefly look into some of the atrocious behavior of men toward women in world history. Although some of these examples are no longer legally practiced, they survive in local communities or exist through our collective unconsciousness.

## Patriarchal Traditions in the East and the West

### Confucian Principles: Seven Eligible Grounds for Divorce

It is called *Chi-chu-chih-e* in China, *Chil-Guh-Chi-Ach* in Korea, and *Shichikyo no sei* in Japan: beginning under the Ching dynasty (1644-1912) in China, there have been seven grounds under which a man could arbitrarily divorce his wife:

1. If she behaves disobediently to her parents-in-law.
2. If she fails to give birth to a son.
3. If she is talkative.
4. If she commits adultery.
5. If she is jealous of her husband's concubine.
6. If she carries a malignant disease.
7. If she commits theft.[24]

Married women in China, Korea, and Japan have suffered under such unfair rules. In contrast, their husbands could have extramarital sexual relations, keep concubines, commit theft, and be talkative. In a case of failing to give birth to a son, a husband's parents usually pressured him to divorce the wife. Since a divorced woman was rejected by her own family and her husband's family, as well as by society, most women were willing to accept everything to keep their marriage, including concubinage.

### Confucian Principles: Women's Three Virtues of Obedience

The three virtues of obedience (*sam-chong-ji-ui*) were also implemented in these countries. According to this rule, a woman must acquiesce to:

1. Her father when she is young.
2. Her husband when she is married.
3. Her son when she is old.[25]

This rule required of women thorough obedience to men throughout their lives. It indicated that women were completely dependent on men and had no free will to exercise. This dependence was well demonstrated in the fact that a married woman was not known by her name, but as someone's wife, a certain child's mother, or the person of a certain hometown. Some women did not even have their own names. This custom of women's anonymity is still practiced in some parts of Korea, China, and Japan, where women have no identity apart from men.

### Mothers-in-law

When a woman is married, she engages in what is called *Si-jip Gahn-Da*, which literally means "going to her husband's family home." The patrilocal residence is a norm in Far Eastern countries. In this arrangement a daughter-in-law lives under the harsh, twenty-four-hour control of her mother-in-law. Almost all married women in China, Korea, and Japan undergo this harsh treatment by the mother-in-law. Jealousy of the daughter-in-law's claim to her son's affection is one of the main reasons for this ill treatment. The mother-in-law's desire to avenge the injustice she herself has suffered as a daughter-in-law is also a factor.[26] It is absurd that such a vicious circle of misplaced vengeance continues throughout history. Such oppression by the mother-in-law is the work of the accumulated unconsciousness of han. The negative explosion of han is scarcely controllable by the power of mind (consciousness), for unconsciousness overpowers consciousness. This practice still continues widely in China, Korea, and Japan. To overcome this oppression of daughters-in-law, both mothers-in-law and daughters-in-law must *understand* their own entangled reality of han and determine to resolve it.

### Foot-binding

This was exclusively practiced in China with no connection to Confucian teachings. It is believed that the practice of foot-binding started in the tenth century. The custom is derived from the imperial harem of the Tang dynasty in its training of court dancers' manner of stepping. It steadily spread from the court to the commoners, and by the early twelfth century it was widely practiced throughout China.

The actual foot-binding was performed by wrapping a long piece of cloth bondage around a young girl's feet, gradually increasing the tightness of the cloth day by day until the feet were permanently molded into a "golden lotus" form.[27] Every mother who desired her girl to grow beautifully and respectably would, under the social pressure, start binding her feet at the age of four or five. The effects of the foot-binding "are extremely painful. Children will often tear away the bandage in order to gain relief from the torture; but their temporary removal, it is said, greatly increases the pain by causing a violent revulsion of the blood to the feet."[28] To many Chinese men, these compressed feet are sexually arousing. A man said, "Every time I see a girl suffering the pain of footbinding, I think of the future when the lotuses will be placed on my shoulders or held in my palms and my desire overflows and becomes uncontrollable."[29] The bound feet symbolically and literally confine women to their place—their own rooms—because walking with bound feet means an awkward gait, and the pain that follows. Women would thus seldom dare to go outside except when carried on sedan chairs.[30]

The irony of this is that women carried out the practice of foot-binding! To satiate men's sadistic sexual appetite, women who experienced foot-binding bound their own daughters' feet. Foot-binding provides a vivid example of how the oppression of the world has been carried out. The oppressed women perform the "dirty work" and are blamed for it, while the true oppressors sit behind. This is part of the paradoxical structure of the world, which is han, in which the oppressed victimize other oppressed individuals and peoples who are defenseless and vulnerable.

### Infanticide

The infanticide of girls is widespread in Asia and elsewhere. Since the Chinese government has enforced the population control policy of "one child for one family," penalizing two-children families by depriving them of their various benefits, most families that prefer infant boys to infant girls on the grounds of the succession of the family and supportability for the family murder their infant girls.

This is true in India as well. U.S. researchers, at an American Association for the Advancement of Science meeting in Chicago, reported on February 8, 1992 that 72 percent of all deaths of infant girls in a rural southern India region were the result of infanticide.[31] The researchers revealed that one in every 10 female births in rural areas of Tamil Nadu state ended in infanticide, and suspect that a much higher rate of infanticide actually takes place. The Indian subcontinent and China have *60 million fewer women* than would normally be expected.[32] In Europe and the United States, there are about 105 women for every 100 men; in Africa and Latin America, the numbers of men and women are about equal; in the Indian subcontinent and China, there are approximately 94 women for every 100 men.[33] It is an observed fact that infant mortality due to natural causes is higher among male babies, and that it is normal that there are more women than men in the world. Thus, this report indicates that there is an alarming rate of female infanticide in the Indian subcontinent and China and that it occurs in Latin America and Africa as well!

The stories related to these sad killings fill the hollow hearts of parents in China and India. The story of Ah Ching is a very sad one epitomizing the tragedy of what is going on in China. A journalist told the following story to Pui Lan Kwok, a theologian in Hong Kong:

> Ah Ching is a little girl who lives in a village in China. Her parents are hard-working peasants. Ah Ching's father likes the little girl but he wants to have a son. One night when Ah Ching was asleep, she suddenly felt a heavy blanket pulling over her and she could hardly breathe. She struggled and yelled, 'Mama, Mama, help, help me!' To her amazement, she found out the one who tried to suffocate her was her father! She cried and prayed that her father would let her go and promised to be a nice girl.
>
> Ah Ching was so afraid that when the dawn broke, she escaped from the farm house and she went to seek rescue from her old grandma. When the grandma heard the story, she was so sorrowful that tears began to run down her wrinkled cheeks. The night came, grandma put Ah Ching to bed and comforted her. But at midnight, grandma, summoning all her strength, suffocated Ah Ching with an old blanket with her trembling hands.[34]

This han-ful situation is reality in present-day China.[35] Numerous girls have been slain since the government put into law the regulations concerning the size of families. No word can describe the agony of girls and their families involved in infanticide. In this we see the han of the entire human family. Until we change patriarchal values, we too are conspirators in these silent murders. Under the patriarchal value system, many of those who survive infanticide will be abused, molested, raped, and exploited.

### "Crime of Honor"

The disparity of the marriage relationship between males and females is outstanding in Brazil. While women's matrimonial fidelity is jealously demanded, their husbands' extramarital affairs are generally tolerated in this society, as in others. But one evil patriarchal custom is particular to Brazil: the "crime of honor" committed by husbands. A wife must avoid any act that might be construed by a jealous husband as an act of infidelity. If she is caught in flagranti, both she and her "gigolo" might be murdered by the furious husband. When unable to commit such a "crime of honor," the husband loses his status in society.[36]

The worst part of the unwritten law is that after killing their spouses, if they declare that they have killed their wives to defend their "honor," they go free in court. Brazilian feminists have claimed that instead of spending money on divorce fees and dividing posses- sions, some husbands choose the inexpensive way of eliminating their wives: hiring professional assassins. Such cases are increasing. Be- tween 1980 and 1981, 722 husbands who killed their wives claimed their rights to a "crime of honor" in Sao Paulo alone.[37] Since the early 1980s, Brazilian feminists have protested against this vice with the slogan: "True lovers do not murder." Pressured by women, Brazilian state governments have installed 71 special police stations for wom- en's defense since 1985. In 1988, one of the six special police stations in Sao Paulo received 7,000 reports of "crimes of honor."[38]

Although the Supreme Court of Brazil recently declared the crime of honor illegal, husbands' violence seems to continue. This crime of shame against the whole of humanity must be exposed to the world and must be stopped. The women who have been murdered by their husbands have died in their unspoken han.[39] The first step to abolish this diabolic custom is not only through the legal enactment of criminalization but also through Brazilian women's vehement rejec- tion of such a crime, if possible in alliance with Brazilian men. Since Brazil is a Catholic state, the church must delve into the crime of honor, closely connecting the issue with the doctrine of salvation. The traditional doctrine of salvation has been preoccupied with the doc- trine of justification (Protestantism) or the unity of justification and sanctification (Roman Catholicism)—but both centering around the forgiveness of sin. True salvation should include the healing of the han of abused wives and their families, as well as the forgiveness of the sin of their husbands.

## Witchcraft

A conservative estimate of the number of witchhunts throughout the history of the European continent and the British Isles is nine million.[40] Most accusations of witchcraft occurred in rural environ- ments. Typically, the accused were destitute old women and mid- wives, since babies' deaths or family sicknesses were ascribed to their curses.[41] Other marginal women in society were blamed as social scapegoats and were executed because of their visibility and their defenselessness. This was the reason the majority of accused witches were women. In addition, ancient misogynistic prejudices of the Christian tradition reinforced the aforementioned social realities.[42] The deeply embedded Christian prejudice against women, derived from the belief that woman yielded to the temptation, made people blame women again for witchcraft.

58

*The Rite of Sati*

*Sati* is the rite of self-immolation of widows in India when their husbands die. It is called "self-immolation," but it is hardly voluntary.[43] The rite was regarded as the ideal for widows, their supreme religious duty; by this practice, they elevated not only themselves, but also their husband to heaven, were they in hell.[44] *Sati* had become pervasive in the country when the British came to India. In spite of the fact that it was banned in 1829, the custom still lingers. In the name of religious custom, thousands of women were forcibly burnt to death.

Another example of patriarchy in India has been the practice of child marriage, in which many young girls around the age of ten are compelled to marry older men before the building of their personalities, thus allowing their older husbands to mold their young wives' characteristics according to their own program. Indian patriarchy treated women no better than the lowest caste, the Sutra. Women have been used as slave-wives, deprived of their self-dignity and various kinds of human rights.

## Reflection

One of the sources of women's han is that mothers educate their young daughters in the way of patriarchy. Human knowledge, tradition, and communal values were exclusively created by men. Women had no chance to develop their own body of knowledge and value system to pass on to their daughters. As they themselves had been trained, they trained their own daughters. They bind their daughters' feet to please men, and they persecute their daughters-in-law. The complex structure of han lies in the fact that wounded older women keep spinning the wheel of the vicious cycle of evil by inflicting patriarchal wounds upon vulnerable young women.

Women also rear their sons in ways that further the patriarchal value system. The tragedy of this situation is that sons trained by women exploit and oppress women. They give life to sons to whom they will be subjugated. In spite of their revulsion toward the patriarchal system, they become the channel that sustains the oppressive system of patriarchy. This fact is the twisted source of women's han.

Chinese footbinding, *sati*, infanticide, the crime of honor, and unfair divorce practices are legally prohibited, yet they are illegally practiced here and there or reappear in the form of collective unconsciousness, on the basis of which women and men operate their daily lives. Negative han, unconsciously accumulated for a long time, often explodes toward the wrong people. Women who have been oppressed in turn victimize their powerless, defenseless daughters and daughters-in-law. They have no intention of doing so, but they are often caught up in the unconscious power of patriarchy. Unless we work through the individual and collective unconsciousness of the patriarchal value system, patriarchal expressions of oppression will continuously emerge in different forms. In the contemporary world, we see these expressions in anti-abortionism, autocratic behavior, and jingoism. When a person suffers from repression, she or he may go to a psychotherapist for healing. When a culture suffers from the repression of collective unconsciousness, it needs religious, cultural, and social transformation, reformation, and revolution, moving toward the resolution of collective han.

## RACIAL AND CULTURAL DISCRIMINATION

Another major cause of han in the world is racial and cultural discrimination. When I say "cultural," I include social and religious aspects. Almost every nation has struggled with racial and cultural discrimination. Discrimination within the human family on the grounds of race, religion, or sociopolitical background has produced racial conflict, violence, slavery, and genocide throughout history.

A few conspicuous historical examples of extreme racism are the genocide of the native peoples of North and South America, the slavery of Africans in North and South America, the Turkish genocide of the Armenians,[45] the Nazi holocaust, the Japanese Nanking massacre,[46] South African Apartheid, and the recent Iraqi massacres of the Kurds.

### Prejudice and Discrimination

Racial discrimination differs from racial prejudice. While racial prejudice is a predispositional attitude toward a group of people, racial discrimination is the harmful treatment of a group.

*Prejudice* makes prejudgments about people which are not based on actual interaction with them. Ethnic prejudice is an antipathy built on an inflexible generalization.[47] Ingredient to prejudice are certain attitudes which operate from a *stereotype*, an oversimplified, distorted conception or image which attributes certain social characteristics to a group. A stereotype presents a positive or negative image, yielding favorable or unfavorable judgments. Prejudicial stereotypes are characterized by an unfair and harmful rigidity of attitude toward the groups in question.

*Discrimination* makes a distinction in favor of or against a race on a categorical basis rather than according to actual merit. Discrimination is distinctive treatment. Aaron Antonovsky defines it thus: "Discrimination may be defined as the effective injurious treatment of persons on grounds rationally irrelevant to the situation."[48] He does not perceive it as a particular individual act but as a unit of social relations. In other words, discrimination is the behavior that reinforces a discriminatory system.

While prejudice can take place without any contact between groups, discrimination requires contact. Prejudice is indirect; discrimination is direct. Their differences are more a matter of degree than of structure. It is commonly believed that attitudinal prejudice causes behavioral discrimination, but in actuality they do not relate to each other in such a simple cause-effect fashion. Their relationship is more complex than to say that attitude causes behavior. There is prejudice without discrimination, discrimination without prejudice, prejudice caused by discrimination, and discrimination caused by prejudice.[49]

## The Causes of Racism

Why does prejudice exist? Some theories answer from a historical perspective, dealing with the facts of slavery and colonialism. Some theories emphasize the individual sources of discrimination and prejudice, highlighting the authoritarian personality. Some theories focus on the cultural factors in relation to their traditions. Some theories shed light on the economic factors of prejudice in order to secure exploited labor forces. Some theories blame urbanization, industrialization, and dehumanization. All these theories testify to the complex causes of prejudice.

There are at least four factors that explain the development of prejudice. The first is a personality dynamic which explains prejudice on the basis of the need of individual personalities for self-expression. The second is a structural aspect that produces prejudice in intergroup conflict and hostility. The third is culture, which passes on group prejudices to children.[50] The fourth is the religious factor.

### Personality Aspect

A personality view emphasizes the psychodynamic aspect of racial prejudice and discrimination derived from individual attitudes, values, and needs. We need, however, to see the individual neither as the isolated cause of prejudice nor as a simple symptom of other causes. Individual propensities and structural elements are the major sources of prejudice and discrimination. Some personality theories perceive prejudice as a product of frustration. When individuals' attainment of desired goals is blocked, they release their frustration and hostility by attacking scapegoats. When one cannot retaliate against the actual frustrating agent, displacement of this hostility and frustration onto minority-group members takes place.[51]

Some theories attribute prejudice and discrimination to biased types of personality. According to the interview data of Frenkel-Brunswik, individuals with high scores on prejudice tests manifest rigidity of outlook (inaccessibility to new experience), intolerance of ambiguity, pseudoscientific or antiscientific attitudes, suggestibility and gullibility, and autistic thinking in goal behavior.[52] Prejudice is also correlated to many other personality predispositions to particular styles of politics, religion, and sexual behavior.[53] These people commonly share the authoritarian personality. T. W. Adorno and his colleagues state in their *The Authoritarian Personality* that persons who are insecure, "ego alien," and suffering from feelings of anomia and powerlessness express prejudice and hostility toward minority groups and underpin authoritarian types of political movements.[54]

*Structural Aspect*

Prejudice and discrimination are more than individual attitudes and behaviors. They are interconnected with social structures and systems. The problem of racism will not go away by changing individual attitudes and behaviors alone. We need to pay attention to the structural causes of racism.

While personality theories can tell why certain individuals of a dominant group are tolerant or biased, they cannot explain why prejudice is directed against certain groups. A structural view can help us analyze why prejudice and discrimination, produced in particular social systems, are directed toward certain groups of people.

Structural racism rises from intergroup hostility, which is built into the basic structures of society. Intergroup hostility is an expression of the struggle for power, income, and prestige.[55] In the struggle, power arrangements regarding who makes economic, political, and religious decisions determine which groups are advantaged or disadvantaged.

A basic attitude underpinning prejudice and discrimination is ethnocentrism. To bolster their claims to power, income, and prestige, groups often use ethnocentrism—belief in the unique value and rightfulness of one's own group.[56] Ethnocentrism as a group weapon serves a group and an individual best in group conflictual situations. Ethnocentrism brings forth an attitude of group superiority within a society and undergirds discriminatory acts against ethnic minorities. Ethnocentrism feeds the structural dimension of racism. In order to do away with structural racism built on ethnocentrism, societies must revise discriminatory employment practices and housing laws presently protected by political, social, educational, and religious sanction. It is necessary as well to revise individual attitudes, since individual insecurity and group advantage nurture each other to implement discrimination.

Economic discrimination, used as a means of maintaining a cheap and perpetual labor force, is part of structural racism. In Oliver Cox's view, "race prejudice in the United States is the socio-attitudinal matrix supporting a calculated and determined effort of a white ruling class to keep some people or peoples of color and their resources exploitable."[57] Prejudice assists ruling groups to justify their course of action and deflects the attention of the majority lower classes from their powerlessness. The ruling groups maximize their power to exploit and to increase the "surplus value" they can extract from ethnic workers.[58] They covertly practice economic policies of racism to exploit minority groups.

A good example of economic racism is *redlining*. Redlining is the practice of banks denying loans on the basis of race, where the purpose of the loan is to finance the purchase of a home or the opening of a new business in an integrated neighborhood. A federal law, designed as a step toward abolishing redlining, requires all lenders to show that they are following affirmative action programs in assisting home loans to low income neighborhoods.[59]

In spite of the federal law, the redlining practice of banks is conspicuous in African-American ghettos such as Harlem in New York and Watts in Los Angeles. Money slips out of depressed redlined zones, but no investment money flows back into these areas. Banks and stores move away from redlined zones, perpetuating the cycle of economic depression and neglect.

"Institutional racism" is part of structural racism.[60] Institutional racism refers to the legalized forms of discrimination which obstruct the equal opportunities for ethnic minorities. The clearest example of widespread institutional racism in U.S. history was the period subsequent to Reconstruction in the American South just after the

Civil War.[61] Institutional racism successfully turns the prejudiced values of a society into discriminatory acts sanctioned by law.

When legislation renders institutional racism illegal, structural racism continues the pattern of discrimination without its prior legal sanction. Structural racism is the residual discriminatory effect of institutional racism.[62] Structural racism with some social sanction involves covert discrimination and segregation within quasi-legal boundaries.

### Cultural Aspect

Another major cause of racism is cultural prejudice. Each race has a belief system which it passes along to its new generation regarding other groups. This belief system is part of the folkways of a group or race.[63] It communicates to the group's young such things as belief in the superiority of one's own group, observation of status differentials among the races, opinions regarding the inappropriate speech and action of others, and group histories. Culture shapes individuals' prejudice against other groups without having actual encounters with them. Individuals in subcultures are frequently trained in how to treat other racial groups in the absence of actual experiences.

While the cultural element does not explain the origin of prejudice as part of a group's culture, it does help us understand how a biased attitude toward minority groups can be passed along as part of culture and tradition.[64] The study of personality needs and group conflicts can explain the origin of prejudice and discrimination, but it cannot analyze why prejudice is exercised toward a particular group. The direction of prejudice toward a group or groups in society arises from historical intergroup conflicts that have been engraved in culture and tradition.

To produce prejudice and discrimination, all three factors—biased personality, structural factors, and culture—must interact. Persons who grow up in a culture of prejudice, who engage in intergroup conflict for economic gain and the acquisition of political power, and who are personally frustrated, will develop intense racist attitudes and demonstrate racially discriminatory behaviors.[65] These factors mutually buttress individual, social, and cultural prejudice and discrimination.

### Religious Aspect

Religion has played an important role in the development of racism. Religion is the soul of culture. Religion integrates the beliefs and values of society and provides the sense of the goal of society. If a religion is prejudiced, its culture becomes racist, and vice versa.

The Christian Church has, on many occasions throughout its history, offered positive endorsement of racism. In European history, religion sanctioned racism and colonialism. In the name of divine mandate, the church evoked the spirit of anti-Semitism, allowed the ruthless conquest of infidels, and espoused slavery systems.

The church has often promoted the perception among its (usually white) members that they are superior to adherents of other religions, and this has in turned often been extended to perceptions of racial superiority as well. Even in contemporary churches in the United States one finds a deep-seated racism. It is said that the hour of worship between eleven and twelve o'clock on Sundays is the most segregated time of the week.

The church is also guilty of apathy toward racial matters, which is itself a sophisticated form of racism.[66] Apathy holds the attitude that the church has "dealt with the problem of racism already" and that nothing more need be done. Apathy is the basic problem of those Christians who are opposed to racism in principle, but do very little to change the structure of racism. "Doing nothing is in fact doing something."[67] These Christians reinforce the system of racist beliefs and values in society.

## Reflection

Racism is a religion, one with its own belief system. Its major dogma is the superiority of a race or races over other races. Racism is the policies of a group or government which favor an allegedly superior race and disfavor an allegedly inferior race. It is also discriminatory behavior and hatred of one race toward another. Ruth Benedict defines racism as "the new Calvinism which asserts that one group has the stigmata of superiority and the other has those of inferiority."[68] Racism is a determinism based on a fixed idea of racial stereotypes.

Racism contradicts the first and second Commandments of the Decalogue and the work of the Trinity. It is an idolatry which makes a god of one's own race. In racism, ethnocentrism wins out over theocentrism. It worships skin rather than God. Further, racism disproves the image of God in all races. It refuses to accept the fact that God created humanity according to the inviolable image of God. The belief in the image of God in everyone will elicit respect for every human being, regardless of race.

Finally, racism rejects the reality of God by debunking the work of the Trinity. Racial discrimination denies the order of creation which God installed. God did not create the order of superior or inferior races. Racial prejudice means the denial of God's magnificent creation of human beings. Racism also nullifies the reconciling work of Christ by setting races against one another. Christ came into the world to break down the dividing wall of hostility between Jews and Greeks (Eph. 2:14). Christ is the symbol of God's emphatic desire for racial reconciliation. Jesus himself defied racism in his mission by talking with a Samaritan woman at Jacob's well (Jn. 4) and by healing the daughter of a Canaanite woman (Mt. 15:21-28). Although the Jews looked down upon Samaritans and despised Canaanites, the ancestral enemies of the Jews, Jesus cared for them beyond the boundaries of national and racial hatred (Lk. 10:30ff). Furthermore, racism contradicts the Holy Spirit's work of bringing forth unity. We are one in the Spirit of God (I Cor. 12:13; Eph. 4:3-6). Racism sows dissension among races. Where the Spirit is, there is unity. But where racism is, there is faction. Racial discrimination in practice negates the *raison d'être* of the Trinity, the core of the Christian understanding of the divine. Thus, racism cannot co-exist with the Christian gospel.

# CONCLUSION

We have explored the sources of han in the world: capitalism, patriarchy, and racial discrimination. Capitalism has waged its war against the dispossessed and the weak. It has faithfully implemented the principle of Social Darwinism: evolutionary selection of the fittest.[69] Social Darwinism has disrupted the order of creation in the world of animal and nature, the system of family, and racial relations. "Dominant" humans destroy natural environments and exterminate animal species, "dominant" parents abuse and molest their children, and a "dominant" race exploits an ethnic group. The capitalist spirit of Social Darwinism undercuts the natural process of life, ravaging others not only for the sake of survival, but for the sake of additional accumulation. It does not operate on the basis of the principle of "need and supply," but on the ground of "demand and supply." The capitalist produces an ivory necklace for the rich, instead of making a loaf of bread for the hungry world. This capitalist spirit, the vortex of han, is "the principalities," "the powers," "the world rulers of this present darkness," and "the spiritual hosts of wickedness in the heavenly places," against which Christians should contend (Eph.

6:12). As a means of resisting the destructive tendencies of capitalism, Christians should focus on a new alternative vision of society that will promote the advancement of God's reign.

Patriarchy has made us believe the Freudian dictum that "anatomy is destiny." This deep-seated unconscious notion is the principle of survival of the strongest. Men oppress and exploit women, not because of their inferiority, but because of their vulnerability. Men take advantage of women's physical vulnerability to dominate them.

The way men have treated women in the domestic and industrial spheres is not much different from the way they have treated slaves. Men have exploitatively lived on the unpaid labor of women at home and their cheap labor at work. The mentality of the ancient and modern slavery system pushed into men's collective unconsciousness has reinforced the exploitation of women in the patriarchal world. Thus patriarchy, which bestows upon men the power to exploit women by reason of their sex, is little different from the practice of slavery.

Sexism is the sin of worshiping anatomy. More concretely, it is a form of phallic worship. The name of its god is *dynamikos* (power). Sexism rejects the God who became *sarx* (flesh)—not *soma* (body)—and served the marginalized, including women. To sexism, God as revealed in Jesus of Nazareth is inferior to the masculine god of Might. The principle of sexism is thoroughly opposed to the proclamation of the gospel of Jesus the Christ.

Racism indicates that race or ethnicity has been used as an initial excuse to separate and subjugate ethnic groups. Through racial discrimination, dominant groups have benefited in the psychological, economic, and cultural aspects of life. The principle of survival of the fittest can be seen in racism, depriving ethnic groups of their basic human rights.

The anti-human and anti-Christian spirits of capitalism, sexism, and racism have strengthened one another and have denigrated both the dominant groups in society and their victims by destroying their true humanity. Such spirit has spawned han in women, ethnic groups, and the downtrodden. The sources of han in the structure of society, as well as in the dynamic intrapersonal reaction of the mind, must be exposed if han is to be resolved.

# The Intertwining of Sin and Han

In this chapter our discussion will shift from the world of han itself to the application of the concept of han in Christian theology. To begin this task, one must first contrast the reality of han with its theological counterpart, sin.

Traditional Christian understandings of sin, repentance, and forgiveness have all but unilaterally focused on the sinner. They have emphasized the magnitude of sin to such a degree that only through repenting of sin to God would the sinner be saved by God's grace. By listening and responding to the assuring Word of God, the sinner's sin is forgiven and his or her guilt is removed. These concepts of sin and salvation are of limited utility in addressing the problems of human evil and suffering. It is my contention that a reinterpretation of sin and salvation in light of the concept of han will yield a more complete basis upon which to understand and respond to these problems. What follows will describe the interrelation of sin and han, the problem of original sin, the idea of *original han*, and guilt and shame in relation to the universality of sin and han.

## SIN AND HAN

Both sin and han itself are causes of han. The two contribute to each other in a cyclical relationship, often overlapping in many tragic areas of life.

Sin is of the oppressor; han is of the oppressed. The sin of the oppressor may cause a chain reaction via the han of the oppressed.

The han of the oppressed in its active mode can seek retaliation against the oppressor in a form which is often itself unjust. The oppressor will in turn react in a way that is yet more harsh and unjust. As a consequence the vicious cycle of violence continues. Since the han-ful reaction of the oppressed is not sinless, the line between sin and han becomes blurred in their action and reaction.

Although for convenience I have divided the sin of the oppressor and the han of the oppressed, most people experience both sin and han. This is not to play down the difference between the oppressed and the oppressors, but to point out the complex entanglement of sin and han in the reality of life.

In order to analyze the problem of human evil, sin and han must be discussed and treated together. To a large degree, sin and han are indivisible in their cause-effect relationship. Some kinds of han, however, are not caused by sin but by natural disasters or self-drive. We can sin against ourselves by exaggerating or excessively suppressing the self. The sin against oneself results in self-derived han. Christian salvation (wholeness) encompasses the reality of sin and han interwoven at the intrapersonal, interpersonal, and social levels.

## The Contemporary Understanding of Sin

How do people understand the reality of sin in the present world? The answer to this question will aid our discussion of the intertwining of sin and han. Frederick R. Tennant (1866–1957), an exponent of liberal theology at the turn of this century, defined sin as "moral imperfection for which an agent is, in God's sight, accountable."[1] It is "an activity of the will, expressed in thought, word or deed, contrary to the individual's conscience, to his notion of what is good or right, his knowledge of the moral law or the will of God."[2] Tenant treats sin as an evolutionary residue of our animal origin, reducing it to sensuality.[3]

Believing that most liberal theologians have understated the gravity of sin, neoorthodox theologians stress its seriousness. Reinhold Niebuhr centers his discussion of anthropology in the doctrine of sin, depicting "man as sinner." For him, sin is primarily *pride* and secondarily *sensuality;* to avoid the anxiety produced by the insecurity of freedom, we commit either the sin of pride by denying the limit of our freedom or the sin of sensuality by giving up the insecurity of freedom. Niebuhr subdivides pride into the pride of power, intellectual pride, moral pride, and spiritual pride. Similarly, sensuality is comprised of lust, gluttony, and drunkenness. To him, all these sins are based on *self-love.*[4]

Karl Barth's doctrine of sin is unique in terms of its placement with the doctrine of reconciliation. For him, only through Jesus Christ do sinners become aware of their sinful nature. As a ray of sunshine reveals dirt in a dark room, so does Jesus reveal our sin in our hearts. He sees *rebellion* against God's eternal grace in Jesus Christ as the fundamental sin. Sin takes three forms: *pride, sloth,* and *falsehood.* Pride is "exalting oneself" to be like God: "evil action." Sloth means to fall into the morass of stupidity, inhumanity, and anxiety: "evil inaction."[5] Falsehood is opposing the truth of Jesus Christ. Its mature form is idolatry, which replaces God with an idol of false religion.[6]

Paul Tillich contends that the heart of sin is *estrangement* from God. Estrangement occurs in the transition from essence to existence. The story of the Fall symbolically portrays the reality of the estranged state. The marks of estrangement are threefold: *unbelief, hubris,* and *concupiscence.* Unbelief is to remove one's own center from the divine center; hubris is to turn toward one's own center as the center of one's self and one's world; concupiscence is to draw everything into one's own center. Therefore, these sins are derived from *self-centeredness.*[7]

Rudolf Bultmann, influenced by Martin Heidegger's discussion of authentic and inauthentic existence, regards the root of sin as *existence without faith.* It manifests itself in *ingratitude, unbelief, slavery, surrender to the world,* and *bondage to death.*[8] Ingratitude is complaining about God's providence in the past and distrust of divine guidance in the future.[9] Unbelief is the opposite of faith in the sense of trustful waiting upon God. It is life "according to the flesh" (*sarx*; Rom 8:4) in contrast to life "according to the Spirit."[10] Slavery is the state where one clings to his or her world and security in his or her own fallenness. The bondage of human existence is total.[11] Bondage to death as the outcome of sin makes a human being end his or her life at his or her quest for life.[12]

Against this existentialist interpretation of sin, political theologians (Dorothee Soelle, Johannes Metz, Jürgen Moltmann, and Frederick Herzog) stress the social dimension of sin. Soelle articulates her concept of sin as *collaboration* and *apathy,* the sins of accommodation and indifference to a structurally founded, anonymous injustice.[13] For her, "The Protestant consciousness of sin is innocuous and distresses no one in its indiscriminate universality, for it identifies sin, not theoretically but *de facto,* with a universal human fate comparable perhaps to smallpox, against which we are protected by vaccination."[14] She rejects the view that sin is simply a private matter that happens primarily between individuals, within a family, or even among the personal relations at one's place of work, choosing instead to understand it as an essentially political and social concept.

Latin-American liberation theologians also revolt against the individualistic views of sin, preferring to present sin in its sociohistorical actuality. Gustavo Gutiérrez, an exponent of this movement, addresses the threefold nature of sin: *economic and sociopolitical oppression, historical determinism,* and *spiritual sin.* Similarly, feminist theology points out that most concepts of sin are sexist in their definitions. For feminist theologians, women's sins are different from men's.

As this review of twentieth-century thinkers reveals, theologians have analyzed the problems of the world from the perspective of the doctrine of sin. For them, sins are moral imperfection, rebellion, pride, estrangement, slavery, collaboration, determinism, and oppression. The individualistic interpretation of sin lacks an awareness of the sociohistorical reality of human sin. The sociohistorical interpretation of sin employed by political, liberation, and feminist theologians includes the various strata of the issues of sin, but it has articulated the notion of sin only from the perspective of sinners, in spite of the fact that some have attempted to point out the shortcomings of the doctrine of sin by adopting the perspective of the oppressed.

## Han

There is a fundamental problem in the Christian way of thinking about sin: it has been oriented almost exclusively to sinners. Christianity has been preoccupied with the well-being of sinners/oppressors and has devoted little attention to their victims. This lopsided proclivity reflects itself in all other levels of Christian life, even in such charitable activities as almsgiving and other social services, because these activities are often seen from the viewpoint of the spiritual growth of the sinner/oppressor.

This sinner/oppressor-centered thinking arises from the very way Christian theology has cast the doctrines of sin and salvation. Christianity has thoroughly analyzed the issue of sin, the way of conquering the power of sin, the way of repentance, the doctrine of reconciliation, justification by faith, sanctification, glorification, and Christian perfection. It has thus delineated a complete map for the salvation of sinners, while at the same time devoting little or no theological analysis to the oppressed, the victims of sinners. The latter have been regarded simply as recipients of pity, compassion, and mercy.

The problems of the victims of sin have been relegated to pastoral counseling or to other psychological therapies; their pain is simply to be cured by counseling or therapy. The issue of victims has not been taken seriously at the level of theological doctrine. I am not suggesting that pastoral counseling and other kinds of therapy are not serious disciplines, but that the han of victims needs to be attended at the doctrinal level. The han of victims must not be treated simply as a pathological problem. The han of victims is a vital element in our understanding of the problems and the salvation of the world.

We need a theological *revolution*—a Copernican revolution in the doctrine of sin and salvation. The unilateral perspective of Christian doctrines must be changed into a bilateral one. Subject-object divisional thinking must be overcome. In this one-sided scheme, it seems that everything, including God, exists for the well-being of the subject. Victims are the objects whose salvation is outside the concern of the subject. Even neighbors whom the subject should love are necessary only that he or she might be sanctified.

A subject must meet another person as a subject. In this intersubjective relationship, the doctrine of sin can be complemented by the doctrine of han; the doctrine of repentance by the doctrine of victim's forgivingness; the doctrine of justification by faith by the doctrine of justification by love; the doctrine of personal sanctification by the doctrine of social sanctification; the doctrine of static salvation by the doctrine of dynamic salvation.

Several theologians have defined sin as selfishness or self-centeredness (e.g., W. Rauschenbusch, H. R. Mackintosh, Reinhold Niebuhr, P. Tillich, and William Temple). But it is the doctrine of sin itself that is self-centered; it is concerned about and focuses almost exclusively on the sinner/oppressor.

The present form of the doctrine of sin is inadequate to diagnose and address the world's problems. For instance, at a collective level the racial confrontation between Palestinians and Israelis cannot be adequately explained with the concept of sin alone. Apart from the han-ridden history of Israelis and the han-ful experience of Palestinians, their fight will not be fully understood. Beyond the conscious level of history, the conflict must be interpreted from their collective unconscious han and be resolved from the depth of their han. The resolution of the problem only through political negotiations can simply touch the problem on the surface. On an individual level and on a community level, they need to work on the problem of han in addition to that of sin.

While the doctrine of sin is of limited utility in addressing the problems both individuals and communities face, the notion of han, because it deals with the collective conscious and collective unconscious dimensions of conflict and oppression, can better plumb the depths of wounded and antagonistic communities. Since han sometimes causes individuals and communities to sin against the enemy, the doctrine of sin must be seen in relation to han. Sin and han are intertwined in the dynamic reactions of inimical communities. To stop the vicious cycle of sin and han, both the problems of sin and the collective conscious and unconscious han of opposing communities must be dissolved. Collective conscious and unconscious han will be resolved only by the *understanding, envisagement,* and *compassionate confrontation* of involved communities.[15]

## Han in Western Theology

Western Christian theology has long held a partial, implicit understanding of the consequences of human sin, and this partial understanding can be more fully articulated by introducing the idea of han. The following will review the content of han in the history of the doctrine of sin.

In spite of sometimes quite rigid understandings of sin on the part of most Western theologians, even a person such as Cyprian could speak of the results of original sin as "wounds," *vulnera,* which can be construed as han imprinted on the self.[16] For Cyprian, Christ suffered for our sins and healed the wounds received by Adam: "For when the Lord at His advent had cured those wounds which Adam had borne, and had healed the old poisons of the serpent."[17] His concept of wounds which we inherit from Adam is strikingly similar to the concept of han which is transmittable from parents. Han can be engendered within one generation by the sin and han of the previous generation.

Thomas Aquinas is another Western theologian who, although not aware of the concept itself, addressed issues related to the notion of han. The reason, hampered by sin, manifests four types of wounds: the wound of ignorance (*vulnus ignorantiae*), the wound of malice (*vulnus malitiae*), the wound of weakness (*vulnus infirmitatis*), and the wound of concupiscence (*vulnus concupiscentiae*).[18] The Fall left behind these wounds in our soul, which are intensified by our actual sin. These wounds speak of the permanent structure of han in every human being, which needs to be healed. Thomas's writing could be interpreted as addressing the notion of the universality of han and its growth in actual sins. Thomas, however, attenuates the gravity of han by generalizing it. The universalization of han indicates the equality of han for everyone. Unless involved in a han-ridden relationship to their parents or the society around them, all babies would not automatically take on these wounds to their nature. Further, Thomas provides no special attention to healing these wounds because he makes no distinction between the wound and the concept of sin. Yet treating the problem of sin alone will not cause these wounds to disappear.

Hegel's "unhappy consciousness" (*das unglückliche Bewusstsein*) approximates a form of han.[19] It is self-conscious conflict and alienation in the world. The Fall as a form of alienation consists of the loss of our natural happiness, and is an indispensable part of the process of being human and being united with God. The "unhappy consciousness," the Fall, enables humans to join God, who declares that humans become "one of us" at the Fall. This "unhappy consciousness" is a necessary means to the actualization of human potential in Hegel's dialectic understanding of history. In contrast, han is partially "unhappy consciousness," but is not an ontological entity required in the scheme of salvation. Hegel postulates the universality of "unhappy consciousness" just as Thomas dilutes our necessary attention on the han of the afflicted. Han *is* unhappy consciousness, but it is not universal. It is not something ontologically demanded for joining the Absolute Spirit in history. While Hegel speaks of the universal experience of "unhappy consciousness," han is the particular unhappy consciousness of the oppressed.

As mentioned before, the contemporary views of sin held by liberation and feminist theologians are quite similar to the concept of han. Gutiérrez posits the threefold nature of sin. His concept of sin as the historical and socioeconomic bondage of human freedom attend to the issue of collective han. In line with the Social Gospel movement and political theology, his achievement of freeing the concept of sin from the individual-centered theology has been a milestone in the contemporary theological world. I must respectfully say, however, that his perspective does not rise above the subject-centered orientation of the doctrine of sin. A change of perspective from his notion of sin to that of han will bring a greater contribution to the transmutation of the world's pain and wholeness.

The feminists' idea of sin has undertaken a shift of perspective from a male-centered understanding of sin to a female-oriented notion of sin. In the view of Saiving, women's sin is different from men's. The former is not pride but *distractibility, the lack of self-centeredness*, and *the negation of the self*:

> For the temptations of woman as *woman* are not the same as the temptations of man as *man*, and the specifically feminine forms of sin—"feminine" not because they are confined to women or because women are incapable of sinning in other ways but because they are outgrowths of the basic feminine character structure—have a quality which can never be encompassed by such terms as "pride" and "will to power." They are better suggested by such items as triviality, distractibility, and diffuseness; lack of an organizing center or focus; dependence on others for one's own self-definition; tolerance at the expense of standards of excellence; inability to respect the boundaries of privacy; sentimentality, gossipy sociability, and mistrust of reason—in short, underdevelopment or negation of the self.[20]

Saiving refuses to accept the doctrine of sin as it has been traditionally interpreted by male theologians. She indicates that the sin of the oppressor must be distinguished from the sin of the oppressed. Women and men suffer from different ills. Judith Plaskow has furthered this feminist critique of the male-centered doctrines of sin, especially those of Reinhold Niebuhr and Paul Tillich. For her, women's sin is *self-sacrifice and obedience*.[21] The feminist critiques of the traditional doctrine of sin are revolutionary in the history of Christian thought. While their altered concept of sin is laudable, it is still murky, failing to articulate the distinction between sin itself and the result of sin.

Distractibility, diffuseness, lack of an organizing center, self-sacrifice, and obedience are not sin. For want of a better term, feminist theologians call them sin. But in point of fact, they are expressions of han. Sin involves the volitional act of offense against God or others. A character trait which has been developed by the infringement of outside forces cannot be called sin. It is instead han, the seat of the wound of victims.

Another issue involved here is whether feminist theologians can completely replace the male-centered concept of sin with women's distractibility, lack of an organizing center, and self-sacrifice. Are women then free from the possibility of committing sin? Do they remain the victims of male encroachment only? As Saiving acknowledges, women are capable of sinning, but the temptations of women are different from those of men. Her point is not to assert the sinlessness of women, but to reject the male-centered interpretation of sin. This indicates that while women's basic problem is han, they

76

nonetheless can commit sin. As we have seen, they often do so by perpetuating patriarchal structures and practices at the expense of other women, spinning the wheel of sin and han yet more.

The idea of han does not deny the concept of pride or self-centeredness as sin. Nonetheless, sole reliance on the doctrine of sin cannot produce answers to the problems of women and other victims of sin because the male-defined idea of sin is in no way as universal as claimed. The notion of han complements the limited view of the doctrine of sin while at the same time transforming its distorted notion of the inherited element of original sin. The concept of han undergirds the possibility of its structural inheritance from parents, but rejects the biological inheritance of guilt.

These theologians and philosophers are aware of something missing in the traditional doctrines of sin. They express it in terms of wounds, unhappy consciousness, oppression, historical determinism, the lack of organizing center, and self-sacrifice. What they intend to express might better be explained by means of the idea of han, the reality of the shadow of sin. The notion of han may help them to transcend the doctrine of sin's one-dimensional approach to the problems of the world. Without a shift of perspective away from the sinner/oppressor-oriented doctrine of sin, Christian soteriology will be helplessly trapped in egocentrism.

While sin is basically a Christian concept, han is a universal one. Accordingly, sin presupposes the religious meaning of salvation, while han presumes multifaceted meanings of human wholeness. Sin may be forgiven by the repentance of the oppressors, whereas han can be resolved through the reconciliation of oppressors and oppressed by means of the healing of the latter.

## Original Sin and Original Han

The classic theological tradition regards original sin as "the universal and hereditary sinfulness of man since the fall of Adam."[22] Original sin is implicit in the Bible and was debated by the early church Fathers. It was Augustine, however, who made this idea a doctrine of the church. For Augustine, in Adam all have sinned. He called humanity a mass of sin, *massa peccati*. After the Fall, Adam and Eve procreated their progeny. Since they were corrupted, they could not bear an innocent child. The Fall created a wounded condition in human nature. Their sinful nature was transmitted to their children through two channels: imperfection (*vitium*) and guilt (*reatus*). Adam's posterity inherits not only original sin but also original guilt.

Augustine's formulation of the concept of original sin rested on a mistranslated exegesis of Rom. 5:12. Ambrosiaster, an anonymous contemporary of Augustine and Ambrose, misinterpreted the passage with a wrong Latin translation which Augustine accepted. The Latin version mistranslates the Greek phrase *eph ho pantes heimarton* (for that all sinned) as *en ho pantes heimarton* (in whom [*in quo*] all sinned).[23] Ambrosiaster read a Latin version, "In whom, that is, in Adam, all sinned . . . From him therefore all are sinners, because from him are we all."[24] Augustine quoted this passage in formulating his doctrine of original sin. The passage means that death passed to all, inasmuch as all sinned, not "in Adam all sinned."

Protestant liberal theologians generally refuse to accept the doctrine of original sin, while neoorthodox theologians appropriate the doctrine because it points to the universal sinfulness of human nature. Neoorthodox theologians, however, deny the literal interpretation of original sin derived from the story of the Fall. For example, Barth accepts the doctrine of original sin which shows us the reality of evil human nature, but he rejects the concept of hereditary sin. Tillich says that the doctrine of original sin is a symbol to show the reality of estranged human existence. For Niebuhr, the story of the Fall is a myth which expresses a higher dimensional truth of human nature. He contends that the myth depicts the paradoxical truth of both the inevitability and the "unnecessity" of sin, and thus human responsibility for it.

Traditionally, the concept of sin has been divided into *actual* and *original* sin within Protestant theological circles. It is identical with the Catholic distinctions between *formal* and *material* sin, and between *reatus* (guilt) and *vitium* (imperfection). The one type of sin (original, material, *vitium*), is universal so that no personal involvement in its act is necessary. This sin is unavoidable. It involves collective, but no personal, guilt.

The other type of sin (actual, formal, *reatus*), is individualistic, involving moral actions. It is a willful choice of action which can be averted. In this setting, individual guilt results from one's own sinful action.

F. Tennant refuses to accept the first type of sin, because we are not responsible for it. He regards sin as moral imperfection for which human beings are accountable. He rejects the separation of the religious idea and the ethical idea of sin. For him, there is no sin for which humans are culpable except the ones they commit.

Against the Catholic and Protestant views which hold two types of sin, and against Tennant's view which supports only actual sin, Emil

Brunner says that the two forms of sin are as inseparable as a tree from its fruits. He holds that these two types of sin exist in a dynamic relationship of tension. He espouses the idea that humans are sinners and thus they sin; they are both enslaved by the power of sin and produce actual sins.[25]

The separation of original sin from actual sin creates a problem concerning guilt. If we attempt to hold on to the doctrine of original sin, it will be difficult to repudiate the "original guilt" which results from original sin. And if we are indeed to be considered guilty for sin we have not committed, such logic breaks down divine justice. The concept of original guilt undermines the guilt of oppressors by universalizing the guilt of humanity. The idea of original sin inevitably projects the idea of original guilt.[26]

The predominant view of the Eastern church denies the theory of original sin and universal guilt, while accepting a debilitation of human nature in the Fall. Most Greek Fathers do not regard this enfeeblement as sin and refuse to accept any real innate depravity or sinful proclivity as the outcome of the Fall. They affirm the relatively free and spontaneous will of humans. By advocating the reality of human freedom, Eastern views of sin focus on the actual sin and hence the actual guilt of individuals. The Western view develops the doctrine of original sin, the depravity of human nature, the universality of guilt, and the bondage of the will. The Eastern view speaks more closely to the reality of han than the Western view. The universality of sin and guilt weakens responsibility for actual sin by treating sinners and their victims without discrimination before God.

Original sin as the actual reality which needs to be forgiven contradicts God's justice. This idea has misdirected the course of Christian theology by placing a smoke screen before the reality of the suffering of the wronged; it has created the han of the suffering in the church. The doctrine of original sin cannot be justified for the following reasons:

1. It is not logical. Sin is something one commits and for which one is responsible. That someone else committed a sin for which we are yet called to be accountable is illogical and irrational.[27] Original sin does not fit any of the categories of sin. Sin involves a willful act. It is not sin if it is inherited. Sin is not a disease; it cannot be transmitted.

2. Original sin generalizes, and hence dilutes, the reality of human sinfulness. Newborn babies may have a proclivity to sin, but they do not and cannot sin. Without volition it is

impossible to sin. No baby has ever been convicted of a crime in a human court, nor would God judge them as sinners. In Augustinianism and Calvinism, they are regarded as sinners. It seems that the dogmatic thinking of the church has made some theologians blind to the reality of the world.

3. The concept of original sin dilutes the distinction between sinners and their victims by regarding both as equally sinful. The equality of original sin is good news for the wrongdoer but bad news for the wronged.

The doctrine of original sin, however, has attempted to make a very important point: the solidarity of the human family in the interwoven strands of human misery. This fact points to the reality of han. Sin is not passed on to posterity, but han does pass through the channels of human existence and social tradition. When the sinful propensities of parents are transmitted to their children, it is not sin, but rather han which they inherit. Children are neither responsible nor punishable for these propensities, but they may suffer from their consequences. The complicated fact of the unfair transmission of parents' unfavorable proclivities to innocent posterity is the very structure of han.

The transmission of han is fourfold. First, it is biological. Han is transmittable through biological channels. Some of the parents' biological defects or sinful nature may be transmitted to children as han, but not as sin.[28] For example, if a child inherited the genes of a cardiac disease from a parent, the child may also suffer from cardiac disease. Children of alcoholic parents have a high probability of developing alcoholism. The child inherits the seat of han, not the parent's han itself. This can be called "the transmission of the structure of han."

Second, the transmission of han is mental and spiritual. Children are bequeathed parents' mental and spiritual han in general. "Mental" here can also mean conscious; "spiritual" means unconscious. Thus, when parents are han-knotted in the soul, children become heirs to the seat of their parents' han. Deep-seated parental melancholy, bitterness, and resentment can be transferred to children at the mental and spiritual levels.

Third, the transmission of han is social. Children inherit their social environments: patriarchy, hierarchy, racism, ethnic conflict, and violent life-styles. Walter Rauschenbusch, an exponent of the Social Gospel movement, asserted the social transmission of original sin in the channel of social evils.[29] The transmission of original sin to which he referred is the transmission of han.

Fourth, the transmission of han is racial. Children inherit their ethnic ethos. The collective han of race is transmitted to children. Forms of the historical traumas of a race are imprinted in the memory of posterity. These forms constitute ethnic ethos. A particular racial spirit runs down generations through the ethos of racial han.

The doctrine of original sin rightly tries to portray the solidarity of the human race, but it needs to be superseded by the concept of "original han," which is caused by the unfair transmission of the first parents' sinful nature. The idea of han may be a way to save and preserve the doctrine of original sin, whose principal intent is to describe the deep and connected dimension of the human predicament.

## GUILT AND SHAME

The notions of sin and han are closely related to the concepts of guilt and shame. We can say, by and large, that while sin incurs guilt, han brings forth shame. But guilt and shame can overlap the arenas of sin and han. By examining these concepts, we will understand their relationship with sin and han.

There are two types of guilt: subjective and objective. To psychologists, guilt is neither a legal, nor an ethical, nor a religious feeling, but an experience of living. This is not *guilt* in the precise sense, but rather *guilt feelings*, which are subjective. Guilt feelings are defined thus: "Sense of wrong-doing, as an emotional attitude, generally involving emotional conflict, arising out of real or imagined contravention of moral or social standards, in act or thought."[30] These guilt feelings are *subjective guilt*.

To theologians and philosophers, guilt as a moral state, rather than simply a mental experience, is a concomitant of our relationship with God or our authentic existence. For Barth, "sin is guilt."[31] Guilt is an unfailing sign of total depravity. For Tillich, guilt is a sign of our sense of estrangement from God.[32] For Heidegger, guilt is a sign of our "nothingness."[33] Our sinful state and estrangement from God is *objective guilt*. This universal guilt in which all human beings ontologically participate is problematic. Is it guilt or simply human existence? Can we be guilty for the sin which we have not committed?

## Guilt and the Universality of Sin

Guilt arises from the exercise of freedom. The universality of sin precludes the exertion of freedom. Thus, the Augustinian idea of original sin as universal has created a contradictory situation with the reality of guilt. There is no easy way out of this conflict between the universality of sin and the guilt of the sin. Augustinians should deny either the universality of sin or its guilt.

Reinhold Niebuhr attempts to settle this conflict through *the equality of sin* and *the inequality of guilt*. He holds that all human beings equally are sinners in the sight of God, as the Scriptures and orthodox Christianity have claimed. Niebuhr feels uncomfortable however in admitting that there are no preferences "between the oppressor and his victim, between the congenital liar and the moderately truthful man, between the debauched sensualist and the self-disciplined worker, and between the egotist who drives egocentricity to the point of sickness and the moderately 'unselfish' devotee of the general welfare."[34] He rejects both the Barthian ultimate religious fact of the universality of sin, which destroys all relative moral judgments, and orthodox Catholic moral casuistry, which derives relative moral judgments merely from the presuppositions of its natural law. His answer to the contradiction is "an ascertainable inequality of guilt." As his paradoxical statement on sin as "inevitable but not necessary" indicates, he holds that sinners must be responsible for their sin, and thus for guilt, the objective historical consequence of sin. In specific acts of wrong-doing, he upholds the inequality of guilt as much as the equality of sin.[35]

Niebuhr's equality of sin points to the ontological reality of sin we do not commit. He contends that our actual sins have impact on the intensity of our guilt. This idea weakens the actuality of han in relations between sinners and their victims by maintaining the inevitability of sin. His idea of the equality of sin and the inequality of guilt is an oppressor-oriented perspective rather than oppressed-oriented, because it levels the various degrees of sin and only permits various grades of guilt. By stressing the universality of sin, Niebuhr and other neoorthodox theologians have overlooked the issue of the suffering of sin's victims. If we say that they are the same before God, we prove that our dogma does not reflect reality.

The universality of sin can blur the distinction between the sins of the oppressors and those of the oppressed. Niebuhr's idea of the inequality of guilt indicates that there are various intensities to the act of sin. If there were not, why would there be an inequality of guilt?

Niebuhr mixes the guilt derived from original sin and the guilt that arises from actual sin. His "inequality of guilt" comes from actual sin. But if he wants to cling to the universality of sin, he should also advocate the universality of guilt. Neither the universality of sin nor the universality of guilt is rational and logical from the perspective of han.

This Protestant concept of universal sin must be reassessed in light of the rationale of the diversity of guilt. If we stress the universality of sin, it may dilute the importance of actual sin and the significance of han. Nevertheless, Niebuhr's idea of guilt is appropriate for the discussion of han, for his concept of guilt corresponds to the intensity of the offense of sinners, which may result in han in victims.

## Guilt and "Disgrace Shame"

Guilt cannot be discussed in the absence of shame. In *Shame, Privacy and Exposure,* Carl Schneider, a psychologist, distinguishes "disgrace shame" from "discretionary shame."[36] "Disgrace shame" is a dynamic psychological force that can paralyze us developmentally, render us socially dysfunctional, and bring forth spiritual enfeeblement. This shame warps our self-image, on the basis of which we may perceive others wrongly. Discretionary shame underwrites virtues of propriety, modesty, privacy, and prudence, and plays the positive role of watching over our insolent behavior that may infringe the dignity of others. Schneider contends that the former shame is more predominant in Western culture than the latter.[37] According to Robert H. Albers, the dynamics of disgrace shame appear as:

1. Disgust with the self. Any situation which may contribute to public humiliation can discharge a sense of disgrace shame. According to Karen Horney, the discrepancy between one's ideal self and the actual self would yield a sense of disgust with the self.

2. Deficiency in one's person. Deficiency in one's person is the "inferiority complex" in Alfred Adler's term. Appraising oneself in comparison with others and finding oneself wanting triggers the sense of deficiency.

3. Feelings of abandonment or desertion. The threat of separation provokes a fear of abandonment in the world. In Otto Rank's concept, it is equivalent to the anxiety occasioned by separation. Controlling spouses may use the threat of deser-

tion to constrain their partners into remaining in abusive situations.

4. Defectiveness. Physical anomaly, physical handicap, or physical illness might result in a sense of being defective.

5. The sense of defilement. The sense of defilement comes with the traumatic violence of incest or rape. Victims may feel despoiled or desecrated.

The disgrace shame Albers mentions is a form of the actuality of individual han. The victims of offenders and social derision suffer from disgrace shame rather than from guilt. Thus in general we can say that guilt is the experience of oppressors, while shame in the form of disgrace is the experience of the oppressed.

It is customary to treat guilt with forgiving words and absolution. Shame is usually treated with therapeutic counseling. Albers rightly warns us not to confuse guilt and shame when the pastoral action of forgiveness and absolution is conducted. He believes that the guilt of offenders which has not been addressed by honest repentance, coupled with a resultant possibility for forgiveness and restitution, may turn into shame. Thus, counselors must distinguish whether the problem of a client is guilt or disgrace shame, and treat shame first and guilt later.[38] The disgrace shame of offenders as expounded by Albers differs from the disgrace shame of victims, which is han-ridden. The former is derived from embarrassment; the latter from the experience of helplessness and powerlessness.

It is my view that the guilt of the oppressor is not a matter to be resolved through the unilateral proclamation of forgiveness and absolution by a priest or a pastor, without regard to their victims. Forgiveness must take place in cooperation with victims and must involve offenders' participation in the dissolution of their victims' han-ridden shame. The one-sided forgiveness proclaimed by any authority is not forgiveness, but false comfort. Even though true forgiveness involves sinners' participation in the dissolution of their victims' disgrace shame by making restitution, such restitution does not guarantee that their victims will forgive them. An offender is required to have the sincere intention to love the victim, repent his or her sin, and assist the process of the restoration of the victim's dignity. Forgiveness is not a mechanical process resulting from an offender's repentance, but a dynamic relational fruit yielded through the work of grace. Devoid of genuine intention to repent, all the work of full restitution turns into futile ostentation. The end of authentic forgiveness is reconciliation. Not with full restoration, but with the initiation of authentic forgiveness, does reconciliation begin. Reconciliation does not occur in the full compensation of damage but transpires in the cooperative construction of a better quality of life for both perpetrators and their victims.

Han-ridden shame cannot be resolved through forgiveness alone. The act of forgiveness may help to turn around the direction of a victim, but in actuality it is limited in its ability to resolve the shame of han because of the unconscious dimension of shame. Working to transform a han-causing social order will gradually consume the sense of han-ridden shame. The processes of forgiveness and reconciliation must surpass a cognitive level; they require the active involvement of sinners and their victims in the process of mutual transformation. Sinners' guilt and their victims' shame need not be treated separately. They can be understood in their dynamic distinction and correlation, and be unraveled in their cooperative venture for building up their community in unity.

# Unjustifiable Justification by Faith

In this section, we will examine some problems with traditional concepts of repentance, forgiveness, and justification, from the perspective of han. I propose to do so by first recounting briefly the history of penance. Then I will look at the concept of forgiveness, with a view to the distinction between divine and human "forgivingness" and between the "forgivingness" of the wronged and the "forgiven-ness" of the wrongdoer.[1] Concluding this chapter will be an examination of the doctrine of justification from the perspective of the wronged.

## REPENTANCE

Repentance is a step toward reconciliation. In the history of Christian thought, the church has delineated the doctrines of repentance (penance) and reconciliation for the salvation of the oppressors (sinners), but not for the salvation of the oppressed. The church has formulated these doctrines on the basis of sinners' relationships with God, and not with their victims. To achieve a more holistic view, we need to shift our perspective from sinners to their victims.

Augustine established the outline of the church's subsequent teachings on canonical penance. Before him, the church had dealt with human efforts to overcome actual sins. With Augustine, however, the church began to struggle with *original sin* as well as actual sins. Since even the baptized commit sins, Augustine divided sin into *peccata* and *crimina*. *Peccata* are daily occurrences, which can be remitted by the offering of good deeds; *crimina* are serious falls from divine grace, which can be removed only by prayer, baptism, and penance.[2]

Thomas Aquinas further consolidated the framework of penance; his ideas were subsequently adopted by the Council of Trent and used until Vatican II. For him, the sacrament of penance consists of four parts. First, and most important, comes *contrition,* an interior change or *metanoia.* Here the heart sorrows for having committed sin and determines not to fall into it again. The second part is *confession,* a complete avowal to a priest of all the sins one remembers. The third is the act of penance or *satisfaction*; acts of reparation assigned by the priest, mainly fasting, hymns, prayer, or actions such as alms-giving. The fourth is the *absolution*—a declaration of pardon by a priest.[3] This sacrament elicits reconciliation with God and thus salvation. In Aquinas's system, these four parts are divided into *matter* and *form.* The matter of penance consists of contrition, confession, and satisfaction; its form is absolution.[4] He held that *absolution* can alter *attrition,* a fear of punishment, to *contrition,* the deep sorrow for sin that causes divine forgiveness.[5]

During the period of the Reformation, Luther retained the sacramental nature of *absolution,* whereas Calvin rejected it. Luther explicitly accepted the three sacraments in his early writing: baptism, the eucharist, and penance.[6] Nonetheless, he later hesitated to confirm the sacramental character of penance, regarding it as a return to baptism.[7] To Calvin, penance was not a sacrament because its ceremony was not instituted by the Lord for the confirmation of our faith.[8] Both Luther and Calvin criticized the three acts of penance—contrition, confession, and satisfaction—choosing instead to emphasize the doctrine of justification by faith through God's grace alone. For Luther, true contrition is impossible for a sinful human being. Only God's grace makes it possible. Calvin stressed that the Latin term *poenitentia* refers to both *repentance* and *penance.* To him, repentance meant conversion, whose character was fourfold: "A real conversion of our life unto God, proceeding from sincere and serious fear of God, consisting in the mortification of our flesh and the old man, and the quickening of the Spirit."[9] In this scheme, confession is not necessary. The act of penance and absolution by a priest are not required for reconciliation with God. Only through faith in Jesus Christ do we come to repentance. While rejecting penance as a sacrament, Calvin supported voluntary private confession, which might be valuable for advice, compassion, and mutual comfort.[10]

For the Reformers, the act of penance consists of absolution, and not contrition, confession, and satisfaction. It resides in the faith of the penitent rather than in the works of *reparation*.[11] To Luther and Calvin, faith precedes repentance.

Repentance, *metanoia*, is a key concept to reconciliation with God in both the Roman Catholic and Protestant traditions. It is sorrow and regret for one's own wrong. The doctrine of repentance is foundational to other doctrines such as justification, salvation, and sanctification. This brief review of the history of "penance/repentance" enables us to make three points. First, the Protestant traditions have defined and confined repentance to a psychological "turning." The Protestant understanding of repentance hardly speaks of its social implications. Since faith precedes repentance, repentance centers on the meaning of faith in Protestantism. The Roman Catholic tradition had emphasized the privatized meaning of penance until Vatican II. Post-Vatican II theologies have shifted from the individualistic notion of penance to more communal ones.[12] Second, the Protestant tradition has stressed the development of the doctrine of repentance before God but has played down the concept of repentance before the wronged. The Roman Catholic view had been in the same situation until Vatican II redirected this tendency. Third, both Roman Catholic and Protestant theologians have described the doctrine of penance from the perspective of the oppressors but not from that of the oppressed. The assurance of pardon concerns only the restoration of moral freedom to sinners, not to victims.

# COGNITIVE REPENTANCE
# AND SOCIAL REPENTANCE

In the New Testament, *metanoia* means "a change of mind." This is an interior transformation. It is an act of will involving emotional and intellectual elements. It takes place not only in the beginning of the Christian life (conversion) but also throughout the whole life (sanctification). This notion of *metanoia* is pivotal in the life of Christians.

If "change of mind" is at the heart of *metanoia*, a question arises: How does one come to the state of changing one's mind? I believe that it involves more than a confession of sin. True repentance is not a cognitive regret alone, but an orthopraxis for the rectification of the wrong.

In the perspective of han, the profound interior change which is *metanoia* occurs via sinners' participation in the transformation of an unjust world order. True change of mind does not happen in an interior reformation but only when we are involved in the change of wrongs in interpersonal and/or institutional relationships. Our cognitive level of change will be fully actualized in our engagement with transforming the injustice we have afflicted on others. This idea of repentance as participation in social and political justice is rather well described in the term *shuv* in the Old Testament. *Shuv* means a "returning" to God and obedience to God's commandments.[13] More specifically, it is a turning from idolatry, injustice, and inhumanity to the God of Abraham, to justice and compassion for the needy and the downtrodden: the widow, the stranger, the fatherless, the poor (Deut. 14:24, 16:11, 17:19).[14] Christians should retrieve this spirit of *shuv* along with the notion of *metanoia*. *Shuv* is a socioeconomic and political turning, while *metanoia* is a cognitive change. Both are important, but in Christianity the socioeconomic dimension of repentance (*shuv*) has been less emphasized than the cognitive conversion (*metanoia*). It is time to redress the imbalance between these two biblical concepts.

A han-perspective affirms the socioeconomic and political dimensions of repentance, which brings forth true profound interior change. Without being involved in sociopolitical changes for the down-and-out, our repentance remains a solely cognitive level of change. In other words, only by partaking in changing the reality of the victims' world (han) can sinners experience true interior transformation, turning away from sin toward God.

## DIVINE AND HUMAN FORGIVINGNESS

So far we have discussed the repentance of sinners and its impact on sociopolitical spheres apart from their victims' state. Let us now turn to the issue of the *forgivingness* of the wronged and the *forgivenness* of wrongdoers. To alleviate their guilty consciences, sinners may perform what they think they ought to do for their victims out of obligation. This sort of repentance may turn out to be no more than self-gratification. Even sinners' participation in social transformation for the well-being of the needy may not escape being only the wrongdoers' self-complacence.

Until now, the church has shown little concern for victims' forgivingness in the doctrine of repentance. The doctrinal focus of the church has been on the forgiven-ness of the offenders, not the forgivingness of their victims. It emphasized God's forgiveness of our sin. If the divine forgivingness is a necessary condition for the reconciliation between God and sinners, why can we not extend this reality of forgivingness to the human victims against whom the offenders have sinned?

The perspective of han suggests the inclusion of the other side of repentance—the *forgivingness of victims*. True repentance will transpire only when wrongdoers change their way of thinking and life against the wronged *and are forgiven by them*. Without the forgivingness of the wronged, the reconciliation between the wronged and the wrongdoers and between God and the wrongdoers is incomplete.[15] Because we have ignored this aspect of repentance and reconciliation, the doctrines of justification, sanctification, and salvation have centered on wrongdoers, and have forgotten the wronged.

We can find the concept of the forgivingness of victims in Jesus' teaching: "And forgive us our debts, as we also have forgiven our debtors" (Mt. 6:12); "For if you forgive men their trespasses, your heavenly Father also will forgive you; but if you do not forgive men their trespasses, neither will your Father forgive your trespasses" (Mt. 6:14-15). In this case "we" are offenders to God and victims to our fellow human beings at the same time. An important element in this teaching is that Jesus focuses on victims. According to the Matthean author, by using the term "us," Jesus develops his theology of repentance from the perspective of the oppressed (6:12). The writer of Matthew also indicated that in the Lord's Prayer, Jesus also affirmed this by teaching us that the victims' forgivingness of the offenders is a prerequisite for the attainment of forgiveness by God (6:14-15). In the prayer, the offended are the focus of attention. Jesus' ministry itself focused on the offended and not the offenders.

The church, however, has shifted its attention in the opposite direction. The forgivingness of God's mercy has been taught, but the notion of the forgivingness of the offended has been removed from the doctrine of repentance in the history of theology. From the perspective of han, this aspect of victims' forgivingness should be included not only in the field of pastoral counseling, but in our very understandings of the theological doctrines of salvation and reconciliation.

Repentance, in light of the concept of han, is not a momentary event with a set beginning and culmination; nor do we move automatically from an instant of repentance to justification for our salvation. It is an open-ended process which continues throughout our relational life. But unfortunately, the church has underscored the sufficiency of our repentance toward God for our salvation to such a degree that it has omitted the significance of the forgivingness of the offended. From the point of view of han, repentance involves not only a vertical aspect of relationship with God, but also a horizontal aspect of relation to other human beings. No one can have true repentance by turning to God without also turning to his or her neighbor.

## A DOCTRINE OF THE FORGIVINGNESS OF VICTIMS

The second issue is how we care about the wholeness of victims along with the repentance of sinners. Wrongdoers should move beyond their preoccupation with their own turning away from sin to God and begin to see the side of those they have wronged, genuinely caring about their pain and seeking forgiveness from them. However, this is not enough. From the perspective of the offended, the church must develop a doctrine which corresponds to the doctrine of repentance for the offenders. The church, rather than simply individuals, should work to bring forth the wholeness of victims. This we might term a doctrine of forgivingness. Victims' forgivingness (*kaphar* or *áphesis*), is a major theme of Scripture. The rebuking commandment (Lk. 17:3; Mt. 18:15-17) can provide us a more complete picture of this theme.[16] It delineates what the offended can do to the offender: "Take heed to yourselves; if your brother sins, rebuke him, and if he repents, forgive him" (Lk. 17:3). More concretely, the author of Matthew writes:

> If your brother sins against you, go and tell him his fault, between you and him alone. If he listens to you, you have gained your brother. But if he does not listen, take one or two others along with you, that every word may be confirmed by the evidence of two or three witnesses. If he refuses to listen to them, tell it to the church; and if he refuses to listen even to the church, let him be to you as a Gentile and a tax collector (18:15-17).

According to this rebuking commandment, the wronged is to seek to bring the wrongdoer to repentance. The first act is a private challenge. The second act is a small-group challenge. The third act is a church challenge. The fourth act is ignoring the wrongdoer, effectively banning him or her from the community. If the church were to encourage victims to follow this series of steps in response to their victimization, it could prevent many tragically sinful offenses within family, church, community, and nation. The church needs to develop a doctrine for victims in conjunction with the doctrine of repentance. Successful reconciliation requires the cooperation of both the wrong-doers and the wronged. A granting of forgivingness and a reception of forgiven-ness must transpire if the wholeness of both the wronged and the wrongdoer is to be restored. The present doctrine of repen-tance is incomplete in its structure. The doctrine of repentance should not be independent of the doctrine of victims' forgivingness.

There are also several scriptural references on the power of forgiving sins. The power of binding and loosing was bestowed upon Peter (Mt. 16:19), other apostles, and to the Christian community (Mt. 18:18; Jn. 20:23).[17] Matthew 18:19-20 may well have been shaped by a Christian group organized in direct opposition to the leadership and authority of a synagogue.[18] The granting of the power of forgiv-ingness to the entire group accords well with Matthew 23:10-12.[19] But, obviously, the power of forgiving sin was not given to the offenders. The Roman Catholic church has exclusively designated this power to the priest. The power of forgivingness should not be monopolized by a priestly group, but rather must be shared by the Christian commu-nity. It seems natural to me that the wronged rather than a priest should forgive the sin of the wrongdoer. The traditional doctrine of absolution by priests needs to be reinterpreted in light of this discus-sion.

## PROBLEMS WITH JUSTIFICATION BY FAITH

The concept of justification has been a pivotal theme in church history. While the Roman Catholic church has confirmed that justifi-cation means the actual making of the sinner righteous, the Protestant traditions have asserted that justification by faith means that, by God's grace, we are accounted to be righteous even though we continue to be sinners. Saint Thomas, representing the Roman Catholic position, states that we are justified by faith, yet the faith is a gift of grace informed by love that leads us to good works. Thus "justification by faith" means to be actually righteous before God. In Roman Cathol-icism, the infusion of supernatural grace removes sin, regenerates the soul, and sanctifies it, making it worthy of communion with God. This is done by the gift of *actual grace* at the preparatory stage and by the gift of *sanctifying grace* through the sacrament of baptism.[20] By partic-ipating in the sacraments, the sinner is infused with supernatural grace.

Luther, however, insists that, on account of justification by faith, through God's grace sinners are imputed to be righteous even though they are not actually so. The attempt to be righteous before God by our own efforts is the sin he desires to avoid. Thus we remain at the same time justified yet sinful (*simul justus et peccator*).

To him, faith signified a much more profound dimension of Christian life than the definition of "faith" held by the scholastic theologians who, following Augustine, held that faith must be informed by charity. Luther wrote that "Faith is something done to us rather than by us (*magis passio . . . quam actio*) for it changes our hearts and minds."[21] In Luther's scheme, faith meant the full turning to God of one's heart and life, a total entrustment of one's being to God. Thus Luther preferred the word *fiducia* for faith to the term *assensus; fiducia* points away from us, *assensus* points toward us.[22] The bishops at Trent did not realize the deep meaning of Luther's "faith"; they equated it with the Augustinian and scholastic understanding of faith as merely the beginning of justification, whereas Luther's was the beginning, middle, and end of justification.[23] To him, human efforts had nothing to do with conversion and justification.

The followers of the Reformers also deny the meritorious dimension of justification by saying that God accepts sinners as they are, not according to their own worth or merit. "Justification by faith through grace" signifies that neither good works, nor intellectual works, nor believing in a set of doctrines, would save us.

Bultmann, in his effort to demythologize the New Testament, elucidates the doctrine of justification by faith in this manner: "The man who wishes to believe in God as his God must realize that he has nothing in his hand on which to base his faith. He is suspended in mid-air, and cannot demand a proof of the Word which addresses him. For the ground and object of faith are identical. Security can be found only by abandoning all security, by being ready, as Luther put it, to plunge into the inner darkness."[24] Adopting an iconoclastic stance, Bultmann urges us to abandon all security we depend on for our salvation, including our knowledge of faith, if we are truly to embrace the doctrine of justification.

Tillich believes that we cannot reach God by the work of right thinking or by a sacrifice of the intellect or by a submission to the doctrines of the church and the Bible.[25] For him, justification is first an objective event, an eternal act of God manifest in the New Being in Christ. Its subjective side is the act by which we accept that we are accepted by God. To him, the expression "justification by faith" is misleading, for it gives the impression that faith is our act by which we earn justification.[26]

Against the message of the Reformation, the six sessions of the Council of Trent declared that justification can be reached by faith, but only faith informed by love and infused with hope; it is part of the preparation for justification.[27] Good works can increase justification.[28] God freely forgives sinners' sins, but is unable to have communion with them in their sinful state.

Roman Catholics consider the Protestant principle as legalistic and forensic, on account of its involving no actual transformation on the part of the sinner. Protestants regard the Roman Catholic view as magical and a form of works righteousness because justification depends on the actual merit of the sinner and the transforming power of sacraments. In what follows I would like to suggest an alternative to these two positions.

The doctrine of justification by faith is a necessary part of Christian theology for the wrongdoer, yet it has three shortcomings. First, the doctrine views the matter of justification from the perspective of the wrongdoer. Second, it speaks little if at all to the salvation of the wronged. Third, it focuses solely on our relationship with God, diminishing the significance of our relation with our neighbor.

First, this most important doctrine of Christianity (or at least of Protestantism) delineates how the wrongdoer can be saved, but omits how the wronged can be saved. For example, note Tillich's threefold character of salvation: *regeneration* (salvation as participation in the New Being), *justification* (salvation as acceptance of the New Being), and *sanctification* (salvation as transformation by the New Being). To him, regeneration precedes justification. It has subjective and objective dimensions. The objective side is "the relation of the New Being to those who are grasped by it." The subjective side is participation in the New Being itself. "The objective reality of the New Being precedes subjective participation in it."[29] His concept of regeneration does not articulate the necessary relation of the wrongdoer with the wronged if the former is to be regenerated. His idea of regeneration is designed for the salvation of oppressors, irrespective of the oppressed. His concepts of justification and sanctification are for the oppressors also. The wrongdoer is justified by the objective act of God manifest in the New Being in Christ, and the subjective side of the acceptance of the New Being as Jesus as the Christ, and further is sanctified by "being received into the community of those who are grasped by the power of the New Being."

95

Obviously, I do not object to sinners being justified and sanctified. I do wonder, however, whether justification and sanctification are exclusively between themselves and God, apart from any consideration for their victims. The Protestant principle of justification by faith especially connotes "being made just" by God's mercy, in spite of the fact that our sinful nature can defeat the very purpose of the Gospel, "setting the oppressed free."

Roman Catholicism's justification by faith informed by love seems more inclusive in the relation between the oppressors and their victims than the Protestant view, yet its orientation remains fundamentally toward the oppressors. Roman Catholicism believes that sinners are made righteous and sanctified by God's grace acting upon them in the sacraments. Like Protestantism, Roman Catholicism has been mainly concerned with the actual state of the righteousness and sanctification of oppressors, but has ignored the fair state of the oppressed. The doctrines of justification and sanctification must not be understood as stages of life, but as qualities of the relationship between oppressed, oppressors, and God.

In this sense, the author of Matthew reported that Jesus said, "If you are offering your gift at the altar, and there remember that your brother has something against you, leave your gift there before the altar and go; first be reconciled to your brother, and then come and offer your gift" (5:23-24). Jesus insisted that one is only worthy of worship after he or she has been reconciled with the neighbor.[30] The terms *justification* and *sanctification* make sense only in our right relationship with the victims of our sins.

In brief, the doctrine of justification by faith has misled Christians into a one-sided understanding of salvation for hundreds of years. Christianity must reevaluate its oppressor-oriented notion of salvation and reinterpret it in light of a dynamic reconciling action between the wronged and the wrongdoer.


## JUSTIFICATION BY LOVE

The true meaning of justification by faith, according to the Reformers, was not that we are saved by our own faith, but that we are saved by God's grace alone. Therefore there is virtually nothing we can do for our own salvation but depend on God's mercy. Even having faith is not our own work; it is the provision of God's grace. This humble understanding of faith before God has added to Protestant piety, but has also leaned it toward determinism; we have nothing to contribute to our own salvation. By God's grace we are "justified," yet our sinful nature remains as it is.

With this kind of attitude toward justification by faith, Protestantism has endeavored little to change "sinful human nature." This understanding of justification by faith is not only debilitating for sinners, but also hurts the victims of sin by ignoring their wounded hearts. Constant confession of sin before God and putting our faith in God have been the primary focus of religious life. Within this dogmatic agenda, the justification of the wronged has been pushed aside. The sinners are busy with their own sin, repentance, and justification by God's mercy; their victims have to find their own way to salvation. The justification of sinners by faith is an egocentric view, if the doctrine shows no concern for the victims of sin. This type of understanding of salvation through justification by faith is based on a static view of salvation.[31] It considers salvation simply an external change of status from so-called "sinners" to "saints."

The idea of han helps us reorient the meaning of salvation to a doctrine of justification by love in three ways. First, sinners should understand justification before God in connection with their victims. A new comprehension concerning justification must take place in order to bring salvation into our midst. Sinners' justification is not simply a matter of being justified before God, but the genuine willingness to care about the wronged. In this mode of thinking, persons are not engrossed with their own justification but with the healing of others' han. Their concern becomes the removal of all han-causing evils from their roots. They no longer seek simply their own justification but pursue justice for the victims.

Second, the idea of han stresses that genuine human efforts to transform the world's problems are based on God's grace. In the traditional doctrine of justification by faith, human beings can do nothing to achieve their own justification, for what humans do for salvation contradicts what God does (grace). But from the perspective of han, all human efforts to bring forward God's realm take place according to God's full grace. For Rahner, since God is the source of human freedom, the more we depend on God, the more free we become. In the same manner, since God is the source of human efforts, the more we depend on God, the more we extend our efforts to change the han-ful situation of the world. In other words, God's grace is the foundation of our efforts to improve the world's conditions.

Third, this view holds that the other side of faith is love. Without love, faith is empty; without faith, love is blind. We are not simply justified by faith alone. This doctrine has misled thousands of Christians into a self-centered journey of faith. Faith in Jesus Christ alone cannot stand by itself without involving the afflicted, for we know Jesus Christ, not in abstraction, but in and through those who suffer. The love of Jesus Christ is the core of Christian faith. When we have faith in Jesus Christ, we come to love the afflicted for whom Jesus lived. It is not feasible to change our status before God from sinners to saints without changing our natures. With such unchanged nature, we will never experience God's peace and salvation, for salvation is not a *status* but a *state of our nature*. If we are supposedly justified by our faith, yet live in sinfulness, that justification helps no one in actuality and loses its significance. When we change our perspective from our self-centeredness to a victim's view and live in love with others, we come to *justify* our existence and abide in salvation. Our loving nature, brought about by an altered perspective which has shifted from the self to the downtrodden, is eternal life, salvation.

I have pointed out above the shortcomings of the traditional doctrine of justification by faith. In reality, however, justification by faith is interpenetrated by justification by love. The message I have attempted to articulate is that the doctrine of justification by faith has been rigidly dogmatized in the church and that it has led Christians to a house of salvation that is empty. Only when the justification of sinners coincides with the justice of victims, and justification by love joins justification by faith, does a true feast of salvation transpire in the house of God.

# Han and Salvation

The doctrine of salvation is the heart of Christian gospel. It is at the same time one of the most confused and complicated doctrines in the church. Atonement theories, justification, redemption, and the meaning of salvation are all interconnected with this doctrine. In what follows I will attempt to bring a degree of clarity to this confusion by concentrating on the meaning of salvation from the perspective of han.

What is salvation? In the Old Testament, *salvation* is described as "safety" (*yesha*) and "peace" (*shalom*).[1] The term *salvation* in the Greek (*soteiria*) means "deliverance" from enemies in the New Testament, and "health" in an extra-biblical sense.[2] In Latin, *salvation* (*salus*) means "soundness," "health," and "welfare."[3] The English term *salvation* was derived from the Latin.

Traditionally, the church has perceived salvation from three basic perspectives, corresponding to the three major branches of Christianity: Eastern Orthodoxy, Roman Catholicism, and Protestantism. For the early Greek church, salvation meant *freedom from death and error*. For the Roman Catholic Church, salvation denotes *freedom from guilt and its outcomes* in this and the next life (in purgatory and hell). In classical Protestantism, salvation signifies *freedom from the law and its anxiety-producing and condemning power*.[4] These definitions focus on the freedom from the power of sin, guilt, and death. In all of them we see that the meaning of salvation has been defined from the perspective of sinners.

Some contemporary theologians have attempted to define the concept of salvation from fresh perspectives. For Karl Barth, "salva-

99

tion consists in the occurrence of reconciliation, and therefore in healing; in a healing of the rent, a closing of the mortal wound, from which humanity (and openly or secretly every man) suffers. It consists in the removal of antitheses; the antithesis between God and man; then the antithesis between man and man; and finally the antithesis between man and himself. In this sense salvation means peace."[5] All these conditions of salvation are actualized in Christ as *Immanuel*. Barth's understanding of salvation partially resembles the perspective of han in its idea of healing broken relationships. However, he makes no distinction between the wound inflicted by the oppressors and the wound belonging to the oppressed. Thus, he little surpasses the traditional sinner-oriented stance of salvation.

Bultmann, concurring with Heidegger's idea of salvation, construes it as the move from inauthentic to authentic existence.[6] His idea of salvation is ontological and sinner-oriented, regarding it as a state of existence. Reinhold Niebuhr finds salvation, the restoration of the *justitia originalis,* in *self-transcendence* actualized in the life of faith, love, and hope. The heart of self-transcendence is the moment when we realize our finitude: "It is in this moment of self-transcendence that the consciousness and memory of original perfection arise. For in this moment, the self knows itself as merely a finite creature among many others and realizes that the undue claims which the anxious self in action makes, result in injustices to its fellows."[7] His concept of salvation centers on a cognitive understanding of human finitude. Tillich perceives salvation as the healing (*salus*) through, and participation in, the New Being, acceptance of the New Being, and transformation by the New Being.[8] His perception of salvation stands on its ontological understanding.

Karl Rahner defines salvation as *God's self-offering to the whole of humankind,* but it must be followed by human acceptance or rejection of the offering.[9] In other words, salvation is both transcendental and historical; it is always engaged in the divine self-communication and the human response to it (transcendental); transcendence takes place in and through historical events and our response to the divine self-offering is a daily encounter (historical). For Gutiérrez, salvation is liberation. There are three interdependent levels to his interpretation of salvation: first, liberation from socioeconomic and political oppression; second, liberation from historical determinism; third, liberation from sin and the restoration of communion with God and with fellow human beings.[10] His theory is dynamic and communal; his concern is not only for the oppressors but for the oppressed, although he speaks little to the relational nature of salvation between the two.

For Rosemary Ruether, salvation is the original wholeness of humanity presented in Mary, and the establishment of an integrative feminist vision of society built on ecological and nonpatriarchal ideas.[11] Her interpretation of salvation is holistic and relational.

These theologians' concepts of salvation have contributed to interpreting the multifaceted dimensions of the reality of salvation from existentialist perspectives (Bultmann, Tillich), from a Christocentric perspective (Barth), from a realist perspective (Niebuhr), from a transcendentalist perspective (Rahner), from a liberation perspective (Gutiérrez), and from a feminist perspective (Ruether). Gutiérrez's notion of salvation emphasizes its social dimension beyond the individualistic interpretation without underrating the significance of its spiritual dimension. Ruether's "salvation" moves beyond most male theologians' patriarchal and anthropocentric concepts of salvation.

Gutiérrez's and Ruether's doctrines of salvation overlap with the idea of salvation found in the concept of han, for they deal with the pain of the poor, the oppressed, and women. But a subtle difference exists between their perspective on salvation and that of han. Since they operate on the basis of the concept of sin, and not of sin and han together, their concepts of salvation are not clear about the relation between the sinners and their victims, in terms of forgiving sin and resolving han. While Gutiérrez and other liberation theologians have stressed the liberation or salvation of the oppressed from the reality of sin, and Ruether and other feminist theologians have highlighted the liberation of women from the male-centered notion of sin, han-thinking specifies salvation as freedom from han for the oppressed and freedom from sin for the oppressors.

From the perspective of han, salvation can be seen as *participatory dialectic.* I use the term *dialectic* to describe a method that analyses and synthesizes dualities in conflict and contradiction. Such a use of *dialectic* is thus more similar to Hegel's than to Kierkegaard's.[12] This dialectical salvation is the relational, dynamic, and affective interaction between sinners and their victims, and the cooperative efforts of the two to dissolve han and sin. In this salvation scheme, the oppressors dialectically participate in the well-being of the oppressed. Both are interpenetrated in an indivisible dialectical destiny. The oppressors (sinners) cannot be saved unless the oppressed (victims) are saved or made whole, and vice versa. In other words, no one is fully saved until all are saved. Salvation is wholeness, and no one can actualize wholeness by him or herself.

I presuppose that salvation comes to us as a divine gift. All human efforts to work for the reign of God derive from the divine life; divine grace through creation and redemption underlies all human endeavors to dissolve the han of the world. There is nothing humans can claim as their own in doing good, since all bona fide human efforts flow from divine grace itself. I believe that the following discussion will add to the contributions of liberation and feminist soteriologies by treating the reality of han for the purpose of constructing a holistic view of salvation.

The participatory dialectic to which I refer is the engagement in divine life, which is "eternal life." This eternal life is not something one can attain; it is not our possession, but our *true life itself. Life, including eternal life, is not for having* but for *living.* Eternal life is eternal joyful *living.* The content of salvation is the dynamic and loving relationship one enjoys with others in God. In what follows I will treat the issue of the content of salvation rather than that of the theories of salvation (soteriology). The premise of the following discusssion is that where God is, there is salvation. Salvation is not a ✓ *type of state*, but the *quality of the intensity of divine presence* in relationships.

# HEALING PROCESS: SUBSTANTIAL OR RELATIONAL

The participatory dialectic is the healing process which can take place between sinners and their victims. Han requires healing. The important point is, "Whose healing is it?" Traditionally, salvation has meant the healing of sinners from the pain of guilt, fear, and death. The han way of thinking is concerned about the healing of the victims of sinners. This way of thinking does not lessen the importance of the healing and freedom of sinners from their sins, but rather accentuates the meaning of salvation by including the healing of victims in the picture of salvation. Salvation cannot be obtained by sinners alone before God. According to the traditional substantial notion of salvation, such an assumption is reasonable. In the relational corporate notion of salvation, it is impossible. In the efforts to heal the victims of their sins or the sins of others, sinners can experience salvation. It has been held in the church that sinners could achieve salvation by faith through confessing and feeling remorse for their sins. Such a concept of salvation presupposes a substantial view of salvation; it assumes that there exists a substance of salvation that can be secured or attained apart from relationship. Salvation is not something one can hold on to or some place one can enter. The idea that sinners can achieve salvation by confessing their own sin regardless of the welfare of their victims is a narcissistic illusion.

Salvation is a relational event. It is a process of healing and freedom which transpires between sinners and their victims, and sinners and God. Salvation as a unilateral healing of sinners defeats the very meaning of salvation the Christian gospel intends to bring forth. Sinners may suffer their guilt, but they do not suffer from the injury of their victims. By excluding the healing of the injury of the victims, the salvation of sinners loses its intrinsic meaning.

In some Protestant traditions justification by faith has become a mechanical formula. Such faith stresses repentance over reconciliation, thus underscoring the fact that we are not justified for our righteous state, but justified by God in spite of our sinful nature. This tendency to be preoccupied with one's salvation through justification by faith has fostered an egocentric religion. Even the doctrine of sanctification underpins this egotism by concentrating on the spiritual growth of sinners without involving the healing and spiritual growth of their victims.

In contradiction to this egotistical preoccupation, the parable of the prodigal son shows the bilateral character of salvation. From the son's view, salvation is "justification by faith" through the grace of the father. From the father's view, salvation is the resolution of han. This story shows us that salvation lies in the healing of the relationship between the father and the son. We have ignored the dimension of salvation needed for the father, the victim of sin.

In the framework of the concept of han, the subject and the object are not separated in the reality of salvation. More accurately, salvation emerges (as per Buber) from the restoration of an "I and Thou" relationship. In this view, there is no clear separation between *me* and *you*: I am part of you and you are part of me; I am with you and you are with me; I am in you and you are in me. Julian Jaynes claims that three thousand or more years ago, our foreparents were not able to make the subject-object distinction; they had no "I" consciousness.[13] When they suffered their first "nervous breakdown," they became aware of themselves as "I," a separate entity. Whether this theory is right or not, the subject-object separation is not a healthy one, for there is no *self* without *others* (in the first case, without parents). The *self* must thus be understood in a trinitarian relationship. We need to understand that I am not an *ego* in a subject-object relationship, but rather that I come into being in an intersubjective relationship. In this sense, *we* describes the relational actuality more precisely than *you.* Thus, the I and We relation bespeaks more pertinently our actual situation than I and Thou.[14]


# PERSPECTIVAL ALTERNATION: STATIC OR DYNAMIC

It is important here to distinguish between a static and a dynamic view of salvation. A static view considers salvation a fixed or stationary state of bliss bestowed by the divine. A dynamic view indicates that salvation is a lively participation of the human being in the activity of history. According to the philosopher of religion David Roberts, a static view of salvation denotes a changeless state of the human being through total dependence on divine mercy:

> Perhaps it may seem paradoxical to call such an interpretation of Christianity "static" when it places exclusive stress upon the judging and redeeming activity of God. Yet from man's standpoint the situation is static because his norms for living and his salvation are conceived of, not in terms of discoveries and dynamic changes with him, but in terms of an alteration of his status before God—a shift from condemnation to justification in the light of what Christ has done.[15]

In this static view, a sinner can have no claim to share in the inner repentance, but can only depend on God's initiative and God's completion. Human autonomy finds no room in such a view, as it is crowded out by God's exclusive accomplishment.

Roberts names four consequences of the static view of salvation. The first is *hypocrisy.* A sinner's salvation comes from God's mercy, regardless of his or her life. Thus, there are discrepancies between the professed norm and actual living, and this view perpetuates hypocritical living. A second possible consequence is *self-righteousness.* A highflown self-image of being "saved" persuades the person that he or she has reached the height of human existence. This vision induces self-righteousness. A third possible consequence can be *unresolved despair.* In spite of the consciousness of self-righteousness, the fact remains that despair is unresolved within the sinner, for he or she could abandon hope in human, temporal efforts to change the world. A fourth possible consequence is *extreme self-repudiation.* Since every expression of self-assertion is sinful, the sinner cannot discriminate between egocentric selfishness and a sound form of self-love.[16] Roberts uses Erich Fromm's work to distinguish between these two assessments of the worth of the self. In *Man for Himself*,[17] Fromm demonstrates that identifying self-love with egocentricity is misleading. For Fromm, the capacity to love others is "conjunctive with" the capacity to love humanity in one's own person. This self-love in the form of self-acceptance is healthy, while egocentricism is pathological.[18] The confusion of these two reproduces "endless self-castigation." Roberts concludes that this static view of salvation may drive people into paralyzed hopelessness or cynicism by mainly focusing on their shortcomings.

Against the static view, Roberts presents a dynamic conception of salvation, one which enables people to resolve conflict. In this understanding, salvation means to live our life more abundantly through faith in God and Christ:

> So far as Christianity is concerned, this conception implies that its saving purpose is to give men a faith and a mode of life which will make them no longer ashamed of themselves. It cures guilt not by putting forward ideas which assure men willy-nilly that they are "all right," but by releasing a power which removes the *causes* of guilt.[19]

Roberts considers salvation primarily as a "dynamic transformation" that removes moral evils at the source by changing people.[20] He rejects any view which regards salvation as conditions exclusively fulfilled by God, affirming instead a dynamic view which empowers people to actualize existing resources in human nature for resolving evils.

Even though I basically accept Roberts' distinction between the static and dynamic views of salvation, I differ from him on one decisive aspect: Roberts' concept is still sinner-oriented. Roberts describes well the dynamic salvation for sinners, but his perspective has not been concerned about the salvation of victims. For the victim, salvation is the resolution of han. His dynamic view remains in the perspective of sinners, whereas a dynamic view in participatory dialectic understands salvation from the perspectives of both sinners and victims.

The dynamic construction of salvation which a participatory dialectic envisions can be described by the phrase *perspectival alternation*: a transposition of vision from a sinner's to a victim's and vice versa. Truth is perspectival in quantum theory. A beam of light can be recognized as constituted either by particles or by waves, depending on an observer's perspective.[21] According to Werner Heisenberg, we cannot find the *location* and *momentum* of a particle at the same time.[22] If we pin down its position, we are totally uncertain about its momentum. If we follow its momentum, we cannot be certain about its position. Thus, reality is uncertain and perspectival. Salvation is the uncertain reality that is not static but perspectival. When we locate the reality of salvation, we lose its living spirit. When we lose it for the sake of others, we find its heart. The former is static salvation, the latter dynamic salvation.

Salvation never means the transcendence of the self above others nor security for the self. There is no *definite boundary of the self*. In our life of perspectival conversion between the self and others, salvation as wholeness eventuates. It is similar to John Dunne's idea of "passing over" in the context of interreligious dialogue: "Passing over is a shifting of standpoint, a going over to the standpoint of another culture, another way of life, another religion. It is followed by an equal and opposite process we might call 'coming back,' coming back with new insight to one's own culture, one's own way of life, one's own religion."[23]

Perspectival alternation, however, is different from "passing over." While "passing over" comes back to one's own position with new insight, perspectival alternation continuously attempts to see through a shared view, not being able to come back to the original position. It dialectically participates in the shared view. Salvation is not the perspectival move itself, but takes place in its process. This perspectival alternation is not egolessness nor mere self-transcendence in opposition to self-centeredness. It is a dynamic transpositional view of the self and others. The perspectival shift indicates a continual transposition by which we find our true self and others. In other words, salvation through perspectival alternation not only transcends but also affirms the true self and others.

This shift converges with Gadamer's "fusion of horizon," which refers to the unity of dual views such as the historical consciousness of the past and the present horizon, text and context. For Gadamer, "The horizon is the range of vision that includes everything that can be seen from a particular vantage point."[24] Having a horizon is necessary if we are to transpose ourselves into a situation. Transposition signifies neither the empathy of one individual for another nor the subordination of another person to one's own position, but "rising to a higher universality that overcomes not only our own particularity but also that of the other."[25] The horizon of the present cannot come into being without the horizon of the past. "*Understanding is always the fusion of these horizons supposedly existing by themselves.*"[26]

Gadamer contends that understanding the past is analogous to understanding another person as a Thou, insofar as placing oneself in the other's place never means disregarding oneself.[27] Mere transposition would not bring about the true understanding of the subject matter; the hermeneutical consciousness must maintain a tension between the historical consciousness of the past and the present horizon. It indicates that only through a dynamic tension between I and Thou do both come to understanding.

Salvation through a perspectival shift agrees with Gadamer's "fusion of horizons," but moves beyond its level of tension for understanding Thou. "Salvation" requires the tension plus humility. A perspectival shift can take place in transposition, but with humility. As the word *understanding* indicates, when we *stand under* Thou, we come to see him or her as a whole. The humility involved in the perspectival shift denotes seeing Thou not only from an external mode of existence, but from an internal one—we perceive the deep pain of the victim, which is the structure of the person's han or the conscious or unconscious agony of the sinner, which arises from dehumanizing a victim. Perceiving as well as sharing Thou's reality of han, we come to embrace Thou, in the process of which we experience salvation. In this context, humility is never self-debasing nor self-amputating, but self-involvement in affirming Thou in depth. Furthermore, salvation as understanding does not separate its end from its means. Understanding is not a mere hermeneutical method to achieve salvation through knowing Thou, but is the way of humble living in which we experience salvation itself. This life of humble understanding is the content of a participatory dialectic in perspectival alternation.

## COMPASSIONATE REALIZATION OF POTENTIAL

Salvation is neither ontological nor deontological. It is not a state of attaining eternal life nor is it the observance of moral imperatives. All ontological and static categories of salvation should be reevaluated in light of the relation between sin and han.

We have defined salvation as the relational healing process and perspectival alternation between the wronged and the wrongdoers. Healing connotes restoring an original state, indicating a recollective movement. Salvation is more than a recollective restoration; it is as well a forward-moving event. It is the actualization of potential. True healing takes place when people's potential, which has been blocked by han and sin, becomes free to be fulfilled. Healing and the actualization of potential coincide in salvation. Nevertheless, self-actualiza-

107

tion cannot be identified with salvation. Participation in maximizing others' unawakened potential is an act of salvific self-actualization. When we help others thrive in their lives, we experience our own "rich" moments of life. All these participatory efforts of healing others' wounds, understanding their perspectives, and actualizing their potentialities turn into the moments of kairos only when we implement these out of care for people. If we perform these in order to be saved, we will lose our salvation. This type of teleological intention produces superficial participation in others' han, healing, and the actualization of others' potential, for those with such intentions cannot be fully present in others' healing. Salvation is thus a full participatory dialectical relationship with other's in-depth experience of pain and healing.

Nor can salvation occur in the deontological performance of moral imperatives. For Kant, *oughtness*, moral duty, or that which he called "categorical imperatives" should lead our life.[28] According to him, carrying out "categorical imperatives" is the fulfillment of the purpose of human existence. Following the dictation of the categorical imperatives, however, will not bring us to salvation, but only to rigidity of life. His deontological concept of salvation takes place solely within the inward experience of persons. Salvation should not be characterized by what we ought to do, but how much we care about the welfare of others. For Kant, what we ought to do is universal.[29] But from my perspective, this idea is not grounded in reality. The categorical imperatives of people vary according to their upbringing, culture, tradition, and religious values. Consequently, "what I ought to do" may be performed with no regard for others' conditions and needs.

A participatory dialectic mode of salvation can avoid this difficulty by bridging the gaps between the moral categories of various individuals and communities through dialogical understanding. In the fulfillment of moral obligation, one's moral satisfaction may arise but salvation does not yet occur. Salvation begins not with connectedness alone, but with a *compassionate* connectedness. In true salvation, "what we ought to do" changes into "what we love to do." This change emerges from understanding—a deep participation in others' pain. Relationships derived solely from moral obligation can be exhausting; but relationships which arise from the genuine heart of care are a true blessing for the people involved. All the relationships we develop without genuine love are stressful and extinguishable. Teleo-deontological relationships may yield the moral satisfaction of fulfillment, but not salvation. Relationships which result from pure compassion in God's love bring forth salvation. All the work for dissolving others' han on the grounds of the deontological injunction of moral obligation will be laborious and tiresome.

Salvation has been conceived as freedom from death and error (the Eastern church), guilt (the Roman Catholic Church), and law (the Protestant church). All these views emerged from sinners' perspectives. Han-thinking proposes salvation as "freedom from sin and han" and "freedom to eternal life" in the dialectic relation between sinners and their victims. This mode of salvation is a participatory dialectic in eternal life. The eternal life I am speaking of is not for possessing, but for dialogical, dynamic, and compassionate living.

# The Wounded Heart of God

Can God suffer? The church has long debated whether God can suffer like a human being. The passibility of God was condemned as heresy in the orthodox tradition of the church. In the early third century, patripassianists such as Praxeas, Sabellius, and Noetus advocated the birth, suffering, and death of God in the person of Jesus Christ. Their intention was to stress the unity between God and Christ. Against this idea, orthodox theologians emphasized the trinitarian distinction of God and Christ. Tertullian, in his *Against Praxeas*, refuted the idea of patripassianism by asserting that God the Father cannot suffer with the Son on the cross. This denial of God's suffering was due to the influence of Stoicism, whose highest virtue was to achieve the state of *apatheia*, being above passion or emotion. Tertullian was influenced by Stoicism. Clement and Origen, the Alexandrian Fathers, supported the idea of divine impassibility through the method of the *via negativa*, and Augustine and most scholastic theologians followed suit.[1]

There have been, however, many theologians who have held to the idea of God's passibility, even though they have denied patripassianism. Among them, I would single out Saint Anselm, Luther, Kitamori, and Moltmann as strong advocates of the concept that God can suffer. Their ideas concerning God's pain will be briefly discussed, and then I will present my understanding of God's "han." The notion of God's han implies a further dimension of God's reality, the issue of whether even God needs salvation.

I support the idea of God's passibility, although I too reject patripassianism. The focus of my argument will be the suffering of

God manifest on the cross of Jesus Christ, as well as in Jesus' whole life. The meaning of the cross must not be exclusively construed as God's suffering *for* humanity, but also as God's protest against the oppressor.

## ANSELM OF CANTERBURY

In his monumental work *Cur Deus Homo?* (Why Did God Become Human?), Anselm investigates the purpose of the incarnation, which he explained as follows: Sin is an offense against the honor of God. In spite of God's almightiness, mercy, and goodness, God could not pardon sin without compromising God's honor and justice. It was equally impossible for God to demand that humanity compensate for the offense of sin, for the degree of offense against an infinite God is itself necessarily infinite. Since sinful humanity could not compensate for its sin and make restoration to the infinite, offended honor of God, God should punish humanity with eternal condemnation. This would defeat God's own purpose, the happiness of creation. Anselm held that there was only one way to escape the dilemma without affecting God's honor: some kind of "satisfaction" must be made. Since the offense of humans was too great for any finite human being to redeem the sin of humanity, an infinite being who represents the human race to God was necessary. Thus, God became a human being in Jesus Christ; Christ suffered and died on humanity's behalf and made satisfaction to God by restoring God's injured honor.[2]

One of Anselm's outstanding notions of sin is that sin injures someone else. Beyond the violation of laws or regulations, it hurts somebody. By breaking God's law, we dishonor and injure God: "He who does not render this honor which is due to God, robs God, robs God of his own and dishonors him; and this is sin."[3] Anselm's "deprivation of required justice" as original sin involves dishonoring God. Sin is "nothing other than not to render to God what is due."[4] We owe to God undivided and full honor. Dishonoring God is sin.

Anselm, however, insisted on God's impassibility as well. Since God's *existence* is the same as God's *essence,* God cannot suffer injury. Suffering implies imperfection: "Nothing can be added to or taken from the honor of God. For this honor which belongs to him is in no way subject to injury or change."[5]

Although God's honor is perfect, immutable, incorruptible, and infrangible, and even though nothing can be added to or subtracted from God's honor, humans dishonor God; they disturb the order and the harmony of God's creation by refusing to subject their will to God's governance.[6] Human sin somehow injures God:

> Therefore man cannot and ought not by any means to receive from God what God designed to give him, unless he return to God everything which he took from him; so that, as by man God suffered loss, by man, also, He might recover His loss.[7]

Although Anselm affirmed the impassibility of God, he also acknowledged that God was dishonored and suffered by sin, for sin creates anguish and injury in God.[8] Anselm's Platonic presuppositions could not admit the suffering of God, while his biblical understanding of God allowed for the divine passibility on humanity's behalf. God is compassionate. To the sinner doomed to eternal torments, God uttered: "Take my only begotten Son and make him an offering for yourself"; or : "Take me, and ransom your souls."[9] The God who is impassible is compassionate toward the sinner! That is the gospel, the good news. Anselm's incarnate God is compassionate, and thus passible:

> How, then, art thou compassionate and not compassionate O Lord, unless because thou art compassionate in terms of our experience, and not compassionate in terms of thy being.
> Truly, thou art so in terms of our experience, but thou art not so in terms of thine own. For, when thou beholdest us in our wretchedness, we experience the effect of compassion, but thou dost not experience the feeling. Therefore, thou art both compassionate, because thou dost save the wretched, and spare those who sin against thee; and not compassionate, because thou art affected by no sympathy for wretchedness.[10]

Here lies the han of God, that the impassable and invulnerable God suffers for humanity! To Anselm, the ontological aspect of God is incapable of being passible for human wretchedness, but the soteriological aspect of God is capable of being passible for the wretched. Here we see the struggle between Anselm the philosopher and Anselm the theologian. The latter seems to win out when he asserts that at least within the boundary of our experience, God is passible.[11]

Anselm was the first prominent theologian to mention the reality of *the han of God*. Human sin had dishonored God, *which caused the wounded heart of God*. The dishonor requires satisfaction and the injury demands healing. Anselm finds the satisfaction of the divine dishonor in the atoning work of Jesus Christ. The injury Anselm describes is the deep anguish of God. In a sense, the cross of Jesus Christ is both the satisfaction for as well as the expression of the wounded heart of God. Anselm knew the reality of han caused by the pang of sin. The anguish incurred by sin either in God or humans must be resolved through restoring the victim's honor and satisfying the victim's dishonor. He also mentioned the necessity of the resolution of han at a human level: "For as one who imperils another's safety does not enough by merely restoring his safety, without making some compensation for the anguish incurred; so he who violates another's honor does not enough by merely rendering honor again, but must, according to the extent of the injury done, make restoration in some way satisfactory to the person whom he has dishonored."[12] He applied this principle of *resolving han* to the divine level. The idea of this *divine wound* is the key to Anselm's theology, particularly his soteriology. Anselm made a great contribution to theology by highlighting the divine injury, God's han, in relation to human sin. But unfortunately he claimed that God could be satisfied only through the work of Jesus Christ. He missed an important point: *through the repenting work of the sinners who have injured God,* God could be satisfied. He thus reduced the significance of human work in the drama of salvific history by focusing solely on the work of Christ.

## MARTIN LUTHER

After Anselm, Luther was the first major theologian to address the issue of the pain of God. In speaking of the wrath of God, Luther said that sin is the enemy of God, since God loves righteousness; every sin *insults* and *wounds* God, whose very existence is righteousness.[13] Toward sin, God responds with wrath. Using an Old Testament term, Luther presented God as the God of jealousy. God's nature, however, is nothing less than pure love; he is not a God of wrath but a God of grace.[14] He indicates that the wrath of God is not an expression of God's essence but the undeniable relational entity existing between God and sinners. For him, wrath is God's "alien work" against God's "proper work"; through a dialectical operation wrath prepares the proper work as in law and gospel.[15] The injury of God by human sin coincides with the idea of han. Wrath is not essential to God, but is rather an existential expression of God's han. Yet God's han is different from what Luther understands as the divine wrath, which sinners perceive as divine reality. God's han arises from divine love, not from divine wrath.

Luther treated the issue of God's injury (divine han) in his "theology of the cross." He employed the terms *theologia crucis* and *theologia gloriae* (theology of the cross and theology of glory) to describe the knowledge of God.[16] In the Heidelberg Disputation of 1518 he regarded *theologia crucis* as the essence of true theology and *theologia gloriae* as its opposite.[17] A *theologia gloriae* characterizes the knowledge of God attained from the basic philosophical principle of scholastic theology, while *theologia crucis* refers to the knowledge of God derived from the crucified Christ. The theology of the cross delineates *Deus crucifixus* (the crucified God) and *Deus absconditus* (the hidden God). In the biblical references Romans 1:20ff. (God's invisible nature in creation) and I Corinthians 1:21ff. (God's visible foolish side in the cross), the theology of glory and theology of the cross can be seen respectively. Romans 1:20 shows a human effort to grasp the invisible nature of God from the works of creation through reason. From this attempt, one can only know the *Deus gloriosus*, the glorious God, in such divine metaphysical attributes as omnipresence and omnipotence.[18] First Corinthians 1:21ff. shows God's wisdom and power in the cross of Jesus Christ.

The theology of glory perceives God from the divine works in creation, while the theology of the cross understands God from "divine sufferings." The former directly seeks God in divine power, wisdom, and glory; the latter paradoxically finds God in the divine weakness, foolishness, and suffering. The theology of glory makes humans stand before God on the foundation of their moral righteousness, whereas the theology of the cross destroys human self-righteousness and leads humans to pure receptivity.[19]

The theology of the cross is a main subject of Luther's thought. For him, the "wisdom of the cross" is the standard of all genuine theology.[20] The cross is the symbol of divine judgment over human beings which declares the culmination of all human efforts to have fellowship with God. It destroys both natural theology and self-righteous moral theology. The cross hides God, yet reveals the hidden God not in might, but in lowliness and helplessness.[21] God's power is God's helplessness, God's life is God's death.[22]

In his *Table-Talk* Luther rejected the argument that, because the Godhead can neither suffer nor die, in Christ only the human nature suffered. Against this he contended that not only the human nature but the divine nature had suffered and died for us.[23] Luther furthermore affirmed that "To be born, to suffer, to die, are characteristics of the human nature, of which characteristics the divine nature also becomes sharer in this Person."[24] For Luther, we cannot know God except through the cross.[25]

The knowledge of God is not theoretical knowledge but involves the entirety of human existence. It is impossible for us to view the cross as an objective reality in Christ without knowing ourselves as crucified with Christ. The cross signifies God's meeting us in the death of Jesus Christ only when we experience Jesus' death as our own.[26]

To Luther, the cross is the expression of the divine injury. To unbelievers, God appears to be wrathful and angry, but to believers, God reveals Godself in "weakness" and "suffering." The cross ends all speculation about the divine character, including the wrathfulness of God. It enables people to know God in experience. The cross, the expression of the divine han, cannot be understood in the absence of the human experience of han. Only the victims of sin would know the hiddenness of God in the cross, which is the divine pain caused by human sin and the divine participation in human suffering.

Nevertheless, there is a problem in Luther's approach to divine knowledge. He overemphasized the cross of Jesus Christ as the only way to the knowledge of God. In reality, not only through Christ's death, but also through Christ's life do we come to know God. Even in the event of the incarnation, we find the *agony* and *wound* of God. The divine helplessness is shown throughout the life of Jesus Christ. It is impossible to separate Jesus' life from his cross. They are interpenetrated in suffering. Our knowledge of God must derive from a balance between the life and the cross of Jesus Christ.

Jesus' life—his birth and ministry—reveals parts of the divine "helplessness" and "suffering." Even before the event of the cross, Jesus daily bore his cross and suffered in life. When he said, "If any man would come after me, let him deny himself and take up his cross and follow me" (Mk. 8:34), he indicated that he lived the life of bearing his cross. Jesus' life was a cross-bearing, a han-ridden one.

## KAZOH KITAMORI

Kitamori, a Japanese pastor and theologian, is a Lutheran thinker who conspicuously spoke about the suffering of God in his *Theology of the Pain of God.* In 1946, after the painful defeat of Japan in World War II, he articulated the essence of God as pain.[27] People related the motif of the book with the defeat. To a certain extent, he wrote this book in response to the tragedy of the war—a fact which he mentioned in his preface to the third edition.[28] Kitamori, however, asserts that the theme of the pain of God is the "heart of the gospel."[29] Using Luther's concept of the wrath and love of God, "God fighting with God" at Golgotha, Kitamori united God's wrath and love within a "tertiary"—the pain of God.[30]

To him, the essence of God is the divine pain and is revealed at the cross: *The essence of God can be comprehended only from the 'word of the cross'.*[31] For him, the essence of God means the heart of God, which is pain.

Kitamori found the term "pain of God" in Jeremiah 31:20 ("My heart is pained") in a Japanese translation. The Hebrew verb *hamah* means anguishing, moaning, groaning in the painful condition of the human heart. He extends this state of heart to God.[32]

Kitamori was critical of Western Christianity's preservation of the idea of divine impassibility influenced by Greek philosophy. One of his theological tasks was to "win over the theology which advocates a God who has no pain."[33] His task was twofold: to advocate the all-embracing nature of God and to include the pain of God in the all-embracing divine nature. The all-embracing God is "'God embracing completely those who should not be embraced'—that is, 'God in pain'!"[34] Through God's pain God resolves human pain and through God's own pain Jesus Christ heals human wounds.[35] How does God heal human pain? Kitamori believes that God heals us through our own service of God's pain. To him, "Take up your cross and follow me" means "Serve the pain of God through your own pain."[36] By serving God through our pain, our pain is healed in sharing divine salvation.[37]

Kitamori, however, held that pain as God's essence cannot be interpreted as substance. It is a mode of understanding God in relationship. In the preface to the fifth edition (1958), he says: "The theology of the pain of God does not mean that pain exists in God as *substance*. The pain of God is not a 'concept of substance'—it is a 'concept of relation', a nature of 'God's love'."[38] In suggesting this relational model, he rejects the accusation of patripassianism by accusing his detractors in turn of asserting a non-relational model of God. Furthermore, pain as "the essence of God" should be comprehended in historical contexts: "I myself do not find the necessity of using the 'pain of God' as a theological term any longer, since this term has served its purpose adequately in stressing the mediatory and intercessory love of God over against the immediate love of God."[39] When we understand the pain of God which leads to the love of God, the term "pain of God" is not indispensable in our theologizing.

Kitamori's pain of God speaks to the issue of the han of God. Without understanding the pain of God, we would not understand the cross of Jesus Christ. Without understanding the cross of Jesus Christ, we would not understand the heart of God. Surely human sin hurts God and God's pain is understood in the event of the cross.

Nevertheless, unlike the term "pain of God," "God's han" will not have any moment in history when its existence will abolish itself. As long as people commit sin, the idea of the han of God will be used to describe the injury done to God by human sin. Kitamori was ambiguous when he said that the use of the term "pain of God" was no longer necessary. I wonder whether this means that he need not use this term in his understanding of God, or God's "pain" is no longer "essential" in relation with God's creation.

The han of God is not God's *essence*, but God's *existence*. God's han is produced by the tension between God's essence in divine nature and God's existence in the world. It is fully revealed in the incarnation and crucifixion.

## JÜRGEN MOLTMANN

Moltmann attained his eminent theological reputation with the publication of *Theology of Hope* in 1964. This volume concerns the meaning and hope of history found in Christian eschatology. Moltmann's book began with the *resurrection* of Christ. Some accused him of being one-sided with Christ's resurrection, regarding it as a kind of medieval theology of glory, neglecting the aspect of Luther's theology of the cross. The publication of *The Crucified God* in 1972 balanced the one-sidedness of his previous work by stressing the *crucifixion of Jesus Christ* in conformity with the *theologia crucis*.

For Moltmann the cross of Jesus Christ is the center of all Christian theology, for all theological themes have their focus in the crucified God.[40] It reveals who God really is and who Jesus is. At the cross, "Jesus died abandoned by God."[41] The cross exposes God's self-abandonment and self-identity.

Moltmann bases his theology on the cross and the resurrection of Jesus Christ. The event of the crucifixion, particularly Jesus' loud cry, is the center of his theology and life: "Jesus died crying out to God, 'My God, why hast thou forsaken me?' All Christian theology and all Christian life is basically an answer to the question which Jesus asked as he died."[42] In the godforsakenness of Jesus, we see God crying out against God, the true identity of God. Moltmann understands the death of Jesus on the cross as God's active suffering. That is, "God not only acted in the crucifixion of Jesus or sorrowfully allowed it to happen, but was himself active with his own being in the dying Jesus and suffered with him."[43] Moltmann's concept of God allows Godself to be crucified in Jesus. God takes upon Godself the judgment for human sin and shares humanity's destiny.[44] Along with other theologians he criticizes the traditional insistence on the impassibility of God and defends the idea of God's suffering. To some his approach seems to be a kind of patripassianism or Sabellianism.[45] He does not, however, equate Jesus' suffering with God's. Jesus' death was not God's death as believed in patripassianism: "Jesus' death cannot be understood 'as the death of God', but only as death *in* God."[46] By positing that Jesus suffers dying and God suffers Jesus' death, Moltmann circumvents patripassianism.[47] The reason God suffers is due to God's love for the Son. "God's being is in suffering and the suffering is in God's being itself because God is love." God is not compassionless power, but "is known as the human God in the crucified Son of Man."[48] God is affected by the human situation.

Following Luther's theology of the cross, Moltmann avoids using the epistemology of natural theology.[49] He advocates the true knowledge of God only through Christ the crucified, while not rejecting the possibility of the indirect knowledge of God manifest in the world: "Christ the crucified alone is 'man's true theology and knowledge of God'. This presupposes that while indirect knowledge of God is possible through his works, God's being can be seen and known directly only in the cross of Christ; knowledge of God is therefore real and saving."[50] Moltmann contends that we cannot reach the true knowledge of the Trinity, the heart of the reality of God, through the indirect knowledge of God in God's works. Christ is the true way to the reality of the Trinity: "The place of the doctrine of the Trinity is not the 'thinking of thought', but the cross of Jesus."[51]

But a question arises: how do we know God through the event of the cross? Both Luther and Moltmann hold that we first understand the event of the crucifixion by our participation in Christ's death, which provides us the knowledge of the suffering of God. How, then, do we participate in Christ's death and suffering? While it is clear that we cannot experience Christ's suffering directly, we can have an indirect experience of Jesus' suffering by taking part in the suffering of the downtrodden. The direct knowledge of God through the Cross which is so important to Moltmann is impossible, unless he presumes it to be found in mystical experience.[52] Without knowing the suffering of people in the world, we cannot understand the cross of Jesus Christ nor the reality of God nor the knowledge of the Trinity. We will find Christ's crucifixion *in the world* through the oppressed. If we fail to encounter the crucified God in the hungry, the naked, the oppressed, and the imprisoned, we will never meet God crucified. Thus, Moltmann's insistence on the vertical knowledge of the cross of Jesus Christ needs to be modified in light of the horizontal revelation of God in the history of the suffering world. God's direct revelation through the cross must be understood in terms of our indirect experience of the divine revelation through the crucified of the present world.

Furthermore, Moltmann's understanding of the cross as the divine passion for sinners needs to be seen from the other side. For him, " . . . what happened on the cross must be understood as an event between God and the Son of God . . . He is acting in himself in this manner of suffering and dying in order to open up in himself life and freedom for sinners."[53] Moltmann overlooks the other side of the cross: the side that epitomizes han, the agony of the victims of sinners. The cross should not be seen as freedom for the oppressors only, but as the oppressed's decisive defiance of sin and evil. The cross means not only that God passes judgment on the sin of people upon Godself,[54] but also that God passes judgment upon the oppressors.

# THE WOUNDED GOD

Divine impassibility is problematic. Influenced mostly by Stoicism, patristic and medieval theologians asserted that God is perfect and thus cannot change, for any change for the perfect God means a move to an inferior position.[55] This conclusion is solely the outcome of their own speculation on the reality of God. It does not say anything about the reality of God revealed in the Christ-event. They produced their own image of perfection by saying that the perfect God suffers nothing. But how do we know what the perfection of God is? Is it not true that whatever God does is perfect (William Occam)? We know that what God did on the cross was perfect, provided that Christ is the ultimate manifestation of God. Thus, we can say that the perfect God can suffer.

## Human Sin and Divine Han

Sin hurts God and one's fellow human beings. Every sin which is committed against others wounds God, for God created and has loved those against whom we have sinned. As Anselm asserted, God is not passible, yet God suffers with human beings. God suffers not because sin is all powerful, but because God's love for humanity is too ardent to be apathetic toward suffering humanity. No power in the universe can make God vulnerable, but a victim's suffering breaks the heart of God. For Moltmann, God's suffering in Christ on the cross is due to God's love for the Son. To me, God suffers for the Son on the cross not only out of God's love for the Son, but also God's love for humanity. God's love for humans suffers on the cross. The cross represents God's full participation in the suffering of victims. That is, Jesus's death was the example of an innocent victim's suffering in which God was *fully* present. Yet every victim's suffering also involves God's presence.

As Luther stated, God meets us in suffering and death. The cross is the meeting place between God and us. Another way to say this is that han is the point of encounter between God and humanity. The cross is the place where God experiences human suffering and the place where humans understand God's agony. Sin forced Jesus Christ to be crucified on the cross. Sin forces people to suffer the anguish of han. The divine agony which brought forth the Incarnation can be identified with han. The Incarnation was an expression of the divine han, which was fully manifested at the crucifixion-event.

### Does God Need Salvation?

God's han, the wounded heart of God, is exposed on the cross. Here an important issue is not whether God is passible, but what is the meaning of Jesus Christ's suffering on the cross. The cross of Jesus Christ can be interpreted from a human perspective and a divine perspective. It is not only the symbol of God's intention to save humanity (human perspective), but also the symbol of God's need for salvation (divine perspective).

The cross of Jesus is a symbol of God's crying for salvation (*Eli, Eli, lama sabach-thani?*),[56] because God cannot save Godself. If salvation is relational, then one cannot save oneself. *God needs salvation!* This sounds ridiculous and blasphemous. But if we understand salvation from a holistic perspective, God yearns for salvation because God relates to human beings.

This idea is biblical. The divine han can be seen in the Old Testament, where, in contrast to Aristotle's notion of a god who is metaphysically immutable, the God of Israel suffers sorrow and affliction. God is "grieved at his heart" because God has created a race that has morally corrupted itself (Gen. 6:6); the soul of the Lord is described to be "grieved for the misery of Israel" (Jud. 10:16).[57] The most poignant image of God in the Old Testament appears in Deutero-Isaiah, where the prophet portrays God as a woman in labor: "For a long time I have held my peace, I have kept still and restrained myself; now I will cry out like a woman in travail, I will gasp and pant" (Is. 42:14). This image of God as a woman in travail strongly depicts God in tremendous pain, groaning, gasping, and panting. In the midst of the turmoil of ancient empires, God suffers the plight and darkness of Israel. Israel's suffering was not the true will of God. While Israel suffered under the exceedingly heavy yoke of the Babylonians, God restrained Godself (Is. 47:6). But the time of the restrained silence is over and God cries out like a woman in birth pangs. God as "a woman in travail," the boldest figure employed by any prophet, conveys a sense of the deep intensity of God's suffering.[58] This is the clear biblical image of God who suffers with humanity and craves for salvation.

Another prominent image of God in the Old Testament is God as husband. Hosea compared God to a loving husband, while he compared Israel to an unfaithful wife. In the book which bears his name Hosea's wife has deserted him. Hosea realizes that if he forgives and loves his deserting, unfaithful wife, God is even more loving and forgiving of God's people. Like Hosea, Jeremiah employs the analogy of the marriage relationship between God and Israel: "Surely, as a faithless wife leaves her husband, so have you been faithless to me, O house of Israel, says the Lord" (Jer. 3:20). God agonizes and grieves over her unfaithfulness and wantonness. As the betrayal of a woman pierces the heart of her lover, so suffers God the betrayal and disloyalty of Israel.

The prominent Jewish philosopher Abraham Heschel has argued that in the prophets God reacts with pain and sorrow to the Hebrews' breaking of the covenant, and that the prevalence of anthropomorphic descriptions of God in the prophetic writings are central to the entire biblical message.[59] God does not impassively judge the deeds of humans in an attitude of cool detachment. God's judgment is imbued with a feeling of intimate and loving concern. God's love or anger, God's mercy or disappointment is an expression of the profound divine participation in the history of Israel and all the nations. Heschel believes that this is the essential message of the biblical prophets.[60]

As life is a partnership between God and humanity,[61] so is salvation. Creation is God's covenant with humans and indicates the divine commitment to the well-being of humanity. Until humanity is made whole, God will be restless. God cannot be detached from the griefs and suffering of humanity. The Old Testament, especially the prophets, bespeaks the indivisible covenantal relationship between God and Israel: "In all their affliction he was afflicted" (Is. 63:9). When the people of God rejoice, God rejoices too. The destiny of God involves the destiny of humanity. The salvation of humanity is interpenetrated with the salvation of God.

In the New Testament, the picture of the prodigal son's father who waits for his lost son day and night depicts the divine han (Lk. 15:11-32). In the parable, the father's heart is broken on account of his younger son and yearns for his return. The father's heart is crucified by his son's departure. In this image of the waiting father, we can see the passive dimension of the divine han, while in most of the prophets' image of God, we find its active aspect. The crucified heart of God is the divine han revealed through the Christ-event and history. In this parable, we see Jesus' image of a God who desires the repentance of sinful humanity. Until the prodigal returns, God is restless. This biblical God is never a God of aseity[62] or self-complacence. The parenthood of God suggests that God is not well when God's children are not well. Until the last prodigal returns home, God's mind and body are nailed to the cross.

Our speculative image of an almighty, impassible God has been shattered by the Incarnation and crucifixion.[63] The all-powerful God was crucified. The cross is the symbol of God's han which makes known God's own vulnerability to human sin. The cross and the parable of the Prodigal indicate that God desires full human participation in divine salvific history. On the cross, God demands the healing of the wounded heart which has been inflicted by sinful human beings. The healing involves the repentance of sinful people. The cry of the wounded heart of God on the cross reverberates throughout the whole of history. God shamefully exposes the vulnerability of God on the cross, demanding the healing of the han of God.

The cross is God's unshakable love for God's own creation. Like parents who give birth to and then love their children, God is wrapped up in a creational love with humanity. The divine love of creation is much more profound than the parental love of childbearing. God's *agape* toward both the han-ridden and sinners will not be fulfilled without their healing and return. In other words, God cannot save Godself apart from the salvation of humanity. God needs human beings if God's salvific history initiated with creation is to be fulfilled. God's creation was the divine declaration of God's relationship with humans. God's participation in history connotes that God is in a vulnerable relationship with humans. The ultimate symbol of God's need for salvation is manifest in the Incarnation and the cross of Jesus Christ.

## The Cross as the Symbol of God's Protest

The cross is not only the expression of God's love for humanity, but also the protest and wrath of God against oppressors. Jesus' suffering epitomizes God's love made available to sinful people and God's historical determination to save them. The crucifixion-event shows God's full participation in the suffering history of the oppressed—which is not a superficial involvement but a true incarnation in the innermost part of human agony. The divine involvement in human suffering is the beginning of the healing of the oppressed. Hope may flow from the future eschatological event of the general resurrection (Pannenberg) or from the Promissory Word of God (Moltmann). But from the perspective of han, the actuality of divine participation in human suffering is the fountainhead of human hope in history.

The cross is the center of God's han erupted in the middle of history, telling the oppressors "Enough is enough." Unlike Peter Abelard's "moral influence theory," which presents the cross as persuading and luring sinners into voluntary repentance, a han ✓perspective perceives the cross as God's strongest protest against oppressors. To Jesus Christ, calling the Pharisees "children of vipers" was a harsh challenge to them. In like manner the cross is the ultimate challenge to oppressors to make their choice between repentance and eternal death (Jn. 3:18-20).

In brief, the cross of Jesus Christ commands oppressors to repent of the sins which have caused God's han and the han of others. It is the ultimate divine negation of human evil. When the cross of Jesus Christ is seen from the perspective of the oppressed, it signifies God's suffering *with them*; seen from the perspective of oppressors, the cross means God's suffering *because of them*.

## God's Han in Jesus' Life

It is not right to limit the crucifixion of Jesus Christ to the three hours of suffering on the cross. The crucifixion of Jesus must be understood as extending to his whole life. Jesus lived the life of taking up his cross everyday. It was not only Jesus' suffering that caused God's han; all human beings' pain is engraved in God's suffering.

Even a sparrow's falling is remembered by God. Whitehead attributed God's unforgettable memory of all sufferings to the consequent nature of God.[64]

Not only did the cross express the han of God; so also did the thirty-three years of Jesus' living.[65] We have concentrated on the cross of Christ as God's suffering. But we have neglected the suffering aspect of Jesus' life. Jesus' birth bespeaks of the han of God for the children of the poor. According to the birth story, there was no room at the inn and Mary delivered the baby in a manger (Lk. 2:7).[66] Even in the present world, there is no room in hospitals for the babies of the poor. The han of God persists in the fact that there is no room available in the world for thousands of babies whom God has created. Every minute thirty children die for want of food and inexpensive vaccines around the world.[67] Every day more than 25,000 persons, most of them children, die for lack of clean drinking water.[68] Every baby's death causes the implosion of God's han. The act against God's creation of new lives crucifies the heart of God.

Jesus was born poor, worked as a carpenter (Mk. 6:3),[69] and journeyed as a preacher. He taught the crowd, healed the sick, and protested the injustice of religious leaders. As a man of sorrows, he underwent grief, crying with the bereaved. He was a friend of the friendless, the untouchably unclean, and the despised. He was mocked as a drunkard, was measured by his association with friends of low status, was called a Samaritan, was accused of being a lunatic possessed by the Devil (Jn. 8:48), and was excommunicated by his religion (Jn. 9:22). He was acquainted with the deep han of human beings.

Furthermore, Jesus, the Lord of freedom, had to live under the √ law of Moses. The human regulations and traditions almost suffocated him and obstructed his work. Jesus' suffering for three hours on the cross was one thing; his many years' suffering with smothering religious stipulations was another. The latter was a profound source of Jesus' han. Compared with at least three years' suffering from humiliation, mockery, false accusation, religious inquisition, the three hours' suffering was rather light. The church has overemphasized Jesus' suffering on the cross, for Jesus' crucifixion signifies God's redemptive power. But Jesus' teaching, preaching, healing, and serving were redemptive as well. The unbalanced stress on the suffering of Jesus on the cross is one of the reasons why the church has encouraged "worshiping Jesus" over "following Jesus." We need to maintain a balance in the way we value these two types of Jesus' suffering.

## The Knowledge of God

A crucial issue in this theological discussion is the knowledge of God. My premise is that we come to know the reality of God only in the midst of experiencing han in the world. Hearing this, one might well ask: "Is it necessary to experience han to know God?" While I do not believe that one should intentionally seek the experience of han in order to know God, in our participation in the han-ridden life of the oppressed, we come to know God with the crucified Christ and the downtrodden. All our speculative knowledge of God crumbles down before the deep human agony of han in the life of Jesus and the downtrodden. Han is the point of contact between Jesus Christ and suffering humanity and between Jesus Christ and God. Christ represents the han of the downtrodden to God and the han of God to the downtrodden. Christ is the expression of the divine han and the epitome of the han of the oppressed.

The wounded heart of God can be glimpsed when the impassible God suffers for the pain of humanity (Anselm). The wounded heart of God is shown when God embraces those who cannot be embraced (Kitamori). We can meet the wounded God at the cross through participating in Christ's death (Luther, Moltmann). In the life of Jesus, God exposes God's wound which requires salvation. The divine wounded healer makes God's own wounds available as the source of healing.[70] This wound of God is the true strength of salvation in history.

The traditional knowledge of God's attributes such as "omnipotence," "omnipresence," and "omniscience" needs to be reevaluated in light of the han-ful life of Jesus Christ. These attributes are quite meaningless to us, unless they speak to our lives. They are abstract, for we are not in the position of judging the actuality of omnipotence, omnipresence, and omniscience. They are beyond our comprehension and experience.

Christ sheds new light on the attributes of God through his actual divine life (theo-praxis). Jesus Christ has taught us that God is crucified everywhere we are oppressed (omnipresence); God knows our deepest sorrow (omniscience); God's vulnerable love shown on the cross and in the death of Jesus is more powerful or persuasive than anything known to us (omnipotence). Christ's teaching and life have revealed to us the wounded heart of God, which feels with the han of the oppressed and suffers the sin of the oppressors. This wounded God in Jesus Christ is truly powerful, wise, and salvific. This wounded

God shapes and reshapes the course of history in the form of the hungry, the imprisoned, the naked—the *han-ridden*.

The salvation of the wounded God and of the oppressed and of the oppressors is the crux of the knowledge of God. To know God is to have an intimate relationship with God. In the past God has been the object of knowledge. But God does not exist apart from our living. Knowledge is not for just contemplating (Aristotle), nor understanding (Hegel), but for living (Kierkegaard). Only by living in God do we come to know God. For Christians, God is not an abstraction, but the God of han in history, Jesus Christ. By participating in the life of Jesus Christ and his historical mission, people come to know the true meaning of life; in such true knowledge of life, the oppressed dissolve their han and the oppressors eliminate their sin; human participation in actualizing the purpose of the Creation and Incarnation accomplishes the healing of God's wounded heart.

# Han: The Point of Interreligious Dialogue

Sin is a uniquely Christian concept which has been a major way of understanding the troubles of the world in Christian, Jewish, and Islamic traditions. One does not find such a notion of sin in Eastern religions such as Buddhism, Hinduism, Confucianism, Taoism, and shamanism.

But the notion of han can be found in every major religion, even though it is implicit and expressed in modified forms. Han, the pain of victims, can be a focal point of interreligious dialogue for all major world religions. In what follows I will suggest that han can thus become a significant point of contact for interreligious dialogue.

## THE PRESENT TREND
## OF INTERRELIGIOUS DIALOGUE

There are basically five views of interreligious dialogue in Christian theology.[1] The first is an *exclusivist* view. This holds that only Christianity possesses the truth. Karl Barth represents this view. There is no true revelation of God in history, but only in Jesus Christ. To him, all religions are the expressions of unbelief. They are human efforts to reach God. Even Christianity as an institutional religion is a form of unbelief. Under the true revelation of God through Jesus Christ, all these religions, including Christianity, are subject to judgment.

The second is an *inclusivist* view. It contends that all human beings can find salvation in Jesus Christ and that Christ is at work everywhere. Thus, salvation takes place all the time and everywhere. This approach accepts the event of salvation in other religions, but interprets it in light of the norm of Christ. Karl Rahner represents this view. He believes that there are "Christians without a name" in other religious traditions. Christ is the gate through which all enter into salvation. Thus, salvation can be found within other religions, based on the saving grace of Christ.

The third is a *pluralist* view. It abandons the claim that Christ is the norm of salvation and that Christianity is superior to all other religions. John Hick is an exponent of this position. He holds that the Christian term *God* refers to the "ultimate Reality" to which other great religions (Judaism, Islam, Hinduism, Sikhism, Taoism, and Buddhism) also point and respond.[2] Calling this "Ultimate" by different names such as "Allah," "Yahweh," "Nothingness," "Brahman," or "God," these religions conceive of the ultimate either in a personal or a nonpersonal way. The real importance in expressing the "Ultimate" is not a matter of the superiority of one religion over others, but a matter of "the transformation from self-centeredness to Reality-centeredness."[3] To Hick, the superiority between these religions can be measured by "examination of the facts."[4] There are two ways to measure the fruits of each religion: individual and social transformation. At the individual level, we can do it by examining how much "sainthood" each tradition has fostered; at the social level, we can gauge it by examining the work of a religion in the promotion of the welfare of humanity. He says that even though it seems impossible to make any quantitative value judgments upon these matters, no religion can be singled out as manifestly superior in its output for sainthood and social transformation.[5] They are just about equal in their achievement. In this model, conversion from one to another religion is inappropriate. Only converting nonbelievers to any religion will be relevant.

The fourth is a *transformationist* view. This approach affirms the continual transformation of religions through self-critical reflection and interaction with other traditions. John Cobb, Jr., has defined this view in such a way as to avoid the errors of what he calls an essentialist view or a conceptional relativist view. The essentialist view assumes that "there is an essence of religion," and that this universal essence of religion undergirds all religions.[6] Conceptual relativism upholds a pluralism of norms so that "each tradition is best by its own norm and there is no normative critique of norms."[7]

Cobb starts from the premise that each religion is unique. Thus, he advocates the uniqueness of Christianity and rejects the position of the pluralist view in order to affirm "a much more fundamental pluralism."[8] While the pluralists perceive all major religions embodying the same ultimate reality, Cobb views each of them as unique and different from one another. Consequently his position is a form of Christocentrism from which he moves out to dialogue with other traditions; without one's own position, a dialogue with others is impossible. But the Christocentrism he advocates does not espouse Christian superiority or its normative value toward other religions. For him, Christ is a radical openness which does not exclude other religious traditions. Christianity can enrich itself through incorporating truth from other religions as Augustine did from neoplatonism. Through interreligious dialogue, he intends to elicit mutual transformation.

The fifth is a *liberationist* view. This view is not mainly concerned with the recognition of the universal reality of religions nor with the historical relativity of religions, but the removal of human sufferings and problems through interreligious dialogue. Rosemary Ruether and Marjorie Suchocki represent this approach from a feminist perspective; other proponents include Aloysius Pieris and Paul Knitter. Ruether and Suchocki dispute the superiority of Christianity to other religions on the basis of the irrelevancy of religious chauvinism. For them, as male chauvinism in Christianity is absurd, so is religious chauvinism in an interreligious context. Ruether stresses the need for cooperation among feminists of different religions for bringing justice. Suchocki urges that interreligious dialogue shift its focus to the concreteness of human suffering, human welfare, and justice. Being keenly aware of the diverse values of justice in various traditions, she opts for using the phrase, "openness to self-development and self-determination within the context of community."[9] Carefully examining both christology and buddhology, Pieris concludes that they are meant to work in cooperation and complement each other in the struggle against human misery and poverty. Knitter holds that worldwide human suffering calls for a worldwide interreligious dialogue for worldwide liberation from social, economic, and militaristic evils. All these, as well as other liberationists, advocate liberative praxis and a "preferential option" for the poor and the needy through interreligious dialogue.

## HAN AT THE CROSSROADS OF RELIGIONS

Since the reality of han is shared by all major religions, I would like to make two comments regarding the usefulness of the concept of han in interreligious dialogue. First, current interreligious dialogue must change its focus from a discussion of the answers which each religion offers to the logically prior issue of the world's concrete problems. This means a shift from debating the particular or universal truth of religions to treating the problems of particular cultures or religions (particular han). In the absence of the concrete problems each religion faces, our interreligious dialogue tends to move toward speculating abstract truths or comparing dogmatic differences. Concerning the contact point of interreligious dialogue, Panikkar says, "If fundamental theology is to have any relevance in our time of worldwide communication, it has to address itself to a radical cross-cultural problematic."[10]

Han as the suffering of victims can be a cross-religious problem. Most religions strive to deal with the reality of han. In Christianity, Christ came into the world to bear the griefs and the sorrows of humanity (Mt. 8:17, I Pet. 2:21-24) and to take away the sin of the world (Jn. 1:29). Hinduism holds that the chief goal of human beings is their emancipation from the bondage of finitude and mortality. This goal, called *moksha* (emancipation), points to a state of blessedness beyond all the misery and limitations of the human world. Buddhism emerged to defy *dukkha* (suffering) and to attain *nirvana* or *satori*. Buddhism has uniquely focused on the issue of han.

Judaism has struggled to find the meaning of its faith since the Nazi holocaust took place. The inexplicable suffering of the innocent has been a focal point of its religious inquiry. Islam has emphasized social equality and justice. Islam's genuine commitment to racial equality has gained it adherents in many regions of Africa, particularly since Christianity was viewed as a disguise for white racism.[11] Shamanism is a religion that arose to treat the han of the common people. Shamanism in a narrow sense prevails in the region from the Bering Strait to Siberia, but its reality as a primitive religious phenomenon has existed in wider regions—central, north, and southeast Asia, Polynesia, North and South America.[12] It has been with humanity for many thousands of years. The term *han* was derived from Korean shamanism and its resolution is the chief purpose of the existence of shamanism in Korea.

The actuality of han stands at the crossroads of the real concerns of various religions. All religions should be united in their efforts to overcome the suffering of humanity. Each can pursue its own social responsibility for the alleviation of the world's suffering. But when they organize together in cooperation for a global plan of opposing dehumanization and the destruction of nature, the thickness of the power of evil will eventually be broken. However idealistic it may sound, cooperation between religions is required to bring forth the future of humanity. In some parts of the world, such collaboration between religions has been partially realized. In Korea, against the military dictatorship, some Christians and Buddhists worked together to elicit justice and democracy during the 1980s. It was called the *minjung* (downtrodden) movement. During the Japanese occupation, leaders of major religions—Buddhism, Chundokyo, Christianity—coordinated their efforts to bring forward the independence declaration of 1st March 1919. Faced with the han of the loss of their country's independence, these leaders transcended their religious differences and were united in their effort to resist the unjust Japanese occupation.

Second, interreligious dialogue needs to combine the dynamic dialectic of interreligious orthodoxy and interreligious orthopraxis. As the separation of orthodoxy and orthopraxis within a religion is unwholesome, so is the separation of these two aspects in interreligious dialogue and life. The present state of interreligious dialogue is unilateral, emphasizing the discussion of interreligious orthodox doctrines.

I believe that philosophical and doctrinal dialogue helps mutual understanding and enrichment. Nevertheless such a dialogue has its limit. As the result of such a dialogue, we may reach the conclusion of finding either the one ultimate reality of our religions or some fundamental divergences of religions lying beyond dialogue. If the outcome of a dialogue does not bear the fruit of cooperation for dispelling the power of evil in the world, all these efforts will turn out to be a childish play for seeing what new things others have. My point is not that interreligious dialogue must bear the practical fruit of cooperation at the end of long interlocution, for there is no guarantee that such theoretical dialogue on interreligious orthodoxy would culminate in cooperative interreligious orthopraxis. I would insist instead that a dialogue for interreligious orthodoxy and a cooperation for interreligious orthopraxis must concur to alleviate the suffering of creation. There is no reason to waste our time waiting until interreligious dialogue concludes to begin interreligious cooperation for the removal of the world's suffering.

While religions engage in dialogue at the doctrinal level, they also need to be engaged together in helping suffering humanity and disrupted nature. For example, in terms of our growing ecological crisis, we may literally not have enough time left for full discussion of our doctrinal differences, for we are crossing the second threshold in our environmental crisis, and invaluable human beings, other species, and nature itself are being destroyed irrevocably.[13] Humanity lives on time borrowed from future generations. Religions cannot enjoy the luxury of exclusively doctrinal dialogue for an indefinite time. *Now* is the time to cooperate for building up broken humanity and the world.

## MOTHER TERESA

I believe that the reality of han is a good starting point for practical interreligious dialogue whose goal is to analyze the reality of the world's suffering and engage in actual teamwork for the transformation of the reality of han into constructive energy to build up the world. Mother Teresa's life eloquently bespeaks the essence of interreligious dialogue. The following story was told by the late professor Asish Mondal at Bishop's College in Calcutta, who was familiar with the beginning of Mother Teresa's mission in that city.

> An Albanian nun from the Sisters of Loreto had a conversion toward the poorest of the poor while she traveled India by train. She had seen many human beings dying on the streets without human dignity. She (Mother Teresa) came to Calcutta to help the poorest of the poor, and established the Missionaries of Charity. She received permission from the city government to use an old *Kali* temple. In lieu of a nun's habit, she and her sympathizers wore *sari*, the principal outer garment of Hindu women, and helped the dying so as to die in human dignity. They washed the faces of the dying and were present at their deaths, so that they knew someone was caring for them.
>
> People of the community thought that she was doing the service to convert people to Christianity, in spite of the fact that she and her co-workers did not evangelize nor serve the poor in the name of Christ. One day some members of the community attacked the temple by hurling stones at the mission. Windows were broken and flying pieces of broken glass cut some workers' bodies. Yet they did not move but kept caring for the dying by wiping their faces and giving them drink.
>
> Since there was no response from inside, these attackers, consisting of Hindus, atheists, and communists, walked into the mission holding stones and clubs in their hands to find out what had hap-

pened. They were deeply moved by the unshaken will of Mother Teresa and her co-workers at the scene. The leader of the group dropped his clubs and said to Mother Teresa, 'I do not believe in the God you believe in, nor the Jesus you preach, nor the Christianity you brought in, but I believe in what you are doing'. Then he helped her and her sisters in cleaning up the mess. Other attackers followed suit. After this incident, they became Mother Teresa's ardent supporters.[14]

She has not endeavored to proselytize the local Hindus and has not preached Jesus Christ to people, but has simply lived out Christ's teaching by helping the helpless and dying. The healing of the han of the poorest of the poor has been the focus of her missionary work.

In the collaboration of transforming the han of the oppressed, the dispute over the supremacy of a particular religion disappears. The category of supremacy comes from the idea of competition, not from the toil of cooperation. The inquiry into the ultimate reality of religions will be resolved in compassionate, humble work for suffering people. The pivotal questions of doctrine in interreligious dialogue will be fully answered when religions engage in harmonious work for removing han in the world.

# CHAPTER 9

# The Resolution of Han

We have discussed the han of human beings and of God. The issue to which we turn in this final chapter is the resolution of this han. The han of human beings is not a Christian matter, but an interreligious, interracial, and intercultural matter. The divine han will be resolved when the han of the oppressed and the sin of the oppressors are resolved, for the wound of God has been inflicted through the affliction of the human family.

To disintegrate the han of the human race and the world,[1] the church needs to develop the way of the resolution of han as well as the forgiveness of sin. The Christian gospel can be good news, provided that it is not only for the absolution of the sin of sinners, but also for the resolution of the han of their victims. In the beginning, Christianity was largely a religion of the lower strata of Roman society—the down-and-out. But since the conversion of Constantine, √ Christianity has been the religion of sinners—the oppressors. This does not mean that the church has not had among its members the oppressed, but rather that it has been led by elite groups whose theology has dominated the church. Consequently, it has not been concerned about the han of the downtrodden, but about the forgiveness of the sins of King David. I do not object to the church's concern with the forgiveness of sin, but I do object to the fact that the church has not developed any doctrine for the resolution of han. My purpose here is not to delineate such a doctrine, but to suggest some steps which might be taken in resolving the han of the world.

To unravel han, we need to comprehend its nature. Han is frozen energy that can be unraveled either negatively or positively. If it

137

explodes negatively, the han-ridden person may seek revenge, sometimes killing oppressors. If han implodes negatively, the han-ful person can slip into a fatalism that might develop into mental disorders or suicide. If han is unraveled positively, it can be converted into the fuel for transforming the social injustice which causes han in the first place and for building up a new community.

How can we unravel han in a positive way? There are four steps: *awakening, understanding, envisagement,* and *enactment.* These are no more than limited guidelines for the positive disintegration of han.

## AWAKENING

The han-ridden need two kinds of awakening: one to the reality of their own han and the other to the causes of han. It is common that people do not acknowledge the pain of han in themselves; even if they are aware of it, they deny its pain until its severity will allow them to deny it no longer. Han quite often operates at an unconscious level, and as such is invisible and unrecognizable. People need to recognize their han, or the deep pain of suffering. At this point, the dissolution of han begins.

The next step for the han-ridden is to awaken to the matrixes which engender han in the world. They need to identify han-causing vortices at a personal level as well as at the collective level. The personal level of han is generally derived from family relations, personal traumas, and job-related issues. They are in general interconnected with the collective level of han. Various collective han-generating centers exist—e.g., militarism, political tyranny, economic exploitation, and social discriminations. As we have already seen, the capitalist global economy, patriarchy, and racial and cultural discrimination are the primary centers of collective han, from which many others emerge.

## UNDERSTANDING

Upon standing under others' perspective (the root meaning of the word *understand*), we are able to see the entirety of the other. When we thus stand under others, we appreciate them.

Pain that is shared is pain no more. The han that is understood is han no more. When we understand the han of the afflicted, the han

138

begins to melt away. Understanding has been perceived as a rational process of thinking only. It is, however, more than mere rational comprehension. Han cannot be fully understood in mere objectification. Understanding takes place when we participate in others' rational, emotional, and corporeal dimensions of life. I use the term *understanding* in a much broader meaning than is common. The understanding of han will penetrate the entirety of its reality, hence setting in motion its resolution.

Understanding is not the same as a transpositional perspective which denotes seeing things from the other's viewpoint. Understanding indicates standing under the other's perspective and seeing the world. Understanding connotes humility in interpersonal and intra- ✓ personal relationships. This humility is different from the humility to which feminists and liberationists object, the humility imposed upon the humiliated. To the oppressed, humility implies low self-respect, low self-esteem, and denial of the worth of the self. For instance, the Korean people, having been humiliated by their Japanese occupiers, had a hard time understanding the virtue of humility commanded by the Christian gospel.

The humbleness that I am proposing never denotes subjugation or abasement, but an act of emptying the self. To those who have been denied by others, the injunction to self-emptying sounds inhumane. That is why Valerie Saiving has said that women's sin is not pride or will-to-power but distractibility, the lack of an organized center, and diffuseness. Judith Plaskow backed up this claim by saying that "women's sin is precisely the failure to turn toward the self."[2] Feminist theologians strive to affirm the self rather than deny it.

My presupposition, based on the insights of Nicholas of Cusa and Luther, is that God resides in the deepest center of the self. Nicholas of Cusa said that the divine is the center and periphery of everything. For Luther, God is nearer to all creatures than they are to themselves.[3] The self-emptying, or *kenosis*, which lies at the heart of what I mean by humility, means negating the self negated by others. The more one empties one's own self, the more transparent the divine center of the self becomes. Without negating the negated self, it is impossible to know oneself or to build a true self. Any efforts to find self-identity devoid of self-negation end up in futility. In this sense, any efforts to find the true self by building a deformed center will be unfruitful, because one endeavors to build the true self on the basis of a distorted self which has been wrongly projected by repression and oppression. Even though women and minorities suffer from lack of pride and of organizing center, they need to empty their present selves to find their true selves. True self-emptying is true self-fullness. When we empty the denied self, we can begin to appreciate, enjoy, and love ourselves and others. In Mahayana Buddhism, self-emptiness enables us to join the universal self; in Christianity, self-emptiness, *kenosis,* enables us to be with God—not God the Almighty, but the crucified God. As we empty our denied self, we come to see the crucified God more clearly in the deepest center of our self. In the Crucified, we find the meaning of our existence and the true courage to overcome both our spirit of resignation and our hatred toward our oppressors. The Crucified is the ultimate symbol of human han and, at the same time, the human courage to rise above it.

To understand—and hence to resolve—han, we need to view it from three perspectives: rational, intuitive, and incarnational. Where there is true understanding of han, han begins to dissolve itself.

## Rational Understanding

When our rational faculty grasps the totality of han in connection with the reality of the world, han becomes resolvable. Our rational faculty functions to find the knots of han in entanglement. Let us assume that someone has deeply hurt us and we have developed han toward the person. How do we resolve the han? Only when we comprehend why the person acted in such a way will our antagonism and abhorrence toward that person begin to melt away. In the same manner, when we comprehend the reality of our han, we begin to see a way to resolution.

Such rational understanding is not simply an analytic ability to grasp the meaning of han, but a more synthetic capacity to comprehend the whole spectrum of han-producing situations.

Some philosophers' concepts of *understanding* will be helpful for our discussion. The notion of understanding has been regarded as an analytic or cognitive faculty only. Instead of treating it as such, I will maintain that understanding is a synthetic faculty in attaining knowledge.

For Kant, our knowledge derives from *understanding* and *sensibility,* two fundamental sources of the mind. *Understanding* is the power of the active mind to know an object. *Sensibility* is the capacity of passive receptivity of knowledge. Their cooperation is required of all attainment of knowledge: "If the *receptivity* of our mind, its power of receiving representations insofar as it is in any wise affected, is to be entitled sensibility, then the mind's power of producing representations from itself, the *spontaneity* of knowledge, should be called the understanding. . . . To neither of these powers may a preference be given over the other."[4] Rationalism emphasized the side of reason or understanding in gaining knowledge independent of experience, while empiricism stressed the reality of experience or sensibility independent of reason. In Kant, continental rationalism and British empiricism converge.

As the above indicates, Kant separates understanding, the faculty of spontaneity, from sensibility, the faculty of receptivity. In contrast to this, I would suggest that understanding is the faculty of integrating reason and experience. Reason alone or experience alone is insufficient to grasp the reality of the world. Kant provides no integrating entity for both reason, or understanding, and experience. I use the term *understanding* to unite these two faculties.

In Hegel's thought, understanding (*Verstand*), is separated from reason (*Vernunft*). "Understanding is the power of distinction but it cannot bind together again the concepts it has distinguished. . . . The power of synthesis, the combination of thesis and antithesis into a higher unity is speculation."[5] Reason is the power of synthesis via speculation. Understanding, the faculty of abstraction, grasps its objects through abstract ideas and sees its opposition and contradiction. Reason, the faculty of synthesis, overcomes contradictions and opposition by means of the dialectic movement, which "continually allows concepts which negate one another to arise and be united again."[6] To Hegel, understanding is incapable of integrating contradictions, but is capable only of distinguishing one from another. Yet I would insist that reason is not as capable as Hegel believes. It does not have the power to comprehend and integrate all things, for there are many matters which reason neither comprehends nor penetrates—such realities as God, the dynamic interaction of unconsciousness, and curved time and space. Tillich regards such all-embracing Hegelian reason as hubris.[7]

Understanding, which may not comprehend all the reality of the world and beyond, is able to integrate things around us through its rational, intuitive, and visual perspectives and through the acceptance of its own limits. Understanding is not as ultimate as reason in Hegel. It is an initial, inaugural avenue to true knowledge.

Rational understanding is our faculty to analyze and integrate things at the level of the intellect. With this, we can comprehend the entanglement of han in the world of absurdity, contradiction, and injustice. Han can be disentangled via rational understanding at an individual as well as a collective conscious level. At an individual conscious level, rational understanding functions to discern the reason why aggressors commit offenses. Rational understanding also discloses the interconnection of individual han with the root causes of han.

When the offended probe into the motives of offenders, they come to comprehend han-producing situations. For example, the han of a victim begins to move toward its healing and resolution when the victim begins to grasp why the offender has committed such an offense. However, if the case is child molestation, the offense needs to be understood at the collective level of patriarchy and hierarchy. When child molestation is seen within the larger picture of sociocultural structure, the han of child molestation will have a chance to be resolved. Without the pertinent rational grasp of the offender's deed, the hard feeling of the offended toward that person cannot begin to melt.

Sometimes the offended are not given a chance to comprehend their offenders' oppressive actions. In such an instance the offended need to confront their offenders without avoiding the pain of facing this reality. As the offended reason with their offenders in an attitude of understanding, the offended find some ways to unravel their han in the midst of such an honest challenge.

To resolve the han of victims to a fuller extent, collective rational understanding is necessary. The more people who are aware of and comprehend the reality of the victim's han, the lighter that han will be. Han can be more easily resolved when it is treated by collective efforts. Such public understanding of han would call for public cooperation in its resolution and would alleviate the burden of han.

Rational understanding also enables victims to perceive others' han through their own han. Their han can serve as the lens through which they view and come to understand the han of others; in so doing, they transcend the preoccupation with their own han only. Their han can also become the ground of self-critical reflection. For instance, the victims of racism often turn out to be the imposers of other oppression—e.g., sexism, child abuse, and religious persecution. Reflecting on their own han, they can realize that they are offenders as well as victims.

Rational understanding plays an important role in helping victims understand the cause of their han by allowing them to delve into the complexity of the structure of han in order to grasp the connection of individual han with collective han, in providing a reference for a self-criticism of the generation of han, and in helping to rise above the egocentric fixation on one's own han.

## Intuitive Understanding

Rational understanding is engaged in the conscious level of han. Intuitive understanding deals with its unconscious level. Rational understanding is limited in its ability to penetrate the totality of han. Intuitive understanding enters the unconsciousness of han where the majority of our han is submerged.

Spinoza distinguished three levels of knowledge: *imaginatio* (imagination), *ratio* (reason), and *scientia intuitiva* (intuitive knowledge).[8] The first level of knowledge, imagination or opinion, emerges from the affections and their reflective ideas. Since these are mere composite images drawn from various human experiences, they are "inadequate," "subjective," and "confused," and are unable to provide scientific knowledge of things.[9] This sensory knowledge frequently leaves us open to domination by external influences. Spinoza regarded this first type of knowledge as "the only cause of falsity."[10]

The second level of knowledge, *ratio*, derives from "common notions and adequate ideas of the properties of things."[11] The common notions are properties common to all bodies—e.g., extension and motion. They are indispensable due to the fact that they offer the basis for science, mathematics, and metaphysics. For Spinoza, an "adequate idea" has all the internal signs of a true idea without reference to the object.[12] This rational knowledge gradually liberates us from bondage to our sensory passions by helping us to see impersonal and determined causes of events. His metaphysical foundation for the adequacy of ideas is the human mind as part of the divine mind: "The human mind is part of a certain infinite intellect."[13] While *imagination* is personal and arbitrary, *reason* is universal and necessary.

The third level of knowledge, *scientia intuitiva*, arises from the second level of knowledge. This knowledge is obtained in its essential relation to God rather than in isolation: "Since all things are in God and are conceived through Him, it follows that we can deduce from this knowledge many things which we can know adequately, and that we can thus form that third sort of knowledge."[14] If an adequate knowledge of God is attained, it satisfies the full content of the emotional and intellectual need and brings us the peace of understanding: "As each person therefore becomes stronger in this kind of knowledge, the more is he conscious of himself and of God; that is to say, the more perfect and the happier he is."[15] The highest good and virtue of the mind is the knowledge of God. This intuitive knowledge as direct awareness of the cosmic order makes us feel truly ourselves, part of that cosmic order—God. For Spinoza, intuitive knowledge is the highest way to know ourselves and God.

The intuitive understanding of which I speak is similar to Spinoza's in terms of espousing direct awareness of ourselves, others, and God. But it is different from Spinoza's in its emphasis on the nonhierarchical notion of knowledge. While he mentions three levels of knowledge, I would uphold three aspects of understanding. Intuitive understanding can unlock our han and that of others, opening the gate to the world of unconsciousness and its chaotic dynamics. The rational function of understanding is limited in its ability to analyze the realm of unconsciousness, but the intuitive and immediate perception of understanding comprises the underside of han. By accepting han, the intuitive understanding apprehends the depth of its unconscious dimension.

Intuitive understanding includes an emotional component. Rational understanding cannot grasp the emotional dimension of han. Spinoza also stressed the importance of emotional dynamics. He speaks of two emotions: passive and active. Passive emotions come from the feeling of pleasure and pain associated with external things. Those arising from "inadequate" or "confused" ideas become the source of human bondage and misery. Passive emotions depend on external things. Active emotions are "strength of mind" and "generosity." They are the desire to be oneself and to help others—e.g., temperance, mercy.[16] Active emotions are the source of human perfection and happiness. He believes that reason can free us from bondage to passive emotions.[17] Through detachment from the external causes of our misery, he suggests a way to overcome the inadequacies of the passive emotions. Spinoza's passive emotions are quite similar to the notion of han. But the control of passive emotions by reason is at variance with the rational understanding I have described. Although I agree with his basic tenet regarding the nature of passive emotions, I do not see it as something to be controlled but to be rechanneled for positive causes. No emotion can be destroyed or eliminated, but it can be transferred to another form.

Intuitive understanding surpasses the rational realm of understanding. It ceases to try to explain or reason with the reality of han, but rather walks into the sanctuary of han to embrace its agony. In this healing process, a paradigm of han can operate to correlate one's own han to that of others. Here the idea of the "wounded healer" can be an effective way to understand another's han and be fully present in it.[18]

Intuitive understanding includes empathy, the intellectual and emotional identification with another person. But it goes beyond empathy in that it encompasses the realm of intuition independent of any reasoning process. It affectionately cares for the unconscious side of han. Unqualified acceptance is the main characteristic of intuitive understanding. In the process of intuitive understanding, the person who understands and the person who is understood both experience mutual penetration, mutual enrichment, and mutual transformation toward healing.

## Incarnational Understanding

Rational understanding grasps the conscious level of han, while intuitive understanding perceives the unconscious level of han. Incarnational understanding is humble and compassionate participation in the reality of han. It integrates the rational and intuitive understandings by implementing them in daily life. While the rational and intuitive understandings are cognitive, incarnational understanding is attitudinal. Rational and intuitive understandings are limited in their ability to dissolve han. Incarnational understanding will fully enhance us to complete the task of the dissolution of han. Analytic and perceptive understandings cannot grasp the wholeness of reality. Incarnational compassionate understanding, on the other hand, will help us grasp the full knowledge of reality. Reality does not fully disclose itself to us when it is scrutinized by the observer. At the most, reality shows its partial aspect when it is analyzed or is perceived objectively. But when an observer participates in reality with compassion, it opens itself up and shows its nature. The reality of han does the same. When han is embraced by the observer with compassion, it begins to open up to be dissolved. Incarnational understanding is to participate in the reality of han with the attitude of compassion and humility. In an incarnational understanding, the wound of han begins to heal itself.

Incarnational understanding is one of the key notions in comprehending the Christ-event. God encounters humanity in an *in-carnation* (literally "en-fleshing") to understand the affliction and infirmity of the flesh. There are two Greek words used to express our physical existence: *soma* (body) and *sarx* (flesh). Both terms were disdained by Hellenistic civilization, *sarx* more than *soma*. The Johannine author intentionally used the term *sarx* to describe the Christ's "incarnation" (Jn. 1:14). In a world where Stoicism and Platonism's influence led to a denigration of the "fleshly," the "incarnation," the divine dwelling

145

in *sarx*, was a shocking proclamation. The world of the Platonic "Idea" treated *logos* as something that never materialized. Stoicism held that *logos* enjoyed *apatheia*, "passionlessness." In the midst of these traditions, the Christian gospel declared that the divine *Logos* became *sarx*. We can grasp the incarnation-event only in perspective of the divine *kenosis* (self-emptying), the act of true divine understanding (Phil. 2:3, 7). The main message of the incarnation is that, having taken on flesh and becoming human, God now understands the depth of human suffering.

Jesus' life was connected with events of incarnational understanding. The miracles followed his perception of the suffering of people. With compassion for the hungry, he fed more than five thousand people. Seeing the widow who lost her only son at Nain, he was moved to revive her dead child (Lk. 7:11-17). Having a compassionate heart toward the sick man who had been ill for thirty-eight years, he healed him in spite of breaking the sabbath law (Jn. 5:2-18). He became a friend of the down-and-out: Mary Magdalene, a former prostitute; Zacchaeus, a chief tax collector; the Samaritan woman, a person of scandalous reputation. His life was a true incarnation in their lives of affliction. He underwent their suffering in incarnational understanding. He never *performed* miracles[19]; the miracles took place on the basis of his incarnational understanding of the suffering.

His crucifixion meant undergoing a thorough experience of human misery and agony, one of the most painful and humiliating ordeals of human experience. The crucified Jesus exposed the despair, agony, and helplessness of human existence. In the crucifixion, both the divine and human natures of Jesus meet to understand the depth of human suffering. The cross of Jesus represents the han of humanity, especially of the innocent. God is nailed down and participates in the pain of the abused and molested children, and the agony of the victims of patriarchy and genocide.

His resurrection can also be interpreted from the perspective of incarnational understanding. He arose to understand the disciple who betrayed him. He arose to transform his han-ridden disciples who were frozen in fear and in despair. He arose to resolve the han of the oppressed. He arose to vindicate the death of the innocent and lift up the downtrodden.

The Johannine author particularly emphasized a theology of incarnational understanding. After the resurrection, Jesus appeared before his disciples by the Sea of Galilee. He asked Peter three times whether Peter loved him. As this scene is played out, the Johannine writer changes the Greek term for *love*. According to John Marsh, the two words for love—*agapaō* and *phileō*—are not synonymous in this passage.[20] This change was not accidental, but intentional for the Johannine writer.[21] At first, Jesus asked, *agapas me?* That question meant whether Peter loves him unconditionally. *Agapē* is "the strong, new, and typically Christian word for love."[22] Peter answered, *philō se* (I love you conditionally; I love you as a disciple who followed you for three years. But I am unable to love you at the level of *agapē*).[23] As these comments indicate, *agapaō* is the stronger word than *phileō*.[24] The second time, Jesus asked Peter, *agapas me?* Peter could not answer except by stating his own honest feeling: *philō se*. The third time, Jesus changed the words and asked, *phileis me?* (Do you love me as your brother and friend?) Jesus did not insist on his own way but came down to Peter's level of love.[25] Peter's third answer was grievous: *su panta oidas, su ginōskeis hoti philō se* (You know all things, you know that I truly love you at the level of brotherly love).[26] According to Plummer, "In the third question Christ takes him at his own standard; he adopts S. Peter's own word." [27]

Even after betrayal the resurrected Jesus sought to understand Peter at the Sea of Galilee and did not impose his own unconditional love upon him, choosing instead to come down to Peter's level. In the mind of the Johannine author, Jesus truly stood under Peter's condition.[28] When understood by Jesus, Peter's life was radically transformed. Incarnational understanding involves the whole personality of participants. It is not a mere mental exercise, but a total commitment to the resolution of others' han.

The han of the offended will begin to disintegrate when he or she *understands* the offender. In a true sense, the offended himself or herself can heal his or her own wound. The offender can only help the healing of the wound by participating in the process through his or her own *metanoia*. Jesus the betrayed sought Peter the betrayer to forgive his sin and transform him. The offender is locked in and only the offended can open the door. The offender dehumanizes himself or herself in the act of dehumanizing others to such a degree that his or her distorted existence cannot make others' wounds whole.

## ENVISIONMENT: A VISION OF A NEW WORLD

To resolve han in the world, we need a new worldview, one which will reform the systems that have produced han in the world. Although it is not my intention to draw a concrete picture of a new world order, I would like to suggest a long-term project for a new world order, which will reduce the han of the world. Such a project has two points: a new way of thinking and an alternative global community.

## A New Way of Thinking: A Cosmic Eucharist

Individualistic ways of thinking, egocentric ideas, and hierarchical attitudes are predominant in this world due to false worldviews. I suspect that the Newtonian worldview has contributed to the promulgation of such attitudes. During the nineteenth century, the Newtonian mechanistic worldview seemed so certain that no scientist could think differently from it. This worldview is still upheld by many people. David Bohm, a prominent quantum theorist, sums up the spirit of the mechanistic view in three points. First, the world consists of basic elements in the form of particles. Second, these elements are external to and independent of one another. Third, because the elements are mechanically connected, the forces of interaction do not affect their inner natures.[29] In this view, individuals, like "particles," are independent of one another and are only externally connected. This way of thinking is also the basis of the individualistic understanding of sin and salvation in Christianity.

Against this Newtonian mechanistic worldview, a new idea has emerged in the contemporary scientific, philosophical, and religious world. That is the *principle of interpenetration*. Interconnectedness has been strongly espoused by quantum theory, process theology, and the Bible. A strong voice for the interpenetration of all things is quantum theory, which offers a nonmechanistic worldview. According to David Bohm, there are four main points in quantum theory. First, "all action or all motion is found in a discrete indivisible unit called a *quantum.*"[30] Electrons jump from one orbit to the other without passing the space in between. Second, "matter and energy have a dual nature; they manifest either like a wave or like a particle according to how they are treated in an experiment."[31] Third, things are connected with other things without the property of locality and without the bond of the connection. This is the principle of nonlocal connection. Fourth, "the whole organizes the parts, even in ordinary matter."[32] In brief, quantam theory stresses the internal relationship between the parts and the whole. David Bohm calls this *unbroken wholeness.*[33] The theory of relativity props up strict continuity, strict determinism, and strict locality, but quantum mechanics reverses all these principles, replacing them with discontinuity, indeterminism, and nonlocality. In the mechanistic picture, the parts are only externally connected to one another. But in the quantum picture, external relatedness is a secondary and derivative truth, while internal relatedness is the primary truth.[34]

One strange quantum phenomenon is that particles somehow appear to "know" what other particles are doing and seem to know it at speeds faster than the speed of light.[35] The particles can simultaneously communicate themselves instantaneously across entire universes beyond the speed of light—the maximum speed of the universe. This alludes to a principle of "nonlocality": "Nonlocality means that we cannot discuss the different parts of space independently. Yet we cannot get hold of whatever connection there is between the two different regions of space," explains John Bell, a physicist of the European Laboratory for Particle Physics (CERN).[36]

The parts are so closely interconnected that their very characteristics emerge from the connections, and thus one can only understand the universe by seeing it as a whole. According to the S-matrix theory, "In the new worldview, the universe is seen as a dynamic web of interrelated events. None of the properties of any part of this web is fundamental; they all follow from the properties of the other parts, and the overall consistency of their mutual interrelations determines the structure of the entire web."[37] This theory renounces the essentialist worldview which believes in the existence of fundamental constituents of matter. Reality in locality is only a partial truth, if not a distorted illusion. "Man has always been seeking wholeness—mental, physical, social, individual. The notion that all these fragments are separately existent is evidently an illusion, and this illusion cannot do other than lead to endless conflict and confusion," writes David Bohm.[38]

In another light, the prominent process philosopher Alfred North Whitehead coined the term *causal efficacy* to describe this same interconnectedness. In this mode of looking at reality, we find "a direct perception of those antecedent actual occasions which are causally efficacious both for the percipient and for the relevant events in the presented locus."[39] This mode exemplifies "its participation in the general scheme of extensive interconnection, involved in the real potentiality."[40] John Cobb, Jr., and David Griffin expound this as a mode of immanence and of participation: "Insofar as we influence one another, we participate in one another, and through all sorts of complex patterns all of us influence one another. . . . The starvation of an Indian peasant will be felt to diminish each one of us."[41] Process theology stresses *event thinking* in contrast to *substance thinking*. The latter regards relations as external to substances. The former understands relations as internal to events. No event occurs without its interconnection with other events.[42] All events are internally connected and signify their interdependence.

The concept of interconnectedness is also the core teaching of Scripture. Its teaching concurs with that of quantum theory, but the Bible explains the reality of interconnectedness further. While quantum theory points out the mysterious interpenetration of particles, the Bible explicates the affectionate interconnectedness of all creation, ascribing it to *the divine love*, which is the gravity that sustains the interconnectedness of the universe. The church is the extension of the body of Jesus Christ (I Cor. 12:12-26). This body metaphor denotes the unity of the church as an organic whole. There are various parts, but they are only one body. The Pauline epistles uphold this view of the unity of the church (Rom. 11; Eph. 4:4f). The ones who realize this unity in Christ are called the church. The Johannine writer confirms this unity of Christ's followers and the unity between God and Jesus Christ (Jn. 17:11, 21). They are fundamentally indivisible, although each may act differently from the reality of the unity. The function of the church is to assist people to realize their unity in Christ, enlarging its circle of the awareness of that unity.

Holy Communion is the rite which reaffirms this indivisible unity of the human family. By sharing the consecrated bread and wine, we recognize the interpenetration of our individual beings. The Johannine writer describes this interpenetration between God and Christ: "That they may all be one; even as thou, Father, art in me, and I in thee, that they also may be in us, so that the world may believe that thou hast sent me" (Jn. 17:21). The writer of the book of Revelation also confirms the interpenetration between Christ and us: "If any one hears my voice and opens the door, I will come in to him and eat with him, and he with me" (Rev. 3:20). The Eucharist means that the body of Christ is one, but is broken in order to restore the oneness of humanity. We need to take this rite of Eucharist seriously in our daily living and extend it to a cosmic level. Paul's vision of *all in all* refers to a cosmic view of the Eucharist (Eph. 1:22-23).

What does this idea of the cosmic Eucharist in relation with interconnectedness signify in the world of han? First, it debunks the bifurcation of dualism. The separation between "we" and "they" in racism and sexism is an illusion. It does not imply that we are all the same and no distinction exists between us. Duality does exist, for unity presupposes duality. Unity without duality makes no sense; duality without unity is false. Only in the unity of duality do we truly know ourselves and others. In other words, we do not understand who we are until we understand our interpenetration with others.

In the past, a group of people or a race has endeavored to find its belongingness or identity by excluding others. This negative way of self-identity has always offered a false image of others and itself and has brought forth group, racial, and sexual conflict. With the new way of interconnected thinking, we can find our own belongingness by including others. Through opening and enlarging our boundary of identity, we come to see our personal and group identity. We are windows to one another. Only through windows are we able to see the beauty of the blue sky, the green pastures and trees, and mountains outside our limited room. When we realize this interconnectedness, we wholeheartedly appreciate the existence of other groups and races, instead of depreciating it.

Second, the interconnectedness of the universe unmasks the erroneous structure of hierarchism. Dualism does not simply divide for the sake of division, but does so for putting down another. Hierarchism exploits many human relationships, including sexual and racial ones. It supposes that authority flows from above. In reality, authority is not in the hands of rulers, but in the hands of those who accept authority. A ruler may assume that he or she has authority. But if people reject this authority, it no longer exists. The ruler may have external power over the people, but he or she only has as much internal authority as they are willing to grant.[43]

True power is not the will to control others. True power is the strength to help others to become what they can be. This strength does not presume women to be what they ought to be, projecting their stereotype. This does not remind ethnic people what they used to be. Those who understand this strength will seek to actualize to a full extent the potential of others as well as their own. They will actively seek to promulgate the success of others. They realize that they are meant to help others if they are to succeed in the life of interconnectedness. Those who desire to control others experience agony themselves. They have no joy and no peace. The will to control others necessarily involves the restraint of one's own freedom; the heart to control others curbs one's own freedom first.

The realization of interconnectedness is pivotal in resolving the han of the world. In the realization that others' han is our han and vice versa, we enter into a new dimension of true human nature. In fact, we know little of our han unless we know the han of others. If we realize our indivisible interconnectedness, all, including the oppressors, can cooperate to dissolve the han of the oppressed.

Third, interconnectedness points to the unity of mutual respect and love. Mere interconnectedness is not the goal of our relationships. This interpenetration recognizes the creative distance necessary to mutual respect and love. Without this creative distance, true interpenetration cannot exist. *Kyoung*, reverence, is the heart of neo-Confucianism. It elicits the appreciation and adoration of all existences.[44] It is loyal to all forms of beings. In neo-Confucianism, all beings should be interrelated in this *kyoung*, which is vertical in attitude and horizontal in relationship. The vertical dimension of interrelationship is reverence and the horizontal dimension is love.

Catherine Keller, a feminist process theologian, points out that in Whitehead's organicist vision, the interrelatedness of all beings is coupled with a concept of *mutual transcendence.* She warns that love, derived from the intuition of interconnection, is vulnerable to criticisms of narcissism if it falls into mere immanence. For her, "Such loving need not eliminate transcendence and individuality."[45] The true unity which occurs in interconnectedness is different from mere immanence; it flows from the appreciation of, enjoyment of, and affection for one another's presence at a creative distance (*kyoung*).

I would suggest that mutual reverence brings forth the transcendent dimension of life. Love binds up (immanence) while mutual respect builds up (transcendence). Not passive connectedness, but active connectedness can create true unity. There is something in the active connection which ties us together. That is the goal, the vision of interconnectedness, whose center is love and whose periphery is reverence. The dynamic dialectic of love and reverence will elicit joy and peace through the qualitative life of dialogical unity.

## An Alternative World Order: A Global Church Community

In this extremely complex world of sociopolitical and economic systems, it seems that no single institution is committed to drawing a big picture for a future world. One might expect the university to take such a role in planning for the future, but reductionism has led its various disciplines to academic isolation so that it is incapable of presenting an integrated vision of the future. The church as a global institution ought to take a leadership role in reshaping a future world. The church is meant to envision "a new heaven and a new earth." If it does not dream of tomorrow's world, transnational corporations and governments will keep shaping the world by making capitalistic and nationalistic decisions for the future.

Capitalism is an unplanned economic system, in which private individuals or corporations chiefly own the means of production, investment, distribution, and the exchange of wealth. It has been operated on the principle of the survival of the fittest. We know that the spirit of capitalism is not harmonious with the teaching of Jesus, as particularly shown in the parable of the laborers in the vineyard (Mt. 20:1-16). In God's vineyard, all the laborers who came to work different hours are paid equally.

Since Martin Luther's idea of the two kingdoms came to rule Western society, the church has retreated into an isolated world of religion. According to Luther, God has established two kingdoms, one ruled by the law and the other ruled by the gospel. As popularly understood, Luther's theory connotes that Christians should not expect the state to be ruled by the gospel, and rulers must not rule over the kingdom of the gospel. This idea of dualism has imbedded itself in the civilization of the Western world and has separated the realm of religious life from secular life.

This dualistic idea has created the strange phenomenon of the separation of the Christian kingdom and God's kingdom. For example, of the 350 million Latin Americans, 90 to 95 percent of the people consider themselves Christians.[46] 92 percent of the population of the Philippines are Christians.[47] But these countries are far from approximating the reign of God, suffering some of the most deep-seated injustice in the world. The dualistic traditional mission strategy which focuses on saving souls yet ignores the other needs of the evangelized must be readdressed if the church is serious about the establishment of God's reign on earth.

The church cannot afford to leave the matter of the whole world in the hands of rulers. This does not mean that the church should be directly involved with the politics of the world. The church, however, needs to maintain a vision of the future reign of God in its long range-strategy of mission. Just waiting for God's intervention into history to establish God's kingdom cannot be an option for the church. The church should concretely prepare for God's reign. It should radically shift its theological reflection from "when the eschaton comes" to "how the eschaton can come."

The world suffers today from a profound lack of visionary leadership. Political scientists such as Jack Behrman and Robert Brosse have analyzed the deficit of leadership among nations. For them, no country is fit to take the leadership role of the world.[48] Government leaders are preoccupied with the welfare of their national companies, despite their transnational characteristics. Transnational corporations have not exercised their leadership; they have not "carried into their decision making any other values than the pragmatic one of efficiency."[49] The managers who run these transnational corporations are not educated to be leaders, but to be effective and efficient administrators. Thus the world has suffered a vacuum of leadership.

President Bush announced a "New World Order" to come in his U.N. speech in 1990: "We have a vision of a new partnership of nations that transcends the Cold War: a partnership based on consultation, cooperation and collective action, especially through international and regional organizations; a partnership united by principle and the rule of law, and supported by an equitable sharing of both cost and commitment; a partnership whose goals are to increase democracy, increase prosperity, increase the peace and reduce arms."[50] The phrase has conjured up expectations that this vision would lead the world out of the disorder produced by an astonishing international change. Almost three years later, however, it has become clear that such a notion is no more than a catch phrase to describe the post-Cold War era.[51] It seems that the world is drifting without a vision of its future.

The church should boldly dream of a new global order, one which will heal and prevent the han of the world. We recite the Lord's Prayer continually: "Thy kingdom come and thy will be done on earth as it is in heaven." If we take this prayer seriously, we need to envision how we might realize the petition for the coming of God's kingdom. The vision of the future is the important task God has given to the church. The church is a unique institution whose global network can work toward such a universal vision.

As Robert McAfee Brown, a leading North American liberation theologian states, the good news is that we don't have to search for a foundation to start building a global community. The church at its best is a global community already.[52] The final loyalty of the church is not to any single nation, nor to anything else—including its own institution—but to God above all other gods.[53]

The church must take a leadership role in this exploited and confused world where capital and profit become gods due to the code of the wild: survival of the fittest. In this regard the church needs two movements: self-renewal and strife for the establishment of God's commonwealth. Self-renewal is necessary for its reformation within. The church is required to take off the old divisive clothes of hierarchy and patriarchy and unite in the body of Christ. The church also needs self-critical reflection on itself for continual renewal. If it is to advance

God's reign, the church must challenge injustice and absurdity even within its own walls.

Simultaneously, the church must strive to envision an alternative community of cooperative living, in order to lead the world to God's reign. More concretely, the church is meant to be a community of economic democracy, of corporate social responsibility, and of corporate political power—a living community, not a mere religious community of individuals.

## Economically Democratic Community

In capitalist society, democracy in a strict sense cannot be fully implemented because economic imbalance between the rich and the poor influences various factors of our democratic life. Bertrand Russell addresses this point in his *Political Ideals*:

> Institutions and especially economic systems, have a profound influence in moulding the characters of men and women. They may encourage adventure and hope, or timidity and the pursuit of safety. They may open people's minds to great possibilities or close them against everything but the risk of obscure misfortune. They may make a man's happiness depend upon what he adds to the general possessions of the world, or upon what he can secure for himself of the private goods in which others cannot share. Modern capitalism forces the wrong decision of these alternatives upon all who are not heroic or exceptionally lucky.[54]

The capitalist global economy as a source of han promotes competition, social isolation, violence, poverty, and individualism. Its rise, allegedly derived from the Calvinist work ethic, opposes the underlying idea of the gospel, yet the church has proposed no alternative vision of a socioeconomic system.

John B. Cobb, Jr., and Herman E. Daly recently published a monumental book on a new vision of a global community: *For The Common Good: Redirecting the Economy Toward Community, the Environment, and a Sustainable Future*. This impressive cooperative opus between a theologian and an economist suggests the need for "a community of communities." They provide one of most thorough visions for an alternative society based on the Whiteheadian interpretation of Christian principles. The "community of communities" they envision is to decentralize the economic and political power of government to a local level and to move toward a self-sufficient society, environmentally sustainable and socioeconomically achievable.[55] They contend that decentralization of political power will occur through decentralization of the economy. Their emphasis is on the economic dimension of reformation.

As possible steps for redirecting the economy, Cobb and Daly present three: "The very first step toward redirection must be a widespread recognition that something is wrong, that present policies do not work, that the wild facts must be taken seriously.... The second step is a widespread recognition that most of the problems faced by humanity today are interconnected and indeed have a common source.... The third step is the recognition that human beings still have the possibility of choosing a livable future for themselves and their descendants."[56]

Although basically agreeing with their vision of "a community of communities," I perceive it from a different angle: a vision of the global church community, of economic democracy as the starting point of the economic reformation of the world and its emphasis on corporate lifestyle. While they stress the significance of a local community, I would accentuate the role of the global church community in implementing the vision and lifestyle of an economically democratic community.

The church has been a primarily religious community, delimiting its scope of fellowship and activity basically to the religious realm. The church should move toward being a cooperative living community rather than strictly a religious community. If we take the Eucharist and our commitment to the advancement of the reign of God seriously, we need to share our economic and sociopolitical activity together. The church should be more than a Sunday community. If we share an eternal hope, we should share our lives in the effort to bring that hope to fruition.

The early Jerusalem Christians had "breaking of bread" daily in private houses (Acts 2:46). One purpose of this practice was to support the needy. "Breaking of bread" signifies a continuation and a reminder of the Lord's Supper.[57]

I believe that the church is the community which shares *both* faith and bread together. It is the community of believing *and* living. To satisfy these two elements, the church should exemplify its responsibility of corporate living in this world. In spite of the church's fragmentation, I would suggest that a possible way of living for Christians would be "a democratic church community."

### Corporate Lifestyle

The idea of "a global religious community" in the economic sphere necessitates an economically democratic society. It envisions an alternative system to capitalism and socialism, embracing the strengths of both systems. While capitalism advocates the investment and ownership of the means of production and distribution by private individuals or corporations, socialism strengthens the ownership of the means of production, capital, and land by the community as a whole. The idea of a religious economic community upholds capitalism in terms of the private ownership of property and capital. In terms of sharing the means of production, it resembles socialism. This idea corresponds to that of the *moshav* in rural Israel.

In Israel, there are two outstanding rural community lifestyles: the *kibbutz* and the *moshav*. The *kibbutz* is a cooperative, self-sufficient, and egalitarian community. Members possess no private property and receive no wages. Instead, their needs for housing, health care, education, vacations, and pocket money are supplied by the community. All members participate in decision-making, budget allocation, and alterative lifestyles. There are over 260 *kibbutzim* in Israel, comprising nearly 3 percent of its population.[58]

The *moshav* is a democratic and self-governing community based on the idea of the delegation of authority. In it, each family as the basic unit possesses its own household and farms its own land, but major economic and social needs are cooperatively met. The cooperative system deals with marketing and supply collectively, and provides education, medical, and cultural services. There are approximately 450 *moshavim*, constituting 4 percent of Israel's population. Each *moshav* is comprised of about 60 families.[59]

While the *moshav*, being popular, flourishes, the *kibbutz* declines in its financial strength. The 280 *kibbutzim* owe $4 billion.[60] Like communist countries, the *kibbutzim* suffer from the inefficiency of cooperative work. *Moshavim* flourish because they are basically private enterprises.

Some important principles of the *moshav* are: (1) comprehensive, coordinated, and integrated agricultural planning; (2) planning and implementation at the village level, including everyone in the settlement; and (3) settlements based on family-sized farms.[61] The first of these, comprehensive agricultural planning, connotes that all services are available to farmers at the village level: planning for their production program; credit for obtaining specified inputs; all the production services (irrigation, drainage, pruning) to put the production program into effect; and marketing services. Coordinated agricultural planning also means the harmonization of local planning at the regional and national levels, the vertical coordination of planning. Integrated planning indicates that the main goal of planning is its

157

implementation at the village and farm levels. The second principle means that the center of planning and implementation is the village with all its farms rather than the individual farmer. The third principle indicates that the family-type farm may be the most efficient for various types of culture and the most adaptable to the development milieu. Collective farming has generally not been a success because of the lack of incentive to work hard. The structure of the *moshav* allows for a combination of individualism and cooperation.[62]

Even though the *moshav* is a rural farming system, the church as a religious economic community can appropriate some of its strong points. The church does not have to be a commune, but it can open itself to a more cooperative lifestyle than is currently the case. If we take the Eucharist seriously, the church should be a *living-believing* community rather than just a *believing* one. Communal lifestyles of living have a long tradition in Christianity, particularly conspicuous in the monastic movement and diverse religious communities. As such a corporate lifestyle for celibates is optional, a semicorporate lifestyle for families should be optional in church life. The *moshav* is a viable, functioning system, and the church can draw a few guidelines for forming such a semicorporate community.

First, the family is the basic and independent financial unit. The church community can share comprehensive, coordinated, and integrated agricultural or urban planning. Such urban planning may range from child caring to job search and training at the local, regional, and national levels. Second, the church community implements the planning. It includes sharing the tools and equipment of productions and reproductions. In an agricultural setting, the means of production can be tractors, combines, trucks, and other kinds of machinery. In an urban setting, this connotes sharing transportation, housing, and housing construction projects. Third, such a religious community espouses all efforts to empower a local community such as "a community of communities." These efforts include starting or supporting a co-op type of environmentally oriented supermarket which sells local vegetables and products. In the U.S., "The average food item travels 1,300 miles from where it is grown to where it is consumed. Shipping a truckload of produce across the country costs up to $4,500. In addition, a dollar spent on local foods circulates in the local economy, generating $1.81 to $2.78 in other business."[63] The local co-op type of community-centered system not only enhances the self-reliant economy of a local community, but also boosts energy conservation. The purpose of the economically democratic religious community is not to procure its own growth, but to galvanize the co-op type of a self-sustaining local community in the vision of a new way of living. However ideological it may sound, we need to strive to implement a more corporate lifestyle for the advancement of God's reign on earth. The church has not attempted the task of living together as a serious mission (with the notable exceptions of monastic and certain other communities) since the time of the primitive Christian community, but instead has retreated into the realm of a "religious" community.

*Church Banking System*

One of the ways to alleviate the han of the world is to create church banking systems. Admittedly, such an idea involves risk and vulnerability. Although most denominations have their own credit unions (which can be expanded to build banking systems), they are basically self-serving financial organizations. The churches are lacking in a vision of a new economic world order for the advancement of God's reign in the global dimension of economic life. The credit unions of the two largest American Protestant denominations demonstrate such lack of a global vision. The purpose of the ministers' credit union of The United Methodist Church is as follows: "The credit union is a group of people with a common bond who pool their savings and lend the money to each other at moderate rates of interest."[64] The purpose of the Southern Baptist Credit Union is to be "a financial institution which provides for the insured investment of your savings into the lives of Southern Baptist Churches, ministers and church members. It is not owned by an individual or company. It is owned and operated by its members."[65] The intentions of these credit unions are good, but they are not good enough to change the economic structure of our society. The churches should envision a new economic world order and slowly move toward it. If the church does not endeavor to plan for God's full reign in our economic life, who will? We Christians cannot afford to leave our financial resources in the hands of commercial banks which exist for their own profits and have exploited the poor and the downtrodden. We must manage our financial resources wisely for the advancement of God's reign on earth. With the vision of restructuring financial institutions in order to stop exploiting the poor and to help the needy, we need to strengthen and redirect the present systems of credit unions or create church banks. There is no reason why Christians should support commercial banks which illegally practice redlining, invest their money in South Africa, and support unethical companies. If a majority of Christians and sympathizers were to join church credit unions or banks and endeavor to restructure world financial systems, we could make a radical impact in the world of injustice, poverty, and hunger.

Such credit unions or banks could invest their funds in the redline zone and in new factory openings in slums, and spend their profits for scholarships. For example, a month after rioting ravaged much of Los Angeles' inner-city in 1992, some African American-owned banks planned to ask African Americans to participate in the rebuilding effort by drastically increasing their deposits in their three institutions: Family Savings Bank, Broadway Federal Savings & Loan, and Founders National Bank. These three institutions have combined assets of $300 million, while a number of the state's larger banks individually secure assets of $1 billion or more.[66] Leaders of these institutions contend that they have a better record than nonminority banks in lending in inner-city and integrated neighborhoods, but they need to increase their assets greatly to be more effective. To reach that goal, they plan to announce a campaign—in cooperation with African American churches—to persuade African Americans to shift $10 to $15 million in deposits from mainstream banks to African American banks.[67] This plan is backed by a coalition of about 85 percent of the city's African American clergy, who will urge their parishioners to shift assets to these institutions.[68] It is my hope that other Christians and concerned citizens will join African Americans in this historic effort to galvanize African American financial institutions and help to rebuild the devastated city. As Rev. Edgar Boyd of Bethel African Methodist Episcopal Church says, "This is the first step toward economic empowerment."[69]

As Christian financial institutions grow larger, they can even invest their capital to improve the quality of life in poor nations. They can provides loans and assistance for economic self-sustenance projects in poor nations. The World Bank (The International Bank for Reconstruction and Development) is supposed to perform this job by financing long-term (15–20 year) development projects. In a way, the World Bank has improved the quality of life in poor nations, but with many shortcomings. The donor nations exert leverage on the economies of recipient nations. Thus, a development project the World Bank supports sometimes serves the purposes of the donor nation more than those of the recipient.[70] The practical goals of the assistance of the World Bank have not been the self-sustenance of poor nations but their economic development for the further profitable investment of donor nations. For example, western corporations need highway, electric, and communications systems if they are to operate in third-world countries. A survey of World Bank projects through 1970 reveals that of the $14.3 billion allocated for development projects for third-world countries, $9 billion were in the areas of transportation and electrical power.[71]

Christians have supported various commercial banks that have gone out to invest their money in the wrong places, pursuing their own profits alone. Christians have not wisely utilized their financial resources to defy ghettoization, injustice, poverty, and world hunger. The organization of church financial institutions, which could make a great impact on the life of the poor and the hungry, is overdue. However risky it seems to be, our Christian discipleship calls for such a venture of Christian commitment to the advancement of God's full reign.

## The Community of Global Social Responsibility

As a global community, the church can challenge the irresponsible actions of transnational corporations in both the first and third worlds. Most often our individual voices are not heard by large corporations and governments, but such organizations are keen to hear the church's voice as it represents the global community.

The church has tremendous sociopolitical power in the world. Accordingly, it has much social responsibility for the justice of the world. The church must exert its power and social responsibility efficiently if it is to transform the world toward God's full reign.

For example, the Interfaith Center for Corporate Responsibility (ICCR) in the United States has exerted the financial muscle of mainline churches to pressure many major transnational corporations to address questions of workers' rights and other justice issues since 1976.[72] Currently, ICCR is primarily concerned about promoting the withdrawal of transnational corporations from South Africa, enhancing affirmative actions, alleviating the international debt crisis, and striving for the improvement of working conditions for third-world women hired by U.S.-based companies. For instance, when the Tandy Corporation, operators of Radio Shack, closed down a Korean plant in 1989 without paying severance, ICCR campaigned to pressure the company either to reopen the plant or to make severance payments. "We are also calling on management to recognize the principles of fair treatment to workers—including adequate wages, health and safety standards, and the right to organize," says ICCR staffperson Dara Demings.[73]

ICCR, consisting of more than 200 religious congregations and agencies, frequently works in coordination with labor, community, and other religious groups. One such campaign is directed at Manufacturers Hanover Trust, a bank with over $210 million invested in the South African economy. ICCR calls on the Trust to demand rapid repayment of these loans, coordinating its efforts with religious groups in West Germany, Switzerland, France, and Britain, whose major banks also hold extensive South African debt.[74]

Since the church is loyal to God and to the welfare of God's creation, it can operate in the interests of the global community, not simply individual nations. In the case of a plant closure the church can protest against the closure via its global network system. The Steel Valley Authority can serve as an example of the church's involvement in a plant closing. In response to the massive unemployment that had a devastating effect on the industry's traditional center (the tri-state region of eastern Ohio, western Pennsylvania, and northern West Virginia), church leaders, steelworkers, other trade unionists, community activists, and unemployed workers united to form the Tri-State Conference on Steel in 1979. Its primary concern was the patronage of community ownership and control of steel facilities. In 1986, it succeeded in establishing the Steel Valley Authority (SVA), a public agency, in Mon Valley, Pennsylvania. Local municipalities empowered the SVA to take over plants through eminent domain when private owners refused to keep them open (eminent domain is the power the government can exert to take over property required for public purposes by compensating the property owner for its fair market value). Thus plants taken over by the SVA can be sold to suitable private buyers, worker-owned cooperatives, or publicly owned industrial cooperatives.[75] The SVA can be a role model for a local response to plant closures.

Our social responsibility is the establishment of economic democracy in the world. We have seen that laissez-faire capitalism leads the world to the virtual economic dictatorship of the rich. In a world where 40 million people are dying each year from hunger and hunger-related diseases,[76] the monopolistic control of wealth is no less evil than the Nazi dictatorship. German theologian Ulrich Durchrow compares this with apartheid and the atrocities of Nazi Germany:

> My question is whether apartheid is not just the tip of the iceberg. We inhabitants of industrialized nations, together with a few tiny elites in the countries of Asia, Africa and Latin America, are exploiting the majority of the world's population just as systematically as the white South Africans exploit the majority of the people in South

Africa. The demon of profit for the few at the expense (i.e. the impoverishment) of the many has the whole world economic system firmly in its grip, with all the side-effects in the shape of discrimination and the suppression of human rights. The forty million or more deaths from starvation per year, the direct result of the workings of the present global economic system, require of us just as clear a confession of guilt as the murder of the six million Jewish men, women and children in Nazi Germany and as does the deprivation of twenty million people in South Africa of their rights today.[77]

We are participating in an economic system which lets forty million people die of hunger and hunger-related disease each year. If we do little to change this system, we come to participate in the present evil structure of the world, just as did those who overlooked the Nazi holocaust. Our social responsibility is pivotal for the well-being of the world. Our negligence of it involves many deaths. Christian faith emerges from a community of faith; it is communal and corporate. Thus, Christian faith denotes social responsibility. Christian social responsibility involves our accountability for wealth. In fact, the prerequisite of Jesus' discipleship is the sharing of one's own wealth with the poor (Lk. 18:18-30). The management of wealth is directly connected to Christian discipleship and faith. We cannot serve God and mammon together (Mt. 6:24). We cannot serve this capitalism which worships money made by our hands. The church must suggest a new economic order and take corporate social responsibility to change the system. Capitalism goes hand-in-hand with economic totalitarianism, not with the Christian faith.

Our concern for social responsibility should arise from our compassionate action for han-ridden people. In spite of enormous tasks before us, we don't have to be anxious or despairing; what we are required to do is not to resolve all social problems, but to be faithful to God's call for our responsibility for society.

## Politically Democratic Community

When I speak of the church as a political community, I do not mean that the church is an institution for conducting political affairs, but that it is an institution which uses political strategies to present its own ideas.

With the economic vision ("economically democratic church community") alone, the full reign of God cannot be established on earth. A theocentric democracy will advance the full reign of God, in which the divine will concurs with the will of the human family and with the will of all creation; the divine will penetrates the human will, and is expressed through the human will. Equity, freedom, peace, and love are fully actualized in the community of God.[78] A politically democratic church community reflects these features at a substantial level. The features of a politically democratic church community are equity and freedom.

Equity means the quality of fairness and justice, in contrast with the notion of equality which implies the same in quantity, degree, ability, and merit. In equity, people develop their potential and contribute to society according to their capacity and their ability. Equity is measured with reference to well-being rather than with reference to equal distribution: "Any scheme of distribution which provided equal incomes to all persons would be radically unjust," according to Catholic economic ethicist John Ryan.[79] Equity is the idea of the parable of the laborers of the vineyard (Mt. 20:1-16). Those who come to work in the morning receive the same wages as those who come in the afternoon. The parable points beyond equality in quantity. Equity consists of equality, fairness, and humanity.

Freedom denotes the authentic realization of one's own gifts endowed by God. For Reinhold Niebuhr, "Their [humans] highest good consists in freedom to develop the essential potentialities of their nature without hindrance."[80] The ideal possibility for humans at a social level involves freedom and equality. But freedom creates a tension with equality in Niebuhr's idea. If one's freedom to achieve his or her potential conflicts with that of others, justice demands a balancing of power between them. True freedom is incapable of infringing on the freedom of others. Based on God's freedom, true freedom encourages the freedom of others to be maximized in God. The expansivist definition of freedom, which is necessarily offensive to others, is not freedom but indulgence.

Political democracy without economic democracy is only nominally democratic. The two democracies form each other, but the latter is more fundamental. In this sense, we hardly see the true practice of democracy in the world. The church has its mission to bring forth true democracy in its own structures, as well as in the media, families, societies, nations, and the world.

*Democratic Mass Media*

The United States, the nation most fervently dedicated to freedom and democracy in the world, has been more undemocratic than most people have thought. If democracy denotes the rule of the majority, the socioeconomic and political structure of the United States and other countries is undemocratic in the sense that only the

164

powerful minority rules the majority via misinformation and the control of information. The Vietnam deception, Watergate, the Iran-Contra covert operations, and the Savings and Loan scandals have eroded democracy in this country.

In particular, the U.S. mass media are so in the hands of rich and powerful corporations that we scarcely ever receive free and independent information, according to sociologist Michael Parenti:

> Ten business and financial corporations control the three major television and radio networks (NBC, CBS, ABC), 34 subsidiary television stations, 201 cable TV systems, 62 radio stations, 20 record companies, 59 magazines including *Time* and *Newsweek*, 58 newspapers including the *New York Times*, the *Washington Post*, the *Wall Street Journal*, and the *Los Angeles Times*, 41 book publishers, and various motion picture companies such as Columbia Pictures and Twentieth-Century Fox. Three quarters of the major stockholders of ABC, CBS and NBC are banks such as Chase Manhattan, Morgan Guarantee Trust, Citibank, and Bank of America.[81]

Thus, it is highly questionable whether the U.S. mass media are able to report independently of the interests of the corporations that own them. The institutions that constitute the mainline press are not simply sympathetic to big business; they *are* big business.[82] In addition to the major corporations, the U.S. government has the ability to manipulate public opinion through distorted information and control of information. The war against Iraq in 1991 can serve as an example of the media bias controlled by corporations and manipulated by the government. NBC is owned by General Electric, one of America's biggest military contractors. GE manufactured or supplied parts for nearly every major weapons system used by the U.S. during the Gulf war, including the Patriot and Tomahawk cruise missiles, the Stealth bomber, the B-52 bomber, and the AWACS plane. When correspondents and paid consultants on NBC television praised the performance of U.S. weapons, especially that of the Patriot missiles, they were extolling equipment produced by the very company that pays their salary.[83] At the same time, the U.S. military provided the networks with high-tech bombing videos that were tailored to avoid images of mutilated victims. With few exceptions the public was shown a bloodless and antiseptic conflict.[84] At least 100,000 Iraqi soldiers died, and the Allies held up to 175,000 prisoners.[85] We know that in addition to these estimates, many women, children, and other civilians died in the war.

The church has, as part of its mission, the promotion of accurate information to the public, which will enhance true democracy in the world. The gospel is good news not only because it shares the saving power of God, but also because it confronts the power of distorted news. Without knowing what is truly happening, the church is unable to raise its prophetic voice against social evil. Proper biblical interpretation requires the dialogue between text and context (Paul Tillich). If our information on the context is distorted, our biblical interpretation will be contorted.

The church should change the present mass media system, support alternative information systems, or develop its independent information networks for Christians and the public. The church as a global institution needs to disseminate truthful news of the world as well as the good news of Jesus Christ. The church information networks must be different from the traditional networks of propaganda. They must be reliable, truthful, and responsible.

## The Church

The Christian church is one of most nondemocratic institutions in the world. Its hierarchical separation between clergy and laity underlies other types of social hierarchy. Some denominations are better in this regard than others, but in general the doctrine of the priesthood of believers enunciated by the epistle of Peter (I Pet. 2:4) and defended by Martin Luther has never been fully implemented in the Christian church. The class struggle between laity and priests has marred the advancement of the full reign of God. Unless the ordained abolish their own special class status, democracy in the church will be obstructed by their hierarchical structure of consciousness.

The Roman Catholic Church lags especially behind in the social reality of democracy: "Among us, Roman Catholicism has always been incompatible with democracy."[86] Roman Catholic hierarchies have contributed to Latin American dictatorships as Confucian hierarchies have upheld the dictatorships of Far-Eastern countries.[87]

The priesthood must arrive at a functional self-definition, rather than a structuralist or ontological one. Christ's friendship with us (Jn. 15:15) abrogates priestly hierarchies, making all human beings one human family. God's full rule will arrive with this understanding of friendship in the life of democracy.

## Family

Home has been the planting ground of human development. When the family is genuinely democratized, democracy at the social level takes place easily. A hierarchical relationship between husband and wife will create an undemocratic community at home as well as in society. When children are abused and molested at home, they tend not to learn how to treat others with respect. The family is the true community where people learn and practice democracy.

The church is closely interrelated with the family system. In describing itself, the church relies heavily on concepts drawn from the family: "the children of God," "the Son of God," "honoring parents," "brethren," the idea of "God as Father," the idea of "the Trinity." Consequently, the notion of the family shapes the reality of the church's teachings. An anti-democratic rule of the father generates a totalitarian image of God or distorts the idea of the Trinity. Those who are molested by their brothers would not associate warm feelings with the use of the term *brother* to refer to a fellow Christian. Furthermore, the children of authoritarian fathers have difficulty conceiving of the image of genuinely democratic political leaders. The church as a global community needs to work for the democratization of the family, as this is crucial for its own self-understanding and the image of the advancing community of God. The church, interconnected with the family, is the most appropriate institution to work for the democratization of the family system.

## Ecologically Sound Community

*Economy vs. Ecology*

Just as suddenly as the Soviet brand of communism has crumbled irreparably, so can an ecological catastrophe occur.[88] The world cannot deplete its resources through economic development indefinitely. According to Lester Brown, there are two contrasting views of the state of the world: economic views and ecological views. Economic views are concerned about savings, investment, and economic growth. They are concerned about the expansion of economic opportunities more than natural constraints on human economic activity. This type of view prevails in the worlds of industry and finance, national governments, and international development agencies.[89]

Ecological views, on the other hand, care about the relationship of living organisms toward one another and their environments. According to such a perspective, all growth processes should be circumscribed within the natural parameters of the earth's ecosystem.[90] Ecological views contend that continuing the single-minded pursuit of economic growth will eventually lead to economic collapse.[91] Before it is too late, we should adapt an ecological view without deserting the poor in their plight.

The human family needs to shift the focus of life from economic growth to a new mode of measuring the improvement of civilization. One such alternative is "humanizing progress." The present way of economic growth does not resolve the problem of poverty but increases it by widening the gap between the wealthy and the poor. "Humanizing progress" shifts the goal of development from growth in economic wealth (vertical growth) to growth in the equitable distribution of wealth and in human and environmental health (horizontal growth). It proposes global economic improvement within the boundaries of environmental self-sustenance.

In the past, economic growth was the sole indication of the advance of a nation. At the present, new ways of measuring progress are being developed. According to Lester Brown, there are two interesting recent efforts in this area: the Human Development Index (HDI) devised by the United Nations; and the Index of Sustainable Economic Welfare (ISEW) designed by Herman Daly and John Cobb. The Human Development Index is a combination of three indicators: longevity (life expectancy at birth), knowledge (literacy rates), and command over resources required for a decent life (gross domestic product).[92] The Index of Sustainable Economic Welfare considers not only average consumption but also distribution and environmental degradation.[93] After treating the consumption component of the index for distributional inequality, ISEW factors in several environmental costs related to economic mismanagement, such as natural resource depletion, loss of wetland, loss of farmland, the cost of noise, and air and water pollution. It is the most sophisticated indicator of progress available for the status of life in the United States.[94] A third way is *grain consumption per person*, a particularly sensitive measure of changes of well-being in low-income countries.[95] We need to find more wholesome ways to measure progress for low-income countries with such categories as drinking water supply, availability of basic medical service, and housing.

This progress in humanization denotes not only improving human living conditions, but also the humane treatment of animals and care for nature. Our motif of ecological care should be based not simply on the fear that human annihilation will occur if environments are destroyed, but on a genuine concern and love for God's creation.

*International and National Green Taxes*

Heavy international and national taxes on carbon dioxide emissions, the generation of other greenhouse gases and toxic waste, and emissions which cause acid rain will discourage the production of such pollutants. Many countries already tax various pollutants. A survey of the members of the OECD (Organization for Economic Cooperation and Development) turned up more than fifty environmental charges, including levies on waste, noise, and air and water pollution, as well as various pollutant product charges.[96] Revenues from green taxes could be used to clean up environmental pollution.

*Population Explosion*

According to Noel Brown, North American director of the U.N. Environment program, we have a full-occupancy planet, and today 80 percent of deforestation results from population growth.[97] World population is growing by 92 million people each year, roughly equal to adding another Mexico annually.[98] By 2050, the present world's population (5.4 billion) will double (10 billion).[99] With the present population growth rate, by the year 2050, the U.N. estimates that an additional 5.9 million square kilometers of land (the total size of today's protected natural areas) will have to be turned over to roads, urban uses, and farming.[100] Two thirds of the human family is hungry, partly because of inequitable distribution (85 percent of the world's income goes to 23 percent of its population; by contrast, more than 1 billion people living in absolute poverty survive on less than $1 a day),[101] but increasingly because of falling per-capita food production.[102] Despite the fivefold rise in world economic output since 1950, 1.2 billion people—more than ever—live in absolute poverty today.[103] Since the beginning of the 1990s, the ranks of the hungry have increased.[104]

Family planning is one of the best ways to deter the population explosion. Under the pressure of the political far right, the Reagan administration withdrew all U.S. funding from the International Planned Parenthood Federation and the United Nations Population Fund.[105] Religious resistance to population control in the Roman Catholic Church, some Protestant churches, and many Muslim societies has helped foster rapid population growth. To overcome this obstacle, the redirection of the religious resistance to population control should concur with the education of the poor on family planning.

*The Ecological Bible*

The creation story in Genesis 3:17-19 reveals our humble origin; *adam* (humankind) is made of *adamah* (soil, dust), tills *adamah* (field), and then goes back to *adamah*. The sequel is *adamah–adam–adamah*. We are composed of soil. When soil dies, we die too. The earth is not made only for the human family. After creating living creatures on the fifth day, God saw that it was so good that God blessed them and declared: "Be fruitful and multiply and fill the waters in the seas, and let birds multiply on the earth" (Gen. 1:22). John Macquarrie has pointed out the significance of the priestly tradition's survival alongside the dominant prophetic tradition of the Old Testament. A passage arising from the priestly religion which brings to light its nonanthropocentric perspective is the story of Noah. After the flood, God made a covenant with the human race and with every living creature: "Behold, I establish my covenant with you and your descendants after you and with every living creature that is with you, the birds, the cattle, and every beast of the earth with as many as came out of the ark" (Gen. 9:9-10).[106] Further, whereas most of the psalms laud the mighty work of the Lord in history, the priestly psalms observe the work of the Lord in nature: "The heavens are telling the glory of God." (Ps. 19:1).[107]

Human beings are neither the center nor the master of the earth. We are the most intelligent among creatures, receiving the image of God (Gen. 1:23). We are, however, very apt to misinterpret the image of God and become entrapped in anthropocentricism. As some Israelites misconstrued the chosen as God's special favor for them, we may mistake the image of God for God's exclusive love for the human family. Just as the chosen meant that the Israelites were first elected to spread God's mercy and love to others, so does the image of God denote that humans have been selected as God's instruments to share God's mercy and love with other creatures and nature. The New Testament testifies to Christ as the image of God (Col. 1:15, II Cor. 4:4). The image of God that Christ disclosed to us is not the image of a tyrannical and exploitative god, but a God of self-giving, care, mercy, compassion, and self-transcendence. As we grow in the image of God, we become more caring, cherishing, and loving of the whole creation. To fulfill God's purpose of creation, we must envision a global wholeness in which all of God's creations live in respect, harmony, and love, rejoicing in one another's company.


# ENGAGEMENT:
# COMPASSIONATE CONFRONTATION

We have discussed the process of *understanding* and *envisagement* as necessary steps for the resolution of han. *Understanding* is compassion and *envisagement* is hope. By themselves they are not enough to dissolve han. The two must meet in the *engagement* of action, which is faith (James 2:26). This last step for the resolution of han is *compassionate confrontation.*[108] Confrontation without understanding will cause unnecessary, hostile conflict. Compassion without confrontation will result in ineffective transformation. Confrontation with the heart of compassion for the oppressors will genuinely change their heart through creative tension.

Understanding and envisagement empower the people of han to take action in dismantling han-causing elements in the world. The disentanglement of conscious han is different from that of unconscious han. While conscious han is resolved in an effort to transform the world of han, unconscious han is dissolved in an attempt to transcend the irreversible world of han. Engagement in resolving conscious han signifies the transformation of the reality of han-causing people and evil. Confrontation is the will to action, the determination to face this reality rather than escape from it. Engagement in resolving unconscious han means transcending the painful event of whatever caused han. The han that lies beyond the reach of our conscious efforts can only be transcended. This indicates that there is an unresolvable dimension of han. The transcendence of unconscious han transpires as a gift when the person of han is engaged in a task of converting han-causing people and removing han-causing evil.

## Transformation: Conscious Han

Understanding and envisagement will enable han-ful persons to have the hearts of compassionate confrontation. This confrontation is the courage to call offenders to repentance. If offenders are willing to change their ways, they and their victims can work together toward an alternative vision of society. In this case, the han of the victims will be dissolved in the midst of transforming han-causing elements. At a personal level, a vision may be reunion, restoration of broken relationships, and reconciliation between victims and their offenders. At a collective level, a vision can be a new world order which may inspire victims and offenders alike to change the capitalist global economy, patriarchy, hierarchy, and racism into a *hanless* society—the global community of political and economic democracy, equity, respect, and affection.

In the course of participation in the transformation of the root causes of han, victims experience the dissolution of han, using up han as fuel. Han is the thick energy that is continually collapsing inward.

171

If it is wrongly handled, it will explode and destroy others as well as the han-ful person. If it is rightly unraveled, then it can be used as the positive dynamic energy which empowers victims to reconstruct the reality of the world which inflicted pain upon them.

The understanding of han at the rational, intuitive, and incarnational dimensions begins to melt the han of the afflicted; the vision of the interconnected nature of reality and an alternative society will raise up passive han and avert it from its negative energy. Finally, compassionate confrontation will convert passive and active han into the will to compassion and the will to construction, respectively.

In this process, however, the resolution of victims' han should not be the final goal of all action. The goal should be building the community of God through the mutual transformation of victims and their offenders. Victims can transmute their negative energy of han into a positive one for constructing the community of God; their offenders can cease afflicting others and participate in the establishment of God's community.

But victims must initiate this process of true reconciliation, since the oppressors hardly come to repentance by themselves, as their own wrongs prevent them from seeing reality. Oppressors are often locked in a room where the door has no knob. Their prison is self-centeredness. Many do not even know that they are imprisoned, nor do they know who they truly are. They are trapped in their own prejudice, discrimination, and dehumanization. By circumscribing others, they circumscribe themselves; by oppressing others, they oppress themselves; by dehumanizing others, they dehumanize themselves; by hating others, they hate themselves first. The oppressed can see their oppressors better from outside, knowing where the door is and how they can come out. The oppressed can help them see their own blindness and the effect of their own wrongs. Without the assistance of victims, perpetrators would not see the pain caused by their evil work. Only victims can open the offenders' eyes to see what they have done. Victims are thus able to help offenders convert from their own iniquity.

Compassionate confrontation challenges oppressors to repent and cooperate with the oppressed to advance the full reign of God. The crux of this action is a common vision and task which both groups share together, for which they can cooperate, and toward which they move together.

The following story of the Robber's Cave Field Experiment demonstrates the significance of a common vision and task in resolving the enmity of two groups.[109] An experiment executed by Muzafer

Sherif and his associates involved a group of boys, aged eleven and twelve, who were attending a summer camp. They were psychologically well-adjusted and came from middle-class families. Without the knowledge of the boys, the summer camp was staffed by researchers who steered and observed their aggressive behavior.

Two groups of boys were ushered into separate cabins, each unaware of the existence of the other group. Each group had its own time to organize group activities and to cooperate for mutual tasks, through which the members became familiar with one another. During this period, each group developed its group identity, including its own name, regulations, and jokes.

When the time arrived to introduce intergroup conflict, the two groups were set to compete for a group reward. A series of contests turned good sportsmanship into an ethic of winning at all costs. "Rattlers" and "Eagles" denigrated each other, calling names, picking fights, and ravaging each other's camps. The accelerating hostility between them united each group.

Next, the researchers endeavored to resolve the hostility between the groups. Religious services were conducted to emphasize brotherly love and cooperation, but these helped little in stopping the fights. Introducing a third party to serve as a common enemy temporarily lessened the intensity of conflict, but eventually expanded its perimeter. The groups also rejected the proposal to have conferences between the leaders, fearing that the leaders might sell out their group interests. Even some common activities—meals, fireworks on the Fourth of July, going to the movies—did not work, serving only to further channel the boys' expressions of animosity.

Only through a series of superordinate goals, which necessitated the cooperation of both groups, did the enmity decrease gradually. A breakdown in the water supply line required joint efforts to find the leakage and helped to reduce the conflict temporarily. Further series of joint efforts, such as renting a movie and pulling a food supply truck to get it started, finally melted down their hostility. Each group came to appreciate the other and to develop friendships with their former enemies. At the end, the majority of the boys opted to return home on the same bus; even the winning group treated the loser with the five-dollar prize.

This experiment illustrates the importance of a common vision and task (a superordinate goal) which elicit mutual respect and cooperation. Even though we cannot presume that such an experiment has a universal applicability, we can say that cooperation via superordinate tasks will alleviate tension between antagonistic groups. Likewise, a common vision and task will bring about cooperation between the oppressed and their oppressors. The han of the oppressed will be best reduced in their confrontational action, which will eventually lead the oppressors and the oppressed to a common vision and task. Even if the oppressors refuse to repent and participate in transforming han-causing problems, the oppressed can resolve han in their acts for the compassionate confrontation and for the rectification of social wrongs with a vision of a new community.

Lack of understanding of the world's injustice and lack of a clear vision for the future world precipitate the han of the world. People, whether the oppressed or the oppressors, must be led to see their common tasks. Compassionate confrontational action will empower the oppressors and the oppressed to come out from their own egos and han, and commit themselves to something greater than their own selves.

The compassionate confrontational act is similar to Paulo Freire's definition of praxis, in which reflection and action transform reality.[110] This compassionate confrontation, however, includes all the considerate movements and efforts toward the transformation of the world pain of han, whether they are words, deeds, thoughts, or commitments. In other words, this *act* does not mean to do something physically, but encompasses all the compassionate striving of various people for the transformation and the transcendence of han-inducing situations and han-causing persons. Such endeavors as writers' writings, teachers' teaching, activists' activities, and artists' works of art with the heart of care and compassion are transformative acts. The compassionate confrontational act involves preparatory toil for practice and practice for the meaningful transformation of the world's han. In the midst of participating in a compassionate confrontational act, the people of han can transform the world of han as well as their own han.

## Transcendence: Unconscious Han

While transformation is the key to resolving personal and collective conscious han, transcendence is the door to unraveling personal and collective unconscious han.

The unconscious han of victims cannot be dissolved by removing han-causing elements alone. The han of irreversible events such as tragic death can only be resolved through transcendence. This process is the work of unconsciousness, but can be identified in the expression of joy and peace when it transpires. Transcendence takes

174

place at the "critical point" of which Teilhard de Chardin speaks. It involves a change of state—"the curve doubles back, the surface contracts to a point, the solid disintegrates, the liquid boils, the germ cell divides, intuition suddenly bursts on the piled-up facts."[111]

How can we arrive at the point of transcendence? At a personal level, transcendence occurs when victims face their irreversible traumas through recollection. They need to confront their own abysmal dread of traumas. At a collective level, it takes place when a group of victims identifies their han together, and hopes and works for an alternative society.

At an individual level, the victims of traumas tend to bury their painful memories of these events. The point of transcendence can be reached only when victims work through the reality of such painful events. For example, in the *han-poori* of a drowning victim in Korean shamanism, a possessed shaman replays the process of the drowning step by step and shows the bereaved and friends the way the victim was drowned. The shaman speaks and acts as if she or he were the victim, reliving the traumatic accident.[112] This ritual, called *soo-mang-koot*, helps the bereaved and friends recognize the han-filled reality of the accident and the uselessness of fostering han, and seek positive ways to divert their energy from han into the prevention of a future drowning. In the midst of watching the reenactment, the bereaved and friends experience the point of transcendence. Recognizing the reality of the painful han and determining the diversion of han-energy are the avenues by which one transcends the unconscious level of han. The moment when a person of han realizes his or her own limitations and new possibilities is the transcendent point.[113]

The moment of self-transcendence occurs at a collective level when a group of the han-laden sees its han-ridden situation together and projects a new society.

Younghak Hyun, professor of religion at Ewha Womans University, looks into the Korean mask dance to understand how the han of the oppressed can be disintegrated. In the mask dance, the oppressed (actors and actresses) become free to be themselves behind a mask, making a caricature of a ruling class. Through laughter and dancing, the performers and the audience become united and reach the point of "critical transcendence" of the world's injustice. The suppressed feeling of the *minjung* (people of han) in the performance is released into concrete body language in which the *minjung* become conscienticized. Such critical transcendence never arises from the biography of an isolated individual, but rather from the sociopolitical and historical biography of the *minjung*.[114] The experience of transcendence enables the *minjung* to transcend present history and gives a momentum toward the change of oppressive situations.

Collective transcendence occurs when we see the reality of han together as a group and when we have an alternative vision of society. The recollection of traumas elicits the transcendence of han, and the circle of the resolution of unconscious han is completed in the compassionate confrontation of these traumas.

# CONCLUSION

We have examined here the meanings of both the Christian doctrine of sin and the Asian cultural concept of han. As we have seen, sin has been understood as pride, concupiscence, self-centered-ness, unbelief, hubris, falsehood, sloth, ingratitude, slavery, death, and collaboration. One thing that is missing from the traditional Christian doctrine of sin is concern for and understanding of the victims of sin. As a result, the church has adopted a one-sided emphasis on the moral agency of sinners and focused primarily on their forgiveness and their salvation.

My purpose has been to demonstrate this shortcoming in the doctrine of sin and to suggest its complement through the notion of han, in the hope of bringing forth a holistic vision of the salvation of both sinners and their victims.

The Christian gospel cannot afford a parochial vision in the world of God's creation. Envisaging the wholeness of the universe, we must go beyond the problem of sin and grapple with the han of the world. To understand the depth and breadth of the world and humanity's han, theology as a discipline which integrates the structure and meaning of all beings (as per Tillich) must not hesitate to use information and perspectives from other disciplines. While the doctrine of sin is theological, the concept of han is broader in scope. The analysis of sin is insufficient to give a comprehensive picture of the world's problems. The notion of han is needed for a proper perception of the complex trouble of the world. By treating the issue of sin alone, we are not able to grasp and cut off the vicious cycles of abuse, violence, exploitation, and oppression which plague the planet and its inhabitants. The original intention of the Jesus movement was not to establish a religious institution, but to bring about the wholeness of creation. Christianity needs to enlarge the scope of the doctrine of sin—its primary means of diagnosing the world's wrongs—to include the idea of han. When the doctrine of sin and the idea of han cooperate to unravel the depth of the human predicament and the pain of the world, a new dawn of salvation will begin to arrive in history.

# NOTES

## Introduction

1. Reinhold Niebuhr, *The Nature and Destiny of Man*, 2 vols. (New York: Scribner's, 1941–43), 2:6.

2. The Children's Defense Fund, a Washington-based child advocacy organization, reports that *every day* in the United States:

One child in five wakes up in poverty and 100,000 go to bed homeless.

1,849 children are abused and 3,288 run away from home.

2,989 children see their parents divorce.

Nine children die from gun-shot wounds, six are murdered, seven commit suicide and 684 attempt suicide.

1,629 teenagers are in adult jails.

Ron Harris, "Children's Lack of Power Leaves Needs Unmet," in a series entitled "Growing Up in America," *Los Angeles Times*, 16 May 1991, p. A8.

3. One out of every four girls and one of every ten boys in the United States are believed to have had some sort of sexual experience with an adult by age eighteen. State of California Health and Welfare Agency and Department of Social Services, *Child Sexual Abuse* PUB 106 (8/87).

4. Reginald S. Moxon, *The Doctrine of Sin* (New York: George H. Doran Co., 1922), p. 40.

5. Ibid., pp. 41–46.

6. Valerie Saiving, "The Human Situation," in *Womanspirit Rising*, ed. Carol Christ and Judith Plaskow (New York: Harper & Row, 1979), p. 37.

7. Gustavo Gutiérrez, *A Theology of Liberation*, trans. and ed. Sister Caridad Inda and John Eagleson (New York: Orbis, 1973), pp. 25–37.

8. Van A. Harvey, *A Handbook of Theological Terms* (New York: MacMillan Publishing Co., 1964), p. 220.

9. J. C. O'Neill, "Sin," *The Westminster Dictionary of Christian Theology,* ed. Alan Richardson and John Bowden (Philadelphia: Westminster, 1983), p. 539.

## Chapter 1

1. Han is *hen* (hate) in Chinese, *kon* (to bear a grudge) in Japanese, *horosul* (sorrowfulness) in Mongolian, *korsocuka* (hatred, grief) in Manchurian, and *hân* (frustration) in Vietnamese. *Matthew's Chinese-English Dictionary* (Cambridge, Mass.: Harvard University Press, 1963), p. 310; Andrew N. Nelson, *The Modern Reader's Japanese-English Character Dictionary* (Tokyo: Charles E. Tuttle, 1962), p. 400; Eun Ko, "Han ui Kuek-Bok ul We-Ha-Yuh" (For Overcoming Han), *Han ui Yi-Ya-Ki* (The Story of Han), ed. David Kwang-sun Suh (Seoul: Borhee, 1988), pp. 33–34.

2. Tong Hwan Moon, "Korean Minjung Theology," unpublished paper, 1982 (typewritten). The *minjung* are the people who have been politically oppressed, economically exploited, socially alienated, culturally despised, and/or religiously rejected. They are the people of han.

3. Peter Burke, a social psychologist, studied the dynamics of a small group and attained this hypothesis via persuasive evidence from the small group laboratory. Peter J. Burke, "Scapegoating: An Alternative to Role Differentiation," *Sociometry* (June 1969): 156–68.

4. Ibid.

5. Jürgen Moltmann, *Theology of Hope,* trans. James W. Leitch (New York: Harper & Row, 1967), pp. 15–26.

6. Mary Louise Bringle eloquently argues that despair is neither sin nor sickness but a symptom of both, pointing to the brokenness in the world. *Despair Sickness or Sin?* (Nashville: Abingdon, 1990), pp. 178f.

7. "The essential preliminary to a supernova explosion is the generation by silicon fusion of a massive iron core. Under enormous pressure, the free electrons in the stellar interior are forcibly melded with the protons of the iron nuclei, the equal and opposite electrical charges canceling each other out; the inside of the star is turned into a single giant atomic nucleus, occupying a much smaller volume than the precursor electrons and iron nuclei. The core implodes violently, the exterior rebounds and a supernova explosion result." Carl Sagan, *Cosmos* (New York: Random House, 1980), pp. 238–42.

8. Ibid.

9. Andrew Sung Park, "Theology of Han (Abyss of Pain)," *Quarterly Review* (Spring 1989):50–51.

10. Meister Eckhart, *Breakthrough: Meister Eckhart's Creation Spirituality in New Translation,* Introduction and commentaries by Matthew Fox, O.P. (New York: Doubleday, 1977), pp. 213, 226–27, 238.

11. Erik H. Erikson, *Childhood and Society* (New York: Norton, 1950), pp. 251–52.

12. Ibid., p. 251.

13. See Samuel Beckett, *Waiting for Godot: Tragicomedy in 2 acts* (New York: Grove Press, 1970). *Godot* signifies a God who is forever absent, who never appears to us.

14. Karl Schoenberger, "S. Koreans Just Love to Wax Lyrical," *Los Angeles Times,* 16 December 1988, part I, p. 36.

15. Nam-Dong Suh, "Towards a Theology of Han," in *Minjung Theology,* ed. Yong Bock Kim (Singapore: The Christian Conference of Asia, 1981), p. 59.

16. Karl Schoenberger, "S. Koreans Just Love to Wax Lyrical," p. 36.

17. Ibid.

18. David Kwang-sun Suh, "A Biographical Sketch of an Asian Theological Consultation," in *Minjung Theology,* p. 27.

19. Nam-Dong Suh, "Towards a Theology of Han," in *Minjung Theology,* p. 58.

20. Younghak Hyun, "*Minjung,* the Suffering Servant, and Hope," paper presented at Union Theological Seminary, New York, 13 April 1982.

21. C. S. Song, *Theology From the Womb of Asia,* (New York: Orbis, 1986), p. 70.

22. Ibid. p. 71.

23. They are Go-Un, Nam-Dong Suh, Won Sang Han, David Kwang-sun Suh, Younghak Hyun, Soon Tae Moon, etc.

24. *Marah* was the first camp of the Israelites after the passage of the Red Sea. Because of the bitterness of the brackish water, it was named *marah* or bitterness. Moses cast a tree into the water which was then made sweet (Ex. 15:23).

25. *The Compact Edition of the Oxford English Dictionary: Complete Text Reproduced Micrographically,* 2 vols. (London: Oxford University Press, 1971), 2:3830.

26. According to Soon Tae Moon, a *minjung* writer, "han is the wound of the heart in a passive term and the blood occlusion. The former is the knot of the mind and the latter is the knot of the spirit." Soon Tae Moon, "Han yi Rhan Muut Inga?" (What is Han?), in *The Story of Han,* p. 141.

27. Nam-Dong Suh, *Minjung Shinhak ui Tamku* (Exploration of Minjung Theology), (Seoul: Han-Gil Sa, 1983), pp. 351–53. The translation is mine.

28. I am indebted to the late Prof. Nam-Dong Suh who inspired me to see the similarity of Jesus' and Tae-il's deaths. Ibid., pp. 350–53.

29. Concerning the identity of the Servant, there are various interpretations: the collective interpretation (Baudissin, Budde, Smend, Wellhausen, König, Eissfeldt, and Lods), the individual interpretation (Sellin, Kittel, Gressmann, Engnell, Gunkel, Weiser, and Elliger), the collective and individual interpretation (Nyberg, North, and Rowley), the idea of Israel's worldwide mission (Lindblom), and cult-mythological features and royal features (Gressmann, Engnell, Lidhagen, Böhl, and Kaiser). Georg Fohrer, *Introduction to the Old Testament,* trans. David Green (Nashville: Abingdon, 1968), pp. 377–81.

30. Elie Wiesel, *Night*, trans. Stella Rodway (New York: Hill & Wang, 1960), pp. 111–13.

31. Elie Wiesel, "Recalling Swallowed-Up Worlds," in *Theologians in Transition: The Christian Century "How My Mind Has Changed" Series*, ed. James M. Wall (New York: Crossroad, 1981), pp.127–33.

32. Even though restrained in its round-up of some alien Japanese, the Department of Justice did act much more harshly toward Japanese nationals than toward German nationals in term of numbers interned. Roger Daniels and Harry H. L. Kitano, *American Racism: Exploration of the Nature of Prejudice*, (Englewood Cliffs: Prentice-Hall, 1970), p. 58.

33. Ibid., p. 57.

34. Ibid., p. 62.

35. Violet Masuda, "Amazing Grace," in *The Theologies of Asian Americans and Pacific Peoples: A Reader*, ed. Roy Sano (Berkeley: Asian Center for Theology & Strategies, 1976), p. 2.

36. Her case is quite similar to the condition of original sin; we must be accountable for the sin which we have not committed. Chapter 7 treats this issue more fully.

37. Violet Masuda, "Amazing Grace," pp. 2–3.

38. John Lee "The Discriminated Fingers: The Korean Minority in Japan," *Monthly Review*, January 1987, p. 17.

39. "Trial of Missionary Scheduled," *Japan Christian Activity News*, 25 September 1982, p. 7.

40. John Lee, "The Discriminated Fingers: The Korean Minority in Japan," p. 22.

41. *The Dong-A Daily News L.A. Edition*, 15 August 1989, p. 1.

42. Nam-Dong Suh, *Minjung Shinhak ui Tamku* (Exploration of *Minjung* Theology), p. 326.

43. Su-nam Pak, *The Other Hiroshima: Korean A-bomb Victims Tell Their Story*, trans. Greg Barrett et al., (Kanagawa, Japan: self-published, 1982), pp. 7–10. The italics are mine.

44. Recently, the Korean government interceded for A-bomb victim survivors living in Korea (1,564), asking Japan to compensate $2.3 billion to them. *The Dong-A Daily News L.A. Edition*, 15 August 1989, p. 1.

45. St. John of the Cross (1542–1591) uses the term "the dark night of the soul" to describe his spiritual journey to the state of perfection. Experienced as if it were at night, the journey in darkness consists of two parts: the first night is the purgation of the sensual part of the soul; the second is of the spiritual part. I use the expression "the dark night of the soul" to indicate the double negation forced upon the Koreans in Japan: psychosomatic and social denial. They have experienced a crucifixion without the hope of resurrection. See E. Allison Peers, ed. *The Complete Works of Saint John of the Cross*, trans. E. A. Peers, 3 vols. (Westminster, MD.: Newman, 1953).

46. D. J. West, ed. *Sexual Victimization: Two Recent Researches in Sex Problems and Their Social Effects*, (Vermont: Gower, 1985), p. 1

47. Ibid., pp. 6–7.

48. D. E. N. Russell, "The Incidence and Prevalence of Intrafamilial Sexual Abuse of Female Children," *Child Abuse and Neglect*, vol. 7, pp. 133–46. quoted in West, *Sexual Victimization*, p. 7.

49. L. Newman, "The Terrors of Sexual Abuse . . . Behind Closed Doors," *19*, September 1982, pp. 34–36.

50. L. Newman, "Sexual Abuse Within the Family," *19*, May 1983, pp. 35–39.

51. Elizabeth Ward, *Father-Daughter Rape*, (New York: Grove Press, 1985), pp. 50–59.

52. Ibid.

53. Ibid.

## Chapter 2

1. David Kwang-sun Suh, "A Biographical Sketch of an Asian Theological Consultation," pp. 27–32.

2. *The Korea Times (Supplement)*, 23 February 1991.

3. J. L. Barkas, *Victims* (New York: Scribner's, 1978), pp. 14–15.

4. This refers to a theory formulated by Melanie Klein (1882–1960), pioneer of child analysis and research into depressive and schizoid states. She remained a Freudian. Melanie Klein, *Contributions to Psycho-Analysis* (London: Hogarth Press, 1948).

5. Cf. Barkas, *Victims*, pp. 14–15.

6. See Chapter 1

7. Suzanne M. Sgroi, ed. *Vulnerable Populations*, 2 vols. (Lexington: Lexington Books, 1989), 2:46.

8. Freud introduced the concepts of "life instinct," *eros*, and "death instinct," *thanatos*. The life instinct, the sexual instincts, are perpetually attempting and achieving a renewal of life, while the death instinct leads what is living to the extinction of life. Sigmund Freud, *Beyond the Pleasure Principle*, vol. 17 (London: Hogarth Press, 1920).

9. Sigmund Freud, *The Interpretation of Dreams*, in *The Basic Writings of Sigmund Freud*, trans. and ed. A. A. Brill (New York: The Modern Library, 1938), p. 544.

10. Ibid., pp. 491, 544.

11. Friedrich Nietzsche, *The Genealogy of Morals*, trans. Francis Golffing (New York, 1956), pp. 168–69. For Nietzsche, Christian love is the product of resentment. The inferiors love even their superiors who are their enemies because of their fear of the latter's power.

12. During the Soviet leader Mikhail Gorbachev's visit to Beijing on May 15–18, 1989, a million people demonstrated, demanding democratic reforms and the change of political leadership including that of Deng. On June 3–4, army troops entered Beijing and crushed the pro-democracy protesters. Tanks and armored personnel vehicles moved into Tiananmen Square where the main demonstrations and hunger-strikes were staged, rolling over the protestors and opening fire upon them. It was estimated that about 5,000

were killed, 10,000 were injured, and hundreds of students and laborers were arrested. Mark S. Hoffman, ed. *The World Almanac and Book of Facts 1991* (New York: Pharos Books, 1990), p. 699.

13. "Beijing Credits Stability to Use of Force," *The Los Angeles Times*, 10 April 1991, p. A6.

14. Richard Rubenstein, *After Auschwitz* (Indianapolis: Bobbs-Merrill, 1966), p. 152.

15. Ibid., p. 225.

16. T. Walter Wallbank and Alastair M. Taylor, *Civilization Past and Present*, 2 vols., 4th ed. (Chicago: Scott, Foresman and Co., 1961), 2:558.

17. Richard Reeves, "A Land of Widows and Orphans Remains U.S. Enemy," *Los Angeles Times*, 31 March 1991, p. M2. Richard Reeves, author and syndicated columnist, published this article on his return from Cambodia and Vietnam.

18. Ibid.

19. Carl G. Jung, *Analytic Psychology: Its Theory and Practice* (New York: Pantheon, 1968), p. 44.

20. Carl G. Jung, *Letters*, ed. G. Adler (Princeton: Princeton University Press, 1973), p. 408.

21. Ibid., p. 283.

22. Philip W. Goetz, ed. *The New Encyclopaedia Britannica*, 29 vols. 15th ed. (Chicago: Encyclopaedia Britannica Inc., 1988), 1:567.

23. Georg Fohrer, *Introduction to the Old Testament*, pp. 266–68. *Their Sitz im Leben* is cultic. The cultic form of lamentation, however, is not separable from a mournful situation shown in Jeremiah's "Lamentations."

24. Ibid.

25. Cf. Hun-Young Yim, *Han-ui Moonhak kwa Sa-Hwe Ui-Sik* (Han Literature and Social Consciousness), In *The Story of Han*, pp. 104–6.

26. Plato in the *Timaeus* presents the mythical idea of the creation of the world whose soul and body are made by the Demiurge according to the Form of the ideal living creature.

27. Lester R. Brown and Sandra Postel, "Thresholds of Change," in *State of the World 1987*, ed. Lester R. Brown (New York: W. W. Norton & Co., 1987), p. 14.

28. Ibid., p. 14.

29. Ibid., p. 6.

30. Sandra Postel and Lori Heise, "Reforesting the Earth," in *State of the World 1988: A Worldwatch Institute Report on Progress Toward a Sustainable Society*, ed. Lester R. Brown (New York: Norton, 1988), p. 85.

31. Sandra Postel, "Denial in the Decisive Decade," *State of the World 1992*, ed. Lester R. Brown (New York: Norton, 1992), p. 3.

32. Edward O. Wilson, *The Diversity of Life* (Cambridge, Mass: Harvard University Press, forthcoming), quoted in *State of the World 1992*, p. 3.

33. Ibid., quoted in *Time* 1 June 1992, p. 51.

34. A quote from the Nature Conservancy, in *50 Simple Things You Can Do to Save the Earth*, The Earth Works Group (Berkeley: Earthworks, 1989), p. 14.

35. Lester R. Brown and Christopher Flavin, "The Earth's Vital Signs," *The State of the World 1988*, p. 5.

36. Ibid., *p. 5.*

37. Lester R. Brown and Sandra Postel, "Thresholds of Change," *The State of the World 1987*, p. 4.

38. Sharon Begley et al., "A Gaping Hole in the Sky," *Newsweek*, 11 July 1988, p. 22.

39. Michael D. Lemonick, "The Ozone Vanishes," *Time*, 17 February 1992, p. 60.

40. Lester R. Brown and Christopher Flavin, "The Earth's Vital Signs," p. 6.

41. Arthur Schopenhauer asserts that wherever he looks, whether in the inorganic or organic sphere, he detects the manifestation of the one individual Will in the phenomena of attraction and repulsion, in gravitation, in the impulse by which the magnet turns to the north pole, in animal instinct, in human desire and so on. Frederick Copleston, S.J., *A History of Philosophy*, 9 vols. (Garden City: Image Books, 1963), 7:37.

## Chapter 3

1. I use the term "evil" as the reality that appears as the result of sin. I do not treat it as an ontological or a teleological entity. John Hick's answer to theodicy is teleological. He views the world as a "vale of soul-making." John Hick, *Evil and the God of Love* (New York: Harper & Row, 1966), p. xii. David R. Griffin's process theodicy explains evil in the God of process thought who cannot unilaterally prevent all evil. His theology denies the traditional idea that God is omnipotent. David Griffin, *God, Power, and Evil: A Process Theodicy* (Philadelphia: Westminster, 1976), pp. 279–80.

2. Ibid., p. 11.

3. Edna Bonacich and Lucie Cheng, "Introduction: A Theoretical Orientation to International Labor Migration," *Labor Immigration Under Capitalism: Asian Workers in the U.S. Before World War II*, ed. Edna Bonacich and Lucie Cheng (Berkeley: University of California Press, 1984), p. 10.

4. Ibid., p. 13.

5. Ivan Light and Edna Bonacich, *Immigrant Entrepreneurs* (Berkeley: University of California Press, 1988).

6. Light and Bonacich insist that the cheap labor in Korea has been absorbed U.S. immigration policy. But this rationale for Korean immigration is an oversimplification of the issue of Korean immigration. Byong Gap Min, a Korean-American sociologist, is a voice against their simplistic diagnosis.

7. Ivan Light and Edna Bonacich, *Immigrant Entrepreneurs*, pp. 426–29.

8. Some launched their own businesses with the money of co-investment; others with money accumulated through long, hard labor; others with financing from relatives or friends in the United States or Korea.

9. Ibid., pp. 427–28.

10. Cf. Ivan Light and Edna Bonacich, *Immigrant Entrepreneurs,* pp. 427–28. Their figures 5 & 6 are very thorough.

11. Max Weber, *The Protestant Ethic and the Spirit of Capitalism,* trans. Talcott Parsons (London: G. Allen, 1930).

12. Refer to Chapter 6.

13. Confucian *Analects,* Vii, xvi. quoted in *The I Ching,* trans. James Legge (New York: Dover, 1963), p. 1. The basic text of the *I Ching* seems to have been prepared before 1,000 B.C.E., according to James Legge. This is one of the five Classics Confucius edited. Legge inferred from this passage the existence of the *I Ching* before the time of Confucius.

14. *The I Ching,* Appendix V, 4. pp. 423–24.

15. Karen Warren, "Feminism and Ecology: Making Connections," *Environmental Ethics* 9 (1987): 3–20.

16. Rosemary R. Ruether, *Liberation Theology* (New York: Paulist Press, 1972), p. 115.

17. Rosemary R. Ruether, *New Woman/New Earth* (New York: Seabury Press, 1975), p. 74.

18. Ibid.

19. *Sexism and God-Talk* (Boston: Beacon Press, 1983), p. 72.

20. Ibid., pp. 161–62.

21. Reinhold Niebuhr, *The Nature and Destiny of Man,* 2 vols. (New York: Scribner's, 1941), 1:180.

22. Ibid.

23. Jean Baker Miller, *Toward a New Psychology of Women* (Boston: Beacon Press, 1976), p. 1.

24. Aline K. Wong, "Women in China: Past and Present," in *Many Sisters: Women in Cross-Cultural Perspective,* ed. Carolyn J. Matthiasson (New York: The Free Press, 1974), p. 235. Takashi Koyama, Hachiro Nakamura, and Masako Hiramatsu, "Japan," in *Women in the Modern World,* ed. Raphael Patai (New York: The Free Press, 1967), pp. 291–92. Yung-Chung Kim, *Women of Korea: A History from Ancient Times to 1945* (Seoul: Ewha Womans University Press, 1976), pp. 52–53. Sung-Hee Lee, "Women's Liberation Theology as the Foundation for Asian Theology," *East Asian Journal of Theology (EAJT)* 4 (Feb. 1986): 7.

25. Takashi Koyama, et al, "Japan," p. 292. Sung-Hee Lee, "Women's Liberation Theology as the Foundation for Asian Theology," p. 7.

26. Aline K. Wong, "Women in China," p. 234.

27. Howard S. Levy, *Chinese Footbinding, The History of a Curious Erotic Custom,* (New York: Walton Rawls, 1966).

28. Ibid., p. 52.

29. Ibid., p. 179.

30. Aline K. Wong, "Women in China: Past and Present," pp. 232–33.

31. Thomas H. Mauch II, "Researchers Find Widespread Infanticide of Girls in India," *Los Angeles Times* 9 February 1992, A12. This is the first documented evidence of the extent of infanticide in India.

32. Ibid.

33. Ibid.

34. Pui Lan Kwok, "God Weeps With Our Pain," *East Asia Journal of Theology*, vol. 2, No. 2 (October 1984):228. Quoted in Mary Elizabeth Moore, "The Unity of the Sacred and the Public Possibilities from Feminist Theology," *Religious Education* 84 (Summer 1989): 396–97.

35. In South Korea, many parents who prefer infant boys abort female fetuses after finding out their sex via amniocentesis tests. At the present, elementary schools have a problem with an unbalanced number of boys and girls. This is a different way to murder baby girls—"fetuscide."

36. Levy Cruz, "Brazil," in *Women in the Modern World*, p. 215.

37. *The Korea Times Los Angeles Edition,* 19 April 1991, p. C1.

38. Ibid.

39. This "crime of honor" is preposterous in such a country as Brazil where a young boy is encouraged to seek maximum satisfaction in sexual activity as early as possible via the custom of *virility*. In the custom, the boy of puberty is promoted by his parents and relatives to have sexual relations because male virginity is ridiculed. Yet girls' virginity is absolutely required by the same people. Levy Cruz, "Brazil," pp. 214–15.

40. Andrea Dworkin, *Woman Hating* (New York: E. P. Dutton, 1974), p. 130.

41. Joseph Klaits, "Who's To Blame? An Examination of Witchcraft," in Jacqueline Scherer and Gary Shepherd, eds. *Victimization of The Weak* (Springfield: Charles C. Thomas, 1982), pp. 39–40.

42. Ibid., p.41.

43. The first scattered cases appeared in the post-Vedic period. The inauguration of the post-Vedic period (after 300 B.C.E.) was crucial in determining the present status of women in India. The practice was revived around 700 C.E. by the two lawgivers Angira and Harita. The systematic compilation of Hindu law took place at that time. Vatsala Narain, "India," in *Women in the Modern World*, pp. 23–24.

44. Ibid.

45. The genocide of the Armenians took place on April 24, 1915. The religious and intellectual leaders of the Armenian community in Constantinople were arrested in their beds, imprisoned, tortured, and killed. Armenians in the Turkish army, already segregated into "labor battalions," were also massacred. Armenian men were then roped together, marched to nearby uninhabited locations, and killed. After a few days, the women and children were deported from Anatolia to the Syrian Desert, where they were left to die. It is estimated that the number of those killed ranges from four hundred thousand to over a million; the actual number is probably more than eight hundred thousand. Ervin Staub, *The Roots of Evil,* (Cambridge: Cambridge University Press, 1989), p. 10.

46. The Nanking massacre occurred in December 1937. As the Chinese armed forces evacuated Nanking, the Japanese troops advanced into the city, raping women and slaughtering helpless prisoners and civilians, an atrocity which shocked the world. Estimates of the number killed are about 200,000. Kenneth Scott Latourette, *The Chinese: Their History and Culture,* (New York: The Macmillan Company, 1934), p. 351; National Council of the Churches of Christ, "A Resolution on U.S. Pressure Toward Remilitarization of Japan and Textbook Revision by the Government of Japan," New York, 1982, p. 4.

47. Gordon Allport, *The Nature of the Prejudice* (Cambridge, Mass.: Addison-Wesley, 1954).

48. Aaron Antonovsky, "The Social Meaning of Discrimination," *Phylon* (Spring 1960):81.

49. George Simpson and J. Milton Yinger, *Racial and Cultural Minorities* (New York: Plenum Press, 1985), pp. 22–23.

50. Ibid., pp. 41–45.

51. John Dollard, et. al., *Frustration and Aggression* (New Haven: Yale University Press, 1939). Peter J. Burke, "Scapegoating: An Alternative to Role Differentiation," *Sociometry* (June 1969):159–68.

52. T. W. Adorno et. al., *The Authoritarian Personality* (New York: Harper & Row, 1950), pp. 753ff.

53. Ibid., p. 971.

54. Ibid.

55. George Simpson and J. Milton Yinger, *Racial and Cultural Minorities*, p. 41.

56. William G. Sumner, *Folkways* (Lexington, MA: Ginn, 1906), pp. 13–15.

57. Oliver L. Cox, *Caste, Class and Race: A Study in Social Dynamics,* (New York: Doubleday, 1948), p. 475.

58. Marios Nikolinakos, "Notes on an Economic Theory of Racism," *Race* (March 1963): 43–54.

59. The Community Reinvestment Act or Title VIII of the Housing and Community Development Act of 1977 became effective November 6, 1978. Cleveland *Plain Dealer,* 4 February 1979, p. 7-1.

60. Louis L. Knowles and Kenneth Prewitt, *Institutional Racism in America* (New York: Prentice-Hall, 1969).

61. Joseph Hough, Jr., "The Problem of Racism—Another Look," Claremont, CA (Typewritten.)

62. Ibid., p. 5.

63. George Simpson and J. Milton Yinger, *Racial and Cultural Minorities*, p. 43.

64. Ibid.

65. Ibid.

66. Joseph Hough, "The Problem of Racism—Another Look," pp. 8–10.

67. Ibid., p. 9.

68. Ruth Benedict, *Race: Science and Politics* (New York: The Viking Press, 1945), p. 98.

69. Social Darwinism uses Darwin's evolutionary theory to argue that evolutionary selection empowers those with more talent to survive better than the less talented. Thus, it holds that inequality in social classes demonstrates the natural differences among people. For a further study, see William Graham Sumner, *What Classes Owe to Each Other* (New York: Harper & Row, 1903).

## Chapter 4

1. Frederick R. Tennant, *The Concept of Sin* (London: Cambridge University Press, 1912), p. 245.

2. Ibid., p. 242.

3. Frederick R. Tennant, *The Sources of the Doctrines of the Fall and Original Sin*, second ed. (New York: Schocken, 1968).

4. Reinhold Niebuhr, *The Nature and Destiny of Man*, 1:178–240.

5. Karl Barth, *Church Dogmatics*, ed. G. W. Bromiley and T. F. Torrance. 13 vols. (Edinburgh: T. & T. Clark, 1969), 4:2:403.

6. Ibid., 4:3:448.

7. Paul Tillich, *Systematic Theology*, 3 vols. (Chicago: University of Chicago Press, 1951–63), 2:44–55.

8. Rudolf Bultmann, *Primitive Christianity*, trans. R. H. Fuller (New York: Living Age Books, 1956), pp. 55, 189.

9. Ibid., p. 55.

10. Rudolf Bultmann, *Theology of New Testament*, trans. Kendrick Grobel, 2 vols. (New York: Scribner's, 1951 and 1955), 1:127.

11. Ibid., p. 246.

12. Ibid.

13. Dorothee Soelle, *Political Theology*, trans. John Shelley (Philadelphia: Fortress, 1974), p. 89.

14. Ibid.

15. Refer to chapter 9 for the steps of resolution.

16. *De op. et eleem.* 1.

17. Ibid., 2:26.

18. Thomas Aquinas, *Summa Theologiae*, ed. & trans. Thomas Gilby (New York: McGraw-Hill, 1967), I-II.85.a.3, Reply, p. 91.

19. Georg W. F. Hegel, *Phenomenology of Spirit*, trans. A. K. Miller (Oxford: Clarendon, 1977), no. 752.

20. Valerie Saiving, "The Human Situation," in *Womanspirit Rising*, p. 37.

21. Judith Plaskow, *Sex, Sin and Grace: Women's Experience and the Theologies of Reinhold Niebuhr and Paul Tillich* (Washington: University Press of America, 1980), p. 2.

22. Van A. Harvey, *A Handbook of Theological Terms*, p. 221.

23. Norman P. Williams, *The Idea of the Fall and of Original Sin* (New York: Longmans, Green and Co., 1927), p. 308.

24. Ibid.

25. Emil Brunner, *Man in Revolt* (Philadelphia: Westminster, 1947), pp. 147f.

26. The concept of original sin, however, refers to the inheritability of han.

27. For Kierkegaard, sin is an illogical jump from God's order to irrational human existence. He attempted to save the concept of sin by pointing out its irrational nature. In fact, his understanding of sin is closer to the concept of han.

28. Han can be formed not only as the consequence of sin, but also as the results of natural events such as natural disasters or disease.

29. Walter Rauschenbusch, *A Theology For The Social Gospel* (Nashville: Abingdon, 1945), pp. 59ff.

30. James Drever, *A Dictionary of Psychology* p. 111. Quoted in John G. McKenzie, *Guilt* (Nashville: Abingdon, 1962), p. 22.

31. Karl Barth, *The Epistle to the Romans*, trans. Edwyn C. Hoskyns (London: Oxford University Press, 1933), p. 170.

32. Paul Tillich, *Systematic Theology*, 2:44.

33. Martin Heidegger, *Being and Time*, trans. John Macquarrie and Edward Robinson (New York: Harper, 1964).

34. Reinhold Niebuhr, *The Nature and Destiny of Man*, 1:220.

35. Ibid., pp. 221–27.

36. Robert H. Albers, "Shame: Theological and Pastoral Perspectives," A research paper presented at the School of Theology at Claremont, 1989. (Mimeographed) The following discussion owes much to Prof. Albers' article.

37. Ibid.

38. Ibid.

## Chapter 5

1. I use the term "forgivingness" for describing the forgiveness of the wronged toward the wrongdoer, and the term "forgiven-ness" for the forgiven state of the wrongdoer.

2. St. Augustine, *On the Gospel of St. John*, in *Nicene and Post-Nicene Fathers of the Christian Church*, ed. Philip Schaff, 14 vols. in 2 series (Edinburgh: T &T Clark, 1986), 1:7:230-35. See also *On the Creed*, ibid., 1:3:374-75.

3. Thomas Aquinas, *De fidei articulis et septem sacrementes*, ed. Mandonnet, in *Opuscula omnia S. Thomae* (Paris, 1927), 3:16.
Quoted in Max Thurian, *Confession*, ed. G. W. H. Lampe, trans. Edwin Hudson (London: SCM, 1958), p. 23.

4. Ibid.

5. B.C. Poschmann, *Penance and the Anointing of the Sick* (New York: Herder and Herder, 1964), p. 178.

6. In *De captivitate Babylonica*, he affirmed the sacramental value of *penance*. See *Luther's Primary Works: Together with His Shorter and Larger Catechism*, trans. & ed. Henry Wace and C. A. Buchheim, (London: Hodder & Stoughton, 1896), p. 294.

7. He hesitated to confirm the sacramental character of absolution because of the insufficiency of a divine sanction and held that penance is a renewal of baptism. See *Luther's Primary Works*, ed. Henry Wace and C. A. Buchheim, p. 408.

8. John Calvin, *Institutes of the Christian Religion*, trans. Henry Beveridge (Grand Rapids: Eerdmans, 1989), IV.19.15,17.

9. Ibid., III.3.5–8.

10. Ibid., II.4.12–13.

11. Max Thurian, *Confession*, p. 38.

12. Kenan B. Osborne, O.F.M. *Reconciliation & Justification* (New York: Paulist, 1990), pp. 182–83, 208–20.

13. *The Englishman's Hebrew and Chaldee Concordance of the Old Testament*, 5th ed. (Grand Rapids: Zondervan, 1975), pp. 1238–45.

14. Paul Tillich, *Systematic Theology*, 3:219; Joseph Haroutunian, "Repentance," in *A Handbook of Christian Theology* ed. Marvin Halverson and Arthur A. Cohen (New York: New American Library, 1958), pp. 321–22.

15. Some may ask: "Does forgiveness by God depends on our victim's forgivingness? If the victim refuses to accept our repentance, what will happen?" I believe that the *forgiven-ness* of an offender depends on his or her sincerity of the heart in repentance. This is "internal forgiven-ness." If this internal forgiven-ness concurs with the external forgivingness of the victim, that will be ideal. If the victim does not forgive, the offender should live with the internal forgiven-ness alone.

16. James Orr, ed. *The International Standard Bible Encyclopaedia* 4 vols. (Grand Rapids: Eerdmans, 1960) 2:1133.

17. Ibid.

18. Stephenson H. Brooks, *Matthew's Community*, (Sheffield: JSOT Press, 1987), p. 106.

19. Ibid.

20. Van Harvey, *A Handbook of Theological Terms*, pp. 135–36.

21. G. Yule, "Luther's Understanding of Justification by Grace Alone in Terms of Catholic Christology," in *Luther, Theologian for Catholics and Protestants* (Edinburgh: T. & T. Clark, 1985), p. 15.

22. Kenan B. Osborne, O.F.M. *Reconciliation & Justification*, p. 145.

23. Ibid.

24. Hans Werner Bartsch, ed. *Kerygma and Myth* (New York: Harper & Row, 1961), pp. 210f.

25. Paul Tillich, *The Protestant Era*, trans. James Adams, Abridged Edition (Chicago: University of Chicago, 1957), p. xi.

26. Paul Tillich, *Systematic Theology*, 2:178–79.

27. Kenan B. Osborne, O.F.M. *Reconciliation & Justification*, p. 190.

28. Ibid., pp. 193–94.

29. Paul Tillich, *Systematic Theology*, 2:177.

30. A similar text occurs in Mk. 11:25 ("And whenever you stand praying, forgive, if you have anything against any one; so that your Father also who is in heaven may forgive you your trespasses"). The Matthean text supposes knowledge of temple sacrifice, whereas the Markan text is set in the worship of the community and retains no reference to the temple cult. Stephenson Brooks, *Matthew's Community*, pp. 30–31.

31. See Chapter 6.

## Chapter 6

1. Donald G. Bloesch, *The Christian Life and Salvation* (Grand Rapids: Eerdmans, 1967), p. 40. *Shalom* means primarily "soundness," "health," but also signifies "prosperity," "well-being" in general in relation to both humans and God. It indicates the material dimension of welfare. James Orr, ed. *The International Standard Bible Encyclopaedia*, 4:2293.

2. William F. Arndt and F. Wilbur Gingrich, *A Greek-English Lexicon of the New Testament* (Chicago: University of Chicago, 1957), pp. 808–9.

3. D. P. Simpson, *Cassell's Latin Dictionary* (New York: Macmillan, 1959), p. 532.

4. In Pietism and revivalism, salvation means the defeat of the godless state through conversion and regeneration; in ascetic and liberal Protestantism, the overthrowing of special sins and progress toward moral perfection. Paul Tillich, *Systematic Theology*, 2:165–66.

5. Karl Barth, *Church Dogmatics*, 4:2:314.

6. Rudolf Bultmann, "New Testament and Mythology," *Kerygma and Myth I*, ed. Hans Werner Bartsch (New York: Harper & Row, 1953), pp. 27, 33.

7. Reinhold Niebuhr, *The Nature and Destiny of Man*, 2:277.

8. Tillich, *Systematic Theology*, 2:166, 176–80.

9. Karl Rahner, *Foundations of Christian Faith* (New York: Seabury, 1978), p. 143.

10. Gustavo Gutiérrez, *A Theology of Liberation* (New York: Orbis, 1973), pp. 36–37.

11. Rosemary Ruether, *New Woman New Earth* (New York: Seabury, 1975), pp. 58–59.

12. While Hegel's dialectic stresses the unity and continuity between conflictual dualities—appearance and reality, temporal and eternal, the world and God—Kierkegaard's emphasizes the disunity and discontinuity between them.

13. Julian Jaynes, *The Origin of Consciousness in the Breakdown of the Bicameral Mind* (Boston: Houghton Mifflin, 1976), Chs. 3 & 6.

14. It is difficult not to use "I and Thou," for we are accustomed to describing the relation between subject and object in this mode. Nevertheless, it is necessary to point out that "I and We" is truer to reality than "I and Thou."

15. David E. Roberts, *Psychotherapy and a Christian View of Man* (New York: Scribner's, 1950), p. 125.

16. Ibid., pp. 125–28.

17. Erich Fromm, *Man for Himself* (New York: Rinehart, 1947).

18. David Roberts, *Psychotherapy and a Christian View of Man*, p. 138.

19. Ibid., p. 129.

20. Ibid., p. 132.

21. Fred Alan Wolf, *Taking the Quantum Leap* (San Francisco: Harper & Row, 1981), pp. 3–6.

22. Werner Heisenberg, *Physics and Beyond* (New York: Harper & Row, 1971). Richard L. Liboff, *Introductory Quantam Mechanics* (San Francisco: Holden-Day, 1980), pp. 51–53.

23. John S. Dunne, *The Way of All the Earth* (New York: Macmillan, 1972), p. ix.

24. Hans-Georg Gadamer, *Truth and Method*, trans. Joel Weinsheimer and Donald Marshall (New York: Crossroad, 1989), p. 302. The italics are mine.

25. Ibid., p. 305.

26. Ibid., p. 306. The italics are Gadamer's.

27. Ibid., pp. 358–62.

28. Kant classifies all moral laws as either *hypothetical* or *categorical imperatives*. For him, "If the action would be good solely as a means to *something else,* the imperative is *hypothetical*; if the action is represented as good *in itself* and therefore as necessary, in virtue of its principle, . . . then the imperative is *categorical*." Immanuel Kant, *Groundwork of the Metaphysic of Morals,* trans. and analyzed H. J. Paton (New York: Harper & Row, 1948), p. 82.

29. Kant believes that we do not know beforehand what a hypothetical imperative will be. But we know at once what a categorical imperative contains, for it is a universal law. For him, there is only "a single categorical imperative": "*Act only on that maxim through which you can at the same time will that it should become a universal law.*" Ibid., p. 88.

## Chapter 7

1. J. K. Mozley, *The Impassibility of God: A Survey of Christian Thought* (London: Cambridge University Press, 1926), pp. 28–52.

2. Anselm of Canterbury, *Saint Anselm: Basic Writings,* trans. S. W. Deane, intro. Charles Hartshorne (La Salle: Open Court, 1962), p. viii.

3. Anselm of Canterbury, *Cur Deus Homo* I:xi, ibid., p. 202.

4. Ibid.

5. Ibid., I:xv, p. 208.

6. Ibid.

7. Ibid., I:xxiii, p. 232.

8. Ibid., I:xi, p. 202.

9. Ibid., II:xx., p. 286.

10. Anselm of Canterbury, *Proslogium* VIII; ibid., pp. 13-14.

11. I do not know how he knows that God does not experience the feeling in being. That conclusion is too speculative to be cogent.

12. Ibid., I:XI, p. 202.

13. *Luther's Works*, ed. H. T. Lehmann, 55 vols. (St. Louis: Concordia, 1955-1986; hereafter abbreviated as LW), 14:316.

14. LW 12:336.

15. LW 2:134.

16. Gerhard Ebeling, *Luther*, trans. R. A. Wilson (Philadelphia: Fortress, 1972), p. 226.

17. Paul Althaus, *The Theology of Martin Luther*, trans. Robert C. Schultz (Philadelphia: Fortress, 1966), p. 25.

18. Gerhard Ebeling, *Luther*, p. 227.

19. LW 31:55.

20. LW 14:305, 309.

21. Paul Althaus, *The Theology of Martin Luther*, p. 30.

22. Ibid., p. 34.

23. J. K. Mozley, *The Impassibility of God*, p. 122.

24. Ibid.

25. LW 31:55.

26. Paul Althaus, *The Theology of Martin Luther*, p. 28.

27. Kazoh Kitamori, *Theology of the Pain of God* (Richmond: John Knox Press, 1965).

28. Ibid., p. 12.

29. Ibid., p. 19.

30. Ibid., p. 21.

31. Ibid., p. 47. The italics are Kitamori's.

32. Ibid., pp. 8, 151-52.

33. Ibid., p. 22.

34. Ibid., p. 12.

35. Ibid., p. 20.

36. Ibid., p. 52.

37. Ibid., p. 53.

38. Ibid., p. 16.

39. Ibid., pp. 16-17.

40. Jürgen Moltmann, *The Crucified God*, trans. R. A. Wilson and John Bowden (New York: Harper & Row, 1973), p. 204.

41. Ibid., p. 69.

42. Ibid., p. 4.

43. Ibid., p. 190.

44. Ibid., p. 193.

45. Sabellianism flourished in the early third century. It stressed the unity of God without the distinction of the Trinity. Such terms as "Father," "Son," and "Holy Spirit" simply refer to three modes of divine action; there are no substantial distinctions within the divine. Thus, Sabellianism was virtually indistinguishable from patripassianism which held that God suf-

fered on the cross because the crucified Jesus was none other than God Godself.

46. Moltmann, *The Crucified God*, p. 207.

47. Ibid., p. 243.

48. Ibid., p. 227.

49. Ibid., pp. 212–14.

50. Ibid., p. 212. These two sentences are his interpretation of Luther's position, and he supports Luther's idea on the exclusive manifestation of the knowledge of God through the crucified Jesus.

51. Ibid., p. 240.

52. He disparages medieval mysticism. Ibid., p. 213.

53. Ibid., p. 192.

54. Ibid., p. 193.

55. Mozley, *The Impassibility of God*, p. 38.

56. Mk. 15:34. For Moltmann, this outcry expresses Jesus' agonizing death marked by a deep sense of being abandoned by God: Godforsakenness. *The Crucified God*, pp. 126–53.

57. J. K. Mozley, *The Impassibility of God*, p. 3.

58. Abraham J. Heschel, *The Prophets* (New York: Harper & Row, 1962), p. 151.

59. Ibid., p. 11.

60. Abraham J. Heschel, *The Insecurity of Freedom: Essays on Human Existence* (New York: Schocken, 1959), p. 160.

61. Ibid.

62. In scholastic and especially in Thomistic thought aseity denotes the identity in God of existence and essence, since God is the ground of God's own being, and thus marks God out as "pure act." R. A. Norris, "Aseity," in *The Westminster Dictionary of Christian Theology*, ed. Alan Richardson and John Bowden (Philadelphia: Westminster, 1983), p. 47.

63. Some may raise a question on the resurrection of Christ as the proof of God's almightiness. But that is not the final triumph of God in history. St. Paul indicates that the Holy Spirit of God worries and grieves over human affairs. Symbolically we are living between the "Third day" (resurrection) and the "Seventh day" (sabbath).

64. For him, there is another aspect of God: the primordial nature of God. It primarily dreams of the future of the world, while the consequent nature reaps the harvest of the "tragic Beauty" of the past. Alfred North Whitehead, *Adventures of Ideas* (New York: Free Press, 1933), p. 296.

65. This does not indicate that Jesus never had joy, peace, and pleasure in his life.

66. There was room only on the cross for Jesus.

67. Jack Nelson-Pallmeyer, *The Politics of Compassion* (New York: Orbis, 1986), p. 99.

68. Ibid.

69. The readings of *tekton* diverge on whether carpenter was Jesus' or his father's occupation. Hans Conzelmann, *Jesus*, trans. J. Raymond Lord, ed. John Reumann (Philadelphia: Fortress Press, 1973), p. 28.

70. Henri J. M. Nouwen, *The Wounded Healer* (New York: Doubleday, 1972), p. xiv.

## Chapter 8

1. Paul Knitter, "Preface" to *The Myth of Christian Uniqueness*, ed. John Hick and Paul Knitter (New York: Orbis, 1988), pp. vii-xii. I am greatly indebted to John Cobb for the following discussion.

2. John Hick, "The Non-Absoluteness of Christianity," *The Myth of Christian Uniqueness*, p. 34

3. Ibid., p. 23.

4. Ibid.

5. Ibid., pp. 23–27.

6. John Cobb, Jr., "Beyond 'Pluralism,'" *Christian Uniqueness Reconsidered*, ed. Gavin D'Costa (New York: Orbis, 1990), p. 81.

7. Ibid., p. 85.

8. Ibid., p. 84.

9. Marjorie H. Suchocki, "In Search of Justice," *The Myth of Christian Uniqueness*, p. 160.

10. Raimundo Panikkar, "Metatheology as Fundamental Theology," *Myth, Faith, and Hermeneutics* (New York: Paulist, 1979), p. 325.

11. John Hutchison, *Paths of Faith*, pp. 454, 493. In Islam, *thàr*, the vendetta, is similar to the concept of active han. It was a tribal ordinance of great antiquity. Its content is that *wali*, the male next-of-kin of a slain person, has the right to avenge the killing on the actual murderer. The Koran is explicit about it; the same book, however, recommends mercy on the murderer. H. A. R. Gibb, "Islam," in *Living Faiths*, ed. R. C. Zaehner (Boston: Beacon 1959), p. 189. The Koran also emphasizes the relief of the poor and needy, the freeing of slaves and prisoners and other charitable work.

12. Mircea Eliade, *Shamanism*, trans. Willard R. Trask (New York: Pantheon, 1964).

13. According to Lester Brown, we have passed the first natural threshhold—the limit of the stress of nature. If we cross the second one, there is no way we can avoid a catastrophic ecological disaster.

14. The late Dr. Asish Mondal told me this story at Berkeley, California, in 1983. He was professor of church history at Bishop's College in Calcutta, India.

## Chapter 9

1. Since human beings cause the pain of the world, the resolution of human han is a way to resolve the han of the world.

2. Judith Plaskow, *Sex, Sin and Grace*, p. 151.

3. Luther said, "God has found the way that his own divine essence can be completely in all creatures, and in everyone especially, deeper, more internally, more present, than the creature is to itself and at the same time nowhere and cannot be comprehended by anyone, so that he embraces all things and is within them." Quoted in Paul Tillich, *A History of Christian Thought*, ed. Carl E. Braaten (New York: Simon and Schuster, 1967), pp. 248, 373.

4. Immanuel Kant, *Critique of Pure Reason*, trans. Norman K. Smith (New York: Random House, 1958), p. 61.

5. Erik Schmidt, *Hegel's Lehre von Gott* (Gutersloh: G. Bertelsmann, 1952), p. 91. Quoted in George F. Thomas, *Religious Philosophies of the West* (New York: Scribner's, 1965), p. 271.

6. Ibid., pp. 87f. Hegel's reason differs from Kant's. While Hegel's reason passes from the knowledge of phenomena to the knowledge of noumena, Kant's reason is circumscribed in the realm of phenomena.

7. Paul Tillich, *A History of Christian Thought*, pp. 411–14.

8. Baruch Spinoza, *Ethics* (London: J. M. Dent & Sons, 1910), Pt. II, Pro. XL.

9. Ibid., Pt. II, Pro. XXXV.

10. Ibid., Pro. XLI.

11. Ibid., Pro. XL.

12. Ibid., Definition IV.

13. Ibid., Pt. II, Pro. XL.

14. Ibid., Pt. II, Pro. XLIII. For Spinoza, God is nature.

15. Ibid., Pt. V, Pro. XXXI.

16. Ibid., Pt. V, Pro. LIX.

17. Ibid., Pt. V, Pro. XXX.

18. Henri J. M. Nouwen, *The Wounded Healer* (New York: Doubleday, 1972).

19. He refused to *perform* miracles (Mt. 4:1–10).

20. John Marsh, *The Gospel of St. John* (Baltimore: Penguin Books, 1968), p. 669.

21. A. Plummer, ed., *The Gospel According to St John* (Cambridge: Cambridge University Press, 1913), p. 352.

22. John Marsh, *The Gospel of St. John*, p. 670.

23. The term *philia* as used in the New Testament usually means brotherly love. The word *agapē*, according to Anders Nygren, is the unmotivated and unconditional love that God pours out upon the sinner (Jn. 3:16). Anders Nygren, "Eros and Agape," in *A Handbook of Christian Theology* (New York: Meridian, 1958), pp. 96–101. See also Anders Nygren, *Agape and Eros* (London: SPCK, 1953).

24. John Marsh, *The Gospel of St. John*, p. 669.

25. For Plummer, Peter's choice of *phileō* was doubly intelligible: "(1) it is the less exalted word; he is sure of the natural affection which it expresses; he will say nothing about the higher love implied in *agapaō*; (2) it is the

warmer word; there is a calm discrimination implied in *agapaō* which to him seems cold." A. Plummer, ed., *The Gospel According to St. John*, p. 352.

26. John Marsh, *The Gospel of St. John*, pp. 670–71. It is debatable whether the two different words, *agapē* and *phileō* are distinguishable. While Bernard, Barrett, Bultmann, Hoskyns, Lightfoot, Mastin, and Brown see no real difference of meaning in the variation of the words, Westcott, Plummer, and Marsh find differences. Barnabas Lindars, ed., *The Gospel of John* (London: Butler & Tanner, 1972), p. 634.

27. A. Plummer, ed., *The Gospel According to St. John*, p. 352.

28. Westcott contends that Jesus gives up the idea of loftiest love and adopts the word which Peter used, since Peter cannot live up to the highest demand of Jesus' love. The Johannine author foretells through this encounter that Peter will ultimately reach the height of love when he imitates the Lord in his death. Brooke F. Westcott, *The Gospel According to St. John* (London: James Clarke & Co., 1958), pp. 303–4. It should also be noted here that Jesus used Aramaic. In Aramaic and Hebrew, there is one basic verb for expressing the different types of love. It seems that the Johannine author reinterprets this incident according to his own theological understanding.

29. David Bohm, "Postmodern Science and a Postmodern World," in *The Reenchantment of Science*, ed. David Ray Griffin (New York: State University of New York Press, 1988), pp. 60–61.

30. Ibid., p. 63.

31. Ibid.

32. Ibid., p. 64.

33. Ibid., p. 65.

34. Ibid., p. 66. For more on Bohm's philosophical examination of the concept of wholeness, see David Bohm, *Wholeness and the Implicate Order* (London: Routledge and Kegan Paul, 1980).

35. Rushworth M. Kidder, "Living Proof of the Strange Quantum Ways," Third in a Five-Part Monitor Series, *The Christian Science Monitor*, 15 June 1988, p. B4.

36. Ibid.

37. Fritjof Capra, *The Tao of Physics: An Exploration of the Parallels Between Modern Physics and Eastern Mysticism*, Second Edition (New York: Bantam, 1984), p. 276.

38. Rushworth M. Kidder, "Living Proof of the Strange Quantum Ways," p. B4.

39. Alfred North Whitehead, *Process and Reality*, ed. David Ray Griffin and Donald W. Sherburne (New York: Free Press, 1978), p. 169.

40. Ibid., p. 168.

41. John B. Cobb, Jr. and David Ray Griffin, *Process Theology: An Introductory Exposition* (Philadelphia: Westminster, 1976), p. 154. The other mode of perception is that of presentational immediacy, which is a supplemental phase of experience. The interplay between the two modes is described as *perception in the mixed mode of symbolic reference.*

42. Charles Birch and John B. Cobb, Jr., *The Liberation of Life: From the Cell to the Community* (Cambridge: Cambridge University Press, 1981), p. 88.

43. See Chester I. Barnard, *The Functions of the Executive* (Cambridge, Mass.: Harvard University Press, 1968).

44. Ha-Tai Kim, *Tongsuh Chulhak ui Mannam* (The Encounter of East and West Philosophy), (Seoul: Chongro Sujuk, 1985), pp. 116, 134.

45. Catherine Keller, "Feminism and the Ethic of Inseparability," in *Women's Consciousness, Women's Conscience,* ed. Barbara Hilkert Andolsen, Christine E. Gudorf, and Mary D. Pellauer (New York: Winston, 1985), pp. 260, 262.

46. Esther and Mortimer Arias, *The Cry of My People* (New York: Friendship, 1980), p. 2.

47. *The World Almanac and Book of Facts 1991,* p. 743.

48. Jack N. Behrman and Robert E. Grosse, *International Business Governments: Issues and Institutions* (Columbia: University of South Carolina Press, 1990), pp. 414–16.

49. Ibid., p. 417.

50. Robin Wright, "World View: Old Ways Falling but 'New World Order' is still Murky," *Los Angeles Times,* 25 June 1991, p. H1.

51. The Bush administration has avoided the use of the term since then. National Security Adviser Brent Scowcroft, who crafted the phrase during an afternoon of fishing with President Bush in the early weeks of the Gulf crisis, joked in an interview at the White House: "I told you more than I know about it." He seriously retorted, "I think you're putting too much specificity into it. . . . It is the notion of a new opportunity that's opening up with the ending of the East-West confrontation and how . . . the United States and its allies and friends can take advantage of it to improve the way the international order works." Ibid.

52. Robert McAfee Brown, *Making Peace in the Global Village* (Philadelphia: Westminster, 1981), pp. 20–21.

53. Ibid., p. 31.

54. Quoted in Robert Elias, *The Politics of Victimization* (New York: Oxford University Press, 1986), pp. 98–99.

55. Herman E. Daly and John B. Cobb, Jr., *For The Common Good* (Boston: Beacon, 1989).

56. Ibid., pp. 355–56.

57. Williston Walker, *A History of The Christian Church,* rev. Cyril C. Richardson, Wilhelm Pauch, and Robert T. Handy (New York: Scribner's, 1959), p. 22.

58. Ministry of Foreign Affairs, *Facts About Israel* (Jerusalem: Information Division of Ministry of Foreign Affairs, 1985), p. 13.

59. Ibid.

60. Daniel Williams, "Capitalism Sprouts at Kibbutzim," *Los Angeles Times,* 22 June 1991, pp. A1, A16, & A17.

61. Maxwell I. Klayman, *The Moshave in Israel* (New York: Praeger, 1970), p. 250.

62. Ibid., pp. 250–53.

63. Sam Passmore, "Hendrix Turns to Arkansas Produce," *Arkansas Gazette* 10 June 1987, quoted in Herman E. Daly and John B. Cobb, *For The Common Good*, p. 361.

64. Methodist Ministers Federal Credit Union, *Handbook of Services for Members of Methodist Ministers Federal Credit Union*, a booklet (Montclair, California: Methodist Ministers Federal Credit Union, 1989), p. 1.

65. *Southern Baptist Credit Union*, a brochure (Brea, California: Southern Baptist Credit Union, 1991).

66. George White, "Rebuilding, With Interest," *Los Angeles Times* 28 May 1992, p. D4.

67. Ibid., p. D1.

68. Ibid.

69. Ibid.

70. Suzanne C. Toton, *World Hunger* (New York: Orbis, 1982), pp. 40–41.

71. Bruce Nissen, "Building the World Bank," in *The Trojan Horse*, ed. Steve Weissman (San Francisco: Ramparts, 1974), p. 53.

72. Rachael Kamel, *The Global Factory: Analysis and Action for a New Economic Era* (Philadelphia: American Friends Service Committee, 1990), p. 69.

73. Ibid.

74. Ibid.

75. Ibid., pp. 26–27.

76. Jack Nelson-Pallmeyer, *War Against the Poor: Low-Intensity Conflict and Christian Faith* (New York: Orbis, 1990), p. 10.

77. Ulrich Durchrow, *Global Economy: A Confessional Issue for the Churches* (Geneva: World Council of Churches, 1987), pp. 92–93.

78. To avoid a sexist connotation, I prefer "the community of God" to "the kingdom of God" for describing the full reign of God.

79. John A. Ryan, *Distributive Justice* (New York: MacMillan, 1927), p. 213.

80. Reinhold Niebuhr, *An Interpretation of Christian Ethics* (New York: Living Age, 1956), p. 134.

81. Michael Parenti, *Inventing Reality: The Politics of the Mass Media* (New York: St. Martin's, 1987), p. 27.

82. Jack Nelson-Pallmeyer, *War Against the Poor*, p. 61.

83. *Convergence*, Summer 1991, p. 8.

84. Ibid., p. 10.

85. U.S. intelligence issued these rough estimates. Mark S. Hoffman, ed. *The World Almanac and Book of Facts 1992*, (New York: Pharos, 1991), pp. 37, 66.

86. George P. Howard, *Religious Liberty in Latin America?* (Philadelphia: Westminster, 1944). Quoted in José Miguez Bonino, *Doing Theology in a Revolutionary Situation*, ed. William H. Lazareth (Philadelphia: Fortress, 1975), p. 11.

87. Some branches of the Roman Catholic church, such as in the Netherlands and United States, are more progressive on social, economic, and political issues and are less guilty of this characteristic.

88. Sandra Postel, "Denial in the Decisive Decade," in *State of the World 1992*, p. 3.

89. Lester R. Brown, "The New World Order," in *State of the World 1991*, p. 5.

90. Ibid.

91. Ibid., p. 6.

92. Ibid., p. 9. See also U.N. Development Programme, *Human Development Report 1990* (New York: Oxford University Press, 1990).

93. Ibid., p. 10. See also Herman E. Daly and John B. Cobb, *For The Common Good*, appendix.

94. Ibid., p. 11.

95. Ibid., p. 9.

96. Sandra Postel and Christopher Flavin, "Reshaping the Global Economy," in *State of the World 1991*, p. 182.

97. Eugene Linden, "Population: The Uninvited Guest," *Time* 1 June 1992, p. 54.

98. Sandra Postel, "Denial in the Decisive Decade," p. 3.

99. Eugene Linden, "Population," p. 54.

100. Ibid.

101. Sandra Postel, "Denial in the Decisive Decade," p. 4.

102. Lester R. Brown, "The New World Order," p. 16.

103. Sandra Postel and Christopher Flavin, "Reshaping the Global Economy," p. 188.

104. Ibid.

105. Lester Brown, "The New World Order," p. 17. Ironically, as a result of the U.S. fund withdrawal, more women in low-income countries are rejected access to family planning services and forced to resort to abortion. National Family Planning and Reproductive Health Association, "The 1980s: Decade of Disaster for Family Planning," Washington, D.C., April 1990.

106. John Macquarrie, "Creation and Environment," *The Expository Times*, (October 1971), p. 6.

107. Ibid.

108. For Howard Clinebell, growth takes place in the tension and interplay between caring and confrontation. H. Clinebell, *Growth Counseling* (Nashville: Abingdon, 1979), Ch. 2.

109. Muzafer Sherif et al., *Intergroup Conflict and Integration: The Robber's Cave Experiment* (Norman, Oklahoma: University of Oklahoma Press, 1961).

110. Paulo Freire, *Pedagogy of the Oppressed*, trans. Myra Bergman Ramos (New York: Seabury, 1974), p. 91.

111. Teilhard de Chardin, *The Phenomenon of Man* (New York: Harper & Row, 1955), p. 78.

112. Teagon Kim, *Hankook Mushok Younku* (A Study of Korean Shamanism) (Seoul: Chip Moon Dang, 1981), pp. 355, 394, and 400.

113. For Reinhold Niebuhr, self-transcendence happens when one realizes one's own limits.

114. Younghak Hyun, "A Theological Look at the Mask Dance in Korea," in *Minjung Theology*, ed. Yong Bock Kim (Singapore: The Christian Conference of Asia, 1981), pp. 43–50. The *minjung* are the politically oppressed, economically exploited, socially alienated, culturally despised, or religiously condemned.

Printed in the United States
41219LVS00016BB/8

9 780687 385362

# Voices of the
# Undocumented

Val Rosenfeld and Flor Fortunati

Published and Distributed by
First Edition Design Publishing, Inc.
P.O. Box 20217, Sarasota, FL 34276-3217
www.firsteditiondesignpublishing.com

Library of Congress Cataloging-in-Publication Data
Rosenfeld, Val, Fortunati Flor
    Voices of the undocumented / written by Val Rosenfeld and Flor
Fortunati.
    p. cm.
    ISBN 978-1506-900-54-4 pbk, 978-1506-900-55-1 digital

1. BIOGRAPHY & AUTOBIOGRAPHY / Cultural Heritage. 2. Personal
Memoirs. 3. POLITICAL SCIENCE / Public Policy / Social Policy. 4.
SOCIAL SCIENCE / Emigration & Immigration

V8897

# CONTENTS

*….. we are and always will be a nation of immigrants. We were strangers once, too.*

Barack Obama

# Introduction

For more than seven years, I have been teaching ESL ("English as a second language") as a volunteer at the Day Worker Center in Mt. View, California. When I first came to the Day Worker Center, I did not recognize its full purpose. I was retired and taking Spanish classes and was looking for an opportunity to practice the language. The Day Worker Center was a volunteer opportunity to get some real life Spanish experience and to contribute to the community at the same time. I soon discovered that very few of my friends knew about the Center or that such an organization even existed, let alone exactly what the Center did and whom it served.

A day worker center is a community-based organization that helps workers find day jobs. Although the center does not restrict who can register for their services, in the San Francisco Bay Area it primarily serves a Latino immigrant population. There are approximately 70 such day worker centers throughout the United States. While these centers vary in their locations and administration, each center aims to provide jobs for service workers - to help such workers, who would otherwise stand on street corners, come in off the streets into a supportive environment. Employers in the area are then encouraged to hire their day workers from the centers, rather than off the street.

Over these seven years, I have been responsible for two ESL classes a week at the Day Worker Center of Mountain View – a beginning class and an advanced class. During this time, I have heard small parts of many of the workers' life stories. As I got to know the workers better, I found that I wanted to hear their whole stories – where they came from, how they got here, and how they found their place in this country and community. Since many of the workers have limited proficiency with English, I realized that they needed to tell their stories in their native language in order to convey all the details and the associated emotions. When Flor Fortunati, who is from Argentina and thus fluent in Spanish, joined me as a volunteer teacher at the Day Worker Center, she felt the same draw to the workers' stories that I had experienced. Together, we had the ability to interview the workers and to hear their stories in their own language and in their own words.

We selected men and women from a variety of Latin American countries to interview. At first, many of the workers were reluctant to talk about their pasts. Perhaps, the workers worried that by telling their stories, they would endanger their status in the Unites States, as many of them are undocumented. Perhaps the workers worried that middle-class Americans would not understand their hardships and experiences. But, once Flor and I started interviewing them, they quickly opened up. They wanted someone to be interested, someone to understand what they had experienced in their efforts to create new lives for themselves and their families. As the workers became increasingly comfortable speaking of their pasts, we discovered how moving their stories were and how justifiably proud the workers were of their accomplishments. And, at the same time, we found that knowing the details of their lives made us feel closer to them as students and as people and neighbors.

We recorded all of the interviews in Spanish, transcribed them and then translated them into English. We have made every effort to allow each worker to tell his or her story in his or her own words. To preserve the integrity of their stories, we have presented them as a narrative, as the workers have told them to us. Only first names have been used and some names and locations have been changed, and pictures omitted, at the request of the worker. We believe this documentation of oral history is important. You must know the stories to truly know the people.

# A Brief History of the Day Worker Center

In the San Francisco Bay Area, the cities of Palo Alto, Mountain View and Los Altos, along with local police departments, openly support the Day Worker Center. This has not always been the case, however.

In 1994, California voters overwhelmingly approved Proposition 187, also known as Save Our State. Proposition 187 was a ballot initiative to establish a state-run citizenship screening system and prohibit undocumented immigrants from access to health care, public education and a range of other social services. The proposition passed by a wide margin and its passage immediately resulted in wide-spread opposition. Legal challenges to the new law soon followed. Three days after the passage of Proposition 187, a federal judge entered a temporary restraining order blocking the enforcement of the law. Within a month, a permanent injunction was issued finding the proposition unconstitutional and blocking all provisions of the law. Specifically, the judge found that the law infringed on the federal government's exclusive jurisdiction over immigration-related matters.

The injunction against Proposition 187 did not change the community's attitude toward day laborers, unfortunately. Around the same time, residents in the California cities of Mountain View and Los Altos, along with their police departments, complained about immigrants congregating on the street corners in search of job opportunities. In an effort to address these divisive issues, a community lawyer in the area brought together people from various constituencies, including, elected officials, religious leaders and residents, to create a focus group to develop the concept of a physical day worker center. The initial Center operated within the rectory of a small church, but, after its initial success, moved to another building in a more central business location in Mountain View. It operated there until 1999, when the cities of Los Altos and Mt. View each passed an ordinance banning employers from picking up day workers from street corners, thereby making it illegal for residents and businesses to hire a large segment of the undocumented worker population seeking employment.

While the Center aimed to get workers off street corners, its fate remained uncertain as well. When the Center's lease expired in 2001, the landlord elected not to renew it. With the loss of the lease, the Day Worker Center literally disappeared. Virtually overnight, there was no Center, no computers, no telephone, no work opportunities, nothing. During the next few months, the organizers of the Day Worker Center collected signatures, held marches, and went to the city councils. Finally, the Center's organizers found assistance with a large law firm in Palo Alto, California. Lawyers from Morrison and Foerster and MALD (Mexican American Legal Defense), working together, were able to successfully challenge the city ordinances. The cities were forced to pay the Center's legal fees and to compensate the organization for all the damage it had sustained. This success served as an important victory for the Center and for undocumented workers' rights.

In 2002, after this successful legal victory, the Day Worker Center re-opened. Throughout the next nine years, the Center operated from various rooms in local churches. By 2011, the Center had raised enough funds through private donations to purchase a former laundromat in Mountain View, where it established its new headquarters as a non-profit, 501(c)(3) Corporation. The Center refurbished the building to include an office, a greeting area, a great room (with tables and chairs, a library area and computer area), a kitchen, and a classroom. The Center currently employs a paid director and two assistants and has an annual budget of approximately $150,000, which is funded through a combination of grants and private donations.

Today, 60-80 day workers use the Center's service. Approximately 10% of the workers are non-Latinos, primarily from Ethiopia and other parts of Africa. Another, smaller portion of workers were born and raised in the United States, but have turned to the Center in search of day employment. Regardless of the worker's origins, the Center has become part of their lives.

Despite the success of the Center, numerous immigrants still look for work on street corners. Some of these workers wish to negotiate for jobs by themselves, preferring to avoid the rules of the Center, such as wearing a "uniform" (workers are required to wear a Day Worker T-Shirt to all jobs) and participating in the obligatory English classes. These workers prefer to handle it themselves. They want to be outside and feel strong enough to communicate with employers on their own.

Finding jobs for the day workers remains the primary goal of the Center. Each morning, workers put their names on a list (the first ones to arrive are first on the list) that is used to assign jobs. When employers call or come by the Center, the workers who arrived earliest get priority. Employers typically seek workers for manual labor: moving, cleaning, gardening and some minor construction. These are some of the hardest, most grueling jobs and are poorly paid. Hourly wages are $12 - $15 (depending on the skills necessary for the job) for a minimum of 4 hours.

In addition to its job-finding function, the Center has become a community center for immigrants. Workers come to the Center and ask basic questions, such as: "Can you please translate this document?" "Can you help me find a school for my children?" "Where can I find medical care for my family?" "How can I find an apartment to rent or a room to share?" The Center strives to create an environment in which the workers feel safe asking for help and sharing their problems and concerns. The Center offers workshops on consumer rights, tenant rights and civil rights. Families are also welcome, including children. The workers can come and eat here, share a meal, and talk to other people while they wait for work.

Many workers leave their spouses and children in their home countries, not wanting to raise their children in the U.S. Most of the workers just want to make enough money to support their families and, eventually, return to their countries of birth. They miss their homes, their families, and their own culture. Unfortunately, these workers often arrive with unrealistic expectations of their opportunities in the U.S., believing they can stay a few years, and pay back all of the money they owe (often thousands of dollars paid to the coyotes for bringing them across the border) and save some additional money for their family. They think that a year's work will allow them to return to their families in their native countries with enough money to start a business. Expectations are that workers will be able to send back a few hundred dollars a month – which is a great deal more than they can earn at home. They are willing to live five or six men to an apartment, skip meals, and wear second hand clothes in an effort to save money to send home.

But the years go by. One year turns into two and then three. The passage of time often erodes family relationships, which simply cannot stand the huge time, distance and financial burdens placed on them. Workers' expectations prove unrealistic. The husband comes with dreams and hopes. The wife stays back home, waiting for money. The workers try and stay connected to their families, but often a feeling of impotence and shame arises when they cannot provide adequately for them. Then, their families just disappear. It is a very common story, and happy endings are rare.

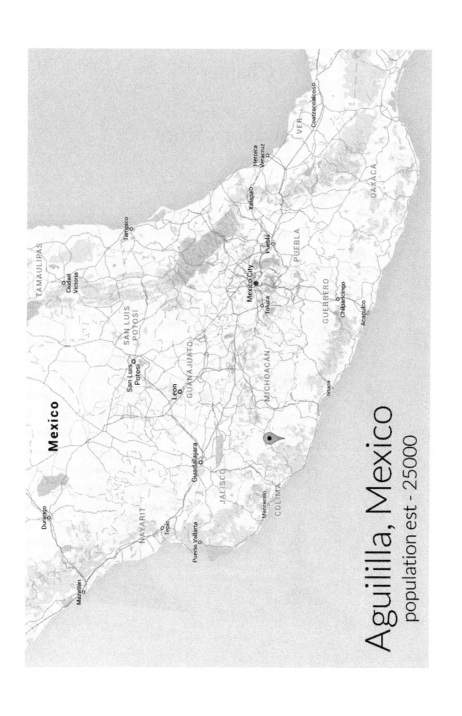

Aguililla, Mexico
population est - 25000

# Chapter 1

## Salvador's Story

"In Mexico, where I lived, there was a great deal of violence. This was the main reason I decided to try to go to the U.S. The authority is for sale in Mexico. I've seen people murder my friends in front of me. I've seen them fall. Once a friend of mine was killed beside me. These guys arrived, and when I looked and saw who was coming, my friend was right beside me. He had told me what was going on, and as soon as I moved, they shot him. I moved so that they wouldn't shoot me and the bullet flew right beside my head. It was a problem concerning 'skirts'. My friend had told me everything that was going on and said 'my friend will come to kill me' and after a while, we saw him coming and my friend said, 'there he comes, there he comes,' and a minute later, he was dead.

"On another occasion I saw soldiers kill four men. The soldiers have authorization to shoot anyone that opposes them. Because if the soldiers come and try to disarm you and you show them your gun, you'll get shot and killed. That time, four friends went down the street with loud music and bearing guns; they were criminals. The soldiers waited for them on the corner and as they arrived the soldiers told them to raise their hands. One of the friends, his name was Rogelio, without more ado, took his gun and shot the commander. He shot and hit him. When he showed his gun, he was told, 'raise your hands,' he shot the officer, he shot the lieutenant, and hit him in the chin and shoulder. But the soldiers were aiming their guns at the men. Then, when the gun thundered, the soldiers shot. All four friends fell.

"There were also a lot of drugs when I was growing up. Yes there was, yes. But there was not the slaughter of people like there has been since ten years ago. There were drugs in the hills and the soldiers went and brought a lot of drugs and a lot of people tied up, from the mountain, from the hills. But there weren't as many murders as there have been in the last ten years. We didn't have that. Drugs, yes, lots and lots. I'm more afraid to go back home right now. It scares me because now they pick people up and one walks to the truck and the next day or in two days' time you are already dead in a ditch or on the mountain. They kill and ditch them, so that scares me now."

Salvador is 64 years old. Although he describes himself as the smallest in his large family, he is 5 feet 11 inches tall, 185 pounds and solidly built, with a strong jaw, salt-and-pepper hair and a full moustache. He was born in 1950 in Aguililla, in the state of Michoacán, in western Mexico. To the east is Mexico City; to the west, the Pacific Ocean. The name 'Michoacán' is from Nahuatl, a Uto-Aztecan language spoken in central Mexico since the 7th century AD, and it means 'place of the possessor of fish,' referring to those who fish on Lake Patzcuaro.

Today Michoacán is a region of drug production, sex-trafficking, oil theft, kidnapping, gun running and extortion. But in 1950, when Salvador was born, Augililla was a sleepy little village in central Michoacán. "Although I was born in Aguililla, my family moved to a ranch after I was born and stayed on the ranch, called Reparito, for three years. My dad worked planting corn. Then we went back to the town, to Aguililla, and then from Aguililla we went to another ranch, La Laja. We lived in La Laja possibly fifteen years. We went back and forth from the ranch to town, depending on the situation. In May, we would go to the ranch to plant and in December, after the harvest, we went back to the town. We did this for many years and then in 1969 we returned to the village of Aguililla and stayed.

"My father had rented the land on the ranch but owned a house in town. The house had a dirt floor. It had no bathroom and did not have any electric light. I remember we used candles or oil lighting. My grandfather, my mom's dad, and my mom's mom lived in the same town. The town of Aguilla was very limited - eight or ten houses at most. But when one is young you can have fun with everything. Even if you don't have anything to eat tomorrow, a child is happy, having fun. As an adult, it changes and when you are old, it changes more.

"All the families were very large. My mother stayed at home. We were nine children, five boys and four girls and I was the fifth child. My uncle, the brother of my mother, had eleven children! Another uncle had 14, and yet another brother of my mother, 10, and another brother, 6. They all lived nearby in the village. In Aguililla, I met a lady with 26 children; 26 from the same man and they all became adults. They are not all alive now, some have been killed, and some are miscreants. But their parents saw them all till adulthood. It is amazing.

"The first part of life is the most beautiful. We had little money, I wore patched clothes. I wore shoes for the first time at age 20. I used to wear *guarachitas*. I owned only one pair of shoes, that's all, and few clothes, two or three changes only. And my mom patched my clothes over and over.

4

"I only went to school for a little time. I had an aunt who taught me and my dad paid her. Three of my brothers and two of my sisters went there to learn. My dad was paying her per month, but only for a short time - five months and no more. I grew up speaking Spanish. I can read Spanish a little, not very fast, but I read. My younger siblings went to the government school. It was easier then, when we lived in town, because when we lived on the farm, there was no school. There were only four houses on the ranch, and there was another ranch far away. It took an hour of walking to go to school. Two younger brothers went to school, but the biggest, no, they didn't.

"I began working, when I was 10 years old, - less than 10 years. My dad earned money by sowing seed, and also herding mules and cattle. We went with my dad to plant corn, and then also helped with the horses, too. I learned how to ride horses and mules. I also worked during harvesting, herding mules loaded with corn and gathering the *breña* to burn, too. There was always work to do. When we were in town my dad would bring firewood on mules to sell, and we helped. And when we were back in town, some of us would be hired for the day. Sometimes when I went to work there were unpleasant odors and thorns, but it was only a day. It passes, it passes. A hot day, but it passes, it passes. It's all good. All my sisters stayed home and helped in the kitchen. Two of my sisters made clothes, with sewing machines, and people paid them to make clothes.

"In the village, after we worked, we played at night, in the center of the square. My many cousins and I ran around over there under the trees, and we threw stones at the animals. I liked to go play with nuts as balls. There's a tree that bears nuts in the center of the square and we gathered some nuts to play. Nuts, if you gather some and store them where there's no sun and don't get them wet, they last 10 years and you can eat them. They last a long time and nothing happens, nothing happens. A grain of corn or rice too, if you keep it dry, walk away, 50 years later, you plant it and it grows corn. They last long, last long, 50 years. We played with walnuts, and since there were plenty, we filled large bags, and we kept them there.

"One year, in December – December 12th, it was a holiday and there was a party in Aguililla, and I was penniless. My dad had cornfields and harvested and sold and collected all the money to sustain a large family. My dad would not spend the money on himself; no, we were nine, plus my dad and my mom. We all ate, all eleven, we all spent; the crops were for our house. Two days before the 12th, a friend of mine asked me, 'Will you help me harvest? We'll finish in a day.' 'Uh, really?' I said. I did not have any money and I had a girlfriend who was my first girlfriend. Well, I'll work because I don't want to be penniless on the 12th. We went to work and started early in the morning and ended when it was getting dark. The next day was December 12th. I got home and I went to bathe at night in a river, a river in December is cold, but anyway, I bathed there in the cold river. My friend lived in a small house near me. He told me, 'After a while I'll bring you the money.' 'Okay.' I bathed, returned, and he did not show up. The next day, on the 12th, I met him there and he said, 'You know what? The man that was going to pay me gave me nothing. He did not pay me.' I had no money to go for a walk with my girlfriend, or to invite her for a soda. But, I didn't get angry, I did not blame him. I got paid, but two or three days afterwards. But that beautiful day, there was nothing. These are little things that one remembers.

"I never served in the army. No, no, no. It was an option, but my dad was a bit closed. Two of my older brothers went marching. But I did not. One day I told my dad, 'I'm going to subscribe for military service' and he said: 'No! That does not work, that's no good.' And that was it. It was not mandatory, well I never heard anyone say: 'They took them to the military.' No, I've never heard it. Maybe in other times, maybe, but I do not remember them taking anyone. My dad was closed-minded. He also did not know how to read; he could read in Spanish a little bit because he taught himself a little when he was older.

"My dad would not let us go to work for a government company. He said, 'No.' In Mexico, there are large companies, where there are military soldiers protecting the company and the company pays them compensation. My dad was opposed to 'those companies from the government.' My dad was like that. But after I asked him five hundred times, I told him, 'I'm going to work' and he decided. 'Ok, go.' My dad always had those ideas about companies with the government. He thought that it does not work. But my dad was wrong.

"So eventually we all worked for large companies - my four brothers and my dad. With all of us working, our economic situation changed. My brothers went to work in construction, building houses. Then I went to work at a road construction company. After that, I went to work at a sawmill and worked there for three years, cutting wood to make tables.

"Life changed; it became a little bit better. As it improved we were able to add a bathroom to the house, as well as lighting, and wooden floors and a stove. Everything was a bit better.

"However, after three years, the sawmill closed. It was a big company, with a very large sawmill, with a huge production. When it closed all the workers got money, this much for you, this much for you. For a short while I worked fixing truck tires. I would fix the tires that were punctured. The company was a sawmill, but it also had truck maintenance and I was in charge of that. I was the *llantero*. They hired me for that, because I had worked for three years, and at the mill they heard I was out of work and they looked for me and hired me.

"And that was the last job there in Mexico, and that was it and then I came here. That is how I got the money to come to the United States. I had wanted to come to the U.S. for many years, but I did not have enough money. So what stopped me was the economic situation. I did not dare to borrow money to come here. After I worked at the sawmill, when it was over, they gave money to everyone and I said to myself, 'this money, is for this,' and with that money I came to the U.S. But I wanted to come, 8, 10 years before I finally came. I told my dad, 'Well, I'm leaving tomorrow,' and he asked where I was going? I said, 'To the U.S.' He said, 'But what are you going to do there, just go and open your mouth there?' 'No, well, I am leaving.' 'Okay, Okay,' he said. My mother was sad, but my dad wasn't. He was sad, he just didn't show it. My mother cried, but my father didn't.

"I came to the U.S. illegally in May, 1979. I took a bus to Tijuana from Aguililla. It took two days. I only had the clothes I had on, and one change of clothes in a bag. In Tijuana, I paid a coyote on the border $250 to help me jump the fence and cross over into California. Back then there wasn't a big fence like right now. Back then there was a regular fence, a wire fence; it was low, and you jumped over it. It was barbed wire, but it was low. Right now the fence is 12 feet high, and made of steel – so it's difficult now. After we climbed the fence, we walked a little, one hour, maybe two. Then we got to a house on the U.S. side of the border - a house the coyote controlled. We remained hidden in the house for four days. After that, a car was sent to pick us up; we got in the trunk of the car and went to Los Angeles in the trunk, lying there. The money I paid the coyote brought me across and included everything. After I crossed, they brought me up to Redwood City (California), on the Greyhound bus. I came across the border four times, as I will explain later. Each time was slightly different. Once I paid the coyote only to Los Angeles, and went from Los Angeles to the Bay Area on the Greyhound. Other times I paid to Redwood City, and it was included in the coyote's, price.

"It was not difficult to cross. Just a little bit of walking. We just walk and hide, and walk again for 30 minutes and hide, but it was not long. Some people come by Arizona, and they walk for 10 hours. We were a group of 25, 30 people and children. The guide there was ahead. One by one we followed. It was dark, at night. In the evening, at 8:00, as it got dark, we crossed, and after a while we hid. We could see a plane above us, but it did not see us. There we would wait till dawn. We were picked up in a car, two or three cars because there were many of us, and from there we drove to Los Angeles. That was the first time.

"The United States was just as I thought it would be. They told me that it was clean, beautiful, lighted streets, and cement sidewalks, impressive stores, very different from Mexico. It ended up being as I thought it was. It was what I expected. "The most difficult time was the first year I came. I came to Redwood City, penniless and knowing nothing. I brought one pair of shoes. One or two weeks later, a cousin asked me to go to K-Mart to shop. They are in Redwood City and here in Santa Clara there were some. My cousin asked me to come; he was with his wife, and we were neighbors here. He said, 'Come to K-Mart.' We went together, and when we got in the store my cousin started shopping with his wife there. I only had one U.S. dollar. There were some shirts hanging there at 99 cents, but when I go to pay, because of the tax, it was more than one dollar. Ninety-nine cents, but with the tax, it cost slightly more than one dollar I had. Well, I could not buy it. I left the store and my cousin stayed there.

"I got out and I walked. I knew where to wait for the bus. I knew where I was walking and I arrived at Middlefield Road. There in Redwood City, there was a gentleman, sitting there, a Chilean, sitting there, 'Hey! Is the truck (bus) about to arrive?' He said, 'It is,' and I sat and waited, but since I left the store I was thinking and thinking about the situation that I was in, and thinking and thinking. And as I sat there I was crying, I was crying, thinking I did not have money. And the Chilean said, 'What's wrong? Are you crying?' 'No, no, I'm not crying. I have dust in my eyes.' 'Hey you're crying!' he said again. 'Yes, I'm crying, yes, I'm crying' 'What's wrong?' 'Look, I have no job, nor do I have money. I went to buy a shirt and I did not have enough money.' He said, 'Are you sick?' 'No, no, I'm not sick.' He said, 'Do not worry, you've got your health, you're young, do not worry.' Well yes, I thought. I'm not sick, I can work. And that helped me a lot. He helped me a lot.

"After that, I was working two or three days a week as a day worker. Then I had no more work and then in a few more days there was more work. It was very limited. I saved and saved. Rent was $60 per month. When you don't have a job, it's a lot, a lot right? I earned $90 in total. They paid $2.90 per hour and at that time I did not pay taxes. I didn't pay anything else. $90. It was limited, limited living. I was never hungry, but there were times when you didn't get to eat until late at night.

"I was here 6 months and then I was caught. When one is arrested, it's a horrible thing. Immigration caught me in the park. I lived in Redwood City and came to see volleyball games in a park in Mt. View. I like that a lot, watching volleyball; every day I went to watch, almost every day. I had just arrived there at Rengstorff Park and Immigration was there gathering people. They were heading out and we ran into each other. So I came here to the park and as I was arriving here, they were catching people and they caught me. There was a big truck and two or three small trucks. The truck stopped and the driver of the truck got off the truck and the others who were with him arrived fast and they got out their guns. The driver cried, 'Amigo! Amigo!' and I stopped. I had a friend who had a similar van. That particular day I went there because he needed help fixing a detail on it, and when I looked I thought it was my friend with his van. But it was Immigration. They asked for my papers – I had none. I got on the truck; there were 22 people.

"They arrested me on Sunday and I was taken to Santa Rita. They moved me on Monday afternoon. We got to the line in downtown Mexicali; we stayed a while longer and then were sent by bus to Guadalajara. There they let me go and from there it took six more hours to get to my village, Aguililla. I went by bus, I had some money and I bought the ticket there, for $24.

"The Border Patrol did not take anything away from me, they just searched me. They treated me very well. I had very few things, only the clothes I was wearing, because all of my things were in my apartment. I had only a few things there - six months' worth of things. I called a cousin of mine and asked if she were coming back to Mexico, please bring me the things that I have there in the apartment. She brought me my clothes. I would have lost it all, but then it was only two or three shirts and clothing. I was lucky, though. I had a check for $150 in my pocket when they caught me. $150 in a check and $150 in cash. $300 with the check and the cash. I had them with me because I got paid on Saturday and I pocketed the check and was walking around and they caught me and I had the check on me and $150 in cash. Thankfully I didn't have to return to Mexico without any money.

"I crossed back to the U.S illegally again. The second time, it was the shortest stretch. We walked for two hours. A car picked us up and took us to Redwood City. And the third time was also short. We went by car. The third time, after crossing, we went into a house and spent 2 days there. In the house, there was food and water. We were four or five people. And the fourth time, because I got to jump 4 times, in 1979, 1980, 1983 and 1985, four times. The last time we walked during the day, we were lucky. We ran like 30 minutes, and bam! We got to the car, fast; it was two in the afternoon, it was the easiest. There are always many animals, but I am not afraid of animals, I was not scared.

"Well, I had a cousin in the Bay Area and I spoke to him and he asked, 'How are you coming?' 'In a Greyhound.' 'When you arrive, I'll be there waiting, here in Redwood City,' and he was waiting for me. Well I got luckier when I came back the final time in 1985. It changed because I got here and a bit later I got a job. I started to work after three days and that work was for two years. Then I left, by then the situation had changed.

"I met Esther, originally from DF Mexico City, in 1985. I was 35 and she was two years older, 37. She worked in Cupertino, and I worked and lived in Redwood City. We met on the #22 bus. It was Sunday and I came from Redwood City and was going to San Jose. She got on the bus at San Antonio and El Camino. When we met, we started talking, and continued the conversation until today. No, we're a couple, but not married; we've been together for about 25 years. She was 38 when my baby, Alicia, was born in the United States.

"By amnesty, in 1987, I became a resident. Esther got her residency later. When I met her she was illegal–she had over-stayed her visa. I was a resident when I met her and she was illegal, but when I met her she was applying for residency and then managed to get it, but many years after I met her.

"Then, in 1990, I could not work for a few years. I had been working for a roofing company for about a year when I had an accident and I burned my hand and arm with that black tar that you throw on houses–that is why I have all the scars on my right arm. The pain wasn't too bad, but in my mind I was traumatized by what I saw. As soon as the firemen arrived I got an injection and the pain was over. But in my mind it was horrible. I had to have surgery - a skin graft. I was 40. The ambulance took me to the hospital and I stayed for fifteen days in the hospital. The company gave me $800 per month for eight months while I was out of work–State Compensation. Two checks of $400. It was very little. When I was out of the hospital, I contacted a lawyer about the accident. He took the case but it did not help. I only got $6000 after 5 years. I was sent back to work after eight months. But I was not well, so I did not go to work. The doctor gave me a letter and said, 'Take it to the company where you work,' but I didn't take it because I did not feel competent. So the allowance was cut. I did not go back to that job. I never went back.

"When Alicia was five months old, Esther went to Mexico because her father became ill. She went to Mexico because she had originally come to the U.S. with a visa, and she came and went with a visa. Except the visa was now expired. She stayed in Mexico for 5 months and told me, 'I'll arrive at SFO [airport], wait for me at the airport. I'm taking a few things for you to help me with.' I arrived at SFO, 30 minutes earlier than her arrival. The plane arrived, people kept coming and she didn't come through the gates. I said to a woman: 'Is a lady with a one-year-old girl coming?' She said, 'She has been stopped there and they are asking her many questions.' It was immigration services, at the airport. Then the immigration worker from the airport came and said, 'Salvador! Come here to say hello to her, because we are sending her back.' And he asked me for my green card. I showed it. My wife was already there, and crying. They made her go back to Mexico with the baby, but it didn't affect her green card application. It was lucky they didn't reject her application. Then he said, 'You can talk to her for 15 minutes, because we are sending her back right now on the same plane she came.' And we were talking and the officer said, 'Time for you to go,' and gave me the things she brought for me. She spent three months there and came back by paying a coyote. Before she returned, I met Esther in Tijuana. Alicia was born here, in the U.S., so she had no trouble passing. She gave me the girl there, in Tijuana, and later she paid a coyote to cross. Afterwards, Esther got her green card, because she hadn't lost her status.

"We live together in Santa Clara. First in an apartment for a while and right now we have lived for eleven years in a three room house that we own. Esther cleans houses and does housekeeping. She works Monday to Saturday usually and Sunday occasionally. Now I work as a day worker. We divide the expenses between my daughter, my wife and me, and more or less we manage. Our main expenses are the house payment. The food is not so expensive. Food is really more expensive in Mexico than here, more expensive in comparison to what one makes. Because here, an ordinary day for a worker is $100; not too bad. With $100 I'll eat 10 times, I'll go to eat at a restaurant, but not a fancy restaurant. In Mexico, one day's pay equals two times eating in a restaurant. Look, what a comparison, twice to ten, it's a big difference, big difference, so the food is not such a big expense–it is the rent.

"We were able to buy a house because my wife had money for a down payment. In Mexico, my wife had a license to rent space in a building that held a market. When she came to the U.S. she sold the license for that building space. From there she got the money for the house's down payment, $100,000. We make monthly payments to the bank of $2,000. We do not pay much, because we gave $100,000 as a down payment. My wife wanted to put $200,000 down. We have paid for the first 11 years out of 25.

"Esther wants to be herself. I will put up with everything that I can, because I have patience. Look, when you have an issue with your husband, it should be discussed just between the two of you. When my daughter was three years old, Esther kicked me out. She kicked me out for three days. Those were bad days, the days I felt most alone in life. One day we were talking, we sat down to dinner at the table, and I cannot remember what we were arguing about, not that I wouldn't want to tell you, but I do not remember. We had an argument. I do not feel it was a strong argument, but she slaps me across my face. It was not an argument, it wasn't strong, but the emotions were strong, so I slapped her back. More or less the same way she hit me. She said nothing - I just saw her face, angry, she got up and went into the room. Then I had dinner and I got up and she was crying there. 'Go away,' she said 'Get out of here.' I pretended not to hear.

"The next day I was not working because I was incapacitated by the roofing accident. My girl was about three years old then. The next day, Esther got up early, she worked every day, seven days a week then, and she went to work. I was there in the house. At six, seven o'clock, in the evening she arrived, and said, 'Hey, didn't you hear what I told you last night? You need to get out of here.' The next day she went, as usual, to work. That day I went to walk my baby down the street and I was crying and walking, and my child asked, because my little girl learned Spanish and English very well from the beginning, she said, 'Hey Dad, are you crying?' 'No, my daughter, I am not crying, there's dust in my eyes.' I walked and my girl asked me again, 'Are you crying, Dad?' 'No, it's just dust.' But she noticed. That was at noon, my wife was working, and I arrived with my daughter, from a little walk of half an hour. I started to wrap my stuff there, make a packet of clothes, a small package. My sister lived in Redwood City, and I called her and asked if my brother-in-law was there. Her husband was my friend. ' Ask my friend, when he arrives, if he can call me?' A few hours later, I called again, and when I called he was there. 'My friend, what happened?' he asked. *Compadre*, I want to ask you for a favor, without prejudice. Can you give me permission to stay there in your house alone, because my wife gave the apartment back and she's going to Mexico with my girl?' I said that, but it was a lie. So I said, 'And if you do me the favor to receive me, please come get me right now, I have everything packed,' because I had only a few things.

"I didn't even have $5.00. I didn't have a job, and the help I had, the monthly payment from the accident, had been cut. I got there at night and cried all night long. I was there three days. And then Esther calls the house. She also knew how to cut hair, she learned in Mexico. She said to my brother-in-law 'Hey *compadre*, it's been a long time since I gave your children haircuts, how are they?' 'Oh! They look awful,' he answered. 'No one has cut their hair other than you when you came.' She said, 'I am coming over to cut their hair.' But she just wanted to go where I was. She arrived there and we started talking, and after five hours, she had cut the kids' hair. 'We're leaving, *compadre*,' she said. 'Come here,' she said to me, in the other room, because there were people there. 'Come over here,' and we went into the other room, 'What do you want?' I said 'Hey, I want you to forget what happened, I want you to forget it, and I want you to come back.' I was not deaf, either. Those three days were heavy. These are things one remembers, as you know.

"Anyway, I never drank, not young nor old. Yes, I like drinking, but I do not like it when I see what one does when he's drunk. I've been drunk twice in my life, once in Mexico and over here the year I came here. I got drunk there once and four years later I got drunk for the second time here. Since then, I've said, 'No more.' It's been 34 or 35 years of that. Never again. Why? Because a person who is drunk will spit out words like an old guitar. A person, when he's drunk, demands things that make no sense at all. If I'm drunk I'll say: 'Hey! That day I found you, you did not greet me.' What kind of claims are those? 'Hey! The other day I asked for a cigar, you had one and refused me.' This is not an appropriate demand, these things are simple things, but claims have been made. So they are claiming things without sense, without a case, this has led me to not drink.

"Our daughter, Alicia, is now 24 years old and lives with us. She went to school in the U.S., but only up to high school. She speaks English very well. She didn't want to continue studying. She is probably sleeping right now. What time is it right now? Is it 1:00 in the afternoon? She's still in bed right now. She attended high school and didn't want to study anymore. She wanted to work in a salon. She went to school in a beauty salon - it cost $12,000, for one year. To finally finish the course, she had to go live in Southern California. It was the last assignment, and she didn't do it. She did not get a certificate, and the money, I had to pay $12,000, was wasted. Because if you do not have the certificate, what do you have? Nothing, really.

"Then Alicia started going to people's homes to do odd jobs, and nothing else. She then started to work in San José, in security for a company called Sysco. She worked for 5 years there, at night. But one day they found her sleeping, and they told her not to sleep on the job. Another day, they found her sleeping again, and they told her that it is work, not sleep. The third time, bye, they fired her. Now she's got nothing. And she's not looking, because she says she won't until her unemployment runs out. I told her, 'Look honey you drive, you're young; you can get a job anywhere. You are 24 years old and know English and Spanish.' But she's not looking, she isn't looking. She doesn't want to work, because she's very comfortable. I tell her to get a job in whatever she has experience. Her mom bought her a car and it cost $14,000. It's not a new car. She asked for the car and asked, and asked. Well, after a lot of insistence my wife said, 'I'll buy her a cheap car.' She bought it and gave it to her. She got a license soon after that, and that's when she went to work for the security company. She just doesn't want to work. It is a problem.

"Alicia also has a son, Eli, three years old. And who knows where the father is. Eli lives with us, but he doesn't go to school, yet, he's too young. He speaks English. My daughter tells us not to talk to him in Spanish, but since I do not know English, I always speak Spanish. And my wife speaks English to him, so the kid barely knows any Spanish, hardly anything.

"In my family, I am the one's who's economically less. My brothers and sisters are working, doing great things. There is a brother who does bridge construction, by contract, and has a great job. My other brother can do that, but no longer wants to work in the sun so now he makes bathrooms, inside, but he makes good money, because it's by contract. Another brother lives in Seattle. He learned how to draw in Mexico. At first he painted players' shirts and then he worked in Mexico for Banamex, the National Bank of Mexico and Pemex, the state owned petroleum company, drawing pictures – making plans for roads. He is in Seattle right now. He moved to Seattle from San Francisco and right now he works at universities, doing painting and drawing. He also paints on cars. He has a very good job, but what he doesn't have is money. Because he spends it all, he spends it all.

"Out of nine children, there are eight of us left, five men and three women. My sister would have been 72 right now, two years in between, my following brother is 70, a sister is 68, another brother 66, then there's me at 64 and two by two to finish 9! Only the first one died, – she was walking and fell, from heart failure. The doctor told her one day, 'You are ill, I can see a spot in your heart and you will die quickly, you will not suffer.' She was told that she would die quickly and she did, she did not suffer.

"It was many years before I came to the Day Worker Center. I had been in the States 30 years when I came here. This center has been in many places. I first saw it when it was on El Camino Real, near Walmart. I watched as the workers entered, but I never entered. I watched as I passed. From there they moved to California Avenue. I walked in front of it many times, but I never entered. I started coming to the Center when it was on Mercy St., near Castro St. in Mountain. View. I had worked in a carpentry company, Harmon Construction, beginning in 1995, for 12 years, building houses. Then I stopped working there and I came to the Day Worker Center. We moved to the new Center on Escuela Avenue three years ago.

"What I like to do most is digging, because before I worked in a carpentry company, I worked for 12 years in a company doing excavations for foundations. That's where I made more money - that is where I made the most. In the Day Worker Center there are fewer options, only jobs like moving, painting, or gardening. That is what's most abundant here. Yes, I like it; it beats having nothing. It's better. Now I work possibly four or five days a week - even more, sometimes. Four days for sure, whole days. Yes, many employers call me. On Monday, I worked 8 hours, on Tuesday I did not work because I went to the clinic, but I worked yesterday for eight hours. I work almost every day.

"Every day after work I go to see volleyball in the park. But I don't go with Esther. Volleyball, it's fun. It amuses me and affects me a little, because I bet and I lose. $20, $40, $60. Sometimes I win and sometimes I lose, but I lose more than what I win. On Saturday, I won about $40, but lost $60 on Sunday! So no, it is not a good business. Eventually, I'll stop working. But I'm never home. I go outside and spend time walking around. Because if there are no people in the house I do not like being there alone and if there are people in the house I don't like it either, so I'm not very adept. Sometimes, I come to the Day Worker Center at half past 6 in the morning, 6:20 to 6:30. Sometimes, if I am not at work at two in the afternoon, I stay until 5:00 and then I go out to San Jose to watch the volleyball game. I arrive home at 9:00 p.m. I leave early and arrive late.

"I often go to Mexico – I have gone many times by bus and plane. I have an ID and a green card, but I could not get a driver's license. I have been on planes, but I do not like it, I am scared of flying. I do not like it, but I've done it. When my father died I flew home; when my mom had surgery for the first time, too. Three times I've flown, but I went by plane and returned by bus. About two years ago, the director of the Day Worker Center and several of the workers went to Washington D.C. for immigration reform. I was invited, but I didn't want to go. I don't like airplanes.

"But I'll stay here in the U.S permanently. I have no capital, neither here nor there. Being poor there or being poor here, it's better here. But I am happy I came. I only want to go to Mexico for three weeks and then return – that is what I want. I'm going to apply for U.S. citizenship. After five years of being a resident, a person can be a citizen. I haven't done it before, well just because you say, 'Tomorrow, tomorrow, tomorrow.' I will have to take the exam. It's not hard. It is difficult, but only because I do not know English. But at my age I can take it in Spanish. Fifty-five years or more, you can take it in Spanish, so for me it is not hard. I just leave it for tomorrow, tomorrow, and tomorrow.

"What I want out of life is to work eight hours, five days a week, a steady job, not six or seven or ten hours a day, no, just eight hours and five days. Simple, nothing else. I also want good health, and to have no enemies. I don't have any now, but I wouldn't want to, ever. My dad told us to try to live well, not be spiteful, that if ever a person insulted us, not to mind. It'll pass; it will pass, because if one pays attention to every little problem one would always have problems. If someone walked by me and was drunk and pushed me and insulted me? Ah, don't mind, don't mind. Others go for the gun and they find each other and kill each other. I've seen things like that. So if one paid attention to all these little things we'd already be six feet under. We'd be in prison; we'd have lost an eye from a punch. It's better to be a bit of a coward than a little bit brave, because in Mexico there is all of that violence all the time. Your brother killed my brother, I seek your brother and I don't find him, but I find you, pum, pum, pum, only because your brother killed my brother and that should not be, it should not be. That happens a lot in Mexico – revenge. Families are killed. It's horrible.

"Now I'm healthy. I'm not missing an eye. I'm not missing a hand, a foot. And what else… Who knows? So hopefully my daughter will find a job tomorrow. She says she'll find one and work, but she says that every day, but she is not looking for it. I pay taxes every year. But, I do not know if I can retire now, because if I do not keep putting money into social security, it won't increase anymore. If you give me $5 right now for retirement, if I don't work it's going to be the same, it will not grow, right? And I am ready to apply for retirement, because I am 64.

"When one gets older I feel everything closes up a bit. I'm going to be walking around dragging a foot and maybe with a blind eye; I feel like I'll get to that. Because I don't know how long I will last. But you never know in life, will it be 20, will it be 30, will it be 2 will it be 1, or tomorrow we don't know, but I do not analyze it.

"Life has taught me many things. I have gotten to know many things, good and bad, because life shows you everything. It was all good, because I never, when I was here or there, or young or old, have fought with another person. If anyone ever throws a punch at me they will break my jaw because I know nothing. So that's why I have not had bad experiences. I have learned not to fight. That's what I learned, a good point. Look I trust everyone. We live better when we trust. I'd like to be remembered as good people."

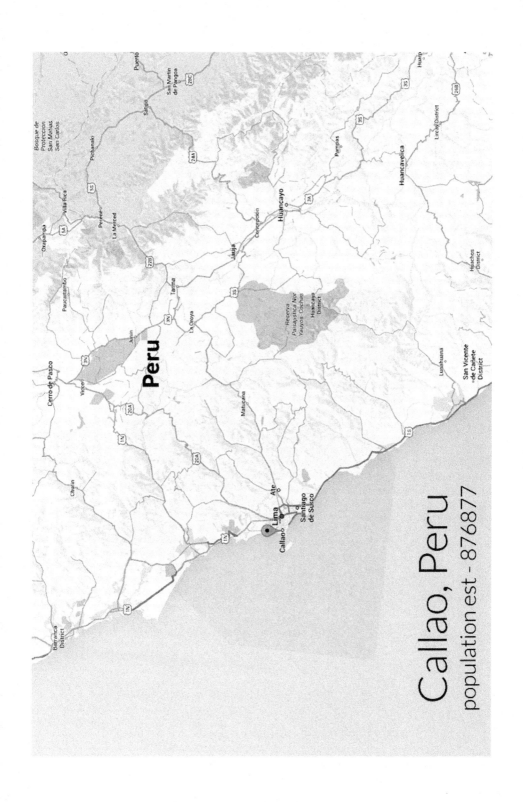

# Callao, Peru

population est - 876877

# Chapter 2

## Ernesto's Story

"It is a bad time in my life, a difficult time. Because right now I do not have documents to work and, indeed, I am illegal in the United States. My visa expired, because I entered legally on a tourist visa and stayed. I overstayed. And I cannot get a job that matches my skills and my education.

"I'm from Callao, Peru. That is the port of Lima. My journey has been from Peru, to Japan and finally the United States. Why Japan? Because in the 1990's - in 1992 or 1993, the situation in Peru was very critical. There was so much terrorism and the terrorist group 'Sendero Luminoso' (Shining Path) was a Maoist insurgent organization that had surrounded Lima. It was a civil war – they were trying to establish a dictatorship of the proletariat. It was a brutal organization and used violence against peasants, trade unions, elected officials and the general civilian population. We all knew people that had been killed by violence and bombs. It was a very dangerous country in those years, but there was also the opportunity to travel by visa to Japan. The president of Peru was a descendant of Japan and so the two countries had a relationship. Also, at that time, Japan had a need for a lot of workers. So I decided to leave Peru.

"I was born on 26 March, 1953. I am old - 61 years old. My dad is also named Ernesto. I do not like my middle name - Braulio. It comes from a saint. At the time that I was born it was common to use names from the calendar. My dad was born in Lima, itself. My mom was born north of Lima, in another department - Chimbote, which is a fishing port. My mom came from the countryside. My father was a city man, who hated countrymen. You know the term 'Indians.' Well, in Peru, you call them 'Cholos'. He hated the Cholos. Cholos in Mexico is another thing. In Mexico cholo is a gang member. In South America, Cholo is Indian, dismissive. 'That Cholo crap!' My mom always told me that my dad was mean to her. Sometimes, he would say 'Hey, Chola ...' and you know, they had fights.

"My grandparents were Italian and Spanish and came to Peru. At that time it was difficult to live in Europe because of the war, the famine. I did not know them. They died before I was born. My father and my mother were both orphaned when they were children. So I do not know what it is to have grandparents. My dad was raised by his grandfather, and my mother by her older siblings. She was the youngest of the siblings.

"My dad was white. He was the son of Italians and had light eyes, lighter than mine and he looked a lot more 'gringo', whiter than me, you could say, so he felt entitled. There is racism in our countries. I look just like my dad, but my dad was whiter. In terms of personality it's a bit complicated. I sometimes say I am becoming more and more like my dad, because I like drinking. My father drank in the street and he would call me. 'Son! Son! Come and see!' I would hide. I think in that way I had a traumatic relationship with my dad.

"My mother separated from my father when I was three years old. Well, as I said, the first three years of my life we lived in Callao. My father was a merchant and the port was there. He collected the merchandise that was imported from everywhere. I lived there until I was three. We lived in a home, but my parents sold it later. There were three bedrooms, living room, and kitchen. A normal house - two bathrooms as well.

"From there we went to live in Lima. It's not a long trip - twenty minutes. We began to live in a rented house. I was living with my mom and my two siblings – my older sister, and my younger brother.

"I almost do not remember Callao, as I was only three when we left. Lima is a cosmopolitan, big city. Similar to Mexico City. It has 10 million inhabitants. I lived in the midst of the city, in the concrete jungle. I have never lived in the countryside. I do not even like the countryside. Well, maybe for a day, to walk a little, but then I get bored and mosquitoes start biting and I just return to the city.

"My mom did not work. My father never paid alimony to my mom. When they got divorced, my mom said it was very hard. She had a little savings here and there. He just went away. My dad went to the United States - to San Francisco. A few years later, he returned to Lima. He said he missed his children, his three children. But when he returned he had a drinking problem. He lost his business and everything else. I do not remember him from when I was a kid. I remember him as an older man, when he approached us apologetically. I do not resent him. I even buried him.

"When I was ten or so, my mom remarried. My stepfather was a United States police colonel. She created another home and we lived with him in Lima. I called my stepfather 'dad'. He brought us up practically. My mom and stepfather had a son - my stepbrother – who now lives in the United States. He is a U.S. citizen, because his dad was from the U.S.

"In my youth I got in trouble. I had a crazy youth. In the 1970's, I was a hippie. Long hair and drugs. Yes, I had problems; do I have to tell you? I don't need to hide it from you, I smoked marijuana as a boy. It was illegal, of course. My mom would pick me up from the police station. Eventually, I went to school and I calmed down. My brother, however, was more serious. I'm the black sheep of the family.

"I went to college, at the Metropolitan Higher Institute of Lima, where I learned technical drawing. It is a technical degree, a career in middle management. In the Metropolitan Higher Institute of Lima I did two years of drawing and then became a civil construction technician. It applies to a very wide range of jobs, to be a helper of a civil engineer. His right hand, like a master builder.

"When I was twenty years old, I taught. I volunteered in the church and taught literacy to people who could not read back in my country. And I liked it. I taught writing, everything. I like teaching. I like to teach many people. Sometimes, now, I will correct when some colleagues say an incorrect word; then I correct them. I teach them real Spanish, Castilian, which is what we speak.

"I didn't serve in the military. It was mandatory at that time. I went and, as I was a bit shortsighted, I said, 'I'm blind, I cannot see.' 'Okay, go over there.' I was exonerated. It was quite easy. At that time they sought you. There were raids to find young people to get them by force to join the army.

"I married at age 20. I got a girl pregnant when I was 20 years old. Precisely at that time I stopped partying a bit and I had to work. I really wanted to apply to the Faculty of Architecture, which was what I liked. I couldn't continue my studies because I had to start working as an engineer. She was really young, too. We got married in Peru, in Lima. We got married in a church. She was, you would not believe this, 15 years old. And her dad was a cop. In the United States they put you in jail for something like that. In Peru, you get a choice: you have to marry or go to jail. Anyway, that was the hardest time of my life. I had to work and my aspirations for a career in architecture or civil engineering were gone. From then on, I've been working my entire life.

"I had already worked in the construction company, drawing plans for architecture and construction for about 20 years when I decided to leave for Japan. By then, I had divorced my first wife. A few years before I decided to leave for Japan, the construction company I worked for sent

23

me to work in Cuzco, Peru. Machu Picchu is there. I went there to work on the renovations of a hotel, the best hotel in Cuzco at the time, a tourist hotel. There I met my second wife Anabella. My second wife is from Cuzco. I stole her away and brought her with me to Lima, where we got married. A few years went by, four years, but we had no children. We still didn't have any children by the time we left Lima to go to Japan. I thought one of us might have problems, might be infertile, that we couldn't conceive. We came to Japan and she became pregnant. I do not know what happened, maybe the climate change, I do not know. It must be the change in hemisphere. Anabella was very young. I was already 34 and she was 20. There we had a child - my daughter - who is now 20 years old.

"We lived in Japan for 14 years. My daughter was born there, she speaks Japanese, and she behaves like all Japanese. She also speaks perfect Spanish, because we spoke to her in Spanish, but she is Japanese. She lives there with her mom.

"Living in Japan was very difficult at first. In the first year, second year, I suffered a lot. To communicate I had to sign a lot. Sometimes you were told 'You're a fool' and you didn't even realize. You would have said 'arigato, arigato, sayonara' and they were saying, 'You are stupid,' 'arigato, sayonara.' Eventually I learned to speak a little Japanese. I'll tell you one thing, the one thing that happens in Japan is that the Japanese are not very friendly to you. They are not rude or angry, they don't resent you; they are scared of you. If you talk to them in English, they are scared of you. Furthermore, when they have a few drinks and want to talk to you, you can say you're Chinese or Spanish but they will believe that you speak English. They always believe that the foreign language is English - it's amazing. But the Japanese do not speak English, they don't know how to speak English, they are afraid of English. The only place where English is spoken is at the counters at the international airport. It's the only place. Not like here.

"In Japan, I had two different jobs, the first with auto parts. I worked for two years in a factory. Auto parts from that factory were exported all over the world to the United States from Toyota, Nissan. Japanese cars are all pretty much the same; they have nothing different from each other. If you check your car, Toyota has the same piece, a capacitor or whatever, it has the same piece as a Nissan, Mazda, that is, the car is standard, and there is no car that is better than the other. Now, it may be better because of the engine or the power, but no worse or better in quality. You can never say that a Toyota is better quality because they are the same parts; it's the same factory. In the factory, I worked in the press making tubes for air conditioning on cars. Everything there is machine controlled. I have also gone to the factories where they make the cars themselves. For example there are doors, doors, doors, shelves, chassis, chassis, and chassis. What a rich country, I really miss that country. In the U.S. there are car factories, but they are far away. I think cars are made in Detroit in the United States.

"From there I went to work at a paper mill company. They made countless types of paper. We made giant spools of two tons of paper. From there, they then send the spools to another site, where they cut it and make it into legal size, and other sizes of paper. I drove a forklift. When the warm paper came out, something like a giant two-ton or three-ton spool, I came with the forklift. It was a special forklift. And you know who would throw the paper? A robot. A giant robot labeled the paper, everything. I grabbed the spool, and you had to have great technique, because if you grabbed it in the wrong way, some of the paper would be ruined. A small mistake could scrap some 100 layers of paper and they would have to be sent to recycling. The paper was worth hundreds of dollars. It was hard, but sometimes I even did it when I was sleepy, or drunk, it was an automated thing.

"In Japan I made $3000 - $ 4000 per month. I could even afford to have three girlfriends! I was a 40 year-old man in the prime of my life. There were plenty of women there that were not Japanese - Russian, Romanian, Ukrainian, Eastern European, blondes with blue eyes, as well. You didn't even look at the Japanese. What's more, if you like brunettes more – there were women from the Philippines up for grabs. It is very difficult for Japanese women to accept you, and for the family to accept you and for her to consider you as a boyfriend.

"I was a womanizer. I would go out all the time in my car. My wife got tired, and me, too. Then we split up. I started living alone in Japan when I separated from my wife. I felt alone and I used to go clubbing. I knew all the discos in Japan. In Japan there is a building, and it's so well done that you see a door that looks like a flat, open the door and it's a nightclub, another door, another nightclub. Licensed, everything. Japan's nightlife is incredible, it's unbelievable. I've never seen anything like it. Many things are legal there. I'm not going to lie.

"We spent a few years separated like that. She took my daughter, but we lived near each other. I didn't miss anything. My daughter's school was close to my house. If she wanted to come to my house, she had a key to my little apartment, and she came and opened the door. 'Hello daddy, hello, hello.' We were like friends.

"But the time came when I had to renew my visa - there are no permanent visas in Japan. There are permanent visas, but not like here, where you have the green card and you're done. Over there you renew it every three years. I went to the immigration office to renew my Japanese visa. I knew what was going to happen. They asked: 'Where is your wife?' 'She is not here.' 'She has to come.' 'Why?' Because my wife was giving me the visa - she was a Japanese descendant and she was giving me the visa. They said, 'Oh, no, but the wife has to come.' 'But I am divorced and I have a child that was born here.' 'Yeah, that's fine, but hey, I'm sorry, sayonara!'

"I regret the madness. I regret what I did in Japan. I mean, going out with women and stuff. I lost my home and my wife. Yes that's the saddest thing. Because she's a good woman. She got married again, to a Japanese man.

"I cannot go back to Japan. I cannot go back because immigration laws are very strict there. I was told to leave. I wasn't expelled, that's good; if not, I would not have been able to enter the United States. And Japan's foreign policy remains the same. The border is even more closed. They no longer accept immigration, not even if I am the Peruvian son of Fujimori, the former president.

"Since I could not stay in Japan, I called my nephew in California and said, 'Hey I have problems with Anabella.' He knew that we had separated. The problem is that immigration is asking me where my wife is, but I have no wife and then I will not be able to renew my visa. You have to be careful, because Japan is a very dangerous place to go without a visa, because police in Japan ask for documents at any time of the day. Also, I had become bored with Japan - too much partying.

"My nephew, who is a U.S. citizen, is the son of my sister. He is an architect by profession, but is not practicing right now. He practiced in Peru. In the U.S. he has a job that has nothing to do with architecture, in one of those medical technology companies. He said, 'Come here uncle, here's the place to be. We'll make it.' In the end I came to the U.S. and everything was just talk. 'No, uncle, the thing is, employment is low, wait;

be patient.' I arrived just when the economic crisis hit the US. There were no jobs, no work in 2008.

"I came to the United States on a tourist visa from Japan. I stayed with my nephew, who lived in Palo Alto, California. He said, 'Yes, uncle, don't worry uncle, we'll make it.' I came with some savings, about $ 4000. I spent six months not working. Then the money ran out. But I was lucky - I met a friend who introduced me to someone who said, 'Hey! There is the Day Worker Center where you can get work.' But wait, I went to the Center, hanging around, but nothing happened. After about three months I went to Utah to see my stepbrother, who is married to an American. Then I spent a year in Utah in Salt Lake City. Everywhere pure snow - how awful!

"I worked in Utah eventually, but the worst was that there was practically no work and the weather was horrible. Horrible. In California you may not have a job, but here you are with friends, there's sun, vegetation. There, it's horrible - and there are only Mormons. Utah is the state of the Mormons, it's a state created for them. Everyone is a Mormon. My brother is a Mormon.

"My family has not helped me. My older sister married an American and she'll become a citizen, too, one of these days. She has not submitted any papers for me yet. She has not submitted a single request for my green card or anything. She says, 'Ahh, but wait! Do you have the money?' Because you have to go pay a fine, something for forgiveness, I am not sure what it is.

"It was the same thing with my brother who lives in Utah - the son of my stepfather. My mom is living in his house and is 82 years old. She talks to me every day. She will become a citizen also. Because she's been here for five years and is over 70 years old, she is not asked to know English. Showing that your child is a citizen is all you need. And she can request it for me, if she doesn't die before that, poor thing.

"From my mom and dad we are my sister, then me, and my recently deceased brother. He died at 56 or 57 years old. He was a professional public accountant. His daughters had a great education, one is an industrial engineer, and the other one studied business administration. He lived in Peru. My brother traveled around the world for conferences. He went to India, to England. He was the chief auditor. Auditors are accountants, well, a certain specialty job for accountants. He traveled the world and seemed well positioned; he had a home and everything, and he had a heart attack. Younger than me. He was my younger brother by one year and died at 59. We had even studied at school as if we were twins as young children, in the same school year. We celebrated birthdays together, just to save a bit on the party. Our birthdays were only one week apart. We'd celebrate on a Sunday with cake and all. Our cousins would come. Those are beautiful memories.

"My son by my first wife is now 40 years old and lives with his mother in Canada. He is a Canadian citizen. They live in Quebec, Montreal and speak French. Their children also can speak Spanish, because at home they speak Spanish. Now I get along well with my first wife, the mother of my son. My son went to law school and became a lawyer. He studied in Peru when he lived there, but when he arrived in Canada, he was told he would have to go back to school to practice. He decided not to study in Canada, and so he does not practice the profession. My boy already has his life - he has given me three grandchildren, he is married, and just bought a house in Canada. He said that there is a room for me for when I decide to go. He wanted me to go and live there. But I wouldn't get used to it and I do not want to bother them. I don't want to be a burden. They say it is terribly cold there, 20 degrees below zero in the winter; the pool freezes. It's horrible. I like California. I think it's the best climate in the world.

"My daughter is 20 years old and lives in Japan with her mother. My daughter speaks Spanish and Japanese. But I cannot decipher her Facebook page. She doesn't want to be my friend on Facebook, but I can see her photos and she'll write in Japanese, so I cannot understand. I sent her a friend request, but she does not want to be my friend.

"My daughter is a problem. She's young and I wanted her to go to continue with school. She was studying languages. But now she has started to work and stopped going to college. She bought a car. In Japan anyone can afford a car. It's like here, too, all the sons of Americans have their own cars. She bought the car with her salary, go figure. In Japan, a girl of 14 or 15 years if they already have more or less a certain body height can be given permission to work. They work in cell factories or things of that sort.

"About four years ago, I went to the Day Worker Center. It has helped me a lot – helped me to survive. Now I do the simplest work - a bit of carpentry, gardening. I don't like to paint, I hate painting! Every time I have started to paint, I lost my jeans or spoiled my clothes. We get to the center 'Come! Ernesto! You are leaving! You have to go to work! You're going to paint this,' and I did not bring the right clothes. I am not a professional painter. You end up painting yourself. I have to keep working until I get tired. I have no social security here. There are people at the Day Worker Center who are nearly 70 years old and continue to work, and come here. It is heavy work. It can be shoveling, moving.

"Right now, I work part time in a warehouse of Moroccan handicrafts. I earn $15 per hours and I work three times a week, for eight hours – 24 hours a week. I do many things – I store, I pack, unpack. The warehouse is very big, and it has big shelving full of products, lamps. It is called Casablanca Market. It had a shop on Castro Street in Mt. View, but now I do not know where they are selling. The owners hired me from the Day Worker Center. They went to the Center and looked for a person to help them, and then another person, and another one; but the lady was very particular. She did not put up with them. 'OK, bring another, bring another,' until I went and she liked me and I have been working there for a year and a half. And I speak a little English, because the others did not speak any English. The owners say, 'Do this' and the other workers would go to sleep. They know that I am not here legally. However, the owner likes how I work. I get paid in cash – outside of the books.

"I've had false papers, but now I don't have them. I think only 5% of the people have false documents. I have been offered fake IDs, - but no, – I do not want to do those things. I've had a California driver's license, but it's expired. The police stopped me twice while driving and the fine for each ticket was $472. So from that day on I had no car. I don't want to be working just to pay the DMV, so I do not drive anymore. I don't have any social security. To find work I go to the Day Worker Center. You are waking up to the reality here. I've never had a problem with the law here. Especially since I do not look like an immigrant. There once was a raid and I watched how they took Mexicans away, but to me they said nothing, not even the time of day.

"I am very outgoing and I know many people from many countries. I worked 14 years with Brazilians. I speak Portuguese. I have worked with Filipinos, with Japanese. Now, from time to time, with Americans, Moroccans, with Hindus who constantly go to the Center to request a worker. They all like me. Sometimes I hear the other men say, 'Ernesto always has help from the office.' They say that every day I go to work. But sometimes people come and, for example, nobody wants to work with

Hindus. They say 'No, that does not pay well,' but to me, Ernesto, they come to get me, calling me directly on my phone, to work. 'Hey, why do Hindus always ask for you? You get sent by the office, right? 'No!' 'It's one thing in which I differentiate from the others. These men, Mexicans, Central Americans, think that it's about being strong, but they do not speak, do not have the gift of conversation. When I go to work with employers I start to talk in English. I say, 'I'm from Peru. Where are you from? 'Then,' 'Ah! Yes! Peru? Machu Picchu!' And so I don't get heavy work and they become my friends. Now I work almost every day, and the rest of the men do not. They have a different mentality. So I think my gift is to be outgoing with people of all cultures.

"No, sometimes people don't like me - they think I'm a smartass. That I act like I know a lot. But I think I have a certain level of culture. Of culture, not of intelligence - I'm talking culture. I know many things, many people. I think that's my strength and I think that's what happens with employers. Employers call me back. 'Ernesto, come!' And there have been employers who have gone to find me at the Center and I was not there and do you think they took another worker? 'Oh no, tell him to see if he can come on Saturday. I'll come back on Saturday to see if he can come, or whenever he can.' Or they'll call me. They have my number and everything. Which does not happen with others there in the center.

"No one gives me a job just like that. They give me work because, as I said, they know me and have taken a liking. But just imagine if it ends. Do you know what the problem is, too? In winter, the work in the Day Worker Center is low; it slows a lot. People go to work once a week, once a week. How can you live on $ 100 a week?

"Now I rent a room in a house in Mt. View. It is a home owned by a Mexican family and I rent a room. Five people live in the house. There is another room that is also rented. Before I was renting alone, $700 just for a room. But I had to get a roommate, because the bills went up. I met my roommate at the Center. Bernardo is from Chile. He no longer comes to the Center these days. He works elsewhere. He comes to the Center occasionally, but when he gets a job, he usually works for a month. He is a good carpenter, a house carpenter. Not furniture. Because in our country the carpenter makes furniture, but here a carpenter makes frames for houses. Yes, in Peru houses are built with brick, concrete.

"When I am not working I go to a club around here on Castro Street in Mt. View. I go with my Mexican friend Daniel to the disco. I go drinking with my friends. I go to San Francisco and go to a restaurant with my family in Palo Alto. I also play the guitar. We have a group at the Day Worker Center and sometimes we perform in the local communities or restaurants. We play for tips.

"I've reached a ceiling. I'm hoping to retire. I'm going to officially retire in Japan, and they'll send money to me here. I already got an advance. It was three years ago, I was sent a check, and I'll receive a Japanese pension, because I worked more than 14 years in that country. So I contributed, paid taxes; they deducted 25% of what I earned. If you earn $4000 almost $1000 went for retirement. And I always had good health care. When I got sick, I received the best medical care in hospitals. While I was in Japan, I had back problems. By doing nothing. I do not know why I had this problem. Maybe by being on the lift, the movement, the discs of the vertebrae became damaged, and I gained weight. Because the work was actually easy. When there was no production left, the boss would tell us to go for coffee, rest.

"I could go back to Peru, if I get papers in the United States. But the truth is that since my brother died, I have no family there. That's another thing, there are people who tell me 'Hey! Buy a car!' No! I do not want to get a fine and I want to have a clear record, enough with the expired license. 'No! But what?' 'You know who tells me that?' Those people who do not mind having fines, or do not care, because they are sending money home and then plan to stay in their own countries. In their country they are building their houses. I have to be more careful. I have to watch myself because I want my bones buried here, to be buried here.

"I want a dignified old age. Not like some people older than me that are at the Center. I would like a decent old age, perhaps working in a softer job. I aspire not to make a lot of money, but as I say, a dignified old age. Working perhaps as a clerk in a store, something such as Fry's Electronics, so to speak. Something to be in contact with people. But I have to improve my English.

"Most importantly, I want to meet a mature woman and get married. Because I had a child at 20, my second daughter at 40, and I'm 60 now and I need a third wife. Marrying for the company and also the papers, too. Why should I be a hypocrite? Because even if my sister asks for a green card for me, or my brother asks for a green card for me, until I get the green card it will be at least 15 years. Instead, with a marriage to a

U.S. citizen, in three years, No! In six months you have a green card and in three years you can be a citizen. That's how it works here.

"So I'm looking for a girlfriend. I have a special friend – Ludmila - but it's nothing official. A friend with benefits. She is a Russian-American and lives in Saratoga. She has been here for 10 or 15 years. I met her at a barbecue. She is about 63 years old. She was a teacher in Russia. She is Jewish and Jews get visas to enter and before long, become citizens. It's like the Cubans - it is almost impossible to find a Cuban illegal. Because when a Cuban is on American soil, in a month they give them a green card.

"The government - I do not know how it's done - but the government pays Ludmila - gives her an apartment. I do not know why the government helped her for being Jewish. Policy. It is as if she has political asylum, but that was then. This is not the era of Stalin. What happens is that it is a political issue. Why help the Jews? Why do Americans give weapons to the Jews? Give logistical support? But that's another problem, they do not want to see it. Hitler died, Stalin died and why do the Jews need so much help? But it's very easy, very easy. Because, basically, all it is a political issue. Why for the Latinos, is it not easy and it is easy for others? They come from Russia, Ukraine, even countries like Pakistan, India, because it is a political game. The United States is not interested in Latinos. If you go to Mountain View, it is the same - pure Chinese, because here they get a visa easily.

"I wanted to marry Ludmila out of convenience. She is my official girlfriend - I introduced her to everyone, and she knows my family. I introduced her to my brothers and even to my mom when she came to visit me. So you can say that she was my official girlfriend. She also wanted to get married, but the problem is that when I asked her to marry me she went to find out about our situation.

"She went to city hall and she learned she would lose some benefits by marriage and said, 'No, let's go on like this.' She didn't leave me, but said, 'Let's live together, but we cannot get married, because the government will take my pension, will take this, take that, and my apartment will become more expensive.' She even gets paid retirement. They would reduce it. She receives a check for $900 monthly. If she married me she would no longer receive the $900. Her brother said, 'Ah, you want to marry this man? He should provide for you.' She worked in the U.S. for only five years and paid taxes. Americans do not know these things because they are never interested in knowing. It's like they live in another world.

"If I do not marry Ludmila, I will try and find another woman to marry. I keep both options in mind. Now I have a new girlfriend – Lucia. She is a friend - a good friend. I met her in Mountain View. I was walking with a friend and he introduced us. Even though I am old, I have some social activity. She is also working - she is Mexican. But I have no interest in getting married, because she does not have a green card. She is in the same situation as me, but right now she is legal, here with a tourist visa, comes and goes, comes and goes.

"I am an old man. That's the uncertainty that I have. Suddenly, I'm too old, I'm not going to get anything, and I will not get a partner. Suddenly, I do not know, I could get a heart attack. That's my insecurity, that's what worries me. Well, you learn from your mistakes, too, I'm going to say. There are things that can no longer be undone. It's already done. But it leaves a mark. But one learns."

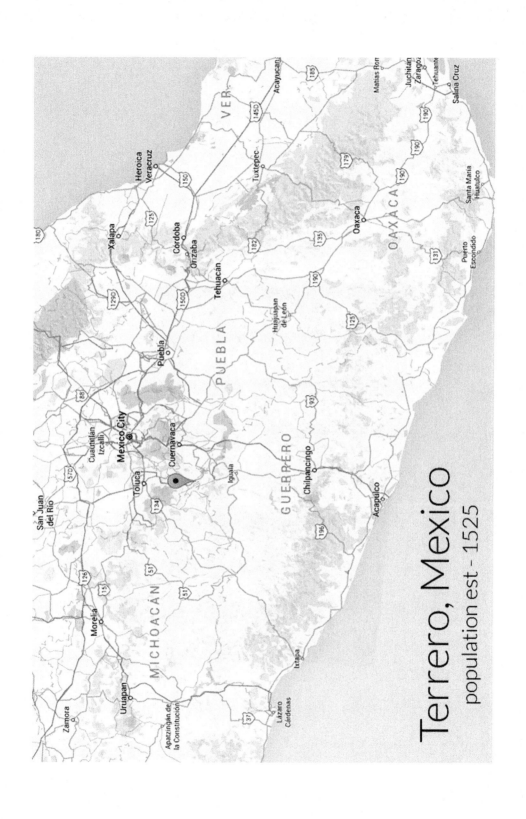

# Terrero, Mexico
## population est - 1525

# Chapter 3

## Lucía's Story

"I was born in Mexico, in 1965, in Terrero, a town about two and a half hours south of Mexico City. I lived in a tile house in the very center of the village; everything was close. About three blocks away there was the church, opposite that the government building, across from that was the bank, on the other block were many restaurants.

"We lived in our own house. My father told us that when he planted onions, he would sell them and when he did well, he used the money to buy the land and gradually built the house. We only had two rooms and a kitchen and a corridor. We had no bathroom. We had a space in the back yard that we called a 'corral' where my dad had a horse and he had chickens. My dad never let his daughters ride the horse - only my brothers. I remember that although at first we were allowed to keep animals, at some point it was forbidden. Once, you could have pigs, but then you no longer could. So my father had to move his horse; he took it away, up on a hill. He had some land there; he put up a roof for protection, and that's where he left his horse.

"My mother worked in the house. She was always at home, taking care of us. She was very dedicated, I remember when I was younger, I didn't have to do anything. Only my oldest sister used to help out, she'd make tortillas, she'd do groceries. My other sister too, one would wash and the other would iron, and so on. They'd distribute the work between them.

"My father worked mainly as a day worker, as his father had done. He usually worked by seasons. During the rainy season he'd plant crops. He grew corn, planted onions. Our family earned money only by my father's jobs. We never went hungry, but my parents could not buy many needed things for us.

"My grandparents were also born in Terrero. I remember my grandfather; we called him *abuelito*, my mother's father. He dedicated himself to doing this thing called *chiquihuites*; by weaving reeds and *otate* he made some type of baskets, squared and round ones. People bought them; they were called *tapaderas*. A cloth was placed on them and then they were meant to store tortillas. My grandmother, his wife, stayed at home. Sometimes, she also helped him in that she would sweep the streets of people that would ask her and then paid her. She also helped make meals - it was not a restaurant, it was called a *fonda*, she'd go there to grind chili in a mill. She was a good cook.

"My mother had two children that died when they were babies. One came after my brother Javier. My mom said he caught some kind of cough. *Tos hogona* is what they called it at the time and he died. I guess, I think it would have been bronchitis, or something like that. But back then my mom used to say that he died of *tos hogona*. It was when children caught a bad cough and couldn't stop coughing. She told me he was about a year old. I never met him.

"Then after me another girl was born, but she died. She didn't die during the pregnancy; she got to the end of the pregnancy. I do not know if she was born sick and then died or if she was actually stillborn.

"In all, I have three sisters and six brothers. I am the sixth sibling – two brothers live in Minneapolis, I live in California and the rest live in Mexico. I haven't seen my siblings since I've moved to the United States. But we talk over the phone. Sometimes I send them some money, but not always. I only send money when someone is ill. Right now, one sister is sick with diabetes. She's sick, and her husband is a day worker in Mexico. I do not know how much they pay him right now, maybe 120 or 150 pesos per day. He is only a day worker and there are times when it rains, there are times when there's no work. There is more work is the rainy season, when many people want to plant. But sometimes, if it rains too much, there is no work.

"All my brothers and sisters and also my cousins liked to go play together outside at the side of our house. We played there in the afternoon when there weren't many cars on the street. We liked to play with different things and different games. It is not like now - with smartphones and video games. No. Playing hide and seek, 'the black man,' 'the birds,' and 'the onions.' When we played the birds we gathered a lot of children. One would sell birds and the other bought them and the one selling had all the kids lined up and would give each person a special name, a name or a color. Then when the buyer came he would ask, 'Can you sell me a bird?' 'What color?' And he would say, 'Green' 'No, no, there are no green left' so then he'd say, 'Blue' 'Oh! This one is blue.' And 'How much does it cost?' The buyer would pay him and the bird would run away and the buyer would have to catch him; if he didn't it was no longer his.

"When I turned twelve, I helped out in the house, too. I had to sweep the kitchen or the street. Every day we would sweep out the side of the street from the house. I went to school, too. My parents would only send me to primary school. After going to school, I helped my mom in the house. I wanted to learn to knit, because some ladies in the village, some women, came together to weave thread, called estambrón. My sisters also knitted; they got paid for the work they did. They made shawls, but shaped like triangles. I learned how to knit, a little, but since then I've forgotten how to do it. Well that's what I did, nothing else, knitting. We would knit all week and on Saturday we had to deliver what we did.

"My school was quite a big school and after I left they remodeled it and made it larger. There were several grades, many first and second grade classes. I was walking distance from school - close by. It was about two blocks away. I lived close to most things in the neighborhood. The market, church, bank, office, and school.

"I finished my sixth year in school. It was the neighborhood school. I was more or less a good student. I would get eights out of ten. You could pass with a six, but you were barely making it through then. What I liked most was Spanish – language class.

"I wanted to be a nurse, but never studied it. I always think about that - I did not know why my parents were that way. That is why I tell my children, 'Study, here you have the opportunity to study.' I encourage them to make an effort and continue studying. Because they have opportunities to study, and we did not get them, and would have liked to.

"My mom did not force us to continue studying. She didn't encourage us to go to school after primary school. When I was about 17 years, I told my mom I wanted to learn something else. In our town, situated next to the government building, was a special trade school. There, in that school, many courses were taught - there was sewing, making clothes, a knitting course and cooking classes. There was also a nursing course. You only had to pay before one entered - as a contribution or something - but it was not much and it was once, for the whole year. I told my mom, 'I am going to that school to study' and she said, 'No, you're not going anywhere.' 'Why?' 'Because all those women that say they are going to study just go to meet guys,' and she never allowed me to go. Back then one always obeyed their parents. When we were older, our father wouldn't even let us go out, he forbid it and said, 'No.' 'Where are you going? What will you do?' And just, 'No.' Sometimes, we left in secret and then when we got back, we got in trouble.

"My mom died in 1998 – the year before I came to the States. She got ill. She had a severe stomachache, and after a while her back started hurting, too. We took her to the doctor because it got to a point where it hurt just to walk. Wherever she was, if the pain started she'd have to sit down, and when it passed she could keep walking. She went to the doctor and got a few tests and x-rays. The doctor told her that she had a tumor, but said they were going to operate on it. She had the surgery, but they couldn't remove the tumor completely - it was already too large. When she had surgery, they only took a piece and that was sent for analysis to see what kind of tumor it was. They told us nothing came out. She remained like this for a while and when her back started hurting again my brother took her to the doctor. The doctor told my older brother and my sister and my other brother who died later, that she had no more options; that she would not heal. Then we did another x-ray and a shadow showed up in her lung, she had lung cancer. A month later, almost a month after that, she died.

"When my mother had passed and it was only my father in the house, he would give me money for household spending. I would cook and do everything. He'd give me money for the food. Also, my brother who stayed there, when his wife left him, lived there in the house. He'd work and between both of them they paid me. They gave me say fifty or sixty dollars and gave me half each. Then, when I wanted to buy soap I would tell them I needed money for soap, because I also washed and ironed for them. I would also work for others, if anyone would ask me to help out in their house or even wash or iron. I only cooked in our house.

"After my mom died, my dad did not want to be alone, so he was with another woman. He would leave on Fridays and would go to Taxco, a city where he would make a lot of money. He would go there to sell things, such as onions, cilantro, and carrots. He'd sell it all. He'd travel on Friday and return on Monday night or Tuesday morning, at about eight o'clock. While he was there, he was with another woman.

"And I was home with my brother. My brother who'd begun drinking daily and kept drinking and no longer worked. He was really lost. Then he got into AA and I was left alone in the house. My sister-in-law lived in the same house, but on the other side of the yard - because where the animal pen used to be, since we didn't have any animals left, they leveled the ground and made a small house for themselves.

"In 2002 my brother died. He drank a lot and he started suffering from cirrhosis. He recovered, but then was told he couldn't drink again. He lasted two or three years without having a drink, but then began to have a beer every once in a while... and so on. He got sick again and was in the hospital for about a month.

"My dad died in 2005. I was already here - in the States. He died because of all his drinking. He suffered from high blood pressure, because of the drinking. He didn't want to quit, maybe sometimes he'd quit for a few days and he did not drink a lot or only drank a beer. He did not understand he shouldn't drink at all and finally he got sick from it and started getting very slim and his belly got really big, it filled up with water. He was so sick and got admitted into the hospital. He got better and they'd discharge him, until one day they didn't.

"I thought about getting married. I was going to get married at about 28 years old, but I was a lot older when I got married. I used to think that I would get married and have children; for me it was nice to have children, but not too many. I thought that I'd have four tops, but I'd probably have three and I ended up having just two – two sons Leandro and Pablo.

"I met my future husband, Tomás, in Mexico, there, in my town. I met him because he was from Guerrero state. His family came to live in my village, where I lived. I did not know them very well. My husband's brother married my sister. After they got married I got to know them, and that's how we met. So they got married first. This happened long before we got together. We already knew each other but we were not together yet. We got to know each other in Mexico. After his father and mother died he left and came to the States in 1993 for a better life. I stayed in Mexico and we spoke on the phone. He kept saying he was going to return soon, but he did not. When he had been in the States for six years, he said he was returning to Mexico but that he was coming back to bring me to the States.

"Well I decided I wanted to come to the States because I always thought, 'I have to go to the U.S.; at least I have to visit it.' I was going to come with my brother but as my mother had died, only my dad was left. I asked my brother to help me come to the U.S., and he said, 'Yes, but with permission from my dad, you have to talk to him and if he gives you permission, then yes, I'll help you. If he says no, I cannot help you.' I talked to my dad then and he said, 'Yes, that he gave me permission.' I told my brother and my brother said, 'Tell him I want to talk to him, that this day I am going to come and talk to him.' I told my dad. When my brother was going to speak to him, I told my dad again, 'My brother wants to speak to you' and he said, 'You know what? I have said yes, but I already thought about it and you're not going anywhere.' He just refused. I was an adult - I was 34, but still he refused; he said, 'No and no.' And I asked him, 'But why not? Just for a few months nothing else! To get to know the country and come back.' 'No I told you you're not going to go anywhere, you will not treat me as if I'm clueless. You're going to go and you're not going to come back.'

"In 1999, I told my future husband, Tomás, I was coming to the U.S. and that I was going to come with my brother. My brother then said he would not help me, because my dad did not give me permission, so he was not going to help. I talked to Tomás and he said, 'OK, if you want to come I'll help you. Then I won't have to go over there to return with you, I can just save that money and help you come here. If you come then I'll help, I'll pay for all expenses and everything.'

"Then I got in touch with a person I knew was bringing people over to the U.S. I came with a man who brought people from our town over the border. It wasn't just me - there were many of us. There were 15 or 20 people from my town alone.

"I took a bag, a backpack with a change of clothes and money that was in my pocket in the inside of my pants. We traveled from my hometown to Mexico City by car, after that we took a plane in Mexico City to the border near Arizona. We crossed in Aguaprieta. That was not where the plane left us, I can't remember the name of that place, and we had a short drive to the border town. We did the whole trip in many small pieces. When we got there, we stayed one night. We got in late at night, so we stayed in a hotel that night and the next day, at six in the evening, or at seven, they picked us up and took us to a hill and we started walking to cross the border. At first we were 15 or 20 people, but then there on the hill many more came. We were like 30 in the end. We walked from 7:00 p.m. to 6:00 a.m. the next day. It was the month of October. It cost me $1,200. I had to pay extra.

"After we went over the hill we waited all day for someone to pick us up. Someone was supposed to pick us up and take us to Arizona. So we were there all day and we had nothing to eat, because we did not carry anything. We had a little bit of water, but by nighttime we had finished it. We no longer had water. At around 3:00 or 4:00 p.m., the person who guided us, communicated with another person, then this other person came and brought us a few gallons of water and some sandwich bread with mayonnaise – nothing else. That's all we ate. From then on we waited for someone to pick us up, but we didn't get out of there until the evening.

"Then at around 7:00 or 8:00 p.m. people started coming for us, but each of them picked up only a few of us. I ended up riding in a car, in a van, one of those that have tarps on the back. All of us who would fit got in there, we were covered with the tarp and we took off. We were taken to the ranch of a person who was in contact with the man who brought us. Once we got there we had dinner and they let us bathe there. We slept in that house and the next day we left. Finally the car left me in Santa Ana, California. Only a few of us got to California, many others were going to Chicago. Different cars would pick them up.

"I came with two girls - two men brought us in a car. We arrived in Santa Ana and they wanted to drop me off in Los Angeles. But, Tomás, who was in communication with the coyotes, said, 'No.' He asked them to bring me up to the Bay Area. The man said that they could not bring me up here and said he was going to leave me there in Santa Ana, but he said that if my husband wanted to, he could send me by plane to San José, California. When the coyote spoke to Tomás, he told him to send them money to buy me a ticket for the plane. That was on top of the $1,200. They bought me a change of clothes just because I was very dirty. They bought a T-shirt and trousers for me and took me to an airport and left me there. I came to San José and Tomás was waiting for me.

"When I came here I had just turned 34 years old. Tomás and I got together at that time, but nothing more. We started living together, and then we had our children. I think when our first child was four or five years old we finally got married. My husband and I are Catholic, but we were not married by a church.

"By the time I arrived in the States, Tomás had been in the U.S. for a while. He worked in a pizzeria. He worked there for 19 years. It is two years since he stopped working there, because they closed the restaurant. Now he does day work. He does yard and garden work and assists doing floors or masonry. But he does not know how to do that on his own – the company he works for tells him what to do and he does it.

"When I first got to the U.S., I started cleaning houses; but later on, when I already had children, I no longer worked. Tomás told me not to work. He said he did not know how we would look after the children if I worked. He thought that any money I'd made would be spent in day care.

I'd end up working for no money. He told me that I shouldn't work until they were old enough, until they were in school. I started attending adult school, because I said, 'I do not work and have time to study, I should go to school.' I went to adult school when my younger son started going to kindergarten and my older one was in elementary school. I learned a lot, because when I came, I knew nothing. I could count numbers only to eleven and knew no more. I didn't know the letters of the alphabet. I finished three years of adult education.

"After eleven years in the States, I wanted to work again. I had met some friends who told me that they were going to the Day Worker Center in Mt. View, California to work and that they were finding jobs. I was not working. I asked my husband, 'What if I started going to the Day Worker Center? I was told one could get a job there.' 'Well, go there if you want, just go.' So I started going there. Through the Center, I've worked cleaning houses and sometimes babysitting. I like everything. I have two houses I clean on a regular basis. I go once every two weeks to each. Sometimes when the owner has people over, she asks me to come every week. Since they employed us through the Center we get paid $12 an hour. But if I work for six or seven hours she gives me $120.

"If my husband works in the morning, I'll work in the afternoon. Our children go to school from 8:00 a.m. to 3:00 p.m. Tomás usually takes Pablo to school. On Wednesday morning I walk him to school. Sometimes he tells me he's going with other boys, but it's not common. He always asks me to walk him and he calls me to tell me if is he is coming back or to see if his dad did not go to work so that he'll pick him up. Leandro walks or rides his skateboard or bicycle.

"My older son, Leandro, likes skateboarding. The younger liked the scooter. One Sunday the family went to a park and on that day my son said, 'Can I bring the scooter?' 'Take it.' We went through the park and down a bridge. As we were descending, the older boy had already been there, and on that day the younger one was wearing flip-flops and he said, 'Lend me the scooter, I can take it' and he gave it to him. I said, 'No, no, do not go, you're going too fast and you can fall.' He grabbed the scooter anyway and was going really fast and fell when he was going down the hill. I was afraid he'd fall on one side and continue rolling down. He fell and he could not stop; he wanted to stop with his foot, lower it to break, and I think the flip-flop made him fall. He scraped his arm, knee, face, and forehead. He was crying and no longer wanted to use the scooter.

"The younger son, Pablo, is now 13, and the older, Leandro is turning 15. He's a year and a half older. We speak only Spanish to our children. They started to learn English when they started to go to school. The younger boy started going to preschool and learning his first few English words. He would sing in English. Then in kindergarten, they learned more English. Pablo is a good student, but the older boy finds it harder. Leandro says he does not like school. He keeps asking, 'Why was school invented?' I tell him, 'How do you ask that! If there were no school ... ' He is attending high school now. He says he does not like it, he thinks it's boring. I tell him he must study so that when he is older he can be whatever he wants. He says he wants to be a football player. He likes to play and wants to be a professional football player. I tell him, 'To be that you also have to keep studying.'

"On weekends, sometimes, we go to the movies. I do not like the movies very much, but the older boy does. Because he likes those movies and I do not like them, I fall asleep in the cinema. I do not like the films that he likes best, so I ask his dad to take him. Even if he doesn't like them, he takes him. My son will tell you over and over that he wants to go. The younger one doesn't. Sometimes he says he will go too but then says: 'No, I'll go another day to see a movie that I really like.'

"I want them to be smart kids and really become something, for them to have good families and get along. I want them to have wives and children and also be a good parent, for them to live well when they build their families. They used to fight a lot before and right now Leandro plays tricks on his younger brother, but they play. As soon as they start playing I know how it will end. So I say, 'Please peace, peace please!' And then comes the younger one and says, 'Leandro did this to me!' 'You wanted to play with him too,' I say.

"Well, I think I am a good mother to my children and they listen to the advice I give them. Although they sometimes do not want to hear it or they don't understand it yet, in the end I'd like them to think that it was good advice I was giving them. They are good kids and I am proud to have them be my children. They are already so big, they are growing and I say that when they're little, one says 'Oh! And I want them to grow!' and now when they are older, 'Oh! I wish they were babies!' And then I see pictures of when they were young children and say, 'Oh! Look at how beautiful they are!'

"Right now, we live in an apartment in Sunnyvale, CA. It is a two-bedroom apartment, and like every other apartment it has its living room, kitchen, bathroom; it has a balcony. The boys share a room. We rent it for $1,650 each month. Our biggest expenses are rent, food and bills.

"To help make the rent, we rented our sofa in our living room, to a person that we trusted. That person said that we were like family to him and we also thought of him as family. He was a 32 year-old man. We met him because he lived with some friends of ours, and he said he wanted to move out of there because it was too expensive and he had to share the room. There were about five people in the room and he did not want to stay there because they charged a lot.

"We already had someone sleeping on our sofa, but when that person vacated, the man asked my husband again, and Tomás told him we were moving. We had already been asked to move because the apartment was going to get remodeled. They asked us all to leave. My husband said, 'If you want to come you can, but in a few days we're leaving.' 'Yes, I'm going there' and he came to live in our house. We spent fifteen days in the old apartment and then we moved and he continued living with us for about two years.

"One day, this past year, Pablo realized that his brother had left his Facebook account open, on the computer. He told me about the account being open. He said, 'Leandro said he doesn't have a girlfriend, but he has a photo with this girl.' I asked, 'How do you know?' 'He left his Facebook page open.' 'Did you close it?' 'No.' I wanted to see and I started to look at his Facebook page - but it already seemed to me like something was off. When we looked at the computer we understood that the man renting our sofa was abusing him. He lived in our house! It was the hardest thing for our family.

"The day I realized what was happening, because my younger son showed me, Leandro was not home. We had given him permission to stay overnight at the home of one of his friends. Before he went, I talked to his friend's mom - the boy's mother. My son did not know we knew anything at the time and, as the man was single, we did not tell him anything when we realized the situation.

"I used to leave Leandro with that person and take the younger one with me, on Saturdays when I had to go downtown or anywhere. When they didn't have to go to school, I'd take Pablo with me. I thought then that the guy is a male and the child was a boy, too. I thought nothing could go wrong in that case.

"And then a day came when I had a bad feeling about it. I do not know why, but I already sensed something, because I thought, 'Oh! I hope he's not teaching him bad things.' I started wondering what they might be doing. As the day came, the day when I realized, something came to my mind. I thought that he may have messages or conversations with this person and I started to look for that on Facebook and there were a lot where he would threaten the boy. My husband and I were so shocked and so ashamed for our family.

"When I saw everything, I took the computer away because I was in my son's room, and I did not want Pablo to see. I went to the kitchen and my younger son asked, 'Why are you going out there?' 'I'm tired of sitting here in bed. I'll go there to the table in the kitchen.' I went and there I began to see everything. Then I told my husband 'Come, come, I want you to see this!' 'What is it?' 'I think, this is wrong' 'But what?' 'I want you to see it yourself, sit down and see this.' I felt like I was filled with rage, I do not know, I felt my body, inside, I was shaking. We did not know what to do! 'What should we do? This is not right, this is wrong.'

"At that time the man was not home so my husband told me, 'I'll talk to him when he gets home.' 'You know what, if you talk to him, do you know what he will do? He is going to go away and what if he remains in contact with Leandro?' 'Yes, how should we do it, then? Should we talk with the two of them together?' And I said, 'What will happen then is that he is going to go away from here; I do not want him to be here.' We found ourselves not knowing what to do, because if we kicked him out he would go but he could still be in contact with Leandro or he could do something to him.

"Two days passed and then the boys were on vacation from school one week and then on that day, Monday, it was a holiday, and everything was closed. We told the child's godparents what was happening and they suggested we go to a community-counseling center and ask to see someone who could help us there. When we arrived, we were told it was only by appointment. But when they saw us, when we told them what we were going through, that it was urgent and we wanted advice, they saw us. We showed them the computer, where we had the proof of everything.

"When we showed the counselor, she said she had to call another office, Child Protective Services. They said that what was happening was a crime, what that person was doing was a crime. The man was of age and that Leandro was just a child. Then we talked to this other person, who asked, 'Are you willing to let the police intervene?' We said, 'Yes. We must do that.' They said they were going to call them and let us talk to them. We talked there and told them what was happening and the police said, 'Go home. In a few minutes a person will come by your house and talk to you.' and we were told to stay in the house, a person would come.

"When Leandro wanted to leave the house, we told him, 'You're not going to go anywhere.' 'Why?' 'Because a teacher will come to talk to you.' 'What did I do?' 'I do not know. We want to know, too.' In reality, we did not want to tell him anything.

"Later that evening the police arrived, one detective and a social worker. The detective and the social worker spoke Spanish. They talked with Leandro who said nothing, because the man had threatened him and told him, 'You can't say anything, anything.' Then the detective took my son to the police department, because he would not talk very much at home. The detective said she was going to take him, so that they could talk privately, so that my son could talk more freely, if we gave them permission, and if we wanted to, we could also go.

"We all went to the police department. We waited for my son and finally, the man was detained. He is still in jail. Leandro is better, but what I am afraid of is that when the man is freed, I don't know what is going to happen. We do not know how many years he'll be given, because the case is still not closed, because the man has not declared himself guilty. He does not have papers here. He is still in prison, and we don't know what will happen. We are still scared.

"I have been in the United States for 15 years. My children were both born here and are citizens. Right now, I have no papers to go to Mexico, so I have to stay. I would like for something to get done so that we would have papers to be here, that we could at least get a work permit. My children can apply for green cards for us, but they cannot do that until they are 21 years old. By that time, I think we'll be old.

"Our challenge is to learn to speak English, because in many places where there is work they want you to know English. I communicate, but not very well. It depends on the type of work and what you need to do. They usually ask for us to be able to communicate with the employer well. Of course our children speak English well. And if we mispronounce things, they laugh. They say, 'You do not know, do not know,' and that is why we are learning. Anything we don't know we then ask them, 'How would you say this?' and then they tell us.

"If I had papers I'd like to go back home to visit, but I would return. I want to live here. I would be here and there, on both sides. Because I don't think my children want to go and I'd rather stay here with my children. My children are the most important thing, my family and work. Work to keep on getting by, at least. If someday, something happens to me and I get sent back to Mexico, I will not be able to get back to the U.S. It is harder to pass through the border now.

"In a few years I think that I will no longer be able to work. 'What shall we do?' I think about what will happen when we're old folks and if we are still here in the States. I do not know if my children will want us to be living with them. I think if they do not want us to be living with them, then it would be better if we were in Mexico. But life is better here."

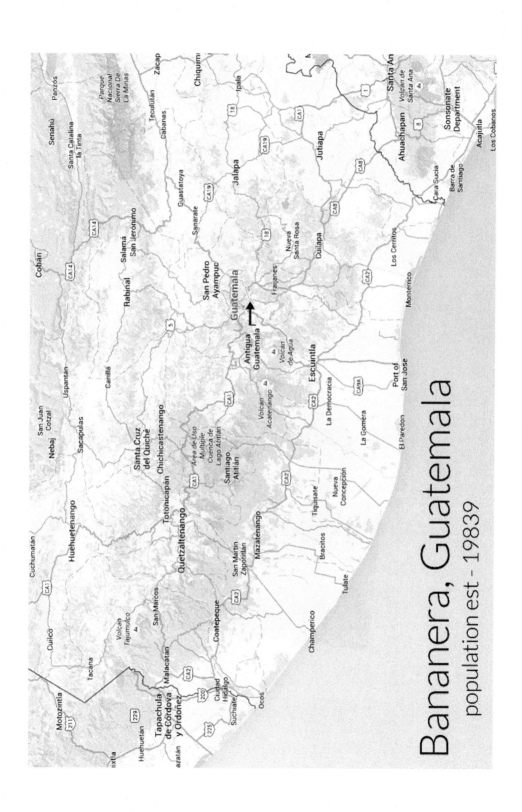

# Bananera, Guatemala

## population est - 19839

# Chapter 4

# Ruben's Story

"I am not unhappy, but I am not happy. I'm from Guatemala City, the capital of Guatemala. When I came to the U.S. in 2002, the rest of my family was already in the States and they were all American citizens. I had a wife and two small children, who were living with me in Guatemala. My mom, who was also living in Guatemala, got sick. My siblings in America wanted my mom to come and spend Christmas in the U.S. But my mom did not want to go if my children, her grandchildren, and my wife didn't come with her.

"We were doing well in Guatemala. I always had good jobs. I worked with my head, nothing physical. But, to please my mom, I requested three visas, one for my wife and two for my children. After a while I received them. Then I presented my passport. I had been coming to the U.S. since the 1980's on work related trips. I never liked the U.S. as a place to live. But that time, as I said, my mom would only travel if my wife and my children traveled with her. Since everyone had their visa, I only had to give them the money to fly over and spend Christmas and New Years in the States. I did not travel with them because I was working as an industry supervisor. After three months in the U.S., my family did not want my mom, or my children, or my wife to return to Guatemala. They wanted me to travel to the States. That's why I'm here. I do not regret the decision for them, I regret it for me.

"So when I entered the U.S. I had a visa. The owner of the company I worked for in Guatemala cleared me because I had I traveled with him to the U.S. and other Central American countries to buy spare parts for machinery. I knew a little English, because it was necessary to know a little English to buy machinery.

"I stayed - overstayed. I don't have a green card. My brother started the paperwork for me to be legal. I had to pay $700 to start the process. The papers are still being processed - they entered them in 2001, and right now, one month before 2001 is being processed (2000). It's a matter of time, nothing else. I talked to the lawyer and he explained, I can fix those papers, but you would have to leave the U.S. and live in Guatemala for 10 years. The lawyer advised me, 'No, do not go, you better wait here because laws change here. Sooner or later the law will be changed here and you'll be able to arrange your papers here. There'll be no need for you to leave.' I asked what advantages or disadvantages I'd have if there were reforms, and he told me that I could only get advantages, because all my information has been submitted, and there is no need to look for anything else.

"I was born in Guatemala, in a place called Bananera on January 9, 1953. My dad told me he went for a walk with me, and did not know what to name me. 'The first friend to greet me, that's what I will name him.' He met a man who was big, and called Ruben Pena. 'I'm going to name him Ruben,' and so he did. I only have one name.

"I take after my dad. He was of Spanish descent, but was born in Guatemala. My mom was from Mazatenango, Guatemala. They met at a baseball game and they stayed together. They lived nearly 65 years together and got married after about 40 years of being together, after having built their family. We were already grown when they got married.

"We are 5 siblings - three females and two males. Now the oldest is 69. She's called Argentina. Followed by Leticia, who is 66. Then Graciela, she is 64. Then me at 61, and Robert, 56 years old. All five alive and kicking. My sister Argentina lives in Palo Alto, CA. The other sister, Leticia, is staying with them, because she is on vacation here. She lives in Guatemala. My brother also lives here in Palo Alto, CA. The three live together in an apartment. I also live in Palo Alto, but not with them.

"My dad worked to provide for us all. He was fine carpenter of furniture. He worked for a company and also did rustic pieces, but his specialty was fine carpentry. I remember my dad a lot - for me he was not only my father, he was also my friend. My mother as well, but with my dad a little more, because he was a man. One relates more. We played ball, etc. I waited for him as 'water in May ' (an expression in Guatemala, the rains that everyone is waiting for to plant), so I waited for my father to play ball.

"I spent my childhood in Bananera, until I was 25 years old. It gets confusing for me: Bananera, Guatemala City, the U.S. ... all of it together. In Guatemala we begin working when we are very young. As my father was my friend, I went to work with him. 'I'll help you,' he said, and he gave me a few pennies, and I was happy. Seeing my father work too much was difficult for me. In our town, at the age of 18 years, one could legally work. I had to talk to the mayor and ask him to add a year to my age. I wanted to begin working to help my dad. In those places it is hard to live. I said, 'I do not want to live like my father lived.'

"When my dad was working, when I was young, we lived in a small wooden house. As I grew older, I told my dad that I wanted to make a house where he and my mom could have a room with a bathroom inside, where I could have a room with a bathroom inside, and about three more rooms for when my family comes to visit from U.S., for them to live here. I started designing it on paper. It was going to be a comfortable house. I laid everything out. I was the architect of this house. I had seen a house I liked, and I made some scribbles and then I drew it the same as the one I liked. I gave the drawing to the mason, and he made it.

"Our home was in a very good neighborhood. Where we lived, if you did not have sugar that afternoon to sweeten your coffee you could go to anyone in the neighborhood and say, 'Could you lend me a cup of sugar?' And they would lend it to you, and you would return the favor some other time. Over here, in the U.S., you can lend but it won't be returned.

"In primary school, I liked going to school in the morning. I returned home at noon and we had to do our homework; we couldn't play until we finished. When we finished our homework we had lunch, and ran out to play ball. We helped my mother to do the housework, because we each had our tasks. It's your turn to bring water, your turn to sweep, your turn do the dishes ... we all had our chores. But everyone had a good time doing our tasks. There were no fights over it - it was all in order. I wash the dishes, you sweep, we didn't leave everything for my mom to do, because as I said, we were 5 children, and leaving everything for my mom to do was too heavy for her.

"Everyone else said, 'I will go to the U.S. to help my children make it.' But my dad did not think that, my dad said, 'I will help my children here.' He had another mindset, but a good one. And he helped us get through. When we got older, his first child moved, and then another and in the end three went to the States and two stayed in Guatemala. I did not leave my dad and my mom. I got married and had my dad and my mom with me. My father died; he is buried in Guatemala. My mother became ill, and came here (to the States). And then I came. My mother died in 2003, she is buried here in a cemetery in the U.S. That is the problem and that is one of the reasons why I'm still here. And what's done is done and one cannot take it back.

"The most important thing for my parents was to help their children be successful. I completed primary, secondary and some years in a school for a teaching career. It did not seem long. The company my father worked for provided education and health insurance for primary school. It was one of the best schools in Guatemala. It was called Dolores Bedoya de

Molina and my father's company paid for it. After that, I went to a private school, where he had to pay for our education.

"I liked mathematics. I learned from my dad. I did well, and was a good student in mathematics. I read a story of Socrates, where he had to add a list of numbers. First he added pairs and then the odd numbers he left behind. When he finished adding the even he would just grab the odd points. In Guatemala when you bought something, the shopkeepers wrote it down in their little booklets. When the shop owner grabbed the calculator, my dad would tell him, 'You know, tell me the numbers and I'll do the math.' 'Okay'. The owner would tell him 2.13, 5.22, 4... And my dad said, 'It is this much.' And the other man would begin adding with the calculator, 10 minutes later ... he got the same number... And that is how I learned from my dad how to operate with numbers. I have worked in establishments and companies in purchasing and sales and was scolded by a supervisor because of how I add to and fro looking for pairs, leaving the odds. And when I finished with the pairs I see a 5 and another 5 and another 5, I say 15 once, I don't say 5 plus 5 plus 5 ... if there is four 5's I just add an even 20. He did not care, and the supervisor scolded me and said, 'That is not how you add.' And I said, 'While the result remains the same, you can add however you want.' And that is good.

"I started attending the teaching college, although I did not get to the end of it. That's when we moved to Guatemala City. I studied for 11 years of elementary school, 3 of high school and 3 more of teacher's school. 17 years in total. I was still young and if I had a little more schooling it would have been better.

"I would have liked to be an asphalt engineer, because I realized that many numbers and calculations are used in that field. In meters, logs ... everything is achieved through numbers. And, as I said, I have always liked numbers. But it didn't happen. At that time, pursuing that type of career was very expensive. And I started to work and I liked the money. When I started, my first job was to sweep. You swept for a while and then were moved to a better spot. I swept the whole factory for three months. Then the most sophisticated machine in the factory caught my attention. During my lunch hour, my free time, I would help the other workers, and the owners noticed and moved me to the largest machine. What I learned in the first factory where I worked sweeping, I put to good use. After a while, another company called me and asked me to help make their factory work.

"I worked in Guatemala in the companies Corrugadora Guatemala, Cartones de Guatemala, Empaques San Lucas, Cajas y Empaques de El Salvador, and Empaques de Costa Rica. Everything about cardboard. When I focus my attention on one thing, I like to solve it. It is certain that there are engineers who are engineers, perhaps, because they buy their diploma. I am not an engineer, but I was better than the engineers. Because I already came with my ideas, and said, 'This is not true, so let's do this better.' They would say, 'I studied for this.' 'Well, I did not, but I have many years of work in this industry and I know it like the palm of my hand, so let's do it this way, it is better.' And it was.

"In the last factory I worked in, we were in a village or town, and we went to lunch by plane - from that village to the city, 20 minutes, just to go to lunch. We were the owner, supervisors, and me. Six of us went to lunch. When we returned, everyone who worked for me, fifteen men, told me, 'Why don't you eat with us?' They ate there in a humble little dining room. I spoke with the boss and said, 'I'm not going to go to lunch with you; I'll go to lunch with my workers. The boss said, 'Well then go, all we can do is pay for your lunch.'

"My wife only completed elementary school, when we were coming to the States. I had requested visas for them. The first thing the embassy asked for was for a letter of recommendation and we asked an evangelical pastor and the evangelical pastor denied us. He told us that they could not lie. I said, 'Then say she works for you, that she is your secretary.' 'I cannot lie,' he said. 'Well, thank you very much.' I went to another priest and explained my problem and asked, 'Can you help me?' 'Sure,' he said. Because the other priest denied me; I could not lie to the second priest. He said, 'If I knew that what I do is for you to use it in something bad, that is one thing, but you are not going to do anything wrong, you will use it for something good.' He did it. The problem was when he came to the embassy with us, they asked my wife, 'You are the secretary?' 'Yes.' 'Here you have a computer, press the L.' My wife put all her fingers together and pressed every key. The consul was a good person because he realized why she did that and approved the visa. At least I can use the computer; I got my first diploma typing. I did it years ago. I have not forgotten where the letters are.

"So I did not come to the U.S. to make money. Money was never a problem. I didn't have too much, but I always had money. I never used a checkbook or credit card in Guatemala; I used cash. I liked to carry no less than 15 thousand quetzales in my wallet, whenever I was traveling. It was my decision was that my mother, my wife and my two children should come to the States. And they never returned. I joined them, but the reality is, that I am not very happy to be in the U.S. I wish I had stayed in Guatemala. I haven't lost hope of returning. The owners of the factories over there are still calling me. When they call me they say, 'Where are you working?' and I lie, I tell them I'm in a factory that I used to work at. I'm not going to say I'm gardening, or cutting trees, that's my business.

"When I came to U.S. I went to my sister's home - my mother, my wife and my two children were there. They all are American citizens. Only my wife, my children and I are not. I started working in construction on a building in San Francisco. My nephew got me the job. My nephew worked there and asked me if I wanted to work with him and I said, 'Yes,' because I was out of work. He would drive me there and back. But those are temporary jobs, the house was completed and the work stopped.

"When that job finished, I started caring for a gentleman here in Palo Alto. He was a millionaire. I worked with him and he paid very well. I earned around $10,000 a month. I took care of him from 4:00 p.m. until 10:00 a.m. the next day, Monday through Friday. On Saturday I started working at 4:00 in the afternoon and left on Monday. So, I spent all night Saturday and all day Sunday until Monday morning at his home and then left again. He would even say, 'This weekend come with your wife and two children,' as he had enough room. He was alone; his whole family lived in New York. I had a good time with him. Unfortunately, he was too sick and I only worked with him for eight months before he died. He used to give us his credit card to pay for everything in the house. Of course, we had to send the receipts to his children so they could see how everything was being handled.

"He died, and his children were very good people, and gave me a good settlement. When I finished that, I lost my job, and as I had some money I said, 'Well, let's take a break.' But the money runs out, and I started to look for work, I kept searching and searching... until they told me about the Day Worker Center. That is how I got here and I have been here ever since.

"At the Day Worker Center they have a variety of jobs for us. They ask us to work and we don't even know what kind of work we are going to do. It's not like when you have your work, for example, as a chef. Every day you know that you are going to cook. Not at the Center. Here it is 'I need two workers for one thing,' and the next day it will be for something else. When they come to tell me that there is work, I ask, 'What is it?' If it is electrical work, I better leave it for someone else. I'd like a system here in the Center where businesses can come to give us more work, because here we sometimes spend whole days doing nothing.

"Sometimes I get jobs I don't even know how to start. All I know is that I will finish it, and before I know it, when I look up, I didn't know where to start and I am already finished. Once a man who lived nearby hired me, and told me, before you start I want you to watch these videos on the computer. And we sat at the computer and began to see the videos. He wanted me to plant some grass, but artificial grass. And I asked, 'Where am I going to do that?' 'There.' But the place where he wanted to do it was a dump. I had to clean it up, remove branches, garbage, clean it; it took me almost eight days to do everything. After I finished, it turned out really nice and I said, 'What a change!' He took a photo before and an after picture when the work was finished. There was a difference, quite a difference.

"I like gardening and moving mostly. In summer there is a lot of yard work, but in winter it stops. An hour ago I was called for a job. If I had time, they would send me to do some gardening. But as I had this commitment for this interview, I told them no, I couldn't right now. Send someone else or I can go after the end of the interview or maybe tomorrow, since we had agreed on this a while ago. I did not want to miss it.

"I get up at about 5:00 a.m., I shower; I do not like staying in bed. It is not for me. They say that when one is already an adult, resting is just a way to wait for death. My dad, at three or four was already up. He did not sleep or let my mom sleep, because he would go to the kitchen and start making coffee. And it is true, we all go through that, eventually. At 7:00 a.m. I am already ready to come to the Center. I have had breakfast. I even watch the news. I see many people at the Center who drink their coffee here because they had no time at home. There is always time, it's just that they don't make the time, because there is time for everything.

"If I don't go to work, I am at the Day Worker Center until 2:00 in the afternoon. For those who do not work, life here is hard. If I do not work I have to try and figure something else out. And, it gives me no pain or shame to admit it, I go to the parks to find cans, bottles, recycling. I save. I will wash cars. I hope that someone recommends me to another person. Three days a week, I teach a few ladies English. They are studying English at the park. There is a public school where they teach English, but the English they teach is a bit advanced. So these women do not understand much, and they have asked me to help them, and they pay me. I earn my pennies here and there. I earn my cents. I'm not lazy.

"Full time work is very difficult to get right now without papers. Especially at this time. A year ago, I got a job as a dishwasher. I had already worked as a dishwasher in another restaurant, but they had closed because the owner sold the place and when the new owner arrived, he fired us all. So I got the job as a dishwasher in another restaurant and they didn't even have to teach me, I already had the experience. What a great experience! Right? Putting dishes in the machine and removing them. Well, I did the cleaning and then I had time to take a break. The owner told me, 'Look Ruben, I think you should come to work every other day.' I said, 'But why? Every other day? One day in and a day out?' 'Because I see that you have enough time to rest. Better that the day you do not come to work all those dishes will accumulate for the next day and you will have enough work to do.' I told him 'I'm sorry, but you want me to work a two-day job in one day? I rest because I work fast. If you do not want me to rest, I will work slower.' 'No, I'd rather you only came every other day.' 'No, you know what? Pay me for the days I have worked and thank you very much.'

"The truth is that here in the Day Worker Center, one is lucky. If you work with Americans, you can establish a little life here at the Center. Sometimes you get to work for different kinds of people. There are Americans, Hindus and Chinese. The truth is, I do not know if it's good to say, but there are people who are not good. For me, the best people to work for are Americans. They realize the work you do, which is very easy but they cannot do it and they take it into account. But there are other people watching you work and saying, 'I could have done that myself.' I say, 'But then why didn't you? I wouldn't have needed to come here.' There are all kinds of people. Last week I could only work for two days, but one American lady was good and she paid us as if we had worked all week.

"I do not have friends, real friends, at the Day Worker Center. I have acquaintances. I wanted to find a friend here in the United States, but have not found one yet. I've realized that a person, who has enough, does not want me to have as much as him. Even among us, there is selfishness.

"If I do not have work, I come home, unless my wife wants me to run errands. Then I go to the park to see what I can find. I wait until night to see if I'm going to teach the ladies I told you about. And, literally, that is it. Last night they brought me to a child to babysit. Another night I cared for another lady's child. I get paid $25 a night just for the child to fall asleep there. I'm watching him, sleeping next to him. At six in the morning they pick him up. Here you have to do everything you can to earn money. You have to do everything.

"I met my wife, Romelia Arevalo in Guatemala. When I built the large house I designed, her family rented our small house next door. It was love at first sight or love at last sight, but well, that was how I met her. As our houses were next to each other, when I returned home from work, I do not know if by chance or if she knew my time to arrive, she came to the door of the house where they lived and I greeted her. It was every day and I said, 'This is not a coincidence,' and already my heart had begun to beat a little faster and that's how we began a relationship that has continued to where we are now.

"Because of the jobs I've had, there were women who wanted to be with me. Because I was an important person in business, I drove around in my own car and when I worked for the company they would put me in a company car, with my driver. And women then realized, 'If I stay with him I'll be fine.' But at that time I did not think of finding a woman for me. I dated them, but not to formalize a life. Until my wife was the one who got me. And here I am, 22 years later, still with her. And sometimes I ask her, 'Aren't you bored of me by now?' 'No,' she says.

"The truth is that I have been with my wife 22 years, but we were not married for many years. As I told you before, my brother who lives in the U.S. filed the paperwork for us to stay here. I had to marry her in order to be eligible to stay. We got married in 1999.

"My wife taught me many things. Before I met her, I did not have any meaning in my life. If I wanted to, I would come home early or come home late, or not come home. Now I try my best to get home at 2:00 in the afternoon. Many at the Center say, 'Why would I want to go home? If I am at my house I'm alone. The apartment owner does not want us to be there during the day because we make noise.' I agree with them. They are right. They have no one to take a piece of bread to. They are alone. If I were alone I would also spend my time on the street, but I'm not alone. I have someone to see. Even though, as in every home, there are a few discussions. It is healthy to argue a bit.

"As I mentioned, I have two children. The female, Wendy, is the oldest; she was born on May 12, 1994, the boy, Julio Ruben was born on April 12, 1996. They have gotten so big already. Right now my son is working selling donuts. My daughter's husband will not let her work. He works at a car dealership.

"The pride that I have right now is that my daughter got married and made me a grandfather. And my son, that is 18, has not gotten married, yet, but he is living with a girl, and also gave me a grandson. Two grandchildren one month apart. My grandchildren are both boys. My daughter's son is Abraham and my son's is named Antonio. Right now the most important thing for me, as a proud old man, are my grandchildren. Always in good times and in bad, we are there for each other. Especially now with these two grandchildren, I'm more united than I am alone.

"Five of us live together - my wife, my son, his girlfriend, my grandson and me. We live in an apartment in Palo Alto. My daughter lives with her husband in Sunnyvale. The apartment where we live charges us $1,200 per month in rent. It has a bedroom, a living room, a kitchen and bathroom. The cheapest thing you can have. And they are charging that because we have been renting there for quite a while. I take care of the rent. My son is responsible for food and bills, along with my wife, because she works, too. She works at The Donut Shop. My son also works at The Donut Shop. My wife worked there, and a boy resigned, and my son was looking for work and my wife had several years working there. She spoke to the boss and the boss hired our son. They get paid in cash.

"My main problem right now is economics. What I care about is income. Sometimes there is not enough income, and my son and wife help me with the rent. I think not only me, but also all the people at the Center have trouble paying the rent. Well, I'm beating it, because, as I say, I'm here, I'm there, I'm here, there. If I sit waiting to see if money will fall from the sky, it won't. That's the hardest part. In the U.S. you can find food anywhere. Clothes, you find anywhere. Where to live is the most difficult. If I have enough for the rent, I do not worry. Half the time I do not have enough, and I have to find a way.

"When I am not working, I like to read, mostly the Bible. I like to read and watch television. At least from what I understood when I was watching the History Channel, there are forty generations before ours. All these unknowns are things I like. I like to learn. I like to cook; I do not know if you know that meat we call *ranchera*. They are a few slices of steak and I like to throw them on the grill with all their concoctions, flavors, to release the scent. Some onions, rice, and some chili. I usually do it on Sundays.

"Sometimes we go to parties. I drink a couple of beers, but I like to be careful who I do that with, because sometimes there are people who may have something bottled up inside. When there are some beers involved it comes to light. And, for me, I never liked it.

"I also do things with my wife. Sometimes I say, 'We got old!' 'Let's go out, just the two of us. Let´s see if we remember anything from when we were young!' And we leave together and go to a restaurant to eat. Because all the rest of the time we are taking care of everyone else. We get along well. Of course in the Bible it says, 'Therefore, a man leaves his father and mother' and the woman also says the same thing 'and will join her husband and they will become one person.'

"I believe that there is one God. I trust, really trust, in God. I also depend on him and on myself because I'm not hopeful to be sustained by someone else. On Sunday, I go to a Protestant church. Not to kill time but to listen to the minister, and I listen to the good advice he gives, because even though the minister is human and he might not say all good things, I take the good and discard the bad. Protestant gospel. Most people in Guatemala are Catholic. My parents were Catholic. The truth is that I changed because of where I want to get to in life. After a Catholic baptism, there is a party, beer and liquor. They start to fight - men with men, women with women. That does not happen in the religion in which I am now. There are baptisms, too; they dip the baby in the water, and we all eat quietly, no beer, no liquor, no nothing. That was my reason why I changed. I even have a friend who sent for her dad to Guatemala to celebrate a Catholic baptism. Her father came to the States and to this date he is in prison, because at the party he had an argument with my friend, and killed him and he is in jail.

"I have faced my life and solved problems. I do not know how I did it, but I think I've solved them well. In my future I would like to improve, I'd like it to improve from what I'm going through right now. When I am gone, I would like to be remembered for the good things, not bad things. For even though one has been bad, you know very well that a dead man is never bad. From the moment he dies people say, 'Poor thing, he was so good!' - even if he was the worst person.

"I intend to return to Guatemala and my dad at some point. My family does not want to, but I can't adapt here. You might live next to someone and not even know them. Not there. In Guatemala, the neighborhood is your family. Something happens to you in the morning, knock on the neighbor's door and the neighbor will help you. Here, if something happens at dawn, you knock on your neighbor's door ... he is either asleep or he will not open the door, and the next day you go and talk to them and they tell you, 'You should have knocked harder.' The truth is, I've noticed that people are selfish - mostly those that are doing well. They do not want those who are doing worse to catch up with them. In other places where I've been, it's never like that.

"The problem is that my only family still living in Guatemala, is my sister. Everyone else is here. And as we have always been united, we want everyone to be here. My family tells me to be patient. With papers I can go back to Guatemala and then I can return to the U.S. My wife likes it here. She is happy here, because she has her two children, two grandchildren, and her little job. I say, 'I know that you are well here, because you were never okay there in Guatemala.' But if I went back to Guatemala, I could work for one of the same companies as before.

"Maybe I am too old for change and improvement. Not only here, even in Guatemala they're telling me that no one will give you a job once you are over 30. As I say, both in Guatemala and here in America, if you have friends, you get a job, but without friends you cannot get work. I have a nephew here, an American citizen, good English, and he spent years without working, sending letters here, sending letters, applications, and nothing. Until at last he spoke to his sister-in-law and through her he got a job. Now he is the manager of a hotel. But, he is a citizen, he has good English, and it was still hard. Let alone one being illegal, it's even harder.

"One thinks about it, but as we say, the future is not known. To God one day is as a thousand years and a thousand years is one day. I would like to be a nice old man, a kind old man. I do not want to ever be prostrated. The culture we have in the U.S., which our children have been learning, is that when one gets old they want to put you into an asylum. I would not like that, because in our culture, the grandparents come first, his coffee cup, his sweet bread, everything for him first. Not here. Here grandpa is a burden.

"To regret, regret, what's done is done. I regret having come to the United States. Well, life has taught me many things, both good and bad. I tried to ignore the bad and keep the good. But sometimes, as the apostle Paul says, 'Why do I do what I should not do and what I should, I do not do.' Every mind is a world on its own, we are human, and we make mistakes."

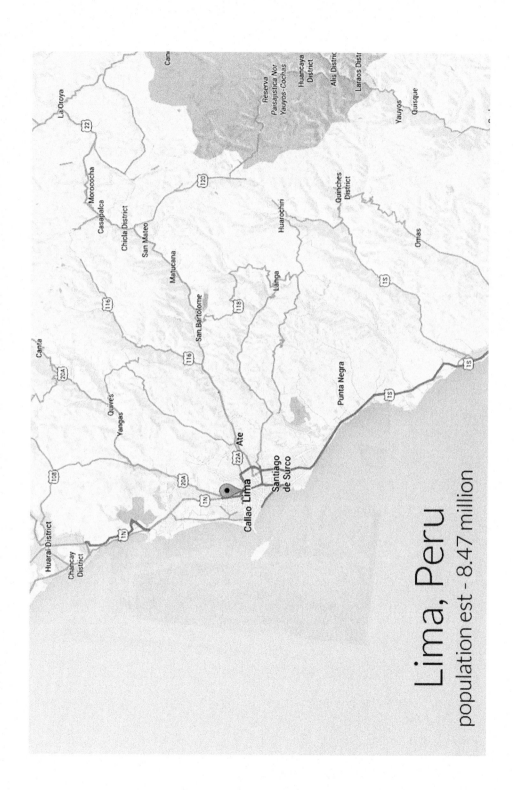

# Lima, Peru
## population est - 8.47 million

# Chapter 5

## Aurora's Story

"In 1999, my son Andrés, who lives in the United States, sent me a letter of invitation, asking me to come visit him in the Bay Area. He is really not my son, he is my nephew, but I raised him since his childhood. I am like a mother to him. He calls me mom because I raised him since he was a small boy. My sister died and his father was already dead, so I kept my nephew and raised him as my own child. Since I was single at the time, I was the only one who could take him. My other sisters were married and living away from home outside of Lima, Peru.

"My nephew was in the Peruvian military when he came to the States. At that time, the situation in the country, with the rebel group Shining Path was very difficult. Andrés sought and obtained political asylum and has his papers. He lives in a rented house in Los Altos, California and works for NASA, doing maintenance. He married and had two daughters. When they were young girls, Andrés brought his daughters to me in Lima. He took them to me because, according to him, the education was better in Peru.

"When Andrés invited me to the States, I was able to obtain a tourist visa for 6 months and flew from Lima to Dallas, for a stopover, and then to San Francisco. I brought my nephew's daughters back with me to the States. I brought them back to their parents when the oldest was 15 years old.

"My life in Lima was okay – I could not complain. I had a steady job and earned a little money. I could just support myself. When my nephew Andrés sent me the ticket to the U.S., my desire wasn't to stay here. I asked my employer for six months' leave without pay and vacation. I wanted to go back to Peru, because I had work there.

"After I arrived, I did not want to be here doing nothing for 6 months. Everyone in the family went out – to work or school - and I was alone in the house. So I thought, to entertain myself, I'll go to work and will work until I leave. I turned in job applications and was called and started working almost immediately. I thought I could use the money to pay for my ticket back or other expenses.

"I worked for a lady, taking care of her five year old child. The woman was a teacher, so I began work at 7:00 a.m., and came home at 3:00 pm. I also got a job at a movie theater at the Shoreline Theaters in Mt. View, California. At that time, they were not so concerned about immigration papers or work visas. I worked from 4:00 p.m. until closing at 2:00 a.m.

or whenever the last showing ended. The last film sometimes started at 12:00 a.m., and because we still made popcorn or coffee or whatever, we had to stay until it was over. We had to leave everything clean when we closed.

"I slept little, because I had to get up at 6:00 and go to work. I was used to it because in my country I worked in a hospital and sometimes I had the shift from 7:00 a.m. to 7:00 p.m. and sometimes 7:00 p.m. to 7:00 a.m.

"At Shoreline Theater, I worked the cash register and worked in the cafeteria. I would refill the condiments for the snack bar. So I had to open large cans of ketchup, mustard and jalapeños and put the contents in smaller containers. I worked for them for several months and was going to let them know I was leaving my job, since I was going to return to Lima the next day. I already had my return ticket.

"But I had an accident! I cut my hand, tendon and nerve. I had always opened the cans before with no problem. But that day, when the can I was holding was tough to open, I pressed hard, and the can, one of those large, round ones, slipped and deeply cut my left wrist. I was bleeding a lot and the company called emergency. They took me to the hospital and they stitched my wounds superficially.

"I even called to postpone my ticket... I thought that in eight days they'd take the stitches out and I would be fine. But no, when they took the stitches out, I had lost all mobility in my hand. I couldn't move it, not even my arm. My tendon and nerve had been cut through.

"So I did not plan to stay. My story was not to be here, because I had my work in Lima. Even though I earned very little, it was a steady job. But I stayed because I had to have surgery again. The company and I saw a lawyer and I told the lawyer what had happened to me. I told her I had to travel and she said, 'Do not travel! You'll stay handicapped. You need surgery.'

"I had surgery and was in rehabilitation for 6 months. I had to work with the lawyer, but at that time, I did not know not to use a lawyer from the company. The company paid for all my medical expenses and gave me $5,250 aside as compensation. They helped me get cured and all, but I did not get much compensation. Others tell me that if I had another lawyer I would have gotten more money, because, even today, this hand does not work for me. This happened when I was 54 years old. So that is why I stayed in the U.S., in the Bay Area, after my visa expired. I am glad I stayed, but it took me away from my family and my children.

"My son Pavel lives in Arizona. After my surgery, I left my nephew's home and went to Arizona for three years. There was no work there and I had no benefits in Arizona – all the expenses were on my son. Also, I did not like the weather there – it was very hot - too hot! The sun leaves spots on your skin. I decided to return to California.

"When I arrived back from Arizona, I began living with a friend, Natividad Rosales, in a small house in Mt. View, California. I met her at the Adventist Church we both attended. We share the expenses - $900 for rent plus other expenses, like water and electricity. Rent is the main expense. First, when I work, I save for the rent. I do not spend anything. And once I have enough for it, I go to Costco and buy things there wholesale, like paper towels, toilet paper and vegetables.

"We each buy our own food and we share meals. Every time we cook we make different food. We tire of the same thing. Sometimes she cooks, sometimes I cook. We usually cook for three days and put the rest in the freezer. We are friends and go out together. We leave our house and travel. We get to know other places, go for a stroll, go out to eat.

"I had heard about the Day Worker Center from others in the neighborhood. I came and signed up. Now I do housecleaning. It is difficult to work with my hand that still does not work well. I usually work once or twice a week. It is not enough and with that alone I would starve. But I also have other work – outside the Center. I have three houses I clean on a regular basis. The pay is usually $12 per hour. Some people are good and pay $15 or even $20 per hour. But some want to pay less!

"I like cleaning homes, but the liquid cleaners are strong. I wear gloves, but I still get the smell of the products on me. Often times, people use pure Clorox and it feels as if I have an allergy. My eyes burn and cry and it's bad for the throat, too. Sometimes you get splashed. I have spotted jeans from splashes of bleach while cleaning showers.

"The Day Worker Center helps–it is a very good place to get work. It gives people who are unemployed an opportunity. I have many co-workers that I see regularly. But they are not my friends. Friends come to your house on the weekend. I only see the workers at the Center. I see faces, but sometimes I don't even know their names.

*****

"I was born in Lima, Peru in May, 1946 and I considered myself an 'orphan.' My mom, who was 42 years old, died in childbirth when I was born. My older sister raised me–she is the only mother I knew. I called my sister 'mama.' She was already married when I was born. She was the oldest, so she promised my mom she would take care of me. So I always called her mother, even after I got older and got married.

"All together we were eight siblings. There were four boys and four girls. Of course, since my mom died, I am the youngest and last female. I only have two brothers left, the others died. My brothers still live in Lima.

"My real mom was a descendant of the Japanese – her mother, my grandmother, was Japanese - but of course I did not know her. My father descended from the Spaniards. He was tall, white and thin. He worked in a cement factory, called Portla Cement, in San Juan de Miraflor. We lived in company housing. My father also bought land to build another house for himself. So I did not grow up with my dad–he was there sometimes, but he had his own house. I lived in the factory house with my mom (older sister) and her husband. It was a big house - it had 5 rooms and a store. We had a warehouse and we sold produce. My mom worked in the store. And on weekends, we helped. My dad would come and make a balance of the profits. He'd take us to buy clothes, shoes, whatever we needed, with the profit.

"My mother (older sister), her husband and my dad always told us to go out. They said, 'Go to play! But when the factory signals the day is over you must be back.' He was a very strict and very, very quiet man. He only played with me occasionally. That's what I remember of him. And then he passed away.

"It was good growing up in San Juan de Miraflores. At least it was when I was a small child. All my neighbors got together at night and played *ronda*. Sometimes I went to my neighbor's house, Mrs. Filomena, and we played 'theater'. When we played at theater, we did poetry or sang or acted. We also invented characters. We invented games and played house and cooked. We played making food. I would steal things to cook from my mom. Or I would climb to the tops of trees and bring down the fruit. We had tiny pots and had a kitchenette that we called *ronera* (rum). We put the food in the pots and pans. We had everything – the whole set.

"I attended the company school. It was a private school, because the company paid for the school. Basic, elementary education and then from there I went to high school. I went until I was 16 years old. I was not the best student, but I was more or less a good student. I loved language and history and geography.

"As I got older, I learned to knit, sew and cook. I liked it. I started with babies. I liked knitting small clothes and at school we were taught sewing. I also liked to embroider all types of bed sheets. I first made them for dolls and then I started making them for myself. I remember we had a sewing machine – a 'Singer' machine, but it was manual – you had to step on the pedal to make it move. I sewed just for me – and then for my children. Not for anyone else. I liked making little clothes for babies. Mixed clothing with bows and things like that.

"I helped my mom. She cooked during the week. Saturday and Sunday we washed clothes at our house. Her husband said so, and so we did. On Saturday, we had a half day of school and then in the afternoon, I washed clothes, then ironed them on Sunday – both my uniform and my dad's before he died.

"I had wanted to pursue a career – to enroll in military service. I had a dream to be a paratrooper, but it didn't happen. Once my father died, I had no help. I actually finished high school at night, working during the day shift. I did not study English, at all. We didn't learn it in high school; those who attended night did not get to study English. If you attended during the day, you would get the English course. Same thing with job training, sewing – all of that is suppressed during the night shift.

"After high school, I studied at a technological institute. I became a medical assistant. I worked in the hospital with patients and in emergencies. I knew how to take temperature, pulse and respiration. I'd give patients intravenous injections; I prepared and read medical diagrams.

"Then my mom (older sister) died in an accident! Everyone said she was a good person. Many people came to her burial. They showed up and kept coming. People cried. She was always willing to give. I even remember when I was very little, there was an insane woman, a *loquita* begging for food. My mom always had a container with food to give her. I had to take over the care of her son, Andrés, and his sister.

"I married at age 22 and had five consecutive children – all male – in addition to raising my sister's son and daughter. So seven in total. They were all born in Peru. I met my husband, because he was one of my sister's college teachers. I adapted so that all I did was go from work to my children. I had an aunt who helped me before I went to work.

"My husband and I divorced many years ago. I had a problem with him, because I am not one to put up with much. I can't put up with a man who cheats on me. So we divorced and I do not keep in touch. I am not sure if he remarried or even where he is living.

"My children range in age from 42 (oldest) to 36. The eldest, Yuri, lives in Spain; Yakov Moises lives in Peru and has an eight-year old daughter – my only grandchild. My son Nikolai is married and does not have any children; my son Vladimir lives in Orlando. Pavel, my youngest, lives in Arizona. All my children have been successful. They are all professionals and have their life ahead of them. One studied mechanical production; one is a pastor of a church and has written a few books. The children are now scattered - living all over the world. One is in Spain, one in Florida, one in Arizona, and two in Peru. Besides my nephew and son in the U.S., I no longer see my other children. We speak by phone, but it is different. We do not see each other anymore.

"The most important thing in my life is my children. I have struggled for them so they can do something in life. I worry that they are well. It is everything I want. Even if they do not give me anything, as long as they are okay, it is the most important thing. I wish them to have a tranquil life. If they get sick, I worry. Last month, I was concerned and nervous, because my married son, Nikolai, who lives in Lima, was in a coma from a generalized infection. I thought he would die. We're so far away, so I did not know much about the situation and no one explained it to me. His wife didn't explain it. She only told me he had a generalized infection. He took a while to come out of the coma – three months. The infection was strong and affected his throat, ears and stomach. He could not eat and was fed intravenously. But he recovered and told me 'he feels good now.'

*****

"As I said, I was not thinking of staying in the U.S. I wanted to return. But I had to stay. I have now lived in the States for 16 years. I have my Peruvian passport, but it is expired. To renew it, I need to go to the consulate in San Francisco. I pay taxes yearly. I have an ITIN number and pay tax as a self-employed person, because I am not working for a company. The IRS does not care about my immigration status, as long as I pay taxes on my wages. I do not earn much, so I will not have to pay anything extra.

"I would love to fix my immigration situation in the U.S. That way I can return to Peru. I am retired in my country. I have to go through some paper work to get my pension. I worked there for 23 years. I only needed two more years for a full pension, but they have to give me something. I have already received the documents at my house that tell me I can make withdrawals. However, I have to fix it from here. Since I haven't been able to do the paperwork, I can go to the Peruvian consulate and authorize my son that lives in Lima to take care of it. It will take about a year and a half to do it.

"I would like to live a quiet life, without problems, but things are not always so. I do not want to hurt anyone or have anyone hurt me. No harm, no evil thought for others. To want for others what I want for me. If one gets into someone else's life, you get in trouble. It brings you problems – don't intervene. Each person as they are accounts to God personally.

"My family was Christian, but we did not go to church. I started going to church, a long time ago, when I was already an adult. Now I am very religious, a Christian Apostolic. My religion helps me live peacefully. Every day the first thing when I wake up, I entrust my path to God. For him to guide my children and me. I do that every day. So my confidence comes from God. If I have problems, I pray and tell God. I trust him and the problem is solved. It is the tranquility I have because I rely on him. When my son was ill, I asked my church to pray for him. And now he's well. We leave it in God's hands, and if something does happen, then it is because he permits it. Then it was his time.

"I do not have any goals left for me. I am an old lady. I do not know if I will stay here or return to Lima. I leave it in God's hands. As he says, 'Do not think of what has to be tomorrow, because every day brings its desire.' So I think every day, my future will be whatever God chooses for me."

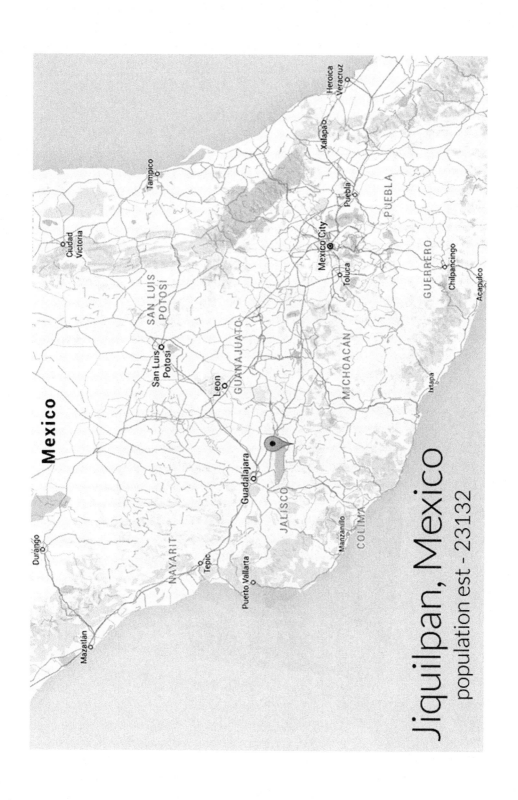

# Jiquilpan, Mexico
population est - 23132

# Chapter 6

## José Luis's Story

"The town where I'm from, Jiquilpan in Michoacán, Mexico, is where one of the most famous presidents of Mexico was born. He was called General Lázaro Cárdenas del Río. He was famous because he took back oil wells from the United States. America used to be the owner of Mexican oil. The General knew that if he fought the United States, the U.S. was going to win. He decided to make an agreement with them. The story says that the United States government said, 'Ok, if you want it back you have to pay us something.' I do not know if it's true; it is said that the General paid with animals, oxen, cows, with chickens, with pigs, with whatever they had, to recover the oil.

"General Cárdenas del Río is famous. Many Americans might not have liked him, because it was a lot of oil. They must have thought, 'We've already taken their land, we don't want them to starve.' Then the General was respected and the oil returned.

"This president, the one that paid them, was born in the city where I was born. And it's a small town, about a quarter of a million people. Two Mexican presidents came from the town and are acknowledged by history. Two good presidents from one small town are not easy.

"In our national histories, all of our presidents have been corrupt. For example, if a president were from Colima, he would intentionally give a lot to the people of his town, his state. If a president were from Chihuahua, he'd grab money to benefit his people and make them rich. This president was asked, 'You are ending your period serving as president and what will you leave your people, if you have not done anything in your town? You have not built factories, you have not given them anything like other presidents have done.' He did not want to steal or be corrupt. He said, 'I'm going to leave something that the people are never, ever going to forget. I'll leave education for them.' He built all the best schools in the country in his city. Then others said, 'But there are no factories,' and he said, 'Yes, but the people in my village will be the ones owning the companies, managing the companies. They are the ones who will make all of you earn more money, but they will be managers.' And he did just that.

"In my town, most people are well-educated. There are many people from Michoacán who have not been to school, but there are many options to go to school there. Cárdenas built the largest technology college across the country. It included a language lab, gym, tennis, separate football fields, soccer fields, basketball, volleyball, everything, with nothing to envy from a first world school, a school similar to those found here in the U.S. - a great school. It was a finishing school, like a college, but was technological. That was what he wanted. 'I do not want my countrymen to be workers, I want them to be professionals.'

"I was born on January 7, 1963. I was named José Luis after my uncle who lives in Fresno, California. My mom was born on a ranch called La Lagunita. It's about 20 km from the village where we were born. My dad is from the same town where I was born, Jiquilpan. They were both from in the state of Michoacán. We are eight in total – two brothers, my brother and me, and six sisters.

"I didn't meet my grandfather, my dad's dad, because he died before I was born. He died in an accident - a train ran over him. He was a construction worker. The train caught him and he died. My grandmother married another man, my father's stepfather. He lived with his family, his sons. When I was growing up, we always visited them. My grandmother helped me, because I was her favorite grandchild. Secretly she was always giving me money and sometimes my cousins would ask her, 'Why? He is not even our cousin and you always give him.' 'Because he never asks for anything! You are always asking me. He comes here and does not even ask for bread.'

"My step-grandfather's name was Ramon and when he died they did not tell me until about a month after it happened, because they said, 'If we had told you, you would have wanted to come back.' He loved me more than his own children. His family went to his home only to grab things and people would say, 'You never have to watch José Luis, you don't need to watch over him.' 'No, I know, I can let him in my house and he never touches anything. I have to be careful with all the rest of you.'

"My grandmother, my mother's mother, died when she was 114 years old. She was really old. When she died the same thing happened. My mom did not tell me until after some time. When people close to me died, I used to go back home, but mainly when I was single. Sometimes. I would have had just returned to the States. 'Do not tell him, he just got back.' And they wouldn't tell me until later.

"My grandfather, my mother's father, still lives. He was younger than my grandmother who died at 114. Right now he must be around 104 years old. Do you know why? Because they live on his ranch. They live healthily. I would go to visit them and they said, 'Well, right now I'm going to make a chili.' And my grandmother would go to the back of their farm and bring onions, tomatoes, cilantro she had just harvested from her garden.

"My dad was always the type of person who worked. He was humble and honest. A word to describe him is illiterate. He never went to school. He did not study anything, but he was a very intelligent person. He could not read or write, signed with crosses and numbers, but he knew a lot. He made his own bills when he signed contracts, because he was not going to work just for the day. He had contracts to build houses. My dad was our provider. He was not a person who declared his love for others. We knew that he loved us and he made every effort to give us the best.

"One of the things I remember most about him is that when I was three years old, we lived in a poor area. It was very difficult to get by and I do not know how he managed, but he got me a tricycle. Everyone envied me and borrowed it. And mind you, rather incredibly, what one remembers when you were little and I remember when I was three. And I remember things as if I were seeing them right now, with my grandmother, my mom, and my dad. Things that happened and that stayed with me and left their marks. I remember that day my cousins were fighting to get to ride my tricycle and my mom said, 'Don't let them, they will break it.' I said, 'No, they don't have one, let them ride it.' My son now behaves like me. It was moving because, I bought a battery car for his birthday and most adults said, 'No, do not let them climb on your car, they're going to break it.' 'Why not? They are poor and they do not have money to buy one; their parents can't buy it.' I had to go buy an extra battery, because it would end up with no charge when he was playing alone.

"My mom took care of our home. She was a strong character and that was very good for us. My mom was hard with us. She'd tell us to do homework, homework, homework. To eat properly. My mom went to school for a very short time; it was like three or four years. She was of humble origin and people of her origin did not care about education. No, let us be donkeys. For them, work, work and work. No, my mom made sacrifices, washed and ironed outside the home. She'd go to work as a maid, cleaning houses to get money to give us what we needed. My dad sometimes did not make enough.

"The first memory of my childhood is sad. All the children where I lived were part of my family. Back then, everyone thought the only future was coming to the U.S. That's what they told you. If you were big and strong you would come to work here to send money to your parents. My parents saw that I was brilliant at school and I liked going to school. My mom said, 'No, if we stay here we are going to be the same, and I see you are quieter than everyone else, you do not move in the same circles as them.' So my mother convinced my father to move the family to a different town where there would be more opportunities. In the community of Jiquilpan, there was violence between the same family, domestic violence. Families are wrapped in the same problems and that's why my mom saw that she did not want to go to that extreme with my dad. She wanted to leave that place because, you know, when mothers and sisters are involved it becomes a big problem. And I saw that my dad was very different from his brothers and his family. My mom convinced him that we should move to another area.

"People in our new neighborhood were quite different from those where we lived with the family. They had also separated from those areas and wanted a different kind of life, a humble but different life. The area where we had lived was like a closed neighborhood where we all lived together. Once we moved, we lived in our own house, by ourselves. Each house was separate from the others. Humble houses, but everyone had their home.

"Sometimes it makes me sad, because you see people coming to the U.S. and one hears their stories. Many say, they came here and fell in love with an apartment because it has carpet, or because it has a bath, where one can bathe with hot water or that they have a toilet. We had all this stuff, but we did so humbly. Even though my dad never went to school, he was a successful construction worker. He made a great effort to be able to give us those things. Even if he could only afford a battered old car, we'd have a car. He made a lot of sacrifices, and my mom, too. My mom's main responsibility was to get us to stay in school and study, study, study. My dad brought in the money. We used to help in whatever we could. When we were little, I remember, there was a river near my house and to start making the foundation for our new house, we would carry stones. Everyone carried stones. At that time my siblings were tiny; the younger ones were four or five years old and they carried a pebble.

"In the area where we moved, we begin to think in a different a way. Things changed. Now it was not growing up to come to the United States, but to find a way to progress in the country. Study. School, school, school. My parents started noticing improvement with all my siblings. I was a bit better in school than others, but they sent us all to school. When they wanted to send me to a paid school, I said, 'No.' They were sacrificing too much for me. I thought we all should have the same opportunity, because we were brothers and sisters. I did not want them to continue paying for me, so I went to a public school. I thought if I wanted to go to a school farther away it would be due to my own merits. So I started making my own way. I began to excel in class. I received a full scholarship. We got free vacations all the time then and we all dedicated ourselves to studying.

"I was good at school. I mean, because my friends would say, 'Hey, but you never study and always do well.' I never liked to miss classes and I paid attention. I also practiced doing math. While listening, I was practicing and doing math and just studied the day before an exam. My strategy was that I related numbers, dates, names, everything to things. Each one of us has his own tips. I like sports; so I related it to someone or something famous. The names and dates. It was always very easy for me.

"When I was not in school or studying, I played soccer. Always. My team was called America. My dad wanted me to play baseball and that was one of our arguments, because I didn't like baseball. If I had stayed in the area, I would have played baseball, because he had bought me equipment. But I did not like baseball and the area where we moved to, we all played soccer.

"When I was young, my idea was to be a soccer player. In fact, I could have been one, if I had not come to the U.S. I had a chance to play. When I came to the U.S., I was paid to play on certain teams. I was paid for playing on teams that played well. To me, if I stayed in Mexico, I possibly could have played soccer professionally. When I got here too. To me soccer has always been a hobby. I would never say it would be my business, because I had friends who were good and ended up with some defects, or foot injuries. I thought, that's not going to sustain me for life, and I started to do other things.

"When I was on vacation from school, my dad taught me electricity. Then in the houses he built, I did the electrical installations, ever since I was very young. I was in high school and I had to do the installations. I had people working with me at that age. They would do things I could not do, such as making holes in the walls. My dad said, 'You have to pay people before you will get your money. I do the work, you get paid and you pay your people. Take the money you make, put it in the bank so you'll never have to ask us for money for school.' I never asked them for any money. Sometimes, my mom never told me, but I knew that money was tight. There was always some bill, light, water or something. Without her knowing I would get the bill paid. Later when the collectors arrived to the neighborhood, they would tell her, 'No Doña Lola, your son already came and paid the bill!' She'd scold me. 'Why? You never ask for money, you never ask!' 'No, mommy, I have what I need.'

"My dad said that since he worked in construction, he wanted me to be an engineer. That was another problem that I had with him. Engineering was well suited for people who liked to deal with numbers, like I was. However, mom wanted me to do something quieter, close to home, like being in an office or something. I did what she wanted. When I finished high school, my parents gave me as a trip to Manzanillo, Colima as a graduation gift. We had family that lived there. When I returned, my mom had enrolled me in administrative sciences. So I went, I did my tests and everything and people would tell me 'Hey! You are such a good student, you will go to waste in science, come here.' 'No, my mom says there and I'm going there because it will cost her, and I will not have much time to be working.'

"I did not go into the military. I have led a blessed life, really. When I went to submit my application, after high school, it turned out that the general of the division shared my name, José Luis. When I arrived, they said: 'You don't need to do anything.' He signed my application, and I left. It depended on the year you were born; my generation had to enroll.

"After secondary school, I attended a technological school. My favorite subject was math. I was studying for a Bachelor of Accounting. Numbers, numbers. I came up to the U.S. a year before finishing. In fact I had planned to return to finish my career, but no, I didn't do it. I was studying in the technology school. During the holidays, in 1985, my brother, who knew I was a good student, and was living here in the U.S., in California, said, 'As payment for your good grades and all your efforts, come to the U.S. Then you can earn some money for your studies, for you to continue.'

"For me, everything was fine while I studied. It was a very difficult life change to come from Mexico to the States, mainly because you live your whole life studying over there. You come here and you cannot do that, because you are old enough to work. If I had been born in the U.S., it would have been different, since I liked studying. I think I would have done something.

"It took me two days by bus to reach the border. It took two days, because the buses can only go the speed limit. I went through the hills, with a person who had an agreement with the coyotes. He was given money and asked to help people across. At that time it was cheap. He charged me roughly $300 and my crossing was easy. We went through San Ysidro, the border town near Tijuana. We were all going to go together in a car. The coyote saw us all and said to me, 'OK, you're going to go through sitting in the passenger seat of the car.' I got some glasses and I got a newspaper and I went through the line and everyone else was hidden below, inside the car. An American was driving and Immigration just said, 'Okay' as we passed. It was not very difficult. The driver just said, 'He is my friend and we came to visit' and he told me, 'Don't talk and pretend to be asleep.' And so we went through the border.

"Once I crossed, I was in San Juan Capistrano, a city near the border. When we arrived there the guy said, 'Let's eat at McDonald's' and we went to eat at McDonald's. I said, 'Hey, we better go and eat on the way, because my friends are down there in the car.' They didn't get out. They were hidden in the bottom of the car. They knew how to do it. There is a cover below, and they traveled beneath it. People cross in many different ways. I did not have to live through that. I sat, comfortably. That is how I crossed the first time.

"I came in 1985 and worked in the fields, in Santa Maria, California. I worked there for 4 or 5 months. In the field picking strawberries. It was hard work. I earned about $60 per day – they paid per box. When I went to the U.S., it was only for a period of 3 to 4 months, to earn some money and then go back to Mexico. I saw how hard the work was, so I told my brother, 'I will not return to the United States ever, because it is very hard work.' At that point I had made, for that time, a lot of money. I said to myself, 'If I ever return to the United States I'll come on a plane, not running down the hill.' I told him, 'If I come back, it'll only be on those terms.' I returned to Mexico. When I returned, I went by car with my friends. They took me by car all the way back to Michoacán. It took us around 36 hours–we all drove.

"The following year my brother said to me, 'Do you want to come back?' I was attending the technological school and I said, 'I'll only go on the conditions I said before. I do not want to go through the hills.' My brother sent me money and I went to apply for a visa at the U.S. Consulate in Guadalajara. As I was an excellent student, I applied for a student visa. I took my notes with me to the interview. I was only planning on coming to the U.S. for the holidays. I was going to go for the second time, but they did not know I had been there before. They granted me an indefinite visa, for life, as a student, but on vacation. So the second time I came to this country was in 1986 with a student visa. My brother paid for the round trip airfare. When I came here, the second time, it was easy. I arrived in Los Angeles and my family was waiting for me; my cousins, my uncles, my brother all came to fetch me at the airport. And I stayed. I did not return.

"I came to the Bay Area because my brother lived in San Jose and my cousins lived in other parts of the San Francisco Bay Area. My uncle lived close to Fresno on a ranch. The rest of my cousins lived in Los Angeles. My brother told me that there were many jobs available. I had come during my vacation time. I had only come for the holidays, really, so we went to Disneyland, to the Studios; we visited San Francisco, the Golden Gate and everything else. At that point I thought I was only staying for the holidays. Once they were over, I would return, because I had my ticket back and I was twelve months – just two semesters, away from completing my college degree. So I came and then, no. I started working and I started making money.

"People asked me, 'Why didn't you finish college?' I regret that. When I arrived in Fresno, my uncle told me, 'Go to school to learn English. Here you won't have money, but you'll have a house, and you will not pay rent.' And I ignored him, because I did not want to live on a ranch and I came over here and I can't regret it.

"I began working in the strawberry fields again. A man who worked for the company saw me and took an interest in me. He saw I was quite different. He saw I was not dressed like the others. I wasn't wearing a hat or a cap. I looked like a city boy. He saw me and said, 'Don't you think this job is too heavy? Too rough for you?' 'Yes, but this is where I am earning my money.' 'Okay, I have an easy job for you. Do you know how to drive?' 'Yes.' Then I started to help move trucks around inside the ranch. I drove trucks and fork lifts in his cellar where fruit was stored. I started to do different activities, but not in the sun.

"When I came the second time, I stayed longer. My brother told me, 'I was making it.' This was in 1986, when Silicon Valley was strong. There was a lot of work, hard work. Back then companies were open 24 hours. You worked as long as you wanted. I worked 14 or 16 hours daily.

Then the Amnesty came. I did not know what the rules were. I found out that if I worked more than ninety days in 1986 - and yes, I had worked, around 100, 120 days, - then you qualified for amnesty. So I stayed. I already wanted to go back, but my brother said I had a chance if I stayed in the U.S.

"My parents were sad when I went to the U.S., although not at first. At first they thought I was only coming here for the holidays, and when I told my mom I was staying. My mom was always hard on us, but she was very brave in other things. I said to her, 'You know what, mom? I'll be staying there,' and she said, 'I'll feel sad, but only God knows why he does things in this way. Maybe your future is there.'

"I had complained about this country. We come here almost like slaves. I didn't like that. Then I thought, well, I'm here anyway. If I do not do well, I can return. I used to visit my friends in Los Angeles. When I went to visit them, they were working, selling hamburgers at McDonald's, in Burger King, or working in hotels. I thought, maybe this will be my future and I will end up staying here like them. My friends could not get papers and they always had to come over with a coyote. Here is my chance - because the visa I had only allowed me to come on holiday, not to work.

"My brother said, 'You have an option; you can file your paperwork. Get your green card and when you want to return to Mexico you'll be able to come and work with your papers, and forget about your visa. You'll have your papers.' I went and paid $185. This happened when Ronald Reagan was president. He was the one who established this law, the famous amnesty program. I filed my papers. At that time, the U.S. government was afraid of AIDS. It was a serious problem at the time. I had to take a test and if you tested positive they would not give you papers. I did everything. It went well and in November, 1990 I became a permanent resident.

"I met my wife, Alicia, at a party, in a dance center the first time I came to the U.S. She loved to dance. At that place, the man that received the admission tickets was from the same town as me. He invited me and I saw her and I asked her to dance with me. We started to get to know each other. She was my girlfriend and then I went back to Mexico. Then later, when I returned, we began seeing each other again. She became pregnant almost immediately. That was 19 years ago.

"In Mexico I had been married before, but it did not work. I married a girl who was an applied chemical drug biologist, the best student in the whole country. She was from my hometown and she studied at Instituto Tecnológico de Morelia, in the University of Michoacán of San Nicolas de Hidalgo. I married her when I was 25 years old. I had it all planned. I said, 'I'll have two children, a boy and a girl and I'm going to get married at 25.' And when I was 25 years old, I got married. I was used to being in the U.S. and I thought she could continue studying at any university she wanted, being an excellent student. So I said, 'Go study at Stanford, and that's where we will live.' But her family got involved and she paid more attention to her family. Her family wanted her to go to Harvard. Neither of us gave in. We had no children, we got divorced. We were legally married, but hadn't had our ceremony, yet. So the marriage got annulled, because I came here. I was going to go back to get married in church, but I didn't. We talked. We lived two completely different lives, and we would not agree on many things. We decided to cut our losses and remain friends. She still visits my family. She got married and remained friends with my mom and my sisters.

"Then I started living with Alicia. We got married after we had children, to solve her immigration status. We lived in Redwood City and eventually bought a house. My children were born in the U.S. When I was single, I went out. I was here, I was there, I had no commitments. I had girlfriends, I traveled, this and that. My life changed the day my daughter was born. When my wife became pregnant, I said, 'No!' because she was talking about having an abortion. My mom called me, because she found out. My wife had called my mom in Mexico and told her and she must have thought I was going to do what everyone does, run away. My mom told me 'No, I do not want that. If you do that, do it, but I do not want to see you at home ever again.' It wasn't necessarily that, because I still had it in my head that maybe I'd go through with it, but I wanted her to be born. She was born in Sequoia Hospital in Redwood City. When I held her for the first time, I felt moved. When I held my daughter and hugged her, there was nothing else. She is 18 years old now.

"Since my daughter was born, I changed a lot. When my friends looked for me, they would say, 'You are a wimp.' 'Well, yes I am. Look, here's the reason, my daughter!' Wherever I went, I brought my daughter. I took her everywhere. There are lots of pictures. My friends would say, 'Hey! You only live for your daughter.' 'Yes, I live for my daughter' and when I got angry with my wife and everything and she'd ask, 'Will you leave?' 'No, I will not leave because of her.' And then my son was born and my life got even better. My son will be 16. He was born two and a half years or so after my daughter.

"When my daughter was in elementary school, she started liking numbers. 'But how will I do it daddy?' At that time we rented a large house in Redwood City. I used some big cardboard signs to make the multiplication tables. It's not very common here and I wore them and said, 'Review them.' Tables from 1 to 10 and from 1x1, 9x7, and so on. She advanced a lot in math after that. My son does not like it. My son had a problem at birth. He almost died. He pooped when he was about to be born, something got to his head. But it's okay. It's not bad, but it takes him longer to remember things. He just needs helpful tips. For the things he likes, he has learned everything without problem. He likes soccer and knows all the names and everything there is to know of all the teams worldwide. Whatever he is interested in, he knows perfectly. But things like math and school in general - not so much. When you push him a little, he moves forward. He'll say, 'You know what Daddy? I want these tennis shoes, but they cost this much.' I respond, 'I have no money now to pay for them. We will calculate the card payments, but you have to promise me that you'll do better, because I see that you are not doing well in school.' After some time he'll come back and say, 'No, on these I did great, here is this one' and shows me. My wife scolds him. She is stronger but does not know how to read or write. I'd tell her, 'Leave him. He made an effort, and we will not punish him.' She says to him, 'No, but look at your sister, how excellent she's doing.' 'No, no, shut up with that! No, you can't say something like that.'

"My daughter makes me proud. It is said that genes are inherited and I think she has inherited my genes. Of course, everyone speaks the best about their children. My children are very noble. When I do well here, when they are going somewhere, I say, 'Do you need money?' And they are not like other kids that always want money. They'll answer, 'I don't need any, I still have some.' They are honest; they are noble. I am proud of that. I do not treat them as if I were a general or anything. My wife is harder on them, but I am not. Everyone is educated differently, because my wife wants things exactly as she says. I like freedom; they decide for themselves, but of course, one tries to teach them the things that you think are not appropriate on the way. I trust my children, because I have taught them. Even when something bad happens, nothing matters. If it's something they broke, we will repair it. We can deal with anything; we don't need to hide anything.

"I like to be organized. Sometimes people say, 'You have everything written down, all that you need to do every day.' I just like to be organized with my stuff, and I try to do it at home with my children, but children don't. They get into their rooms and make a mess. I say, 'Go tidy your room,' because sometimes my son makes a mess in his room; my daughter leaves her shoes in the bathroom or leaves a shirt on our bed. 'Try to be organized.' My wife argues with our children and I tell her, 'You know what? Do not get upset. Shut the door and do not look inside. They'll have to clean it up when it's their turn.' They clean up each week. I try to be quiet, calm, because I've seen things I would not like them to go through. I try to be patient with them as much as I can.

"I'm also very practical. For example, my daughter started driving. She gives everyone rides and I say, 'You know Sandra, don't give rides to everyone, because people will get used to it, and everyone will start asking you to do it, and when you don't have time people will think you are mean for saying no.' It's happening. 'Daddy, you told me this would happen.' 'I just told you, now you're seeing it for yourself.'

"I want my children to study as much as they can. My daughter may go to Foothill College. She has not decided yet. She has a few options. She wants to go to Texas and has a scholarship to go there. She also likes another school in Monterey; I'd like that, it's closer. What I tell her is that if she likes numbers she should look for something related to them. It seems as if she likes dentistry, because I see her books and they are related to that. My son wants to be an athlete, but he is not very dedicated. I have to be more careful with him, because he is very attached to home. I feel he has slightly less capacity for school. Especially if he is not so good at something, you at least have to dedicate your time to do that and not other things. He doesn't like school, and then they start doing other things, wandering the streets. Watching them grow and seeing that they stay on track, is very important to me. I am aware, especially in this age, it is important to know what they are doing, especially with their friends, because that's where they deviate. I live to see my children grow up.

"While my children had been growing up, I first worked in assembly in the company Zircon where my brother worked. I stayed there for 5 years and then the company relocated to Mexico. Then I worked in a similar position for three years at Qualtronics. And then for a company called GM Resound. They made devices for people who could not hear well. I tested the devices with a computer. I ran a test to see if they were working well, to send them to the client. But the company moved to Minnesota - it used to be in Redwood City – and my wife did not want to move with the company. And so we stayed in Redwood City. That decision greatly affected our lives.

"It was a good job and after we chose not to move with the company, I could not find another job like that one. Then we lost everything. We lost our house when the economic crisis came. We had been paying for the house for six years. We lost it when I lost my job and my wife was deported. We had no money to pay. My work decreased a lot. We were living on unemployment and things got ugly. We had to move to a place where we'd pay less. Once we moved, it wasn't so bad and after some time I thought, it's better this way. We were just thinking about the mortgage payment all the time and we confined ourselves, and those who were suffering the most were my children. There was no money for eating out, no money for McDonald's and we couldn't go to Great America. Everything had stopped because of the house payment. When we ended up losing the house, it took the stress off. We couldn't even have lunch out. Everything had to be cooked at home and everything we bought was the cheapest we could find. After we moved out of the house, I knew what we had to pay. We had more possibilities to do more things. We started to rent and now we rent an apartment belonging to a church in San Jose. The apartment has two bedrooms and cost about $1,200 per month.

"After losing the house I began drinking a lot. Once, I saw that my son was hiding because he could see how wasted I was. That's the saddest thing - I remember that. When I was into the habit of drinking, I got as far as going to the street and wanting to live in my car for a while. People came to find me, 'You don't need to be like this.' My brother gave me phones twice, to be able to communicate with me, and I lost them. I did not want to know anything about anyone. I just wanted to be there, doing that. I realized if I carried on in this way I would lose my family, I would lose everything. Not my family - my children, what is most important to me.

"Like I said, after we lost our house, I began to drink a lot. Eventually, I went to the Victory Outreach Rehabilitation Center for 10 months. After I came out, I came to the Day Worker Center, because I had friends there – I knew Mauricio and Francisco from Venezuela. I met them while I was in the rehabilitation center. I was about to begin looking for a job, but I went to the Center to look for them. When I came to the Day Worker Center to look for them, I talked to one of the people that worked for the Center. I told her I'd I come to look for my friends and she said, 'But then do not go looking for work - why don't you fill in an application?' 'Okay, I'll fill one in just in case.' I did not find my friends that day. The next day I came back. I intended to just go and visit. I just wanted to see them and greet them and ask for their phone numbers. But when I came the next day the Center asked me, 'Do you want to go to work? You will make more or less this much, for about three or four hours.' And I said, 'Well, I can do this while I wait for my friends to return from their jobs.' I worked, and decided to stay. It is two years since I came here. It has been since then that I have not done taxes because I did not know what records they kept at the Center and I thought I just had to ask for them, but I couldn't. I did not know how all of this was handled. This year I'll be a little more prepared.

"At the Center, I work at whatever happens to come my way. Whatever is offered. If there's moving, gardening, anything. It's manual labor more than anything. The Center sometimes has a little more appreciation for me on some things. For example, in organizing the work. Almost always, if we're three or four workers, I get the instructions and deliver them to others. Tell them what they will have to do. No, I cannot do any electrical work, because is a bit different here than it was in Mexico. The materials, especially the type of construction and everything. It's not that hard, actually; I just need to catch up. I would like to do something like that in the future. Because an electrician is well paid. At our home I used to do some electrical work, but not now since we rent.

"Yesterday, Sunday, there was a job through the Center, and the director, was a little annoyed at me; she said, 'Hey, there's that work,' and I said, 'I always go to work, but only eight hours on a Sunday.' It had been already three Sundays that I had not been with my son. 'I will not ask him,' I told the director. I couldn't. I can work 8 hours, but starting early. The other day I was at this event for more than 16 hours from 9:00 a.m. to 3:00/4:00 a.m. in the morning the next day. But it's money. Money is necessary; but sometimes ... there are other important things too – like watching soccer with my son.

"I come to the Day Worker Center because I don't have any other work. There are a few citizens at the Center. I have my application on Call Jobs. I've been to interviews, but they do not call me. I think it is because of what I'm looking for - because on my resume there is the kind of work I actually do. These jobs are new to me. Physical work is new for me. My previous jobs were doing the kind of work that was not as hard. I have a lot of experience with electronic assembly. Some companies have called me, but I go and do the test, and then, as usual, 'We'll call,' and they do not call me. I'm hopeful, maybe, you never know. I went all the way to Hayward and Fremont, where most of these companies are now located. I have a lot of experience in assembly, especially welding. I know it's difficult, because all those jobs have been taken, and are being done in other countries. I do want one of those jobs so that I can have my 40 hours. It is more stable.

"Even though I have lived here for more than 24 years, I have not become a citizen. I have to do that, but have not because I haven't filed taxes in the last few years. I have not filed because I've only had jobs like this – day labor jobs. That's the problem. I paid taxes for many years and I only owe the last three years. I need to get a lawyer and tell him about my situation. That's what I intend to do, but I have not done it yet because of the economy. It would cost about $600; that is not much in itself, if you are single and living alone. I can come up with the money, but the problem is that I have my family. I have my daughter, my son, my wife, and I have to contribute to pay our expenses. I can't, I can't. That's why I have not done it yet, but my record is not bad. I could do it. I have always filed tax returns. Because I made very little, I always got refunds of up to $8,000. I did not include, as many who do not have papers do, many dependents. The government does not return almost anything in that case. I included only myself and one dependent. So I got money returned.

"Now that I'm living life differently, I do not need other things to be okay. I'm glad I found that out. I always say people here get materialistic, thinking only about the money, and I do not think in the same way. I sometimes have arguments with my wife because she is thinking about money all the time. I say that, because I am comfortable. When it's Father's Day, my son will come and tell me, 'Here Daddy, I don't have anything else to give. I know, you do not work.' And he'll give me a card, and it's worth more than anything to me.

"I have good memories of Mexico. Although I still have a little anger against my dad because my dad left my mom when we were older. I do not know, in the end I cannot say if it was a bad thing to do. Each person has his own thoughts - but he left my mom. My mom gave him all the best years in her life and everything. Women like those you cannot find anymore, a woman of only one man. She stayed at home and he went away. He wanted part of the house and everything. We all had to provide a little money to give to him so that he'd leave my mother alone. My mom stayed in his house.

"My brother, my cousins all live here in the States. We all send my mom money. She doesn't really need much, but still. For her to pamper herself once in a while. I send her what I can, depending on how I do here. At least $100 per month, that's what I can send her most of the time. My mom still lives in our house. She does not want come to live here. She has her visa. She comes to visit twice a year, but it is hard for her because she has to travel. When she comes here, she has to visit her children in Los Angeles, Modesto, Hayward, San Jose and New York. We can meet here. But she has to travel to Los Angeles and then to New York. If she has enough time she'll visit all three places. We each have to pay for her to travel to our house.

"Before, I was the one that was better off, economically, than everyone else in my family. I had good jobs and everything. But when everything slowed down, I did not follow the company that hired me, because of lack of support from my wife. But anyway, we are all here and everything is good. Economically everyone is able to bring my mom over whenever they want. I am the only one who can't. That is why I give her some money each month. She does not want to live here. She is at home and at home is where she wants to be. Someday I'd like to reunite everyone. Sometimes I think, 'If one day I hit the lottery', which is the only way I would be able to have enough money, I would buy a home and we would all live there, my whole family.

"I'll be honest - It's hard. Here, in the Day Worker Center, most people are alone; many have wives in Mexico. I live with my wife. We don't have a good relationship, and sometimes we have problems - she is very difficult. There have been occasions when I've left home. It is very difficult when you know that they are doing something wrong and they say, 'I know I'm doing something wrong, but that's me and I will not change.' You can't do anything with that. I said, I'd stop drinking, but she has a problem also ... she loves casinos. You can't get her out of there. She wanted us to live in Las Vegas. I have an aunt in Las Vegas who offered us a studio and she said, 'Let's go there.' I told her, 'No, I do not want to go to Las Vegas, because you won't be able to get out of the casinos; if we move there it is going to be worse.'

"Maybe, taking refuge in this I'll go back to drinking. Right now I'm fine and calm, without doing so. I have spent almost three years without drinking. I did it alone. I walked away from where Mauricio and Francisco were, and I did it for me. I lasted 10 months in rehabilitation, and I kept thinking... 'My children need me, need my money, whatever I can give them. I'm going home.' I've kept myself sober without going to those places. I haven't even gone back to church.

"I believe in God. I like to meditate. Occasionally, I go to church. I have no specific religion. I've been through Catholicism and other forms of Christianity. To me, God is only one, and he is where you go and is with you always. Everything depends on how you fulfill your commandments. To me, the most important book in church is the commandments. If you try to respect them, to the best of your abilities, it will show you a good path.

"Even after all the errors I've made, I consider myself a person who has not made mistakes. I do not say, 'I regret this or I am ashamed of this.' In truth, even though one sometimes might say, 'Oh, I am ashamed of this,' or 'I feel bad', it is not so. If you start thinking that way, you start doing it to yourself and you'll end up traumatized. Even right now, when I'm riding the bus, people would come to me and say, 'Hey, but if you have a car, why are you standing there waiting for the bus?' 'Because I am now living my life in this way and I feel comfortable this way.'

"I have always been a peaceful person. There are people who still appreciate me because of it. I've been involved in trouble and everything and through dialogue I have avoided problems. There have been people, for example, that would have fought and I told them, 'You know what?' Talk, talk, and this can be arranged, because sometimes it is only gossip or this or that or there are misunderstandings about everything or sometimes they are drinking or something and I always avoided fights. A person that knew me used to say, 'Is José Luis here?' 'Yes.' 'There will be no fights, he convinces them, and they do not fight.' Sometimes they even talk until they end up embracing each other. These are misunderstandings; there is nothing to be fighting about. Lately I told someone, 'Okay, remember, as things stand, if there is a dispute, you'll have problems. You will have a problem, end up in court, and if the police come, you will end up in jail or deported. That's how it's going to end, and remember that you have your commitments!' 'Oh, yes, you are right - just talking.'

"I wonder how I will be remembered. I would like to be thought of as a quiet person, who makes common sense of things. Right now, what worries me the most is our economy. Sometimes there is not enough. Sometimes I get home and did well. But something always comes up. Like now, the rent increased $200. Because supposedly the church is going to make some repairs - so they say. I had already planned something, and I had told my son, 'Mexico will play against Chile in the next few days and we're going to watch the game together.' But with this increase, 'Forget about the game.' Our plans get changed."

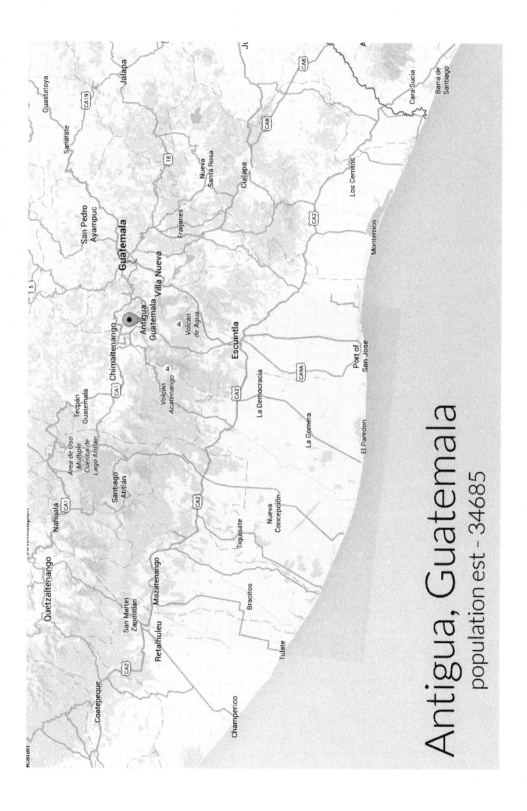

# Antigua, Guatemala
population est - 34685

# Chapter 7

# Laura's Story

"I came to the United States from Antigua, Guatemala with a tourist visa. I brought my six-year-old daughter María Belén with me. I decided to quit my job and leave everything I had in Guatemala and come to the U.S.

"The process to obtain a U.S. visa is very difficult; they have many requirements. You have to own property: a home, a car, have a bank account and have economic solvency, in order to show that you can pay for your expenses in the United States. First, you make a phone call to the embassy to make an appointment. They then give you an appointment about a month later. After that month has passed you go to the appointment. Once in the embassy, you have to pay. When I got my visa, 10 years ago, I paid 1200 *quetzales*, (about $170). The type of visa you get depends on your financial status. Some get it for five years, others for 10 years, others are granted a visa indefinitely. My visa expires in 2018, but is only good to visit the U.S. for six months at a time - and then I need to return to Guatemala. But I am planning to stay – I do not intend to return.

"I had a good job in Guatemala. I worked in security, for the Vice-President of the country. Since I was working for the Guatemalan government, my employer handled all the paperwork for the visa. I used to travel a lot with the Vice President.

"The organization I worked for is called 'SAAS' - Secretary of Administrative Affairs and Security of the Presidency. Earlier, in 1996, peace agreements were signed in Guatemala. There are versions that say that there was a genocide, others that state there was no genocide. Before the Peace Accords were signed in Guatemala, the State, which was the army, was the one who protected the president of Guatemala. When peace was signed, the army was removed from that function and the SAAS was funded. They no longer wanted the military to look after the president, so trained civilians were assigned the job. So, that's where I started, where I began. I had no previous training; they trained me. It was a year-long intensive training, and in the process, I have protected first ladies, daughters of presidents, government ministers. I have protected both men and women. I was always a bodyguard. I have been doing this for 14 years.

"It was great. I liked my job very much, because I got to know a lot of people. You learn many things, and that never gets boring. You have no idea who you might meet that day, or where you're going. They give you the agenda the day before and say, 'Tomorrow there will be an interview at this hotel, with the Vice President, the President ...' or 'We're going to San Marcos, traveling with the first lady to give toys to children ...'

"Usually things went fairly smoothly. But once, in the area of Panajachel, a very beautiful lake in Guatemala, we had a bad experience. The first lady was coming to Panajachel the following day. I was in the advance department, and we came before and prepared everything. We would take a look at the road, determined where she was going to sit, who would be next to her, if she was going to receive a souvenir or a gift. We checked and organized all these things before she arrived.

"That day, we were in three cars, and were not wearing the suits we usually wear, because this was the day before the arrival. We would wear the suits the following day. We were armed with guns and everything, though. Then, halfway there, we had to board the cars onto a ferry to cross the lake. We did not want to board cars, because we had many things on them, even the dogs, the K9 unit and other things that we were using, for example, the white paint to make a heliport for our helicopter to land. So we didn't want to go by ferry, and decided to go around the lake, by land. We were on our trip when three men appeared in the middle of the road, standing in front of our cars, wearing ski masks, dressed as military and wearing hats so that we could only see their eyes. They were armed with AK-47s. We knew what weapons they had, because we were trained on weapons. They did not say anything to us. They thought we were tourists, because many Americans go through there, and these men steal their cameras. They use AK-47s to frighten, to intimidate. Many times they had no ammunition and after robbing people, run away towards the banks of the ravine. But on that occasion, they shot at us first. I was in the first car, so I saw them head on. They started firing, and my partner was the first to shoot back. He made me react. We got our guns out and started shooting. We got out of the car and started chasing them on foot. We found their safety area - they had food there, and even had a place to store things. We found things there, but we couldn't catch them. These men knew the area perfectly and knew where to hide. We didn't. That same day we notified the authorities of SAAS, so that the next day they had assigned people from the military to guard the perimeter of the road.

"Depending on the person I was protecting, they'd allow me to enter their house. When the person trusted me, and I had many that did, I was allowed to be inside. They even gave me a room to stay in. Those allowed inside the house were usually the kitchen crew and me. Then, when the Vice President needed something, she would say, for example, 'I need you to go buy this.' She would just say it to me, and then I would have to send someone. I received the orders and then, in turn, coordinated the staff that was outside the house. I also learned to cook and make desserts while I was working. The cooks that worked for the people I protected, taught me on the job.

"My problem is that I had a partner, my ex-husband, who was violent. He has a military career, and also has a career as a lawyer. I met him when I worked in security. He was from Escuintla, Guatemala. I married at age 21 and was married for 16 years. We had two daughters, born eleven years apart. I liked being a mother - it is exhausting but rewarding.

"The life that we had together was very good. We both worked for the government; the two of us had a good salary and we traveled a lot. I know all of Guatemala, the whole of Guatemala City and every town and city within Guatemala. We lived very comfortably with only one child. I felt that I was old. In Guatemala people get married at a very young age. Not here. Here it is very different. I was 32 years old, and I said, 'I'm old; let's decide to have one more child and I'll get an operation. We can only have one more, because I'm too old.' And then we had another baby. The fact is that we traveled a lot for work, and we didn't have more time to dedicate to more children.

"But then, my husband met a young lady, very pretty, much younger than me. He fell in love. He changed a lot, and went so far as to hit me. He was not like this before, never in his life had he hit me before. During that time, I reported him twice in for violence. I never went to the hospital for that, because the hospital that we went to was a military hospital; it would have been a problem for him. I did not want him to get in trouble, because I wanted to get a pension from him.

"I have physically endured violence with my ex-husband and in my job. However, I feel what hurt me the most is the verbal violence. Because words affect you a lot. I cried a lot, for a long time. I thought that I was to blame. My self-esteem was very low, and I went through a very difficult situation. I tried to be strong for my daughters. I tried not to show them the pain I was going through. When I was not feeling well, when I felt my self-esteem decline, I could just go to the salon and lift myself up again. But it took time for me to say, 'I can no longer deal with this life.'

"I lodged two complaints about my situation. Both reports were discarded halfway through, because my husband was a friend of the judge; he was friendly with those who handled the case. My reports were dismissed - they didn't follow them through. That was the end of the relationship, when everything finally broke. I got tired and I found no other way, so I divorced and came here. I just left. I have been divorced 3 ½ years. I never got a pension.

"The justice system in Guatemala relies heavily on corruption. If you have money, and you have power, which is the driving force in Guatemala, you can have a case. If you are just one more of the common people and have no power or powerful friends, then the justice system will not do anything for you. My ex-husband has a tourist visa and he can travel and he can be armed. He can come and go. In fact he has. But he does not know I'm in California; he knows I'm in the US, but not where I am. He is interested in finding me; he has tried to contact me, but I don't want to talk to him. I don't know if he remarried or not. I know nothing about his life; I do not care.

"The difficult thing is that I think many men cheat on women. I don't know if it happens here, but at least in Guatemala. And sometimes women forgive them. But I felt I had the means to sustain my daughters, go to the beauty salon, grab my car and go to the beach. I had independence. So I did not have to suffer him hitting me. I did not have to endure him coming home with another woman's smell. I had no reason to put up with that. I am a strong woman.

"In Guatemala, if I had had any other job, if I didn't work for the government, it would have not given me the economic solvency to provide for my daughters. I have two daughters. My husband doesn't pay any alimony. There is no child support there, as there is here. The laws in Guatemala are different. If you have the means, raising children anywhere in the world it can be easy.

"When I left my country, I flew from Guatemala to Denver; I went looking for my dad, who lived in Colorado – I will tell you about him later. Then from Denver I flew to San Francisco. I didn't like the climate in Denver. I do not like snow. I didn't enjoy the weather. And it is harder to find a job in Denver - there are more Americans than Latinos. When I was in Denver, I could barely speak and communicate with people, because they all speak English.

"I decided to come to the San Francisco Bay Area. I had already been here - I had traveled here before, as a tourist, for a week or two, with my bosses. There is a big Latino community here. It felt great that in stores you can be assisted in Spanish.

"As I told you, I managed to come here with my little girl, on a visa. It was a blessing that I could bring her with me, because many people don't have their children here. They wish to bring them. My oldest daughter, Camilla Inez, was 18 years old and stayed in Guatemala. She lives on the university campus. She stays at my mom's house on weekends She is studying industrial engineering, in Guatemala, in a private university and is in her third year. She only has two years left to finish college. She is very smart and loves math, like I did. She already knows more than me. Since she attends a private university, I also had to pay for her tuition.

"The situation was very hard when I arrived in the United States. I did not have a job with which I could afford food, clothing and all our expenses. I did not know the rent would be so expensive here in the Bay Area. And then my daughter, María Belén, got sick. She got pneumonia; she had a terrible cough and started coughing a lot. I took her to the doctor and they prescribed an antibiotic for her, but the antibiotic did nothing. Then it got worse. She started coughing blood, and her nose started bleeding; she developed a high fever. And I had to work. I have no family here, and I had just arrived. I had no friends or acquaintances at that point. I had no one to leave her with and the people I usually took her to said, 'She can't come here today, she is ill and she might be contagious. She might get other children sick.' I couldn't work, I had to look after her and it was very difficult. I then decided to send her back to Guatemala to live with my mother. My daughter returned to Antigua and likes living with my mother. She misses me and misses my cooking.

"She is healthy now, but I miss her like crazy. I hope I can bring her back here later on if things are better. That is what gives me courage, strength. I hope I eventually get a stable job here, get settled so that she can return.

"I ignorantly thought I was safe here in the States. Nothing bad ever happened to me in Guatemala. I came here, and in two and a half months, I have suffered two robberies here in the U.S. First, I bought a bike to move around; I left it locked outside of my work, and when I got back the bike was gone. People say that Guatemala is dangerous, but nothing of mine ever got stolen there.

"The second robbery happened when I accompanied a woman, my landlady, to East Palo Alto. There were a lot of dark people there. The landlady had to meet with a lawyer, so we went there, because there's something like a communication center for lawyers. I was filling out a job application, and she said, 'If you want to, you can stay in McDonald's, because there is WI-FI there.' Well, I was there in McDonald's while she went to fill out the paperwork she needed, and she said, 'I will pick you up.' I put my computer on the table; I finished my application and closed it. I was then checking my phone and a dark-haired boy approached me and said, 'You running fast?' And I said, 'Yes, I'm running fast.' Then he said, 'I do not think so,' and he grabbed my computer and ran away.

"I'm still upset about the theft and my child, and because I feel that in Guatemala I had a good life. I had my house and my car. Here I have no car. I have no house, and my daughters are my main concern. I do not like living here in the U.S. I do not like that rent is so expensive, and for that reason I have to share a home. You cannot come and rent an apartment for yourself, or your family. That was one of my biggest fears also when my daughter was with me, because you share a place with people you don't know, and when you have a 6 year old girl ... But for working, there's a lot of job opportunities here.

*****

"I was born on September 24, 1975 in Guatemala City, the capital of Guatemala. I grew up in a big house - It had 7 bedrooms, two bathrooms. I lived in an area of the capital city, a nice area with my parents, who were born in San Marcos, Guatemala. My grandparents also lived in San Marcos. We went from Guatemala to San Marcos to visit them often. They had a business, a grocery shop. I loved going there with my brothers, because we used to eat things from the store, sweets.

"My dad worked in a hosiery company, called Nylon Tex. He did that and also sold cement, pebbles, sand ... building materials. He had his own business. My mother took care of the business. On weekends, my dad determined what was missing in the business and would bring it.

"My parents bought the house I grew up in. It was a nice home; it was home with principles. I have no sisters but I have 3 brothers. My parents treated all four of us equally. We all had to help around the house; we all had chores; girls and boys equally, everyone had a job.

"But then my dad came to U.S. with the idea of starting a business to help the family. But while he was in the U.S – in Denver Colorado, my dad fell in love with another woman and got married. He never returned to Guatemala, even though he can travel - he is a U.S. resident. I was 14 years old when my dad came to the States, which was a very difficult stage of my life. I was the only girl in the family and my dad loved me. He protected me more than my brothers. Then when he came here, I cried a lot for my dad. My parents haven't gotten a divorce, but they've been separated for 30 years. The lady he lives with is from El Salvador. They have visited El Salvador, but not Guatemala.

"After my father left, my home as I knew it disintegrated. My mother sold the house where we lived and we moved to a small house in Antigua, Guatemala. Our neighborhood was very quiet. They were simple, humble, ordinary houses. We could play outside, around the block, with the other children in the neighborhood. There was none of today's technology, of course. I thought it was weird, because I didn't have any sisters, I only had brothers. During Christmas or for birthdays I got dolls; I wouldn't even take them out of their boxes, I liked them but I was not interested in playing with them. I had three brothers, and when they were playing with their remote control cars and racing, I always wanted to play with them.

"Two of my three brothers stayed in Guatemala. The oldest, Alejandro, lives in Zacatecas, Mexico. He is 40 years old; we are two years apart. After me, is my brother Gonzalo who lives in Antigua, Guatemala. He is married and has a family. The youngest brother is called Daniel. He also lives in Antigua. I used to live in Antigua, near the entrance to the city, but now I live in California. The two brothers that live in Guatemala are in the army; they are military officers. One of my brothers, the one that comes after me, Gonzalo, is still guarding the President's son. The other one, Daniel, was recognized as outstanding and is sent to different provinces for 20 days at a time. He then returns home for a week and then goes back. He commands a platoon of over 30 soldiers.

"I have a bachelor's degree in electricity and am an electronics expert. Both in electricity and electronics. I had many colleagues, but I was the only woman. I have seen that women here learn a bit about electronics in high school, but in Guatemala it was rare, unusual. I was the only woman and had about 60 male classmates. I was a good student - I did well. I liked math and electronics takes a lot of math skills, like linear algebraic equations. I also completed 6 semesters of law school. I did not finish. I had two years left. I left because I could not pay for college.

"I dreamed of becoming a professional person, and have a nice, stable, safe home, and have a normal family, with a husband and children. When I came here I felt very alone. I had some money, and thought I would rent an apartment for my daughter and me, but all I could rent was a room. We found where to stay right away. I cried because I did not like the family that we lived with. In the laundries there are ads: 'Room for rent,' 'Living room for rent' or 'Shared room' without knowing anyone, and I thought, 'I must find a place to rent.' I saw the ads in the local laundromat and I immediately rented a place. And the family that lived there with me, the men drank a lot and the lady hit her children. It was a horrible environment, and I did not like it there. I did not like it, but you do not know the people you rent from.

"It was very ugly, especially the first night, because I had not brought enough blankets; I had a blanket, but it was very cold, we suffered the cold. I put a lot of sweaters on my daughter. Then I moved because I did not like it there. I moved about two weeks later. Now I share an apartment on a street behind Target. I live with a lady from El Salvador and a lady from Mexico. It is a three-bedroom 2-bath apartment. I have my own room and share the bathrooms and kitchen. I have to pay $600 per month in rent.

"After I arrived, I had to walk, and look for work, and look for any opportunities. We were hungry. I was filling out applications - nowadays everything is online. Since I did not have a computer, I went to the library, and in the library, a lady told me, 'You must go to the Day Worker Center, and they can help you find a job.'

"When my daughter came here for a month, she went to school, to Castro School. When I was looking for a school, I met three women. They had a car but they did not drive. I can drive, but I had no car. Latina women who know how to drive have learned here; I learned in my country. I can also ride motorcycles, and most women here can't.

"I will do anything here to get by. I don't look for work that I like; I look for anything I can get. Now I clean houses, and in the evenings I work in Safeway and in Target from 3:00 a.m. to 7:00 a.m. and then I come to the Day Worker Center. In Target I work restocking products. I get paid $10.55 per hour. At Safeway, I help with packing at the register, like the work little children do and get paid $10.00 per hour. I do not have a social security number but I have an ITIN number from the IRS. Every check I receive from Target or Safeway has taxes deducted from it. I send $200 each week to my mother for my daughter. Sending my daughters money and my rent are my two main expenses.

"At the Day Worker Center, you get a number every day. You have to be consistent and come all week. If you went out to work today, you go to the back of the line, and you're last the next day. And tomorrow, if there is only work for two people, only those with the number one and two get it. Even if they come in late. When I started coming here I thought, 'The early bird God helps' and I would arrive here at 7:00 a.m. But it was not true; the one with the number got the job. Typically, in a week, you can work two times through the Day Worker Center. In general the work for women is housecleaning.

"There was a day at the Center when someone came in to ask for someone who could sew. They needed to make some things for horses or ponies, some flags or pennants for horses. You had to know how to use a sewing machine. Of the women at the Center, no one knew how to operate a sewing machine – but I knew. So I went, and I had gone to work a day earlier, so in that case I was lucky. Because I knew how to sew.

"I have two days off in both jobs at Target and Safeway. I have Monday and Thursday. On Monday and Thursday I clean houses. So people look at me there in Safeway ask me, 'You work here, how did you get this job?' It is not usual. And I work with my given name. I know it is unusual, many people here told me. Many Latinos, who have seen me here in the Center, have told me that. In both places, at the entrance, there was a sign saying, 'Now Hiring.' Inside Target there are a few computers, and I applied there. I believe I was I hired because I knew some English, and because I was better educated; many immigrant women never went to school.

"Now that I am settled, I have a bit more time. I start in the afternoon, at 4:00 p.m., at Safeway, and at 3:00 a.m. in Target. Then during the day, if I have time, I take advantage and come to the Day Worker Center. I have acquaintances there, but not friends who I trust. I really like the English classes in the Center because that is a way of investing my time. If I'm not in English class, I'm cleaning houses. But I don't have any free time to go and have fun. I cannot go amuse myself if my daughters are over there. I'm better now, but do not have any friends. But I do not mind so much, because I just arrive home after work and I go to sleep.

And I do not have to worry about going to work and my child staying in the apartment alone.

"Every morning and every night, I pray for my children. I call my daughters every day. I want them to have a good family, and a nice home. I would just like to be with my daughters; I do not care if it's here or there. I do not want to be there and be miserable, and I do not want to bring them here to suffer. My desire is to do well, nothing fancy, just well. To be able to provide for them.

"After my divorce In Guatemala, there were two men who tried to get closer to me; but I would not accept anything because my children are small. I said, 'First I will get my daughters through this, and then I will see what I will do with my life.' I may marry again. Maybe. When I came here, I felt very alone. I saw that life is much easier as a couple, because if you are married, the husband pays the bills and the wife helps with the food, the clothing, etc. I am by myself... I need someone to help me and support me.

"I would like to stay in the States long enough to raise money to return home to Antigua and start a business. People have told me, 'This country is the land of opportunity.' I still have not seen the opportunities. I want to learn to be a barista, because once I save enough money here, I want to go back to my country and own a bar.

"But I would like to stay in the U.S., if I could become legal. My father, who has legal status, could help me, but I do not know how he can do that. He doesn't know either, even though he has been here for a long time. At least I have learned some English, if only by ear. I do not speak well in past / present / future verb forms, but as little as I know, my dad knows less. He came here when he was older than me, and he never worried about learning English. So he's here, living as though he was undocumented, afraid. But he has a green card. My father told me that if I could, I should find out what can be done; I should get a lawyer, which is what we'd need for him to apply for my green card.

"Well, to go to a lawyer I need money; I do not have any money. I told my situation to the Day Worker Center staff and they gave me the address of a lawyer, who was here in Mt. View, California. When I went, there was no one there. I was sent to Milpitas, where the lawyer had moved. In Milpitas I was told that they didn't cover domestic violence, and they sent me to another place. Then I went to that other place ... I have gone to several places.

"But I am only asking about my situation and not involving my father. I am not going through my dad. After that, I went to another lawyer at Stanford. But they only help you when you are already being deported, so they did not take my case, not if INS isn't already involved. So I have to wait for INS to try and deport me.

"I worked in Guatemala for 14 years and I only had a year to go in order to apply for a pension. With 10 years working in the government you already get half a pension. I can already count on that when I turn 50. But if I return now, and work for another year, I can retire for time worked and not by age. I think in the future, when I become a senior, I hope to be doing well, because I've already worked. I won't have to bother my daughters. If they want to help me, that is fine, but I will not depend on them.

"For my future life, I do not have any concerns. I am concerned about the lives of my children. María Belén has been affected by many changes, the divorce, and then I foolishly brought her over here, to do nothing but suffer. I know this change is very difficult for her. But she is very intelligent. She was only here for a month, and she learned many English words.

"Life has taught me to be very independent. I trust that I can do it, too. 'Come on! You have to work, do something with your life.' I used to exercise a lot in Guatemala. Here I've been eating a lot. I have a lot of anxiety. I cannot sit still. If I have free time, I will run; I like running, sports, and filling out applications ... moving. I want to be an example for other women, and for other women to look at me and say, 'Yes, I can do it.'"

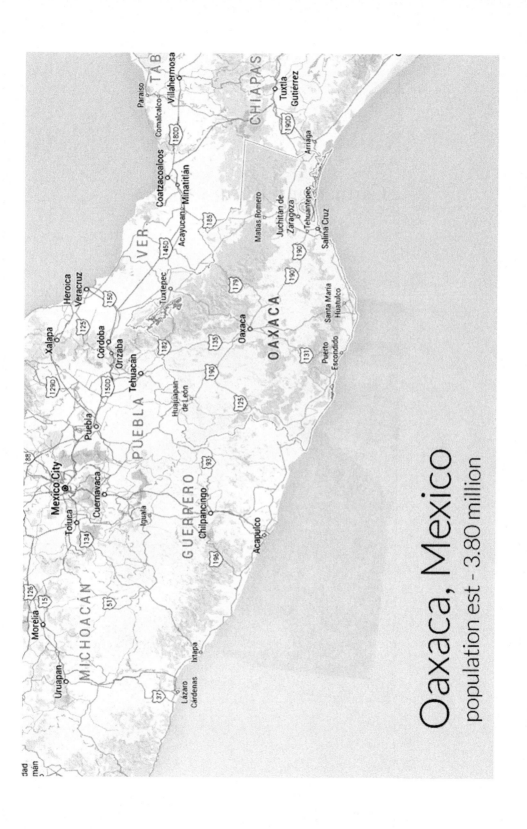

# Oaxaca, Mexico
population est - 3.80 million

# Chapter 8

# Carmen and Rocío's Stories

## *Carmen*

"I have two daughters. The oldest is my adopted daughter - Carmen Rojas. When I was 16, I spent four years working in the fields in Oaxaca, Mexico, planting corn, chilies and tomatoes. I met the Rojas family then - we were neighbors. Of course, I did not suspect that years later, I would adopt their daughter, Carmen, as my own. There is a lot of violence in Mexico. People steal - money, girls, livestock and property. These people killed her mom when Carmen was a young adult. But she hid in the mountains, and stayed hidden for a week. Felicitas, my wife, went to get her. Carmen couldn't speak any Spanish, had no good clothes. We taught her Spanish and sent her to adult school. Carmen is about 39 years old now and very successful. She studied to be a lawyer. She lives in Mazatlán, and she has her own business.

"I was born in the state of Oaxaca on September 28, 1951. I will be 63 this month. I was born in the pueblo of Tlaxiaco, where they speak the local dialect - Mixteco. When I came to the U.S. from Mexico, I brought a birth certificate that said September 28, 1951. However, I lost my birth certificate and I had to send for a new one. Someone made a mistake and put the wrong date on it. They put on the 24th. So that's the date I now use in the U.S. The true date is the 28th. Four days apart.

"I am named Carmen. My dad, who had never gone to school and could not read, heard the name 'Carmen'. He thought, 'All names that end with an 'A' are women's, and of course it doesn't end with an 'A,' so we will name the child Carmen.' That was it. I didn't change my name, or change the date I was born. There are people who do that, because they have problems in Mexico. Then they come here and change their name, or have problems here in the States and get renamed, but not me.

"My grandparents were born in the pueblo of Santiago Nuyoo. My paternal grandfather died very young; I saw him when he was dying. He had a disease similar to cancer and died. My grandmother brought him to our house in her arms. My maternal grandfather was, at that time, a landowner. He had land and cattle, but they had no money; they had property. They had goats, sheep, and chickens. Where they lived, there were mountain lions that ate the goats. So my grandfather had lots of dogs - the good kind, not those that sleep in, those that defend you. Because there was no electricity then, no medical help or medicine, no lamps. Dogs were the guardians.

"My parents were also born in Santiago Nuyoo. In the native language I speak it means 'moon face.' I had three sisters. The oldest died a month and a half ago - she was old and sick and died in Oaxaca, Mexico, where she lived. Another sister now lives in an *ejido*, (communal land ownership) in a place called Plan de San Luis. It is a place where the government hands out large amounts of land to the people who are called *ejidatarios* (co-op members); my third sister lives where my parents were born, in Santiago Nuyoo.

"Tlaziaco was a neighborhood, so to speak. It was spread apart. It was a community of only 4 houses. The homes were not right next to each other. If or when we could not finish the work in the fields, our neighbors came and helped us. And when they were late with their harvests, we would help them.

"As a young child I did not wear clothes. I am from a native race that did not wear clothes. No toys. We played with stones, flowers, frogs, snakes, cockroaches. Plants in the water (clean, not like here, where there is a lot of pollution). When I was five years old, I already worked. Our house was made of grass; from *sacate* leaves, banana leaves. My parents used the leaves to build our house. Ours was a *sacate* home. As it was made from banana leaves, when it rained, we got wet. During the rainy season we used to go live in caves. In the caves, water didn't enter; it was dry. We slept in the cave; the fire was lit, and my mom cooked and the goats we had slept next to us. My dad checked that there were no lizards, snakes, scorpions, mice or raccoons in the cave. It was cold, very cold. There was no bathroom. We did everything on the ground. I remember it all - it seems like yesterday. My mom and dad sowed corn and tomato, chili and beans. We ate that. We didn't go to the store, didn't buy food, nothing.

"We were hungry all the time, but there were plenty of fruits; if you wanted to eat a mango, you went and took it from the tree. To eat meat, my dad had a 22 rifle; he would hunt at night, killing rabbits and raccoons. He hunted and arrived home at 5:00 a.m. and prepared everything. I helped him - I brought water. He speared the game and put it in the fire. Delicious.

"Growing up was really difficult, because there was so little food. My mom gave me five tortillas for five days. She'd say, 'Eat a tortilla on

Monday, and you will get mangos, guavas, bananas to eat. And on Tuesday, another tortilla, and you'll get fruit and drink water.' There was never enough food, and no clothes. I used the same shirt for two years. It broke and my mom would patch it.

"All my parents did was work. When we were little, 5, 6, 7, 8 years old, they worked. My mom made tortillas on a stone. Because we were little, our job would be to put wood on the fire. We had a blower and used it to catch the fire. My dad would go to work, sowing cornfields, banana, and coffee, far away. He worked in the mountains, where there were no other people. He did not like to go too far. He went there to plant coffee. He would arrive home three or four days later. My dad was paid in cash. They paid five pesos for a whole day's work with a machete. Five pesos was a lot of money then. Only my dad worked; my mom took care of the goats, so that they were not eaten by coyotes. We went to school and my dad worked in the fields.

"Still, I saw my dad often. He took me to school. I was the only boy in the family. But I had no shoes. It hurt my feet, but there were no shoes. Only my dad had a pair. I was barefoot. I could not work, because I was too small, but I fetched water from rivers. I retrieved water with a *bule*. It is a gourd like plant that grows in our area of Mexico. We cut it and it has seeds. We let it rot inside, and then took out all the seeds. Like a small pumpkin.

"Saturday and Sunday, I helped my dad plant corn, collect bananas and oranges and go sell it to other people. One time, when I was about nine years old, I walked with him from Santiago Noyoo to Tlaxiaco - from 1:00 a.m. to 8:00 p.m. the same day. Walk and walk and walk with my dad. We carried fruit, bananas and ginger and sold it. My dad was carrying a sack of coffee and sold it and got money. We arrived home at 8:00 p.m., walking all day.

"There was no school close to where we lived, so we went to Santiago Noyoo. I had a tiny battery transistor radio and I listened to music on the way from my house to school. It was four hours each way. I went with my sisters. There was a shift from 8:00 a.m. to 1:00 p.m., and again from 3:00 to 6:00. We went to school all day, both shifts. Right now, the students enter at 8:00 or 9:00 in the morning, but at 3:00 or 4:00 they leave. We stayed at the school from Monday to Friday, because it was far away. We did not live at school. We lived at my grandmother's house. To get to school, we left at 4:00 or 5:00 a.m., when it was still dark and we had no lamps.

"My dad never sent us to school when we could already work in the field. Once I was of age, I helped him collect corn, fetch firewood, cared for the goats and got *chapulines* (they are small insect like grasshoppers that could be sold in to be eaten).

"When we were not in school or helping with chores, we played basketball. Our community bought some balls and gave us the balls to play with at recess. We also played on the swings, to and fro. At home, there was never anything - my dad never bought toys. The toys were rocks, frogs, and grasshoppers, cutting firewood, grabbing a stone and grating it over another one. My sister and I had races - we would run up the mountain, rolling downhill.

"I got to the sixth grade, but I was kicked out of school because I never passed it. I was 16, and should have been in high school, but did not pass. Because I had to walk very far, I hardly went to school. If you didn't do your homework, or didn't answer the question the teacher asked, or if you did not come early, or did not do your homework, the teacher used a ruler - you stretched your hands and the teacher hit you or they would pull your sideburns. Otherwise, they made you stand near the blackboard holding a brick.

"I liked grammar, writing and reading fast, but did not learn in school. I learned very little. The only one who spoke Spanish was the teacher; all the rest spoke indigenous languages. Most of the time, I did not understand what the teacher explained.

"I learned to write and I learned to speak Spanish outside of school. I also learned how to not have fear. I was in town with my dad, when some Americans arrived. My dad told me, 'These people are Americans; they do not speak Spanish, they speak English. They're American, do not go near them.' He was afraid. I don't know why. But they say that for the human being it's better to be afraid, because it's like a defense.

"Because there was no money, when I grew older I joined the Mexican Military. It was very hard, but it was voluntary. I told my mom I did not want to work in the field anymore, because there were so many dangerous animals and poisonous snakes. Once they bite you, bye. I told her I wanted to go into the army to earn money fast. Four months later, when I was 22 years old, I put on my uniform. I made some money, part of which I sent to my mom.

"The Military has a lot of discipline. They make you jump into the thorns, and push you into the water. You learn to climb up towering mountains. You had to jump on cacti. We did many push-ups and learned to walk across the rocks and the mountains. You had to cross a river with the water up to your chest. You couldn't remove your clothing. You had to run Tuesday and Thursday mornings. You had to learn how to jump over a table, from here to there. You had to run from here, jump and fall on the other side. If you fall with your heels, it hurts, but if you fall with the tip of the foot, it's okay.

"The basic instruction for the Mexican Military was four months. They cut your hair, teach you how to greet, teach you how to read books, teach you to disarm and to fire a weapon. After four months, you are the same as a veteran and can now perform a service. After that, you can advance - you can go up in grade and then they pay you more. I reached the rank of sergeant.

"After training, we went to catch bad people. Many would tell me, 'Kill him.' But inside my heart, I couldn't do that. It was not part of my nature. I did not know that, but in my heart I was not born to harm another person. So, the military sent others to kill, and they did it.

"In the Military, I was in Mazatlán and Sinaloa. I worked in the State of Chihuahua, and part of Sonora. I was working all the time and saw a lot of violence. We would go for six months to the mountains where there was drug trafficking. We had to destroy acres of marijuana and poppies. When there was no road, we had to go down with a rope from a helicopter. They lowered a rope and hung us way down, one by one, because the chopper couldn't land where there were only mountains.

"I remained in the army for 18 years. I made a lot of money in the military. I thought, 'If I resign, they will give me a lot of money and I'll make a deal.' Others told me, 'You have two years left until retirement. Wait two more years and you can retire and you are going to make money permanently.' But I didn't wait. I left on April 8, 1990, after 18 years - two years too early to get a pension.

"When I left the army, I stayed for two more years in Mexico. I moved from Tlaxiaco, where I was born, to the city of Oaxaca. In Oaxaca, I worked four months in construction earning good money. Because I was still relatively young, I was accepted to work on a construction site. I did what is called hard construction (it's different from the U.S.). You need to pick up 50 or 60 pounds on your own. Then I went to Mazatlán,

Chiapas, Durango then to La Paz. I did not travel for leisure - I went looking for work in all those places.

"I had wanted to create my own business in Oaxaca, but a friend asked me to come to the U.S. My friend brought me to the United States in 1993, when I was 42 years old. I came with him, alone. I was already married to Felicitas. I met her as a little girl in elementary school. My wife and I are of the Indian race. We got married when we were 27 and 30 years old, in 1982 in Plan de San Luis. We never got divorced. My wife taught me a lot - she taught me how to stop saying swear words, how to make cookies and how to sew with a sewing machine. But, to come to the United States, I left my wife in Tlaxiaco with my daughter Rocío, and my adopted daughter Carmen and came to the U.S. with my friend.

"My friend knew a coyote; he had used him before. He had been in the U.S. before and had left. We traveled by bus for 23 hours from Oaxaca to Mexico City. From there, another 18 hours to Tijuana, Mexico. That is where I crossed. I paid the coyote about $450. We crossed the border walking with the coyote and with about five other people. We walked through the desert. I was in great physical condition, because I had been in the army - so it was easy for me. It took, more or less, on average, five hours of walking, during the day. We left Tijuana at 3:00 a.m. We had a suitcase, a backpack with water, and good shoes. A change of clothes, nothing else. After we crossed the border, a car picked us up and took us to a house, where we bathed, changed clothes, and combed our hair. Then we boarded a plane at the airport in San Diego and flew to the airport in San Jose, California.

"For me it wasn't difficult, because I went through rougher times. I had been in the army for 18 years. I could walk all day without food, with only clean water. I could sleep standing up. I could walk all day while it rained. I could cross a river that could kill you. I could run 10 km with lots of gear, in the sand, at the beach. Uphill and downhill. On the grass and on the pavement. Heat. I was in great physical condition, so walking from Tijuana to the other side wasn't very difficult. With the training they gave us in the Army, everything I saw in Tijuana and during the crossing, I looked at without fear; I had already seen it all.

"Also, while I was in the Army I saw people being murdered, people being kidnapped. While we were crossing the border, we saw dead people and sick people. People crying, children. I had seen all that in Mexico. So, when I was crossing the border, I saw it as something I had experienced before.

"When I arrived in San Jose, California I knew for sure I had work, food, and clothing. I had a friend who lived in Mountain View, California and worked hard. He had come alone from Mexico - had left his wife and children and came here. He got me a job. I didn't struggle to get work, where to sleep, clothing or food. Everything was done. The first day, I arrived and I went to work. Working as a janitor.

"The person who brought me here to America gave me work, but he abused me, hit me, and left me lying there. Do you know San Tomas Expressway? In San Jose, California? He left me there and I did not know anything, - whether to go north or south. I knew nothing. I had worked twelve hours - all night and it was freezing. It was December. He left me lying there in the street. I have not forgotten - bleeding in the face. We had had an argument about a job that was done wrongly in the bathrooms. He had no education and was very big and strong and he hit me and left me. I do not consider him an enemy now; punishment will come on its own. Sometimes I run into him, he lives near here. 'Hi Pedro, how are you? How is your family? Nice to see you, congratulations, keep working.'

"My wife and daughter, Rocío, came to the U.S. in 1998, five years later. I had sent for them, because my wife had worked while I was in the U.S. and saved money. They came with a tourist visa, but overstayed. Then they had to go back, due to a family emergency and could not come back together. They were caught by immigration and separated at the border. But, they were able to reunite in Mexicali at a friend's house. Then I arranged for them to cross separately, but with the same coyote.

"But by then, I was lost in the drink ... I do not like to talk about that, because it does not sound good. I felt most alone in life when I had a drinking problem. Because it's bad. But it is better to live with problems, then to have nothing. From the problems you learn. One's life is like piano keys, there are black keys and white keys, that's life. The black keys are the enemies of us, diseases, debts, problems, and no job. The white keys are the future. But the two go together. The person who has no problems is a weak person.

"When my daughter, Rocío, first arrived with my wife, she was nine years old. I went to get them in Los Angeles. They crossed the border with a visa. They did not walk. They had a tourist visa. My family, my wife's family, my sister's family, no one had gone to college, no one had studied, nothing but the first grade, third grade, nothing more. My wife, Felicitas said, 'If we're going to have a daughter, she will have to study.' My wife and I were both day workers, but we sent our daughter, Rocío, to school.

"We had this dream of us arriving, going to a university, speaking English, and speaking other languages, and visiting other countries. Not having to speak the native language all the time, but learning something. We wanted to take advantage of the opportunity. But we did not know how it is here.

"Let's take an example... a person comes from Argentina. Arrives in the U.S. This is his house and that's his job. From home to work, from work to home, work, home. For 40 years, for 50 years ... knowing that it's the land of opportunity, and not taking advantage of it. That happens to me still. Most people live like that - it sounds harsh but it's true. They do not realize there is an opportunity in this country. There's a lot of money. We're still poor. I do not know how to start a business that you can grow.

"When I first arrived in the U.S., the first 5, 6, 7 years I was happy, but as it progressed I got older; I felt tired. One does not walk fast any more, we do not want to learn English, as well. There are obstacles, but it is not anyone's fault, it's my own fault. I can't blame Obama, the police, my daughter or my wife that I don't know English; it's my responsibility.

"I have a mentor, he lives in Sunnyvale. When I first came, I lost a lot of work, and he told me to come to see him. 'I will not give you money or a job - I'll give you an idea of how to do things. If you want to work, you will cut your nails, cut your hair, use clean clothes, walk fast and walk straight. Greet people. I'll teach you a greeting not to use. This greeting is called, 'dead fish'. It creates distrust, because I'm squeezing the hand. The proper greeting is like this: 'Hello, how are you?' And I corrected everything little by little. If I have a job and the boss leaves, I'd do the work as if he were watching me; I do not feel like, 'The boss is gone, now I can rest.' No, I am not like that.

"I am very reliable - if I have a job, I arrive 20 minutes early. I have been always like this, because the army disciplined me. If you do not arrive on time, you are out. Then I got used to always arriving on time. Do the job well. For you to get work, you have to change your attitude, speak well, say no curse words, cut your hair, wear clean clothes, and walk 25% faster than anyone else. Then they see your good attitude. A lazy person has a bad attitude, doesn't do things correctly, is late, does not bathe or mouths off.

"If the police grabbed me, I'd go willingly, if I'd made a mistake. But stealing, hurting someone or hitting someone, or using a weapon, or using a knife, no. I'll tell you, I will never do it. In this country, if you do things well, no one bothers you. When I worked as a janitor, all night, I was alone and traveled to Los Gatos, San Jose, South San Francisco, and Oakland. I came and worked one day here and a day there. I liked to return home driving on the streets, because all the traffic lights were green. But there always were policemen around. In 2009 I was stopped 14 times at night. I have been driving for about 10 years without a license. The police stopped me, because I was alone in the street. They flashed their lights and said, 'What are you doing at this hour?' 'Working.' 'Where do you work? And your license?' 'I work over there, clean an office and I don't have a license ...' 'Okay, go.' And they let me leave. One day my car turned off and I was stranded in front of the light, red, green, red, green, and the car didn't work. The police came and helped me. They helped me push the car off the street. They never took my car. I have a few tickets for not stopping at a stop sign, turning outside the time, or because of a busted taillight, but not for any serious violations. If the police stop me, I say, 'Sir, here's my license. I did not stop because I did not see it.' Without using profanity. I do not get a ticket. I like it when there are lots of police, because it is their job.

*****

"I am now 63 and my sister from Oaxaca is 64. My sister that died was 65 and my youngest sister is 55. I only speak with the one that lives in San Luis Plan de Oaxaca. She lives there, and she learned to speak a little Spanish, but she speaks the indigenous language beautifully. When I talk to her, it gives me a good laugh, because she has a very nice tone. I talk to her in the indigenous language only. She wants me to come back to Mexico, to her home and eat corn tortillas. I want to go.

"My father died five years ago. My mom died in 1978. My dad was left alone and remarried. He had another son, my half-brother. He came here to the States and settled in Virginia. When my dad died my stepbrother returned to Plan de San Luis, because my dad left him 26 acres to raise cattle. There was no one to take care of the land, so he left the States. I am also his son and I have a legitimate right to the land, too. I can be the owner of these properties, but I have a different idea. It's not

121

something I want. My stepbrother is now caring for the land. It's a lot of ground. It has water, springs and cedar trees.

"I heard about the Day Worker Center from my daughter, Rocío. Since she was a little girl, she liked accessing information and surfing the internet. I had been laid off of work and I was going to return to Mexico, but Felicitas, my wife, told me not to go. We were paying $450 in rent, but my wife told me, 'You have to recycle.' I collected lots of bottles and cans and went to San Jose, Sunnyvale, Mountain View, East Palo Alto, and Menlo Park on my bike and got money from recycling. Then my daughter found the web page for the Day Worker Center in Mt. View. And I came to the Center and have stayed here as a day worker for about six years. At the Center, we get jobs and also have classes. People come and talk about immigration reform. We also get people talking about how to grow a business, how to make money, how to put a business together. People talk about our health care. They give us ideas.

"While I am at the Center, I want to learn gardening and plumbing, but learn from the beginning. Right now, I can't get a job in a company because of my age. But if you get there when you're young, they'll give you a job. As I mentioned, my first job was as a janitor with my friend Pedro. Then I went to a company called Ramirez Janitorial. I didn't like that job, because you do not learn anything, it was very simple. It made no sense. I just cleaned here, dusted and left. But electrical work, plumbing, gardening, and architecture are interesting areas. Sometimes I work as a gardener in the houses around the Center. I like working on the land. I like plants – I was born among them.

"Near the Day Worker Center, there is a lady's place I go to for two or three hours, but she pays me more than $15 an hour, because I arrange her plants pretty well. Whenever I worked there, I would be careful not to step on anything, I'd leave everything spotless, and if there was more, I'd clean more. I'd do it in less time, and when the lady comes out, she looks up and says, 'Hey, you've arranged my garden beautifully.' When I work for this lady, instead of going to work, 2, 3, 5, 8 hours - I go for 2 or 3 hours and she pays me $100. And I do not ask her when she'll pay, or at what time I have to leave. I arrive and do a good job. She likes it.

"One day, through the Day Worker Center, I went to work for a man who had a big garden. He said, 'Get off the machine and go buy grass,' with a nasty tone. 'Then what do I do?' 'Pick up the trash, and we'll go.' He spoke to me like that. You should not talk to a person in that way. If you are working for me, I'm not going to talk to you like that. I'd say, 'Come, let's do this job, let's mow the lawn, and once we finish, you and I are going to take the tools up, and we're done.' Better communication needs to be used. You shouldn't say, 'You do' and 'I won't do it.' The man brought me back to the Day Worker Center. He said, 'Did you like it or not?' but loudly. And I do not use that tone. I told him, 'The reason you have not grown your business is because you have not changed your attitude.' I told him, 'Your business has not grown, you just do the work, physically, all you do is the work. Because you can't communicate with people, you do not know how to treat people.' Serving the people is very different. You should say, 'Come, and you and I will do it together.' You can't say to people, 'Do it, and fast.' I gave him ideas; I didn't scold him. He answered me with swear words, but I didn't scold him.

"I want to learn carpentry and plumbing. I want someone to say, 'Here is a carpentry shop. There's a man who will teach you.' If I had a place like that, I would go. One Sunday, I worked with an architect. I know nothing about how to hold a tool and put in a nail; I don't know how to cut wood. But the man taught me with a lot of patience. The man said, 'Carmen, handle it like this, put the weight of your body behind it, place the nail, put this here and use this tool.' He taught me. I liked it. He was not one of those people who say, 'Move away, I'll do it because you do not know how to.' He told me, 'Pick it up like this, use your body weight as well, mark it with your pencil and use this saw and cut it.' I would like to find a place to learn, not for the money, but to learn.

"The hardest part of my life is that I do not know English and have no close friends - only friends that I drink with. I have some friends from the Day Worker Center. How do you feel when you talk with someone like a friend, with a good attitude? It feels nice. Sometimes, when I talk to the people I know at the Day Worker Center, I tell them a little about my story. I talked to my friend a bit about where I came from. I came here and did not speak Spanish well, and did not understand anything - let alone English. I said that I was very poor, not poor in ideas, poor in the sense that I'm seeing that you're eating, food, breakfast, lunch and dinner and I have nothing. As a child there were people who ate good food and I watched. I was hungry but my dad taught me to never steal.

"Not everyone in my family is like me. I have nothing. Others in my family are architects, doctors. They have properties and they have homes. Not the same life that I have. They have families who are in the States or in Mexico; others are in the army. But they are good, not like the life I had. Felicitas and I were the ones that were out of medicine, food, clothing, education and money to study.

"Now I live in an apartment with my wife and daughter, Rocío, who is 26 years old. We live near the Day Worker Center in a one-bedroom apartment. The reason I rent a one-bedroom apartment is that my daughter is old enough - she needs to have privacy. She said to us, 'You can sleep in the living room.' My wife and I live in the living room and sleep on the couch. We get up to cook in the kitchen. And then we do the cleaning twice a week. My daughter put her office in her room. She's in there and we are here. Everyone has their own bookcase. Rocío has a huge bookcase and I have a bookcase. Felicitas, my wife, has one too.

"The monthly expenses are difficult. Rent is $1,630. But we share it. Our apartment complex is not a place where Latinos typically live. It's in an area where students live, places where Google engineers live. Here, they do not make noise. We pay the rent first. We can run out of food, but rent comes first. I was taught to be responsible with the rent. It is paid on the 25th or 28th of each month. We share the cost of rent. I give the money to my daughter. She puts the money in her account and the rental company automatically removes it from there.

"I want my daughter to become an independent entrepreneur, for her not to work long; I want her to become a free person by the time she is 30 or 35, with spare time (just like some other people), and money and for her to travel around the world, for her not to need to return to work. I don't know if she has a boyfriend. I do not ask. I always say, 'You have to have a family, you cannot be alone. Pretend you are like a flower that will wither on the tree, sad and lonely. You have to find a partner and start a family. Have one or two children and educate your children. Not how I started.'

"I hope she can raise a family, and not rely on a boss that pays you very little money. It's not bad to work, but it's bad to get permanent work, with no money and paying rent. It is better to build a home. People that make their money work for them are free. Success is not having much money, but having style.

"I eventually want to return to Mexico. I am lonely here – I have no true friends. The other day, when I was watching television, I saw that Mexico is not like when I left. The town where I grew up now has many roads, TV, phone, and the internet. There are good homes. There are no *sacate* houses, nothing like that. But it is very polluted. When I was there as a child, the water was clean, there were no cars ... clean. But not now.

"I think, 'Why didn't I study when I was young?' It's not my dad's fault. It is not because there was no money. It is because of me. Even though I am as old as I am right now, I would like to learn. I'm willing to work for no money, but I want to learn, because what you learn is valuable. What helped me was when I switched to the Christian life. I stopped swearing, I stopped drinking. I had no friends. I had friends, but drinking ones. Then I started to write notes and repeated them and practiced with another person. 'If you dress well, that does not count; what counts is the inside, the heart. When you change, you can change the world.'

"To lead a good life is to do good to someone else, help someone else, and give to those that have no food, because money is not everything. There are many people who have a lot of money, but do not have the idea of sharing. But a person who has money and shares, will always live in a quiet place. They will live happily, and give thanks to God for each new day. When you wake up in the morning, give thanks.

"In life there are two paths, there are good ways and bad ways. But we need both. There is a lady who comes to the center, called Lourdes. I ask, 'How are your children?' 'They are very rebellious,' she says. I say, 'No. You are the mirror of your kids, there are no bad kids, and those kids are bad because you raised them. Stand at your bathroom mirror and look at yourself. You are the mirror of your children. A person who has no problems is a weak person.' And, I said, 'Do not give your children many toys, because they will grow weak. Give gifts as they respond, as they grow. If you are a good student, I'll give you a gift. If you are a good engineer, I'll give you a hug, I'll give you my love, give love.'

"To be remembered, you have to do great things. I do not think I'll get a statue or a monument. No. Did you know your grandfather? Your great-grandfather? No, because they didn't do great things, so we do not know them. If they had done big things for future generations, we would be seeing them in a photo and hearing their story. For example, this one was an engineer. This one left an inheritance to his grandchildren; this one was a writer, he left many books. As they did nothing, we do not know them.

"I regret coming here to the United States. For me, where I came from, Plan de San Luis, is a beautiful place. There's no road, but there is a river and the boys who studied with me in primary school made their houses on the banks of the river, and they are bankers or have made a lot money through farming. The river is like a road between the state of Veracruz and Oaxaca. Everything that's produced on one side of the river is sold on the river. All the products that are produced here; they sell it on the river and they've made a lot of money as entrepreneurs. I want to return to Plan de San Luis.

"I told my sister who lives in Plan de San Luis that I'm going to build a house on a mountain where she lives. I'm going to make a house there, because she has a spring. It's like a hole and the water is very clean water. And on this land, I'll get seed, have cattle, have two dogs, big sheep dogs and live there and have a car and be close to children."

# Chapter 8 (Continued)

## Rocío's Story

"I came to the U.S. when I was nine years old with my parents, Carmen and Felicitas. I have no memories of Mexico. I probably do, but I don't think about Mexico that much. My first memory of the U.S. – what surprised me the most – was the roads – they were so long. Because after we crossed the border, we drove from Los Angeles to the San Francisco Bay Area. The first time I came was with a visa that eventually expired. We were here for a year or two. Then, we decided to go back to Mexico to try and figure out a way to come into the States legally – but it didn't work. We could not get a return visa, so my parents paid a coyote and we came over the border again. I remember it was very difficult to adjust to the culture and learn the language. Very, very difficult."

Rocío is a petite young woman with long dark brown hair, tan skin and a bright smile. She speaks eloquently and intelligently about growing up as an undocumented person and attending school in the Bay Area. Rocío's father describes her as "a very restless person. A person who wants to invent something and would make millions of attempts to achieve it."

When she arrived in 1998, she lived in East Palo Alto and attended public school. Her teacher in public school thought she excelled beyond other students, and contacted her parents to recommend that she apply to Eastside College Preparatory, a middle school and high school in East Palo Alto, CA, a lower income area located halfway between San Francisco and San Jose, CA., within several miles of Stanford University. The school was started by a Stanford graduate as an independent, tuition-free school for students from 6th through 12th grades who have shown promise of becoming the first in their families to attend college. At this time, over 60% of the student body is Latino. The school is sponsored by local real estate developers, venture capitalists and other wealthy individuals.

"I was very lucky in that I actually went to private school. That was my first opportunity. During the time I was at Eastside, I had a mentor - Chris. This is a person I have stayed in touch with, even since I graduated. Having a mentor like her was the beginning of everything for me. She was really more than just a mentor and friend. She was an advocate – like a parent. With her guidance, I started traveling while I was in middle school. With her help, I went to D.C., I went to Atlanta, and I went to all these conferences on journalism and other subjects. And I remember, Chris always prepared me – she took care of my flights – not financially, but she gave me guidance – what to expect – things you would normally, as a kid, get from your parents. Many parents have been through it–for example, they know when you need to apply for college so you do not miss the deadline. My parents and most immigrants did not have that kind of experience to impart to their children.

"I worked hard and graduated Eastside Prep with a 4.0 GPA. I had an interest in journalism and theater. I was accepted into several very good universities. I received a scholarship from the Rotary Club of Menlo Park and attended Columbia University in New York City.

"College was difficult. I became depressed, but I could not tell my parents. My parents would not understand the pressures I was going through. I was no longer the A student and I was at the bottom. My mentor, Chris, from Eastside Prep, took me by the hand and helped me through the situation. I feel better now.

"My mentor was like a parent and opened up her whole network to me. Her husband happened to be a very well-known executive back in the day. And, because his wife had faith in me, he also opened his network to me. Especially when I was applying for jobs – wow, that makes a difference. I remember, I was applying to Deloitte. I had submitted my resume and her husband made this call to this acquaintance or friend that he had in Deloitte, and the following day there was a follow-up call and the interview happened right away. The same thing happened with McKinsey. I have always realized that it makes an incredible difference in your career, your life, to have these kinds of advocates help open doors.

"The other part is that the mentoring also helped my social life. There were things that I didn't know going into Columbia – like the Homecoming – because I never had that. I went to a really tiny school. We didn't even have a prom. It was invaluable, having someone who exposed me to dining out and country clubs. I could be at the same level as the other students at Columbia.

"While I was at Columbia, I was making zero money. Every summer, it was a struggle to find an internship, because of my immigration status. Even if I could work for free, for example, in the United Nations in N.Y., I could not afford to rent an apartment in NYC for the summer. So I had to come back here to the Bay Area. I remember that during that time, in the summer, my parents were sharing a two-bedroom apartment with another family. They only had one room. I remember that summer made a big difference for me, because while I was living in the room with my parents, I could actually save up the money I made from my internship in the place I worked. I could spend that money during the school year. That was better than living in N.Y. during the summer, and spending for food and all that. And it helps, because I got the internship experience – it is on the resume – and on the other hand, I had money for the year. That's what was really important.

"I graduated from Columbia University with a degree in economics in 2011. Because of my illegal status, I could not go into investment banking, which is what I wanted to do. So I had to be creative about what to do. I started doing marketing for a real estate company here in Silicon Valley - a company in Palo Alto. I didn't know this at the time, but I remember, what drew me into marketing wasn't necessarily the branding, or the things in design, or putting the catalogues together, the pamphlets, but it was the database. The company had a huge database with many real estate contacts. Basically, we would bombard people with email. For me, that was very annoying, because I thought, wait a minute, why are you sending the same email to all these different people. They have different needs. One is looking for a condo and one is looking for a house. Someone is looking under one million dollars and someone is looking for something more expensive. And it bothered me. So I organized all their data.

"Later on, I could legally work under a program called DACA (Deferred Action for Early Childhood Arrivals). This program started in 2012. People like me – children of undocumented workers - can get two years of work authorization and they can renew it every two years until they are 30 or unless the government decides to end it. It is not a law, it is not an executive order, but it is just a temporary relief program – a memorandum authored by the Obama administration and implemented by the Department of Homeland Security. It is basically a grant of deferred removal action and does not confer lawful immigration status or provide a path for citizenship. It can end when the President leaves office or at any time.

"When I got my DACA permit, I could apply for any job. I actually decided to go into technology. I stayed in marketing and I started doing business cases for different marketing programs at Cisco Systems. I wasn't happy with it and then finally, by serendipity, I was thrown into a stretch assignment. I always knew that I liked to understand people, understand behavior. And this was the perfect opportunity, because it allowed me to do design for the first time. That's how I started discovering that I really loved to understand behavior. And then, through experiences I had at work, I began to realize that there was actually something called user experience. And I can do this on a full time basis. I am thinking about changing to that. Within or outside of Cisco – we'll see.

"I would like to remain in design - design experiences for products and services. But the thing that drives me, especially now, is that I finally found what makes me passionate. It is basically that, in design, you are conveying an idea. A simple idea. And that idea can potentially change people's lives. But in order to get to that idea, you need to be able to communicate so well – so proficiently. I think that people like Steve Jobs were able to do this so well. Of course he would curse and do all these things, but ... to be able to have that level of simplicity and convey it through your design, that's beauty.

"My perspective is that there is actually something interesting that is happening in Silicon Valley. There are people like my parents who came here in the 1990s and work here in janitorial or service types of jobs. And immigrants like my parents bring their kids as well. Then the kids grow up here and they become Americanized. Later on, some of these children go on to college and then they are able to become a guide for their parents.

"Here in Silicon Valley, immigrant parents are relying more on their kids. Especially in this particular area, because this area is very expensive. The younger people that are moving here for technology jobs are pushing up the house prices - and the rents. For example, I was actually in East Palo Alto this week and went to drop my mom off and I was just looking at East Palo Alto. I had not been there for 4 years, since 2010. I kept seeing along the street, houses for sale. I was actually curious to see how much the price was. Surprisingly, the house that I was looking at was half a million dollars –this is in a low-income part of the Bay Area. The demographics will definitely change because of these price increases. The population will probably become more Asian and less Latinos and African Americans.

"So what happens is that people like my father, who is a day worker and probably makes $200 to $400 per week - that honestly doesn't mean anything, but it still helps them a lot. Then, you find the next generation is carrying on or supporting the family, as well. Because the lifestyle, here in Silicon Valley, has definitely gone up and it will continue to increase over time as more people are coming in. And then, you find that more immigrant families are moving south to Sunnyvale, San Jose, and Gilroy. But East Palo Alto is the only place that has rent control in the Valley. So there are really not many places that people like my parents – day workers – can go. It is going to be a challenge, because they are serving the community here in Silicon Valley, in Palo Alto, Los Altos, Los Altos, Hills, and Mt. View. There is going to be a commute. The commute will take longer. And there have to be trade-offs, because some of these families have kids. Do I go to the Day Worker Center or drop off my kid at school that now happens to be 40 minutes south of here and there is traffic in the morning? That is definitely a trend. It is already happening and we will continue to see it intensify over the next few years.

"So the challenge is, we need to understand these families and understand where they are coming from and what they can contribute. Actually, here is the beauty. And I do not think many people see it yet. There are families like my parents that are undocumented and they are immigrants and they are service people, but they brought a child with them. And that child somehow happened to go to school and then to college. And some children of immigrants are working in technology and other industries. Well, as more families have the same success, they are bringing their kids and they may, at some time, be able to contribute to the business world. Which right now, I have to say, is only one perspective.

"I am a designer. And when we think about design, especially in the company where I work, the perspective is to think about the typical person; to understand his wants and needs. The typical person is a Mike or a Rachel, someone who is the typical American. But the reality is the demographics are changing. And we need people like myself or children from these immigrants, who can reflect that this technology is not only going to be used by Caucasians, but is also going to be used by Latinos and African Americans.

"Someone who happens to live in a more affluent community and owns a house needs someone to realize how important his support is for day workers. He needs to see that someone is coming to do his gardening at $12 per hour, but that person may have a child and they are putting him through school or just that they are paying rent. And it makes a big difference that you are giving them that money.

"I remember at one time, my dad was working at the Day Worker Center and I do not remember what my mom was doing. But I remember him doing the Day Worker jobs, plus he was also doing recycling. And he did not even have a car, so he was using his bike to carry big bags of recycled goods. In 2007-2011 - that was in the middle of the financial crisis. But rent was about still $1000 per month – it was still quite a lot for them. Now a one bedroom is more expensive - around $1800. We live in a one-bedroom place now and my parents sleep in the living room. It is expensive – it is almost $1900 for our one bedroom. I help my parents with the rent, of course.

"I just received my new DACA card, so that will be valid until 2016. That gives me another year. My parents will be fine here in California. What worries me most is how the area is changing so fast. It is kind of turning against them; not against them like throwing them out; just that rents are increasing and it is hard to find service jobs. So I actually have been considering moving. I don't know yet. I will probably be moving at some point in my life. The challenge is taking my parents with me. I've been to the East coast, I've been all over and I have not found a place like the San Francisco Bay Area. In the sense that people here are very generous, and they are actually willing to help you if you tell them what you need. But it is still so hard.

"It will be up to the next generation to support and help out. Just like I am doing right now. That's the other thing this area – we have done a great job bringing in profits and making products that have changed people's lives. The next level is we need to educate young kids in less advantaged neighborhoods, like East Palo Alto and East Menlo Park (lower income areas) that you do not have to do what your parents did – which is get a job and stay with a company 20 years. We need to show them the alternatives.

"Marc Zuckerberg, the founder of Facebook, was teaching an Entrepreneur101 class in one of the middle schools in East Menlo Park. And when he went there, he asked the kids in the class what were their dreams and aspirations. One of them raised his hand and said 'I really can't do this, because I am undocumented.' And that's when it hit him – this is something that worries this community. Zuckerberg's non-profit organization is called 'FWD.us' and is trying to bring awareness to immigration reform. However, even this organization is about immigration reform in the context of we need more HV1 Visas for the technology community, not necessarily the whole comprehensive immigration reform.

"Unfortunately, it is going to take time. For example, even at Cisco Systems, I am one of the few Latinas in the company directory. Looking at the marketing organization – which is around 1500 people, I am one of the only Latinas, except for the assistants or the janitors. It is shocking. I was looking at Fortune 500 companies and I would have thought that by now they would have taken advantage of the diversity card. Unfortunately, the level of qualification is part of it. Also, they don't take risks when they hire people - especially because they have to answer back to shareholders. But I think, if you can get this idea to kids – to take risks, it can make a big difference. For example, they can begin their own start-up; if you do have an idea, you need to go for it. But the problem is that immigrant parents don't have much knowledge about possibilities, because all they have known all their lives is that you do this and then you get paid and that is how you pay the rent. But there has to be some sort of way to show them that there are alternative paths to the American dream.

"I was reading this book by Christian Rudder; he is one of the co-founders of OkCupid – a free online dating service. His whole book is about all the data they have accumulated on his web sites. When I was reading through that book, I compared myself to what's expected of a Latina. I do not fit there. I probably fit more on a white spectrum. That's why, when I think of my mentor, Chris, I realize she helped me get into that spectrum. Not 'get' – she exposed me to it, so I could be better prepared, and actually gain advantage.

"I would like to become a citizen, but I am not sure that will happen anytime soon. I do not think the President will do anything–he is too nice. He is not willing to take risks. We'll see.

"The company I work for cannot do anything for me – there is really no way. I know it sounds really depressing, but there is really no way. I was talking to a friend a while back and he asked me why don't I get an HV1 visa. Or why don't you do 'x..y..z?' I was trying to explain to him that there is no way. We broke the law. We came here illegally. And if we were to go back, we would face a ten-year ban and we could not come back into the States. Anyone who is here illegally – even if you came with a visa and overstayed that visa. You broke the law. So you go back and you face a ten-year ban. I am not really into politics, but I can't help saying this: The system is just not working anymore for the 21$^{st}$ century. They really need to revamp it. Even while I was waiting for my DACA worker authorization to come in, it took a while, and I was thinking to myself, why does this take so long? Homeland Security runs the DACA program. The company I work for does not do anything to help me. They just know that I have this temporary work permit. They don't care. They do check status and I have a social security number. And I pay taxes As an outsider looking in or an insider looking out, the system just does not work anymore. While I was preparing the paperwork for DACA, I was thinking to myself, it is kind of like the DMV. It is painful, but you have to go through it. And unfortunately there is no competition, so you really can't innovate. I was thinking to myself, Oh God, this is sort of the same. I think to myself why is it so hard? Because if you just follow the rules, nothing gets done.

## *Chris*

"I was a volunteer at Eastside Preparatory School in East Palo Alto. I know that Rocío had heard about Eastside while she was in primary school and very much wanted to go there. Eastside was well known in the public schools in East Palo Alto. It is the dream school of many Hispanic families.

"Rocío is a person who seeks out what she needs. It is the most amazing thing. In fact, if I were writing a story about her, I would say it is central to the story - that she makes her life happen. And she finds the people in her life that will make it happen. She is very proactive. And, so, I think that once she and her teacher talked about the possibility of Eastside, she said, 'I really want to go there.'

"Initially, I wasn't even working with her group. The way it is organized at Eastside is that, if you were volunteering there, you would get seven children to yourself and you would teach them their entire English program - literature, parts of speech, and vocabulary. The curriculum is very rigid so that everyone was delivered exactly the same program. So I was working with seven other seventh graders. Suddenly Rocío came to me and said, 'Would you help me? I am writing a book.' And her English was not what it is today. She said, 'I need to practice the English language, so I am writing a science fiction story.' She was on page three hundred and something. She asked, 'Would you edit it for me?' That's a lot of work to do, so I told her that I would just help her on the part of the book she was working on right then. 'We'll just work together on that,' and so we did that after class. She got transferred into my group. There were suddenly openings; two students moved from my group and I may have said, send Rocío to my group, since we are already talking and working together. As soon as she got there, we sort of took off working, on the side, as well as doing all the work in class.

"I only worked with her one year - in seventh grade. She was the star pupil. She just achieved at everything. I worked there another few years and, as she went up the grade levels, she would come to me and talk to me about what was going on. Our interaction after the first year was as friends. She was a sponge. She was the class leader. She was very serious about it and not particularly social. She was kind of a loner.

"This little girl, who was walking home to a house you or I would not want to live in, in East Palo Alto, living with 17 people. They shared the house in order to pay the rent. There were no other children in the home.

"She was already relating to her teachers more at Eastside than to her parents. And then you have two people at home who are very, very simple people. Her mother may not have gone to school at all and her father may have gotten up to the sixth grade. That is not a very stimulating situation at home. Everything had to come from within Rocío. And she would walk home from school on winter nights, down by the Dumbarton Bridge. She would never complain about it. She was a very determined little girl. Determination is key to understanding her.

"So after that first year, and as I said, she was the shining star, it became clear to me that she was going places. We just kept talking the other years I worked there. One of the things she wanted to do was to take extracurricular activities that would help her with her English. So she would challenge herself by joining the journalism team to write more. She would challenge herself to take leadership classes, photography, or whatever excited her. And this is, of course, a theme for her throughout high school and college. She over does; she picks the hardest curriculum you can have. She would take a regular load and three extra classes, because she was so excited to learn. So, we just became friends. I helped her understand 'first world life' in the Bay Area – that was part of our relationship. She had never even seen the ocean!

"We still talk, because we are friends. It was ongoing that we talked about life and the opportunities that would be available to her with an education. And I always stressed that she was on the right track. She talked about social things with me, but it was mainly that she did not feel truly a part of things. She had no interest in boys at that age.

"We talked about a whole host of things that she did not have the opportunity to talk to her mother or father about. She came to our home while she was in high school and that made a big impression on her. And, I used to take her to her home sometimes after school, and it was a scary situation. She certainly was one of the top graduates in her class. I saw her routinely through high school, but, once she went to Columbia, she would call me and we just kept the connection going. She knew I was there for her.

"Columbia was her number one choice. She got a free ride at Columbia. A total free ride. Her balance was zero every semester. It was extraordinary – food, housing. I think she had only to pay for books. All her classes, everything, was paid for. All the way through for four years. So, my husband and I would give her a little spending money. We also talked to her about budgeting – the same things we did with our children. I had a lot of very serious talks with her about budgeting – I am giving you this amount of money for spending money – and I definitely want you to see a play in New York City every semester She was so serious, she would just work, work, work.

"She was extremely stressed at Columbia. She refused to go to a counselor, which was a bone of contention between us. I really wanted her to reach out at the college for help. She did not feel comfortable with a counselor – it was not in her culture to do that. And her parents had no idea what to say and do to help her. Her parents loved her very much – she comes from a very loving couple. For a while she was more critical of her parents, I think, because of their limitations in education and experience. But, I think she is very appreciative of her parents and their love – she has really matured.

"At some point I thought she would quit college due to the stress. But I said, 'That is not an acceptable option. You have to stay there.' Not harshly. For her, it was lonely and miserable. Columbia is tough. She couldn't have picked a tougher school. She knew it was an elite school and that made her very happy.

"We also discussed planning. Figuring out what her week looked like. How much could she take on and still manage to do well. Those were long talks about making a plan. She wasn't seeing out far enough. She was just so excited about all the different classes offered. She would dabble in things. It was free to her. She took Chinese. She took dance, which has always been a real release for her. She has consistently gone back to it over the many years. It has been good for her social life. But there are huge gaps still in her being able to navigate through this culture.

"Her parents, Carmen and Felicitas, have been to my home. We had a party for Rocío when she graduated college. It was very small, with her parents and the adults in the community that have helped her and a couple of friends. Her parents were not able to communicate with me. It was an extremely moving day, because we had a formal party for her and she said that she had nothing to give us back – for all of us who had helped her. So she danced for us. It was a modern, interpretive dance, set to music that she had choreographed. It was unusual to have someone do that for you, but that is what she was able to give to us. It was beautiful and people were extremely moved.

"Her parents are beyond polite. When I would drop her off at home, they would always say, 'Thank you.' Her father, especially, is emotional. He adores her. Her mother is more reserved. Rocío pointed out that her parents have had no privacy in their relationship until she got them an apartment two years ago. It was the first time her mother has had a roof over her head that is hers. It was an emotional time for her parents – they were beyond grateful to have their privacy. Her mom and dad told her they felt like they were just starting their marriage. Before that, they had either lived apart (when Carmen was in the Mexican Army) or in a house with several other people. The three of them lived in a single bedroom. They had a little hot plate, and they could use the kitchen if they wanted to. She had to live in a room with her parents.

"After graduating Columbia, Rocío was more discouraged than ever. She did not have good job prospects after her unbelievably hard work over many, many years from the time she was twelve. This is a girl who looked on line and found a way to get into Columbia. She was on line constantly looking at all her possibilities. She was very proactive. And then all the work it took in high school and then all the work it took in college. And then she came out and could not get a job, because of her undocumented status. How unbelievably discouraging that was.

"She finally got a job at a real estate agency in Palo Alto. But we were having a long lunch and she told me she had to get out of there. 'I have changed their whole business plan and done everything I can do. I want to be in corporate America so badly.'

"I told Rocío that there was one person she ought to talk to – a friend of mine. Rocío told me she knew her, because she had house sat for her for two or three weeks one summer. I had recommended Rocío to her. This woman was one of the head people at Cisco Systems. I called my friend and asked if she would be willing to meet for coffee with Rocío and told her the situation. I told her she was undocumented. But Cisco was in the process of hiring 200 new young employees and this woman was in charge. I gave her Rocío's number and gave Rocío her number and they met for coffee. She got her an interview at the Company and told the people to get her a job. And she got a job.

"That was all happening while Obama was initiating the DACA program. Cisco was a little nervous and wanted to get the paperwork done. Rocío could not believe it. She got a great salary, she got DACA and she got a driver's license; she bought a car, she got her parents an apartment. It was like a fairy tale.

"Rocío is impatient already at Cisco. I have told her not to even think about making a change for two years. I do not care how bored you are – that paycheck is coming in every month. They like you, they have given you a raise. She has health care for the first time. But she is isolated, again. She may feel isolated, because Cisco is an aging company – it is not a young, dynamic company. And she really was bored there. But I do not think it is a good idea for her to start her own business. She has thought about working for a smaller company, where she would have a little more influence. She has spoken up to her bosses and gotten a few people to state what the problems are in the company. She is an outspoken person.

"I do not think it would be a bad idea if Rocío had to leave the States - for a corporate job - a sophisticated job - somewhere in the corporate world. I've asked, 'What's so terrible?' And Rocío answered, 'My parents.' If her dad wants to go back to Mexico, it could be a blessing in disguise. Her father is idealizing a return to Mexico. I do think he should be very careful about his influence over Rocío. Even if she went back to Mexico, she would get a good corporate job in Mexico City. She is an extremely educated person. And there are a lot of professionals in Mexico. So, she could survive that, and in ten years, it sounds like a million years to her, but if she left at thirty and came back at forty, she would probably marry down there; she would be in her own culture.

"I think she is working to feel part of this culture and to understand it. It will take a lifetime, because she was so excluded from it for so long. So much of your culture comes from your parents, we help our children. Our children have their parents as models. There are so many subtleties about being an immigrant.

"Rocío's social life has really evolved over the last year and a half. I think it is unfortunate that her entry into the U.S. may be through marriage. It colors dating. And she is very inexperienced in the dating world. She did not do any dating until her senior year in college.

"When we see each other, I will ask her, 'What do you think about everything?' I mainly listen. I give her advice where I can. I do think Rocío will come out on her feet. She will find a way. She is not brilliant, but she is just the most hardworking person you have ever met in your life.

"I think her biggest challenge is comfort in communication. She was not communicating well with people until she was at Eastside. So she is way behind. I would just say, Rocío is 'tough' to talk to – it does not flow. Part of this is just her personality – she is an introvert. Social things do not come easily. She works at them like she works at everything else.

"The future is very, very uncertain. She has DACA but only for 4 more years. Congress better do something about immigration. These are the 'dreamers', these are the kids, and they have no control over it."

## *Rocío*

"The lives of the Latinos are not part of the lives of most people, and we have to make it part of our lives. It will come. We are seeing more couples marrying people from different cultures. For example, I probably date more Caucasian men and over time I will probably end up marrying one. People will become aware, because my kids will be hanging out in an upper middle class neighborhood. I can stay here if I marry someone who is a citizen, but I have not found that person.

"Now I need to be more aware of it. I have the pressure because in these next two years I need for my career to take off and bring more awareness to this somehow. And on the other side, I have the pressure to take dating more seriously. I am 26. The people that you socialize with may not necessarily know about the situation. The reason is because we are all so very disconnected. Over time, we are somehow going to start drawing in and then you will see more interracial marriage and, of course, more connection, I think that is when the government will finally do something. But it will take time."

## *Carmen*

"I worry about my second daughter. The adopted girl we have in Mexico, she has her business already. My main concern is with Rocío, She will not last long working for someone else - she needs her own business. Whatever you want, I say to Rocío. I am on my way out, but do not worry a lot. I live with what we know today. Yesterday is past. You are tomorrow."

# Epilogue

We are a nation of immigrants. Our parents, or grandparents or even more distant ancestors, came to this country, carrying with them memories of their past lives, as well as their own personal hopes, not knowing what the future held for them. Perhaps, they have shared their stories with you.

The next time you hear a friend, or relative or neighbor say, "I think all the undocumented workers should be sent back," consider asking, "Have you spoken to your gardener? Have you spoken to your housekeeper? Have you asked them if they are here legally or are undocumented? Have you asked them why they left their native countries? Most importantly, have you asked them about their children, their aspirations and their dreams?"

# Discussion Questions

1. Salvador came to the U.S. with only the clothes he wore to cross the border. How did you feel when he cried because he did not have enough money to buy a shirt? How did you feel when he slapped his wife? Did this change your impression of him in any way? Do you think he will become a citizen?

2. Ernesto worked in Peru and Japan before coming to the U.S. What do you think of his attitude towards other workers? Towards the Japanese? The Mexicans? The Jews? Do you think he will get married to an American citizen and how do you feel about that?

3. In Lucia's story, was she wrong to rent out her sofa? How did you feel about the situation with their son's abuser? Lucia reported the abuse. Do you believe that other undocumented victims of abuse may hesitate to report crimes against themselves? Why?

4. Rubin came to the U.S. to be with his family. Why do you think he is unhappy here? Do you think his support of his unmarried son and his girlfriend and grandchild perpetuates a culture of unmarried parents?

5. Aurora sustained a serious injury while working in the U.S. and received a small settlement. Should that change her immigration status in the U.S.? Would a citizen have received a different settlement? Having worked in Peru, she is eligible for a pension. Should she leave the U.S. and retire to Peru?

6. Jose Luis completed three years of college in Mexico. Why do you think he has had difficulty finding employment in the U.S.?

7. We grant political refugees asylum in the U.S. In Laura's Story, do you think having an abusive husband is reason to grant her asylum? Both of Laura's children are in Guatemala. Should she return to be with her children or try to stay in the U.S. and earn money for the future?

8. Although Rocío's parents only completed a few years of school, Rocío graduated from a prestigious American university. How do you think Carmen and his wife helped Rocío achieve her accomplishments? What is Carmen's perception of his daughter and how does it differ from her perception of herself? Do you agree with Rocío's philosophy regarding day laborers? What should Rocío do if/when her DACA status is terminated?

9. Has this book changed your outlook on day workers? On illegal immigrants? If so, how? Have these stories impacted your views on the current U.S. immigration policy? Do you think it is different for each case? Why?

10. In the San Francisco Bay Area, the Day Worker Center of Mountain View is supported by the community and the police. Do you think that this is a good policy, even though many of the workers are undocumented?

11. There are approximately 11 million undocumented immigrants in the U.S. today. What do you think America's policy should be concerning them?

12. In many of the stories, the workers dream of returning to their home country. Do you think they will? If no, why not?

CPSIA information can be obtained
at www.ICGtesting.com
Printed in the USA
LVOW04s1742011016
506635LV00002B/47/P

9 781506 900544

# CHAMPIONS OF FREEDOM

## The Ludwig von Mises Lecture Series

CHAMPIONS OF FREEDOM
Volume 34

# Great Economists
## of the
## Twentieth Century

Hillsdale College Press
Hillsdale, Michigan 49242

*Hillsdale College Press*

CHAMPIONS OF FREEDOM
The Ludwig von Mises Lecture Series—Volume 34
*Great Economists of the Twentieth Century*

©2006 Hillsdale College Press, Hillsdale, Michigan 49242

First printing 2006

The views expressed in this volume are not necessarily the views of Hillsdale College.

Printed in the United States of America

*Front cover:* (from left to right for each row)
Friedrich A. Hayek, photo © The Nobel Foundation
Ludwig von Mises, photo courtesy of Hillsdale College
John Maynard Keynes, photo © Corbis
Frank Knight, photo courtesy of Special Collections Research Center, University of Chicago Library
James Buchanan, photo © The Nobel Foundation
Milton Friedman, photo courtesy Milton Friedman

Library of Congress Control Number: 2006936138
ISBN-10: 0-91308-03-0
ISBN-13: 978-0-916308-03-2

# Contents

# Contributors

**Robert J. Barro** is Paul M. Warburg Professor of Economics at Harvard University, a senior fellow of the Hoover Institution of Stanford University, and a research associate of the National Bureau of Economic Research. Dr. Barro was recently president of the Western Economic Association and vice president of the American Economic Association. Co-editor of Harvard's *Quarterly Journal of Economics*, he writes occasionally for *The Wall Street Journal*, where he was previously a contributing editor. His current research concerns the impact of rare disasters on asset markets and the interplay between religion and political economy. His recent books include *Economic Growth, Nothing Is Sacred: Economic Ideas for the New Millennium,* and *Getting It Right: Markets and Choices in a Free Society*. He is currently completing a new intermediate macroeconomics text titled *Macroeconomics: A Modern Approach*.

**Bruce Caldwell** is the Joe Rosenthal Excellence Professor of Economics at the University of North Carolina at Greensboro. He is a past president of the History of Economics Society, a past Executive Director of the International Network for Economic Method, and a Life Member of Clare Hall, Cambridge. Dr. Caldwell serves on the editorial boards of seven academic journals and has held fellowships at New York University, Cambridge University, and the London School of Economics. His current research has focused on the writings of the Nobel Prize-winning economist and social theorist Friedrich A. Hayek. He is author of *Beyond Positivism: Economic Methodology in the 20th*

*Century* and an intellectual biography of Hayek titled *Hayek's Challenge.* Since 2002 Dr. Caldwell has been the General Editor of *The Collected Works of F. A. Hayek,* which will be the definitive scholarly collection of Hayek's writings.

**Lee A. Coppock** is an economics professor in the Department of Economics at the University of Virginia. Dr. Coppock has also taught economics and quantitative business courses for several years at Hillsdale College. He received his Ph.D. from George Mason University, where he had the privilege of studying under James Buchanan, the 1986 winner of the Nobel Prize in Economics. Dr. Coppock's current research is on economic growth rates across U.S. states. He has published articles in several journals, including *Economics Letters, The Southern Economic Journal,* and *Constitutional Political Economy.*

**Donald J. Devine** is the Grewcock Professor of American Values at Bellevue University, as well as a columnist, writer, adjunct scholar at the Heritage Foundation, and a political and management consultant. Dr. Devine is also the editor of ConservativeBattleline.com, the on-line publication of the American Conservative Union Foundation. He served as director of the U.S. Office of Personnel Management under President Reagan, as Reagan's deputy director of political planning, and as a regional director in his campaigns. He was senior political consultant for Bob Dole's and Steve Forbes' presidential campaigns, and has been a consultant to Republican committees and many GOP campaigns. For fourteen years, he was associate professor of government and politics at the University of Maryland, specializing in democratic theory and public opinion. Dr. Devine is the author of seven books, including, most recently, *In Defense of the West: American Values Under Siege.*

**Richard M. Ebeling** is president of the Foundation for Economic Education. Dr. Ebeling was formerly the Ludwig von Mises Professor of Economics and Chairman of the Department of Economics and Business Administration at Hillsdale College, and has also served as a vice president of the Future of Freedom Foundation. He is the editor of the three-volume work, *Selected Writings of Ludwig von Mises*—two volumes of which have been published by Liberty Fund Press—which is primarily based upon papers of Mises unearthed in a formerly secret Moscow archive. He edited several volumes in the *Champions of Freedom* series from Hillsdale College Press, as well as other works, including *The Dangers of Socialized Medicine* and *The Tyranny of Gun Control*. His most recent book is *Austrian Economics and the Political Economy of Freedom*. Dr. Ebeling is currently working on an intellectual biography of Ludwig von Mises.

**Steve Forbes** is president and CEO of Forbes and editor-in-chief of *Forbes* magazine. Since he assumed his position in 1990, the company has expanded to include *Forbes Asia*, *ForbesLife*, Forbes.com, Forbes Conference Group, and Forbes Custom Media. Mr. Forbes was born in Morristown, New Jersey, and he received a BA in history from Princeton University. At Princeton, he was the founding editor of *Business Today*, which became the country's largest magazine published by students for students and which is still being published currently by Princeton undergraduates. The holder of more than twenty honorary degrees, Mr. Forbes serves on the boards of the Ronald Reagan Presidential Foundation, the Heritage Foundation and the Foundation for the Defense of Democracies. He is on the Board of Overseers of the Memorial Sloan-Kettering Cancer Center and on the Board of Visitors for the School of Public Policy of Pepperdine University. In both 1996 and 2000, Mr. Forbes campaigned for the Republican nomination for the presidency. He is the author most recently of *Flat Tax Revolution: Using a Postcard to Abolish the IRS*.

**Lord Robert Skidelsky** is Professor of Political Economy at Warwick University in England. Lord Skidelsky is a director of the Moscow School of Political Studies, founding member of the World Political Forum, and a member of the Advisory Council of the School of Advanced International and Area Studies, Shanghai University. He has written numerous articles on the economic and political aspects of international relations, including, most recently, "Keynes, Globalization and the Bretton Woods Institutions in the Light of Changing

Ideas about Markets." The author of *The World After Communism*, he is currently working on a book on globalization and international relations. His three-volume biography of the economist John Maynard Keynes received numerous prizes, including the Lionel Gelber Prize for International Relations and the Council on Foreign Relations Prize for International Relations. Lord Skidelsky was made a life peer in 1991 and elected a Fellow of the British Academy in 1994.

**Mark Skousen**, professional economist, investment expert, university professor, and author of over twenty books, holds the Benjamin Franklin Chair of Management at Grantham University. In 2004–2005, he taught economics and finance at Columbia Business School, Barnard College, and Columbia University. Since 1980, Skousen has been editor-in-chief of *Forecasts & Strategies*, an award-winning investment newsletter. He is also chairman of *Investment U*, one of the largest investment e-letters in the country. He is a former analyst for the CIA, a columnist to *Forbes* magazine, and past president of the Foundation for Economic Education (FEE). He has written for *The Wall Street Journal*, *Forbes*, and *Reason* magazine. His bestsellers include *The Making of Modern Economics*, *The Power of Economic Thinking*, *Vienna and Chicago*, and *Friends or Foes?* In 2006, he compiled and edited *The Compleated Autobiography, by Benjamin Franklin*. In honor of his work in economics, finance and management, Grantham University renamed its business school, "The Mark Skousen School of Business."

# Foreword

For 34 years we have collected the papers delivered at our annual Ludwig von Mises Lecture Series at Hillsdale College into book form, calling the series "Champions of Freedom." This volume, consisting of papers delivered in February of this year, has as its theme the great economists of the twentieth century.

The last of the economists discussed herein is Milton Friedman, winner of the Nobel Prize for Economics in 1976 and recipient of the Presidential Medal of Freedom in 1988. Dr. Friedman pioneered the "Chicago School" of economics, wrote many seminal books, and served as an advisor to three presidents.

Milton has also been a longtime friend of Hillsdale College. Just this past May, he was the keynote speaker at our National Leadership Seminar in San Francisco, which commemorated the 25th anniversary of his and his wife Rose's book, *Free to Choose: A Personal Statement*.

Two weeks ago we were saddened to hear of Milton's death at the age of 94. He will be remembered as one of the most stalwart and influential defenders of individual liberty of our time.

We dedicate this volume of Champions of Freedom to his memory.

LARRY P. ARNN
President
Hillsdale College
November 30, 2006

# Introduction

This volume of Champions of Freedom, the Ludwig von Mises Lecture Series, gives an insider's view of six of the great economists of the twentieth century. The authors who write about Milton Friedman and James Buchanan are not only scholars who have studied the work of these great economists, they know their subjects personally. The authors of the essays on John Maynard Keynes, Frank Knight, Ludwig von Mises, and Friedrich Hayek are renowned experts on the history of economic thought and the works of these economists. The editor of one of the world's premier business magazines discusses the battle between collectivism and free markets, a topic found in the writings of each of the great economists. An eminent political scientist provides insights on recent political trends and the relationship between the advances in economic theory these economists engendered and the translation of those ideas into public policy.

The six economists in this volume cover a range of thought. It includes, for example, John Maynard Keynes, as well as some of his fiercest critics. (Mises once wrote that "Keynes was not an innovator.... His contribution consisted rather in providing an apparent justification for the policies which were popular with those in power in spite of the fact that all economists viewed then as disastrous.")[1] The men discussed in this book include the teacher and mentor to several Nobel Prize winners, Austrian School economists, and the founder of Public Choice Theory. What is common to these six economists is what sets them apart from others: Not only are they all eminent scholars, their collective innovations have had a lasting influence on economic thought and public policy. All iconoclasts of a sort, none were afraid to go against the grain of accepted opinion.

Robert Skidelsky examines the interrelationship among the writings of Keynes, Friedman, and Hayek. While many would think that Keynes and Friedman were polar opposites in their views of the economic system, Skidelsky brings out the similarities in their analyses. The three economists might find common ground in their recognition of uncertainty and information deficiencies in the economy. Keynes was not simply an academic concerned with advancing his reputation among the intellectual elite; he had a passion for putting his theories into practice. His career was marked by extensive public service, both formal and informal. Skidelsky provides insights into Keynes's early training and how he changed the way economists analyze the overall economic system. He relates how Keynes's early work on probability theory is related to his theory of business cycles. Especially interesting is Skidelsy's analysis of the ways Keynes's formulations differed from the existing paradigm, how Keynes rearranged the framework of the business cycle debate, and the extent to which Keynes influenced public policy both during his lifetime and after.

Mark Skousen's essay is an excellent observation of Frank Knight as scholar, teacher, and individual. Knight's many writings provoke thought rather than present a body of consistent thought laid out through a model of economic order. Skousen highlights the side of Knight that would have displeased Harry Truman, who once asked for a one-handed economist because economists always say "on the one hand this, and on the other hand that." Knight's legacy lies in his challenge to readers and students to take his insights as a basis from which to begin to think for themselves. Perhaps this is why he counted three Nobel Laureates among his students.

Richard Ebeling's discussion of Ludwig von Mises benefits both from his personal relationship with Mrs. Mises and from his years of scholarly attention to the writings of the Austrian school. Mises was one of the most prescient economists of the twentieth century. During the 1920s he gave a complete argument for the failure of socialism, logically showing that it cannot provide wealth for the many. In 1927, his small volume, *Liberalism*, countered academic and popular opinion, and essentially predicted the economic collapse brought by the Great Depression, the failure of public works projects to reduce unemployment, and the advent of World War II. Mises demonstrated that capitalism is the only economic system that can create wealth for all, that it is consistent with individual liberty, and that it promotes world peace. Professor Ebeling has been instrumental in keeping Mises's writings alive and carrying on the exchange of ideas that Mises believed would lead to a better society.

Robert Barro's paper is an introduction not just to the works of Milton Friedman, but to the man as well. Professor Barro is able to draw on his long-time friendship with Friedman to give the reader a feeling for the inner workings of the great economist. While Friedman does not believe that an academic economist should attempt to influence policy by accepting a position in government, he is certainly very concerned with the implementation of his ideas. Friedman felt that an academic can best serve by making the case for certain policies by demonstrating the logical correctness of one's argument, testing it empirically, and then explaining it to the mass audience. His book *Free to Choose*, and the documentary based on it, fit within this strategy. In the end, Friedman has had an influence on a raft of issues, such as monetary rules, school choice, privatization of social security, and a flat rate income tax. In each case, Friedman, like the other economists discussed in this volume, stood by his ideas in the face of criticism from the mainstream of his profession and eventually turned his analysis into the accepted wisdom.

Bruce Caldwell, the eminent Hayekian scholar, examines who, among the great economists discussed in this volume, has the broadest scope. Friedrich Hayek's works were initially greeted by the profession as anachronistic and reactionary. Like Mises, he battled hard against the ideas of central planning and delved deeply into the problems of information that condemned central planning to failure. Winning the Nobel Prize almost brought him into mainstream recognition, but even today the wealth of knowledge presented in Hayek's extensive writings is not given sufficient recognition. Reading just the endnotes to his *Constitution of Liberty* provides the reader with a gold mine of information and research.

Lee A. Coppock was a student of James Buchanan at George Mason University, in Fairfax, Virginia, where Professor Buchanan still resides. Coppock's essay covers not only Buchanan's work on Public Choice, for which he is most renowned, but provides enlightenment of a broad range of his important work. Once again we have an economist who challenges the mainstream thought, suffering isolation until his ideas eventually became accepted. Coppock points out that Buchanan, a student of Frank Knight, was somewhat conflicted in his early years at Chicago, describing himself as a Libertarian-Socialist. Buchanan's early work on externalities and clubs undermined the case for government as necessarily superior to markets in the case of externalities and public goods. His *Calculus of Consent* took the issue one step further and addressed government failure as the counterpoint to the work on market failure being done at the time. Buchanan showed that while one may not like the market outcome, one cannot assume a benevolent government that will improve the outcome. One must instead understand how government works, and understand the system incentives that individuals acting as politicians and bureaucrats follow, in order to determine the best policy.

Sherlock Holmes once chastised Dr. Watson by saying, "you see but you do not observe." Steve Forbes is an observer. His essay discusses how the West drifted into acceptance of central planning and the unobserved aspects of market capitalism. In particular, Forbes delves into the morality of capitalism, and presents his argument for how capitalism can gain the moral high ground. As he points out, "philanthropy and business, charity and democratic capitalism are not opposites, but two sides of the same coin." He updates Mises's point that the only way to succeed in a capitalist society is to please others. Rather than decry the advances of capitalism as mainstream media has a tendency to do, Forbes shows how the market process benefits the poor, the environment, and the moral standing of society.

Political scientist Donald Devine examines how the politics of the twentieth century have responded to the great economic debate over socialism and capitalism. Devine questions why the superiority of markets over socialism has been established in the economic community, even as we witness the ever-present growth of government. This is particularly disconcerting when both houses of Congress—as well as the presidency—are under the control of the political party most associated with limited government. Devine believes that because politicians are able to manipulate public opinion, they take advantage of a rationally ignorant public to expand their power base, which is government. As he puts it: Politics trumps economics.

This volume, as well as the conference from which these essays came, lays testimony to the triumph of intellectuals who are willing to overturn the existing paradigm, even if it means being an outcast for much of their careers. While Keynes's ideas were used to expand the role of government, even he thought his theories were a counterpoint to socialism. The rest of the six great economists honored here are staunch defenders of individual liberty and market capitalism as the social order. While Steve Forbes demonstrates that a major media outlet is capable of making a clear and reasoned case for limited government and reliance on markets, Devine believes that the case for liberty needs to be carried forward into the political realm. Readers of this volume will be well-prepared for the task.

GARY WOLFRAM
George Munson Professor
of Political Economy
Hillsdale College

## Note

[1]Ludwig von Mises, *Planning for Freedom*, 4th ed. (Spring Mills, PA: Libertarian Press, 1980), p. 69.

STEVE FORBES

# The Great (and Continuing) Economic Debate of the Twentieth Century

The great economic debate of the twentieth century was between collectivists and free marketers. In one sense, the free marketers won: When the Berlin Wall fell in 1989, it was widely acknowledged that Soviet socialism had been a catastrophic, not to say murderous, failure. But in another sense, the debate continues. Democratic capitalism still has not vanquished the idea of collectivism. Far from it.

At the beginning of the last century, free markets seemed to be on the ascendancy everywhere. But two events gave collectivism its lease on life. The first was World War I. In addition to the slaughter—and to breeding the ideologies of communism, state fascism, Nazism, and even the Islamic extremism we are battling today—World War I served as an intoxicating drug to those in the West who believed that a handful of people in government could manage affairs better than the messy way in which free peoples tend to do so. Massive increases in government powers, coupled with massive increases in taxation, gave many the idea that we can achieve massive increases in produc- tion by commandeering the financial resources of society.

The second event that served as a boon to collectivism was the Great Depression, which was widely seen as a free market failure. This view was false. Misguided government policies were at fault— the Smoot-Hawley Tariff, for instance, which dried up the flow of capital into and out of the country. If you track the stock market crash of 1929, it parallels the course of this tariff bill through Congress. When Smoot-Hawley arose in the fall of 1929, the markets fell; when it looked like the tariff bill was sidetracked in late 1929, the markets revived (the Dow Jones went up 50 percent from its lows in November); in the spring of 1930 it was signed into law, and the rest is history.

There were other factors at work in the Great Depression, of course, such as President Hoover's gigantic tax increases of 1931. But despite the fact that these also involved bad policies, the lesson taken away by many was that economies will implode unless the government manages them. John Maynard Keynes, the intellectual guiding light behind New Deal economics, believed that an economy was like a machine: If you put doses of money into or pull money out at the right times, he thought you could achieve an equilibrium. This idea that government can drive an economy as if it were an automobile has had baleful consequences.

Other leading economists at the time, such as Joseph Schumpeter, recognized that an economy is an aggregate of disparate activities—thus, the idea of achieving equilibrium, while it makes for a neat theory, is nonsense in the real world. A vibrant economy is full of constant disequilibria: New enterprises rise up, old ones decline, and so on. Snapshots of such economies mean very little. In the real world, therefore, free markets operate rationally and efficiently in a way that government regulators simply cannot.

Here in America we came to this realization at the end of the 1970s. Following World War II, we largely bought into the idea that government must play an active role to prevent the economy from going off the cliff. But in the late 1970s, the devastation of inflation and high taxes brought about a reassessment. With the election of Ronald Reagan, the U.S. took a step back from Keynesian economics. Since then, as Western Europe has stagnated—creating, for instance, only a fraction of the private-sector jobs that the U.S. has created—our country has undergone an economic revival.

Nonetheless, democratic capitalism often still seems to be on the defensive. Why?

## Is Democratic Capitalism Good?

One of the great vulnerabilities of capitalism is the perception that it is somehow less than moral, if not positively amoral. A common view of business was depicted in the movie *Wall Street*, in which Michael Douglas's character made famous the phrase, "Greed is good." Capitalism is widely seen as promoting selfishness. We tolerate it because it gives us jobs and prosperity, but many look on this as a Faustian bargain. Charity and capitalism are seen as polar opposites. Thus there is a phrase that is often used today—I myself use it from time to time without thinking—which is "giving back." If you have succeeded in business, it is counted a good thing if you "give back" to the community. Charity is, of course, a good thing. The problem with this phrase is its implication that by succeeding we have taken something that wasn't ours. The same idea is summed up in the cynical saying, "Behind every great fortune lies a great crime." This way of thinking about democratic capitalism is wrong.

In fact, philanthropy and capitalism are two sides of the same coin. To succeed in business in a free market economy, one must meet the needs and wants of others. Someone may have a terrible personality—and be the kind of person who makes babies cry, or who thinks that he or she is only in business to make money for himself/herself—but the bottom line is that such individuals can only succeed if they produce a product or service that people want. This system weaves intricate webs of cooperation that we don't even think about. Someone who opens a restaurant assumes that farmers will grow the food, that processors will process and package it, and that truckers will deliver it (once they have been supplied the fuel to do so by the oil companies, and on and on). These marvelous webs of cooperation happen every day throughout a free economy. No one is commanding it. It occurs spontaneously in a way that economists like Schumpeter understood.

Free markets force people to look to the future and take risks. Misers do not found companies like Microsoft. Nor should we look on it as immoral for people to work for the betterment of themselves and their families. We are all born with God-given talents, and it is right to develop them to the fullest. The great virtue of democratic capitalism is that it guarantees that as we develop our talents, we are contributing to the public good. Statistics show that the United States is both the most commercial nation and the most philanthropic nation in human history. This is no paradox. The two go hand-in-hand.

Another vulnerability of democratic capitalism is that although it leads to progress and to an increase in our societal standard of living, progress is usually disruptive. This allows collectivists to play on people's natural fear of change. We saw this with the rise of industrialism in the nineteenth century. The paintings and writings of that time often depicted a pastoral agricultural past. Then railroads came along to disrupt the canals, and cars came along to disrupt the railroads. Buggy-whip makers and blacksmiths were done for. One can imagine what *60 Minutes* would have been investigating 100 years ago: poor blacksmiths being put out of work by Henry Ford. Likewise, when TV came along in the late 1940s and early 1950s, most movie theaters in the country went broke. Now the Internet is disrupting newspapers and Craig's List is disrupting classified advertising. Disruptions are inevitable in a free market system. The political challenge is to allow these disruptions to take place—they are ultimately constructive, after all—rather than reacting in a way that stymies progress.

In recent decades, collectivists have hijacked the cause of environmentalism to promote their agenda. I am not talking about the desire to have clean water or clean air; we are all in favor of that. One of the great accomplishments of the last century was removing lead from the air we breathe. Saving tigers and elephants from extinction is also a good thing. I am talking about using the mantra of environmentalism to try to control the economy in the way the old-time socialists wanted to, by breathing hellfire and damnation on those who don't subscribe to that new religion. But if the goal is to improve the environment, increasing government regulation and destroying manufacturing is counterproductive. Affluence is the friend, not the enemy, of the environment. As people become better off, they want a higher quality of living, including environmental improvements. And it is new technology that drives such improvements. Consider the East coast of the United States. Even though its population has more than doubled—in some areas, it has tripled—and even though there are more developments, malls, and urban sprawl, there are more trees on the East coast today than there were 80 years ago. Why? Technology allows us to grow more food on less land. Technology is a friend of the environment.

## Additional Collectivist Myths

Three additional myths are used to promote collectivism. One is the idea that demand is the key to economic growth. Collectivist economists often talk about means to increase "aggregate demand," as if that would ensure that the economy will grow. Following Keynes, they assume that the economy is like a machine. But again, the economy is an aggregate of tens of millions of people, millions of businesses, millions of technologies. We don't know how it interacts on a day-to-day basis. We don't know what's going to work or not work. Who could have conceived of eBay 10 to 12 years ago? Today, 400,000 people make their livings on eBay. When Google was launched, there were ten other search engines. Who would have thought another one was needed? But Google found a way to do it better and ended up on top.

Innovation is the key. No matter what the industry—railroads, cars, computers, or the Internet—risk-taking is messy. It is often irrational, and seemingly wasteful. But it is the only way to determine what works and what doesn't.

Another collectivist myth concerns trade. If I were dictator of the world, even though I believe in the First Amendment, I would ban trade numbers, especially merchandise trade numbers. They just lead to mischief. We are given the impression that a trade surplus is like a profit and a trade deficit is like a loss. But trade is not a transaction between countries. It takes place between parties. For example, *Forbes* magazine buys paper. For the 88 years we have been in existence, we have run a trade deficit with our paper suppliers. If you look at just that trade deficit, you might think we are doing poorly. But if you look at the two parties involved, you see that this is not the case. The paper supplier thinks he's going to make money selling his paper. We think we're going to make money by taking the paper and putting print on it, adding value. So it is a mutually profitable transaction, even if it looks like a trade deficit. Or consider the act of having a book printed in Taiwan. Looking at the trade number alone, it appears there is a $2 trade deficit with Taiwan. Yet when the printed book arrives in the U.S., it retails for $24.95. The value is added here. The author gets a cut, the publisher gets a cut, the booksellers get a cut, the distributors get a cut, and the remainder stores get a cut. Something similar happened with the iPod: A lot of its parts are made overseas, but where is most of the value added? Here in the United States. North America has had a merchandise trade deficit for 350 out of the last 400 years, and we have done very well, thank you.

The final myth concerns budget deficits. Milton Friedman said several years ago that if he had a choice between a federal budget of $1 trillion that was in the red and a federal budget of $2 trillion that was balanced, he would take the former. Deficits, in and of themselves, are not evil. Deficits must be put in context, because Washington's inability to curb spending is often used as an excuse to raise taxes.


## Principles of Prosperity

There are five basic principles of economic growth.

First and foremost is the rule of law: Without individual equality before the law, entrepreneurs cannot challenge already existing businesses. Alliances between the latter and government regulators who place barriers before entrepreneurs must be guarded against.

The second essential principle is property rights. We take for granted in this country that if you buy a piece of property everyone acknowledges that you own it. Most countries don't have that kind of uniform property system. A few years ago, Hernando DeSoto, a great economist from Peru, saw that in countries like his, although there is entrepreneurial activity, there isn't the corresponding prosperity found in the U.S. And he wondered why. In his recent book, *The Mystery of*

*Capital: Why Capitalism Triumphs in the West and Fails Everywhere Else*,[1] one of the key factors he cites is the absence of a legal foundation for property rights in so many countries. In Brazil's shantytowns, an individual may know that he owns the house in which he lives, and his neighbors may know it, but the fact is not recognized elsewhere.

Mr. DeSoto was asked by the Egyptian government a few years ago to determine who owns the businesses and residences in Egypt. His finding was that 88 percent of the businesses in Egypt are illegal. Why is that? Here in the U.S., it is possible to set up a business legally in a matter of days. In Egypt, it takes a couple of years. It requires dealing with numerous bureaucracies—and doling out numerous bribes. It makes sense to proceed "informally." On the other hand, running a business outside the law limits its growth. Most "informal" enterprises never grow beyond the level of family enterprises, because if they get too big, they might attract the attention of the tax collector.

DeSoto's group also reported that 92 percent of Egyptian housing is illegal. A family may have a deed to their house, but only a few miles away, that deed won't be recognized. In Egypt, as in so many other places, there is no uniform system of establishing and protecting property rights. As a result, four billion people around the world own $9 trillion of assets that amount to dead capital.

What do I mean by "dead capital"? Remember that in the U.S., the most important source of capital for new ventures is not Wall Street, the local banker, or the venture capitalist. It is the mortgage market. To finance a business start-up, people often increase their mortgage or take out a second mortgage. This is not possible in countries like Egypt. Understanding this was key to Japan's post-World War II economic boom. General MacArthur reformed a feudalistic property system, from one in which the peasants had only an informal system of property exchange into a system with formalized property rights. Immediately, the Japanese economy took off. The importance of property rights is not sufficiently recognized by those of us who take them for granted.

The third principle of economic prosperity is low taxes. Taxes are not just a means of raising revenue for the government. They are also a price. Income taxes are a price paid for working; taxes on profits are the price paid for being successful in business; taxes on capital gains are the price paid for taking risks. In light of this, the importance of low taxes is easy to see: When the price of good things is low—like work, success, and risk-taking—you tend to get more of them. Raise the price of these good things and you get fewer of them. In 2003, tax rates were lowered in the U.S., and the economy started to grow again. As we have seen time and again, tax cuts do not mean a loss of tax revenue. By increasing incentives, the government comes out ahead. Washington's revenues in the last fiscal year were up 15 percent—$100 billion above expectations. Washington's problem is not revenue, but spending.

The fourth principle is making it simpler to launch legal businesses. Getting bureaucracy out of the way will inject a new vibrancy into an economy.

The fifth and final principle is free trade. Expanding markets and creating greater opportunity for trade benefits us all.

The great economic debate continues into the twenty-first century, despite the proven superiority of free markets in terms of delivering prosperity, because misperceptions are keeping democratic capitalism from capturing the moral high ground. Dispelling these misperceptions should be our priority as we carry on that debate in the years ahead.

## Note

[1]Hernando DeSoto, *The Mystery of Capital: Why Capitalism Triumphs in the West and Fails Everywhere Else* (New York: Basic Books, 2003).

Bruce Caldwell

# Friedrich A. Hayek: Economist, Social Theorist, and Philospher of Liberty

My interest in Friedrich A. Hayek, the polymath economist, social theorist, and philosopher of liberty, has turned into fascination.

I did not come to Hayek as a conservative or a libertarian; I came to him as an intellectual historian, a historian of economic thought. There are a number of obvious reasons why a historian of thought might find Hayek interesting.

1. He lived a long time. Born in 1899, he died in 1992: His life spanned the twentieth century.
2. He was a prolific writer. His first significant work was a student essay on psychology, completed in 1920, which became the starting point for his remarkable book on psychology, *The Sensory Order*. His last book, *The Fatal Conceit*, appeared in 1988.
3. His archives are massive. Housed at the Hoover Institution at Stanford, the Hayek archives keep growing; there are now 130 boxes. To give an idea of what this means, his extensive correspondence with Karl Popper fills only two folders in Box 44—and that box contains 29 other folders as well.
4. He was controversial. People either love or hate Hayek, which has given rise to multiple interpretations of his work. Some of these interpretations are very bad, and correcting bad interpretations is what historians of thought try to do.
5. He had a knack for being at the right place at the right time. This point requires some elaboration.

Hayek grew up in fin de siécle Vienna, one of the most fertile places and moments in the history of modern Western thought. He learned economics from Friedrich von Wieser and Ludwig von Mises: the former was his major professor, the latter became his mentor. Among his classmates were people like Oskar Morgenstern, one of the inventors of game theory. After university he went to the United States and, armed with letters of introduction from Joseph Schumpeter, he met the most prominent American economists. He sat in on the American institutionalist Wesley Clair Mitchell's history of economic thought class, and gave the last paper in J. B. Clark's last seminar.

In the early 1930s, Lionel Robbins invited Hayek to the London School of Economics. (As I tell my students, if you go to the main library at LSE today, you are in the Lionel Robbins building.) This led to his appointment, at the age of 32, to a named chair. Upon his arrival he engaged in a series of debates with some of the leading lights of the profession. He debated with John Maynard Keynes and Piero Sraffa over monetary theory and the theory of the business cycle; with Frank Knight and Nicholas Kaldor over capital theory; with Oskar Lange and Evan Durbin over socialism. On his friend Gottfried Haberler's recommendation, Hayek invited the Austrian philosopher Karl Popper to give a paper in his seminar, and was instrumental in bringing Popper to the London School of Economics after the war. In 1950 he moved to the Committee on Social Thought at the University of Chicago, just as the Chicago School of economics was being formed by Milton Friedman, Aaron Director, and, a little later, George Stigler—all of whom Hayek had invited to the first Mont Pèlerin meeting, which he organized in 1947.

Hayek knew all of the best minds of the profession. In telling Hayek's story, one also tells, from a specific point of view, the story of the development of economics in the twentieth century. I say from a specific point of view because Hayek disagreed with just about everyone he came into contact with. If he was always in the right place at the right time, it was usually with the wrong ideas—or so it must have seemed to his contemporaries.

Hayek first began his assault on socialism in the 1930s, when all right-minded people viewed it as a middle way between a failed capitalist system and the totalitarianisms of the fascist and communist variety.

He famously dubbed this mistake "the muddle of the middle." As an Austrian School economist he was suspicious of the use of aggregates in economics because they hide the relative price movements that are so fundamental to the workings of a market. Thus he was a critic of the Keynesian revolution before it had even properly taken place. He was greatly skeptical of the merits of empirical work (a position he shared with Keynes, as well as others), devoting the first chapter of his first book, *Monetary Theory and the Trade Cycle*, to its critique. Because of this, he missed the econometrics revolution. Though he helped introduce general equilibrium analysis to English-speaking economists, he also questioned its usefulness for shedding light on the workings of a dynamic market process: Thus he missed the formalist revolution of the 1950s as well. Just when specialization was sweeping the scientific disciplines, his work was increasingly multidisciplinary and integrative. When not dismissed as reactionary or anachronistic, as was the case with his economic and political philosophy, Hayek's work was ignored, as with the case of his book on psychology. In short, he was a man almost systematically out of step with his time.

Hayek's response to this was classic. He sat down and quietly tried to figure out why so many supposedly smart people got so many things wrong. His answer was very appealing to a historian of ideas: In such works as "Scientism and the Study of Society," "The Counter-Revolution of Science," and "Individualism: True and False," he identified a complex of ideas that had gradually but inexorably led the West to embrace what he called "the scientistic prejudice" or "the planning mentality," both variants of what he ultimately dubbed "constructivist rationalism."

This makes Hayek a fascinating figure. What is truly remarkable, though, is how often over the course of time the *ideas* of this academic gadfly have come to be vindicated.

Hayek is most famous for his critique of socialism, a project that built on the work of his mentor, Ludwig von Mises. Mises had noted that in its purest form socialism calls for the total abolition of private firms, which are replaced by state ownership of the means of production. But if the state owns the means of production, there are no markets in which factors of production are bought and sold. Consequently no prices are attached to them. Mises pointed out that the absence of market prices means that factory managers have no information about which resources are relatively scarce and which are relatively plentiful. He concluded that socialist economies would be much less efficient in using resources than free market economies. Market prices inform market participants about the relative scarcity of goods; by bidding for them, market participants help ensure that resources flow toward their highest valued uses.

Hayek's contributions nicely complement those made by von Mises. He focused on what would come to be called "the knowledge problem"; that is, how to coordinate human action in a world in which knowledge is dispersed. For Hayek, the market system was a key coordinating mechanism. In a market system, millions of agents make millions of consumption and production decisions every day. Their decisions are based in part on the vast array of prices that they confront in the market, prices that give them information about relative scarcities. But in addition, agents have access to particular bits of knowledge that are specific to time and place, some of them tacit. This knowledge shapes the decisions that are made. Because their market activity reflects this local knowledge, the actions these agents decide to make causes this information to become embedded in the array of market prices. In short, market activity is both *price-determined* (prices shape what people do) and *price-determining* (what people do, based on local knowledge, determines what prices are). In this way market prices coordinate the specific knowledge of time and place possessed by millions of market agents. Freely adjusting market prices act as a giant communication network.

Hayek began having these insights in the 1930s, but his clearest statement of them is, perhaps, in his seminal 1945 article, "The Use of Knowledge in Society," which is still quoted today by economists working in the economics of information.

In addition to articulating how markets work, Hayek's arguments undermined the various socialist proposals that were on offer, most of which required some form of price fixing. For those who replaced this with "trial and error" adjustment procedures, Hayek questioned whether such a process undertaken by a state bureaucracy could ever match the speed of adjustment provided by a dynamic market process, fueled as it is by the actions of alert entrepreneurs for whom every error represents a profit opportunity. Still other of his opponents made arguments that went far beyond economics. These socialists promised a society that was not only more efficient than capitalism, but also more just, where individuals have more self-determination and greater political freedom, and where scientific reasoning would be used to improve upon a host of outdated social institutions. To challenge these utopian visions, Hayek needed to develop political, historical, and ethical arguments against them. He did this in what was to become his most famous book, *The Road to Serfdom*.

Against the idea that democratic socialism would bring with it greater political freedom, Hayek countered that planning the economy would soon lead to increased political control. One virtue of a market economy is that it allows people to express their very different tastes and, for those with the means, to get them satisfied. In a planned economy, socialist managers must decide which goods, and how much of them, are produced. Any particular mix of goods will be favored by some groups and opposed by others. Gridlock will ensue. If progress is to be made, even democratically elected socialist regimes will at some point be forced to make decisions for the people, which is much easier to do if political dissension is suppressed. To run a fully planned economy successfully, Hayek claimed that its socialist managers ultimately must secure control of the political process as well. If one looks at the world and examines those economies where top-down central planning has been put into effect, it is clear that restrictions—often severe—on both political and personal freedoms either accompanied the move or followed very soon thereafter.

Though famous as a critic of socialism, Hayek made a number of positive contributions to social theory. In such books as *The Constitution of Liberty* and *Law, Legislation and Liberty*, he made the case for a return to a liberal constitutional democratic market order. I use all those adjectives to signal that Hayek was no Dr. Pangloss about laissez-faire: He believed that a market system by itself holds few guarantees. It is only when embedded in a set of other social institutions—a democratic polity, with strong constitutional protection of a private sphere of individual activity, operating under the rule of law, with laws that are general, prospective, and reasonably stable, with well-defined, enforced, and transferable property rights—would a market system have a chance of working. In these mature works Hayek expounds his philosophy of liberty, describing and defending the complex of institutions, norms, and beliefs that he felt would best promote the discovery, transmission, and use of knowledge so that individuals are able to use that knowledge to succeed in the pursuit of their chosen goals. Hayek's ideas have been taken as foundational by such later Nobel Prize winners as Douglass North and Vernon Smith, whose works in new institutional economics and experimental economics, respectively, seek in their own ways to find the appropriate institutional mix for a free society.

This only touches on some of Hayek's contributions. His work on the informational role of prices is, of course, now considered a seminal insight within economics. His work on complex self-generating and adaptive "spontaneous orders" has piqued the interest of those exploring the relevance of complexity theory, neural network models, and agent-based computational models for economic and social analysis. Philosophers of mind, evolutionary biologists, and neuroscientists have been attracted to his view of the brain as a hierarchical classifier system, as revealed in his remarkable book on the foundations of psychology, *The Sensory Order.*

Most remembered as a philosopher of liberty, F. A. Hayek was also a polymath social theorist. Fascinating in itself, his intellectual journey helps us to better comprehend the contours of the development of twentieth-century social thought. A man of ideas, his life demonstrates the vital importance of ideas in the ongoing battle for liberty.

RICHARD M. EBELING

# Ludwig von Mises:
# The Political Economist of Liberty

Over a professional career that spanned almost three-quarters of the twentieth century, the Austrian economist Ludwig von Mises was without any exaggeration one of the leading and most important defenders of economic liberty. The ideas of individual freedom, the market economy, and limited government that he defended in the face of the rising tide of socialism, fascism, and the interventionist welfare state have had few champions as clear and persuasive as Mises. It is also certainly the case that he was the most comprehensive and consistent critic of all forms of modern collectivism. Furthermore, his numerous writings on the political, economic, and social principles of classical liberalism and the market order remain as fresh and relevant as when he penned them decades ago.[1]

Born in the city of Lemberg in the old Austro-Hungarian Empire on September 29, 1881, Mises came from a prominent family of Jewish merchants and businessmen. A few months before Ludwig was born, his great-grandfather, Mayer Rachmiel Mises, was honored with a nobility title for his service to the Emperor Franz Joseph as a leader of the Jewish community in Lemberg.[2]

Ludwig's father, Arthur, moved his family to Vienna in the early 1890s where he worked as a civil engineer for the Imperial railway system. Ludwig attended one of the city's leading academic gymnasiums as preparation for university studies. He entered the University of Vienna in 1900, and received his doctoral degree in jurisprudence in 1906. In 1909, he was employed by the Vienna Chamber of Commerce, Crafts, and Industry, and continued to work at the Chamber as a senior economic analyst until he left Vienna in 1934 to accept a full-time teaching position at the Graduate Institute of International Studies in Geneva. In addition to his work at the Chamber, Mises taught at the University of Vienna, lead an internationally renowned interdisciplinary private seminar, and founded the Austrian Institute for Business Cycle Research in 1927, with a young Friedrich A. Hayek as its first director.[3]

It was during his years in Geneva, between 1934 and 1940, that Mises wrote his greatest work in economics, *Human Action: A Treatise on Economics*.[4] In the summer of 1940, as the Nazi war machine was finishing its conquest of Western Europe, Mises and his wife made their way from Switzerland to the United States, where he spent the rest of his life continuing his writings and teaching at New York University. He died October 10, 1973, at the age of 92.

In both Vienna between the two World Wars and again in post-World War II America, Mises demonstrated a unique ability to attract intellectually creative students, thus fostering new generations of scholars to continue the ideas of the Austrian School of Economics.

## Ludwig von Mises and the
## Historical Context of His Time

An appreciation of Mises's defense of freedom requires an understanding of the political and ideological trends of the first half of the twentieth century. Throughout most of the nineteenth century, "liberalism" had meant belief in and devotion to personal freedom, constitutionally limited government, the sanctity of private property, as well as freedom of enterprise at home and free trade among the nations of the world.

But even before the First World War many of those who labeled themselves "liberals" were in fact advocates of what a few decades earlier, in prewar Imperial Germany, had been called "state socialism." For almost forty years before the First World War, many of the leading German economists, historians, and political scientists—who became widely known as members of the German Historical School—had argued that the socialists had been correct in their criticisms of free market capitalism. The unregulated market, they said, resulted in the exploitation of workers and a disregard of the "national interest." Where the socialists had gone wrong, they insisted, was in their radical demand for a revolutionary overthrow of the entire existing social order.

What Germany needed instead, they stated, was "state socialism," under which social reforms would be introduced to ameliorate the supposed "excesses" of unbridled laissez-faire. The German Historical School supported and encouraged the imposition of the modern welfare state by the German "Iron Chancellor," Otto von Bismarck, in the 1880s and 1890s. Socialized medicine, state-managed old-age pensions, minimum-wage laws, and government-sponsored public housing and recreational facilities would provide "cradle to grave" security for the "working classes," and would thus lure them away from the more radical proposals of the Marxian socialists.[5]

At the same time, government regulation of industry and agriculture through tariffs, cartels, and subsidies, as well as production and price controls, would assure that the activities of the "capitalist class" would be harnessed to what the political authorities considered to be in the "national interest." Pragmatism and expediency in all economic and social policy decisions were hailed as the highest forms of political wisdom and "statesmanship," in place of "inflexible" constitutional restraints that limited the discretionary power for government intervention.

Members of the German Historical School argued that old-fashioned classical liberalism had been purely "negative" in its understanding of freedom and in advocating that government's role was simply to secure the lives, liberty, and property of the citizenry from violence, aggression, and fraud. Government, they said, had to be more "positive" and active in providing social safety nets for the masses against the uncertainties of life. Hence, they and their "progressive" followers in England, France, and especially the United States soon were referring to their ideas as a newer and more enlightened "liberalism," which would create a truer and more complete "freedom" from want and worry.[6] The concept of liberalism, most particularly in the United States, was changing from a political and economic philosophy of individual liberty and free enterprise under the rule of law and limited government to a notion of political paternalism with an increasingly intrusive hand of government in the social and commercial affairs of its citizens.[7]

The last decades of the nineteenth century also saw the growth of two other modern forms of collectivism: socialism and nationalism. Their common premise was that the individual and his interests were always potentially in conflict with the best interests of society as a whole. The Marxists claimed to have discovered the inescapable "laws of history," which demonstrated that the emergence of the division of labor and private property split society into inherently antagonistic social "classes." Those who owned the means of production earned rent and profit by extracting a portion of the wealth produced by the nonowning workers whom the owners of productive property employed in agriculture and industry.

Eventually this class conflict would lead, through a process of historical evolution, to a radical and revolutionary change in which the workers would rise up and expropriate the property of the capitalists. After having socialized the means of production, the new workers' state would introduce central planning in place of the previous decentralized and profit-oriented production plans of the now expropriated capitalists. Socialist central planning, it was claimed, would generate a level of production and a rising standard of living far exceeding anything experienced during the "capitalist phase" of human history. This process would culminate in a "post-scarcity" world in which all of man's wants and wishes would be fully satisfied, with selfishness and greed abolished from the face of the earth.[8]

The proponents of aggressive nationalism argued that there was, indeed, an inherent conflict among men in the world.[9] This antagonism, however, was not based on social classes as the Marxian socialists defined them. Instead, these conflicts were between nations and national groups. Unfortunately, the nationalist ideologues said, individuals within nations often acted in ways inconsistent with the best interests of the nation to which they belonged. Thus the particular interests of businessmen, workers, and those in various professional groups had to be regulated and controlled for the furtherance of the greater national good. As a result, aggressive nationalism dovetailed quite harmoniously—especially, though certainly not exclusively, in Imperial Germany—with the interventionist and welfare-statist policies of state socialism and the newer "progressive" liberalism.

Commercial and military conflict between the nations of the world was inevitable in the eyes of these nationalists. The prosperity of any one nation could only come at the expense of other nations. Hence, the task of all national statesmen was to foster the power and triumph of their own national group through the conquest and impoverishment of others around the world. Since no nation would willingly accept its own political and material destruction, war was an inescapable aspect of the human condition. Militarism and the martial spirit were likewise hailed as both necessary and superior to the "individualistic" and "pacifistic" spirit of production and trade.[10]

The culmination of these collectivist tendencies was the outbreak of the First World War in 1914, an analysis of the causes and consequences of which Ludwig von Mises offered in his 1919 volume, *Nation, State, and Economy.*[11] The Great War, as it was called, not only brought forth the triumph of the nationalistic spirit; it also saw the imposition of various forms of socialist central planning as virtually all the belligerent nations either nationalized or thoroughly controlled private industry and agriculture in the name of the wartime national emergency. The governments at war also established welfare-statist rationing and regulation of all consumer production since the needs of total war required total state responsibility for the supposed well-being of entire populations.

Out of the ashes of the First World War there arose new totalitarian states, first with the establishment of a communist dictatorship in Russia following the Bolshevik Revolution of 1917 under Lenin's leadership, and then with the rise to power of Mussolini and his Fascist Party in Italy in 1922. Both the communists and the fascists rejected the ideas and the institutions of classical liberalism. Constitutional government, the rule of law, civil liberties, and economic freedom were declared by both variations on the collectivist theme as reactionary hindrances to the success of, respectively, the worker's state in Soviet Russia and national greatness in Fascist Italy. Both communism and fascism insisted that the individual needed to be "reeducated" and made to conform to the wider socialist or nationalist good. The individual was to be reduced to a cog in the machinery of the all-powerful and all-planning state.[12]

Germany's defeat in the war had resulted in political and economic chaos, which culminated in the disastrous hyperinflation of the early 1920s.[13] Many of the social and cultural anchors of German society were unhinged by the war and the inflation.[14] A growing number of Germans longed for a "Leader" to guide them out of the morass of political instability and economic hardship. In 1925, Mises analyzed these trends in Germany and concluded that they were leading the German people toward a "national socialism," instead of either classical liberalism or Marxian socialism.[15] Anticipating the triumph of Hitler and his National Socialist (Nazi) movement in 1933, Mises warned in 1926 that many Germans were "setting their hopes on the coming of the 'strong man'—the tyrant who will think for them and care for them."[16]

In later years, Mises emphasized that while the Marxists in the Soviet Union used the tools of central planning to culturally redesign a socialist "new man" through various methods of indoctrination and thought control, the National Socialists in Nazi Germany took this a step further with their scheme of centrally planning the racial breeding of a new "master race."[17]

## Capitalism, Socialism, and Interventionism

This was the historical context in which Mises published some of his most important works in the period between the two World Wars: *Socialism* (1922), *Liberalism* (1927), and *Critique of Interventionism* (1929). The task he set for himself was to offer a radically different vision of man in society from that presented by the socialists, nationalists, and interventionists. In place of their starting premise of inescapable conflicts among men in terms of "social class," nationality and race, or narrow group interest, Mises insisted that reason and experience demonstrated that all men could associate in peace for their mutual material and cultural betterment. The key to this was an understanding and appreciation of the benefits of a division of labor. Through specialization and trade the human race has the capacity to lift itself up from both poverty and war.

Men become associates in a common process of social cooperation, instead of antagonists with each attempting to rule over and
plunder the others. Indeed, all that we mean by modern civilization,
and the material and cultural comforts and opportunities that it offers
man, is due to the highly productive benefits and advantages made
possible by a division of labor. Men participated in this associative
collaboration in the arena of competitive market exchange.

The confusion, Mises pointed out, is the failure to view this cooperative social process from a longer-run perspective than the changing
circumstances of everyday life. In the rivalries of the market, there
are always some who earn profits and others who suffer losses in the
interactive and competitive processes of supply and demand. But what
needs to be understood is that these changes in the short-run fortunes
of various participants in the division of labor are the method through
which each participant is informed and nudged into either doing more
of some things or less of others. This process brings about the necessary
adjustment of society's productive activities in order to assure that they
tend to match and reflect the market pattern of consumer demand.[18]

Of course, political force can be substituted for the "reward" of
profits and the "punishment" of losses. However, the costs of this substitution are extremely high, Mises argued. First, men are less motivated
to apply themselves with intelligence and industry when forced to work
under the lash of servitude and compulsion, and thus society loses what
their free efforts and invention might have produced.[19] Second, men
are forced to conform to the values and goals of those in command,
and thus they lose the liberty of following their own ends and purposes,
with no certainty that those who rule over them know better what may
give them happiness and meaning in life.

And, third, socialist central planning and political intervention
in the market, respectively, abolish or distort the functioning of social
cooperation. A sustained and extended system of specialization for
mutual improvement is only possible under a unique set of social
and economic institutions. Without private ownership in the means
of production, the coordination of multitudes of individual activities
in the division of labor is impossible. Indeed, Mises's analysis of the
"impossibility" of a socialist order being able to match the efficiency
and productivity of a free market economy was the basis for his inter-

national stature and reputation as one of the most original economists of his time, and was the centerpiece of his book on *Socialism*.[20]

Private ownership and competitive market exchange enable the formation of prices for both consumer goods and the factors of production, expressed in the common denominator of a medium of exchange—money. On the basis of these money prices, entrepreneurs can engage in economic calculation to determine the relative costs and profitability of alternative lines of production. Without these market-generated prices, there would be no rational way to allocate resources among their competing uses to assure that those goods most highly valued by the buying public were produced in the least costly and therefore most economical manner. Economic calculation, Mises demonstrated, guarantees that the scarce means available are utilized to best serve the ends of the members of society.

Such rationality in the use of means to satisfy ends is impossible in a comprehensive system of socialist central planning. How, Mises asked, will the socialist planners know the best uses for which the factors of production under their central control should be applied without such market-generated money prices? Without private ownership of the means of production there would be nothing (legally) to buy and sell. Without the ability to buy and sell, there will be no bids and offers, and therefore no haggling over terms of trade among competing buyers and sellers. Without the haggling of market competition there would, of course, be no agreed-upon terms of exchange. Without agreed-upon terms of exchange, there are no actual market prices. And without such market prices, how will the central planners know the opportunity costs and therefore the most highly valued uses for which those resources could or should be applied? With the abolition of private property, and therefore market exchange and prices, the central planners would lack the necessary institutional and informational tools to determine what to produce and how, in order to minimize waste and inefficiency.

Socialists and many nonsocialist economists claimed over the decades that Mises was "wrong," when he said that socialism was "impossible." They pointed to the Soviet Union and said it existed and operated. However in numerous places in his various writings, beginning from the early 1920s, Mises insisted that he was not saying that a socialist system could not exist. Of course, the factors of production could be nationalized and a central planning agency could be delegated the responsibility to direct all the production activities of the society.

But any supposed rationality and seeming degree of efficiency observed in the workings of the Soviet and similar socialist economies was due to the fact that such socialist planning systems existed in a world in which there were still functioning market societies. The existing market economies provided various "shadow prices" that the socialist planners could try to use as proxies and benchmarks for evaluating their own allocation and production decisions. However, since the actual economic circumstances in such a socialist economy would never be an exact duplicate of the conditions in the neighboring market societies—resources availabilities, labor skills, the quantity and qualities of capital equipment, the fertility and variety of land, the patterns of consumer demand—such proxy prices could never completely "solve" the economic calculation problem for the socialist planners in places like the Soviet Union.[21]

Therefore, Mises declared in 1931, "From the standpoint of both politics and history, this proof [of the "impossibility" of socialist planning] is certainly the most important discovery by economic theory.... It alone will enable future historians to understand how it came about that the victory of the socialist movement did not lead to the creation of the socialist order of society."[22]

At the same time, Mises demonstrated the inherent inconsistencies in any system of piecemeal political intervention in the market economy. Price controls and production restrictions on entrepreneurial decision-making bring about distortions and imbalances in the relationships of supply and demand, as well as constraints on the most efficient use of resources in the service of consumers. The political intervener is left with the choice of either introducing new controls and regulations in an attempt to compensate for the distortions and imbalances the prior interventions have caused, or repealing the interventionist controls and regulations already in place and allowing the market once again to be free and competitive. The path of one set of piecemeal interventions followed by another entails a logic of the growth of government that eventually would result in the entire economy coming under state management. Hence, interventionism consistently applied could lead to socialism on an incremental basis.[23]

The most pernicious form of government intervention, in Mises's view, was political control and manipulation of the monetary system. Contrary to both the Marxists and the Keynesians, Mises did not consider the fluctuations experienced over the business cycle to be an inherent and inescapable part of the free market economy. Waves of inflation and depression were the product of political intervention in money and banking. And this included the Great Depression of the 1930s, Mises argued.

Under various political and ideological pressures, governments had monopolized control over the monetary system. They used the ability to create money out of thin air through the printing press or on the ledger books of the banks to finance government deficits and to artificially lower interest rates to stimulate unsustainable investment booms. Such monetary expansions always tended to distort market prices resulting in misdirections of resources, including labor, and malinvestments of capital. The inflationary upswing that is caused by an artificial expansion of money and bank credit sets the stage for an eventual economic downturn. By distorting the rate of interest, the market price for borrowing and lending, the monetary authority throws savings and investment out of balance, with the need for an inevitable correction. The "depression" or "recession" phase of the business cycle occurs when the monetary authority either slows downs or stops any further increases in the money supply. The imbalances and distortions become visible, with some investment projects having to be written down or written off as losses, with reallocations of labor and other resources to alternative, more profitable employments, and sometimes significant adjustments and declines in wages and prices to bring supply and demand back into proper order.[24]

The Keynesian revolution of the 1930s, which then dominated economic policy discussions for decades following the Second World War, was based on a fundamental misconception of how the market economy worked, in Mises's view. What Keynes called "aggregate demand failures," to explain the reason for high and prolonged unemployment, distracted attention away from the real source of less than full employment: the failure of producers and workers on the "supply-side" of the market to price their products and labor services at levels that potential demanders would be willing to pay. Unemployment and idle resources were pricing problems, not demand management problems. Mises considered Keynesian economics basically to be nothing more than a rationale for special interest groups, such as trade unions, that didn't want to adapt to the reality of supply and demand and what the market viewed as their real worth.[25]

Thus Mises's conclusion from his analysis of socialism and interventionism, including monetary manipulation, was that there is no alternative to a thoroughgoing unhampered free market economy, and one that included a market-based monetary system, such as the gold standard.[26] Both socialism and interventionism are, respectively, unworkable and unstable substitutes for capitalism. The classical liberal defends private property and the free market economy, he insisted, precisely because it is the only system of social cooperation that provides wide latitude for freedom and personal choice to all members of society, while generating the institutional means for coordinating the actions of billions of people in the most economically rational manner.

## Classical Liberalism, Freedom, and Democracy

Mises's defense of classical liberalism against these various forms of collectivism, however, was not limited to the "merely" economic benefits from the private-property order. Property also provides man with that most valuable and cherished object—*freedom*. Property gives the individual an arena of autonomy in which he may cultivate and live out his own conception of the good and meaningful life. It also protects him from dependency on the state for his existence; through his own efforts and voluntary exchange with other free men he is not beholden to any absolute political authority that would dictate the conditions of his life. Freedom and property, if they are to be secure, require *peace*. Violence and fraud must be outlawed if each man is to take full advantage of what his interests and talents suggest would be the most profitable avenues to achieve his goals in consensual association with others.

The classical-liberal ideal also emphasizes the importance of *equality before the law*, Mises explained. Only when political privilege and favoritism are eliminated can each man have the latitude to use his own knowledge and talents in ways that benefit himself and also rebound, through the voluntary transactions of the market, to the betterment of society as a whole. This means, at the same time, that a liberal society is one that accepts that *inequality of income and wealth* is inseparable from individual freedom. Given the diversity of men's natural and acquired abilities and volitional inclinations, the rewards earned by people in the marketplace will inevitably be uneven. Nor can it be otherwise if we are not to diminish or even suffocate the incentives that move men to apply themselves in creative and productive ways.

The role of government, therefore, in the classical-liberal society is to respect and protect each individual's right to his life, liberty, and property. The significance of *democracy*, in Mises's view, is not that majorities are always right or should be unrestrained in what they may do to minorities through the use of political power. Elected and representative government is a means of changing those who hold political office without resort to revolution or civil war. It is an institutional device for maintaining social peace. It was clear to Mises from the experience of communism and fascism, as well as from the many tyrannies of the past, that without democracy the questions of who shall rule, for how long, and for what purpose would be reduced to brute force and dictatorial power. Reason and persuasion should be the methods that men use in their dealings with one another—both in the marketplace and the social and political arenas—and not the bullet and the bayonet.[27]

In his book on classical liberalism, Mises bemoaned the fact that people are all too willing to resort to state power to impose their views of personal conduct and morality whenever their fellow human beings veer from their own conception of the "good," the "virtuous," and the "right." He despaired, "The propensity of our contemporaries to demand authoritarian prohibition as soon as something does not please them...shows how deeply ingrained the spirit of servility still remains in them.... A free man must be able to endure it when his fellow men act and live otherwise than he considers proper. He must free himself from the habit, just as soon as something does not please him, of calling for the police"[28]

What, then, should guide social policy in determining the limits of government action? Mises was a utilitarian who argued that laws and institutions should be judged by the standard of whether and to what extent they further the goal of peaceful social cooperation. Society is the most important means through which men are able to pursue the ends and purposes that give meaning to their lives. But Mises was not what has become known in philosophical discussion as an "act-utilitarian," that is, one who believes that a course of action or a policy is to be determined on an ad hoc, case-by-case basis. Rather, he was a "rule-utilitarian," that is, one who believes that any particular course of action or policy must be evaluated in terms of its consistency with general rules of personal and social conduct that reason and experience have accumulated as guides to conduct. Any action's long-run influences and consequences must be taken into consideration in terms of its consistency with and relationship to the preservation of the institutions essential for successful social interaction.[29] This is the meaning of the phrase Mises often used: the "rightly understood long-run interests" of the members of society.[30]

Thus his defense of democracy and constitutional limits on the powers of government was based on the reasoned judgment that history has demonstrated far too many times that the resort to nondemocratic and "extra-constitutional" means has led to violence, repression, abrogation of civil and economic liberties, and a breakdown of respect for law and the legal order, which destroys the long-run stability of society. The apparent "gains" and "benefits" from "strong men" and "emergency measures" in times of seeming crisis have always tended to generate "costs" and "losses" of liberty and prosperity in the longer run that more than exceed the supposed "short-run" stability, order, and security promised by such methods.

## Classical Liberalism and International Peace

The benefits from social cooperation through a market-based division of labor, Mises argued, are not limited to a country's borders. The gains from trade through specialization extend to all corners of the globe. Hence, the classical-liberal ideal is inherently cosmopolitan. Aggressive nationalism, in Mises's view, not only threatens to bring death and destruction through war and conquest, it also denies all men the oppor-

tunity to benefit from productive intercourse by imposing trade barriers
and various other restrictions on the free movement of goods, capital,
and people from one country to another. Prosperity and progress are
artificially constrained within national boundaries. This perversely can
create the conditions for war and conquest as some nations conclude
that the only way to obtain the goods and resources available in another
country is through invasion and violence. Eliminate all trade barriers
and restrictions on the free movement of goods, capital, and men, and
limit governments to the securing of each individual's life, liberty, and
property, and most of the motives and tensions that can lead to war
will have been removed.

Mises also suggested that many of the bases for civil wars and
ethnic violence would be removed if the right of self-determination
were recognized in determining the borders between countries. Mises
took great care to explain that by "self-determination" he did not mean
that all those belonging to a particular racial, ethnic, linguistic, or
religious group are to be forced into the same nation-state. He clearly
stated that he meant the right of individual self-determination through
plebiscite. That is, if the individuals in a town or region or district vote
to join another nation, or wish to form their own independent country,
they should have the freedom to do so.

There still may be minorities within these towns, regions, or districts, of course, that would have preferred to remain part of the country
to which they belonged, or would have preferred to join a different
country. But however imperfect self-determination may be, it would
at least potentially reduce a good amount of the ethnic, religious, or
linguistic tensions. The only lasting solution, Mises said, is the reduction
of government involvement to those limited classical-liberal functions,
so the state may not be used to impose harm or disadvantage on any
individual or group in society for the benefit of others.[31]


## Classical Liberalism and the General Welfare

Finally, Mises also discussed this question: For whose benefit does the
classical liberal speak in society? Unlike virtually all other political and
ideological movements, liberalism is a social philosophy of the com-

mon good. Both at the time that Mises wrote many of his works and now, political movements and parties often resort to the rhetoric of the common good and the general welfare, but in fact their goals are to use the power of government to benefit some groups at the expense of others.

Government regulations, redistributive welfare programs, trade restrictions and subsidies, tax policies, and monetary manipulation are employed to grant profit and employment privileges to special-interest groups that desire positions in society they are unable to attain on the open, competitive market. Corruption, hypocrisy, and disrespect for the law, as well as abridgements on the freedom of others, naturally follow from this.

What liberalism offers as an ideal and as a goal of public policy, Mises declared, is an equality of individual rights for all under the rule of law, with privileges and favors for none. It speaks for and defends the freedom of each individual and therefore is the voice of liberty for all. It wants every person to be free to apply himself in the pursuit of his own goals and purposes, so he and others can benefit from his talents and abilities through the peaceful transactions of market exchange. Classical liberalism wants elimination of government intervention in human affairs, so political power is not abusively applied at the expense of anyone in society.[32]

Mises was not unaware of the power of special-interest–group politics and the difficulty of opposing the concentrated influence of such groups in the halls of political power.[33] But he insisted that the ultimate power in society resides in the power of ideas. Ideas are what move men to action, that make them bare their chests at barricades, or that embolden them to oppose wrongheaded policies and resist even the strongest of vested interests. Ideas are what have achieved all the victories that have been won by freedom over the centuries.

Neither political deception nor ideological compromise can win liberty in the twenty-first century. Only the power of ideas, clearly stated and forthrightly presented, can do so. And that is what stands out in Mises's books and makes them enduring sources of the case for freedom.

When Mises wrote many of his books in the 1920s, 1930s, and 1940s—communism and fascism seemed irresistible forces in the world.

Since then, their ideological fire has been extinguished in the reality of what they created and the unwillingness of tens of millions to live under their yoke. Nonetheless, many of their criticisms of the free market continue to serve as rationales for the intrusions of the interventionist welfare state in every corner of society. Many of the contemporary arguments against "globalization" often resemble the criticisms leveled against free markets and free trade by European nationalists and socialists of one hundred years ago.[34]

Mises's arguments for individual freedom and the market economy in the pages of *Socialism, Liberalism, Critique of Interventionism, Omnipotent Government, Bureaucracy, Planned Chaos, Human Action*, and many others continue to ring true and remain relevant to our own times. It is what makes his works as important now as when he wrote them across the decades of the twentieth century.

## Notes

[1]On Mises's life and contributions to economics and the philosophy of freedom, see Richard M. Ebeling, *Austrian Economics and the Political Economy of Freedom* (Northampton, MA: Edward Elgar, 2003), chap. 3, "A Rational Economist in an Irrational Age: Ludwig von Mises," pp. 61–99; and Richard M. Ebeling, "Planning for Freedom: Ludwig von Mises as Political Economist and Policy Analyst" in Richard M. Ebeling, ed., *Competition or Compulsion: The Market Economy versus the New Social Engineering* (Hillsdale, MI: Hillsdale College Press, 2001), pp. 1–85; see also Murray N. Rothbard, *Ludwig von Mises: Scholar, Creator, Hero* (Auburn, AL: Ludwig von Mises Institute, 1988), and Israel M. Kirzner, *Ludwig von Mises* (Wilmington, DE: ISI Books, 2001).

[2]On Mises's family background and the cultural climate of Vienna and Austria in terms of the Jews and anti-Semitism, see Richard M. Ebeling, "Ludwig von Mises and the Vienna of His Time," Parts I & II, *The Freeman* (March & April 2005): 24–31 & 19–25.

[3]On Mises's work as policy analyst and advocate in the Austria of the interwar period, see Richard M. Ebeling, "The Economist as the Historian of Decline: Ludwig von Mises and the Austria Between the Two World Wars" in Richard M. Ebeling, ed., *Globalization: Will Freedom or Global Government Dominate the International Marketplace* (Hillsdale, MI: Hillsdale College Press, 2002), pp. 1–68.

[4]Ludwig von Mises, *Human Action: A Treatise on Economics* [1949] (Irvington-on-Hudson, NY: Foundation for Economic Education, [3<sup>rd</sup> rev. ed., 1966] 1996).

[5]Bismarck told an American admirer, "My idea was to bribe the working class, or shall I say, to win them over, to regard the state as a social institution existing for their sake and interested in their welfare." See William H. Dawson, *The Evolution of Modern Germany*, Vol. II (New York: Charles Scribner's Sons, 1914), p. 349.

[6]On the ideas and development of the German welfare state and regulated economy in the late nineteenth and early twentieth centuries, see Ebeling, *Austrian Economics and the Political Economy of Freedom*, chap. 7, "The Political Myths and Economic Realities of the Welfare State," pp. 179–202, especially pp. 179–84; and Richard M. Ebeling, "National Health Care and the Welfare State," in Jacob G. Hornberger and Richard M. Ebeling, eds., *The Dangers of Socialized Medicine* (Fairfax, VA: The Future of Freedom Foundation, 1994), pp. 25–37; see also Mises's criticisms of the German Historical School in "The Historical Setting of the Austrian School of Economics" [1969], reprinted in Bettina Bien Greaves, ed., *Austrian Economics: An Anthology* (Irvington-on-Hudson, NY: Foundation for Economic Education, 1996), pp. 53–76, especially pp. 60–69.

[7]See Richard M. Ebeling, "Free Markets, the Rule of Law, and Classical Liberalism," *The Freeman* (May 2004): 8–15.

[8]Ludwig von Mises showed the inherent flaws and contradictions in the Marxian theory of history and class conflict in *Socialism: An Economic and Sociological Analysis* (Indianapolis, IN: Liberty Classics, 1981 [1922; rev. eds., 1932, 1951]), pp. 279–320; and *Theory and History: An Interpretation of Social and Economic Evolution* (Indianapolis, IN: Liberty Fund, 2005 [1957]), pp. 102–58.

[9]On the evolution and meanings of nationality and nationalism, see Carlton J. H. Hayes, *The Historical Evolution of Modern Nationalism* (New York: Richard R. Smith, 1931); Hayes, *Essays on Nationalism* (New York: Macmillan, 1928); Walter Sulzbach, *National Consciousness* (Washington, DC: American Council on Public Affairs, 1943); and Frederick Hertz, *Nationality in History and Politics* (New York: Oxford University Press, 1944).

[10]Ludwig von Mises, "Autarky and Its Consequences" [1943] in Richard M. Ebeling, ed., *Money, Method and the Market Process: Essays by Ludwig von Mises* (Norwell, MA: Kluwer Academic Press, 1990), p. 138: "Aggressive or militaristic nationalism aims at conquest and the subjugation of other nations by arms. Economic Nationalism aims at the furthering the well-being of one's own nation or some of its groups through inflicting harm upon foreigners by economic measures, for instance: trade and migration barriers, expropriation of foreign investments, repudiation of foreign debts, currency devaluation, and foreign exchange control."

[11]Ludwig von Mises, *Nation, State, and Economy: Contributions to the Politics and History of Our Time* (New York: New York University Press, 1983 [1919]).

[12]See Richard M. Ebeling, *Austrian Economics and the Political Economy of Freedom*, chap. 6, "Classical Liberalism and Collectivism in the 20th Century," pp. 159–78, especially pp. 159–63; on the political and ideological similarities of communism, fascism, and Nazism, see Ludwig von Mises, *Planned Chaos* (Irvington-on-Hudson, NY: Foundation for Economic Education, 1947), pp. 62–79; see also Richard Overy, *The Dictators:*

*Hitler's Germany, Stalin's Russia* (New York: W. W. Norton, 2004); A. James Gregor, *The Faces of Janus: Marxism and Fascism in the Twentieth Century* (New Haven, CT: Yale University Press, 2000); and Francois Furet, *The Passing of an Illusion: The Idea of Communism in the Twentieth Century* (Chicago: University of Chicago Press, 1999); and Richard Pipes, *Russia Under the Bolshevik Regime* (New York: Alfred A. Knopf, 1993), pp. 240–81.

[13]For Mises's analysis of the Great German Inflation, see his monograph, "Stabilization of the Monetary Unit—From the Viewpoint of Theory" [1923], in Percy L. Greaves, ed., *Ludwig von Mises, On the Manipulation of Money and Credit* (Dobbs Ferry, NY: Free Market Books, 1978), pp. 1–49, and Ludwig von Mises, "Business Under German Inflation" [1946], reprinted in *Ideas on Liberty* (November 2003): 10–13; see also Richard M. Ebeling, "The Great German Inflation," *Ideas on Liberty* (November 2003): 4–5.

[14]See Albrecht Mendelssohn Bartholdy, *The War and German Society: The Testament of a Liberal* (New York: Howard Fertig, 1971 [1937]), and Mortiz J. Bonn, *Wandering Scholar* (London: Cohen & West, Ltd., 1949), pp. 273–90.

[15]Ludwig von Mises, "Anti-Marxism" [1925] in *Critique of Interventionism* (Irvington-on-Hudson, NY: Foundation for Economic Education, 1996 [1929]), pp. 71–95.

[16]Ludwig von Mises, "Social Liberalism," [1926] in *Critique of Interventionism*, p. 67.

[17]Mises, *Planned Chaos*, pp. 77–78.

[18]Mises, *Socialism*, pp. 256–78; *Human Action*, pp. 143–76.

[19]Mises, *Human Action*, pp. 628–34.

[20]Ludwig von Mises, "Economic Calculation in the Socialist Commonwealth" [1920], in F. A. Hayek, *Collectivist Economic Planning: Critical Studies on the Possibilities of Socialism* (London: George Routledge & Sons, 1935), pp. 87–130, reprinted in Israel M. Kirzner, ed., *Classics in Austrian Economics: A Sampling in the History of a Tradition*, Vol. 3 (London: William Pickering, 1994), pp. 3–30, and Mises, *Socialism*, pp. 95–194; *Bureaucracy* (New Haven, CT: Yale University Press, 1944), pp. 20–56; *Human Action*, pp. 689–715; see also Richard M. Ebeling, "Why Socialism is 'Impossible,'" *The Freeman* (October 2004): 8–12.

[21]Ludwig von Mises, *Socialism*, p. 102; *Liberalism: The Classical Tradition* (Irvington-on-Hudson, NY: Foundation for Economic Education, [1927] 1996), p. 74; *Omnipotent Government*, p. 55; *Bureaucracy*, pp. 58–59; *Planned Chaos*, p. 84; *Human Action*, pp. 258–59 & 702–3.

[22]Ludwig von Mises, "On the Development of the Subjective Theory of Value" [1931] in *Epistemological Problems of Economics* [1933] (New York: New York University Press, 1981), p. 157.

[23]Mises, *Critique of Interventionism*, pp. 1–31 & 97–106; *Interventionism: An Economic Analysis* (Irvington-on-Hudson, NY: Foundation for Economic Education, 1996 [1941]); *Human Action*, pp. 716–79; *Planning for Freedom* (South Holland, IL: Libertarian Press, 4ᵗʰ ed., 1980 [1952]), pp. 1–49.

[24]Ludwig von Mises, *The Theory of Money and Credit* (Indianapolis, IN: Liberty Classics, 1981 [1912; rev. eds., 1934, 1953]); "Monetary Stabilization and Cyclical Policy"

[1928], reprinted in Kirzner, ed., *Classics in Austrian Economics*, Vol. 3, 33–111; *Human Action*, pp. 398–478, 538–86 & 780–803.

25 For Mises's analysis of the causes and cures for the Great Depression, see Ludwig von Mises, "The Causes of the Economic Crisis" [1931] in Greaves, ed., *Ludwig von Mises, On the Manipulation of Money and Credit*, pp. 173–203; and on Keynesian Economics, see Mises, "Stones into Bread, The Keynesian Miracle" [1948] and "Lord Keynes and Say's Law" [1950] in *Planning for Freedom*, pp. 50–71; for a detailed comparison of the Austrian and Keynesian analyses of the Great Depression, see Richard M. Ebeling, "The Austrian Economists and the Keynesian Revolution: The Great Depression and the Economics of the Short-Run" in Richard M, Ebeling, ed., *Human Action: A 50-Year Tribute* (Hillsdale, MI: Hillsdale College Press, 2000), pp. 15–110.

26 See Ebeling, *Austrian Economics and the Political Economy of Freedom*, chap. 5, "Ludwig von Mises and the Gold Standard," pp. 136–58.

27 Mises, *Socialism*, pp. 58–73; *Liberalism*, pp. 18–42; *Human Action*, pp. 150–53 & 264–89

28 Mises, *Liberalism*, p. 55.

29 Mises, *Human Action*, pp. 664–88; *Theory and History*, pp. 44–61; and Henry Hazlitt, *The Foundations of Morality* (Irvington-on-Hudson, NY: Foundation for Economic Education, 1998 [1964]), pp. 55–61. See also Leland B. Yeager, *Ethics as Social Science: The Moral Philosophy of Social Cooperation* (Northampton, MA: Edward Elgar, 2001), pp. 81–97.

30 Mises, *Human Action*, pp. 664–88.

31 Mises, *Nation, State, and Economy*, pp. 31–56; *Liberalism*, pp. 105–21; *Omnipotent Government*, pp. 79–93.

32 Mises, *Liberalism*, pp. 155–87.

33 See, for example, his essay "The Clash of Group Interests" [1945], reprinted in Ebeling, ed., *Money, Method and the Market Process*, pp. 202–14.

34 See Jerry Z. Muller, *The Mind and the Market: Capitalism in Modern European Thought* (New York: Alfred A. Knopf, 2002), and Ian Buruma and Avishai Margalit, *Occidentalism: The West in the Eyes of Its Enemies* (New York: The Penguin Press, 2004).

ROBERT SKIDELSKY

# John Maynard Keynes:
# Founder of Macroeconomics

## I. Keynes, Hayek, and Friedman

Any evaluation of John Maynard Keynes today is inescapably bound up with the question of what remains of Keynesian economics. Keynes was the first in the field of the three great twentieth-century economists—the other two being F. A. Hayek and Milton Friedman—and his contribution has to some extent been eclipsed by theirs. Today there is a tendency to think of Keynes's "general theory" (GT) as the theory of a deep slump, irrelevant to more "normal" times. This begs the question of the role of Keynesian economics in keeping times "normal." It is certainly arguable that both in 1987 and 2001 heavy deficit finance—the famous "economic stimulus"—warded off depressions. Keynesian attitudes are so built into our system of economic management, we no longer think of them as Keynesian.

There is the interesting question of the relationship between Keynes, Friedman, and Hayek. Friedman is often portrayed as the arch anti-Keynesian, but this is nonsense. In technical economics, monetarism and Keynesianism are first cousins—not surprising since Keynes started his professional career as a monetarist. Both are about the study of aggregates, that is, they are part of macroeconomics, which Hayek never accepted. In his technical economics Friedman is more Keynesian than Hayekian. In his political economy he is closer to Hayek. Both share a mistrust of government and faith in the market system. Friedman's faith in the market is more firmly rooted than is

35

Hayek's in neoclassical equilibrium theory. Hayek's position seems to have been that, even though market outcomes fall short of ideal equilibrium, government intervention will only make matters worse. His greatest contribution to economics was his depiction of the market as a discovery mechanism. Keynes would certainly have agreed with this as a long-run proposition, but would have added that we need a theory of short-run statesmanship to make the long run tolerable. Thus the connections and continuities between the three great economists are as striking as their differences, and we should avoid playing the competitive game with their reputations. The political economy we practice has been profoundly influenced by all three.

## II. A Brief Biography

John Maynard Keynes was born at 6 Harvey Road, Cambridge, England, on 5 June 1883, into an academic family. He was the eldest son of John Neville Keynes, a logician and economist, and Florence Ada Brown, the daughter of a Congregational divine. He had an outstandingly successful school career at Eton College, which was followed by an equally glittering undergraduate one at King's College, Cambridge. There he gained a first-class honors degree in Mathematics, wrote papers on the medieval theologian Peter Abelard and the Conservative political philosopher Edmund Burke, and became President of the Cambridge Union and the University Liberal Club. Of crucial importance to his intellectual and moral formation was his election, in 1902, to the Cambridge Apostles, an exclusive "conversation" society, where he fell under the influence of the philosopher G. E. Moore, and which brought him the friendship of Lytton Strachey. Moore's *Principia Ethica* remained his "religion under the surface" for the rest of his life. It taught that the highest forms of civilized life were friendship, aesthetic enjoyments, and the pursuit of truth.

In 1906 Keynes was placed second in the Civil Service Examination, his worst marks being in economics, which he had studied briefly under Alfred Marshall. After two years in the India Office, in which he wrote a thesis on probability in his spare time, he started lecturing on monetary economics at Cambridge; in 1909, his thesis won him a fellowship at King's College, which remained his academic home for the rest of his life. His membership in the Bloomsbury Group, a commune of Cambridge-connected writers and painters who lived in the Bloomsbury district of London, dates from the start of his friendship with the painter Duncan Grant, Lyttton Strachey's cousin, in 1908. In 1913 he published his first book, *Indian Currency and Finance*, and served on the Royal Commission on Indian Finance and Currency.

Keynes helped to avert the collapse of the gold standard in the banking crisis of August 1914 that accompanied the outbreak of the First World War. From January 1915 to June 1919 he was a temporary civil servant at the Treasury, showing a notable ability to apply economic theory to the practical problems of war finance. He was against military conscription, and would have been a conscientious objector had his Treasury work not exempted him from military service. When Lloyd George succeeded Asquith as Prime Minister, Keynes (in January 1917) became head of the Treasury's new "A" Division, set up to manage external finance. He helped to build up the system of Allied purchases in neutral markets, while chafing at Britain's growing dependence on American loans and the failure to arrange a compromise peace. Keynes was chief Treasury representative at the Paris Peace Conference in 1919, where he tried unavailingly to limit Germany's bill for reparations, and to promote an American loan for the reconstruction of Europe. His resignation from the Treasury on 5 June 1919 was followed in December by the publication of *The Economic Consequences of the Peace*, the book that first brought him international fame. A bitter polemic, informed by both moral passion and economic argument, against the Allied policy of trying to extort from Germany an indemnity it could not pay, it reflected his revulsion against Lloyd George's leadership in both war and peace, and his fears for the future of European civilization. Unless the Versailles Treaty were drastically revised, "vengeance, I dare predict, will not limp."[1]

Between the wars, Keynes's life was divided among Cambridge, London, and East Sussex. He was a spectacularly successful investment bursar of King's College, and, despite some major reverses, made about £400,000 for himself over his lifetime—£12,000,000 (or $22,500,000 in today's currencies)—out of which he financed a fine collection of pictures and rare books and the building of the Cambridge Arts Theatre in 1935. In London, where he rented a house at 46 Gordon Square, he was, at various times, on the boards of five investment and insurance companies, the chief one being the National Mutual Life Assurance Company, which he chaired from 1921 to 1937. Between 1923 and 1931 he was chief proprietor and chairman of the board of the weekly journal *Nation and Athenaeum*, contributing regular articles on financial and economic topics. (He remained chairman of the board of the *New Statesman and Athenaeum* when the two journals merged in 1931.) Between 1911 and 1945, he edited the *Economic Journal*. In the 1920s his ideas on economic policy permeated Whitehall through monthly meetings of the Tuesday Club, a dining club started by his friend and stockbroker, Oswald Falk. In the 1930s, he sought to influence policy through his membership in the Prime Minister's Economic Advisory Council. In 1925, he took the lease of Tilton, a farmhouse in East Sussex, next door to Charleston, where Duncan Grant lived with the painter Vanessa Bell. This move coincided with his marriage to the Russian ballerina, Lydia Lopokova, who gave his life the emotional stability it had previously lacked, and which provided the necessary background for sustained intellectual effort.

In the 1920s, the postwar European inflations, succeeded in Britain by heavy unemployment, formed the background to his two theoretical books, *A Tract on Monetary Reform* (1923) and *A Treatise on Money* (1930), which dealt with the causes and consequences of monetary instability and their remedies. These theoretical exercises were punctuated by two notable polemical pamphlets, "The Economic Consequences of Mr. Churchill" (1925) and "Can Lloyd George Do It?" (1929), the second written with Hubert Henderson. The first attacked Churchill's decision, as Chancellor of the Exchequer, to put the pound back on the gold standard at an overvalued exchange rate against the dollar; the second was a plea for a large public works program. Reconciled to Lloyd George in 1926, Keynes attempted to provide the Liberal Party with a social philosophy of the "middle way" between individualism and state socialism, suitable for an inflexible industrial structure. Regulation of demand, he would later write, was the only way to maintain capitalism in conditions of freedom.[2]

The Great Depression of 1929–1932, together with technical flaws in *A Treatise on Money*, took Keynes back to the theoretical drawing board. What now seemed to be needed was not an explanation of Britain's "special problem" of persisting unemployment, but an explanation of how aggregate output could collapse, labor remain unused, and global depression persist in a world in which resources remained scarce. From the autumn of 1931 to the summer of 1935, Keynes worked on a new book of theory, initially titled "The Monetary Theory of Production." He was helped not just by older economists like Ralph Hawtrey and Dennis Robertson, but by Roy Harrod and a "Cambridge Circus" of young disciples led by Richard Kahn. There was just one major pamphlet in these years—"The Means to Prosperity"—written in June 1933. On a trip to the United States in 1934 to study the New Deal firsthand, he wrote: "Here, not in Moscow, is the economic laboratory of the world."

*The General Theory of Employment, Interest and Money*, published in February 1936, tried to demonstrate both that "underemployment equilibrium" was logically possible and how monetary "fine-tuning" by the central bank combined with an extensive "socialization" of investment could maintain full employment. The first proposition in particular divided the economics profession, since it rejected the "classical" thesis of a self-equilibrating economy. The publication of *The General Theory* confirmed the breach between Keynes and his chief collaborators in the 1920s, Dennis Robertson and Hubert Henderson. At the same time it marked the birth of a "Keynesian school" of economics led by Richard Kahn and Joan Robinson at Cambridge, Roy Harrod and James Meade at Oxford, and Nicholas Kaldor at the London School of Economics. In the United States the *The General Theory* supplied the younger generation of (mainly Harvard-trained) economists with a theoretical rationale for the New Deal. Keynes himself joined in the fierce controversies that his book generated, even though he was severely incapacitated from May 1937 to March 1939 with heart disease. As another European war, and with it, the return to deficit-financed full employment, became increasingly likely, Keynes sought to win acceptance for his revolution by showing how the management of aggregate demand to avert depression could just as easily be used to contain inflation in a war economy.

The upshot was his pamphlet "How to Pay for the War" (1940), which won the approval of his arch-critic Friedrich Hayek and whose logic influenced Kingsley Wood's war budget of 1941. Restored to a semblance of health by his doctor, Janos Plesch, Keynes himself returned to the Treasury in August 1940 as an unpaid adviser to the Chancellor of the Exchequer, and remained its dominating force for the rest of his life. Elevated to the House of Lords as Baron Keynes of Tilton, his influence was felt in the Beveridge Report on Social Security in 1942 and in the Employment White Paper of 1944, which pledged the government to maintain a "high and stable level of employment" after the war. In 1942, Keynes became chairman of the Council for the Encouragement of Music and the Arts (CEMA), a wartime innovation that inaugurated permanent state patronage of the arts. It was transformed into the Arts Council of Great Britain shortly before he died.

The American demand that in return for Lend-Lease Britain scrap its imperial preference system after the war inspired Keynes to his last great constructive effort—his plan for an International Clearing Union (1942). This was designed to shift balance-of-payments adjustments from debtor to creditor countries so as to avoid the externally generated deflationary shocks that had spread depression under the gold standard. The Bretton Woods Agreement of 1944, which set up a system of fixed but adjustable exchange rates and two new institutions, the International Monetary Fund and the International Bank for Reconstruction and Development, fell short of Keynes's hopes. The abrupt U.S. cancellation of Lend-Lease in August 1945 led him to undertake the fifth of his six Treasury missions to the United States in an effort to secure an American grant or interest-free loan of $5,000,000,000. Forced to accept a semicommercial loan for $3,750,000, Keynes gave a brilliant defense of his policy in his last speech to the House of Lords on 7 December 1945.

On 21 April 1946, worn out by his labors, he suffered a fatal heart attack at Tilton, a little short of his sixty-third birthday. In an imposing memorial service at Westminster Abbey, British Prime Minister Clement Attlee headed a list of mourners drawn from all walks of life.

## III. Keynes's Major Contributions

To understand Keynes's contribution to economics, we need to say a word about how economics was done before Keynes. The "classical" theory, which Keynes set out to overthrow, was essentially the theory of a barter-exchange economy, in which Say's Law (that supply creates its own demand) held, and in which money affected only the price level. This barter-exchange model of the economy evolved into the timeless equilibrium models of Menger and Walras, in which everything depended on everything else simultaneously, so that their economics consisted of an infinitely extensible system of simultaneous equations. In these systems, prices, including wages, were infinitely flexible and markets always cleared. This kind of analysis was becoming common when Keynes started doing economics, and it has gained immeasurably as economics has become more mathematicized, eventually marginalizing the Keynesian approach within economic theory, though not in policy.

What led Keynes to challenge this way of doing economics?

First, I would put the influence of Alfred Marshall at Cambridge. Marshall was a kind of bridge between classical and neoclassical economics. He believed that the chief problem in economics was how to model time, and he developed the idea of three periods—the short run, the normal, and the long run—to explain how economies moved through time to adjust to shifts in supply and demand conditions. This was sharply different from the market-clearing simultaneity of the general equilibrium approach. His favorite form of analysis was partial equilibrium—dealing with the economy sector by sector and holding the rest of the system constant as he did so. Also he believed that money altered the economy, and that boom and slump entered the picture through the influence of money on prices. The Keynesian model is best seen through Marshallian spectacles—as a "temporary" or "short-period" equilibrium, with a fuller adjustment coming later, though with no tendency for adjustment to full employment.

Second, Keynes's training in economics was quite limited. In the preface to *The General Theory* he talked of the difficulty of escaping from old ideas "which ramify ... into every corner of our minds." But Keynes didn't have to unlearn as much as some of his contemporaries. What he knew best was the theory of money, both pure and applied, which he taught in his prewar courses at Cambridge. The theory of value, based on the barter-exchange economy, ramified much less extensively. Unlike Hayek, he always viewed the economy from what would now be called a macroeconomic perspective. The whole struggle of his economics was to link up the inherited theory of money with a theory of output in order to explain fluctuations in the latter.

Third, his understanding of economics was strongly rooted in personal experience of financial markets. This was an interest from an early age. His credo was realism of assumptions, and he had no interest in working with models that had no reference to acknowledged facts. "Economics," he wrote in 1938, "is a science of thinking in terms of models joined to the art of choosing models which are relevant to the contemporary world.... Good economists are scarce because the gift for using "vigilant observation" to choose good models, although it does not require a highly specialized intellectual technique, appears to be a very rare one."[3] It was the experience of trying to work with one such model, the Quantity Theory of Money (QTM), which excluded by assumption the phenomena he sought to explain—fluctuations in output—that led him to develop a theory of output.

Finally, his experience working with the QTM led Keynes to insist that assumptions should be consistent with policy. Most economists tacitly abandoned their assumptions when endorsing remedies for slump conditions. Keynes set out to develop a model that justified a certain kind of intervention.

Keeping this in mind, we can group Keynes's main contributions to economics under three heads: the theory of deep economic fluctuations; the theory of effective demand; and the technique of stabilization policy based on the second.

**The Theory of Economic Fluctuations**

This cannot be wholly understood apart from Keynes's distinctive theory of probability, expounded in his *Treatise on Probability* (1921). As he was later to do in economics, he produced a "general theory" of probability, in which statistically based probability—as in insurance markets—was a "special case" of a logical theory of probability. This led him to distinguish between risk, or situations with known probability distributions, and uncertainty, when "there is no scientific basis on which to form any calculable probability." Much of economic life inhabited the second sphere, which is why booms and slumps were endemic. He wrote in 1937: "Thus the fact that our knowledge of the future is fluctuating, vague and uncertain, renders wealth a peculiarly unsuitable subject for the methods of the classical economic theory."[4] This may be contrasted with the modern mainstream view that agents maximize with known probability distributions, so that market-clearing models are the most appropriate for analyzing economic behavior. Keynes himself identified as a tacit axiom of the classical theory of the self-regulating economy that "at any given time facts and expectations were . . . given in a definite and calculable form."[5]

Keynes's theoretical work in the 1920s is devoted to unpackaging the Quantity Theory of Money, which ruled out, by assumption, the possibility that monetary disturbances can have "real" effects on the economy. This might be true in the long-run, Keynes remarked acidly, "but in the long-run we are all dead."[6] Keynes used the quantity of money *equation* to show that changes in the quantity of money can unsettle business expectations and the distribution of income, thereby causing short-run fluctuations in the level of business activity. In doing so, he emphasized the use of money as a "store of value" or hedge against uncertainty, and the distinction between fixed and flexible prices. In the *Treatise on Money*, he argued that the disturbing effects of money can arise not just from inflationary or deflationary policies, but from *autonomous* changes in business sentiment. Much of the *Treatise* is devoted to analyzing the consequences of short-run changes in the "propensity to hoard" or "velocity of circulation," which Keynes identifies, by means of his "Fundamental Equations," with the emergence of windfall profits and losses, and a disequilibrium between saving and investment. Keynes shows how disequilibrium prices produce an oscillation of boom and slump around a (notional) full-employment equilibrium. But such equilibrium is accidentally achieved, in the absence of appropriate monetary policy.

The chief theoretical point that emerges from these two works is the instability in what Keynes would later call the liquidity-preference schedule. His claim was that, in a variety of situations readily encountered in economic life, hoarding money can yield superior utility to investing it, and that this, combined with "sticky" wage and price contracts, can explain quite prolonged lapses from full employment. His contribution up to 1930 was largely a summation of the monetary theories of Irving Fisher and Knut Wicksell, and is properly regarded as a contribution to the theory of economic fluctuations, with increased emphasis on volatile expectations. Like Fisher, Keynes advocated a monetary policy of keeping domestic prices stable; this might be incompatible with adherence to the international gold standard, an institution that Keynes dismissed as a "barbarous relic."[7]

## The Theory of Effective Demand

Keynes's revolutionary contribution to economics lies not in his theory of business fluctuations but in his theory of how aggregate output is determined. This is the subject matter of his *General Theory of Employment, Interest and Money* (1936). The QTM was a theory of the price level, when the levels of output and employment were explained in real, non-monetary terms. Following a suggestion from Ralph Hawtrey, Keynes agreed in 1930 that "it will probably be difficult in the future to prevent monetary theory and the theory of short-period supply from running together."[8] This was the start of Keynesian macroeconomics.

The core of *The General Theory* is the theory of effective demand. Its central claim is that aggregate supply and aggregate demand are reconciled through changes in quantities rather than prices. It is a short-period theory: Prices adjust only after, and as a result of, the fall in output and employment, and even then not completely. In the short-run, the volume of output in an economy is determined by the money demand for that output. The GT is the theory of what determines the level of money demand for output.

In Keynes's notation, $Y = C + I$. This tautology simply means that National Income ($Y$) is equal to the sum of the expenditure on National Output, divided into consumption spending ($C$) and investment spending ($I$). Consumption expenditure is governed by Keynes's "consumption function," based on the "psychological law" that consumption (and therefore saving, which is Y - C) is a stable fraction of total income, and that the marginal propensity to consume is less than unity. In a growing economy the gap between consumption and production must be filled by investment if full employment is to be maintained. The amount of investment is determined by the relationship between the expected profit rate ("marginal efficiency of capital") and the cost of borrowing (rate of interest). The rate of interest is the price of parting with money as determined by the state of liquidity preference. Thus given the interest rate, the amount of investment may fall short of what the community wishes to save. The revolutionary claim of the GT is that when this happens the divergent plans are brought into equality by a reduction in the level of income (output). Moreover, if the consumption function is known, it is possible to show, by a mathematical formula (Kahn's multiplier), by how much the community's income or alternatively employment must change to reconcile divergent saving and investment plans. The novelty of Keynes's treatment, as compared not just with the older theory, but his own *Treatise on Money*, was to demonstrate that an economy might be in equilibrium, with saving equal to investment, and aggregate demand equal to aggregate supply, at less than full employment.

Critics fastened on the most contentious feature of the new doctrine, the theory of "under-employment equilibrium." They denied that this was a genuine equilibrium; it was a disequilibrium state, frozen by the assumption that certain prices were fixed. Flexible prices would always ensure the desired level of employment, whatever was happening to aggregate money demand.

Keynes could have defended his position by saying that his fixed-price assumptions were realistic; but he set out to expose the logical flaws underlying the implicit classical price-adjustment story. He denied, first of all, that the interest rate was, or could be, determined in the market for saving and investment, since the quantity of saving depends on the level of current income. This was the basis of his view that changes in income equilibrate saving and investment plans.

As far as wage flexibility is concerned, Keynes agreed with the orthodox view that the *real* wage is inversely related to the quantity of employment, but denied that real wages are determined in the labor market by money-wage bargains, since an all-round reduction in money-wages might, by reducing the general price level, leave the real wage unaffected. The effect of a "flexible wages policy" thus depended entirely on its impact on the components of aggregate demand—consumption and investment—that might well be unfavorable.

Keynes conceded that, in time, the decline in employment (or money-wage rates) would, by decreasing the amount of money required to satisfy the business demand, lower the rate of interest required to satisfy the "propensity to hoard";[9] he also thought that after a slump a shortage of capital goods would develop that would revive profit expectations.[10] In short, a slump might eventually bring about the price adjustments that according to the classical economists were supposed to prevent the slump from occurring. He doubted, though, whether even longer-run forces would ensure a gravitational pull toward full employment. "We oscillate," he wrote, "round an intermediate position, appreciably below full employment and appreciably above the minimum employment a decline below which would endanger life."[11]

Despite nonacceptance by the leading economists of key elements in Keynes's macroeconomic model (Dennis Robertson, in particular, made a damaging attack on his theory of interest), critics were driven to argue for their positions within the analytical framework Keynes had set up. Macroeconomic analysis became part of the economists' tool kit, even if Keynes's own conclusions were rejected.

Let me try to grasp the vision or intuition that drives the technical analysis, but which is not perfectly captured by it. It is best revealed in answer to the question of why Keynes thought that full employment is unlikely to be the long-run, or normal, state of affairs. His answer is that the rate of interest tends to be permanently higher than the expected profit rate on capital, except in "moments of excitement." This is because money carries a permanent liquidity premium. Thus at almost any time the marginal return to money is greater than to capital goods, because money offers a unique hedge against uncertainty. Technically, there is zero or very low elasticity of substitution between money and goods. Over time, the marginal return to money falls less than the marginal return to goods. All wants are satiable except the desire for money. In this picture of the economy there is a permanent unemployment problem, because money employs no people in its production.

Notice, this would not be true under a *pure* gold standard in which the demand for liquidity would be satisfied by employing people to dig up gold. So we have two states of nature: pure metallic currency systems, which keep people poor but employed, and credit money systems, which enable societies to grow wealthier, but create semipermanent unemployment.

So we come back to the liquidity preference theory of the rate of interest, which is where Keynes's vision and theory meet. Keynes said that the rate of interest is the price people demand for parting with money. The only intelligible reason for demanding this price is uncertainty. With perfect information the classical theory of interest—as the price that savers demand of borrowers—would be true. Logically the equilibrating mechanism could be either income or interest, depending on the information assumption being used. To get Keynesian policy accepted it was enough to admit that the speculative demand for money balances to hold was normally greater than zero.

That subnormal activity is possible because of money's liquidity premium is a powerful intuition. But as a basis for a secure empirical generalization it is very shaky. Intuitively, one would expect the liquidity premium to be quite large at some times and quite small at others. Formally, that is all *General Theory* claims. Empirical data suggest that this is indeed the case, since, as Keynes himself recognized, there have been longish periods, such as the nineteenth century, when money's "own rate of interest" was sufficiently low to allow "a satisfactory average level of employment" under laissez-faire conditions.[12] Certainly there is little real warrant for Keynes's *obiter dictum* that modern societies achieve full employment only in "moments of excitement" when, as he put, "over-optimism triumphs over a rate of interest which, in a cooler light, would be seen to be excessive."[13] So although it would be wrong to call the General Theory the theory of a severe slump, there is little doubt that Keynes's gloomy vision owes a great deal to the Great Depression of 1929–1932.

## Stabilization Technique

Keynes's three main theoretical books were aimed at providing justifications for conscious attempts to stabilize output and employment at a high level. The quest for output stabilization led directly to the development of National Income and Expenditure Accounts, to enable governments to estimate the size of the "output" gap—the gap between what the economy was producing and what it could produce at full employment (or, in later refinement, when it was growing to trend)—that needed to be plugged by extra spending. Keynes also insisted that the aggregate demand and supply framework of the General Theory could be used to work out how much spending needed to be withdrawn from an economy to prevent inflation if aggregate demand exceeded aggregate supply.

In principle, stabilization policy can be either monetary or fiscal, or some combination of both. In practice, Keynes rejected the monetary route to managing demand. He did not deny that investment was interest-elastic. But he thought that interest-rate changes, produced by varying the quantity of bank credit, were too slow-moving in their effects on investment; and he was worried that if interest rates were raised to check a boom it would be difficult to bring them down to check a slump, since the expectation of falling rates would increase the "propensity to hoard." So he advocated a policy of permanently cheap money, to be buttressed by capital controls if required. This left fiscal policy as the main instrument for preventing both slumps and inflationary booms. A shorthand description of Keynesian fiscal policy is that the budget should be balanced over the cycle, that is, government should incur debt during the downswing and accumulate surpluses in the upswing. It is not clear that Keynes ever thought this, or at least consistently. His final position rested on a distinction between current and capital expenditure. The "ordinary" budget should be permanently balanced (even in surplus); capital programs should be accelerated or retarded to deal with the cycle. This assumed that a large proportion of investment would be public investment. As he put it in 1943: "If two-thirds or three quarters of total investment is carried out or can be influenced by public or semi-public bodies, a long-term programme of a stable character should be capable of reducing the potential range of fluctuation to much narrower limits than formerly.... If this is successful it should not be too difficult to offset small fluctuations by expediting or retarding some items in this long-term programme."[14]

Finally, Keynes attached only minor importance to exchange-rate adjustments. His Clearing Union Plan (1942) provided for fixed, but adjustable, rates; this was a feature of the Bretton Woods Agreement (1944). Keynes's attitude—like that of most economists of his day—was governed by price-elasticity pessimism. He preferred countries to use, if necessary, capital controls to protect their balance of payments in the framework of a monetary regime of fixed exchange rates, low tariffs, and automatic creditor lending through international institutions.

Keynes was not an ivory-tower theorist. His theorizing was controlled by real world events. His own investment experience enabled him to identify the "speculative" motive for holding money; his sense of political fragility led him to concentrate on the economics of stabilization; his civil service experience enabled him to turn theories into workable plans. His economic theorizing was less directly, but still importantly, controlled by his philosophical beliefs, particularly by his conception of the good life and of the conditions of just exchange.

## IV. The Legacy

Economics was transformed by its encounter with Keynes. Macro-economics became for many years a dominant part of the subject; macroeconomic forecasting became the main tool of government policy. However, Keynes's doctrines never won universal acceptance, and key aspects of his theoretical and policy legacy have been challenged. The debated issues can be grouped under four headings.

### Acceptance of Keynes's Theory

What Keynes bequeathed was not the same as what was accepted. The first theoretical breach came with demonstrations by Pigou (1942) and by Modigliani (1944) that the Keynesian slogan "quantities adjust, not prices" was true only if money wages were rigid. This became the basis of the "neoclassical synthesis," which grafted Keynesian macroeconomics onto classical theory, but left the rigidities unexplained. Milton Friedman's counterattack was both methodological and theoretical. On the one hand, he argued that it was not acceptable to posit *ad hoc* supply functions. Second, his own application of neoclassical standards of method to Keynes's aggregate equations—seen in his permanent income hypothesis (1957), the stable demand for money function (1956, 1963), and the theory of the "natural rate" of unemployment (1968)—undermined the case for Keynesian stabilization policy. Economies were more cylically stable than Keynes had supposed; multipliers were small, or nonexistent; government manipulation of aggregate demand had no permanent "real" effects, but only raised the inflation rate. These "policy ineffectiveness" propositions were to be hardened still further by the "rational expectations" school of Robert Lucas and Thomas Sargent. The tendency of Friedman's critique (popularly called "monetarism") was to reinsert an updated version of the Quantity Theory of Money into the heart of macroeconomics. It revived the pre-Keynesian notion (adumbrated by Keynes himself in the *Tract on Monetary Reform*) that the most important macroeconomic function of governments was to keep stable the purchasing power of money.

## Acceptance of Keynesian Policy

Contrary to widespread mythology, this was patchy. Both the British and U.S. governments committed themselves to targeting "high" levels of employment, but it is often asserted that U.S. policy became Keynesian only in the early 1960s, and German policy became Keynesian in the late 1960s. Both episodes were fairly brief. Much of this discussion begs the question of what one means by "Keynesian" policy. Running a budget deficit is no more a sign of Keynesian virtue than running a budget surplus in boom conditions is anti-Keynesian. An alternative argument is that Keynes's influence was exerted not so much through national policies as through the willingness of the United States to provide the rest of the world with reserves and liquidity. However, this likewise begs the question of how "Keynesian" this willingness was.

## The Impact of Policy on Events

For a long time, the canonical view was that Keynesian demand-management policies and Keynesian-inspired institutions (the Bretton

Woods system) were mainly responsible for the uniquely successful employment and growth performance of most countries in the 1950s and 1960s. Today most of the credit for that "golden age" is given to opportunities for "catching up" with American technology, recession-proof military spending by the United States, and high levels of "social" spending.

In the 1950s and 1960s it was common to argue that Keynesian policy helped to save capitalism by removing the scourge of mass unemployment. (In Marxist terms, it *legitimized* the capitalist order.) By the 1970s it was being argued that it endangered the long-run survival of capitalism by producing rising inflation, an expanding public sector, and increasingly draconian wage and price controls. Specifically, Keynesian fiscal philosophy, by justifying budget deficits in some circumstances, opened the way, in a democracy, to permanent deficit finance. Alternatively, the Keynesian policy of "fine-tuning" the economy was destabilizing, rather than stabilizing, owing to the existence of variable leads and lags. Keynesian uncertainty, that is, applied as much to Keynesian policy as to the operations of the market economy.

## The Current Debate over Keynesian Economics

According to the monetarist-cum-rational expectations schools, Keynesian economics failed the predictive test: It led to "stagflation." In the 1970s, Keynesian policies were attacked for ignoring the existence of a "natural" rate of unemployment, and (by the Virginia or Public Choice school) for assuming that politicians wanted to maximize the collective social welfare, rather than their own individual utilities. Taken together, these two attacks offered a forceful argument against the use of discretionary fiscal and monetary policy to balance economies.

The use of models of economies with nominal rigidities is still general, but whether these rigidities are to be taken as given is much more questioned than in 1950s and 1960s. The dominant "supply-side revolution" of the 1980s was chiefly concerned to dissolve rigidities seen as institutional by deregulating labor markets. Against this, the "new Keynesians" explained how sticky prices are rational because of transactions and information costs, and how shocks to demand can destroy both physical and human capital. These explanations seemed both to strengthen and weaken the case for Keynesian macroeconomic policy. On the one hand, they gave renewed intellectual respectability to stabilization policy. On the other hand, by explicitly introducing inflation into their analyses, they conceded the existence of a rate of unemployment (the so-called NAIRU or Non-Inflation Accelerating Rate of Unemployment) below which unemployment could not be pushed by manipulating demand. Finally, against the mainstream profession's use of Bayesian statistics and decision theory to model agents' behavior, a minority school of "Post-Keynesians" continues to assert the fundamental nature of Keynes's attack on the rationality axiom.

An interim judgment on the Keynesian Revolution would be that the main body of classical economics was too well entrenched to be overthrown by the frontal assault he mounted. The notion that uncertainty was at the heart, rather than at the financial margins, of economic processes proved too subversive of the science economics claims to be acceptable. At the same time stabilization policy is widely accepted and practiced, in contradistinction to much of textbook theory. So Keynes's hope of an economic science whose assumptions are congruent with economic policy has yet to be realized. Many economists would say today of Keynes what Marshall said of Jevons: "His success was aided even by his faults ... he led many to think he was correcting great errors; whereas he was really only adding very important explanations."[15] Whether this will be the final verdict is still questionable.

## Notes

All references to Keynes's writing are to the *Collected Writings of John Maynard Keynes*, 30 volumes, published by Macmillan/Cambridge University Press for the Royal Economic Society, 1971–1989. Referred to below as *CW*.

[1] John Maynard Keynes, *The Economic Consequences of the Peace*, 1919, *CW*, p. 170.
[2] Keynes, *The General Theory of Employment, Interest and Money*, 1936, *CW* p. 381; "How to Pay for the War," 1940, *CW*, p. 123.
[3] Keynes to Roy Harrod, 4 July 1938, *CW*, pp. 296–97.
[4] Keynes, "The General Theory of Employment," *Quarterly Journal of Economics*, February 1937, *CW*, p. 113.
[5] Ibid., p. 112.

[6]Keynes, *A Tract on Monetary Reform*, 1923, *CW,* p. 65.
[7]Ibid., p. 138.
[8]Keynes to Hawtrey, 27 August 1930, *CW,* p. 146.
[9]Keynes, 1937, *CW,* p. 118.
[10]Keynes, *General Theory*, 1937, *CW*, pp. 317–18.
[11]Ibid., p. 254.
[12]Ibid., p. 307.
[13]Ibid., p. 322.
[14]Keynes, "The Long-Term Problem of Full Employment," 25 May 1943, *CW*, p. 322.
[15]A. Marshall, *Principles of Economics*, 8th ed. (London: Macmillan, 1920), p. 85.

## Bibliography

Davidson, Paul. "Would Keynes be a New Keynesian?" *Eastern Economic Journal* 18(4): 1992.
Harrod, R. F. *The Life of John Maynard Keynes.* London: Macmillan, 1951.
Hicks, J. R. *The Crisis in Keynesian Economics.* Oxford: Basil Blackwell, 1974.
Keynes, John Maynard.
  *Activities 1939-1945: Internal War Finance.* 1940. *CW*, vol. xxii.
  *Activities 1940-1946 : Shaping the Post-War World.* 1943. *CW*, vol. xxvii.
  *The Economic Consequences of the Peace.* 1919. *CW*, vol. ii.
  "The Economic Consequences of Mr. Churchill." 1925. *CW*, vol. ix.
  *The General Theory and After: Part I Preparatio.* 1930. *CW*, vol. xiii.
  *The General Theory and After: Part II Defence and Development.* 1937–38. *CW*, vol. xiv.
  *The General Theory of Employment, Interest and Money.* 1936. *CW*, vol. vii.
  "How to Pay for the War." 1940. *CW*, vol. xxii.
  *Indian Currency and Finance.* London: Macmillan, 1913. *CW*, vol. i.
  *A Tract on Monetary Reform.* 1923. *CW*, vol. iv.
  *A Treatise on Money.* London: Macmillan, 1930. *CW*, vols. v & vi.
  *Treatise on Probability.* London, Macmillan, 1921. *CW*, vol. viii.
Keynes, John Maynard, with Hubert Henderson. "Can Lloyd George Do It? 1929. *CW*, vol. ix.
Leijonhufvud Axel. *Keynes and the Classics.* London: The Institute of Economic Affairs. 1969.
Moggridge D. E. *Maynard Keynes: An Economist's Biography.* London: Routledge, 1992.
Moore, G. E. *Principia Ethica.* Cambridge: Cambridge University Press, 1959.
O'Donnell R. M., ed. *Keynes as Philosopher-Economist.* London: Macmillan, 1991.
Patinkin, Don. *Keynes's Monetary Thought: A Study of Its Development.* Durham, NC: Duke University Press, 1976.
Schumpeter J. A. *Ten Great Economists.* London: Allen and Unwin, 1952.

Skidelsky Robert

*John Maynard Keynes: Hopes Betrayed.* London: Macmillan, 1983.
*John Maynard Keynes: The Economist as Saviour.* London: Macmillan, 1992.
*John Maynard Keynes: Fighting for Britain.* London: Macmillan, 2000.
*John Maynard Keynes: Economist, Philosopher, Statesman.* Abridged. London: Macmillan, 2002.

MARK SKOUSEN

# Frank Knight and the Origin of the Chicago School of Economics

> Frank Knight dominated the intellectual atmosphere... [he] seemed to most of us, to epitomize the spirit of the university.
>
> —James M. Buchanan[1]

> He was clearly the dominant intellectual influence upon economics students at Chicago in the 1930s.
>
> —George Stigler[2]

George Stigler, James Buchanan, and, to a lesser extent, Milton Friedman—all Nobel Laureates linked to the Chicago School—laud Frank H. Knight (1885–1972) as one of three professors who greatly influenced them. The other two are Jacob Viner and Henry Simons.

When Knight died in 1972, the *Journal of Political Economy*, published by the University of Chicago, devoted several issues to him—a rare compliment. Knight's influence has been considered so dominant that some have knighted him "father" or "grandfather" of the Chicago School. Is such a representation accurate?

My basic thesis is that Frank Knight had, on net balance, a positive influence in defending and improving the neoclassical model of Adam Smith in an age when neoclassical economics came increasingly under attack by institutionalists (Veblen), social engineers (Pigou and Keynes), and Marxists. But in criticizing these critics, he had the annoying habit of adopting some of their arguments. It can be difficult to recognize Knight's positive contributions because they can be concealed by his rambling and obscure writings and his inconsistent and sometimes contradictory philosophy.

55

## Knight's Personal History

Frank Knight, the first of eleven children of evangelical Midwesterners, was a skeptic all his life, though he often returned to religious subjects. He once said that if he could come back as anyone it would be Max Weber, the great German sociologist.[3] Knight's younger brother, Bruce, also an economist, tells the story that at services one day their parents had the children sign pledges promising to attend church for the rest of their lives. Returning home, Frank (then age 14 or 15) gathered his siblings behind the barn, built a fire, and said, "Burn these things because pledges and promises made under duress are not binding."[4]

He pursued his doctorate at Cornell, which resulted in his magnus opus *Risk, Uncertainty and Profit* (1921). For the rest of his career, Knight was a voluminous writer of essays that were compiled and published by students and colleagues. He taught courses on price theory, comparative economic systems, and history of economic thought (David Ricardo was his favorite whipping boy) at the University of Chicago, where he spent most of his career, from 1927 until his retirement in 1955. He remained in Chicago the rest of his life, with emeritus status. In 1941 he helped form the Committee on Social Thought, where Friedrich Hayek and T. S. Eliot taught in the 1950s. His tenure at Chicago matched the presidency of Robert Hutchins (1929–1951), where Knight repeatedly defended the use of the modern works rather than the classics by Hutchins and Mortimer Adler (The Great Books series).[5]

Knight was known to enjoy telling risqué stories, sherry in hand, and to have admired the gloomy poetry of Thomas Hardy. As a professor, he was terribly disorganized and, according to Rose Friedman, two-thirds of his students got nothing out of his classes.[6] He was often sarcastic, cynical, and blunt. One student demanded a refund after Knight made negative comments about religion and the Catholic church in his history of economic thought course.[7]

And his writings are famous for their complexity.

When Chicago graduate Larry Wimmer wrote about Knight's emeritus status in the 1960s, he did not paint the picture of a venerated man. "By the time I was in Chicago (1960–1965), Frank Knight was this small, bent-over old man who would shuffle into the economics department offices almost every day, and walk up the stairs. He never took the elevator, never looked up, and surely never spoke to the students. If someone hadn't told you who he was you might have been inclined to believe that it was another of Chicago's homeless trying to find a warm place. He always wore the same tattered coat. A number of us were disappointed that he was not asked to give a lecture or speak to the students. I was in one seminar in which he asked questions. It was the only time I heard him speak. I went to Chicago on a Frank Knight scholarship. I would have appreciated some contact, and today would make the effort. Back then we tended to wait upon faculty to make the moves and rarely did they do so among first or second year graduate students."[8]

## How Much a Chicago Economist?

One wonders if the Chicago Nobelists are rewriting history. On the surface Frank Knight does not appear to be a "Chicago economist" in the standard way we view Chicago economics today. For example, Friedman and Stigler are famous for using the most advanced statistical methods to test rigorously their theories in micro- and macroeconomics. In 1957, Knight admitted, "Price theory on the traditional lines (filled in with empirical-quantitative content) is by far the most scientific of the disciplines dealing with motivated human behavior, and the most usable in guiding social action."[9] Yet he seldom engaged in empirical work! In fact, many of his references to data were unsubstantiated. According to Stigler, "he was extremely dogmatic in his empirical generalizations—all without a trace of proof."[10]

Chicago economists are often thought of as monetarists who apply the quantity theory of money to their analysis of the business cycle. That was Friedman's great contribution. In his long career, Frank Knight wrote only one article on the subject, in 1941, and there he only hints at what constitutes sound monetary policy. Even then he concludes, "The monetary system can never be made automatic."[11] Worse, he appears to support a fundamental Keynesian/socialist notion that there can be no inherent "self-regulating" governor in a free-enterprise system. States Knight: "Its equilibrium is vague and highly unstable. Its natural tendency is to oscillate over a fairly long period and a wide range, between limits which are rather indeterminate."[12] Friedman, of course, came to the opposite conclusion after doing his monetary studies: "It is now widely agreed that the Keynesian proposition is erroneous on the level of pure theory.... There always exists in principle a position of full employment equilibrium in a free market economy."[13]

## Keynesian Economics: Pro and Con

Many Chicago students reported that Knight was an opponent of Keynesian economics in the postwar era. In his 1950 American Economic Association (AEA) presidential address, he debunked Keynes for having "succeeded in carrying economic thinking well back to the dark age."[14]

Paul Samuelson recalls a conversation with Knight at an AEA meeting in the early 1950s where Knight bluntly told a group, "If there's anything I can't stand it's a Keynesian and a believer in monopolistic competition." "What about believers in the use of mathematics in economic analysis, Frank," asked a colleague. "Can't stand it either," he replied firmly.[15]

Knight wrote a largely negative review of Keynes's *General Theory* in 1937, which Henry Hazlitt included in his *Critics of Keynesian Economics*.[16] According to Knight, Keynes's theory of unemployment was "unsubstantiated," adding that he "simply cannot take this new and revolutionary equilibrium theory seriously." And yet—Knight almost always adds the caveats "but," "on the other hand," and "up to a point" to his views—Knight ultimately endorsed one of Keynes's cures for depression and unemployment, that is, "inflation."[17] Knight wisely rejected the "favourite American recipe" of raising wages to revive spending,[18] yet he joined Henry Simons, Jacob Viner, and other Chicago economists in the 1930s to advocate deficit spending and an expansionary monetary policy to end the Depression.[19] This pre-Keynesian counter-classical approach may surprise many conservatives and libertarians, but it is one that Friedman himself endorses during extreme economic conditions. "Keynes had nothing to offer those of us who had sat at the feet of Simons, Mints, Knight, and Viner."[20]

## The Liberal Market Order

James Buchanan says that he was "converted into a zealous advocate of the market order" when he took Knight's price theory course after the war in 1945. Buchanan notes that at the time almost every student, including himself, was a socialist.[21] Knight converted him. Surely that fits into the Chicago mold, which is famous for its market ideology. (I should add that Jacob Viner, who also taught price theory at Chicago, was pro-market. Friedman called Viner's price theory class "unquestionably the greatest intellectual experience of my life.")[22] Knight spent most of his career opposing the efforts of progressives, institutionalists, Keynesians, and Christians (he was known to make negative, sometimes insulting, comments about the Catholic church) who advocated social control in the name of science and morality. "I believe that individualism must be the political philosophy of intelligent and morally serious men.... It is my conviction that any great extension of state action in economics is incompatible with political liberty, that 'control' will call for more control and tend to run into complete regimentation...and finally into absolutism, with or without a destructive struggle for power."[23]

Yet here again Knight's philosophy was not always consistent. His price theory class was largely pro-market, and his overarching theme was favorable toward Adam Smith's "system of natural liberty," but he always insisted that the market system suffered from "imperfections," particularly two major flaws: a tendency toward monopoly power, and greater inequality of income and wealth. "On the other side, there is an undeniable natural tendency toward greater inequality and concentration of power under free enterprise itself, which political action seems the only way of counteracting."[24] His answer was antitrust and progressive and inheritance taxation.[25] His disciple and colleague Henry Simons advocated similar legislation.[26]

In the next generation at Chicago, Friedman and Stigler proved Knight and Simons wrong on both counts. Yet, at regular luncheons with Friedman and Stigler in the 1950s, Knight persisted in advocating these fundamental weaknesses in the free enterprise system. Stigler reports, "In later years at countless lunches this was challenged on both analytical and empirical grounds by Milton Friedman, each time leading Knight to make temporary concessions, only to return to his standard position by the next lunch."[27]

## A Doubting Knight

During the 1930s, Knight lost faith in the "liberal market order" and fell into a deep pessimism from which he never fully recovered. He confessed, "For the first two years or so after the economic crisis of 1929, I was one of the large group of students of economics who condemned the idea that this was fundamentally different from other depressions. But I have become convinced that I was in error, that we are actually in the course of one of the world's great economic and political revolutions."[28] In an essay on "The Sickness of Liberal Society," written after two world wars and a Great Depression, Knight contended that the "free enterprise system of organization" (he preferred this term to the Marxist-inspired word "capitalism")[29] was full of "imperfections" and could not achieve a just and efficient society.[30] While at later times he denounced Marxism as "romantically immoralistic, destructive, diabolical," even "monstrous," and Marx as "a hater" of a "very high rank,"[31] he toyed with the idea of communism as an alternative social order in the early 1930s, at the depths of the Depression, when he gave a series of lectures under the provocative title "The Case for Communism: From the Standpoint of an Ex-Liberal." Rose and Milton Friedman attended one of these lectures, which they felt were "tongue-in-cheek" and aimed at attracting a large crowd. (Milton Friedman recalls that a majority of the students in the social sciences at Chicago at the time were members of the Communist Party or very close to it.) In a published version, Knight insisted that "liberalism, made up of economic laissez-faire and political democracy, is bankrupt." He confessed to contributing $20 to the socialist Norman Thomas and concluded, "What the nations of the world need today is government...a Communist Party dictatorship would be a real government; it would lead, unify and direct social activity and this is rapidly becoming essential to a tolerable existence."[32] Warren J. Samuels explains Knight's temptation with communism by explaining that "Knight was very much taken with freedom. But he was also a devotee of order," which communism provided.[33] Knight later regretted making these speeches: "I wish I could unpublished them."[34]

Yet into the 1960s he constantly preached a middle way between the extremes of Marxism and laissez-faire. "Marxist economics is a tissue of absurdity, but, sad to say, much nonsense has also been published by advocates of *laissez-faire*," he said. "Anarchism … is indefensible. … [S]ocial life sets many limits to freedom," he explained.[35]

## An "Austrian" Economist?

In some ways, Knight can be viewed more an Austrian than a Chicago economist. He was fluent in German, and he corresponded with Hayek. We don't normally think of Knight as an Austrian because of his zestful attacks on the Austrian theory of capital (to be discussed below) and on Hayek's writings on political economy.[36] But there are some similarities. Kenneth Boulding noted that *Risk, Uncertainty and Profit* has a "distinctly 'Austrian' twist" to it, with its emphasis on entrepreneurship, imperfect competition, and decentralized decisionmaking.[37] Like Mises, he seldom used graphs or charts in his writings. His price theory textbook used in the 1930s has only two diagrams, and his chapter on supply and demand contains not a single supply-and-demand graph.[38] He distinguished between the social and natural sciences, and was naturally skeptical of applying mathematical constructs and quantitative analysis to economics. He often belittled the possibility of doing accurate empirical work: "It is not conceivably possible to 'verify' any proposition about 'economic' behavior by any 'empirical' procedure, if the key words of this statement are defined as they must be defined to be used with relevance and precision."[39]

Knight, like Mises and Hayek, offered incisive criticism of the theory of socialism, noting that central planners lack diverse knowledge (a Hayekian theme) and proper incentives to run an economy efficiently. He concludes, "Socialists grossly oversimplify the organization problem …" and while central planners can run "routine operations of a stationary economy," they might have a challenge trying to deal with a "dynamic" change.[40]

In 1948, at a time when England was nationalizing industries and the United States was contemplating the same, Knight worried that government intervention into the economy would led to full-scale socialism: "But it is my conviction that any great extension of state action in economics is incompatible with political liberty, that 'control' will call for more control and tend to run into complete regimentation."[41] In 1950, Mises gave a speech along the same lines, titled "Middle-of-the-Road Policy Leads to Socialism."[42]

Most Austrian was his persistent pessimism—as opposed to the cheery optimism of Freidman and other Chicagoans in the postwar era. Like Mises and Hayek, Knight was not optimistic about the future of capitalism. In his 1950 AEA presidential address, he said he could "find little cause for jubilation," and bemoaned the lack of sound economic thinking by the public and government officials who favored protectionism, cheap money, tax evasion, and price-fixing. "The cards are heavily stacked in favor of centralization," he concluded.[43]

## Knight as the Philosopher of Skepticism

Until now, we have largely focused on Frank Knight the critic, for which he was most famous. In fact, it was this critical eye that students found attractive. Knight was Buchanan's "role model." (Buchanan has only two photos on his wall—one of Frank Knight and the other of Swedish economist Knut Wicksell.) Why Knight? It was his "willingness to question anything, and anybody, on any subject anytime; the categorical refusal to accept anything as sacred; the genuine openness to all ideas, and, finally, the basic conviction that most ideas peddled about are nonsense or worse when examined critically."[44]

This became known as the Knightian trademark: committing economics (and other social sciences) to extremely rigorous and detailed examination, with numerous "ifs," "buts," "whens," "limitations," and the phrases "on the one hand," "on the other hand," and "up to a point." Knight opposed strict rules and formulas. He was the ultimate skeptic, always extremely cautious about the application of scientific methods. His nihilism went so far that he could state, "The only good principle is to have no principle."[45]

Friedman and Stigler picked up this Knightian trait of questioning authority and constant criticism. Knight and his disciples looked upon received theory, including the new theories of Keynes, with a highly skeptical eye. "Frank Knight was a radical critic, who exhibited little respect for the 'classical,' whether in Greek philosophy or in British political economy."[46] He was disdainful of rank and authority. "Challenge everything," he said, that does not have logic or empirical support. "There is no God, but Frank Knight is his prophet."[47]

The timing was right for this kind of skepticism. In an age when nearly everyone on campus was a socialist or communist, Knight's antiestablishmentarianism helped Buchanan become a libertarian. Perhaps Knight had a similar effect on Friedman and Stigler, allowing them to develop sufficient independence and irreverence of authority to question the Keynesian monolith in the postwar era.

Given his dogmatic skepticism, a school of disciples was never possible. (Schumpeter likewise never developed his own school.) Knight did not fit into any particular research program. He was purely an ivory-tower academic who did not consult with the government or the private sector. According to Buchanan, "The world was not there waiting to be 'saved' by his own efforts, and he would have steadfastly refused to give advice to a reforming despot.... His self-assigned task was to expose the absurdities of others and nothing more."[48] He distrusted reformers: "[P]eople have too much faith in positive action."[49]

## Mistrust of Reformers

When it came to public policy, or "preaching," Stigler (though not Friedman) would later follow Knight's path in maintaining a form of agnosticism when it came to influencing legislators and politicians. "My central thesis is that economists exert a minor and scarcely detectable influence on the societies in which they live."[50] Furthermore, democratic institutions do a good job of reflecting voters' interests, and therefore economists should beware of preaching or chastising them for committing bad economic policy: "Economists...should be reluctant to characterize a large fraction of political activity as mistaken."[51] The political apathy of Stigler and Knight may explain the apolitical attitude of graduate economics students at Chicago.

## Knight the Sociologist

Perhaps we can think of Knight ultimately as a sociologist along the lines of the German sociologist Max Weber, who was trained as an economist. As Knight grew older, he showed less and less interest in pure economics and more and more interest in broader questions of law, ethics, philosophy, religion, anthropology, and political science. He taught courses on Max Weber at Chicago, and translated Weber's *General Economic History* into English in 1927. In 1941, he helped establish the Committee on Social Thought, an interdisciplinary program. In general, "Weber was more systematic, Knight an ad hoc sociologist," states Arthur Schweitzer.[52] Knight differed from Weber in methodology; Knight contended that economic laws are universal, Weber argued that laws must be verified with experience and claimed a "cultural science" of sociology based on time and place. One can see the influence of Weber in this statement by Knight on individualism and society: "The individual is largely formed in and by the social process, and the nature of the individual must be affected by any social action."[53]

## Knight's Early Contributions
## to Economic Science

Ultimately, Knight was a better critic than a systemic contributor of new theories. Nevertheless, he did make several important contributions to economic science, especially in countering the critics of the market.

His most famous work, *Risk, Uncertainty and Profit,* published in 1921, was used as a textbook at Chicago, Harvard, and the London School of Economics, and has been reprinted many times. (It is still in print, though not used as a textbook.) Several aspects of this classic work are worth noting.

Knight's book contains his chief contribution to the theory and nature of the role of profits in the competitive model. Essentially, he seeks to legitimize the existence of profits in the market process and to defend it against critics who argued that profits were unjustified and unnecessary. Knight begins by defending theoretical (that is, deductive) economics with the use of "unrealistic" assumptions of "perfect competition." (Knight was the first to outline these basic assumptions.) Under the rigorous assumptions of perfect competition (many buyers and sellers, perfect knowledge, costless transportation, etc.), profit would be nonexistent. Entrepreneurs would move quickly from areas of lowest return to areas of highest return, and profit would disappear. How then can profit be justified?

By relaxing the assumption of perfect knowledge, the element of "uncertainty" becomes a part of the economic game, justifying profits. Here Knight makes a critical distinction between risk and uncertainty. Risk, he notes, is a measurable probability that can be insured against, such as life expectancy. But uncertainty is immeasurable, such as predicting short-term fluctuations in the stock market or foreign exchange rates, or even women's fashions.[54] Knight argued that the entrepreneur, especially in larger business enterprises, is compensated for bearing the uncertainties of the marketplace.

## Critique of Pigou's Welfare Economics

Knight made a seminal criticism of Pigou's social welfare thesis, Keynesian interventionism, and socialist central planning. In an article titled "Some Fallacies in the Interpretation of Social Cost," published in 1924, he rejected Arthur C. Pigou's classic view of *The Economics of Welfare* (1920) that the laissez-faire market mechanism necessarily failed to achieve efficient allocation of resources. One example was road congestion. Suppose, he said, there are two roads connecting two cities. One road is cheap but badly surfaced, the other is narrow but well-graded (with more costly upkeep). Pigou concludes that the better road will be overused and overcrowded. The solution to this market failure would be to impose a tax equal to the difference between the average cost and marginal cost on the well-surfaced road.

Knight showed that if roads were privately owned, road owners would set tolls that would reduce congestion, and therefore no government tax would be required to establish an efficient use of resources.[55] On a broader scale, Knight's pioneering essay demonstrates that a free competitive environment can allocate resources efficiently as long as property rights are clearly identified. Knight's seminal article encouraged disciples, including Buchanan, Armen Alchian, and Ronald Coase, to study property rights and externalities.

## Knight's Pedagogy: A Mix of Austrian and Chicago Economics

Knight came back to Chicago in 1927, and joined Viner in teaching the basic course in economic price, value, and distribution theory. The course is more fully developed in his textbook, *The Economic Organization* (1933), which made a major contribution to methodology.

Like his book, *Risk, Uncertainty and* Profit, Knight began his discussion of economic theory and the "economic man." He recognized the criticism of Veblen and others that economic man is not actually the social man of the world, and "does not include all human interests."[56] But, Knight argued, the theory of economic man, however one-dimensional, is a useful construct, consisting of a consumer maximizing utility and a producer maximizing profits, and therefore optimizing economic welfare and standard of living.

As mentioned earlier, Knight has only two diagrams in his text-book, one reflecting an Austrian view of the macroeconomy and the other representing the Chicago (and later Keynesian) view of the aggregate economy. On page 41 of his book, Knight illustrates the Austrian stages-of-production approach, showing how resources are transformed into final consumer and investment good, with examples of direct and indirect means to satisfying wants.

On page 61, Knight illustrates the "wheel of wealth" diagram, known today as the "circular flow" diagram. Today only Knight's "circular flow" diagram has been adopted by the profession, and with few exceptions the "stages of production" diagram has been omitted from the textbooks. This is due to Knight's decision in the 1930s to reject the stage-of-production model and Austrian theory of capital, which he regarded as unnecessary. His fatal decision has affected two disastrous effects on modern macroeconomics. First, by creating an excessively aggregate model of the economy, the circular-flow diagram has lead to several fallacies in macroeconomics. For example, it leads to the purchasing-power fallacy, that an increase in income through government spending or a minimum wage can stimulate output.

In addition, the Keynesians (Paul Samuelson, in particular) borrowed Knight's invention of the circular flow diagram to create the Keynesian "paradox-of-thrift" diagram, where savings can leak out of the economy and cause depression. In it we see that the key to economic stability and growth is consumer spending, which drives the circular flow of the economy, while savings leak out of the system.

The Austrians have pointed out that the Samuelson/Knight diagram ignores time and the production process. When the economy is driven by saving and investment, consumption (utility) is the effect, not the cause, of production.

It is a pity Knight didn't continue to preach the dynamic capital-using process of market activity.

## Quantity Theory of Money

Knight's critique of the Austrian theory of capital reinforced Friedman's macroeconomics and his quantity theory of money. Knight's own view of capital and production was along the lines of John Bates Clark, who in an earlier era had attacked Böhm-Bawerk's period-of-production concept. Earlier in his career, Knight accepted the Austrian theory of capital: "I completely accepted it for years, taught it in class lectures and expounded it in text materials," including *The Economic Organization*.[57] But in the early 1930s, he abandoned the Austrian theory and echoed Clark's macro view: "In a stationary economy there is no interval between production and consumption."[58]

In 1934, he expounded a Fisherian version of capital and interest as a stock-flow concept, where capital is a permanent asset that yields future income, and criticized the flaws he saw in the time-structural view of a period of production. For Knight, like the circular flow diagram, "all capital is inherently perpetual."[59]

Throughout the early 1930s, Knight attacked Friedrich Hayek and his theory of business cycles, which was based on a Mengerian time structure of production and heterogeneous capital. Knight dismissed Hayek's theory as "worthless." In 1950, in an introduction to Carl Menger's newly translated *Principles of Investment*, Knight attacked one of Menger's fundamental principles of macroeconomics: "Perhaps the most serious defect in Menger's economic system...is his view of production as a process of converting goods of higher order into goods of lower order."[60]

If capital is indeed perpetual and homogeneous like putty, or water (Clark compared capital investment to the Hudson River), then a structural model is unimportant, and the Austrian theory of the business cycle is "useless."

Knight's dismissal of Austrian capital and business cycle theory was so strong that it influenced his students. In the 1950s, so the story goes, Knight would ask his students the following question on tests: "What do you know about Austrian capital theory?" The only acceptable answer was, "Nothing." According to Larry Wimmer, "Any more than that suggested a misallocation of their time and study. This is folklore; I have no idea if it actually happened."[61] Knight's dogma spread. Friedman and Stigler inherited this disdain for Austrian capital theory. (Stigler dismissed the Austrian theory of production and interest in his published dissertation.)[62] Knight's influence on Friedman is even more profound in this regard. Friedman's quantity theory of money is based entirely on a stock-flow model, where an increase in the money supply, like water, spreads evenly through the monetary river. (Friedman prefers to use the helicopter example for inflation.) Because capital investment is homogeneous, the transmission mechanism is simple and straightforward. Ripple effects are unimportant. What matters is that the height of the river rises.

Thus, the official Chicago view of monetary inflation is a simplistic monetary disequilibrium model, where changes in the money supply cause changes in economic activity. There is little concern over structural imbalances, asset bubbles, and interest-rate distortions. They are of secondary importance. The primary emphasis is on monetary trends, either "easy" or "tight" money as measured by the monetary aggregates. It all comes out of Knight.

## Critique of Knight's Macro View

Other economists disagree, including Fritz Machlup and Israel Kirzner. Machlup called Hayek's capital theory an "indispensable" tool of analysis. "There was and is always the choice between maintaining, increasing, and consuming capital," he wrote in defense of Hayek.[63] Kirzner notes, "Because the Knightian view of the productive process emphasizes the repetitive 'circular flow' of economic activity while denying the paramount importance of a structural order linked to final consumer demand, it is possible to simply ignore the Austrian critique of the productivity theory of interest."[64]

The Austrian stages-of-production model is a more complex depiction of economic activity. It focuses on the importance of capital investment, interest rates, savings, and the right balance between production and consumption. It emphasizes the legitimacy of genuine natural savings as the key to economic performance, not increases in the money supply. It warns of asset bubbles and structural imbalances as a result of monetary intervention. It treats capital as heterogeneous, not just homogeneous. (Capital is liquid and homogeneous until it is invested in specialized capital goods.) It tells us more than the simplistic monetary disequilibrium model of Friedman and the monetarists.

There is a way to test which theory is best. What would be the effect of a steady 10 percent increase in the money supply? The Chicago School would say that this would cause inflation, a real rise in prices beyond the long-term growth rate of the economy. Say the economy is growing at 4 percent. Then inflation would be 6 percent, and would stay at around 6 percent as long as the central bank expanded the money supply steadily at a 10 percent rate. The Austrians would argue that there is an inherent law of diminishing returns at work here, that even with a steady annualized increase of the money supply by 10 percent, at some point the booming inflationary economy would collapse and head into recession or worse because inflation is "unsustainable."

## Conclusion

I like to think of Frank Knight as the "knight" of the Chicago school, and I think he would be pleased with this designation. In the game of chess, the knight is not the most powerful piece on the board. Frank Knight is not the king or queen of the social sciences; that belongs to an Adam Smith, a Carl Menger, or a Milton Friedman. But he has a unique status. The knight is the most versatile of players: The horse jumps, can capture an enemy, and plays alternatively on white and black squares. He is the only piece that can move at the beginning of the game before any pawn move has been made. It is usually brought into play slightly sooner than the bishops (Frank Knight would like that), and much sooner than the king, queen, or rooks. To be most influential, the horse should be placed near the center of the board. A horse on the side or corner is ineffective. As chess players say, "A knight on the rim is grim."

Finally, the knight never plays it straight. The horse moves two squares forward and then moves to the left or right. He is a bit unpredictable. Frank Knight was always giving two cheers rather than three for the market.

George Stigler, who embodied much of the Knightian spirit, spoke the following at a 1972 memorial service: "Frank Knight transmitted, to a degree I have never seen equaled, a sense of unreserved commitment to the truth."[65] To which I add St. Paul's comment, "ever learning, and never able to come to the knowledge of the truth."[66]

## Notes

[1]James M. Buchanan, "Frank H. Knight," *Remembering the University of Chicago*, ed. Edward Shils (Chicago: University of Chicago Press, 1991), p. 244.

[2]George Stigler, "Frank H. Knight," *The New Palgrave Dictionary of Economics* (London: Macmillan, 1987), 3: 56.

[3]Arthur Schweitzer, "Frank Knight's Social Economics," *History of Political Economy* 7 (3; 1975): 279.

[4]Stigler, "Frank H. Knight," *New Palgrave Dictionary*, 3: 55.

[5]See Ross B. Emmett, "Introduction," *Selected Essays by Frank H. Knight* (Chicago: University of Chicago Press, 1999), 1: xvii–xix.

[6]Rose Friedman: "We have often remarked that two-thirds of his students never got anything from him, and the rest never got anything out of two-thirds of his remarks, but that remaining one-third of one-third was well worth the price of admission. To this day we find ourselves often prefacing a comment, 'as Frank Knight would say.'" *Two Lucky People* (Chicago: University of Chicago Press, 1999), p. 38.

[7]Stigler comments, "Knight was both a great and an absurd teacher. The absurdity was documented by his utterly disorganized teaching, with constant change of subject

and yet insistent repetition of arguments...." *Lives of the Laureates*, 4ᵗʰ ed., ed. William Breit and Barry T. Hirsch (Cambridge, MA: MIT Press, 1998 [1986]), p. 81.

8Larry Wimmer (Brigham Young University) to Mark Skousen. Private correspondence, December 2005.

9Frank H. Knight, "Preface to the 1957 reprint," *Risk, Uncertainty and Profit* (New York: Harper & Row, 1921), p. lix.

10George J. Stigler, "Frank Hyneman Knight," *New Palgrave Dictionary*, 3: 56.

11Knight, "The Business Cycle, Interest and Money" in *Selected Essays*, 2: 146. Appeared originally in *The Review of Economics and Statistics* 23 (May 1941): 53–67.

12Ibid., p. 145.

13Milton Friedman and David Meiselman, "The Relative Stability of Monetary Velocity and the Investment Multiplier in the United States, 1897–1958," Commission on Money and Credit, *Stabilization Policies* (Englewood Cliffs, NJ: Prentice-Hall, 1963), p. 167.

14Frank H. Knight, "The Role of Principles in Economics and Politics" in *Selected Essays*, 2: 362–63.

15Paul A. Samuelson, *The Collected Scientific Papers of Paul A. Samuelson* (Cambridge: MIT Press, 1997), 4: 886-87.

16Henry Hazlitt, ed. *The Critics of Keynesian Economics* (Princeton, NJ: D. Van Nostrand. 1960).

17Knight, "Unemployment: And Mr. Keynes's Revolution in Economic Theory" in *Selected Essays*, 1: 345, 364–66.

18Frank H. Knight, "Social Science and the Political Trend," *Freedom and Reform* (Indianapolis: Liberty Fund, 1982 [1947]), pp. 26–27.

19J. Ronnie Davis, "Chicago Economists, Deficit Budgets, and the Early 1930's," *American Economic Review* 58 (June 1968): 477–78.

20Quoted in Robert J. Gordon, *Milton Friedman's Monetary Framework* (Chicago: University of Chicago Press, 1974), p. 163.

21James M. Buchanan, "Better than Ploughing," *Recollections of Eminent Economists*, ed. J. A. Kregel (New York: New York University Press, 1989), 2: 282.

22Interview in William Briet and Roger W. Spencer, eds., *Lives of the Laureates* (Cambridge: MIT Press, 1982), p. 83.

23Frank Knight, "Preface to the Reprint of 1948," *Risk, Uncertainty and Profit* (New York: Harper & Row, 1957 [1921]).

24Ibid., p. iii.

25Knight, "The Playful Act," *Freedom and Reform*, pp. 429–30, 451–53.

26Henry Simons, *Economic Policy for a Free Society* (Chicago: University of Chicago Press, 1948), pp. 57 passim.

27Stigler, "Knight," *New Palgrave Dictionary*, 3: 57.

28Knight, *Freedom and Reform*, pp. 27–28.

29Ibid., p. 448.

30Ibid., pp. 451–52.

[31]Knight, "Ethics and Economic Reform" in *Selected Essays*, 2: 34.

[32]Frank H. Knight, "The Case for Communism: From the Standpoint of an Ex-Liberal," *Research in the History of Economic Thought and Methodology* (Greenwich, CT: JAI Press, 1991), Supplement 2: 53, 66, 92, 99, 106.

[33]Warren J. Samuels, "Introduction," ibid., p. 52.

[34]Quoted in Milton and Rose Friedman, *Two Lucky People* (Chicago: University of Chicago Press, 1998), p. 37.

[35]Knight, "Laissez-Faire: Pro and Con," in *Selected Essays*, 2: 437.

[36]Ibid., pp. 442–50. Knight heavily criticized Hayek's *Constitution of Liberty* (Chicago: University of Chicago Press, 1960), especially his treatment of economic equality, progressive taxation, and social justice.

[37]Kenneth Boulding, jacket quote for Knight, *Risk, Uncertainty and Profit*.

[38]Frank H. Knight, *The Economic Organization* (New York: Augustus M. Kelley, 1967 [1933]), pp. 67–95.

[39]Knight, "What is Truth in Economics?" in *Selected Essays*, 1: 382.

[40]Knight, "Socialism: The Nature of the Problem," in ibid., 2: 89, 95–96, 105. Originally published in *Ethics* 50 (April 1949).

[41]Knight, "Preface to 1948 Reprint," *Risk, Uncertainty and Profit*, p. iii.

[42]Ludwig von Mises, *Planning for Freedom*, 4<sup>th</sup> ed. (Grove City, PA: Libertarian Press, 1980), pp. 18–35.

[43]Knight, "The Role of Principles in Economics and Politics," in *Selected Essays*, 2: 361–62, 390.

[44]Buchanan, "Better than Ploughing," *Recollections of Eminent Economists*, 2: 283.

[45]Knight, *Selected Essays*, 1: ix.

[46]Buchanan, "Frank H. Knight," *Remembering the University of Chicago*, p. 246.

[47]Buchanan, Foreword, *Freedom and Reform*, xi.

[48]Buchanan, "Frank H. Knight," in *Remembering the University of Chicago*, p. 251.

[49]Frank H. Knight, "The Role of Principles in Economics and Politics" (his 1950 AEA presidential address) in *Selected Essays*, 2: 390.

[50]George Stigler, *The Economist as Preacher, and Other Essays* (Chicago: University of Chicago Press, 1982), p. 63.

[51]Ibid., 8. Israel Kirzner wrote a scathing review of Stigler's essay on preaching, describing it as "bizarre…disturbing…unfortunate….affront to common sense." See Kirzner in Daniel B. Klein, ed., *What Do Economists Contribute?* (New York: New York University Press, 1999), pp. 125–32.

[52]Arthur Schweitzer, "Frank Knight's Social Economics," *History of Political Economy* 7 (3; 1975): 290.

[53]Knight, *Freedom and Reform*, p. 69.

[54]Knight, *Risk, Uncertainty, and Profit*, p. 233.

[55]Frank H. Knight, "Some Fallacies in the Interpretation of Social Cost," *Quarterly Journal of Economics* 38 (May 1924): 582–606.

[56]Frank H. Knight, *The Economic Organization* (New York: Augustus M. Kelley, 1967 [1933]), p. 4.

[57]Frank H. Knight, "Professor Hayek and the Theory of Investment," *Economic Journal* (March 1935): 79.

[58]Frank H. Knight, "Capitalistic Production, Time and the Rate of Return," *Economic Essays in Honour of Gustav Cassel* (London: George Allen and Unwin, 1933), p. 339.

[59]Frank H. Knight, "Capital, Time, and the Interest Rate," *Economica*, New Series 3 (August 1934): 264.

[60]Frank H. Knight, "Introduction," *Principles of Economics* (New York: New York University Press, 1959), p. 25.

[61]Larry Wimmer to Mark Skousen. Private correspondence, January 29, 2006.

[62]George Stigler, *Production and Distribution Theories* (New York: Macmillan, 1941). However, Rose Friedman did her own dissertation on capital theory under Professor Knight. It has been rumored that her dissertation, never finished, was sympathetic toward the Austrians. When I asked her about this recently, she nodded her head with a smile, but never said a word (perhaps because her husband Milton is staunchly critical of Austrian capital theory).

[63]Fritz Machlup, "Professor Knight and the 'Period of Production,'" *Journal of Political Economy* 43 (5; 1935): 578.

[64]Israel Kirzner, "Ludwig von Mises and the Theory of Capital and Interest," *Economics of Ludwig von Mises*, ed. Lawrence S. Moss (Kansas City: Sheed and Ward, 1976), p. 62.

[65]Quoted in Friedman, *Two Lucky People*, p. 36.

[66]2 Timothy 3:7.

Lee A. Coppock

# James Buchanan:
# Pioneer for Individual Freedom

## Introduction

In 1986, James Buchanan was awarded the Nobel Prize in Economics. This was a vindication of him, of his ideas, and of his method of inquiry because James Buchanan has never been an academic insider. He received his bachelor's degree from Middle Tennessee State Teacher's College; his academic appointments include Chico State in California.

When asked about his status as an academic outsider, Buchanan often stresses that it is important to him because it has enabled him to explore ideas in an almost unconstrained fashion. He has never felt the need to have his ideas conform to some ideal held by a department in which he might reside.

In examining Professor Buchanan's contributions to economics, I will, of course, emphasize his work in Public Choice economics. But I would be remiss if I skipped over his work in other areas. To encompass the variety of his efforts, I will follow a chronology of his accomplishments.

## Chicago

Frank Knight of the University of Chicago, a founder of the Chicago School, was an inspiration, a role model, and a methodological father to James Buchanan. He ascribes to Knight the credit for his continued determination to question everything, to take nothing as sacred in the development of ideas.

When Buchanan arrived in Chicago, he was a self-described "libertarian-socialist." Apparently he had conflicting ideas swimming in his head. As a Southerner, he had an unquestionable distrust of federal government. But he also had a very real mistrust and dislike of large corporations, banks, and inherited money. After six weeks of Frank Knight's classes, however, Buchanan left all of his socialist tendencies behind and embraced the principles of individual liberty—for good.

The other major influence on Buchanan during his days in Chicago was Knut Wicksell, whom he discovered by accident After he passed his German language exams, Buchanan went to the University of Chicago library where he stumbled onto a copy of Wicksell's works, which were written in German. He was absolutely enveloped by Wicksell's ideas. What he saw in Wicksell was the embodiment of much of what he himself had been thinking, but in a logical and written form. Much of Buchanan's work in *The Calculus of Consent* would be based on Wicksell.

Buchanan left Chicago a very competent neoclassical micro-economist with a distinct appreciation for individual liberty—and a determination to question everything. To see how this translated into his research, we will briefly examine two significant contributions Buchanan made in the 1960s that are not specifically Public Choice.

The first is a paper titled "Externality," which was published in 1962. This was Buchanan's attempt to formally address the issues raised by what economists call "externalities," which are one of the classic "market failures" that economists use to justify government intervention in the private marketplace. Externalities occur when some unrelated third party is affected by the behavior of a firm or individual. Economists in the 1960s (and some still today) would assume that the very appearance of an externality is evidence that the market has failed, and that government solutions must be forthcoming.

The classic externality problems are typically presented as negative production externalities. For example, Alsons Corporation, a firm located in Hillsdale, Michigan, produces showerheads. Suppose that in the production of their quality handheld showerheads, Alsons also produces something undesirable—noise. This noise is a negative externality imposed upon the company's neighbors, which include a number of farms.

Let's assume that showerhead production is very profitable and that there is a law against noise pollution. Suppose Alsons' production is so profitable the company can afford to both produce high quality showerheads *and* compensate the farmers for any damages. In other words, Alsons can pay the farmers for enduring the noise pollution and still make profit. In this world, the farmers are no worse off than they were previously and yet we still observe noise pollution. This scenario is not altogether unlikely.

Here is Buchanan's point: "There is not a prima facie case for intervention in all cases where an externality is observed to exist. The internal benefits from carrying out the activity, net of costs, may be greater than the external damage that is imposed on other parties."[1] Of course, his colleague at the University of Virginia, Ronald Coase, would do even more damage to the traditional externality position.

In a paper titled "An Economic Theory of Clubs," published in 1965, Buchanan goes after the second major "market failure." Following Paul Samuelson's paper (1954),[2] it was assumed throughout the economics profession that a public good was simply a requirement for government provision. In addition, the definition of a public good was much fuzzier in 1965. The fundamental characteristic of a Samuelsonian public good was merely "non-rivalry in consumption."[3] This means simply that the good in question can be simultaneously consumed by more than one individual without affecting the consumption (in quantity or quality) of another individual. An example of a public good is something like a levee: It protects several homes as well as it protects a single home. In contrast, an ice cream cone is a private good: Its consumption by one person absolutely affects the consumption by another.

Samuelson's paper essentially opened the door to significant government intervention. The reason is that there really are scores of goods that are, at least to some degree, nonrivalrous in nature. For example, a lecture has a degree of nonrivalry. You could add a few more students to the audience and there would be no real effect on the quality of the lecture that each individual hears. This applies to movies, golf, education, and many other things. In other words, if nonrivalry requires government provision, the role of government would be significant.

Buchanan's point here is simple: Many of these goods are provided (and provided well) privately. Often, these goods are provided in the form of a club. In fact, *as long as exclusion is feasible,* nonrivalrous goods can and will be provided efficiently by private markets. Buchanan's paper was significant in that it shifted the public goods debate to the characteristic of feasibility of exclusion.

Without his contributions to Public Choice economics, Professor Buchanan would certainly be viewed as a fine neoclassical economist and a champion of freedom. However, what earned him a Nobel Prize and what truly set him apart as a great economist was his path-breaking work in Public Choice theory. We turn to that work now, in reference to the seminal book published in 1962, co-written with Gordon Tullock, *The Calculus of Consent.*[4]

## The Calculus of Consent

The basic approach of *The Calculus* stems directly from the work of Knut Wicksell and James Madison (a Virginian). From Wicksell, Buchanan takes the admonition that "economists have got to stop acting as if they are advising benevolent despots."[5] From Madison, he incorporates the skepticism of behavior and motives of politicians that are embodied in the U.S. Constitution and *Federalist Papers.* The basic approach of *The Calculus,* which many take to also be the thrust of Public Choice economics, is that actors in political markets are motivated by the same factors that influence the behavior of actors in private markets.

Economic behavior is rational utility-maximizing selfish behavior. Using this model of individual behavior, economists can explain much of what people do privately, both in their household and in their business firms. However, in the 1960s, economists (and even political scientists) studying government and political markets assumed a different type of behavior on the part of politicians and bureaucrats. The assumption was that individuals acting in political markets (voters, legislators, bureaucrats) act on behalf of their fellow man. However, individuals buying groceries or seeking education for their children or running a business can only be trusted to act out of selfish ambition. This means that one day someone could become the CEO of GM who is a greedy self-serving individual. However, if this person enters the voting booth, or is elected to office, or is nominated to serve as a bureaucrat, that person undergoes an instant transformation into a "public servant."

*The Calculus* uses the language and tools of neoclassical economics to formalize Madisonian insights. This adaptation of Madison to economics is what spawned the discipline that we call "Public Choice Economics." It is what earned Buchanan a Nobel Prize. It seems simple now, and perhaps it is, but at the time, it was nothing short of revolutionary.

When Buchanan recounts the intellectual environment of the 1960s in both the academy and the discipline of economics, he does so with near bewilderment. He can talk about how he and his colleagues— including fellow Nobel Prize winner Ronald Coase—were outcasts both in the discipline of economics and at their own university, the University of Virginia, which we still fondly refer to as Mr. Jefferson's university (isn't that ironic?). Many of their pioneering papers were published in second-tier journals.

In the field of economics, which was dominated by central-planning and the general thought that government can (and will) fix all the problems in the economy, Buchanan and Tullock basically exclaimed that "the emperor has no clothes, and he wants yours."

Here is the fundamental insight of *The Calculus* that led to a field of research: Government officials are just like you and me. They are interested in themselves, and they will use the resources at their disposal to enrich themselves and secure power. What does this mean for economic policy? It means that simple government solutions to market failures may prove worse than the problem.

The focus in the early part of *The Calculus* is on voting rules for collective decisions. There are two rules in particular that are viewed as benchmarks: simple majority and unanimity (which comes straight from Wicksell). What is so special about simple majority? Why is it that we often default to simple majority when making collective decisions? What is so special about fifty percent plus one? If we base collective activity (government action) on simple majority, then it only takes a simple majority to coerce the rest of the populace.

Buchanan and Tullock examine the costs of different voting rules. Imagine a continuum from 1 to 300. Along this continuum, we are measuring the number required to agree on an issue before collective action is taken. Call this the "necessary number." The rule of simple majority implies a necessary number of 151; the rule of unanimity requires a necessary number of 300.

At one extreme, when the necessary number is unity, collective action can be demanded when only one person votes in favor of it. At this extreme, *any* single person can make decisions on behalf of the group, and thus having the ability to require the group to act in certain ways. This sounds great if that person is me. But any person can do this. This is clearly a silly arrangement that would not last long in any society. At the other extreme, collective activity cannot be required without full consent of everyone in the population (unanimity). Somewhere in the middle of these extremes is simple majority (fifty percent plus one vote).

In order to search for an optimal necessary number on any particular issue, Buchanan and Tullock delineate two types of costs associated with changes in the necessary number. (The term "necessary number" is my own concoction. They probably wouldn't like it— too wordy.) That is, they distinguish two types of costs associated with increasing the size of the majority needed to undertake collective activity.

Buchanan and Tullock call the first decisionmaking costs. These rise with the necessary number. If the necessary number is one, these costs are zero, since no time or resources are expended in order to reach a decision. A single voter decides. However, as the necessary number increases toward 300, decisionmaking costs rise, and they rise more quickly as you approach 300. In fact, the costs of securing the very last vote can approach infinity, depending upon the issue, as the last voter realizes his bargaining position. That decisionmaking costs rise with the necessary number is why the rule of unanimity is infeasible for everyday collective activity decisions, such as referenda or decisions in the legislature. But don't worry—Buchanan finds a nice use for the rule of unanimity later.

A key contribution of *The Calculus* was to recognize a second type of cost from collective activity. In ironic fashion, the authors borrowed the classic "market failure" of externality. Because when activity is undertaken on behalf of the group, which by definition means that all must conform, this has the potential to force some into an activity of which they do not approve. For example, the collective activity could be a vote on the provision of a public good, such as a bridge. If a group of 300 has a simple majority rule, and 151 people decide that to fund the bridge redheads must pay a 75 percent marginal tax rate, people with red hair are out of luck. The majority can impose an external cost on redheads, even though no redheads voted for this proposal. There are external costs associated with private *and* public behavior.

But external costs decline as the necessary number rises. If only one person is needed for collective activity, then considerable external costs can be imposed on the rest of the population. However, if unanimity is required—that is, everyone must agree before collective activity is undertaken—then there will be no external costs imposed upon any voter. This is the beauty of the rule of unanimity: All must agree, so by definition, no external costs can be imposed. This is why Wicksell was so enchanted with the concept. If not for the decisionmaking costs, the rule of unanimity would dominate as a rule for collective activity.

Here are two practical applications of this analysis. Recognition of external costs seriously undermines the rule of simple majority. What is so special about this rule? Why is it that tax packages can be imposed upon the entire population with the agreement of only fifty percent plus one? Why is it that a 51 percent majority can require behavior from a 49 percent minority? A society that respects individual liberty should examine this rule carefully.

It is in a second practical application of this analysis that Buchanan finds a home for the rule of unanimity. That is the application to constitutional formation. When Buchanan talks about constitutions, he is simply referring to the rules of the game. These rules are important. In fact, in the years after the publication of *The Calculus*, Buchanan turned his attention to Constitutional Political Economy. Writing a constitution is essentially setting up the rules before the game begins. We do not know how the game will play out and so we do not know, *ex ante*, whether a particular rule will help us or harm us. We all may agree on a rule behind the Rawlsian "veil of ignorance." Here, in the formation of constitutions, Buchanan sees a very real role for the Wicksellian rule of unanimity.

## Limits of Liberty

Moving beyond *The Calculus of Consent*, Buchanan's writings continued to be shaped by what was occurring in the world around him. The events of the 1960s took their toll on Professor Buchanan and they certainly affected his view of the world. He admits that *The Calculus* was written in a period of optimism, in the early 1960s, "as though he was looking at the world through rose-colored glasses." But he cites the turmoil on college campuses, the "purchase of the Presidency," and the Vietnam War as factors that changed his faith in the stability of democracy.

This change is reflected in a little book published in 1975 called *The Limits of Liberty*.[6] In it, Buchanan felt obligated to make the case for collective activity even if anarchy reigned. His starting point is no longer a stable democracy, but a Hobbesian jungle.

Buchanan uses a simple prisoner's dilemma analysis to justify coming together for collective action. Imagine an island with only two occupants and, initially, no laws: Anarchy reigns. On this island the two inhabitants grow their own food and spend most of their time cultivating the land. But they also have an incentive to steal from the land of the other. Both of them do. The incentives are such that if either one farms a little and steals a little, the outcome is easily the best case scenario for that one individual. That is, as long as the other inhabitant is farming exclusively. But since they both face the same incentives, they know that the best they can do is to farm a little and steal a little.

The problem is that if they both farm-and-steal, their society devolves and the outcome is certainly the least desirable for the island. Resources will also be spent on crop protection (staying up all night to guard, building fences). In this world, the equilibrium outcome (without any sort of collective action) is one in which they are both farming and stealing and guarding. This is not an optimal outcome for either of the two island inhabitants. But neither one has the incentive to just farm.

Here is the impetus for collective action, for group agreement. It would be in the interest of both farmers to adopt a constitution that reads: "Any inhabitant caught stealing will lose a finger." They can even come to unanimous agreement on this (as it occurs at the constitutional stage). What this constitution allows them to do is to reach the best possible scenario in which they both spend all their time producing. Thus, the incentives for collective activity arise even in a world where evil pervades and no legal structure exists initially.

## Conclusion

When most people think about Public Choice economics, they cite the many papers built on the insight of *The Calculus of Consent*: the insight that individuals acting in political markets are motivated by the same factors that motivate people in private markets. But for Buchanan, this contribution is not enough. For him, it leaves a void with regard to economic theories of politics. But in fact, there is something positive that economic analysis can add to political theory. This contribution is that voluntary collective action can take place and through voluntary exchange, it is possible to help each member of a polity.

Buchanan cites Madison's *Federalist* 12. In this paper, Madison argues that it will be to the benefit of all states in the union to form a federal government: It will be easier to protect as the numbers of exposed borders shrinks to one. In the same way, Buchanan believes, individuals can come together for voluntary exchange and so form a collective entity and agree on a constitution that can benefit all.

# Notes

[1]James M. Buchanan and W. Craig Stubblebine,"Externality," *Economica* 29 (116; 1962): 371–84, esp. p. 381.

[2]Paul Samuelson, "The Pure Theory of Public Expenditure," *Review of Economics and Statistics* (November 1954): 387–89.

[3]James M. Buchanan, "An Economic Theory of Clubs," *Economica*, 32 (125; 1965): 1–14.

[4]James M. Buchanan and Gordon Tullock, *The Calculus of Consent* (Ann Arbor: University of Michigan Press, 1965).

[5]See http://oll.libertyfund.org/Home3/Audio.php?recordID=0517.23. The podcast is © 2005 The Liberty Fund.

[6]James Buchanan, *The Limits of Liberty: Between Anarchy and Leviathan* (Chicago: University of Chicago Press, 1975).

ROBERT J. BARRO

# Milton Friedman:
# General Perspectives and
# Personal Reminiscences

When my son Jason was an economics Ph.D. student at Harvard in the 1990s, he said: "I have observed that only two economists can push you around, Milton Friedman and Gary Becker." I agreed, but argued that it was a good thing. Everyone needs heroes, and Gary had only Milton. Milton had no one, except Ronald Reagan in the 1980s, but Reagan does not qualify as an economist. Arthur Burns may once have been the economist hero—as an instructor at Rutgers, he apparently helped to persuade the undergraduate Milton not to be an actuary. However, Burns's exalted status ended in 1971 when he went over to the dark side by endorsing Richard Nixon's outrageous price controls. Milton tells me that Frank Knight was also his "god," presumably between 1932 and 1935 when Milton was a graduate student at the University of Chicago and after 1946, when Milton joined the Chicago faculty.

His long-time friend George Stigler told the story of how Milton got his faculty appointment at Chicago. The two were together in 1945–46 on the faculty of the University of Minnesota. In his *Memoirs of an Unregulated Economist*, Stigler says:

> In the spring of 1946 I received the offer of a professorship from the University of Chicago, and of course was delighted at the prospect. The offer was contingent upon approval by the central administration after a personal interview. I went to Chicago, met with the President, Ernest Colwell, because Chancellor Robert Hutchins was ill that day, and I

was vetoed! I was too empirical, Colwell said, and no doubt that day I was. So the professorship was offered to Milton Friedman, and President Colwell and I had launched the new Chicago School. We both deserve credit for that appointment, although for a long time I was not inclined to share it with Colwell.[1]

It was not until 1958 that Stigler left Columbia to accept the lucrative Walgreen Professorship and was then reunited with Milton in Chicago.

The only person to rival Milton for policy influence in the twentieth century was John Maynard Keynes, who had a strikingly different view of the role of government. Keynes advocated more government intervention into what he perceived as poorly functioning private economies caught up in the global depression of the 1930s. In contrast, Milton put the primary blame for the U.S. depression on government failure, especially of the Federal Reserve's monetary policy. Hence, the existence of the Great Depression posed no dilemma for Milton's broad preference for small government, and he found in the Fed's failures to prevent deflation an argument in favor of monetary rules. As the world evolved—with price stability becoming the major mission of central banks and free markets and property rights becoming the key policies to promote economic growth—Milton surely won the intellectual and policy battles.

Being held in high esteem by the economics profession was not always Milton's status, and he had to endure a long march from pariah to priest. This transition culminated in the Nobel Prize in Economics in 1976, a great choice that confirmed the widespread impact of his economic ideas. In contrast, in the mid-1960s, when I started as a graduate student in economics at Harvard, my professors viewed Milton as a right-wing, Midwestern crank. Surprisingly, Milton was most notorious for his work on money, especially for the dictum that "inflation is always and everywhere a monetary phenomenon."[2]

Milton laid out his views on money in "The Quantity of Money— A Restatement" (an essay in the 1956 book, *Studies in the Quantity Theory of Money*) and the epic *A Monetary History of the United States* (written in 1963 with Anna Schwartz).[3] The *Monetary History* explores money-supply determination under different regimes, including the gold standard. Friedman and Schwartz argued that much of the historical variation in money supply was independent of shifts in the demand for money. They used this pattern to argue that the positive association between nominal money and real economic activity reflected primarily causation from money to the real economy, rather than the reverse.

My Harvard teachers argued that even Milton's permanent income theory of consumption, developed in his 1957 book, *A Theory of the Consumption Function*,[4] was flawed. In truth, Milton had constructed a scientifically impeccable model in which consumer demand depended on households' anticipated long-run income. The permanent-income idea is now a core component of all serious economic analyses of consumer behavior.

The odd thing from a current perspective is that Milton's stress on monetary disturbances was viewed in the 1960s as anti-Keynesian. It is true that Keynes in his *General Theory* deemphasized monetary disturbances as a source of business fluctuations, and he was also skeptical about the role of monetary policy as an anti-recession device. However, particularly since the 1980s, self-styled New Keynesians have embraced activist monetary policy as a centerpiece of counter-cyclical policy. Thus, Milton's stress on the business-cycle effects of monetary shocks now fits comfortably—maybe too comfortably—with Keynesian thinking.

Milton refined his views on money in his 1967 presidential address to the American Economic Association (AEA). "The Role of Monetary Policy," which appeared in the 1968 *American Economic Review*, is probably the most important contribution ever to come from this format. Usually presidential addresses and similar speeches cannot be forgotten too soon. A key result—which, along with work by Edmund Phelps, foreshadowed the 1970s Bob Lucas-led revolution on rational expectations macroeconomics—was that only unanticipated movements in money and the price level mattered for real economic activity. However, Milton's monetary framework implied a potentially important role for activist monetary policy in smoothing out the business cycle. Systematic monetary changes had substantial short-term real effects, and wise interventions could improve the functioning of the macroeconomy. Implicitly, the private market was working badly, beset by sticky prices and wages in the short run, and the monetary authority could help by stimulating the economy in recessions and cooling things down in booms. No wonder that this part of Milton's monetary ideas would be embraced by Keynesians in the 1980s.

To go from Milton's monetary framework to an argument for monetary stability, one needs additional features, such as the "long and variable lags" stressed in *A Program for Monetary Stability*.[5] Even more important is the distinction between rules and authorities emphasized by Henry Simons (and subsequently analyzed in a large literature on rules versus discretion). Models with these features can explain why monetary activism often causes more harm than good, even when (or, rather, especially if) monetary shocks have major real effects. Thus, these extensions can reconcile Milton's conceptual framework with the constant-growth-rate rules for monetary aggregates that he favored in practical policy advice.

Milton has been very successful with the broad proposition that monetary policy activism tends to be mistaken. However, his well-known, specific proposal—that a monetary aggregate such as M1 or M2 grow at a prespecified rate such as 2 or 3 percent per year—has problems. In fact, this area is the only one I know of where Milton pretty much reversed his previous position. The problem is that the real demand for money is not that stable, most dramatically in the current, high-tech financial environment, but also over the longer history. Therefore, a constant growth rate for any monetary aggregate does not ensure anything close to inflation stability. One way or another, a monetary policy aimed at inflation stability has to allow the nominal quantity of money to adjust to shifts in the real quantity of money demanded. In modern inflation targeting, this accommodation works through changes in nominal interest rates, which respond to deviations of inflation (or, possibly, expected inflation) from target. As part of this process, nominal money adjusts automatically to shifts in real money demand. (In technical jargon, the nominal quantity of money is endogenous.)

Although these refinements of constant-growth-rate rules are important, the spirit of inflation targeting fits with Milton's general approach to monetary policy. Central banks ought not to be business-cycle doctors; if they can achieve inflation stability, they have more than done their jobs. In fact, and much to my surprise, central banks in most advanced economies have been remarkably successful since the late 1980s in attaining low and stable inflation. Moreover, instead of adverse consequences for output and employment, real performance has probably improved.

Despite his fame in the macroeconomic area, Milton's most important contributions to the policy debate are on the microeconomic side. His over-arching theme is the benefits from free markets and private enterprise. The conceptual framework is in the outstanding 1953 book, *Essays in Positive Economics*.[6] Many of the policy proposals were expressed as early as the 1950s and appeared in *Capitalism and Freedom*. This 1962 book, developed from a series of lectures in 1956, is the classic work on economic ideas for a general audience. I learn something every time I read this remarkable work, and who can forget the opening lines:

> In a much quoted passage in his inaugural address, President Kennedy said, "Ask not what your country can do for you—ask what you can do for your country." ...Neither half of the statement expresses a relation between the citizen and his government that is worthy of the ideals of free men in a free society. The paternalistic "what your country can do for you" implies that government is the patron, the citizen the ward, a view that is at odds with the free man's belief in his own responsibility for his own destiny. The organismic "what you can do for you country" implies that government is the master or the deity, the citizen, the servant or the votary. To the free man, the country is the collection of individuals who compose it, not something over and above them. He is proud of a common heritage and loyal to common traditions. But he regards government as a means, an instrumentality, neither a grantor of favors and gifts, nor a master or god to be blindly worshipped and served. He recognizes no national goal except as it is the consensus of the goals that the citizens severally serve. He recognizes no national purpose except as it is the consensus of the purposes for which the citizens severally strive.[7]

*Capitalism and Freedom* expressed numerous ideas once thought to be radical but now viewed as mainstream. The all-volunteer army has worked well in the United States and other countries for many years, privatized social security lives in Chile and other places, the U.S. earned-income tax credit is a form of negative income tax, the flat-rate income tax prevails in many countries (even Russia), school vouchers work in some U.S. localities and are under active consideration in others, and market-oriented welfare reform was enacted by Bill Clinton of all people. In addition, open capital markets are the norm in the developed world, and flexible exchange rates prevail in many countries. The spirit of monetary stability has also been accepted, though in the more modern form of inflation targeting. Some years from now we may add Milton's recent proposals on the decriminalization of drugs to the list of generally accepted proposals.

Anyone who wants to understand Milton's policy ideas should start with *Capitalism and Freedom* and then go to *Free to Choose*, the bestselling 1980 book from the television show that made Milton a household name. He notes in his autobiography—*Two Lucky People: Memoirs*, written in 1998 with his wife Rose—that France was the only European country never to air the television program.[8] Seems that some things never change. As evidence of the celebrity status conveyed by *Free to Choose*, I recall being on a trip with Milton when, in Chicago's O'Hare Airport, a man noticed my companion. The man was literally beside himself, in the manner of an avid fan coming in contact with a rock star.

I learned from *Memoirs* that Milton's influence was achieved mainly through the force of ideas, not by direct participation in the policy process. Except for work in 1935–1937 in New Deal Washington (when Milton had no academic job opportunities) and during World War II, Milton avoided government service. His key advice to academic economists: "by all means spend a few years in Washington—but only a few. If you stay more than two or three years you will become addicted and will be unable effectively to return to a scholarly career."[9] My only disagreement is that two or three years in Washington are too many.

In any event, Milton probably would not have been an outstanding policymaker. His main output in Washington during World War II involved work on the establishment of income-tax withholding. It may be that no other law has done more to enlarge the size of the federal government. Certainly Milton regrets the existence of income-tax with-holding, but he also says (no doubt correctly) that this institution would be present even if he had never set foot in Washington.

Milton's *Memoirs* contain interesting views on the value of testifying before Congress and of writing popular commentaries. He says: "I long ago decided it was a waste of time to testify before Congressional com-mittees. Spending the same time writing an op-ed piece or giving a talk is a more efficient use of time for the purpose of influencing policy."[10] I always remember Milton's opinion when I receive an invitation to testify before Congress, and I inevitably decline. I am also pleased that Milton regards commentary in popular media as potentially valuable, since I have spent a fair bit of time writing for *The Wall Street Journal* and *Business Week*. Milton's well-reasoned and lively writings in *Newsweek* from 1966 to 1984 are the model toward which any economic com-mentator ought to aspire. In *Memoirs*, he describes his initial nervousness about being able to generate enough topics to fill the columns. Hence, he did not accept *Newsweek's* offer until he had assembled a substantial list of potential ideas. But Milton says he never used anything from the list—something interesting and timely always came up, and he had no problem producing a column every three weeks.

*Memoirs* also verifies a well-known story about Milton's concern, as 1967 AEA president, about the association's accumulation of a sub-stantial surplus. He worried that the money would be spent on some ill-advised project designed by a social do-gooder. Therefore, he suc-cessfully proposed the startup of a new journal (the *Journal of Economic Literature*) without increasing membership dues. The resulting budget deficit used up the endowment in a reasonably quick and nearly harm-less manner. I remembered this episode when I was AEA vice president in 1998. Again, the association had accumulated a large surplus, and I worried about possible ill-advised uses. My proposal at the time (when the AEA already had three journals) was to cut the membership dues until the endowment declined to a reasonable level. However, lacking Milton's talents at persuasion, I failed miserably in this proposal. The problem of the large surplus was not solved until the stock market declined at the end of the Internet boom in 2000.

Milton is often cited, starting with *Time* magazine in December 1965, for the famous quote: "We are all Keynesians now." However, we learn from *Memoirs* that the quote was taken out of context to change the meaning. The full statement reconstructed by Milton in a letter to *Time* in 1966 is: "In one sense we are all Keynesians now; in another, nobody is any longer a Keynesian."[11] Milton explains that the first sense refers to the rhetoric and style of macroeconomic analysis—Keynes essentially invented macroeconomics as a distinct field. The second sense applies to substantive implications; specifically, to the idea that (almost) no one now advocates the simplistic policy activism recommended in Keynes's *General Theory*. Although the second observation is more significant, the first got the most press.

Milton also mentions a Keynes quote attributed in the 1960s to Richard Nixon: "Now I am a Keynesian in economics." This quote may help to explain the awful economic policies that Nixon carried out as president. Aside from price controls, his administration featured a sharp rise in federal spending, especially for Social Security, a large increase in inflation, the Endangered Species Act, the establishment of the Environmental Protection Agency, and the 55-mile-per-hour speed limit. A misery index based on inflation, unemployment, real GDP growth, and nominal interest rates reveals that Jimmy Carter was the only president with worse outcomes in the post-World War II period. As I have argued elsewhere, Nixon surely deserved to be impeached, but more for economic policy than for Watergate.

I cannot resist noting some intriguing personal linkages between Milton and me. First, we both have Hungarian origins, our families both came from territory that is now part of Ukraine. (My mother was from Munkacs, now Mukacevo; Milton's parents were from Beregszasz or Berehovo.) Second, I have the name Friedmann in my ancestry, though from my father's origins in Transylvania. Finally, in 1982, at the start of my second faculty position at the University of Chicago, I purchased the house at 5731 South Kenwood Avenue that the Friedmans had occupied from 1950 to 1962. (Milton once asked me about the fine workbench in the basement, and I told him that it was still there in 1984.)

Despite all these linkages, I regret that Milton's personal advice to me has not always been of the same quality as his policy advice. For instance, when I was Milton's colleague in 1974, I received an invitation to attend the Hong Kong meeting of the libertarian Mont Pèlerin Society. Since Milton was a founding member of the Society, I naturally solicited his opinion about whether I should attend. He replied that the Society ought to be abolished. Following the lines of a speech he gave at the 1972 meeting, he said that the Mont Pèlerin Society came into being after World War II to serve the needs of persons in countries where dialogues with fellow libertarians were impossible. The Society was highly successful in meeting this need through the 1960s. However, with the development of alternative institutions and the spread of global communications, Milton argued that this function was no longer necessary by the early 1970s. More generally, Milton thought that institutions have a tendency to live on or expand long after their missions were accomplished. Thus, he suggested that the Mont Pèlerin Society declare victory and go out of business, thereby setting a great example for other organizations that ought to fade away. My candidate list—which I think Milton would endorse—includes the International Monetary Fund, the World Bank, and the United Nations.

The problem with Milton's cogent analysis of the Mont Pèlerin Society and institutions more broadly is that I took it as personal advice not to attend the 1974 meeting. Therefore, I turned down the invitation. This was a mistake because I missed out on numerous exciting meetings of the Society until I first attended in 1992 in Vancouver.

In a similar vein, Milton advised me in 1973 to relinquish the tenured position I had at Brown University to accept a nontenured post at the University of Chicago. (I was a visitor at Chicago in 1972.) This advice reflected Milton's general antipathy toward the tenure system, some of which seems to derive from bad personal experiences in 1940–1941 with incompetent and hostile senior colleagues at the University of Wisconsin. Basically, Milton viewed tenure as a mechanism to ensure low work effort by many senior professors. (Milton did not explain, however, why tenure was an equilibrium outcome in the higher education market.)

Even if Milton was correct about the inefficiency of tenure as an institution, it was a fallacy of composition to conclude that tenure was unimportant for me individually. But, not making this connection, I took his general argument as personal advice, and I did give up my tenure at Brown. As things turned out, the Chicago debate over my tenure promotion in 1975 was sufficiently political and acrimonious (albeit eventually favorable) that I ended up leaving for the University of Rochester. Although I tried again unsuccessfully at Chicago in 1982–1984 (in a tenured position!), I think that—had I refused their inferior offer in 1973—I would probably be at Chicago today. (Whether this placement would be good for me or the profession I leave for others to decide.)

One of the best things about the University of Chicago environment is the workshop system; Milton was still running the famous Money and Banking Workshop in 1972–1975. He conducted the workshop in a "page-one/page-two" format. Instead of allowing the speaker to present the paper, Milton began by asking "Does anyone have comments on page 1?" The speaker was then allowed to respond to the comments on page 1, and so on for subsequent pages.

In a 1973 workshop, I presented my paper, published in the 1974 *Journal of Political Economy*,[12] about Ricardian equivalence for budget deficits. (In the model, taxes and budget deficits had equivalent economic effects, along the lines expressed by the classical British economist David Ricardo. However, I should mention that no one in the 1973 workshop noted the connection between my paper and Ricardo's.) This was the only time I witnessed a seminar attended simultaneously by the three great pillars of the Chicago School—Milton, George Stigler, and Gary Becker. At one point, Gary and I got involved in a heated dispute on a technical point in the paper. I recall Milton putting his head down, deep in thought for at least a full minute, while the room was silent. Given Milton's mental quickness, this prolonged deliberation was quite unusual, and there was an atmosphere of thick tension in the room. Finally, Milton lifted his head and declared, in an incredulous way, that Gary was wrong (a nearly unprecedented event) and that I was therefore right. For some reason, Gary lacks any recollection of this event.

Milton moved to San Francisco and joined Stanford University's Hoover Institution in 1977. He wrote *Memoirs* with Rose while at Hoover, and his mind remained remarkably nimble even into his nineties. On one occasion, Milton remarked how surprised he was still to be alive at such an advanced age, that somehow it was a contingency for which he had not planned. Nevertheless, we can only be grateful for this outcome.

More generally, we are fortunate that Milton had the good humor and self-confidence to persevere in the face of many years of scorn by left-wing economists and journalists. The tables were turned on his detractors many years ago, and—to paraphrase his misused quote about Keynes—we are all Friedmanians now.

## Notes

[1]George Stigler, *Memoirs of an Unregulated Economist* (New York: Basic Books, 1988), p. 40.

[2]This quote is from Friedman's 1968 essay "Inflation: Causes and Consequences," *Dollars and Deficits* (Englewood Cliffs, NJ: Prentice-Hall, 1968), p. 29.

[3]Milton Friedman, "The Quantity of Money—A Restatement" in *Studies in the Quantity Theory of Money* (Chicago: University of Chicago Press, 1956); and, with Anna Jacobson Schwartz *A Monetary History of the United States* (Princeton, NJ: Princeton University Press [for the National Bureau of Economic Research], 1963).

[4]Milton Friedman, *A Theory of the Consumption Function* (Princeton, NJ: Princeton University Press,1957).

[5]Milton Friedman, *A Program for Monetary Stability* (New York: Fordham University Press, 1960).

[6]Milton Friedman, *Essays in Positive Economics* (Chicago: University of Chicago Press, 1953).

[7]Milton Friedman, *Capitalism and Freedom* (Chicago: University of Chicago Press, 1962), pp. 1–2.

[8]Milton Friedman, with Rose Friedman, *Free to Choose* (New York: Harcourt Brace Jovanovich,1980); and, with Rose Friedman, *Two Lucky People: Memoirs* (Chicago: University of Chicago Press, 1998), p. 501.

[9]Ibid., p. 110.

[10]Ibid., p. 363.

[11]Ibid., p. 231.

[12]Robert J. Barro, "Are Government Bonds Net Wealth?" *Journal of Political Economy* 82 (November/December, 1974): 1095–117.

DONALD J. DEVINE

# Politics Trumps Economics

After Steve Forbe's brilliant defense of economic freedom that begins this volume, one might ask (in great frustration): "Since free market economists had so clearly won this 'great economic debate,' why does Washington not know it?"

I had wondered why a political scientist was being included in this volume, and now I understand only too well. Experts on economists Friedrich Hayek, Ludwig von Mises, John Maynard Keynes, Frank Knight, James Buchanan, and Milton Friedman were invited to present the good news that limited government and free market ideas were superior to their socialist alternatives and had won the day intellectually worldwide. As a political scientist, I was invited to tell the sad truth that this does not make any difference to politicians.

In the wake of the fall of communism and the worldwide movement toward markets, and led by a Republican president, Senate, and House of Representatives, nondefense, nonsecurity spending in the U.S. has increased proportionately more under George W. Bush than it had under any president since Franklin D. Roosevelt. Indeed, the current administration and Congress added the first new large entitlement since Lyndon Johnson's Great Society, the Medicare prescription drug act. As the existing entitlements are already nearing fiscal imbalance, this single act adds a liability of 150 percent to that of all of Social Security's, bringing the total unfunded liability to $50 trillion. And this was done without even a remote idea of how to pay for it. At the same time, government planning soared, as measured by the Competitive Enterprise Institute's count of regulatory additions to the *Federal Register*. Pork-generating earmarks increased from 150 in 1987—when they drew a veto from Ronald Reagan for being excessive—to 1,400 in 1998 and to 6,371 in 2005.

The sad fact of political science is that politics trumps economics—and, unfortunately, always will. Unless one adopts pure anarchism—and even Mises accepted a central role for government in regulating the police power—government rules will structure how economic affairs will operate. They might negatively affect economic activity, and economists demonstrate they often do, but Hayek was unambiguous in insisting that pure laissez-faire never was and never can be. For one thing, markets require private property and property requires legal rules under which to operate. Hayek, following John Locke, required that the rules be "promulgated, established laws, not to be varied in particular cases, but to have one rule for rich and poor" adopted by popular consent, "by themselves or their deputies," with the aim of preserving property, security, and liberty.

Once government is granted the powers to regulate policing of coercion domestically and internationally and to set the rules for property ownership, it is difficult to limit its powers to only those necessary functions. That was a major concern for the economists we have discussed, all of whom in varying degrees went beyond simple economics to matters of law and political science. Indeed, it can truly be argued that Hayek's and Buchanan's major contributions were in politics, even though they won their Nobels in the gloomy science. All of these men had wonderful ideas to limit central power but, as even the U.S. record demonstrates, they have not been embraced in the real world as have their more strictly economic insights, which have often been overridden by political considerations.

Columnist Thomas Friedman has nicely captured the difference between the two different realms with his symbols of "The Lexus and the Olive Tree." The Lexus is in the marketplace and is the domain of economics. The olive tree is a symbol of the family domicile, carefully tended and protectively surrounding loved ones, where all are safe and sound as long as the outside is kept out. But trade introduces the Lexus within the range of the garden and with it comes foreign ideas and images that threaten family and community. In response, clan or tribe or government attempt to block the intruders, who often fight back with their own governmental powers. In such an environment, few are willing to die for their Lexus, but many will die for their family and friends and olive trees, the domain of politics.

Politics trumps economics because the olive tree trumps the Lexus. I like my Lexus, but I love my family and friends. Through Machiavelli, politicians have learned to manipulate such symbols so that they can control economies and their resulting wealth, although the wise prince was warned to respect property because people will fight for their olive trees. Lobbying by businessmen will often win advantage for some market participants, and a political scientist must know this has only marginal effect. But it was not until I became personally and professionally close to a top legislative leader did I learn that, in fact, the influence is the other way around. The legislator manipulates the economic interests to support him rather than being influenced by them—at least most of the time. The politician has his ear closer to the olive tree interests, and those who will actually fight for their rights, than he does to the businessmen who, as Joseph Schumpeter noted, do not have the courage to say "boo to a goose," especially clever and powerful political ones.

A political scientist must predict that with all our greater knowledge of and respect for the market, the economy will get worse because of politics, but especially because of today's realities. The bills for years of political irresponsibility on entitlements will become due as early as 2016, and tax rates will have to increase greatly to pay them. By 2030, Medicare and Social Security will absorb 14 percent of GDP, almost half of it unfunded, requiring a 91 percent increase in the payroll tax, or an 81 percent increase in income taxes, or a 36 percent increase in total federal taxes. This will drastically slow growth, if it does not lead to hyperinflation or depression. As these obligations come due, fewer workers will be available to pay them. There are fewer younger workers available to take the place of the now less productive elderly; and the younger works are having fewer children to eventually support their own retirement.

It takes 2.1 children per childbearing-aged woman to keep the population steady. Europe is already finished. The birth rate is down to 1.4 percent there and heading lower, which soon will lead to depopulation or mass immigration. The U.S. is doing better at 2.0 children per childbearing-aged woman, but only 1.8 for the segment of the population that is of European descent. The immigration that is mitigating the decline in U.S. population to some extent, however, already has created a backlash that might make the demographic problem worse. The geopolitical aspects of the shift might even be greater. Of the 43 countries that will be dealing with declining populations in the next 50 years, 80 percent are European and none are Muslim. Of the ten countries with the world's largest populations today, none are Islamic; but by 2030, half will be. The United States will decrease from 6.3 percent of the world population today to 4.6 percent in 2050, while the world's Muslim population will increase by 100 percent.

No politician is allowed to discuss the coming entitlements-based crisis even though it will begin in less than a decade. Although President Bush raised the idea of Social Security reform, he was stopped cold last year, in fact he was jeered when he mentioned it in his 2006 State of the Union address. The Medicare problems, which are much larger problems, can be discussed by no one. In fact, politicians mostly call for increased taxes, less free trade, more regulation, and additional spending—including President Bush's own incredibly expensive new prescription drug entitlement. At a press conference just before the State of the Union, President Bush declared himself satisfied with the rate of spending under the current Congress, saying it had met his targets (if not his budgets) and that he did not foresee any future vetoes.

Can the coming entitlement crash be avoided if it cannot be discussed? What about birth replacement rates? Try telling American young men and women they must have 2.1 children per family: This would mean three children for most young families—and four or more children in many others to make up for those who do not marry or who prefer the same sex. Medicare reform would seem an easy sell by comparison. If the population were convinced of the need to become more traditionally religious that might help since, as even nonbeliever Hayek said, paradoxically, freedom and markets require a traditional society with traditional moral values developed in sound families and vibrant local communities. Good luck selling that to the Paris Hilton generation.

The specter of politics-future trumps the economic good news that the market has won intellectually. It would take a moral transformation of gargantuan proportions to change these social dynamics. One should urge the new generation to find a way anyway—and the eternal optimist Ronald Reagan would be the soundest guide. But preaching a politics of restraint is not as easy as teaching economics with a Lexus as the prize.

LUDWIG VON MISES

# LORD KEYNES AND SAY'S LAW

## I

Lord Keynes's main contribution did not lie in the development of new ideas but "in escaping from the old ones," as he himself declared at the end of the Preface to his "General Theory." The Keynesians tell us that his immortal achievement consists in the entire refutation of what has come to be known as Say's Law of Markets. The rejection of this law, they declare, is the gist of all Keynes's teachings; all other propositions of his doctrine follow with logical necessity from this fundamental insight and must collapse if the futility of his attack on Say's Law can be demonstrated.[1]

Now it is important to realize that what is called Say's Law was in the first instance designed as a refutation of doctrines popularly held in the ages preceding the development of economics as a branch of human knowledge. It was not an integral part of the new science of economics as taught by the Classical economists. It was rather a preliminary—the exposure and removal of garbled and untenable ideas which dimmed people's minds and were a serious obstacle to a reasonable analysis of conditions.

Whenever business turned bad, the average merchant had two explanations at hand: the evil was caused by a scarcity of money and

Reprinted courtesy of the Ludwig von Mises Institute (www.mises.org). Originally published in *The Freeman*, October 30, 1950, and reprinted in *Planning for Freedom*.

by general overproduction. Adam Smith, in a famous passage in *The Wealth of Nations,* exploded the first of these myths. Say devoted himself predominantly to a thorough refutation of the second.

As long as a definite thing is still an economic good and not a "free good," its supply is not, of course, *absolutely* abundant. There are still unsatisfied needs which a larger supply of the good concerned could satisfy. There are still people who would be glad to get more of this good than they are really getting. With regard to economic goods there can never be *absolute* overproduction. (And economics deals only with economic goods, not with free goods such as air which are no object of purposive human action, are therefore not produced, and with regard to which the employment of terms like underproduction and overproduction is simply nonsensical.)

With regard to economic goods there can be only *relative* overproduction. While the consumers are asking for definite quantities of shirts and of shoes, business has produced, say, a larger quantity of shoes and a smaller quantity of shirts. This is not general overproduction of all commodities. To the overproduction of shoes corresponds an underproduction of shirts. Consequently the result cannot be a general depression of all branches of business. The outcome is a change in the exchange ratio between shoes and shirts. If, for instance, previously one pair of shoes could buy four shirts, it now buys only three shirts. While business is bad for the shoemakers, it is good for the shirtmakers. The attempts to explain the general depression of trade by referring to an allegedly general overproduction are therefore fallacious.

Commodities, says Say, are ultimately paid for not by money, but by other commodities. Money is merely the commonly used medium of exchange; it plays only an intermediary role. What the seller wants ultimately to receive in exchange for the commodities sold is other commodities.

Every commodity produced is therefore a price, as it were, for other commodities produced. The situation of the producer of any commodity is improved by any increase in the production of other commodities. What may hurt the interests of the producer of a definite commodity is his failure to anticipate correctly the state of the market. He has overrated the public's demand for his commodity and underrated its demand for other commodities. Consumers have no use for such a bungling entrepreneur; they buy his products only at prices which make him incur losses, and they force him, if he does not in time correct his mistakes, to go out of business. On the other hand, those entrepreneurs who have better succeeded in anticipating the public demand earn profits and are in a position to expand their business activities. This, says Say, is the truth behind the confused assertions of businessmen that the main difficulty is not in producing but in selling. It would be more appropriate to declare that the first and main problem of business is to produce in the best and cheapest way those commodities which will satisfy the most urgent of the not yet satisfied needs of the public.

Thus Smith and Say demolished the oldest and most naive explanation of the trade cycle as provided by the popular effusions of inefficient traders. True, their achievement was merely negative. They exploded the belief that the recurrence of periods of bad business was caused by a scarcity of money and by a general overproduction. But they did not give us an elaborated theory of the trade cycle. The first explanation of this phenomenon was provided much later by the British Currency School.

The important contributions of Smith and Say were not entirely new and original. The history of economic thought can trace back some essential points of their reasoning to older authors. This in no way detracts from the merits of Smith and Say. They were the first to deal with the issue in a systematic way and to apply their conclusions to the problem of economic depressions. They were therefore also the first against whom the supporters of the spurious popular doctrine directed their violent attacks. Sismondi and Malthus chose Say as the target of passionate volleys when they tried—in vain—to salvage the discredited popular prejudices.

## II

Say emerged victoriously from his polemics with Malthus and Sismondi. He proved his case, while his adversaries could not prove theirs. Henceforth, during the whole rest of the nineteenth century, the acknowledgment of the truth contained in Say's Law was the distinctive mark of an economist. Those authors and politicians who made the alleged scarcity of money responsible for all ills and advocated inflation as the panacea were no longer considered economists but "monetary cranks."

The struggle between the champions of sound money and the inflationists went on for many decades. But it was no longer considered a controversy between various schools of economists. It was viewed as a conflict between economists and anti-economists, between reasonable men and ignorant zealots. When all civilized countries had adopted the gold standard or the gold-exchange standard, the cause of inflation seemed to be lost forever.

Economics did not content itself with what Smith and Say had taught about the problems involved. It developed an integrated system of theorems which cogently demonstrated the absurdity of the inflationist sophisms. It depicted in detail the inevitable consequences of an increase in the quantity of money in circulation and of credit expansion. It elaborated the monetary or circulation credit theory of the business cycle which clearly showed how the recurrence of depressions of trade is caused by the repeated attempts to "stimulate" business through credit expansion. Thus it conclusively proved that the slump, whose appearance the inflationists attributed to an insufficiency of the supply of money, is on the contrary the necessary outcome of attempts to remove such an alleged scarcity of money through credit expansion.

The economists did not contest the fact that a credit expansion in its initial stage makes business boom. But they pointed out how such a contrived boom must inevitably collapse after a while and produce a general depression. This demonstration could appeal to statesmen intent on promoting the enduring well-being of their nation. It could not influence demagogues who care for nothing but success in the impending election campaign and are not in the least troubled about what will happen the day after tomorrow. But it is precisely such people who have become supreme in the political life of this age of wars and revolutions. In defiance of all the teachings of the economists, inflation and credit expansion have been elevated to the dignity of the first principle of economic policy. Nearly all governments are now committed to reckless spending, and finance their deficits by issuing additional quantities of unredeemable paper money and by boundless credit expansion.

The great economists were harbingers of new ideas. The economic policies they recommended were at variance with the policies practiced by contemporary governments and political parties. As a rule many years, even decades, passed before public opinion accepted the new ideas as propagated by the economists, and before the required corresponding changes in policies were effected.

It was different with the "new economics" of Lord Keynes. The policies he advocated were precisely those which almost all governments, including the British, had already adopted many years before his "General Theory" was published. Keynes was not an innovator and champion of new methods of managing economic affairs. His contribution consisted rather in providing an apparent justification for the policies which were popular with those in power in spite of the fact that all economists viewed them as disastrous. His achievement was a rationalization of the policies already practiced. He was not a "revolutionary," as some of his adepts called him. The "Keynesian revolution" took place long before Keynes approved of it and fabricated a pseudo-scientific justification for it. What he really did was to write an apology for the prevailing policies of governments.

This explains the quick success of his book. It was greeted enthusiastically by the governments and the ruling political parties. Especially enraptured were a new type of intellectual, the "government economists." They had had a bad conscience. They were aware of the fact that they were carrying out policies which all economists condemned as contrary to purpose and disastrous. Now they felt relieved. The "new economics" reestablished their moral equilibrium. Today they are no longer ashamed of being the handymen of bad policies. They glorify themselves. They are the prophets of the new creed.

### III

The exuberant epithets which these admirers have bestowed upon his work cannot obscure the fact that Keynes did not refute Say's Law. He rejected it emotionally, but he did not advance a single tenable argument to invalidate its rationale.

Neither did Keynes try to refute by discursive reasoning the teachings of modern economics. He chose to ignore them, that was all. He never found any word of serious criticism against the theorem that increasing the quantity of money cannot effect anything else than, on the one hand, to favor some groups at the expense of other groups, and, on the other hand, to foster capital malinvestment and capital decumulation. He was at a complete loss when it came to advancing any sound argument to demolish the monetary theory of the trade cycle. All he did was to revive the self-contradictory dogmas of the various sects of inflationism. He did not add anything to the empty presumptions of his predecessors, from the old Birmingham School of Little Shilling Men down to Silvio Gesell. He merely translated their sophisms—a hundred times refuted—into the questionable language of mathematical economics. He passed over in silence all the objections which such men as Jevons, Walras, and Wicksell— to name only a few—opposed to the effusions of the inflationists.

It is the same with his disciples. They think that calling "those who fail to be moved to admiration of Keynes's genius" such names as "dullard" or "narrow-minded fanatic"[2] is a substitute for sound economic reasoning. They believe that they have proved their case by dismissing their adversaries as "orthodox" or "neo-classical." They reveal the utmost ignorance in thinking that their doctrine is correct because it is new.

In fact, inflationism is the oldest of all fallacies. It was very popular long before the days of Smith, Say, and Ricardo, against whose teachings the Keynesians cannot advance any other objection than that they are old.

## IV

The unprecedented success of Keynesianism is due to the fact that it provides an apparent justification for the "deficit spending" policies of contemporary governments. It is the pseudo-philosophy of those who can think of nothing else than to dissipate the capital accumulated by previous generations.

Yet no effusions of authors however brilliant and sophisticated can alter the perennial economic laws. They are and work and take

care of themselves. Notwithstanding all the passionate fulminations of
the spokesmen of governments, the inevitable consequences of inflationism and expansionism as depicted by the "orthodox" economists
are coming to pass. And then, very late indeed, even simple people will
discover that Keynes did not teach us how to perform the "miracle ...
of turning a stone into bread,"[3] but the not at all miraculous procedure
of eating the seed corn.

## Notes

[1] P. M. Sweezy in *The New Economics*, ed. by S. E. Harris, New York, 1947, p. 105.
[2] Professor G. Haberler in ibid., p. 161
[3] John Maynard Keynes in ibid., p. 332.

LUDWIG VON MISES

# ECONOMIC ASPECTS OF THE PENSION PROBLEM

## On Whom Does the Incidence Fall?

Whenever a law or labor union pressure burdens the employers with an additional expenditure for the benefit of the employees, people talk of "social gains." The idea implied is that such benefits confer on the employees a boon beyond the salaries or wages paid to them and that they are receiving a grant which they would have missed in the absence of such a law or such a clause in the contract. It is assumed that the workers are getting something for nothing.

This view is entirely fallacious. What the employer takes into account in considering the employment of additional hands or in discharging a number of those already in his service, is always the value of the services rendered or to be rendered by them. He asks himself: How much does the employment of the man concerned add to the output? Is it reasonable to expect that the expenditure caused by his employment will at least be recovered by the sale of the additional product produced by his employment? If the answer to the second question is in the negative, the employment of the man will cause a loss. As no enterprise can in the long run operate on a loss basis, the man concerned will be discharged or, respectively, will not be hired.

Reprinted courtesy of the Ludwig von Mises Institute (www.mises.org). From the *The Commercial and Financial Chronicle*, February 23, 1950.

In resorting to this calculation, the employer takes into account not only the individual's take-home wages, but all the costs of employing him. If, for example, the government—as is the case in some European countries—collects a percentage of each firm's total payroll as a tax which the firm is strictly forbidden to deduct from wages paid to the workers, the amount that enters into the calculation is: wages paid out to the worker plus the quota of the tax. If the employer is bound to provide for pensions, the sum entered into the calculation is: wages paid out plus an allowance for the pension, computed according to actuarial methods.

The consequence of this state of affairs is that the incidence of all alleged "social gains" falls upon the wage-earner. Their effect does not differ from the effect of any kind of raise in wage rates.

In a free labor market, wage rates tend toward a height at which all employers ready to pay these rates can find all the men they need and all the workers ready to work for this rate can find jobs. There prevails a tendency toward full employment. But as soon as the laws or the labor unions fix rates at a higher level, this tendency disappears. Then workers are discharged and there are job-seekers who cannot find employment. The reason is that at the artificially raised wage rates only the employment of a smaller number of hands pays. While in an unhampered labor market unemployment is only transitory, it becomes a permanent phenomenon when the governments or the unions succeed in raising wage rates above the potential market level. Even Lord Beveridge, about twenty years ago, admitted that the continuance of a substantial volume of unemployment is in itself the proof that the price asked for labor as wages is too high for the conditions of the market. And Lord Keynes, the inaugurator of the so-called "full employment policy," implicitly acknowledged the correctness of this thesis. His main reason for advocating inflation as a means to do away with unemployment was that he believed that gradual and automatic lowering of real wages as a result of rising prices would not be so strongly resisted by labor as any attempt to lower money wage rates.

What prevents the government and the unions from raising wage rates to a steeper height than they actually do is their reluctance to price out of the labor market too great a number of people. What the workers are getting in the shape of pensions payable by the employing corporation reduces the amount of wages that the unions can ask for without increasing unemployment. The unions in asking pensions for which the company has to pay without any contribution on the part of the beneficiaries has made a choice. It has preferred pensions to an increase in take-home wages. Economically it does not make any difference whether the workers do contribute or do not to the fund out of which the pensions will be paid. It is immaterial for the employer whether the cost of employing workers is raised by an increase in take-home wages or by the obligation to provide for pensions. For the worker, on the other hand, the pensions are not a free gift on the part of the employer. The pension claims they acquire restrict the amount of wages they could get without calling up the spectre of unemployment.

Correctly computed, the income of a wage earner entitled to a pension consists of his wages plus the amount of the premium he would have to pay to an insurance company for the acquisition of an equivalent claim. Ultimately the granting of pensions amounts to a restriction of the wage earner's freedom to use his total income according to his own designs. He is forced to cut down his current consumption in order to provide for his old age. We may neglect dealing with the question whether such a restriction of the individual worker's freedom is expedient or not. What is important to emphasize is merely that the pensions are not a gift on the part of the employer. They are a disguised wage raise of a peculiar character. The employee is forced to use the increment for acquiring a pension.

## Pensions and the Purchasing Power of the Dollar

It is obvious that the amount of the pension each man will be entitled to claim one day can only be fixed in terms of money. Hence the value of these claims is inextricably linked with the vicissitudes of the American monetary unit, the dollar.

The present Administration is eager to devise various schemes for old-age and disability pensions. It is intent upon extending the number of people included in the government's social security system and to increase the benefits under this system. It openly supports the demands of the unions for pensions to be granted by the companies without contribution on the part of the beneficiaries. But at the same time the same administration is firmly committed to a policy which is bound to lower more and more the purchasing power of the dollar. It has proclaimed unbalanced budgets and deficit spending as the first principle of public finance, as a new way of life. While hypocritically pretending to fight inflation, it has elevated boundless credit expansion and recklessly increasing the amount of money in circulation to the dignity of an essential postulate of popular government and economic democracy.

Let nobody be fooled by the lame excuse that what is intended is not permanent deficits, but only the substitution of balancing the budget over a period of several years for balancing it every year. According to this doctrine, in years of prosperity budgetary surpluses are to be accumulated which have to be balanced against the deficits incurred in years of depression. But what is to be considered as good business and what as bad business is left to the decision of the party in power. The Administration itself declared that the fiscal year 1949 was, in spite of a moderate recession near its end, a year of prosperity. But it did not accumulate a surplus in this year of prosperity; it produced a considerable deficit. Remember how the Democrats in the 1932 electoral campaign criticized the Hoover Administration for its financial shortcomings. But as soon as they came into office, they inaugurated their notorious schemes of pump-priming, deficit spending, and so on.

What the doctrine of balancing budgets over a period of many years really means is this: as long as our own party is in office, we will enhance our popularity through reckless spending. We do not want to annoy our friends by cutting down expenditure. We want the voters to feel happy under the artificial short-lived prosperity which the easy money policy and a rich supply of additional money generate. Later, when our adversaries will be in office, the inevitable consequence of our expansionist policy, viz., depression, will appear. Then we shall blame them for the disaster and assail them for their failure to balance the budget properly.

It is very unlikely that the practice of deficit spending will be abandoned in the not too distant future. As a fiscal policy it is very convenient to inept governments. It is passionately advocated by hosts of pseudo-economists. It is praised at the universities as the most beneficial expedient of "unorthodox," really "progressive" and "anti-fascist" methods of public finance. A radical change of ideologies would be required to restore the prestige of sound fiscal procedures, today decried as "orthodox" and "reactionary."

Such an overthrow of an almost universally accepted doctrine is unlikely to occur as long as the living generation of professors and politicians has not passed away. The present writer, having for more than forty years uncompromisingly fought against all varieties of credit expansion and inflation, is forced sadly to admit that the prospects for a speedy return to sound management of monetary affairs are rather thin. A realistic evaluation of the state of public opinion, the doctrines taught at the universities and the mentality of politicians and pressure groups must show us that the inflationist tendencies will prevail for many years.

The inevitable result of inflationary policies is a drop in the monetary unit's purchasing power. Compare the dollar of 1950 with the dollar of 1940! Compare the money of any European or American country with its nominal equivalent a dozen or two dozen years ago! As an inflationary policy works only as long as the yearly increments in the amount of money in circulation are increased more and more, the rise in prices and wages and the corresponding drop in purchasing power will go on at an accelerated pace. The experience of the French franc may give us a rough image of the dollar thirty or forty years from today.

Now it is such periods of time that count for pension plans. The present workers of the United States Steel Corporation will receive their pensions in twenty, thirty, or forty years. Today a pension of one hundred dollars a month means a rather substantial allowance. What will it mean in 1980 or 1990? Today, as the Welfare Commissioner of the City of New York has shown, 52 cents can buy all the food a person needs to meet the daily caloric and protein requirements. How much will 52 cents buy in 1980? [Editor: 0.17 cent.]

Such is the issue. What the workers are aiming at in striving after social security and pensions is, of course, security. But their "social gain" withers away with the drop in the dollar's purchasing power. In enthusiastically supporting the Fair Deal's fiscal policy, the union members are themselves frustrating all their social security and pension schemes. The pensions they will be entitled one day to claim will be a mere sham.

No solution can be found for this dilemma. In an industrial society all deferred payments must be stipulated in terms of money. They shrink with the shrinking of the money's purchasing power. A policy of deficit spending saps the very foundation of all interpersonal relations and contracts. It frustrates all kinds of savings, social security benefits, and pensions.

### Pensions and the "New Economics"

How can it happen that the American workers fail to see that their policies are at cross purposes?

The answer is: they are deluded by the fallacies of what is called "new economics." This allegedly new philosophy ignores the role of capital accumulation. It does not realize that there is but one means to increase wage rates for all those eager to get jobs and thereby to improve the standard of living, namely to accelerate the increase of capital as compared with population. It talks about technological progress and productivity without being aware that no technological improvement can be achieved if the capital required is lacking. Just at the instant in which it became obvious that the most serious obstacle to any further economic betterment is not only in the backward countries but also in England, the shortage of capital.

Lord Keynes, enthusiastically supported by many American authors, advanced his doctrine of the evils of saving and capital accumulation. As these men see it, all that is unsatisfactory is caused by the inability of private enterprise to cope with the conditions of the "mature" economy. The remedy they recommend is simple indeed. The state should fill the gap. They blithely assume that the state has unlimited means at its disposal. The state can undertake all projects which are too big for private capital. There is simply nothing that would surpass the financial power of the government of the United States. The Tennessee Valley project and the Marshall plan were just modest beginnings. There are still many valleys in America left for further action. And then there are many rivers in other parts of the globe. Only a short time ago Senator McMahon outlined a gigantic project that dwarfs the Marshall plan. Why not? If it is unnecessary to adjust the amount of expenditure to the means available, there is no limit to the spending of the great god State.

It is no wonder that the common man falls prey to the illusions which dim the vision of dignified statesmen and learned professors. Like the expert advisers of the President, he entirely neglects to recognize the main problem of American business, viz., the insufficiency of the accumulation of new capital. He dreams of abundance while a shortage is threatening. He misinterprets the high profits which the companies report. He does not perceive that a considerable part of these profits are illusory, a mere arithmetical consequence of the fact that the sums laid aside as depreciation quotas are insufficient. These illusory profits, a phony result of the drop in the dollar's purchasing power, will be absorbed by the already risen costs of replacing the factories' worn-out equipment. Their ploughing back is not additional investment, it is merely capital maintenance. There is much less available for a substantial expansion of investment and for the improvement of technological methods than the misinformed public thinks.

Looking backward fifty or a hundred years we observe a steady progress of America's ability to produce and thereby to consume. But it is a serious blunder to assume that this trend is bound to continue. This past progress has been effected by a speedy increase of capital accumulation. If the accumulation of new capital is slowed down or entirely ceases, there cannot be any question of further improvements.

Such is the real problem American labor has to face today. The problems of capital maintenance and the accumulation of new capital do not concern merely "management." They are vital for the wage earner. Exclusively preoccupied with wage rates and pensions, the unions boast of their Pyrrhic victories. The union members are not conscious of the fact that their fate is tied up with the flowering of their employers' enterprises. As voters they approve of a taxation system which taxes away and dissipates for current expenditure those funds which would have been saved and invested as new capital.

What the workers must learn is that the only reason why wage rates are higher in the United States than in other countries is that the per head quota of capital invested is higher. The psychological danger of all kinds of pension plans is to be seen in the fact that they obscure this point. They give to the workers an unfounded feeling of security. Now, they think, our future is safe. No need to worry any longer. The unions will win for us more and more social gains. An age of plenty is in sight.

Yet, the workers should be worried about the state of the supply of capital. They should be worried because the preservation and the further improvement of what is called "the American way of life" and "an American standard of living" depends on the maintenance and the further increase of the capital invested in American business.

A man who is forced to provide of his own account for his old age must save a part of his income or take out an insurance policy. This leads him to examine the financial status of the savings bank or the insurance company or the soundness of the bonds he buys. Such a man is more likely to get an idea of the economic problems of his country than a man whom a pension scheme seemingly relieves of all worries. He will get the incentive to read the financial page of his newspaper and will become interested in articles which thoughtless people skip. If he is keen enough he will discover the flaw in the teachings of the "new economics."

But the man who confides in the pension stipulated believes that all such issues are "mere theory" and do not affect him. He does not bother about those things on which his well-being depends because he ignores this dependence. As citizens such people are a liability. A nation cannot prosper if its members are not fully aware of the fact that what alone can improve their conditions is more and better production. And this can only be brought about by increased saving and capital accumulation.

LUDWIG VON MISES

# LAISSEZ FAIRE OR DICTATORSHIP

## 1. What the Encyclopaedia of the Social Sciences says about Laissez Faire

For more than a hundred years the maxim *laissez faire, laissez passer* has been a red rag to harbingers of totalitarian despotism. As these zealots see it, this maxim condenses all the shameful principles of capitalism. To unmask its fallacies is therefore tantamount to exploding the ideological foundations of the system of private ownership of the means of production, and implicitly demonstrating the excellence of its antithesis, viz., communism and socialism.

The *Encyclopaedia of the Social Sciences* may fairly be considered as representative of the doctrines taught at American and British universities and colleges. Its ninth volume contains an article, "Laissez Faire," from the pen of the Oxford professor and author of detective stories, G. D. H. Cole. In the five and a quarter pages of his contribution Professor Cole freely indulges in the use of deprecatory epithets. The maxim "cannot stand examination," it is only prevalent in "popular economics," it is "theoretically bankrupt," an "anachronism," it survives only as a "prejudice," but "as a doctrine deserving of theoretical respect it is dead." Resort to these and many other similar opprobrious appellations fails to disguise the fact that Professor Cole's arguments entirely miss the point. Professor Cole is

Reprinted courtesy of the Ludwig von Mises Institute (www.mises.org). The following essay originally appeared in *Plain Talk* 3(4; January 1949): 57–64.

not qualified to deal with the problems involved because he simply does not know what the market economy is and how it works. The only correct affirmation of his article is the truism that those rejecting laissez faire are Socialists. He is also right in declaring that the refutation of laissez faire is "as prominent in the national idea of Fascism in Italy as in Russian Communism."

The volume which contains Mr. Cole's article was published in January 1933. This explains why he did not include Nazi Germany in the ranks of those nations which have freed themselves from the spell of the sinister maxim. He merely registers with satisfaction that the conception rejecting laissez faire is "at the back of many projects of national planning which, largely under Russian influence, is now being put forward all over the world."

## 2. Laissez Faire Means Free Market Economy

Learned historians have bestowed much pains upon the question to whom the origin of the maxim *laissez faire, laissez passer* is to be attributed.[1] At any rate it is certain that in the second part of the eighteenth century the outstanding French champions of economic freedom—foremost among them Gournay, Quesnay, Turgot, and Mirabeau—compressed their program for popular use into this sentence. Their aim was the establishment of the unhampered market economy. In order to attain this end they advocated the abolition of all statutes preventing the more industrious and more efficient people from outdoing the less industrious and less efficient competitors and restricting the mobility of commodities and of men. It was this that the famous maxim was designed to express.

In occasionally using the words *laissez faire, laissez passer,* the eighteenth-century economists did not intend to baptize their social philosophy the laissez faire doctrine. They concentrated their efforts upon the elaboration of a new system of social and political ideas which would benefit mankind. They were not eager to organize a faction or party and to find a name for it. It was only later, in the second decade of the nineteenth century, that a term came to signify the total

complex of the political philosophy of freedom, viz., liberalism. The
new word was borrowed from Spain where it designated the friends
of constitutional government and religious freedom. Very soon it
was used all over Europe as a label for the endeavors of those who
stood for representative government; freedom of thought, of speech
and of the press; private ownership of the means of production; and
free trade.

The liberal program is an indivisible and indissoluble whole, not
an arbitrarily assembled patchwork of diverse components. Its various parts condition one another. The idea that political freedom can
be preserved in the absence of economic freedom, and vice versa, is
an illusion. Political freedom is the corollary of economic freedom.
It is no accident that the age of capitalism became also the age of
government by the people. If individuals are not free to buy and to
sell on the market, they turn into virtual slaves dependent on the good
graces of the omnipotent government, whatever the wording of the
constitution may be.

The fathers of socialism and modern interventionism were fully
aware that their own programs were incompatible with the political
postulates of liberalism. The main target of their passionate attacks
was liberalism as a whole. They did not make a distinction between
the political and the economic aspects of liberalism.

But as the years went on, the Socialists and interventionists of
the Anglo-Saxon countries discovered that it was a hopeless venture
to attack liberalism and the idea of liberty openly. The prestige of
liberal institutions was so overwhelming in the English-speaking world,
that no party could risk defying them directly. Anti-liberalism's only
chance was to camouflage itself as true and genuine liberalism and
to denounce the attitudes of all other parties as a mere counterfeit
liberalism.

The continental Socialists had fanatically smeared and dispar-
aged liberalism and progressivism, and contemptuously derogated
democracy as "pluto-democracy." Their Anglo-Saxon imitators,
who at first had adopted the same procedure, after a while reversed
their semantics and arrogated to themselves the appellations liberal,
progressive, and democratic. They began flatly to deny that political

freedom is the corollary of economic freedom. They boldly asserted that democratic institutions can work satisfactorily only where the government has full control of all production activities and the individual citizen is bound to obey unconditionally all orders issued by the central planning board. In their eyes all-round regimentation is the only means to make people free, and freedom of the press is best guaranteed by a government monopoly of printing and publishing. They were not plagued by any scruples when they stole the good old name of liberalism and began to call their own tenets and policies liberal. In this country the term "liberalism" is nowadays more often than not used as a synonym for communism.

The semantic innovation which the Socialists and interventionists thus inaugurated left the advocates of freedom without any name. There was no term available to call those who believe that private ownership of the material factors of production is the best, in fact, the only means to make the nation and all its individual citizens as prosperous as possible and to make representative government work. The Socialists and interventionists believe that such people do not deserve any name, but are to be referred to only by such insulting epithets as "economic royalists," "Wall Street sycophants," "reactionaries," and so on.

This state of affairs explains why the phrase laissez faire was more and more used to signify the ideas of those who advocate the free market economy as against government planning and regimentation.

## 3. The Cairnes Argument against Laissez Faire

Today it is no longer difficult for intelligent men to realize that the alternative is market economy or communism. Production can either be directed by buying and abstention from buying on the part of all people, or it can be directed by the orders of the supreme chief of state. Men must choose between these two systems of society's economic organization. There is no third solution, no middle way.

It is a sad fact that not only politicians and demagogues have failed to see this essential truth, but that even some economists have erred in dealing with the problems involved.

There is no need to dwell upon the unfortunate influence which originated from John Stuart Mill's confused treatment of government interference with business. It becomes evident from Mill's *Autobiography* that his change of mind resulting in what he calls "a greater approximation . . . to a qualified socialism"[2] was motivated by purely personal feelings and affections and not by emotionally undisturbed reasoning. It is certainly one of the tasks of economics to refute the errors which deform the disquisitions of so eminent a thinker as Mill. But it is unnecessary to argue against the prepossessions of Mr. Mill.

A few years after Mill, another outstanding economist, J. E. Cairnes, dealt with the same problem.[3] As a philosopher and essayist Mill by far supersedes Cairnes. But as an economist Cairnes was not second to Mill, and his contributions to the epistemology of the social sciences are of incomparably greater value and importance than those of Mill. Yet, Cairnes's analysis of laissez faire does not display that brilliant precision of reasoning which is the distinguishing mark of his other writings. As Cairnes sees it, the assertion implied in the doctrine of laissez faire is that "the promptings of self-interest will lead individuals, in all that range of their conduct which has to do with their material well-being, spontaneously to follow that course which is most for their own good and for the good of all." This assertion, he says, involves the two following assumptions: first, that the interests of human beings are fundamentally the same that what is most for my interest is also most for the interest of other people; and, secondly, that individuals know their interests in the sense in which they are coincident with the interests of others, and that, in the absence of coercion, they will in this sense follow them. If these two propositions be made out, the policy of laissez faire . . . follows with scientific rigour.

Cairnes is disposed to accept the first—the major—premise of the syllogism, that the interests of human beings are fundamentally the same. But he rejects the second—the minor—premise.[4] "Human beings know and follow their interests according to their lights and dispositions; but not necessarily, nor in practice always, in the sense in which the interest of the individual is coincident with that of others and of the whole."[5]

Let us for the sake of argument accept the way in which Cairnes presents the problem and in which he argues. Human beings are fallible and therefore sometimes fail to learn what their true interests would require them to do. Furthermore, there are "such things in the world as passion, prejudice, custom, *esprit de corps,* class interest, to draw people aside from the pursuit of their interests in the largest and highest sense."[6] It is very unfortunate that reality is such. But, we must ask, is there any means available to prevent mankind from being hurt by people's bad judgment and malice? Is it not a non sequitur to assume that one could avoid the disastrous consequences of these human weaknesses by substituting the government's discretion for that of the individual citizens? Are governments endowed with intellectual and moral perfection? Are the rulers not human too, not themselves subject to human frailties and deficiencies?

The theocratic doctrine is consistent in attributing to the head of the government superhuman powers. The French royalists contend that the solemn consecration at Rheims conveys to the King of France, anointed with the sacred oil which a dove from Heaven brought down for the consecration of Clovis, divine dispensation. The legitimate king cannot err and cannot do wrong, and his royal touch miraculously cures scrofula. No less consistent was the late German Professor Werner Sombart in declaring that *Führertum* is a permanent revelation and that the *Führer* gets his orders directly from God, the supreme *Führer* of the Universe.[7] Once you admit these premises, you can no longer raise any objections against planning and socialism. Why tolerate the incompetence of clumsy and ill-intentioned bunglers if you can be made happy and prosperous by the God-sent authority?

But Cairnes is not prepared to accept "the principle of State control, the doctrine of paternal government."[8] His disquisitions peter out in vague and contradictory talk that leaves the relevant question unanswered. He does not comprehend that it is indispensable to choose between the supremacy of individuals and that of the government. Some agency must determine how the factors of production should be employed and what should be produced. If it is not the consumer, by means of buying and abstention from buying on the market, it must be the government by compulsion.

If one rejects laissez faire on account of man's fallibility and moral weakness, one must for the same reasons also reject every kind of government action. Cairnes's mode of arguing, provided it is not integrated into a theocratic philosophy in the manner of the French royalists or the German Nazis, leads to complete anarchism and nihilism.

One of the distortions to which the self-styled "Progressives" resort in smearing laissez faire is the statement that consistent application of laissez faire must result in anarchy. There is no need to dwell upon this fallacy. It is more important to stress the fact that Cairnes's argument against laissez faire, when consistently carried through to its inevitable logical consequences, is essentially anarchistic.

## 4. "Conscious Planning" versus "Automatic Forces"

As the self-styled "Progressives" see things, the alternative is: "automatic forces" or "conscious planning."[9] It is obvious, they go on saying, that to rely upon automatic processes is sheer stupidity. No reasonable man can seriously recommend doing nothing and letting things go without any interference through purposive action. A plan, by the very fact that it is a display of conscious action, is incomparably superior to the absence of any planning. Laissez faire means: let evils last and do not try to improve the lot of mankind by reasonable action.

This is utterly fallacious and deceptive talk. The argument advanced for planning is derived entirely from an inadmissable interpretation of a metaphor. It has no foundation other than the connotations implied in the term "automatic," which is customarily applied in a metaphorical sense to describe the market process. Automatic, says the *Concise Oxford Dictionary*, means "unconscious, unintelligent, merely mechanical." Automatic, says *Webster's Collegiate Dictionary*, means "not subject to the control of the will . . . performed without active thought and without conscious intention or direction." What a triumph for the champion of planning to play this trump card!

The truth is that the choice is not between a dead mechanism and a rigid automatism on the one hand and conscious planning on the other hand. The alternative is not plan or no plan. The question is: whose planning? Should each member of society plan for himself or should the paternal government alone plan for all? The issue is not automatism *versus conscious action;* it is *spontaneous action of each individual versus the exclusive action of the* government. It is *freedom versus government omnipotence.*

Laissez faire does not mean: let soulless mechanical forces operate. It means: let individuals choose how they want to cooperate in the social division of labor and let them determine what the entrepreneurs should produce. Planning means: let the government alone choose and enforce its rulings by the apparatus of coercion and compulsion.

## 5. The Satisfaction of Man's "True" Needs

Under laissez faire, says the planner, the goods produced are not those which people "really" need, but those goods from the sale of which the highest returns are expected. It is the objective of planning to direct production toward the satisfaction of "true" needs. But who should decide what "true" needs are?

Thus, for instance, Professor Harold Laski, the former chairman of the British Labor Party, determined the objective of planned direction of investment as "the use of the investor's savings will be in housing rather than in cinemas."[10] It does not matter whether or not one agrees with the professor's personal view that better houses are more important than moving pictures. The fact is that consumers, by spending part of their money for admission to the movies, have made another choice. If the masses of Great Britain, the same people whose votes swept the Labor Party into power, were to stop patronizing the moving pictures and to spend more for comfortable homes and apartments, profit-seeking business would be forced to invest more in building homes and apartment houses, and less in the production of swanky pictures. What Professor Laski aimed at is to defy the wishes of the consumers and to substitute his own will for theirs. He wanted to do away with the democracy of the market and to establish the absolute rule of a production czar. He might pretend that he is right from a "higher" point of view, and that as a superman he is called upon to impose his own set of values on the masses of inferior men. But then he should have been frank enough to say so plainly.

All this passionate praise of the super-eminence of government action is merely a poor disguise for the individual interventionist's self-deification. The Great God State is great only because it is expected to do exclusively what the individual advocate of interventionism wants to be achieved. The only true plan is the one of which the individual planner fully approves. All other plans are simply counterfeit. What the author of a book on the benefits of planning has in mind is, of course, always his own plan alone. No planner was ever shrewd enough to consider the possibility that the plan which the government will put into practice could differ from his own plan.

The various planners agree only with regard to their rejection of laissez faire, i.e., the individual's discretion to choose and to act. They disagree entirely on the choice of the unique plan to be adopted. To every exposure of the manifest and incontestable defects of interventionist policies the champions of interventionism always react in the same way. These faults, they say, were the sins of spurious interventionism; what we are advocating is good interventionism. And, of course, good interventionism is the professor's own brand only.

## 6. "Positive" Policies versus "Negative" Policies

In dealing with the ascent of modern statism, socialism, and interventionism, one must not neglect the preponderant role played by the pressure groups and lobbies of civil servants and those university graduates who longed for government jobs. Two associations were paramount in Europe's progress toward "social reform": the Fabian Society in England and the *Verein für Sozialpolitik* in Germany. The Fabian Society had in its earlier days a "wholly disproportionate representation of civil servants."[11] With regard to the *Verein für Sozialpolitik*, one of its founders and most eminent leaders, Professor Lujo Brentano, admitted that at the beginning it called no other response than from the civil servants.[12]

It is not surprising that the civil-service mentality was reflected in the semantic practices of the new factions. Seen from the point of view of the particular group interests of the bureaucrats, every measure that makes the government's payroll swell is progress. Politicians who favor such a measure make a *positive* contribution to welfare, while those who object are *negative*. Very soon this linguistic innovation became general. The interventionists, in claiming for themselves the appellation "liberal," explained that they, of course, were liberals with a positive program as distinguished from the merely negative program of the "orthodox" laissez faire people.

Thus he who advocates tariffs, censorship, foreign exchange control, and price control supports a positive program that will provide jobs for customs officers, censors, and employees of the offices for price control and foreign exchange control. But free traders and advocates of the freedom of the press are bad citizens; they are negative. Laissez faire is the embodiment of negativism, while socialism, in converting all people into government employees, is 100 percent positive. The more a former liberal completes his defection from liberalism and approaches socialism, the more "positive" does he become.

It is hardly necessary to stress that this is all nonsense. Whether an idea is enunciated in an affirmative or in a negative proposition depends entirely on the form which the author chooses to give it. The "negative" proposition, *I am against censorship*, is identical with the "positive" proposition, *I am in favor of everybody's right to publicize his opinions.* Laissez faire is not even formally a negative formula; rather it is the contrary of laissez faire that would sound negative. Essentially, the maxim asks for private ownership of the means of production. This implies, of course, that it rejects socialism. The supporters of laissez faire object to government interference with business not because they "hate" the "state" or because they are committed to a "negative" program. They object to it because it is incompatible with their own positive program, the free market economy.[13]


## 7. Conclusion

Laissez faire means: let the individual citizen, the much talked-about common man, choose and act and do not force him to yield to a dictator.

# Notes

Cf. especially A. Oncken, *Die Maxime laissez faire et laissez passer, ihr Ursprung, ihr Werden*, Bern 1886; G. Schelle, *Vincent de Gournay*, Paris 1897, pp. 214–26

Cf. John Stuart Mill, *Autobiography*, London, 1873, p. 191.

Cf. J. E. Cairnes, "Political Economy and Laissez Faire" (an Introductory Lecture delivered in University College, London, November, 1870; reprinted in *Essays in Political Economy*, London 1873, pp. 232–64).

Ibid., pp. 244–45.

Ibid., p. 250.

Ibid., p. 246.

Cf. W. Sombert, *Deutscher Sozialismus* (Charlottenburg, 1934), p. 213. [American edition: *A New Social Philosophy*, K. F. Geiser, trans. (Princeton, 1937) p. 194.]

Cf. Cairnes, "Political Economy and Laissez Faire," p. 251.

Cf. A. H. Hansen, *"Social Planning for Tomorrow"* in *The United States after the War* (Cornell University Lectures, Ithaca, 1945), pp. 32–33.

Cf. Laski's Broadcast, *Revolution by Consent*, reprinted in *Talks*, vol. 10, no. 10 (October 1945), p. 7

11 Cf. A. Gray, *The Socialist Tradition: Moses to Lenin* (London, 1946), p. 385.

Cf. L. Brentano, *Ist das "system Brentano" zusammengebrochen?* (Berlin, 1918), p. 19. The present writer refuted this distinction between "positive" and "constructive" socialism and interventionism on the one hand, and "negative" liberalism of the laissez faire type on the other in his article "Sozialliberalismus," first published in 1926 in *Zeitschrift für die Gesamte Staatswissenschaft*, and reprinted in 1929 in his book *Kritik des Interventionismus*, pp. 55–90.